Volume 2

Artificial Intelligence at MIT

Volume 2

Artificial Intelligence at MIT
Expanding Frontiers

edited by Patrick Henry Winston
with Sarah Alexandra Shellard

The MIT Press
Cambridge, Massachusetts
London, England

This book was printed and bound in the United States of America.

Library of Congress Cataloging-in-Publication Data

(Revised for vol. 2)

Artificial intelligence at MIT.

(Artificial intelligence)
Includes bibliographical references.
1. Artificial intelligence. I. Winston, Patrick Henry. II. Shellard, Sarah Alexandra. III. MIT Press series in artificial intelligence.
Q335.A78713   1990   006.3   90-5540
ISBN 0-262-23150-6 (v. 1)

Contents: Volume 2

Series Foreword

Artificial intelligence is the study of intelligence using the ideas and methods of computation. Unfortunately a definition of intelligence seems impossible at the moment because intelligence appears to be an amalgam of so many information-processing and information-representation abilities.

Of course psychology, philosophy, linguistics, and related disciplines offer various perspectives and methodologies for studying intelligence. For the most part, however, the theories proposed in these fields are too incomplete and too vaguely stated to be realized in computational terms. Something more is needed, even though valuable ideas, relationships, and constraints can be gleaned from traditional studies of what are, after all, impressive existence proofs that intelligence is in fact possible.

Artificial intelligence offers a new perspective and a new methodology. Its central goal is to make computers intelligent, both to make them more useful and to understand the principles that make intelligence possible. That intelligent computers will be extremely useful is obvious. The more profound point is that artificial intelligence aims to understand intelligence using the ideas and methods of computation, thus offering a radically new and different basis for theory formation. Most of the people doing work in artificial intelligence believe that these theories will apply to any intelligent information processor, whether biological or solid state.

There are side effects that deserve attention, too. Any program that will successfully model even a small part of intelligence will be inherently massive and complex. Consequently artificial intelligence continually confronts the limits of computer-science technology. The problems encountered have been hard enough and interesting enough to seduce artificial intelligence people into working on them with enthusiasm. It is natural, then, that there has been a steady flow of ideas from artificial intelligence to computer science, and the flow shows no sign of abating.

The purpose of this series in artificial intelligence is to provide people in many areas, both professionals and students, with timely, detailed information about what is happening on the frontiers in research centers all over the world.

J. Michael Brady
Daniel G. Bobrow
Randall Davis

Preface cum Introduction

Patrick Henry Winston
Sarah Alexandra Shellard

Thirty years ago, Marvin Minsky published *Semantic Information Processing*, a collection of his students' theses, because there were no journals devoted to Artificial Intelligence. Today, we face the opposite problem: research results are scattered widely among highly specialized journals, conference proceedings, and monographs, making it almost impossible to see the general trends emerging from myriad research and development centers. To help address this problem, we are publishing these volumes, which provide an overview of current work in Artificial Intelligence from the perspective of the students, staff, and faculty of the MIT Artificial Intelligence Laboratory.

Fighting Fragmentation

We believe that such an overview is needed because the expansion of the field has led to narrowness and fragmentation. Until recently, people from different subfields attended the same meetings, and ideas moved quickly. Today, however, the once-small AI community has grown large, and people in one subfield are slow to learn about the exciting new results emerging in other subfields.

Yet historically, cross fertilization has been of great value in Artificial Intelligence. The idea of constraint propagation, for example, emerged in formal logic, became popular through Waltz's work on line-drawing analysis, and then settled in as a dominant paradigm in model-based problem solving. Similarly, the notion of frame became part of the AI vernacular in a paper by Minsky that concentrated on the visual world, but subsequently became mostly associated with expert systems that have nothing to do with vision. And the Connection Machine, which was conceived in our laboratory as a machine for searching semantic nets, has become a dominant vehicle for executing early vision procedures, for computing paths for manipulators, and for brute-force database mining. Elsewhere, the Connection Machine is being used for a host of other unrelated applications ranging from weather modeling to lattice gauge theory in high energy nuclear physics.

Who Should Read these Volumes

We believe that cross fertilization should be as common today as it was in the early days. Accordingly, we have assembled these two volumes to stimulate and provoke a new generation of students, researchers, and those who strive to solve practical problems using cutting-edge technology. If you are among them, read these volumes to learn about emerging trends in Artificial Intelligence and to equip yourself with a host of innovative, reusable ideas.

How To Read these Volumes

We do not expect many readers to devour every chapter in these two volumes. After all, forty-three chapters and more than 1200 pages are too many to digest in a day or two.

Consequently, we have written a short vignette to introduce each chapter. Collectively, these vignettes provide historical perspective, explain the key ideas, describe exciting results, and suggest practical consequences. We recommend that you start with these vignettes so as to determine which chapters best suit your own needs and interests.

Expanding Frontiers

Our title, *Expanding Frontiers*, is meant to be a *double entendre*. One reading is that the traditional AI subfields are advancing, as indeed they are, for there has been great progress in the past decade on everything from model-based reasoning to image understanding. Another reading is that Artificial Intelligence is expanding through the addition of new subfields, such as subsumption-based control and neural-net learning, which have joined the traditional subfields.

It would be wrong to suppose that the subfields of Artificial Intelligence are moving further apart. In the following paragraphs, we outline what we believe to be unifying challenges and unifying approaches to those challenges.

Scalable Solutions

In the early days of Artificial Intelligence, nearly all AI work involved a toy problem. Image understanding programs analyzed line drawings of blocks. Learning programs learned about structures made of blocks. And natural language programs attempted to unravel questions about blocks.

Fifteen years ago, some practical programs had emerged, but for the most part, toy problems still filled the literature.

Today, however, it is increasingly hard to attract attention unless your idea seems robust enough to be scaled up to the level demanded by real-world complexities. You do not necessarily need to exhibit a real-world prototype, but it should be clear that the gap between what you have done and what real technology consumers need can be bridged without another breakthrough.

Throughout these volumes, there are many examples of programs that are manifestly scalable because they have already met the challenge of the real world. For example, Sussman, Abelson, and their students have helped oceanographers solve problems in wave dynamics. Lathrop has helped biologists find new patterns for recognizing proteins in the reverse transcriptase class. Katz has helped journalists access information about Voyager 2's Neptune encounter with a program that reads text and answers questions in English. And Grimson has helped production engineers write vision programs for recognition and testing.

Unmodelable and Chaotic Worlds

Most of today's builders of applied AI systems assume that everything can be modeled and that the world behaves according to model-based predictions. Yet some situations, like desk clutter, defy detailed symbolic description because there is just too much to be described. And some dynamic systems, like robot arms or national economies, seem chaotic in that predictions based on models diverge quickly from reality.

Accordingly, many AI researchers have begun to concentrate on unmodelable and chaotic worlds. Some believe that such worlds cannot be handled with the traditional symbolic systems, arguing instead for neural nets and a variety of other nonsymbolic approaches.†

Within our laboratory, many of us believe that symbolic and nonsymbolic systems are both important. As Marvin Minsky said recently, "The trouble with symbolic systems is that they are too fragile, and the trouble

---

†Some critics of Artificial Intelligence even seem to have succumbed to a nonsequitur: there are some kinds of intelligence that cannot be modeled by symbolic reasoning, therefore symbolic reasoning cannot have anything to do with intelligence.

with neural nets is that they are too stupid." One of the great challenges ahead is to learn how to design systems that are partly symbolic and partly nonsymbolic so that they are neither fragile nor stupid.

But what can be meant by *nonsymbolic*? Some researchers work on neural nets because they believe that the road to intelligent machines must travel through biology. Others disagree. But everyone agrees that we need better theories that show what neural nets can and cannot do. Along these lines, Poggio and Girosi have contributed considerably to our understanding of neural net capabilities and limits by exploiting the mathematics of interpolation and approximation.

Other critics of traditional symbolic computation believe that neural nets are not the right thing either. Brooks, for example, advocates his subsumption architecture, which is based on layers of finite state machines and the principle that the world must be its own model.

Learning and Regularity Recognition

Learning is another approach to dealing with the unmodelable and chaotic in particular and the unspeakably complicated in general. As Artificial Intelligence faces harder challenges, it is natural for more AI researchers to include some aspect of learning in their research agendas. Atkeson, for example, not only wants to make robots agile, he insists that robots learn to be agile. Lee not only wants programs to help decision makers, he insists that programs use knowledge from past decisions. Lathrop not only wants programs to help biologists, he insists that programs dig regularity out of big biology databases. And Davis not only wants programs to debug malfunctioning hardware, he insists that programs learn to handle more difficult debugging problems.

Massive Parallelism

We can now process data like bulldozers process gravel, using parallel machines with thousands of processors. Increasingly, this changes the way we think. Minimally, we can do what we have always wanted to do but could not because of computing limitations; more dramatically, we can have thoughts that we could not have had before because our thinking was shackled by what seemed like realistic hardware expectations. Much of the learning work done at MIT would not have been done were there no massively parallel hardware. Similarly, much of computer vision research would be stifled without experiments enabled by massively parallel hardware.

Today, *massively parallel* means the Connection Machine, which, like the Lisp Machine, is part of a long tradition of innovative hardware and software system invention and development in our laboratory. In that tradition, we continue to expand the frontiers of computer hardware and software, especially those frontiers with obvious impact on AI research. Knight, for example, is working on a medium-grain machine that enables ordinary symbolic programs to be run largely in parallel, without the tedium of removing side effects. Dally is working on a fine-grain machine that supports many models of parallel computation, including those that concentrate on message passing. And in the software dimension, Hewitt continues to develop the theoretical and practical aspects of his Actor model.

Content of these Volumes

Many of the chapters are points of intersection with respect to these emerging challenges and approaches. One way to be certain a solution scales up is to put the solution in harness with a learning idea. One way to learn is to do massive computation enabled by parallelism. And massive parallelism offers one approach to dealing with unmodelable and chaotic worlds.

Consequently, ideas about scalable solutions, unstructured environments, learning, and massive parallelism are pervasive throughout our laboratory, just as they are pervasive throughout the six parts of these volumes:

Volume 1:

- Scalable Solutions for Real-World Problems
- Fueling the Next Generation
- Creating Software and Hardware Revolutions

Volume 2:

- Conquering Unstructured Environments
- Jumping through Hoops and Manipulating Objects
- Recognizing Objects and Understanding Images

To be sure, understanding the computations that enable what we call intelligence remains an extreme challenge. Nevertheless, the ideas and results presented in these volumes demonstrate that the frontiers are expanding at an ever increasing rate. We hope that you find these volumes to be stimulating and provocative, and we hope that you share our excitement about the present and our optimism about the future.

Acknowledgments

Funding and Support

Many government agencies, foundations, and companies have sponsored work in the Artificial Intelligence Laboratory. The Defense Advanced Research Projects Agency, in particular, has taken a visionary position with respect to the impact of Artificial Intelligence for many years, along with the System Development Foundation, National Science Foundation, Office of Naval Research, and the Air Force Office of Scientific Research.

Other sponsors who have made it possible to do essential work include: Analog Devices, Apple Computer, Bear Stearns Company, Dana Farber, Digital Equipment Corporation, Draper Laboratory, E.I. duPont de Nemours, Exxon Research and Development Company, Fujitsu, General Dynamics, General Motors Research Laboratories, Hughes Research Laboratories, International Business Machines, ISX Corporation, Kapor Family Foundation, Lockheed Missiles and Space Company, Lotus Development Corporation, Martin Marietta, Mazda, MCC Corporation, McDonnell Douglas, NASA, NATO, NYNEX, Olivetti, Sandia National Laboratory, Sharp, Siemens, Sloan Foundation, Smithsonian, Sperry, and Wang Laboratories.

Preparation of the Manuscript

We are particularly grateful to all the students, staff, and faculty of the MIT Artificial Intelligence Laboratory who contributed to these volumes. Their enthusiastic cooperation and support were invaluable.

Boris Katz helped enormously with the preface and chapter introductions. The manuscript was typeset in YTEX, a local version of TEX written by Daniel Brotsky. Book design evolved gradually during production, which took a full year.

Several people assisted in producing the camera-ready copy: Berthold Horn and Jerry Roylance helped with Postscript; Roger Gilson's *prestissimo* typing was called upon for those manuscripts not available in electronic form and for the index; Joe Snowdon and Gary Bisbee of Chiron Inc. worked around the clock to print the 1300 pages on a Linotronic 300P imagesetter. And, finally, SAS would particularly like to acknowledge E.P.S. Shellard for his TEXnical advice and continual encouragement throughout the project.

Volume 2

Artificial Intelligence at MIT

Part IV

Conquering Unstructured Environments

Highly automated factories are said to be structured environments because pallets and feeders deliver parts to prescribed places where those parts are held in jigs or mated with other parts to form assemblies. Robots do not have to be very flexible in structured environments because built-in mechanical constraints provide severe limits on what can happen. By contrast, most ordinary factories, offices, and homes, along with everything outdoors, are said to be unstructured environments because just about anything can be anywhere at any time. Such environments cripple ordinary robots, but not the experimental robots described here:

- *In the first chapter of Part IV, Brooks describes his subsumption architecture for robots, an architecture in which each new layer provides a new competence without requiring any bug-introducing changes to existing competence layers. The layers-of-competence idea has been tested by constructing a wheeled robot that retrieves empty soft-drink cans as it wanders about.*

- *Next, Brooks explains that in some unstructured environments there is too much potentially important detail to model symbolically. Consequently, systems built according to the subsumption principles use no symbolic models; instead, the world must serve as its own model via direct sensing. The no-model idea has been tested by constructing a six-legged, beetlelike robot that walks over all sorts of desk detritus.*

- *Another approach, especially suited to factory environments, is to use models effectively, not to avoid them. Lozano-Pérez et al. explain how good models enable their HANDEY system to create its own grasp-and-move sequences from its human boss's what-to-do requests, thus performing one kind of automatic programming.*

- *Finally, Lozano-Pérez et al. show how model-enabled planning works at the level of planning for force-controlled part-mating motions, explaining that without force control, jamming and damage are more likely than successful assembly.*

24

What does it take to build a robot that wanders into your office, copes somehow with the disarray, finds an empty soft-drink can, and carries it away?

Ten years ago the conventional wisdom was that a powerful reasoning system would be required along with an elaborate vision system capable of building detailed internal models in support of the reasoning system. The conventional wisdom was that such systems were a long way off.

Such systems remain a long way off, but a basic can-collecting robot has been demonstrated nevertheless. To build such robots, Brooks champions many nontraditional ideas. One is that there should be no powerful reasoning system and no elaborate vision system. Instead, there should be competence layers, each with just enough computing and sensing capability to add one competence to those competences provided by lower layers.

Next, no competence should be fooled with once debugged; instead, each new competence is added as a layer on top of existing competences. Once you can avoid obstacles, then you can wander, but you must not change the procedures that enable obstacle avoidance, for you will surely introduce bugs.

Of course, the layering idea invites comparison with evolved, natural systems. It also invites comparison with well-modularized software systems in which data and procedure abstraction prevent extensions and improvements from producing catastrophic collapse.

A Robust Layered Control System for a Mobile Robot

Rodney A. Brooks

A control system for a completely autonomous mobile robot must perform many complex information processing tasks in real time. It operates in an environment where the boundary conditions (viewing the instantaneous control problem in a classical control theory formulation) are changing rapidly. In fact the determination of those boundary conditions is done over very noisy channels because there is no straightforward mapping between sensors (for example, television cameras) and the form required of the boundary conditions.

The usual approach to building control systems for such robots is to decompose the problem into a series of *functional units* as illustrated by a series of vertical slices in figure 1.

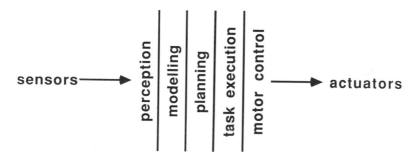

Figure 1. Traditional decomposition of a mobile robot control system into functional modules.

After analyzing the computational requirements for a mobile robot we have decided to use *task achieving behaviors* as our primary decomposition of the problem, and is illustrated by a series of horizontal slices in figure 2. As with a functional decomposition we implement each slice explicitly then tie them all together to form a robot control system. Our new decomposition leads to a radically different architecture for mobile robot control systems, with radically different implementation strategies plausible at the hardware level, and with a large number of advantages concerning robustness, buildability, and testability.

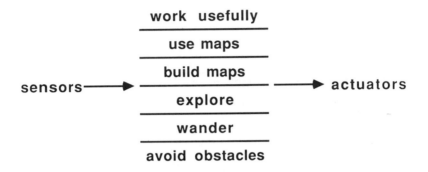

Figure 2. A decomposition of a mobile robot control system based on task achieving behaviors.

Requirements

We can identify a number of requirements of a control system for an intelligent autonomous mobile robot. They each put constraints on possible control systems we might build and employ.

Multiple Goals. Often the robot will have multiple goals, which it is trying to achieve, some conflicting. It may be trying to reach a certain point ahead of it while avoiding local obstacles. It may be trying to reach a certain place in minimal time while conserving power reserves. Often the relative importance of goals will be context dependent. Getting off the railroad tracks when a train is heard becomes much more important than inspecting the last ten track ties of the current track section. The control system must be responsive to high priority goals, while still servicing necessary "low level" goals (for example, in getting off the railroad tracks it is still important that the robot maintains its balance so it doesn't fall down).

Multiple Sensors. The robot will probably have multiple sensors (for example, television cameras, encoders on steering and drive mechanisms, and perhaps infrared beacon detectors, an inertial navigation system, acoustic rangefinders, infrared rangefinders, access to a global positioning satellite system, etc.). All sensors have an error component in their readings. Furthermore, often there is no direct analytic mapping from sensor values to desired physical quantities. Some of the sensors will overlap in the physical quantities they measure. They will often give inconsistent readings—sometimes due to normal sensor error and sometimes due to the measurement conditions being such that the sensor (and subsequent processing) is being used outside its domain of applicability. Often there will be no analytic characterization of the domain of applicability (for example, under what precise conditions does the Sobel operator return valid edges?). The robot must make decisions under these conditions.

Robustness. The robot ought to be robust. When some sensors fail it should be able to adapt and cope by relying on those still functional. When the environment changes drastically it should still be able to achieve some modicum of sensible behavior, rather than sit in shock, or wander around aimlessly. Ideally it should also continue to function well when there are faults in parts of its processor(s).

Extensibility. As more sensors and capabilities are added to a robot it needs more processing power; otherwise the original capabilities of the robot will be impaired relative to the flow of time.

Other approaches

Multiple Goals. Elfes and Talukdar [1983] designed a control language for Moravec's [1983] robot which tried to accommodate multiple goals. It achieved this by letting the user explicitly code for parallelism and code an exception path to a special handler for each plausible case of unexpected conditions.

Multiple Sensors. Flynn [1985] explicitly investigated the use of multiple sensors, with complementary characteristics (sonar is wide angle but reasonably accurate in depth, while infrared is very accurate in angular resolution but not in depth measurement). Her system has the virtue that if one sensor fails the other still delivers readings that are useful to the higher level processing. Giralt *et al.* [1983] use a laser range finder for map making, sonar sensors for local obstacle detection, and infrared beacons for map calibration. The robot operates in a mode where one particular sensor type is used at a time and the others are completely ignored, even though they may be functional. In the natural world multiple redundant sensors are abundant. For instance Kreithen [1983] reports that pigeons have more than four independent orientation sensing systems (for example, sun position compared to their internal biological clock). It is interesting that the sensors do not seem to be combined but rather, depending on the environmental conditions and operational level of sensor subsystems, the data from one sensor tends to dominate.

Robustness. The above work tries to make systems robust in terms of sensor availability, but little has been done to make either the behavior or the processor of a robot robust.

Extensibility. There are three ways this can be achieved without completely rebuilding the physical control system.

1   Excess processor power which was previously being wasted can be utilized. Clearly this is a bounded resource.

2   The processor(s) can be upgraded to an architecturally compatible but faster system. The original software can continue to run, but now excess capacity will be available and we can proceed as in the first case.

3   More processors can be added to carry the new load.

Typically systems builders then get enmeshed in details of how to make all memory uniformly accessible to all processors. Usually the cost of the memory to processor routing system soon comes to dominate the cost of the system (the measure of cost is not important—it can be monetary, silicon area, access time delays). As a result there is usually a fairly small upper bound on the number of processors which can be added (on the order of hundreds for traditional style processing units; on the order to tens to hundreds of thousands for extremely simple processors).

Starting assumptions

Our design decisions for our mobile robot are based on nine dogmatic principles (six of these principles were presented more fully in Brooks [1985]):

1   Complex (and useful) behavior need not necessarily be a product of an extremely complex control system. Rather, complex behavior may simply be the reflection of a complex environment [Simon 1969]. It may be an observer who ascribes complexity to an organism—not necessarily its designer.

2   Things should be simple. This has two applications.

2.1   When building a system of many parts one must pay attention to the interfaces. If you notice that a particular interface is starting to rival the complexity of the components it connects, then either the interface needs to be rethought or the decomposition of the system needs redoing.

2.2   If a particular component or collection of components solves an unstable or ill-conditioned problem, or, more radically, if its design involved the solution of an unstable or ill-conditioned problem, then it is probably not a good solution from the standpoint of robustness of the system.

3   We want to build cheap robots which can wander around human inhabited space with no human intervention, advice or control and at the same time do useful work. Map making is therefore of crucial importance even when idealized blue prints of an environment are available.

4   The human world is three dimensional; it is not just a two dimensional surface map. The robot must model the world as three dimensional if it is to be allowed to continue cohabitation with humans.

5   Absolute coordinate systems for a robot are the source of large cumulative errors. Relational maps are more useful to a mobile robot. This alters the design space for perception systems.

6   The worlds where mobile robots will do useful work are not constructed of exact simple polyhedra. While polyhedra may be useful models of a realistic world, it is a mistake to build a special world such that the models can be exact. For this reason we will build no artificial environment for our robot.

7   Sonar data, while easy to collect, does not by itself lead to rich descriptions of the world useful for truly intelligent interactions. Visual data is much better for that purpose. Sonar data may be useful for low level interactions such as real time obstacle avoidance.

8   For the sake of robustness the robot must be able to perform when one or more of its sensors fails or starts giving erroneous readings. Recovery should be quick. This implies that built-in self calibration must be occurring at all times. If it is able to achieve our goals then it will necessarily be able to eliminate the need for external calibration steps. To force the issue we do not incorporate any explicit calibration steps for our robot. Rather, we try to make all processing steps self calibrating.

9   We are interested in building *artificial beings*—robots which can survive for days, weeks and months, without human assistance, in a dynamic complex environment. Such robots must be self sustaining.

Levels and Layers

There are many possible approaches to building an autonomous intelligent mobile robot. As with most engineering problems they all start by decomposing the problem into pieces, solving the subproblems for each piece, and then composing the solutions. We think we have done the first of these three steps differently from other groups. The second and third steps also differ as a consequence.

Levels of competence

Typically mobile robot builders (for example, Nilsson [1984], Moravec [1983], Giralt et al. [1983], Kanayama [1983], Tsuji [1984], and Crowley [1985]) have sliced the problem into some subset of:

- Sensing
- Mapping sensor data into a world representation
- Planning
- Task execution
- Motor control

This decomposition can be regarded as a horizontal decomposition of the problem into vertical slices. The slices form a chain through which information flows from the robot's environment, via sensing, through the robot and back to the environment, via action, closing the feedback loop (of course, most implementations of the above subproblems also include internal feedback loops). An instance of each piece must be built in order to run the robot at all. Later changes to a particular piece (to improve it or extend its functionality) must either be done in such a way that the interfaces to adjacent pieces do not change, or the effects of the change must be propagated to neighboring pieces, changing their functionality too.

We have chosen instead to decompose the problem vertically as our primary way of slicing up the problem. Rather than slice the problem on the basis of internal workings of the solution, we slice the problem on the basis of desired external manifestations of the robot control system.

To this end we have defined a number of *levels of competence* for an autonomous mobile robot. A level of competence is an informal specification of a desired class of behaviors for a robot over all environments it will encounter. A higher level of competence implies a more specific desired class of behaviors.

We have used the following levels of competence (an earlier version of these was reported in Brooks [1984]) as a guide in our work:

0   Avoid contact with objects (whether the objects move or are stationary).

1   Wander aimlessly around without hitting things.

2   "Explore" the world by seeing places in the distance which look reachable and heading for them.

3   Build a map of the environment and plan routes from one place to another.

4   Note changes in the "static" environment.

5   Reason about the world in terms of identifiable objects and perform tasks related to certain objects.

6   Formulate and execute plans which involve changing the state of the world in some desirable way.

7   Reason about the behavior of objects in the world and modify plans accordingly.

Note that each level of competence includes each earlier level of competence as a subset. Because a level of competence defines a class of valid behaviors it can be seen that higher levels of competence provide additional constraints on that class.

Layers of control

The key idea of levels of competence is that we can build layers of a control system corresponding to each level of competence and simply add a new layer to an existing set to move to the next higher level of overall competence.

We start by building a complete robot control system which achieves level *0* competence. It is debugged thoroughly. We never alter that system. We call it the zeroth level control system, Next we build another control layer, which we call the first level control system. It is able to examine data from the level *0* system and is also permitted to inject data into the internal interfaces of level *0* suppressing the normal data flow. This layer, with the aid of the zeroth, achieves level *1* competence. The zeroth layer continues to run unaware of the layer above it which sometimes interferes with its data paths.

The same process is repeated to achieve higher levels of competence (see figure 3). We call this architecture a *subsumption architecture.*

In such a scheme we have a working control system for the robot very early on—as soon as we have built the first layer. Additional layers can be added later, and the initial working system need never be changed. We claim that this architecture naturally lends itself to solving the problems for mobile robots delineated in the previous section.

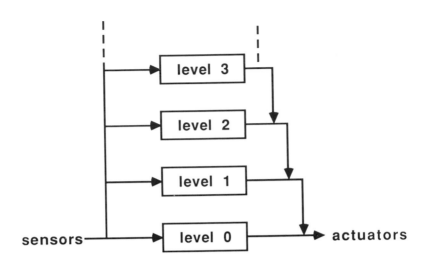

Figure 3. Control is layered with higher level layers subsuming the roles of lower level layers when they wish to take control. The system can be partitioned at any level, and the layers below form a complete operational control system.

Multiple Goals. Individual layers can be working on individual goals concurrently. The suppression mechanism then mediates the actions that are taken. The advantage here is that there is no need to make an early decision on which goal should be pursued. The results of pursuing all of them to some level of conclusion can be used for the ultimate decision.

Multiple Sensors. In part we can ignore the sensor fusion problem as stated earlier using a subsumption architecture. Not all sensors need to feed into a central representation. Indeed certain readings of all sensors need not feed into central representations—only those which perception processing identifies as extremely reliable might be eligible to enter such a central representation. At the same time, however, the sensor values may still be being used by the robot. Other layers may be processing them in some fashion and using the results to achieve their own goals, independent of how other layers may be scrutinizing them.

Robustness. Multiple sensors clearly add to the robustness of a system when their results can be used intelligently. There is another source of robustness in a subsumption architecture. Lower levels which have been well debugged continue to run when higher levels are added, because a higher level can only suppress the outputs of lower levels by actively interfering with replacement data. In the cases that it cannot produce results in a timely fashion, the lower levels will still produce results which are sensible, albeit at a lower level of competence.

Extensibility.   An obvious way to handle extensibility is to make each new layer run on its own processor. We will see later that this is practical as there are, in general, fairly low bandwidth requirements on communication channels between layers. In addition, we will see that the individual layers can be easily spread over many loosely coupled processors.

The structure of layers

But what about building each individual layer? Don't we need to decompose a single layer in the traditional manner? This is true to some extent, but the key difference is that we do not need to account for all desired perceptions, processing, and generated behaviors in a single decomposition. We are free to use different decompositions for different sensor-set task-set pairs.

We have chosen to build layers from a set of small processors which send messages to each other. Each processor is a finite state machine with the ability to hold some data structures. Processors send messages over connecting "wires." There is no handshaking or acknowledgment of messages. The processors run completely asynchronously, monitoring their input wires, and sending messages on their output wires. It is possible for messages to get lost—it actually happens quite often. There is no other form of communication between processors, in particular, there is no shared global memory.

All processors (which we refer to as modules) are created equal in the sense that within a layer there is no central control. Each module merely carries out its function as best it can.

Inputs to modules can be suppressed and outputs can be inhibited by wires terminating from other modules. This is the mechanism by which higher level layers subsume the role of lower levels.

A Robot Control System Specification Language

There are two aspects to the components of our layered control architecture. One is the internal structure of the modules, and the second is the way in which they communicate. In this section we flesh out the details of the semantics of our modules and explain a description language for them.

Finite state machines

Each module, or processor, is a finite state machine, augmented with some instance variables which can actually hold Lisp data structures.

Each module has a number of input lines and a number of output lines. Input lines have single element buffers. The most recently arrived message is always available for inspection. Messages can be lost if a new one arrives on an input line before the last was inspected. There is a distinguished input to each module called **reset**. Each state is named. When the system first starts up all modules start in the distinguished state named NIL. When a signal is received on the reset line the module switches to state NIL. A state can be specified as one of four types shown in table 1.

Output	An output message, computed as a function of the module's input buffers and instance variables, is sent to an output line. A new specified state is then entered.
Side effect	One of the module's instance variables is set to a new value computed as a function of its input buffers and variables. A new specified state is then entered.
Conditional dispatch	A predicate on the module's instance variables and input buffers is computed and depending on the outcome one of two subsequent states is entered.
Event dispatch	A sequence of pairs of conditions and states to branch to are monitored until one of the events is true. The events are in combinations of arrivals of messages on input lines and the expiration of time delays.[1]

Table 1. Specification of a state as one of four types.

---

[1]The exact semantics are as follows: After an event dispatch is executed all input lines are monitored for message arrivals. When the next event dispatch is executed it has access to latches which indicate whether new messages have arrived on each input line. Each condition is evaluated in turn. If it is true then the dispatch to the new state happens. Each condition is an and/or expression on the input line latches. In addition, condition expressions can include delay terms which become true a specified amount of time after the beginning of the execution of the event dispatch. An event dispatch waits until one of its condition expressions is true.

An example of a module defined in our specification language is the
avoid module in figure 4.

```
(defmodule avoid 1
 :inputs (force heading)
 :outputs (command)
 :instance-vars (resultforce)
 :states
  ((nil (event-dispatch (and force heading) plan))
   (plan (setf resultforce (select-direction force heading))
         go)
   (go (conditional-dispatch (significant-force-p
                                resultforce 1.0)
                             start
                             nil))
   (start (output command (follow-force resultforce))
          nil)))
```

Figure 4. Avoid module in Lisp.

Here, `select-direction`, `significant-force-p`, and `follow-force`
are all lisp functions, while `setf` is the modern lisp assignment special form.

The force input line inputs a force with magnitude and direction found
by treating each point found by the sonars as the site of a repulsive force
decaying as the square of distance. Function `select-direction` takes this
and combines it with the input on the heading line considered as a motive
force. It selects the instantaneous direction of travel by summing the forces
acting on the robot. (This simple technique computes the tangent to the
minimum energy path computed by Khatib [1983].)

Function `significant-force-p` checks whether the resulting force is
above some threshold—in this case it determines whether the resulting
motion would take less than a second. The dispatch logic then ignores
such motions.

Function `follow-force` converts the desired direction and force magnitude into motor velocity commands.

This particular module is part of the level *1* (as indicated by the argument "1" following the name of the module) control system described below. It essentially does local navigation, making sure obstacles are avoided
by diverting a desired heading away from obstacles. It does not deliver the
robot to a desired location—that is the task of level *2* competence.

Communication

Figure 5 shows the best way to think about these finite state modules for
the purposes of communications. They have some input lines and some

output lines. An output line from one module is connected to input lines of one or more other modules. One can think of these lines as wires, each with a source and a destination. Additionally outputs may be inhibited, and inputs may be suppressed.

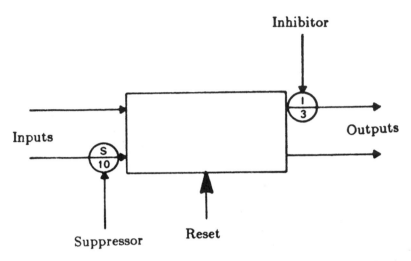

Figure 5. A module has input and output lines. Input signals can be suppressed and replaced with the suppressing signal. Output signals can be inhibited. A module can also be reset to state NIL.

An extra wire can terminate (that is, have its destination) at an output site of a module. If *any* signal travels along this wire it *inhibits* any output message from the module along that line for some pre-determined time. Any messages sent by the module to that output during that time period are lost.

Similarly an extra wire can terminate at an input site of a module. Its action is very similar to that of inhibition, but additionally, the signal on this wire, besides inhibiting signals along the usual path, actually gets fed through as the input to the module. Thus, it *suppresses* the usual input and provides a replacement. If more than one suppressing wire is present they are essentially 'or'-ed together. For both suppression and inhibition we write the time constants inside the circle.

In our specification language we write wires as a source (that is, an output line) followed by a number of destinations (that is, input lines). For instance the connection to the force input of the avoid module defined above might be the wire defined as:

(defwire 1 (feelforce force) (avoid force))

This links the force output of the `feelforce` module to the input of the `avoid` module in the level one control system.

Suppression and inhibition can also be described with a small extension to the syntax above. Below we see the suppression of the command input of the `turn` module, a level *0* module by a signal from the level *1* module `avoid`.

(defwire 1 (avoid command) ((suppress (turn command) 20.0)))

In a similar manner a signal can be connected to the reset input of a module.

A Robot Control System Instance

We have implemented a mobile robot control system to achieve levels *0* and *1* competence as defined above, and have implemented a version of level *2* which brings it to a stage which exercises the fundamental subsumption idea effectively.

Zeroth level

The lowest layer of control makes sure that the robot does not come into contact with other objects. It thus achieves level *0* competence (see figure 6). If something approaches the robot it will move away. If in the course of moving itself it is about to collide with an object, it will halt. Together these two tactics are sufficient for the robot to flee from moving obstacles, perhaps requiring many motions, without colliding with stationary obstacles. The combination of these tactics allows the robot to operate with very coarsely calibrated sonars and with a wide range of repulsive force functions. The robot is not invincible of course, and a sufficiently fast moving object, or a very cluttered environment, might result in a collision. Over the course of a number of hours of autonomous operation, our physical robot has not collided with either a moving or fixed obstacle (see the next section). The moving obstacles have, however, been careful to move slowly.

- The `turn` and `forward` modules communicate with the actual robot. They have extra communication mechanisms, allowing them to send and receive commands to and from the physical robot directly. The `turn` module receives a heading specifying an inplace turn angle followed by a forward motion of a specified magnitude. It commands the robot to turn (and at the same time sends a busy message on an additional output channel illustrate in figure 8) and on completion passes on the heading to the `forward` module (and also reports the shaft encoder readings on another output line shown in figure 8). It then goes into a wait state ignoring all incoming messages. The `forward` module commands the robot to move forward, but halts if it receives a

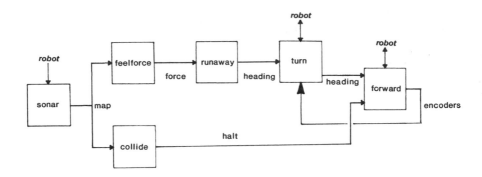

Figure 6. The level *0* control system.

message on its halt input line during the motion. As soon as the robot is idle it sends out the shaft encoder readings—the message acts as a reset for the **turn** module, which is then once again ready to accept a new motion command. Note that any heading commands sent to the **turn** module during transit are lost.

- The **sonar** module takes a vector of sonar readings, filters them for invalid readings, and effectively produces a robot centered map of obstacles in polar coordinates.

- The **collide** module monitors the sonar map and if it detects objects dead ahead it sends a signal on the halt line to the **motor** module. The **collide** module does not know or care whether the robot is moving. Halt messages sent while the robot is stationary are essentially lost.

- The **feelforce** module sums the results of considering each detected object as a repulsive force, generating a single resultant force.

- The **runaway** module monitors the 'force' produced by the sonar detected obstacles and sends commands to the **turn** module if it ever becomes significant.

Figure 6 gives a complete description of how the modules are connected together.

First level

The first layer of control, when combined with the zeroth level, gives the robot the ability to wander around aimlessly without hitting obstacles. This was defined earlier as level *1* competence. This control level relies to a large degree on the zeroth level's aversion to hitting obstacles. In addition it uses a simple heuristic to plan ahead a little, in order to avoid potential collisions which would need to be handled by the zeroth level.

- The **wander** module generates a new heading for the robot every ten seconds or so.

- The **avoid** module, described in more detail earlier, takes the result of the force computation from the zeroth level, and combines it with the desired heading to produce a modified heading, which usually points in roughly the right direction, but is perturbed to avoid any obvious obstacles. This computation implicitly subsumes the computations of the **runaway** module, in the case that there is also a heading to consider. In fact the output of the **avoid** module suppresses the output from the **runaway** module as it enters the **motor** module.

Figure 7 gives a complete description of how the modules are connected together. Note that it is simply figure 6 with some more modules and wires added.

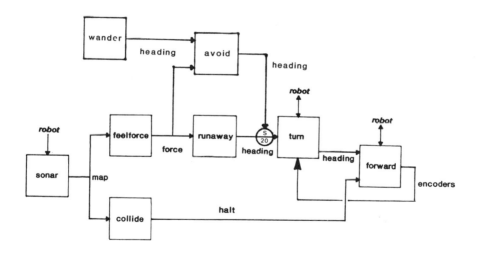

Figure 7. The level *0* control system augmented with the level *1* system.

Second level

Level 2 is meant to add an exploratory mode of behavior to the robot, using visual observations to select interesting places to visit. A vision module finds corridors of free space. Additional modules provide a means of position servoing the robot to along the corridor despite the presence

of local obstacles on its path (as detected with the sonar sensing system).
The wiring diagram is shown in figure 8. Note that it is simply figure 7
with some more modules and wires added.

- The **status** module monitors the **turn** and **forward** modules. It maintains one status output which sends either *hi* or *lo* messages to indicate
  whether the robot is busy. In addition, at the completion of every turn
  and roll forward combination it sends out a combined set of shaft encoder readings.

- The **whenlook** module monitors the busy line from the **status** module,
  and whenever the robot has been sitting idle for a few seconds it decides
  its time to look for a corridor to traverse. It inhibits wandering so it
  can take some pictures and process them without wandering away from
  its current location, and resets the **pathplan** and **integrate** modules–
  this latter action ensures that it will know how far it has moved from
  its observation point should any **runaway** impulses perturb it.

- The **look** module initiates the vision processing, and waits for a candidate freeway. It filters out poor candidates and passes any acceptable
  one to the **pathplan** module.

- The **stereo** module is supposed to use stereo television images [Grim-
  son 1985], obtained by the robot, to find a corridor of free space. At
  the time of writing, a final version of this module had not been implemented. Instead, both in simulation and on the physical robot, we
  have replaced it with a sonar-base corridor finder.

- The **integrate** module accumulates reports of motions from the **status** module and always sends its most recent result out on its integral
  line. It gets restarted by application of a signal to its reset input.

- The **pathplan** module takes a goal specification (in terms of an angle
  to turn, and a distance to travel) and attempts to reach that goal.
  To do this it sends headings to the **avoid** module, which may perturb
  them to avoid local obstacles, and monitors its integral input which
  is an integration of actual motions. The messages sent to the **avoid**
  module suppress random wanderings of the robot, so long as the higher
  level planner remains active. When the position of the robot is close
  to the desired position (the robot is unaware of control errors due to
  wheel slippage etc., so this is a dead reckoning decision) it terminates.

The current wiring of the second level of control is shown in figure 8, augmenting the two lower level control systems. The zeroth and first layers
still play an active role during normal operation of the second layer.

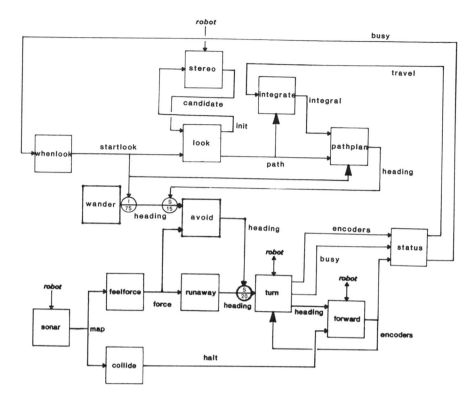

Figure 8. The level *0* and level *1* control systems augmented with the level *2* system.

Performance

The control system described here has been used extensively to control both a simulated robot and an actual physical robot wandering around a cluttered laboratory and a machine room.

A simulated robot

The simulation tries to simulate all the errors and uncertainties that exist in the world of the real robot. When commanded to turn through angle α and travel distance d the simulated robot actually turns through angle $\alpha + \delta\alpha$ and travels distance $d + \delta d$. Its sonars can bounce off walls multiple times, and even when they do return they have a noise component in the readings modeling thermal and humidity effects. We feel it is important to have such a realistic simulation. Anything less leads to incorrect control algorithms.

The simulator runs off a clock and runs at the same rate as the actual robot. It actually runs on the same processor that is simulating the subsumption architecture. Nevertheless, together they are able to perform a realtime simulation of the robot and its control and also drive graphics displays of robot state and module performance monitors. Figure 9 shows the robot (which itself is not drawn) receiving sonar reflections at some of its 12 sensors. Other beams did not return within the time allocated for data collection. The beams are reflected by various walls. There is a small bar in front of the robot perpendicular to the direction the robot is pointing.

Figure 10 shows an example world in two dimensional projection. The simulated robot with a first level control system connected was allowed to

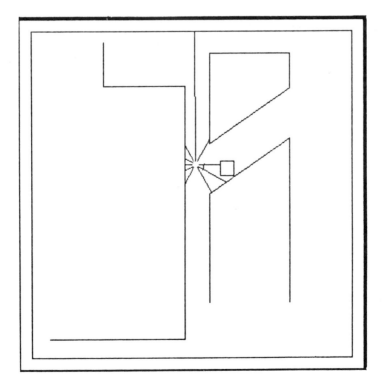

Figure 9. The simulated robot receives 12 sonar readings. Some sonar beams glance off walls and do not return within a certain time.

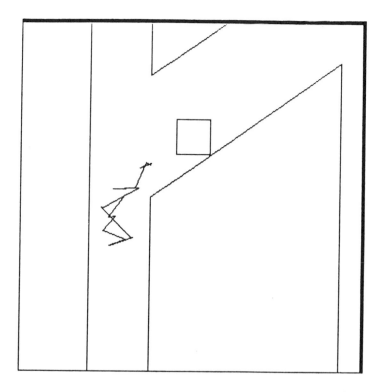

Figure 10. Under levels *0* and *1* control the robot wanders around aimlessly. It does not hit obstacles.

wander from an initial position. The squiggly line traces out its path. Note that it was wandering aimlessly and that it hit no obstacles.

Figure 11 shows two examples of the same scene and the motion of the robot with the second level control system connected. In both cases the `stereo` module was supplanted with a situation specific module which gave out two precise corridor descriptions. While achieving the goals of following these corridors the lower level wandering behavior was suppressed. However, the obstacle avoiding behavior of the lower levels continued to function—in both cases the robot avoided the square obstacle. The goals were not reached exactly. The simulator models a uniformly distributed error of ±5% in both turn and forward motion. As soon as the goals had been achieved satisfactorily the robot reverted to its wandering behavior.

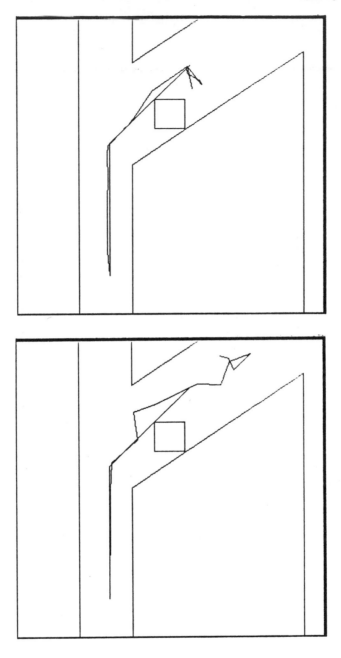

Figure 11. With level *2* control the robot tries to achieve commanded goals. The nominal goals are the two straight lines. After reaching the second goal, because there are no new goals forthcoming, the robot reverts to aimless level *1* behavior.

A physical robot

We have constructed the mobile robot shown in figure 12. It is about 17 inches in diameter and about 30 inches from the ground to the top platform. Most of the processing occurs offboard on a Lisp machine.

Figure 12. The mobile robot, ALLEN.

The drive mechanism was purchased from Real World Interface of Sudbury, Massachusetts. Three parallel drive wheels are steered together. The two motors are servoed by a single microprocessor. The robot body is attached to the steering mechanism and always points in the same direction as the wheels. It can turn in place (actually it inscribes a circle about one cm in diameter).

Currently installed sensors are a ring of twelve Polaroid sonar time-of flight range sensors and two Sony CCD cameras. The sonars are arranged symmetrically around the rotating body of the robot. The cameras are on a tilt head (pan is provided by the steering motors). We plan to install feelers which can sense objects at ground level about six inches from the base extremities.

A central cardcage contains the main onboard processor, an Intel 8031. It communicates with offboard processors via a 12 Kbit/sec duplex radio link. The radios are modified Motorola digital voice encryption units. Error correction cuts the effective bit rate to less than half the nominal rating. The 8031 passes commands down to the motor controller processor and returns encoder readings. It controls the sonars and the tilt head, and switches the cameras through a single channel video transmitter mounted on top of the robot. The latter transmits a standard television signal to a Lisp machine equipped with a demodulator and frame grabber.

The robot has spent many tens of hours wandering around a laboratory and a machine room.

Under level *0* control the robot finds a large empty space and then sits there contented until a moving obstacle approaches. Two people together can successfully herd the robot just about anywhere—through doors or between rows of disk drives, for example.

When level *1* control is added the robot is no longer content to sit in an open space. After a few seconds it heads off in a random direction. Our uncalibrated sonars and obstacle repulsion functions make it overshoot a little to locations where the runaway module reacts. It would be interesting to make this the basis of adaptation of certain parameters.

Under level *2* a sonar-based corridor finder usually finds the most distant point in the room. The robot heads off in that direction. People walking in front of the robot cause it to detour, but still get to the initially desired goal even when it involves squeezing between closely spaced obstacles. If the sonars are in error and a goal is selected beyond a wall, say, the robot usually ends up in a position where the attractive force of the goal is within a threshold, used by avoid, of the repulsive forces of the wall. At this point avoid does not issue any heading, as it would for some trivial motion of the robot. The robot sits still defeated by the obstacle. However, the whenlook module notices that the robot is idle and initiates a new scan for another corridor of free space to follow.

Implementation issues

While we have been able to simulate sufficient processors on a single Lisp Machine up until now, that capability will soon pass when we bring on line our vision work (the algorithms have been debugged as traditional serial algorithms but we plan on re-implementing them within the subsumption architecture). Building the architecture in custom chips is a long term goal.

One of the motivations for developing the layered control system was extensibility of processing power. The fact that it is decomposed into asynchronous processors with low bandwidth communication and no shared memory should certainly assist in achieving that goal. New processors can simply be added to the network by connecting their inputs and outputs at appropriate places—there are no bandwidth or synchronization considerations in such connections.

The finite state processors need not be large. Sixteen states is more than sufficient for all the modules we have written so far. (Actually eight states are sufficient under the model of the processors we have presented here and used in our simulations. However we have refined the design somewhat towards gate level implementation where we use simpler more numerous states.) Many such processors could be easily packed on a single chip.

The Lisp programs that are called by the finite state machines are all rather simple. We believe it is possible to implement each of them with a simple network of comparators, selectors, polar coordinate vector adders, and monotonic function generators. The silicon area overhead required for each module would probably not be larger than that required for the finite state machine itself.

Conclusion

The key ideas in this chapter are:

- The mobile robot control problem can be decomposed in terms of behaviors rather than in terms of functional modules.

- It provides a way to incrementally build and test a complex mobile robot control system.

- Useful parallel computation can be performed on a low bandwidth loosely coupled network of asynchronous simple processors. The topology of that network is relatively fixed.

- There is no need for a central control module of a mobile robot. The control system can be viewed as a system of agents each busy with their own solipsist world.

Besides leading to a different implementation strategy it is also interesting to note the way the decomposition affected the capabilities of the robot control system we have built. In particular our control system deals with moving objects in the environment at the very lowest level, and has a specific (**runaway**) module for that purpose. Traditionally, mobile robot projects have delayed handling moving objects in the environment beyond the scientific life of the project.

References

Brooks, Rodney, A. [1984], "Aspects of Mobile Robot Visual Map Making," in *Robotics Research 2*, edited by Hanafusa and Inoue, MIT Press, pp. 369–375.

Brooks, Rodney, A. [1985], "Visual Map Making for a Mobile Robot," *IEEE Conference on Robotics and Automation*, St Louis, pp. 824–829.

Crowley, James L. [1985], "Navigation for an Intelligent Mobile Robot," *IEEE Journal of Robotics and Automation*, RA-1, pp. 31–41.

Elfes, Alberto, and Sarosh N. Talukdar [1983], "A Distributed Control System for the CMU Rover," *Proceedings IJCAI, Karlsruhe, West Germany*, pp. 830–833.

Flynn, Anita [1985], "Redundant Sensors for Mobile Robot Navigation," *MS Thesis*, Department of Electrical Engineering and Computer Science, Massachusetts Institute of Technology.

Giralt, Georges, Raja Chatila, and Marc Vaisset [1983], "An Integrated Navigation and Motion Control System for Autonomous Multisensory Mobile Robots," in *Robotics Research 1*, edited by Brady and Paul, MIT Press, pp. 191–214.

Grimson, W. Eric L. [1985], "Computational Experiments with a Feature Based Stereo Algorithm," *IEEE Transactions on Pattern Analysis and Machine Intelligence*, PAMI-7, pp. 17–34.

Kanayama, Yutaka [1983], "Concurrent Programming of Intelligent Robots," *Proceedings IJCAI*, Karlsruhe, West Germany, pp. 834–838.

Khatib, Oussama [1983], "Dynamic Control of Manipulators in Operational Space," *Sixth IFTOMM Congress on Theory of Machines and Mechanisms*, New Delhi.

Kreithen, Melvin L. [1983], "Orientational Strategies in Birds: A Tribute to W. T. Keeton," in *Behavioral Energetics: The Cost of Survival in Vertebrates*, Ohio State University Press, pp. 3–28.

Moravec, Hans P. [1983], "The Stanford Cart and the CMU Rover," *Proceedings of the IEEE*, vol. 71, pp. 872–884.

Tomás Lozano-Pérez, Eric Grimson, Jon Connell, and Anita Flynn have all provided helpful comments on earlier drafts of this chapter.

Support for the work in this chapter was provided in part by an IBM Faculty Development Award, in part by a grant from the Systems Development Foundation, in part by an equipment grant from Motorola, and in part by the Advanced Research Projects Agency under Office of Naval Research contracts N00014-80-C-0505 and N00014-82-K-0334.

Nilsson, Nils J. [1984], "Shakey the Robot," *SRI AI Center Technical Note 323*.

Simon, Herbert A. [1969], *Sciences of the Artificial*, MIT Press, Cambridge, MA.

Tsuji, Saburo [1985], "Monitoring of a Building Environment by a Mobile Robot," in *Robotics Research 2*, edited by Hanafusa and Inoue MIT Press, pp. 349–356.

25

This chapter reinforces the ideas introduced in the previous chapter by describing what it takes to build a six-legged, beetlelike robot, about the size of a shoe box, that can walk across your desk, from one end to the other, navigating somehow around or over your telephone, your books, and maybe your lunch.

The six-legged, beetlelike robot is a functioning, physical reality, even though it has to operate in a world that contains more detail than we can hope to get into an internal model. To cope with such worlds, Brooks builds robots in which there is no symbolic description. Instead, the world serves as its own model in that its condition is determined via direct sensing, rather than by reference to something internal. Competence emerges from simple mechanisms interacting with each other and with the world, rather than from a fancy model and a sophisticated reasoning system.

Thus Brooks' six-legged, beetlelike robot may remind you of Simon's famous metaphor of the wandering ant which he introduced almost 25 years ago. Simon's ant follows a sophisticated-looking path, but not because the ant is complicated. Instead, the ant is interacting with a complicated world in which the pebbles and rocks explain the apparent sophistication, not the ant's brain.

A Robot that Walks: Emergent Behaviors from a Carefully Evolved Network

Rodney A. Brooks

In earlier work [Brooks 1986; Brooks & Connell 1986] we have demon-strated complex control systems for mobile robots built from completely distributed networks of augmented finite state machines. In this chapter we demonstrate that these techniques can be used to incrementally build complex systems integrating relatively large numbers of sensory inputs and large numbers of actuator outputs. Each step in the construction is purely incremental. Nevertheless, along the way viable control systems are left at each step, before the next little piece of network is added. Additionally we demonstrate how complex behaviors, such as walking, can emerge from a network of rather simple reflexes with little central control. This con-tradicts hypotheses made to the contrary in studies of insect walking (for example, see Bässler [1983] p. 112).

The subsumption architecture

The subsumption architecture provides an incremental method for building robot control systems linking perception to action [Brooks 1986]. A prop-erly designed network of finite state machines, augmented with internal timers, provides a robot with a repertoire of behaviors. The architecture provides mechanisms to augment such networks in a purely incremental way to improve the robot's performance on tasks and to increase the range of tasks it can perform. At an architectural level, the robot's control system is expressed as a series of layers, each specifying a behavior pattern for the robot, and each implemented as a network of message-passing augmented

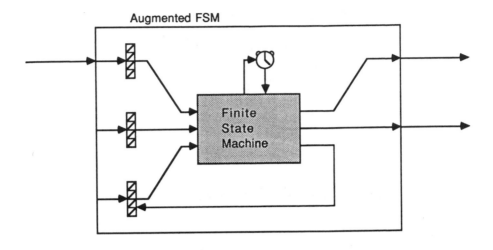

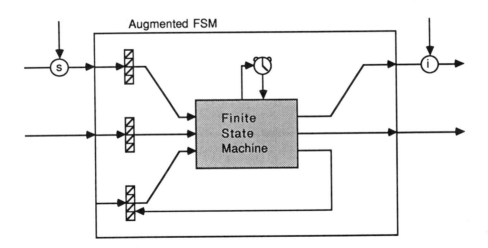

Figure 1. An augmented finite state machine consists of registers, alarm clocks, a combinational network, and a regular finite state machine. Input messages are delivered to registers, and messages can be generated on output wires. AFSMs are wired together in networks of message passing wires. As new wires are added to a network, they can be connected to existing registers, they can inhibit outputs and they can suppress inputs.

finite state machines. The network can be thought of as an explicit wiring diagram connecting outputs of some machines to inputs of others with wires that can transmit messages. In the implementation of the architecture on the walking robot the messages are limited to 8 bits.

Each augmented finite state machine (AFSM), see figure 1, has a set of registers and a set of timers, or alarm clocks, connected to a conventional finite state machine which can control a combinational network fed by the registers. Registers can be written by attaching input wires to them and sending messages from other machines. The messages get written into them replacing any existing contents. The arrival of a message, or the expiration of a timer, can trigger a change of state in the interior finite state machine. Finite state machine states can either wait on some event, conditionally dispatch to one of two other states based on some combinational predicate on the registers, or compute a combinational function of the registers directing the result either back to one of the registers or to an output of the augmented finite state machine. Some AFSMs connect directly to robot hardware. Sensors deposit their values to certain registers, and certain outputs direct commands to actuators.

A series of layers of such machines can be augmented by adding new machines and connecting them into the existing network in the ways shown in figure 1. New inputs can be connected to existing registers, which might previously have contained a constant. New machines can inhibit existing outputs or suppress existing inputs, by being attached as side-taps to existing wires (see figure 1, circled 'i'). When a message arrives on an inhibitory side-tap no messages can travel along the existing wire for some short time period. To maintain inhibition there must be a continuous flow of messages along the new wire. (In previous versions of the subsumption architecture [Brooks 1986] explicit, long, time periods had to be specified for inhibition or suppression with single shot messages. Recent work has suggested this better approach [Connell 1988]). When a message arrives on a suppressing side-tap (see figure 1, circled 's'), again no messages are allowed to flow from the original source for some small time period, but now the suppressing message is gated through and it masquerades as having come from the original source. Again, a continuous supply of suppressing messages is required to maintain control of a side-tapped wire. One last mechanism for merging two wires is called defaulting (indicated in wiring diagrams by a circled 'd'). This is just like the suppression case, except that the original wire, rather than the new side-tapping wire, is able to wrest control of messages sent to the destination.

All clocks in a subsumption system have approximately the same tick period (0.04 seconds on the walking robot), but neither they nor messages are synchronous. The fastest possible rate of sending messages along a wire is one per clock tick. The time periods used for both inhibition and

Figure 2. The six legged robot is about 35 cm long, has a leg span of 25 cm, and weighs approximately 1 kg. Each leg is rigid and is attached at a shoulder joint with two degrees of rotational freedom, driven by two orthogonally mounted model airplane position controllable servo motors. An error signal has been tapped from the internal servo circuitry to provide crude force measurement (5 bits, including sign) on each axis, when the leg is not in motion around that axis. Other sensors are two front whiskers, two four bit inclinometers (pitch and roll), and six forward looking passive pyroelectric infrared sensors. The sensors have approximately 6 degrees angular resolution and are arranged over a 45 degree span. There are four onboard 8 bit microprocessors linked by a 62.5 Kbaud token ring. The total memory usage of the robot is about 1 Kbytes of RAM and 10 Kbytes of EPROM. Three silver-zinc batteries fit between the legs to make the robot totally self contained.

suppression are two clock ticks. Thus, a side-tapping wire with messages being sent at the maximum rate can maintain control of its host wire.

The networks and emergent behaviors

The six legged robot is shown in figure 2. We refer to the motors on each leg as an α motor (for *advance*) which swings the leg back and forth, and a β motor (for *balance*) which lifts the leg up and down.

Figure 3 shows a network of 57 augmented finite state machines which was built incrementally and can be run incrementally by selectively deactivating later AFSMs. The AFSMs without bands on top are repeated six times, once for each leg. The AFSMs with solid bands are unique and comprise the only central control in making the robot walk, steer, and follow targets. The AFSMs with striped bands are duplicated twice each and are specific to particular legs.

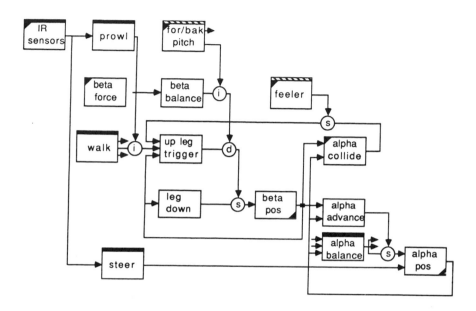

Figure 3. The final network consists of 57 augmented finite state machines. The AFSMs without bands on top are repeated six times, once for each leg. The AFSMs with solid bands are unique and comprise the only central control in making the robot walk, steer, and follow targets. The AFSMs with striped bands are duplicated twice each and are specific to particular legs. The AFSMs with a filled triangle in their bottom right corner control actuators. Those with a filled triangle in their upper left corner receive inputs from sensors.

The complete network can be built incrementally by adding AFSMs to an existing network producing a number of viable robot control systems itemized below. All additions are strictly additive with no need to change any existing structure. Figure 4 shows a partially constructed version of the network.

Standup. The simplest level of competence for the robot is achieved with just two AFSMs per leg, *alpha pos* and *beta pos*. These two machines use a register to hold a set position for the α and β motors respectively, and ensure that the motors are sent those positions. The initial values for the registers are such that on power up the robot assumes a stance

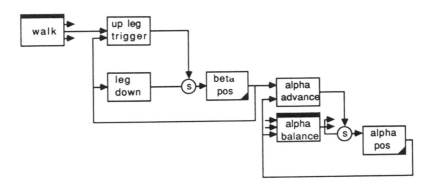

Figure 4. A strict subset of the full network enables the robot to walk without any feedback. It pitches and rolls significantly as it walks over rough terrain. This version of the network contains 32 AFSMs. Thirty of these comprise six identical copies, one for each leg, of a network of five AFSMs which are purely local in their interactions with a leg. The last two machines provide all the global coordination necessary to make the machine walk; one tries to drive the sum of leg swing angles (α angles) to zero, and the other sequences lifting of individual legs.

position. The AFSMs also provide an output that reports the most recent commanded position for their motor.

Simple walk. A number of simple increments to this network result in one which lets the robot walk. First, a *leg down* machine for each leg is added which notices whenever the leg is not in the down position and writes the appropriate *beta pos* register in order to set the leg down. Then, a single *alpha balance* machine is added which monitors the α position, or forward swing of all six legs, treating straight out as zero, forward as positive and backward as negative. It sums these six values and sends out a single identical message to all six *alpha pos* machines, which, depending on the sign of the sum is either null, or an increment or decrement to the current α position of each leg. The *alpha balance* machine samples the leg positions at a relatively high rate. Thus if one leg happens to move forward for some reason, all legs will receive a series of messages to move backward slightly.

Next, the *alpha advance* AFSM is added for each leg. Whenever it notices that the leg is raised (by monitoring the output of the *beta pos* machine) it forces the leg forward by suppressing the signal coming from the global *alpha balance* machine. Thus, if a leg is raised for some reason it reflexively swings forward, and all other legs swing backward slightly to compensate (note that the forward swinging leg does not even receive the backward message due to the suppression of that signal). Now a fifth AFSM, *up leg trigger* is added for each leg which can issue a command to lift a leg by suppressing the commands from the *leg down* machine. It has one register which monitors the current β position of the leg. When it is down, and a trigger message is received in a second register, it ensures that the contents of an initially constant third register, are sent to the *beta pos* machine to lift the leg.

With this combination of local leg specific machines and a single machine trying to globally coordinate the sum of the α position of all legs, the robot can very nearly walk. If an *up leg trigger* machine receives a trigger message it lifts its associated leg, which triggers a reflex to swing it forward, and then the appropriate *leg down* machine will pull the leg down. At the same time all the other legs still on the ground (those not busy moving forward) will swing backwards, moving the robot forwards. The final piece of the puzzle is to add a single AFSM which sequences walking by sending trigger messages in some appropriate pattern to each of the six *up leg trigger* machines.

We have used two versions of this machine, both of which complete a gait cycle once every 2.4 seconds. One machine produces the well known alternating tripod [Klein *et al.* 1980] by sending simultaneous lift triggers to triples of legs every 1.2 seconds. The other produces the standard back to front ripple gait by sending a trigger message to a different leg every 0.4 seconds. Other gaits are possible by simple substitution of this machine. The machine walks with this network, but is insensitive to the terrain over which it is walking and tends to roll and pitch excessively as it walks over obstacles. The complete network for this simple type of walking is shown in figure 4.

Force balancing.   A simple way to compensate for rough terrain is to monitor the force on each leg as it is placed on the ground and back off if it rises beyond some threshold. The rationale is that if a leg is being placed down on an obstacle it will have to roll (or pitch) the body of the robot in order for the leg β angle to reach its preset value, increasing the load on the motor. For each leg a *beta force* machine is added which monitors the β motor forces, discarding high readings coming from servo errors during free space swinging, and a *beta balance* machine which sends out lift up messages whenever the force is too high. It includes a small deadband where it sends out zero move messages which trickle down through a defaulting switch on the *up leg trigger* to eventually suppress the *leg down* reflex. This is a form of active compliance which has a number of known problems on walking machines [Wilson 1980]. On a standard obstacle course (a single 5 centimeter high obstacle on a plane) this new machine significantly reduced the standard deviation, over a 12 second period, of the readings from onboard 4 bit pitch and roll inclinometers. Each inclinometer had a

35 degree range. The standard deviation of the pitch inclinometer fell from
3.592 to 2.325. The standard deviation of the roll inclinometer fell from
0.624 to 0.451 (see figure 5 for details).

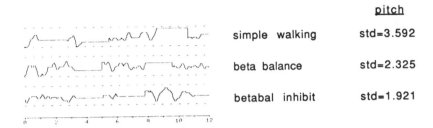

<u>pitch</u>

simple walking   std=3.592

beta balance   std=2.325

betabal inhibit   std=1.921

Figure 5. The robot was set walking across a plane with a single 5cm high
obstacle. The graphs above record the measured pitch during three trials each
for a duration of 12 seconds. The middle of the range of each graph corresponds
to a level body. The upper trace corresponds to simple walking with no force
feedback. The middle trace corresponds to walking with the *beta balance* machine
included. The lower trace corresponds to the walking machine with *beta balance*
inhibited in high pitch situations. The standard deviations for the three trials
are displayed at the right.

Leg lifting.   There is a tradeoff between how high each leg is lifted and
overall walking speed. But low leg lifts limit the height of obstacles which
can be easily scaled. An eighth AFSM for each leg compensates for this by
measuring the force on the forward swing (α) motor as it swings forward
and writing the height register in the *up leg trigger* at a higher value, setting
up for a higher lift of the leg on the next step cycle of that leg. The *up leg
trigger* resets this value after the next step.

Whiskers.   In order to anticipate obstacles better, rather than waiting
until the front legs are rammed against them, each of two whiskers is monitored by a *feeler* machine and the lift of the the left and right front legs is
appropriately increased for the next step cycle.

Pitch stabilization.   The simple force balancing strategy above is by no
means perfect. In particular, in high pitch situations the rear or front legs
(depending on the direction of pitch) are heavily loaded and so tend to be
lifted slightly causing the robot to sag and increase the pitch even more.
Therefore one *forward pitch* and one *backward pitch* AFSM are added to
monitor high pitch conditions on the pitch inclinometer, and to inhibit the
local *beta balance* machine output in the appropriate circumstances. The

pitch standard deviation over the 12 second test reduces to 1.921 with this improvement while the roll standard deviation stays around the same at 0.458 (again, see figure 5).

Prowling.   Two additional AFSMs can be added so that the robot only bothers to walk when there is something moving nearby. The *IR sensors* machine monitors an array of six forward looking pyro-electric infrared sensors and sends an activity message to the *prowl* machine when it detects motion. The *prowl* machine usually inhibits the leg lifting trigger messages from the *walk* machine, except for a little while after infrared activity is noticed. Thus the robot sits still until a person, say, walks by, and then it moves forward a little.

Steered prowling.   The single *steer* AFSM takes note of the predominant direction, if any, of the infrared activity and writes into a register in each *alpha pos* machine for legs on that side of the robot, specifying the rear swinging stop position of the leg. This gets reset on every stepping cycle of the leg, so the *steer* machine must constantly refresh it in order to reduce the leg's backswing and force the robot to turn in the direction of the activity. With this single additional machine the robot is able to follow moving objects such as a slow walking person.

Conclusion

This exercise has successfully demonstrated a number of things, at least in the robot domain. All these demonstrations depend on the manner in which the networks were built incrementally from augmented finite state machines.

- Robust walking behaviors can be produced by a distributed system with very limited central coordination. In particular, much of the sensory-motor integration which goes on can happen within local asynchronous units. This has relevance, in the form of an existence proof, to the debate on the central versus peripheral control of motion [Bizzi 1980] and, in particular, in the domain of insect walking [Bässler 1983].
- Higher level behaviors (such as following people) can be integrated into a system which controls lower level behaviors, such as leg lifting and force balancing, in a completely seamless way. There is no need to postulate qualitatively different sorts of structures for different levels of behaviors, and no need to postulate unique forms of network interconnected to integrate higher level behaviors.
- Coherent macro behaviors can arise from many independent micro behaviors. For instance, the robot following people works even though most of the effort is being done by independent circuits driving legs,

and these circuits are getting only very indirect pieces of information from the higher levels, and none of this communication refers to the task in hand.

- There is no need to postulate a central repository for sensor fusion to feed into. Conflict resolution tends to happen more at the motor command level, rather than the sensor or perception level.

As a last observation, there are a few straight-forward engineering improvements which could be made to the current robot to improve its performance markedly. The first is to add true position sensors to each motor that are accessible to the subsumption architecture. Currently it relies on a knowledge of most recently commanded positions of motors where (especially on rough terrain) this may not correspond well to the actual positions of motors. Second, true force sensing, using strain gauges, would give much more reliable force readings than the rather indirect method we use at the moment: to coarsely time the switching time of the motor current as determined by a built in analog position servo system on each motor.

References

Bässler, Ulrich [1983], "Neural Basis of Elementary Behavior in Stick Insects," Springer-Verlag.

Bizzi, Emilio [1980], "Central and Peripheral Mechanisms in Motor Control," *Tutorials in Motor Behavior*, edited by G. E. Stelmach and J. Requin, North-Holland.

Brooks, Rodney A. [1986], "A Robust Layered Control System for a Mobile Robot," *IEEE Journal of Robotics and Automation*, RA-2, pp. 14–23.

Brooks, Rodney A., and Jonathon H. Connell [1986], "Asynchronous Distributed Control System for A Mobile Robot," *Proceedings SPIE*, Cambridge, MA, pp. 77–84.

Connell, Jonathan H. [1988], "A Behavior-Based Arm Controller," Report AIM-1025, Artificial Intelligence Laboratory, Massachusetts Institute of Technology, Cambridge, MA.

Grinnell More did most of the mechanical design and fabrication of the robot. Colin Angle did much of the processor design and most of the electrical fabrication of the robot. Mike Ciholas, Jon Connell, Anita Flynn, Chris Foley, and Peter Ning provided valuable design and fabrication advice and help.

This chapter describes research done at the Artificial Intelligence Laboratory of the Massachusetts Institute of Technology. Support for the research is provided in part by the University Research Initiative under Office of Naval Research contract N00014–86–K–0685 and in part by the Advanced Research Projects Agency under Office of Naval Research contract N00014–85–K–0124.

Klein, Charles A. [1983], Karl W. Olson, and Dennis R. Pugh, "Use of Force and Attitude Sensors for Locomotion of a Legged Vehicle," *International Journal of Robotics Research*, vol. 2, no. 2, pp. 3–17.

Wilson, Donald M. [1980], "Insect Walking," *Annual Review of Entomology*, vol. II, 1966, reprinted in "The Organization of Action: A New Synthesis", C. R. Gallistel, Lawrence Erlbaum.

26

Today, industrial robots are programmed by telling them how to move, not by telling them what to do, because they cannot translate goals into actions. The reason is that taking things apart and putting them together requires a lot of spatial reasoning. Think about the last time you repaired your car or built a piece of furniture. Or if you are not a mechanic or a woodworker, think about when you played with blocks as a child. In all cases, you have to decide where to put your fingers to pick up things, how to avoid obstacles when you move things, and where your fingers have to be when you place things in their desired positions. Sometimes, there are awkward movements that require different grasp arrangements for pick up and put down.

The key difficulty in solving these pick-and-place problems is that all the decisions are interdependent, making the problem computationally difficult until you learn how to decompose it into nearly independent, computationally feasible subproblems. The design of the HANDEY system embodies one approach to that decomposition. In operation, HANDEY automatically translates what-to-do requests into grasp-and-move sequences even when there is no grasp that works both for pick and for place.

One key enabling idea exploited in the HANDEY system is that of the configuration-space transform, which is to spatial reasoning as the Fourier transform is to signal analysis. In configuration space, obstacles become highly distorted, but objects to be moved become points, which drastically simplifies path planning.

Task-Level Planning of Pick-and-Place Robot Motions

Tomás Lozano-Pérez   Emmanuel Mazer†

Joseph L. Jones   Patrick A. O'Donnell

A task-level robot system is one that can be instructed in terms of task-level goals, such as *"Grasp part A and place it inside box B."* This type of specification contrasts sharply with that required for existing industrial robot systems, which insist on a complete specification of each motion of the robot and not simply a description of a desired goal state for the task. An important characteristic of task-level specifications is that they are independent of the robot achieving the task, whereas a motion specification is wedded to a specific robot.

Task-level robot systems have long been a goal of robotics research. As early as 1961, Ernst's Ph.D. Thesis at MIT attempted to develop such a system. Since then a variety of task-level robot systems have been proposed and several of them have seen some level of implementation. For a survey of previous work in this area see Lozano-Pérez and Taylor [1988].

For the past three years, we[1] have been developing a task-level robot system named HANDEY [Lozano-Pérez *et al.* 1987]. The current system is by no means a complete task-level system; it is limited to *pick-and-place* operations, that is, picking up a part and placing it at a specified destination. The current implementation of HANDEY has successfully carried out dozens of pick-and-place operations involving a variety of parts in relatively complex environments. Figure 1 shows a sequence of intermediate steps of

---

†On leave from LIFIA, Grenoble, France.

[1]In addition to the authors, the following people have contributed to the development of HANDEY: Pierre Tournassoud of INRIA (France), Alain Lanusse of ETCA (France), and Eric Grimson of MIT.

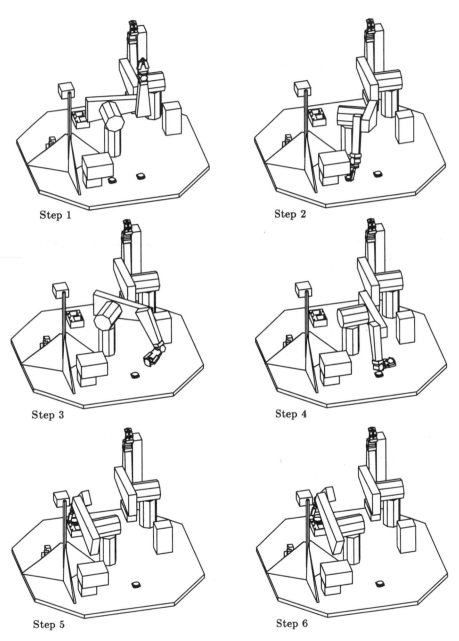

Figure 1. Steps 1–6 in a pick and place operation planned by HANDEY

a pick-and-place operation planned by HANDEY from a specification of the desired final position of the part and geometric and kinematic models of the robot and the environment. The steps illustrated in the figure are:

1   The initial position of the robot and the parts.

2   Grasping a part at a location chosen by the system to avoid collisions with nearby objects.

3   Placing the part on the table.

4   Regrasping the part at a new location compatible with the environment at the destination.

5   Placing the part at the specified destination.

6   Retreating from the destination.

The Pick-and-Place Problem

Consider the overall problem faced by a task-level robot system, given a mechanical assembly task and a single, sufficiently precise[2] robot. The overall assembly planning problem, of which pick-and-place is but a part, can be summarized as follows:

> Choose an order of assembly for the parts,
> Choose initial positions for all the parts,
> For each assembly step,
>> Choose a grasp on the part,
>> Plan a motion to grasp the part,
>> Plan a motion to the assembly location for the part,
>> Plan a motion to extract the gripper.

The pick-and-place problem we have mentioned earlier corresponds to the last four steps above.

Ideally, the assembly problem would reduce to a number of independent subproblems, roughly one per line in the characterization given above. Unfortunately, this is only true in extremely simple cases. In fact, the solutions to all these problems are tightly linked:

- The optimal initial placement of the parts depends on the order of assembly.

- The order of assembly depends on the feasibility of certain assembly steps, for example, whether a subassembly can be inserted into the

---

[2]In this chapter, we assume that the position of all the parts will be known to high accuracy and the robot's positioning accuracy is sufficient to carry out the assembly simply by moving the part to a fixed target position. If this assumption is not satisfied then assembly planning must include *fine-motion* planning, that is, the synthesis of motion strategies that can achieve a desired goal in the presence of sensing and control error. See, for example, Lozano-Pérez *et al.* [1984], Mason [1984], Whitney [1982], Erdmann [1986], Buckley [1987], and Donald [1987].

main assembly in one piece or whether it needs to be assembled in situ.

- The choice of a grasp on a part depends on the environment at the initial location, which depends on the initial placement of nearby parts. The grasp also depends on the placement of parts at the target, which depends on what previous assembly steps have been performed. The choice of grasp depends on the range of motions of the robot; surprisingly many potential grasps will simply not be reachable.

- The choice of a grasp (and ungrasp) motion will depend on the choice of a grasp and on the whole environment, especially near the grasp and destination.

- The choice of an assembly motion will depend on whether a grasp compatible with the assembly has been found, otherwise the part will have to be regrasped.

In short, all the subproblems of the assembly problem are interdependent. This also holds true for the subset of the assembly problem that we are considering, the pick-and-place problem.

One possible approach to the pick-and-place problem, given the interdependence of the decisions, is to treat it as a single motion planning problem with special constraints. In particular, once the object is grasped, the effective shape of the robot has changed and so the constraints on its motion have changed. The problem with this approach is that it runs into significant computational complexity problems. In particular, the additional degrees of freedom in the choice of a grasp add to the robot's motion freedoms. But, it is known that the computational complexity of motion planning problems is exponential in the number of degrees of freedom of the task.[3] Therefore, any practical solution to the pick-and-place problem and the assembly problem must involve decoupling and other forms of dimensionality reduction.

Configuration Space

Robot manipulators are articulated devices made up of a series of rigid *links* connected by one degree of freedom *joints*. Joint motions are either rotational or translational. The positions of all parts of a rigid robot are completely specified by the values of the joint parameters, known collectively as the *joint angles*. Many robots support an alternative specification for desired position, namely, the position and orientation of the robot gripper. But, gripper position is not a unique specification of the complete

---

[3]Motion planning has been shown to be PSPACE-hard [Reif 1987], therefore we expect all complete algorithms for motion planning to have worst-case time-complexity that is exponential in the degrees of freedom but polynomial in the size of the environment.

robot position; there may be many sets of joint angles that place the gripper in the same location.

Any set of parameters that uniquely specify the position of every part of a system, for example, a robot, is called a *configuration* and the space defined by those parameters is the *configuration space, or C-space.* Most algorithmic approaches to motion planning require a characterization of those configurations of the robot that cause collisions (or the complement of that set). We call the collection of configurations that produce collisions the *C-space obstacles* [Lozano-Pérez 1987].

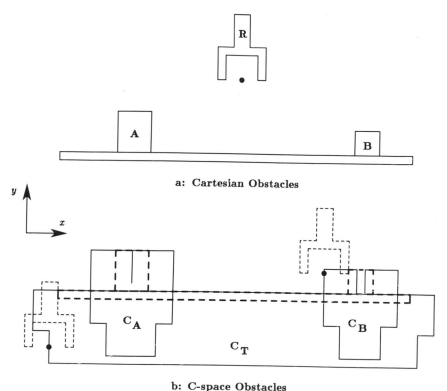

a: Cartesian Obstacles

b: C-space Obstacles

Figure 2. (a) A scene with three obstacles, A, B, and the table. The disembodied robot hand R is capable only of displacements along the x and y axes. (b) The C-space for this hand is the x, y plane. The C-space obstacles corresponding to A, C_A, to B, C_B, and the table, C_T are seen on the bottom figure. The gripper is shown (in a fine dashed line) at two points of the C-space obstacle boundary.

Consider the following very simple case by way of illustration (see figure 2a). In this example, we are limited to a disembodied robot hand capable only of displacements along the x and y axes; we assume that the finger opening remains fixed to simplify the C-space. The C-space for this hand is the

x, y plane. The C-space obstacles corresponding to the objects A, B, and the table in figure 2a are the objects bounded by dark lines in figure 2b. Every x, y point inside one of the C-space obstacles represents and x, y position of R's reference point (the dark circle in figure 2a) that causes a collision. C_A are the configurations that cause a collision between R and A; C_B are the configurations that cause a collision between R and B; C_T are the configurations that cause a collision between R and the table.

Consider a simple robot with two rotational joints, whose joint angles are θ_1 and θ_2, figure 3a. A point in the C-space specifies both of these joint angles and, therefore, the position of every part of the robot. The set of configurations for which the robot is in a collision with an obstacle define C-space obstacles. In this sense, the C-space for the robot is analogous to that of the disembodied hand we saw above, but the C-space obstacles of the robot are significantly more complex than the ones for the hand [Lozano-Pérez 1987], figure 3b. Note that in figure 3b the C-space parameters of the robot are angles. Therefore, the line at the top of the diagram, $\theta_2 = 2\pi$, is the same line as the bottom of the diagram, $\theta_2 = 0$, and the same can be said for the left and right lines, $\theta_1 = 2\pi = 0$. We can wrap the diagram into a tube so that the top and bottom lines meet and then we can wrap that tube into a doughnut (torus) to make the left and right ends meet. Thus, C-space for the two-link robot is really the surface of a torus.

Finding a collision-free path between two specified configurations requires finding some path in the C-space that connects the two specified configurations and does not penetrate into any of the C-space obstacles. Doing this requires characterizing the space outside of all of the C-space obstacles, possibly by a decomposition into disjoint cells. A sample path between the two arm configurations shown in figure 3a is shown in the C-space of figure 3b.

Approximate Approaches to the Pick-and-Place Problem

The crucial step in solving the pick-and-place problem is choosing how to grasp the part. Once this choice has been made, the problem boils down to separate motion planning problems in the C-space of the robot. But, we have seen that the choice of a grasp cannot be made simply by looking at the environment near the part, one has to consider the effect of the grasp on the possibility of finding a path to the goal. Therefore, any attempt at decoupling must consider constraints imposed on the choice of grasp by the environment at the goal as well as that at the origin.

One necessary condition that the choice of grasp point must satisfy is that there be no collisions of the robot with any object at either the initial

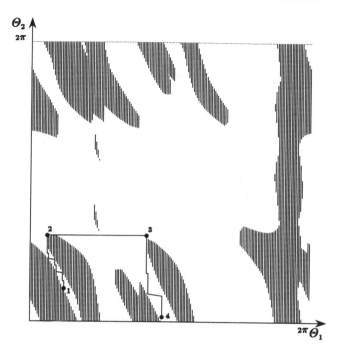

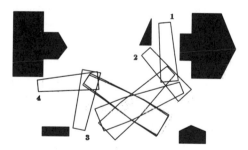

Figure 3. The dark regions (lower figure) are the C-space obstacles for the two-link planar robot and obstacles (top figure). The joint angles are θ_1, θ_2 and these are the labels on the axes of the C-space. A safe path in this C-space is shown, together with four configurations of the arm along the path.

or final position of the part. There are at least two ways of guaranteeing this:

1   Characterize the reachable grasps at the initial grasp position. Then, characterize the grasps that cause no collisions at the destination. The grasps in the intersection of these two grasp sets are collision-free at both positions and reachable at the initial position.

2   Compute the transformation T that maps the grasped part from its

initial to its final location. Apply the inverse transformation T^{-1} to a copy of the obstacles near the final position of the part. Add these transformed obstacles to the obstacles near the initial position of the part. Find a path to any legal grasp that avoids both sets of obstacles (see figures 4 and 6).

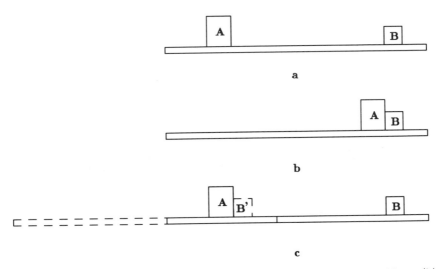

Figure 4. (a) The initial position of A in a simple pick and place problem. (b) The final position of A. (c) The pick and place example showing the obstacles for the final position of part A (shown dashed) superimposed on the obstacles for the initial position (shown solid).

These two methods are not equivalent; the second method will, in general, find fewer grasps than the first method will. In finding a path that avoids both sets of obstacles, we have constrained the problem beyond what is strictly necessary to guarantee finding a grasp that is reachable at the initial position and safe at the final one. Recall that the path we are planning is the initial grasp approach and not the path to the final destination. It is not necessary, therefore, that the *complete* approach path avoid the obstacles derived from the destination, only that the *chosen grasp*, that is, the final position in the approach path, avoid the obstacles.

We have chosen the second method for HANDEY because it does not require characterizing sets of grasps, whether simply collision-free or reachable. Computing these sets can be a burdensome task in the general case. The second method requires only the ability to find a path from a known initial position to some point within a constrained set (legal grasps).

In many cases, there is no grasp with an approach path that avoids both obstacles from the origin and destination. In this case, HANDEY plans a sequence of regrasping steps (placing the object on the table and then regrasping it) that results in a grasp compatible with the target position [Tournassoud *et al.* 1987]. Once again, only the condition that the grasp be reachable without causing a collision at the origin or with the objects derived from the destination is used. In fact, HANDEY does not constrain the grasp so as to guarantee that the destination is reachable once the object is grasped. It chooses the grasp and then attempts to plan a path to the destination with the object in the hand.

Here is a more complete outline of the solution of the pick-and-place problem in HANDEY:

1   Enumerate the possible distinct type of grasps. HANDEY operates in the domain of polyhedral models and robots with parallel jaw grippers, therefore the distinct grasps are limited to pairs of part features (either faces, edges, or vertices) that can be in simultaneous contact with the parallel interior faces of the gripper. Our implementation is currently limited to pairs of parallel faces.

2   Rank the potential grasp faces by the area of intersection of the faces that remains unobstructed after projecting onto the face any obstacles near the face, at both origin and destination.

3   Select a potential pair of grasp faces and pick target points for the fingertips in the unobstructed sections of the faces.

4   Plan a path for the robot gripper, constrained to move parallel to the grasp faces, from a nearby safe point (chosen arbitrarily) to a point close to the chosen grasp point for which there is sufficient overlap between the gripper and the grasp faces. If no path can be found, select a different grasp face and try again. The path must avoid collisions and keep the robot within its legal range of motion.

5   Plan a collision-free motion (using a low-resolution approximation of C-space) for the robot from its current position to the arbitrarily chosen point near the initial grasp.

6   Plan a collision-free motion for the robot, carrying the grasped part (using a low-resolution approximation of C-space) from the initial grasp position to the specified target position.

7   When it is not possible to find a grasp that avoids collisions both at the initial and target positions, plan a sequence of regrasping steps that produce a grasp compatible with the target position. For each required grasp and placement, plan collision-free motions for the robot.

The crucial steps in this formulation rely on being able to find collision-free paths, either between two known points or between a known point and a target set.

The worst-case complexity of motion-planning is exponential in the number of degrees of freedom of the robot; the best motion planning algorithm for a d degree-of-freedom robot has time complexity $O(n^d \log n)$ [Canny 1987], where n is the product of the number of faces, edges, and vertices in the obstacles. Although this bound is polynomial in the environment size, n, this complexity still means that complete motion planning algorithms for real robots are not practical on typical serial computers. Therefore, we have pursued a heuristic decoupling strategy for pick-and-place planning.

Heuristic Motion Planning in HANDEY

Earlier, we outlined an approach to motion planning based on computing C-space obstacles; this approach is described in more detail in Lozano-Pérez [1987]. Although we could use the approximate algorithms described there to solve directly the six degree-of-freedom motion planning problems required for the typical pick-and-place problem, the running times would be too large for practical use, even in experimentation. Instead, we have adopted several heuristic methods of reducing both the dimensionality and the average size of these motion planning problems:

- Using a local motion planner for small motions near obstacles together with a low resolution C-space for large motions farther away from obstacles. The local planner simulates the effect of a body being acted upon by repelling forces from the obstacles and attractive forces from the goal. This general approach is known as the *artificial-potential-field approach* [Khatib 1986].

- Limiting the large motions to the first three joints of the robot, but with the ability to change the values of the last three joints.

- Approximating arbitrary polyhedral obstacles by obstacles with a constant cross section that simplify the computation of the low-resolution C-space obstacles.

The combination of these strategies has resulted in a significant reduction of the running times for motion planning (from a few minutes to maybe thirty seconds) without a significant reduction in HANDEY's ability to solve pick-and-place problems. In the following sections, we describe these methods.

Local planning: The quasi-potential method

In HANDEY, motion near an obstacle happens primarily when the object is being grasped. In those circumstances, the motion of the robot is constrained so that the gripper moves in the plane of the chosen grasp faces. This means that we have a three degree-of-freedom planning problem instead of a six degree-of-freedom problem. But, those three motion freedoms correspond to cartesian motions of the gripper in the grasp plane (x, y, θ) and not to individual joint motions of the robot arm. Therefore, to exploit this reduction in dimensionality, we require a different planner from the one we use for the gross motions of the arm.

We could construct approximate x, y, θ C-space obstacles for the gripper moving in the grasp plane and plan the gripper motions in this space. But, instead, we have adopted a local planner that does not build an explicit C-space. We have two reasons for this choice:

1   In HANDEY, some of the obstacles may not be modeled directly as polyhedra by the system but, instead, they may be represented implicitly by an array of depth measurements. One could attempt to build a polyhedral approximation to this data and use the existing C-space obstacle algorithms for polyhedra. Instead, we chose a method that would deal with the data more directly.

2   Typical cases of approaching obstacles within the grasp plane are very simple and a nearly direct path exists. Local methods have a lower computational overhead in these situations. In difficult cases, local methods will fail to find an answer. In those cases, we can fall back on guaranteed global methods.

Traditional potential methods [Khatib 1986] measure the distance between a number of points on the moving body, the gripper in our case, and obstructions in the grasp plane, compute a repulsive force proportional to a power of the distance, and sum them with an attractive force based on the distance from the gripper to the goal. These total artificial forces and torques acting on the gripper are then used to compute a motion for the gripper via the simulated dynamics of a viscous damper, $f = bv$, where f is the total force/torque vector and v is the resulting velocity vector.

We use a version of this method that effectively uses a potential which is a high power of the distance. Beyond some gripper to obstacle distance, d, the force on the manipulator is 0, within that distance the force is such as to prohibit motion toward the obstacle. The motion plane is represented by a grid and obstacles correspond to filled cells in the grid. The starting point is chosen to be some safe point on the edge of the grid in the same connected component of the grid as the target point.

Surrounding the gripper at a distance, d, and moving with it are *bump lines* (see figure 5). A bump line is a line segment on the grasp plane which is checked each iteration for collisions with filled grid cells. For any position of the gripper, the bump lines represent the locus of points where the presence of an obstacle would constrain the motion of the gripper. *Bump vectors* are vectors perpendicular to a bump line pointing away from the gripper.

In the absence of intervening filled grid cells in the motion plane the motion of the gripper would be a simple translation along the vector connecting the finger and target point. We call the unit vector in this direction the *goal vector*.

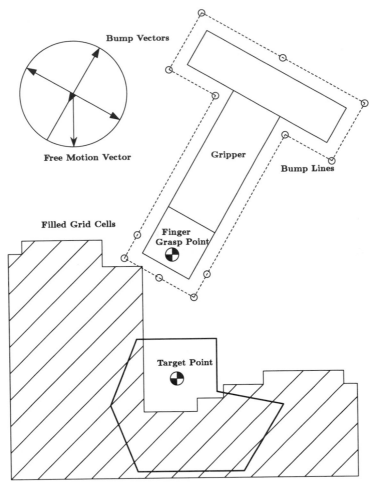

Figure 5. Illustration of the definitions in the quasi-potential method.

After investigating all the bump lines for collisions with filled cells we construct a unit circle and map onto it the goal vector and the bump vectors whose corresponding bump lines have not detected collisions. In figure 5 we show a typical situation. The bump vectors corresponding to colliding bump lines are shown as zero-length vectors, indicating directions in which motion is forbidden.

To compute the translational motion of the gripper we compare the goal vector with the bump vectors. If the goal vector has no component in the direction of a zero-length bump vector, that is, a forbidden motion direction, the gripper is moved in the direction of the goal vector. Otherwise, as in figure 5, the gripper will be moved along the non-zero bump vector closest in direction to the goal vector, down and to the right in the figure.

The bump lines also provide a convenient way to compute a torque to rotate the gripper. Any colliding bump line produces a torque whose magnitude is proportional to the cross product of the bump vector and a vector connecting the finger grasp point with the center of the bump line. We use the center of the bump line rather than the actual point of contact simply to minimize computation on each iteration. The total torque on the gripper is just the sum of torques generated by each colliding bump line.

The gripper is free to rotate about the *finger grasp point* (shown near the finger tip in figure 5). Rotations and translations are limited in such a way that no point on the gripper is moved by more than one grid cell per iteration. This precludes the possibility that any filled grid cells will penetrate the bump lines during an incremental motion.

At each iteration, a check is performed to ensure that a motion in the computed direction would yield a reachable gripper position. If the position is not feasible, then a different direction (if any remain) is tried. Every few iterations the position of the gripper is compared to a previous position. If no significant progress has been made, the path is terminated.

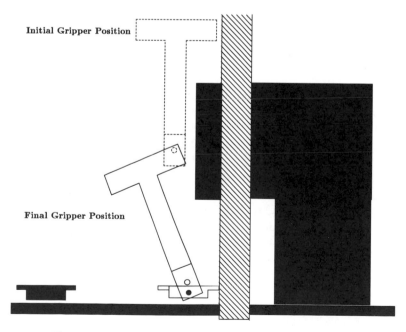

Figure 6. The initial and final position of the gripper for the initial grasp of the example in figure 1. The dark obstacles are present at the pickup point, the hashed obstacle is a copy of the table at the destination where the regrasp is to be done.

At this point the position of the gripper in relation to the target area is checked. If the fingers sufficiently overlap the target, for example, the chosen faces of a grasp, then the path is accepted and returned, otherwise the planner either tries to plan a path from another starting point or tries another pair of faces.

Initial and final positions obtained by the quasi-potential method are shown in figure 6 for the initial grasp of the example in figure 1. Note that the finger grasp point cannot actually reach the chosen target point, but the grasp sufficiently overlaps the target face.

Although this method is not guaranteed to find a solution, it performs reasonably well in many of the cases we have encountered in our experiments. It does fail in some complex cases. We believe that the performance of the method can be enhanced by improving the choice of starting point and by avoiding a reliance on a fixed attraction point. We are currently experimenting with a variation of the method that picks a starting point by finding the maximal clearance translational paths from the target point to the edges of the motion grid. The starting points are the ends of the paths. During each iteration, the attraction point used for computing the artificial forces acting on the gripper will be moved along the chosen path. We hope this will avoid many of the problems of local minima, especially those due to non-convex obstacles.

Global planning: Low resolution C-space

The local quasi-potential method is effective near the target when a nearly direct path is known to exist. For gross motions that span a significant segment of the workspace, local methods are less effective. We use a low-resolution C-space method for these motions. Although the basic method is that described in Lozano-Pérez [1987], the implemented method makes use of several heuristics to significantly lower the average computation time.

One key approximation is to limit the C-space obstacle construction to the first three joint angles of the robot. The planner builds three three-dimensional *slices* of the underlying six-dimensional C-space. One slice is built with the wrist angles fixed at their value at the start of the path, another slice with the wrist angles set at their value at the end of the path, and the last slice for the range of wrist angles between the start and the end. The free-space representation in these three slices is linked up into a single free-space representation that can be searched for a path.

The first two of these three slices are built at high resolution (quantization of one degree), but no attempt is made to build the full three-dimensional slice of the C-space. In fact, every attempt is made to limit the size of the slices. The idea is to move as close as possible to the initial and goal points within the slice that spans the orientations of the wrist

between the initial and goal points. Then, only the final segments need to
be traveled in the remaining two slices. The computation of these slices,
therefore, proceeds in an "on-demand" basis. First, the slice is built for a
very narrow range of the first three angles. If a path is found in this range,
then we stop, otherwise, the range is widened incrementally until a path is
found. This strategy is illustrated in figure 7.

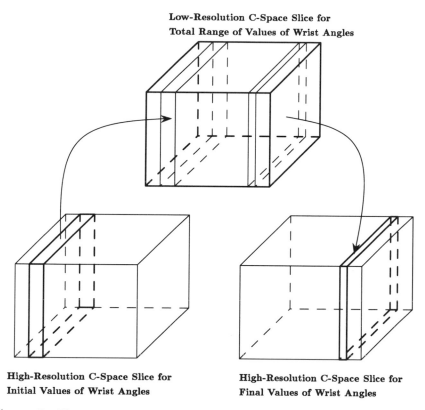

Figure 7. The gross motion planning problem is split into three 3-degree-of-
freedom slices.

The third slice, spanning the range of wrist angles for the motion, is built
to span the whole range of the first three joint angles. But, this slice is
built at lower resolution (eight degrees) and the robot and the obstacles
are approximated to simplify the computation. The idea behind this simplification is to exploit the fact that the computation of C-space obstacles
for planar robots and obstacles is much more efficient than that for solid
polyhedra [Lozano-Pérez 1987]. We can take advantage of the fact that
the Unimation Puma robot that we use in HANDEY has, as do many other
commercial robots, two links that have parallel rotation axes (see figure 8).

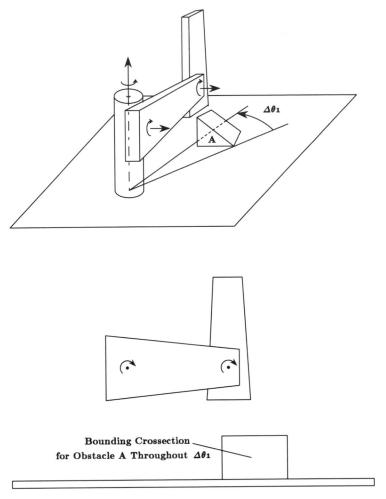

Figure 8. Obstacles can be approximated by tori, centered at the base of the robot, with constant polygonal cross sections in the plane of the second and third links of the robot.

This means that we can approximate the arm as a planar two-link arm operating in a plane determined by the first joint angle. Then, we can approximate the obstacles by tori, centered at the base of the robot, with constant polygonal cross sections in the plane of the second and third links of the robot (see figure 8).

The result of this process is an approximation to the three degree-of-freedom C-space computed using only planar computations. Although this does not affect the asymptotic complexity of the method, it results in a significant speed up.

The interaction between local and global planning

Given a problem, such as a regrasping step, that requires moving from a position close to an obstacle to another position close to an obstacle, HANDEY proceeds as follows:

1   Use the quasi-potential planner to move away from the initial position very near an obstacle. Call this point I'.
2   Use the quasi-potential planner to move away from the final position very near an obstacle. Call this point F'.
3   Use the C-space planner to move from I' to F'.

The current implementation of HANDEY does not choose the points I' and F' with the gross motion planner in mind. In particular, there is no guarantee that these points will be in the low-resolution free-C-space built by the gross motion planner. This is not a requirement, but it would, of course, minimize the amount of computation required to plan the complete path. This connection could be done by marking as desirable targets those grid points (specifying the gripper position and orientation) that map into free-C-space points (specifying the first three joint angles of the arm). Nevertheless, this hybrid local/global approach to planning motions has proven quite effective in our experiments.

Conclusions

HANDEY is unique for being the first task-level system that has received extensive testing in relatively complex tasks. Because HANDEY operates by first locating an obstructed object placed in a random orientation and taking it to any specified location, it must be able to handle quite general motion planning problems. But, for it to be thoroughly tested, it must run in reasonable time. This has forced us to look for simplifying assumptions that do not significantly reduce the generality of the system. We believe that this search for simplifying assumptions will be critical to the development of task-level robot systems.

HANDEY's capabilities are only a small fraction of those required for a comprehensive task-level robot system. Other important capabilities that are not currently part of HANDEY but are important for general task-level robot systems are:

- Planning force-controlled motions to assemble objects in the presence of position error.
- Planning coordinated motions for multiple robots.
- Planning the placement of the parts in the workspace to optimize task execution.
- Planning the nature and order of operations required to carry out a task, for example, the order in which parts are to be assembled.

All these capabilities are currently under investigation within the framework of HANDEY.

References

Buckley, S. J. [1987], "Planning and teaching compliant motion strategies," Report AI–TR–936, Massachusetts Institute of Technology, Artificial Intelligence Laboratory.

Canny, J. F. [1988], *The complexity of robot motion planning*, MIT Press.

Donald, B. R. [1987], "Error detection and recovery for robot motion planning with uncertainty," Report AI–TR–982, Massachusetts Institute of Technology, Artificial Intelligence Laboratory.

Erdmann, M. A. [1986], "Using backprojections for fine-motion planning with uncertainty," *International Journal of Robotics Research*, vol. 5, no. 1, pp. 19–45.

Ernst, H. A. [1961], *A computer-controlled mechanical hand*, Ph.D. Thesis, Massachusetts Institute of Technology.

Khatib, O. [1986], "Real-time obstacle avoidance for robot manipulator and mobile robots," *The International Journal of Robotics Research*, vol. 5, no. 1, pp. 90–98.

Lozano-Pérez, T. [1987], "A simple motion planning algorithm for general robot manipulators," *IEEE Journal of Robotics and Automation*, RA-3 no. 3, pp. 224–238.

Lozano-Pérez, T., J. L. Jones, E. Mazer, A. Lanusse, W. E. L. Grimson, and P. Tournassoud [1987], "HANDEY: A robot system that recognizes, plans and manipulates," *IEEE International Conference on Robotics and Automation*, Raleigh.

Lozano-Pérez, T., M. T. Mason, and R. H. Taylor [1984], "Automatic synthesis of fine-motion strategies for robots," *International Journal of Robotics Research*, vol. 3, no. 1, pp. 3–24.

Lozano-Pérez, T., and R. H. Taylor [1988], "Geometric issues in planning robot tasks," in *Robotics Science*, edited by J. M. Brady, MIT Press.

Mason, M. T. [1984], "Automatic planning of fine motions: correctness and completeness," in *IEEE International Conference on Robotics and Automation*, pp. 492–503, Atlanta.

Reif, J. H. [1987], "Complexity of the generalized mover's problem," in *Planning, Geometry, and Complexity of Robot Motion*, edited by J. T. Schwartz, M. Sharir, and J. Hopcroft, Ablex Publishing.

The work in this chapter was funded primarily by the Office of Naval Research under contracts N00014-85-K-0214 and N00014-86-K-0685. Additional support was provided by an NSF Presidential Young Investigator Award (Lozano-Pérez), the French CNRS (Mazer), and the Digital Equipment Corporation.

Tournassoud, P., T. Lozano-Pérez, and E. Mazer [1987], "Regrasping," *IEEE International Conference on Robotics and Automation*, Raleigh.

Whitney, D. E. [1982], "Quasi-static assembly of compliantly supported rigid parts," *ASME Journal of Dynamic Systems, Measurement, and Control*, vol. 104, pp. 65–77.

27

Think about attaching a nut to a bolt or just opening a door. If you were a robot capable only of position control, you would strip the bolt's threads and rip the door off its hinges were your position sensing or position control even slightly off. People do no damage, however, because people perform such motions by exerting forces, not by forcing positions.

But although force-oriented compliant motions are easy for us humans to perform, they are difficult for us to specify in robot programs. In this chapter, the authors describe a formal approach to the synthesis of compliant motion strategies from geometric descriptions of assembly operations and explicit estimates of sensing and control errors.

One key idea is that of the generalized damper, which makes applied force proportional to the difference between actual velocity and commanded velocity. The generalized damper is heavily involved when goals are achieved by sliding along surfaces.

Another key idea, as in the previous chapter, is the configuration-space transform. Once seen from the perspective of configuration-space, many superficially different path-planning tasks become identical. The problem of inserting a chamfered peg into an unchamfered hole, for example, is the same as the problem of inserting an unchamfered peg into a chamfered hole.

Automatic Synthesis of Fine-Motion Strategies for Robots

Tomás Lozano-Pérez

Matthew T. Mason[†]

Russell H. Taylor [‡]

The central robot programming problem lies in achieving tasks in spite of uncertainty in the robot's position relative to external objects. The use of sensing to reduce uncertainty significantly extends the range of possible tasks. Sensor-based robot programs are very difficult to write, however, as there is little theory to serve as a guide. To make matters worse, programs written for one task are seldom, if ever, applicable to other tasks. These two points make the development of an automatic synthesis strategy for sensor-based robot programs a key priority.

In this chapter, we propose a formal approach to the automatic synthesis of a class of compliant fine-motion strategies applicable to assembly tasks. The approach uses geometric descriptions of parts and estimates of measurement and motion errors to produce fine-motion strategies. Although our description of the approach will be in the form of an abstract algorithm, several implementations based on this approach exist (see [Buckley 1987] [Erdmann 1986] [Donald 1987]). The formalism provides a structured way of thinking about fine-motion strategies and, therefore, may also be helpful to human programmers of fine-motion strategies.

Fine-motion strategies

One important source of the difficulty in robot programming is that the programmer's model of the environment is incomplete and inexact as to

[†] Carnegie-Mellon University.

[‡] IBM T. J. Watson Research Center.

the shape and location of objects. Vision may be used to determine the approximate shape and positions of objects, but generally not with sufficient accuracy for assembly by pure position control. Knowing the object shapes and positions to sufficient accuracy is not enough. Positioning errors inherently limit the tasks achievable by strict position control. Increasing the mechanical accuracy of robots to the levels required for assembly is expensive and ultimately stifling. Instead, one must abandon the paradigm of pure position control for tasks where the allowable motions are tightly constrained by external objects, as they are in mechanical assembly.

The basic method for achieving constrained motion in the presence of position uncertainty is by the use of controlled *compliance* (see [Mason 1983] for an overview of compliance research). Compliant motion meets external constraints by specifying how the robot's motion should be modified in response to the forces generated when the constraints are violated. Contact with a surface, for example, can be guaranteed by moving so that a small force normal to the surface is maintained. Using this technique, the robot can achieve and retain contact with a surface that may vary significantly in shape and orientation from the programmer's expectations. Generalizations of this principle can be used to accomplish a wide variety of tasks involving constrained motion, for example, inserting a peg in a hole and following a weld seam.

The specification of particular compliant motions to achieve a task requires knowledge of the geometric constraints imposed by the task. Given a description of the constraints, choices can be made for the compliant motion parameters, for example, the motion freedoms to be force controlled and those to be position controlled [Mason 1981; Paul & Shimano 1976; Raibert & Craig 1981], or the center of compliance and axis stiffnesses [Hanafusa & Asada 1977; Salisbury 1980; Whitney 1983]. However, it is common for position uncertainty to be large enough so that the programmer cannot unambiguously determine which geometric constraint holds at any instant in time. For example, figure 1 shows some initial conditions that can hold in two-dimensional peg-in-hole insertion. Under these circumstances, the programmer must employ a combined strategy of force and position control that guarantees reaching the desired final configuration from all of the likely initial configurations. We call such a strategy a *fine-motion strategy*.

One of the most widely studied tasks in robotics is the two-dimensional peg-in-hole task. Detailed analyses have been carried out to determine strategies that guarantee successful insertion once the peg is partly in the hole [Drake 1977; McCallion & Wong 1975; Ohwovoriole & Roth 1981; Simunovic 1975; Whitney 1982]. When the initial uncertainty in position is large enough, a strategy must also be devised to ensure that the peg can find the hole [Inoue 1974; McCallion & Wong 1975]. We can illustrate a

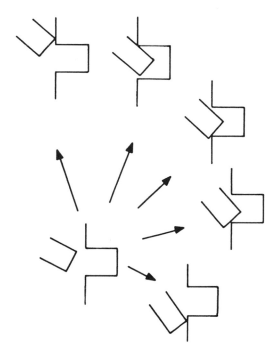

Figure 1. Some possible initial configurations for peg-in-hole insertion.

variety of strategies for one task by considering the ways this problem has been addressed:

- **Chamfers.** Chamfers on the hole entrance and/or the peg tip increase the range of relative positions where the peg can fall into the hole, at least partway. This technique is especially effective if the peg support has lateral compliance [Drake 1977; Whitney 1982].

- **Tilting the peg.** Tilting the peg slightly also increases the range of relative positions where initial entry into the hole is guaranteed [Inoue 1974]. In fact, the geometric effect of tilting the peg is almost identical to providing a chamfer (see the next section).

- **Search.** The simplest strategy is a search by sliding along the top surface until the peg falls into the hole. In general, the search will have to pick an initial direction of motion and, possibly, back up if the hole is not found.

- **Biased Search.** A slight modification to the search strategy is to introduce a bias into the initial position of the peg [Inoue 1974]. This strategy reduces the chances of initial entry into the hole, but it guarantees that the peg will be to one side of the hole.

In this chapter we examine strategies such as tilting the peg and biased search. These are simple strategies employing compliant motion that do not require modifying the task geometry or complicated control structures.

Previous Work

In this chapter we present an approach to the automatic synthesis of a class of fine-motion strategies. We are aware of no previous work with the same goal. There are, however, several bodies of work relevant to this goal. The first of these deals with analyses of geometry and statics of tasks so as to develop conditions that successful fine-motion strategies must satisfy. The second is Simunovic's information approach. The third group deals with attempts to derive strategies starting from partially specified strategies, known as *skeletons* or *plans*. The fourth group deals with attempts to have the robot "learn" strategies from experience and partial task information.

Quite a few authors have analyzed the peg-in-hole assembly task in detail [Drake 1977; Laktionev & Andreev 1966; Andreev & Laktionev 1969; Gusev 1969; McCallion & Wong 1975; Ohwovoriole, Roth & Hill 1981; Ohwovoriole & Roth 1981; Simunovic 1975; Whitney 1982]. In most of the analyses, the assumption is that the peg is initially partly in the hole, possibly at a chamfer. Two important failure modes during insertion have been identified: *jamming* and *wedging*. Jamming is due to misproportioned applied forces; wedging is due to geometric conditions that arise when the parts deform slightly. These analyses have led to the formulation of conditions for successful insertion involving applied forces to relative positions of the peg and hole. As a result, a mechanical device (called the RCC [Drake 1975; Whitney 1982]) has been built that applies the correct forces in response to small initial errors between the peg and hole. A number of heuristic strategies for peg-in-hole insertion have also been formulated, based on more fragmentary analysis. These heuristic strategies have been used successfully in practice [Inoue 1974; Goto, Takeyasu & Inoyama 1981].

Mason's [1982] detailed analysis of pushing and grasping operations in the presence of friction also leads to conditions for successful task completion. These conditions provide the basis for synthesis of operations that succeed in the presence of uncertainty (without requiring sensing).

Simunovic [1979] formulated the information approach to fine-motion based on the principle that assembly is purely a relative positioning task. From this premise he argues that the role of an assembly program is to determine the relative positions of parts during an assembly and to issue position commands to correct the errors. He developed an estimation technique to infer, from a series of noisy position measurements and using knowledge of the geometry of the parts, the actual relative positions of the parts. One problem with this approach is that it requires a very large amount of on-line computation, although this could be handled with special purpose electronics. A more fundamental problem is that the approach assumes only position control and a robot capable of making fine incremental motions. This need not be the case for assembly; by exploiting compliant behavior the robot can achieve high accuracy tasks even with low accuracy position control, for example following a surface by maintaining a downward force. Another problem is that Simunovic's estimation technique requires knowing which surfaces are in contact. This limits the method to situations with relatively small errors; in more general cases, the identity of the contact surfaces will not be known. Our approach is based on a different view of assembly: that the geometric constraints should "guide" the parts to their destination without necessarily having to know exactly where the parts are relative to each other.

One of the earliest explorations in the area of automatic synthesis of fine-motion strategies from *strategy skeletons* was by Taylor [1976]. Taylor developed a technique for propagating the effect of errors and uncertainties through a model of a task. These error estimates were used to make decisions for filling-in the strategy skeletons. For peg-in-hole insertion, for example, the decision whether to tap the peg against the surface next to the hole was based on whether the error estimate for position normal to the surface exceeded a threshold.

Lozano-Pérez [1976] also proposed a method for selecting the motion parameters in strategy skeletons. Each motion in a skeleton was specified symbolically by the relationship among parts that it was designed to achieve. The expected length of guarded moves and their force terminating conditions were then computed from the ranges of displacements that achieved this relationship (taking into account uncertainty in position).

Recently, Brooks [1982] extended Taylor's approach by making more complete use of symbolic constraints in the error computations. The resulting constraints can be used in the "forward" direction to estimate errors for particular operations. But, importantly, they also may be used in the "backward" direction to constrain the values for plan parameters, such as initial positions of objects, to those that enable the plan to succeed. When no good choice of parameters exists, the system chooses appropriate sensing operations (such as visual location of parts) that reduce the uncertainty enough to guarantee success.

Another line of research has focused on building up programs automatically from attempts by the robot to carry out the operations. Dufay and Latombe [1983] describe how partial local strategies, *rules* for a task can be assembled into a complete program by processing the execution traces of many attempts to carry out the task. The method, however, requires knowing the actual relationship between parts achieved by each motion, for example, which surfaces are in contact. This information can be obtained, in many cases, from careful analysis of the forces and positions but, in general, the information is ambiguous in the presence of measurement and control errors. Moreover, the rules used by the system are specific to tasks and must be provided by the user.

A related approach to deriving a strategy from "experiments" is based on the theory of stochastic automata [Simons *et al.* 1982]. The goal is to have the robot learn the appropriate control response to measured force vectors during task execution. The method requires a task-dependent evaluation function so as to judge progress towards its goal.

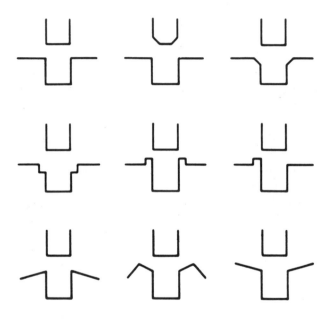

Figure 2. Variations of peg-in-hole require different strategies.

These previous approaches to fine-motion synthesis are based on the assumption that there is a basic repertoire of operations, such as peg-in-hole insertion and block-in-corner, whose geometric structure is known *a priori*. In this view, the task of a synthesis program is to make some pre-defined set of choices among alternative actions, select the values of some parameters, and, possibly, select the order of operations. *In fact, small changes in the geometry of parts can have significant impact on fine-motion strategies.* The different operations shown in figure 2, for example, can all be classified as peg-in-hole, however, they require substantially different programs to insure reliable execution. Similarly, differences in expected position errors will call for different strategies for the same task.

Our approach is motivated by the belief that the set of possible geometric interactions in a task should directly determine the structure of the fine-motion strategy for the task. Thus, for example, the presence of additional surfaces within the region of possible initial contact typically requires a change in the structure of a strategy. The approach we describe in this chapter proceeds directly from geometric descriptions of the parts to a strategy.

Overview of the Approach

In this section we informally outline our approach to fine-motion synthesis using a progression of simple examples. In the next section, we provide a more formal characterization of the approach.

The basic strategy

Consider the simple task of moving the point p from its initial position to any one of the positions in G (see figure 3b). This is a simplified problem but not a completely artificial one. It is equivalent to the two-dimensional peg-in-hole problem in figure 3a, where the axes of the peg and hole are constrained to be parallel. The position of p determines the position of the peg. The boundary of the shaded area represents the positions of p where the peg would be in contact with an obstacle. The transformation from figure 3a to figure 3b corresponds to shrinking the peg to a point and expanding the obstacles accordingly. Note that the sides of the hole have each been moved towards each other by half the width of the peg. In this case, the transformation produces an equivalent problem.

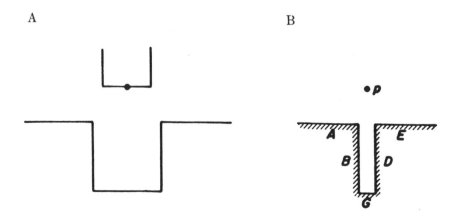

Figure 3. Peg-in-hole insertion: (a) original formulation (b) transformed to point problem.

We postpone a more general discussion of this type of transformation until later. It is the case that problems of moving rigid objects among other rigid objects can be reformulated as equivalent problems of moving a point among transformed objects in a higher dimensional space, called the *configuration space* [Lozano-Pérez 1981, 1983].

The basic step in our synthesis approach is to identify ranges of positions from where p can reach G by a single motion. The directions of such motions can be represented as unit velocity vectors, v_i. For each v_i, we can compute all those positions, P_i, such that a motion along v_i from that position would reach some point of G (see figure 4). We call this range of positions that can reach the goal by a single motion along a specified velocity the *pre-image*[1] of the goal (for that velocity). All we need do to guarantee that p reaches G from any point in any of the P_i is to execute a motion with commanded velocity along v_i.

Figure 4. Pre-image of the goal for different v_i.

If no pre-image of G contains the peg's current position, then we can apply the same pre-image computation recursively using each of the existing pre-images as a possible goal. This recursive process is an instance of the problem solving strategy known as *backward chaining* [Nilsson 1980]. Each pre-image of G, P_i, serves to define a new goal set G_i^1 (the superscript indicates the "recursion level"). This process is repeated until some pre-image P_i^k contains the current position of p (see figure 5). From this chain of pre-images $P_{i0}, P_{i1}^1 \ldots, P_{ik}^k$ we can construct a motion strategy. The two components of the strategy are a sequence of velocity vectors and a sequence of associated termination predicates. Therefore, the strategies may be construed as a sequence of *guarded motions* [Will & Grossman 1975]. Each velocity vector v_{ij} defines a motion that moves from anywhere in P_{ij}^j to G_{ij-1}^j. Whenever p reaches one of the goal regions, the velocity command needs to be changed to that appropriate for the new region, for

---

[1]The rationale for this name stems from viewing motions as mappings from pairs of initial positions and velocities into points along the resulting path.

example, from v_{ij} to v_{ij-1}. The role of the termination predicates is to detect the arrival of p into a goal region. In the simple case we have been discussing, termination predicates simply test to see whether the position is in the goal region. Termination predicates are much more difficult to construct in the presence of position uncertainty. We will discuss this issue in more detail later.

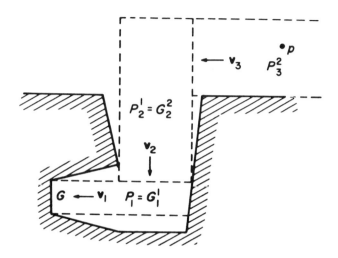

Figure 5. Backward chaining of pre-images.

In summary, our basic approach to fine-motion synthesis is to chain backwards from the goal towards the current position, characterizing at each step the range of positions that can reach the current goal in one motion, that is, the pre-image of the goal. It remains to show how this simple approach is applicable to more realistic assembly problems. Our first step towards this goal will be to discuss the role played by uncertainty in position and velocity. The second step will be to introduce compliant motions. The next step will be to illustrate how friction can be handled. The last step is to show how the notion of configuration space reduces assembly problems for solids into problems involving a point and surfaces in a higher-dimensional space.

The effect of uncertainty

We have assumed thus far that p's position is known exactly at all times and that its direction of motion can be specified exactly. In this section we explore the effects of relaxing these assumptions.

Let us assume that there is error between the actual and the commanded velocity, bounded by ϵ_v. The actual velocity is within a ball of radius ϵ_v in velocity space (the ball of velocities centered on **v** is denoted **B(v)**). Therefore, the path of p is constrained to be within a semi-infinite cone centered on the commanded path and whose apex is the initial position. The angle between the actual direction of motion and the commanded direction is constrained to be less than or equal to $\sin^{-1} \epsilon_v$, which will be approximately ϵ_v for small enough ϵ_v.

The synthesis approach above is based on computing the pre-images of goal regions for particular values of commanded velocity. These are locations from which the goal can be reached by a single motion. In the presence of uncertainty in the actual velocity, we define two alternative pre-images (see figure 6):

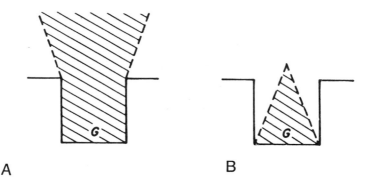

A   B

Figure 6. (a) Weak and (b) strong pre-images of a goal under velocity uncertainty.

- **Weak pre-image.** Locations for which *some* motion within the range of velocity uncertainty may reach the goal.
- **Strong pre-image.** Locations for which *all* motions within the range of velocity uncertainty will reach the goal.

Note that the strong pre-image is a subset of the weak pre-image. In what follows, we will use the term pre-image to mean *strong* pre-image.

In addition to uncertainty in the actual velocity along a motion, there is uncertainty in the position of p. One source of position uncertainty is due to imperfect knowledge of the initial position of the objects in the workspace. Another source of error is due to inherent limitations in the robot's position sensors. For the sake of simplicity, we will lump these two types of uncertainty into a single upper bound on position uncertainty. This assumption does not affect correctness of any derived motion strategies, but might lead to less efficient strategies. In practice, the two sources of uncertainty should be treated differently.

We assume that the actual position is always within a ball of radius ϵ_c centered at the position observed by the robot. All possible observed positions are within a similar ball centered at the actual position. The ball of possible observed positions centered at a position p is denoted $B(p)$. The range of positions potentially traversed by a motion from an observed position along a commanded velocity is depicted in figure 7.

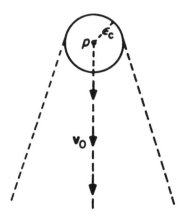

Figure 7. Positions reachable by commanded motion with uncertainty.

Position uncertainty makes it difficult to define termination predicates for motions. A predicate that simply compares the observed position of p against the boundaries of G^i could terminate a motion prematurely. The actual position of p could be anywhere within a ball of radius ϵ_c from the observed position. In order to *guarantee* success *all* possible positions of p must be within the goal. We can think of this effect of position uncertainty as "shrinking" the goal by ϵ_c for purposes of detecting entry. Shrinking G^i removes from G^i any point at a distance less than or equal to ϵ_c from any point in free space not in G^i. This removes from G^i any point that is ambiguous. In many cases, this means that *no* part of the goal is unambiguously identifiable on the basis of position. We will have to rely on the effects of collisions with surfaces or on previous history to identify entry into a goal region. This issue is quite subtle; it is the subject of the next section.

Compliant motion

The example above dealt only with position controlled motions. Due to uncertainty in p's position and velocity relative to the task, this type of motion often leads to empty pre-images. This indicates that the position accuracy is not sufficient for the task. We mentioned earlier that the alternative motion regime is compliant motion. We can visualize the effect of compliant motions as producing sliding on the constraint surfaces derived from the obstacles. Sliding means that the moving object confines its motions to be tangent to the constraining surface(s) [Mason 1981]. When not in contact with a surface, the motion will be along the commanded velocity (to within the velocity uncertainty).

The *generalized damping* model [Whitney 1976] can be used to implement compliant motions with the properties described above. The desired motion is determined by the following relationship

$$\mathbf{f} = \mathbf{B}(\mathbf{v} - \mathbf{v}_0)$$

where $\mathbf{f}$ is the vector of forces acting on the moving object, $\mathbf{v}_0$ is the *nominal velocity* vector, and $\check{\mathbf{v}}$ is the actual velocity vector. In what follows, $\mathbf{B}$ is a diagonal matrix. The role of $\mathbf{B}$ in our usage is primarily to relate the units of force to those of velocity. We assume that the control system implements the above equation and so the behavior of the robot and moving object can be adequately approximated as a damper (for some limited range of operating velocities). The Appendix provides a more detailed treatment of the behavior of a generalized damper.

In practice, because of measuring and implementation errors, there will be a difference between the commanded behavior and the actual behavior of the damper. We summarize these differences by introducing the distinction between the actual nominal velocity, $\mathbf{v}_0$, and the *commanded nominal velocity*, denoted $\mathbf{v}_0^*$. Throughout the chapter, the asterisk will denote measured or commanded quantities that differ from the actual ones because of the presence of error.

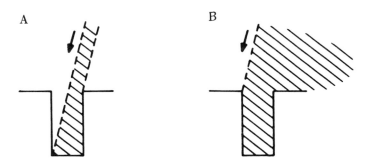

Figure 8. Pre-images for position control versus generalized damper.

The definition of the pre-image of a goal as the set of positions that can reach the goal with one commanded velocity can be retained for generalized damper motions. *Under compliant motion, however, the moving object may reach the goal indirectly by sliding on intervening surfaces.* Therefore, compliant motions typically produce larger pre-images than pure positioning motions. The increased pre-image indicates less sensitivity to uncertainty (compare figures 8a and 8b).

Friction

A crucial consideration in the analysis and synthesis of fine-motion strategies is the effect of friction. A simple model of friction for planar motion without rotation is as follows. We assume that the objects are of a single material with equal coefficients of static and sliding friction, μ. The reaction force from contact at a point on a surface will lie within a *friction cone* with apex at the point of contact and center line along the surface normal. The angle between the normal and the sides of the cone is the *friction angle*, $\phi = \tan^{-1} \mu$. If the applied force points into the friction cone, that is, if the angle of the force vector to the surface normal is less than ϕ, then no motion will result. If the angle of the force vector to surface normal is greater than ϕ sliding will result (see figure 9).

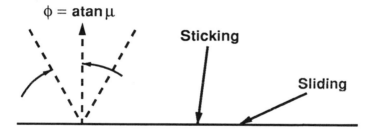

Figure 9. Friction cone.

This model of friction can be extended to include rotations and moments, but the details are beyond the scope of this discussion (see Erdmann [1986]). In what follows, we need only assume that some nominal velocity vectors will cause sticking on a surface and others will cause sliding. We assume, furthermore, that the range of nominal velocity vectors that cause sticking for a surface can be conservatively bounded by a cone, which may be wider than the actual cone. The computation of pre-images must take into account the possibility of "sticking" on a surface. In particular, assuming the motion is generated by a damper (with $\mathbf{B} = b\mathbf{I}$), if the range of nominal velocities for the pre-image contains nominal velocities whose angle to the normal of some surface is less than the friction angle, ϕ, then the motion will stop at that surface (see figure 9 and the Appendix).

Examples

We now have the conceptual tools necessary to synthesize a strategy for the simple example of figure 3. In this section we illustrate one particular approach to synthesis of strategies based on the use of pre-images. The method used in this section is a subset of the general approach described in the next section.

Our goal is to identify some sub-region P of the free space C and a command nominal velocity v_0 such that P is the strong pre-image, under v_0, of the goal surface. Equivalently, P must not overlap the weak pre-image of any surface where motion along v_0 may stick or not reach the goal. We will use this constraint to drive a simultaneous search for P and v_0.

The key problem is in discovering v_0. Our approach here is to narrow in on feasible values of v_0 by progressive refinement. We start with the complete range of possible v_0's and remove from that range any values that can possibly lead to failure (by sticking or not reaching the goal). At each step of the algorithm, we compute the strong pre-image of the goal for the current *range* of v_0's. The strong pre-image for a range of command velocities is the intersection of the strong pre-images for each of the velocities. These are the positions guaranteed to reach the goal for *all* the velocities in the range.[2] This is the same definition that we saw earlier for the strong pre-image in the presence of velocity error. In fact, as long as the velocity ranges used to compute pre-images are greater than $2\epsilon_v$, we need not concern ourselves further with velocity uncertainty. Once the algorithm has chosen a final velocity range, we can pick a specific velocity from the range such that all velocities within the velocity error fall in the chosen velocity range. Narrower velocity ranges will not yield such a safe velocity.

For now we will ignore the need for backward chaining and sketch an algorithm for synthesizing single motions. We will deal with backward chaining presently. The basic algorithm steps are as follows:

1   Compute P, the strong pre-image of the goal surface, for the current range of commanded velocities. If the current range of velocities is split into disjoint sub-ranges, then steps 1 and 2 should be repeated for each sub-range (see figure 10).

2   If P includes an uncertainty ball centered at some starting position, then return P and the current velocity range.

3   Otherwise, if P is empty, pick x to be a surface (other than a goal) where the robot may "stick," that is, such that some velocity in the

---

[2]Note that the weak pre-image for a range of velocities is the union of the weak pre-images for velocities in the range, that is, positions that may reach the goal for *some* velocity in the range.

current velocity range points into the surface's friction cone. If no such surface exists then notify failure and stop.

4   Remove from the range of commanded velocities any velocity pointing into the friction cone of x.

5   Go to step 1.

We can illustrate the operation of this algorithm on our example as follows. Construct a directed graph with nodes for each of the surfaces in figure 3 and one node representing free space (C). A link is directed from node m to node n in the graph if m and n are direct neighbors and m is in the weak pre-image of n for the specified velocity range. That is, there is a link from m to n if some velocity in the current range may cause the robot to move from some point in m (which is not in n) to some point in n (which is allowed to be at the intersection of m and n) without going through points in any other node. In principle, the graph should have nodes representing the vertices; we have left them out for simplicity. This simplification introduces the need for the phrases in parentheses above. See, for example, the link between A and B and B and G (but not vice versa) in figure 10a. We will call this the *reachability graph* for that range of commanded velocities. The reachability graph plays a key role in algorithms for computing the strong pre-image of the goal.

In our example, we start out with a range of commanded velocities including any velocity with a y component less than or equal to zero (we diagram ranges of commanded velocities as sectors of a circle). These are the velocities that will move p from nearby points onto the goal surface G. The reachability graph for this range of velocities is shown at the top of figure 10a. In this figure, we have indicated those surfaces where the moving object may stick (using the electrical ground symbol). The (potentially) sticking surfaces are those whose friction cones overlap the current velocity range. For simplicity, we assume that the contact on surfaces B and D are point contacts.

Figure 10 illustrates the reachability graph and pre-image of the goal each time step 1 is executed. The surfaces used to constrain the range of commanded velocities (step 3) were chosen in the following order: B, D, A, E. The particular order does not affect the final result in this case. The algorithm terminates at the fourth cycle. In figure 10(d), we have shown only one of the two velocity ranges (and corresponding P's) that result from discarding velocities that may stick on A or E. The remaining velocity range leads to a pre-image that is the mirror image (about the hole axis) of the one in figure 10d. Any commanded velocity within either of these remaining velocity ranges will reach the goal from any position within P. Note that the single motion strategy developed by this approach is a biased search (see the previous section). This is a good choice because we have not included chamfers or rotation in our problem definition.

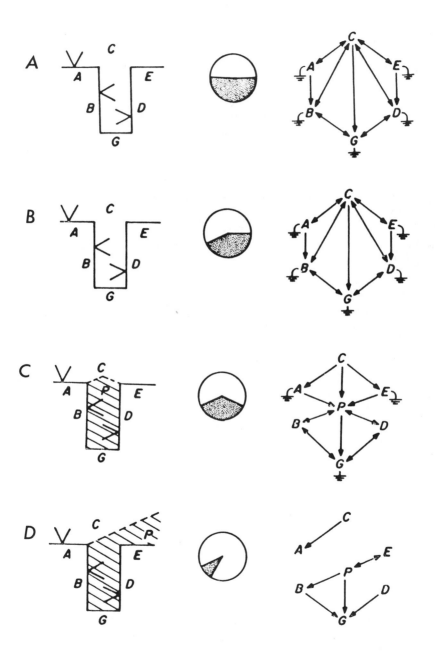

Figure 10. Single move peg-in-hole strategy synthesis.

The example in figure 10 can be done with a single motion (because the friction cones of the horizontal and vertical surfaces do not overlap). We did not require the use of backward-chaining. After step 2 of the algorithm we have a choice of refining the range of directions or of using the current P as the goal for a recursive call to the same algorithm. In principle, we can follow these two paths non-deterministically. In practice, this requires a search guided by considerations such as the number of motions in the strategy thus far and the size of P.

The example in figure 11 illustrates the use of backward-chaining to develop multi-move strategies. In this example, we assume that the first four steps proceed essentially as in the example in figure 10. The final pre-image of the first example now becomes G^1, the goal for the next recursion level. The method applies as before and generates a new pre-image and velocity range. The strategy, then, consists of choosing some velocity from this range, moving until transition into G^1 is detected, and changing the commanded velocity to one of those from the range obtained in the first example.

We noted earlier that, for each commanded motion in a strategy, it is necessary to define a predicate which indicates that the goal has been reached. In multi-move strategies, this condition signals that another motion should be commanded. Three types of basic termination conditions are available:

1 **Position termination.** Terminate if the measured position of p is such that all possible actual positions consistent with the measurement are within the goal region.

2 **Velocity (force) termination.** Terminate if the observed velocity of p is such that all possible actual velocities consistent with the measurement can only occur within the goal region. Note that because motions are generated by a generalized damper, the difference between actual velocity and commanded velocity provides information about reaction forces, for example, contact with a surface.

3 **Time termination.** Terminate if the elapsed time is such that all positions consistent with the commanded motion and observed data are within the goal.

Position termination requires that all actual positions consistent with the measured position be within the goal. This is equivalent to the measured position being in the goal after shrinking it by ϵ_c along its boundary to free space. If any of the dimensions of the goal region are less than ϵ_c, then position feedback is not a reliable indicator of reaching the goal. When the goal is a surface, for example, shrinking will cause the goal region to vanish. In these cases, we must rely on velocity termination which requires that the observed velocities, for example, when landing on or leaving from a surface, be unambiguous relative to surfaces that may be confused with the goal

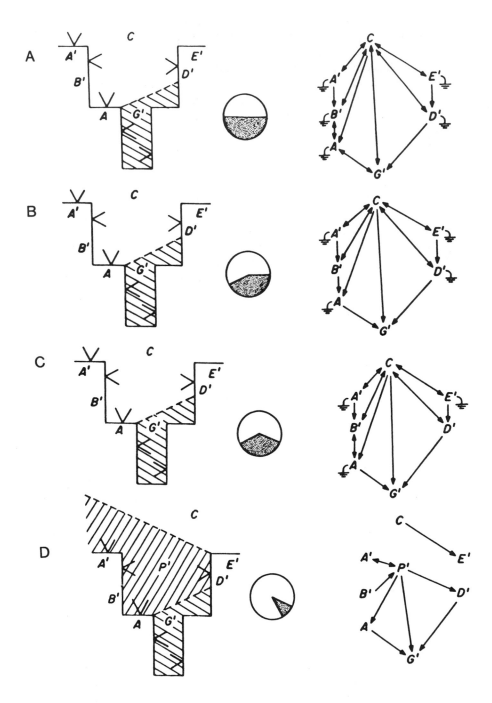

Figure 11. Multi-move peg-in-hole strategy synthesis.

due to position measurement error. Time termination is also useful, when applicable, as it is much simpler to test than position termination.

Velocity termination is the most useful termination condition when faced with large position uncertainty. The strategy synthesized from the example in figure 11. The first motion required by the strategy can be terminated when the x component of observed velocity is zero, that is, when p strikes one of walls on the right of the hole. The second motion can be terminated when either the x and/or y components of the observed velocity are zero, that is, when p is at the left bottom corner of the hole.

These two examples illustrate the class of fine-motion strategies we wish to consider. The strategies operate over a wide range of uncertainty without explicitly computing where the parts are relative to each other. The strategies do not keep any explicit history of previous events although, we will see later, history is implicit in the strategies.

Configuration space

The basic operation in the synthesis method described above is computing the strong pre-image of a goal. To do this, we first transform the input problem, involving a moving object and stationary obstacles, into an equivalent problem involving a point and transformed obstacles. This transformation has a number of advantages. One is that it enables us to represent the pre-images as areas in the transformed space. The key advantage, however, is that this transformation makes the constraints on motion explicit. This is illustrated in figure 12, where an upright peg and chamfered hole are shown to lead to transformed obstacles similar (as far as initial entry into the hole is concerned) to those of a chamfered peg and unchamfered hole and to those of a tilted peg and unchamfered hole. The transformation has served to make explicit the underlying similarity of motion constraints in these tasks. In fact, the transformation reduces tasks involving "arbitrary" geometric interactions between objects to the interactions possible between a point and a set of surfaces.

In this chapter we have limited ourselves to two-dimensional translation. It is possible, however, to extend the transformation approach to more general motions using the *configuration space* of a task [Arnold 1980; Lozano-Pérez 1981, 1983]. A *configuration* of an object is the set of parameters needed to completely specify the position of all points of the object. The configuration of a rigid two-dimensional object, for example, can be specified by two displacements and an angle, that of a rigid three-dimensional object by three displacements and three angles, and that of a robot arm by its joint angles. For concreteness, we will be dealing exclusively with cartesian configurations, for example, (x, y, θ) for objects in the plane, and not joint angle configurations. The space of all possible

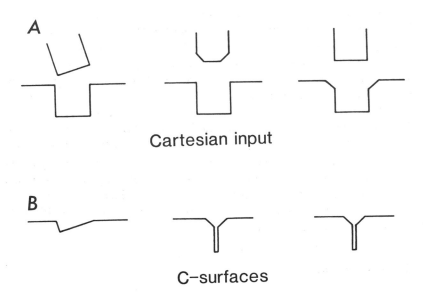

Figure 12. C-space representations make motion constraints explicit.

configurations for an object is known as the configuration space *(C-space)* of that object. An object A is represented as a point in its C-space; the coordinates of that point are the configuration parameters of A.

Stationary obstacles in the environment of a moving object A can be mapped into the configuration space of A. The resulting *C-space obstacles* are those configurations of A which would lead to collisions between A and the obstacles. Configurations on the surface of the C-space obstacle due to B are those where some surface of A is just touching a surface of B. If A and B are both three-dimensional polyhedra, the surfaces of the C-space obstacle for B arise from each of the feasible contacts between of vertices, edges, and faces of A and B (see figure 13) [Lozano-Pérez 1983]. Therefore, each face of a C-space obstacle represents a particular type of geometric constraint on A. A range of positions (and orientations) of A can be represented as a volume in the C-space of A and a motion of A is a curve in the C-space.

As an illustration of the use of C-space surfaces, consider the familiar two-dimensional peg-in-hole problem from figure 3. We can construct a three-dimensional C-space of (x, y, θ) configurations of the peg. In this space, the hole defines an obstacle (see figure 14a). Note that although the resulting surfaces are curved, for each value of θ the (x, y) cross section of the C-space surfaces is polygonal. The surfaces represent one-point contacts and the edges at the intersections of surfaces represent two-point contacts. Line-line contacts also give rise to edges at the intersections of

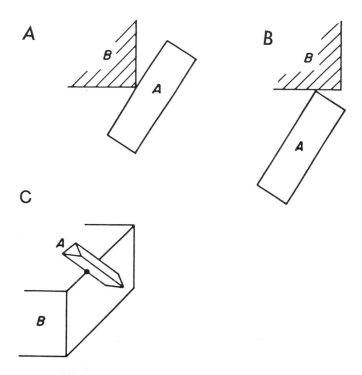

Figure 13. Geometric conditions giving rise to C-surfaces.

one-point contact surfaces. Figure 14b shows cross sections for a peg and chamfered hole.

The C-space representation can be extended to more general kinematic situations. In general, motion subject to geometric and kinematic constraints can be defined as collections of equalities and inequalities that must hold among the parameters that determine the configurations of the robot and the objects in the task. These inequalities represent C-surfaces [Mason 1981]. Take the constraint that a robot hand remain in contact with a crank handle as it rotates. The constraint relating the position of the hand, (x, y), to the position of the crank axis (a constant) and its current angle, α, is a curve (one-dimensional surface) in the configuration space of the task, that is, the (x, y, α) space.

Our goal is to make the detailed analysis of assembly operations algorithmic by casting it in terms of C-surfaces. The purely geometric aspects of the analysis have been exploited in earlier work on obstacle avoidance [Brooks & Lozano-Pérez 1983; Lozano-Pérez 1981, 1983]. C-surfaces also share many of the characteristics of "real" surfaces with respect to force

A

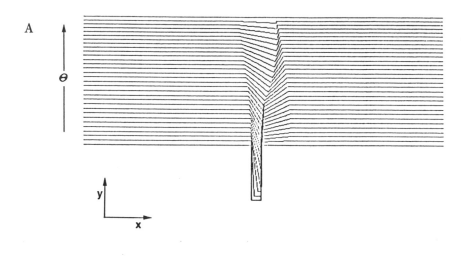

B

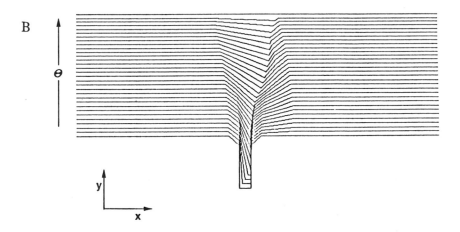

Figure 14. Cross sections of peg-in-hole C-surfaces: (a) no chamfer (b) chamfer.

analyses. This was exploited by Mason [1981] to synthesize compliant motions. The synthesis approach described here also requires a mechanism for computing the effects of friction. Recent work has developed a definition of friction cones for C-surfaces [Erdmann 1986]. Work is under way to show that conditions for avoiding jamming for the peg-in-hole can be re-stated in terms of the relationship of applied forces to these C-space friction cones.

A General Framework

In the previous section we illustrated an abstract planning algorithm for fine-motion strategies. Although that algorithm is representative of our approach to fine-motion synthesis, it is *not* the most general formulation of the approach. In particular, that algorithm embodies a restrictive assumption on the class of single-motion strategies. It only considers strategies obtained by discarding all velocity vectors that point into the friction cones of some subset of the task surfaces. In some cases, further restrictions of the class of velocity vectors would produce a better strategy. The algorithm of the previous section does not provide a mechanism for further restricting the range of velocities. More significantly, we have not provided a criterion for defining what makes one strategy "better" than another.

In this section we will present a more general framework for our approach to fine-motion synthesis. Although the description of this approach takes the form of an algorithm, it is not detailed enough to be considered an effective procedure. Our goal here is to formulate the *correctness conditions* for a class of synthesis algorithms. This framework can be used to elucidate to what extent particular synthesis methods (for the class of fine-motion strategies we are considering) are "optimal." In particular, we are interested in strategies that make the best possible use of sensory data.

Development of the general framework begins with a description of the form of termination predicates for motions, followed by a discussion of the pre-image definition, and of the necessity of passing multiple subgoals to recursive calls of the planner. The rest of the section consists of a formal description of the framework, expressed as an abstract algorithm, and an extended example of its application to the peg-in-hole problem of the previous section.

Termination predicates

Much of the burden of interpreting uncertain information falls on the termination predicate, which must decide when the current goal has been achieved. It is obviously important that termination not be premature; otherwise subsequent motions will proceed on a false assumption. On the other hand, failure to terminate the motion when the goal is demonstrably attained is also bad; the missed opportunity could prevent successful completion of the task (the motion may continue and move away from the goal). Hence it is important that the termination predicate make the best possible use of the available information.

One restriction is placed on the form of the termination predicates: we will exclude predicates which record sensory data for later use. The decision to terminate the motion must be made based on current sensor readings alone. As we shall see below, there is another mechanism which encodes some history, so this constraint is not as debilitating as it may first appear. If later developments suggest that this restriction should be relaxed, the framework can be modified by allowing a state function to be defined along with each predicate.

The form of the termination predicate will be introduced first with the assumption of perfect sensing and control. Consider the situation just after a command has been issued. Given perfect knowledge of the initial position and a perfect controller, and assuming good dynamic models, the planner could predict the subsequent trajectory of the robot. If the position and force sensors were perfect, it would be a simple matter to watch the sensors, or the time, and halt the motion when the robot reaches a goal.

To address more realistic problems, we will first relax the assumption of perfect sensing. The planner still knows what trajectory the robot will follow, but the sensing information cannot be taken at face value. It is necessary to construct an interpretation of the sensory data, which will be the set of all positions/velocities consistent with the sensory data and with the trajectory. Once this is accomplished, termination is again simple—if this interpretation of the sensory data is a subset of a goal, the motion is terminated.

The final step is to relax the assumption of perfect control and known initial position. Suppose we have a set of possible initial positions, and a set of possible nominal velocities. Each different combination of initial position and nominal velocity will give a different robot trajectory. Without knowing which trajectory is the "real" one, the predicate must terminate the motion with a guarantee of being in a goal. To see how this is done, imagine that there is a different robot for each trajectory, that is, when all of the trajectories are being executed simultaneously. For each robot, we can apply the procedure of the previous paragraph: form the set of positions/velocities consistent with sensory data, intersect with the trajectory, check for inclusion in a goal. If the robots all agree that a goal has been achieved, the motion is terminated. This approach guarantees that for any initial position and nominal velocity consistent with the robot's information, and for any position and velocity consistent with observations, termination will occur only if a goal is attained.

When the termination predicate is constructed, it is important to bring all possible information to bear, so that the set of "virtual robots" may be made as small as possible. Thus far we have concentrated on the information encoded in the sensory data, but there is another important source of information. When we formulate a subgoal R and call the planner recursively, there are two important effects. First, the robot will be moved to R. But second, and more to the point, is that when the recursive call returns and the motion is executed, the planner *knows* that the robot is in R. To illustrate the distinction, consider a robot lightly touching a vertical wall, and suppose that the subgoal R is the wall. Although the robot is in R, this fact might not be apparent to the robot if the contact force is small and if the position sensors are noisy. Hence the planner is called recursively to "move" the robot to the wall. Presumably the planner will plan a horizontal motion into the wall. When the motion command is executed the robot will not move, which the termination predicate will interpret as evidence that the "motion" was successful. When the recursive invocation of the planner returns, it will have accomplished its mission, even though it did not move the robot at all.

Another, more familiar, example illustrates the use of this information to construct the termination predicate. Suppose the planner is applied to the point-in-hole problem, with the position sensor giving a position at the lip of the hole (see figure 15). Using the position sensor alone, the planner would have to admit the possibility of the robot being positioned anywhere inside the disc centered on the sensed position. To attain the goal with a single motion would be impossible. However, if the accomplished subgoal R is also consulted, the set of possible initial positions is reduced—the robot must be in the intersection of R with the disc. Starting from this smaller set of possible initial positions, with a command nominal velocity down to the right, it is easy to confirm that all the virtual robots will achieve the goal.

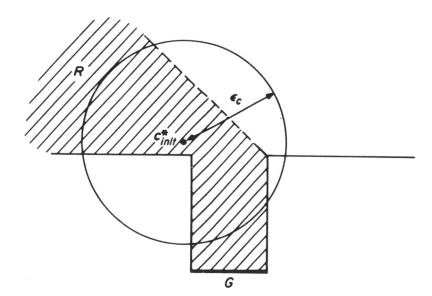

Figure 15. Some history is required to proceed into the hole.

Thus the history of the robot, represented by the accomplished subgoal R, must be taken into account to construct the termination predicate. When the set of feasible trajectories is constructed, initial positions outside the subgoal R should be excluded. That the termination predicate is dependent on the accomplished subgoal R is an important observation, which profoundly affects the ultimate form of the planning algorithm.

Definition of pre-image

The fundamental element in our approach to planning is the ability to construct a pre-image: a set of points from which the goal can be attained in a single motion. In the previous section, the pre-image depended on the goal G and a range of command nominal velocities. By proceeding more formally in this section, we find that the pre-image need not depend on the command nominal velocities, but that it does depend on the accomplished subgoal R.

Conceptually, we can approach this problem as follows: For goal G, and for every possible observed initial position c^*_{init} and accomplished subgoal R, construct the set $S(c^*_{init}, R, G)$ of all command nominal velocities such that the termination predicate, constructed earlier, is guaranteed to terminate the motion. If $S(c^*_{init}, R, G)$ is empty, there is no single motion that can be guaranteed to work for accomplished subgoal R and observed initial position c^*_{init}. If $S(c^*_{init}, R, G)$ is non-empty, then any element of $S(c^*_{init}, R, G)$ is sufficient to attain the goal. Now if the actual initial position of the manipulator is c_{init}, the observed initial position c^*_{init} could be anywhere in the sphere $B(c_{init})$ centered on c_{init} with radius equal to the tolerance on the position sensor. c_{init} should be in the pre-image if and only if every possible c^*_{init} gives a non-empty $S(c^*_{init}, R, G)$. Hence we can define the pre-image $P_R(G)$ of a goal G:

$$P_R(G) = \{c_{init} \in R \mid \forall \, c^*_{init} \in B(c_{init}), S(c^*_{init}, R, G) \neq \emptyset\}.$$

The subscript R is used as a reminder that the pre-image depends on R. Note also that the definition of $P_R(G)$ excludes points outside R. To have a point in $P_R(G)$ but not in R would not make much sense—such a point would be a good place for the robot to be, provided that it was somewhere else!

Recursive calls and multiple goals

When the planner is first called, the robot could be anywhere in configuration space C. If the set of strategies guaranteed to attain the goal G from any point in configuration space $S(c^*_{init}, C, G)$ is non-empty, then the planner can choose and execute one of these strategies. If $S(c^*_{init}, C, G)$ is empty, the planner must construct suitable subgoals and initiate a recursive call to the planner to achieve these subgoals.

Clearly, the planner should specify as subgoals only those sets from which it can achieve the goal, otherwise a recursive call will serve no purpose. To characterize these subgoals more precisely, let us look ahead a bit, and imagine that the recursive call to the planner has just returned. The recursive call guarantees that the robot's position is now in R. Thus the planner must plan a single motion, from initial position c_{init} in R, which attains the goal G. By construction of the pre-image, such a motion exists only if c_{init} is in the pre-image $P_R(G)$. This observation serves to define suitable subgoals—R should include only those points which are also in $P_R(G)$, that is, $R \subset P_R(G)$. Because, by construction, $R \supset P_R(G)$, we can restate this observation: R is a suitable subgoal if and only if $R = P_R(G)$.

Thus, any set satisfying the equation $R = P_R(G)$ is a suitable subgoal. In general, there are a multitude of sets which satisfy this equation. For instance, if R satisfies the equation, so does any subset of R. The question is what to do with this multitude of subgoals. Do we pass them to recursive calls one at a time? Needless to say, the branching factor in this search can be rather large. However, another issue takes precedence. Situations occur for which the planner can be certain to attain one of two goals, but cannot be certain in advance *which* of the two goals it will attain. If the planner were passed either one of the two goals individually, it would fail to find a predicate guaranteed to terminate the motion. With both goals in hand simultaneously, it can plan a motion with confidence that it will ultimately be able to report which of the goals was attained. Hence we will pass all subgoals to the recursive call. This suggests that the approach be implemented without search, but we are not certain whether such an implementation will be possible.

Because the planner will be passed multiple goals rather than a single goal, some adjustment of the notation is required. The set of goals will be written $\{G_\alpha\}$, the set of strategies guaranteed to attain one of the goals for given observed initial position c_{init}^* and accomplished subgoal R will be written $S(c_{init}^*, R, \{G_\alpha\})$, and the pre-image will be written $P_R(\{G_\alpha\})$.

A Formal Statement of the Framework

Nomenclature

c is configuration.

c_{init} is configuration at the beginning of a motion.

v is velocity.

v_0 is nominal velocity.

c^* is observed configuration.

c_{init}^* is observed configuration at the beginning of a motion.

v^* is observed velocity.

v_0^* is commanded nominal velocity.

t is time.

C is C-space, that is, the set of all configurations.

$B(c)$ is the uncertainty ball of configurations; that is, the set of all configurations whose distance from c is within the tolerance of the position sensor.

$B(v)$ is the uncertainty ball of velocities.

$B(v_0)$ is the uncertainty ball of nominal velocities.

$\{G_\alpha\}$ is the current goal set. We wish to move the robot to one of the goals and return the identity of the goal.

$p(c^*, v^*, t)$ is the termination predicate. For each goal in $\{G_\alpha\}$ it returns one of the following: BUG, indicating that no possible trajectory is consistent with any interpretation of the sensory data; CONTINUE, indicating that at least one possible trajectory exists, consistent with the sensory data not just at the goal; or WIN, indicating that all possible trajectories consistent with the sensory data are in the goal.

$S(c_{init}^*, R, \{G_\alpha\})$ is the set $\{(v_0^*, p(c^*, v^*, t)) \mid p \text{ terminates}\}$. By construction of the predicates, guaranteed termination implies guaranteed attainment of a goal. So for a given observed initial configuration and accomplished subgoal R, this gives the set of all winning strategies, where a strategy comprises a command nominal velocity and a termination predicate.

$P_R(\{G_\alpha\})$ is the pre-image $\{c_{init} \in R \mid \forall\, c_{init}^* \in B(c_{init}), S(c_{init}^*, R, \{G_\alpha\}) \neq \emptyset\}$.

$\{R_\beta\}$ is the sets of configurations R such that the pre-image $P_R(\{G_\alpha\})$ includes all of R, that is, $P_R(\{G_\alpha\}) = R$. This is the subgoal set. Satisfaction of an element of this set by a recursive call will allow us to satisfy the current goal set.

R is the subgoal attained by recursive call to the planner.

MotorCommand(v_0^*) execution of this program statement transmits the commanded nominal velocity to the controller, causing the manipulator to execute the planned generalized damper strategy.

$D_{i,j}(t)$ is the actual trajectory; it returns (c, v), the actual configuration and velocity at time t, for initial position $c_{init,i}$ and nominal velocity $v_{0,j}$.

Algorithm

```
Procedure FM({G_α})
   Compute {R_β}
   If C is in {R_β}
      Then R ← C
      Else R ← FM({R_β})
   (v₀*, p) ← choose(S(c*_init, R, {G_α}))
   t ← 0
   MotorCommand(v₀*)
L  {V_α} ← p(c*, v*, t)
      ForEach α Do If V_α = BUG Then Error
      ForEach α Do If V_α = WIN Then Return(G_α)
      Increment t
      Go L
   End FM
```

Example

This section applies the algorithm to the two-dimensional peg-in-hole problem (see figure 16). FM is called with an initial goal set containing the single element G: the bottom of the hole. Let $D_{i,j}(t)$ denote an actual trajectory; it returns (c, v)—the actual configuration and velocity at time t—for initial position $c_{init,i}$ and nominal velocity $v_{0,j}$.

First we construct an example illustrating construction of the termination predicate $p(c^*, v^*, t)$. Such a predicate must be constructed for each (c^*_{init}, v_0^*, R). Here is the predicate for $(c^*_{init,2}, v_{0,2}^*, R)$, assuming that R includes $B(c^*_{init,2})$.

```
Procedure p_{2,2}(c*, v*, t)
   Flag ← False
   For all (c_init,i, v_0,j) ∈ B(c*_init,2) × B(v*_0,2)
      (c, v) ← D_i,j(t)
      If (c, v) ∈ B(c*) × B(v*)
         Then If c ∈ G
            Then Flag ← True
            Else Return(CONTINUE)
   If Flag Then Return(WIN)
      Else Return(BUG)
```

$S(c^*_{init}, R, G)$ is the set of all (v_0^*, p) which are guaranteed to win if executed at a point in $B(c^*_{init}) \cap R$. For our example point, this set is empty. For example, the command nominal velocity $v_{0,2}^*$ is not in $S(c^*_{init}, R, G)$ because trajectories from the left and right edges of $B(c^*_{init})$ will never reach the goal.

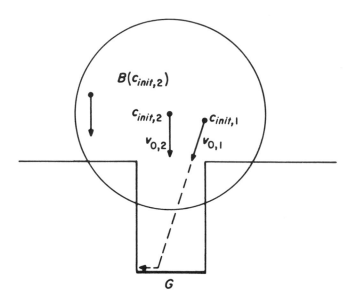

Figure 16. Task illustrating construction of p.

The example predicate will give the behavior specified in sections "Termination Predicates" and "A Formal Statement of the Framework," and is therefore "correct." The form of the predicates is not completely satisfactory, however. The test for goal attainment is done simply by testing whether all possible predicted trajectories have attained the goal. This satisfies the requirements of the formalism because of the way control error is modeled—we have assumed that the control error is constant during a trajectory. A more realistic model of error would yield more robust predicates, combining position, velocity, and time information to detect presence at the goal.

The first step in the algorithm is to compute a set of subgoals $\{R_\beta\}$. Recall that each element R of $\{R_\beta\}$ is a set giving a pre-image $P_R(\{G_\alpha\})$ which is equal to R. The simplest way to begin is to construct the sets consisting of a single configuration. Such a set $R = \{c\}$ is valid if and only if it gives a pre-image $P_{\{c\}}(\{G_\alpha\})$ equal to $\{c\}$. Suppose the recursive call reports the manipulator is at c, then the question is whether a single motion command can move the manipulator to the goal G. This is possible for all configurations c in the shaded region of figure 17. This region is the union of two half-planes and a circular disk [Turk 1983]. A point in one of the half-planes, such as c_3, can move to the hole by selecting a velocity which is guaranteed either to fall to one side of the hole and slide in, or hit the hole directly. A point in the circular region, such as c_4, can move to

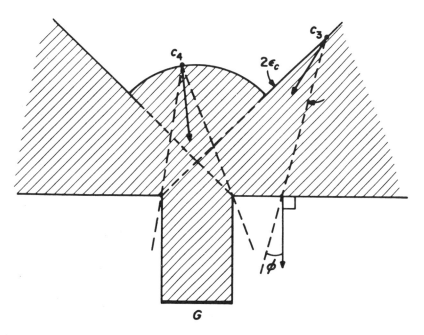

Figure 17. Singleton R's.

the hole by selecting a velocity which is guaranteed to hit the hole directly.

Any set R satisfying $R = P_R(\{G_\alpha\})$ must be a subset of the region indicated in figure 17. The shaded region does not itself constitute a good R, however. For instance, as in the earlier example, the planner might be unable to tell whether the robot is to the left or to the right of the hole. Hence, we must look for subsets R of the shaded region, each of which is equal to the corresponding pre-image $P_R(\{G_\alpha\})$. Three different such subsets are shown in figures 18. Consider, for example, the set shown in figure 18c. There are three different regions in this set: one region to the left of the hole, one region to the right of the hole, and one region in the hole. We can demonstrate that this R is equal to the corresponding $P_R(\{G_\alpha\})$ as follows. Suppose that a recursive call has reported that the manipulator is in R. We now consult the position sensor. If c^*_{init} is to the right of center, the manipulator cannot be in the left region, and the left-sliding command shown for point c_3 in figure 17 will work. Similarly, if c^*_{init} is to the left of center, a right-sliding motion will work. This set works because any "incompatible" subsets—the left and right regions in this case—are separated by a distance of at least $2\epsilon_c$.

The sets shown in figure 19 are *maximal*; they are not subsets of any

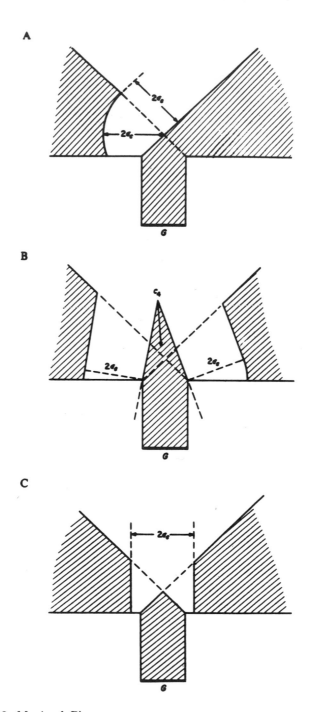

Figure 18. Maximal R's.

other subgoals. Since the subset of any valid subgoal is itself a valid subgoal, it would make sense to pass only the maximal sets to the recursive call. However, situations do occur for which maximal sets do not exist, so we will simply pass all valid subgoals to the recursive call.

Once the subgoal set $\{R_\beta\}$ has been determined there is a recursive call to FM. As in the section "The Basic Strategy," we will use a superscript numeral to indicate the "recursion level." Thus, we write that the recursive call's goal set is the original call's subgoal set by writing $\{G_\alpha^1\} \leftarrow \{R_\beta^0\}$. Construction of a predicate for a multiple goal set is a simple variation of the predicate constructed earlier.

```
Procedure p₁,₁(c*, v*, t)
   Flag  ←  FALSE
   For All α Winα  ←  TRUE
   For All (c_init,i, v_0,j) ∈ (R ∩ B(c*_init,1)) × B(v*_0,1)
      (c, v)  ←  D_i,j(t)
      If (c, v) ∈ B(c*) × B(v*)
         then Flag  ←  TRUE
         For All α If c ∉ G_α Then Win_α  ←  FALSE
   If Flag Then If For Some α Win_α = TRUE
      Then Return(WIN)
      Else Return(CONTINUE)
   Else Return(BUG)
```

Now the recursive call must construct subgoals. In this case, the set of all configurations C is a valid subgoal. No further recursion is necessary, because one of the goals can be attained from any configuration whatever using a single motion command. The recursive call may immediately choose and execute a motion command. When the predicate terminates the motion, the identity of the subgoal attained is returned to the original call, which then chooses and executes a motion command carrying the manipulator to the bottom of the hole.

Conclusion

This chapter has presented a formal approach to the synthesis of a class of fine-motion strategies. The approach operates directly from geometric descriptions of the task and explicit bounds on errors in sensing and motion. The basic method is structured around the computation of the pre-image of a goal region, that is, a set of configurations that can reach the goal using a single compliant motion. We saw that the presence of errors in motion and sensing gives rise to a number of difficult problems in specifying motions and in deciding on termination conditions.

Beyond presenting a specific synthesis approach, the chapter has attempted to:

- Illustrate the usefulness of modeling compliant fine-motion strategies as generalized damper motions that "slide" on C-surfaces (corresponding to geometric constraints).

- Establish correctness conditions for fine-motion programs operating under error in sensing and control.

Our approach to these issues provides the foundation for our synthesis method. Moreover, we hope it may be useful to human programmers engaged in fine-motion synthesis.

The approach in this chapter is part of an attempt to develop a unified approach to robot motion planning, spanning obstacle avoidance [Brooks & Lozano-Pérez 1983; Lozano-Pérez 1981, 1983], compliant motion [Mason 1981] pushing [Mason 1982], grasping [Lozano-Pérez 1981; Mason 1982], and (now) fine-motion strategies. We believe that if sophisticated sensor-based motion strategies are to be routinely used in robotics, the analysis and synthesis of these strategies cannot (or should not have to) be done by human programmers on a task-by-task basis. Moreover, we are in need of a theoretical basis for the development of the programming and control mechanisms best suited for sensor-based motion. For these reasons, there is a vital need for a unified (preferably mechanizable) approach to analysis and synthesis of robot motion. This chapter is a step towards this goal.

References

Andreev, G. Y., and N. M. Laktionev, [1969] "Contact stress during automatic assembly," *Russian Engineering Journal*, vol. 49, no. 11, p. 57.

Arnold, V. I. [1980], *Mathematical Methods of Classical Mechanics*, Springer-Verlag, New York, Heidelberg, Berlin.

Brooks, R. A. [1982], "Symbolic error analysis and robot planning," *Int. J. Robotics Research*, vol. 1, no. 4.

Brooks, R. A., and T. Lozano-Pérez [1982], *A Subdivision Algorithm in Configuration Space for Findpath with Rotation*, Report AIM-684 Artificial Intel-

We would like to thank Rodney Brooks, Steve Buckley, and Mike Erdmann for their helpful comments on earlier drafts on this chapter.

This chapter describes research done in part at the Artificial Intelligence Laboratory of the MIT. Support for the Laboratory's Artificial Intelligence research is provided in part by the System Development Foundation, in part by the Office of Naval Research under Office of Naval Research contract N00014–81–K–0494 and in part by the Advanced Research Projects Agency under Office of Naval Research contracts N00014–80–C–0505 and N00014–82–K–0334. R. H. Taylor was funded in part by IBM while on sabbatical at MIT.

ligence Laboratory, Massachusetts Institute of Technology, (also IJCAI–83 Proceedings).

Buckley, S. J. [1987], "Planning and teaching compliant motion strategies," Report AI–TR–936, Massachusetts Institute of Technology, Artificial Intelligence Laboratory.

Donald, B. R. [1987], "Error detection and recovery for robot motion planning with uncertainty," Report AI–TR–982, Massachusetts Institute of Technology, Artificial Intelligence Laboratory.

Drake, S. H. [1977], "Using Compliance in Lieu of Sensory Feedback for Automatic Assembly," Ph.D. Thesis, Mechanical Engineering Department, Massachusetts Institute of Technology.

Dufay, B., and J. C. Latombe [1983], "An Approach to Automatic Robot Programming Based on Inductive Learning," *International Symposium on Robotics Research*, Bretton Woods.

Erdmann, M. A. [1986], "Using backprojections for fine-motion planning with uncertainty," *International Journal of Robotics Research*, vol. 5, no. 1, pp. 19–45.

Goto, T., K. Takeyasu, and T. Inoyama [1980], "Control algorithm for precision insert operation robots," *IEEE Trans. Systems, Man, Cybernetics*, vol. SMC-10, no. 1, pp. 19–25.

Gusev, A. S. [1969], "Automatic assembly of cylindrically shaped parts," *Russian Engineering Journal*, vol. 49, no. 11, pp. 53.

Hanafusa, H., and H. Asada [1977], "A Robot Hand with Elastic Fingers and its Application to Assembly process," *IFAC Symposium on Information and Control Problems in Manufacturing Technology*, Tokyo, pp. 127–138. Reprinted in *Robot Motion*, edited by M. Brady *et al.*, MIT Press, 1983.

Inoue, H. [1974], "Force feedback in precise assembly tasks," Report AIM-308, Artificial Intelligence Laboratory, Massachusetts Institute of Technology. Reprinted in *Artificial Intelligence: An MIT Perspective*, edited by P. H. Winston, and R. H. Brown, MIT Press.

Laktionev, N. M., and G. Y. Andreev [1966], "Automatic assembly of parts," *Russian Engineering Journal*, vol. 46, no. 8, p. 40.

Lozano–Pérez, T. [1976], *The design of a mechanical assembly system* Report AI-TR- 397, Artificial Intelligence Laboratory, Massachusetts Institute of Technology. Reprinted in part in *Artificial Intelligence: An MIT Perspective*, edited by P. H. Winston, and R. H. Brown, MIT Press, 1979.

Lozano–Pérez, T. [1983], "Automatic planning of manipulator transfer movements," *IEEE Trans. Systems, Man, Cybernetics*, vol. SMC–11, no. 10, pp. 681–689, 1981; Reprinted in *Robot Motion*, edited by M. Brady, *et. al.*, MIT Press.

Lozano–Pérez, T. [1983], "Spatial planning: a configuration space approach," *IEEE Trans. Computers*, vol. C-32, no. 2.

McCallion, H., and P. C. Wong [1975], "Some thoughts on the automatic assembly of a peg and a hole," *Industrial Robot*, vol. 2, no. 4, pp. 141-146.

Mason, M. T. [1981], "Compliance and force control for computer controlled manipulators," *IEEE Trans. Systems, Man and Cybernetics*, vol. SMC-11, no. 6, pp. 418–432. Reprinted in *Robot Motion*, edited by M. Brady, *et. al.*, MIT Press, 1983.

Mason, M. T. [1982], "Manipulator Grasping and Pushing Operations," Technical Report, Artificial Intelligence Laboratory, Massachusetts Institute of Technology.

Mason, M. T. [1983], "Compliant Motion," Reprinted in *Robot Motion*, edited by M. Brady, *et. al.*, MIT Press.

Nilsson, N. [1980], *Principles of Artificial Intelligence*, Tioga Publishing, California.

Ohwovoriole, M. S., and B. Roth [1981], "A theory of parts mating for assembly automation," *Proceedings Ro.Man.Sy.*, Warsaw, Poland.

Ohwovoriole, M. S., B. Roth, and J. Hill [1980], "On the Theory of Single and Multiple Insertions in Industrial Assemblies," *Proceedings 10th Int. Symp. Industrial Robots*, Milan, Italy, pp. 545–558.

Paul, R. P., and B. Shimano [1976], "Compliance and control," *Proceedings Joint Automatic Control Conference*, San Francisco, pp. 694–699. Reprinted in *Robot Motion*, edited by M. Brady, *et. al.*, MIT Press, 1983.

Raibert, M. H., and J. J. Craig [1981], "Hybrid position/force control of manipulators," *J. Dynamic Systems, Measurement, Control*, vol. 102. Reprinted in *Robot Motion*, edited by M. Brady, *et. al.*, MIT Press, 1983.

Salisbury, J. K. [1980], "Active stiffness control of a manipulator in Cartesian coordinates," *IEEE Conference Decision and Control*, Albuquerque, New Mexico.

Simons, J., H. van Brussel, J. de Schutter, and J. Verhaert [1982], "A self-Learning Automaton with Variable Resolution for High Precision Assembly by Industrial Robots," *IEEE Transactions on Automatic Control*, vol. AC-27, no. 5.

Simunovic, S. N. [1975], "Force information in assembly processes," *Proceedings 5th Int. Symp. Industrial Robots*, Chicago, pp. 415-431.

Simunovic, S. N. [1979], Ph.D. Thesis, "An Information Approach to Parts Mating" Mechanical Engineering Department, Massachusetts Institute of Technology.

Taylor, R. H. [1976], "The synthesis of manipulator control programs from task–level specifications," Report AIM-282, Artificial Intelligence Laboratory, Stanford University.

Turk, M. A. [1983], private communication.

Whitney, D. E. [1977], "Force feedback control of manipulator fine motions," *J. Dynamic Systems, Measurement, Control*, pp. 91–97.

Whitney, D. E. [1982], "Quasi-static assembly of compliantly supported rigid parts," *J. Dynamic Systems, Measurement, Control* vol. 104, pp. 65–77. Reprinted in *Robot Motion*, edited by M. Brady, *et. al.* MIT Press, 1983.

Will, P. M., and D. D. Grossman [1975], "An experimental system for computer controlled mechanical assembly," *IEEE Trans. Computers* vol. C-24, no. 9, pp. 879–888.

Appendix: Compliance via Generalized Damping

Generalized damping is a very simple and flexible mechanism for implementing active compliance[3] [Whitney 1977]. The basic approach is to define the desired behavior of the robot by the following relation:

$$\mathbf{f} = \mathbf{B}(\mathbf{v} - \mathbf{v}_0)$$

where $\mathbf{f}$ is the vector of forces acting on the moving object, $\mathbf{v}_0$ is the nominal velocity vector, and $\mathbf{v}$ is the actual velocity vector. In general, $\mathbf{f}$ is a vector of six cartesian forces and torques and $\mathbf{v}$ and $\mathbf{v}_0$ are vectors of six linear and rotational velocities. In our examples here, we limit ourselves to forces and linear displacements in the plane.

Allowing the damping matrix $\mathbf{B}$ to be an arbitrary matrix can produce unusual behavior. One popular example is to relate forces in the $-x$ directions to displacements in the $+y$ direction so that the robot will climb over obstacles. We will, however, limit ourselves to simple damping matrices. In particular, we assume $\mathbf{B}$ to be the a diagonal matrix $b\mathbf{I}$, with $b > 0$. Note that the damper equation is now simplified to

$$\mathbf{f} = b(\mathbf{v} - \mathbf{v}_0)$$

or alternatively

$$\mathbf{v} = \mathbf{v}_0 + \frac{1}{b}\mathbf{f}.$$

Consider an object controlled by a generalized damper with $\mathbf{v}_0$ (at an angle θ below horizontal) on a rigid surface whose normal points along the y axis (see figure 19a). When the object strikes the surface, three possibilities exist:

1   Object slides to the right.
2   Object slides to the left.
3   Object remains motionless.

We can use Coulomb's law to determine which of these three possibilities will occur.

First consider case 1; the object slides to the right, so the velocity $\mathbf{v}$ is horizontal. Coulomb's law dictates that the contact force $\mathbf{f}$ will make an angle $\phi = tan^{-1}\mu$ with the surface normal. Using the damper equation

---

[3]See Mason [1983] for a discussion of generalized damping versus the generalized stiffness and hybrid control approaches to compliant motion.

A

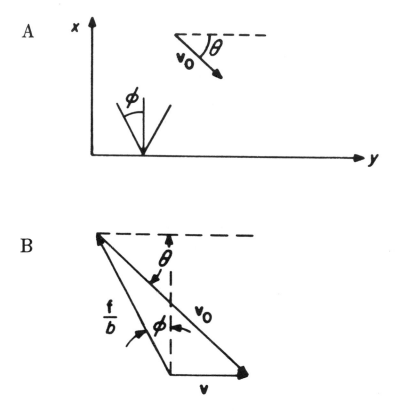

Figure 19. Geometry for generalized damper analysis.

in a simple construction in velocity space (see figure 19b) we see that the nominal velocity angle θ must be less than $\frac{\pi}{2} - \phi$. Case 2, with the object sliding to the left is quite similar and yields the constraint that θ must be greater than $\frac{\pi}{2} + \phi$.

Finally consider case 3; the object sticks, that is, the velocity $\mathbf{v}$ is zero. Coulomb's law gives a constraint on the force:

$$\frac{\pi}{2} - \phi \leq \alpha \leq \frac{\pi}{2} + \phi,$$

where α is the angle which the force $\mathbf{f}$ makes with the horizontal. Again, the damper equation implies a corresponding constraint on θ:

$$\frac{\pi}{2} - \phi \leq \theta \leq \frac{\pi}{2} + \phi.$$

The analysis above yields constraints on the nominal velocity $\mathbf{v}_0$ given the motion of the object. We are also interested in the opposite: given the nominal velocity $\mathbf{v}_0$, what will be the resultant motion. In the present analysis this is easily obtained. If the nominal velocity angle θ is less than

$\frac{\pi}{2} - \phi$, only case 1, right-sliding, can occur. If the nominal velocity angle θ is greater than $\frac{\pi}{2} + \phi$, only case 2, left-sliding, can occur. If the nominal velocity angle θ is in the interior of the friction cone, that is, if

$$\frac{\pi}{2} - \phi < \theta < \frac{\pi}{2} + \phi,$$

then only case 3, sticking, can occur. The only ambiguous cases occur when $\theta = \frac{\pi}{2} + \phi$ or when $\theta = \frac{\pi}{2} - \phi$. These cases are often referred to as "impending motion."

Thus the class of nominal velocities which give a desired motion on a given surface is easily characterized in terms of the friction cone of the surface, making the generalized damper an ideal control function for synthesis of fine motions.

Part V

Jumping Through Hoops and Manipulating Objects

The simple elegance of elementary Newtonian physics can seduce us into believing that our arms and legs are easily controlled. But some of the equations are too complicated to be solved quickly and others involve hard-to-measure parameters. Fortunately, many new ideas are emerging:

- Atkeson and Reinkensmeyer describe how complicated limbs can be controlled, without any sort of dynamic model, as long as there is a way to relate required motions to stored practice motions.

- Singer and Seering demonstrate how to reduce arm vibration by inserting an antivibration filter between arm commands and actuator inputs.

- Raibert explains that his menagerie of hopping, skipping, bounding, pacing, and trotting machines all exploit simple procedures that control height, body posture, and forward motion.

- Hodgins and Raibert show that a mechanical biped can do a forward flip provided that the feedback-free jump, pitch, tuck, untuck, and land movements are done in cooperation with normal locomotion procedures.

- Salisbury et al. describe their insights into the control of the three-fingered Salisbury hand, explaining how that hand can orient objects, hold stiffly, hold softly, feel texture, determine shape, and rearrange its own grasp via controlled slip.

- Salisbury et al. study how we use our arms for pushing, shoving, cradling, cushioning, grasping, and even striking, as well as for carrying our hands around, and they explain why such operations are the forte of the cable-driven Townsend arm.

- Bennett and Hollerbach show that an arm can determine its own limb-length and angle-offset parameters if the arm has at least seven joints.

- And finally, Bennett and Hollerbach show that an arm can determine its own limb-length and angle-offset parameters, even if it has six or fewer joints, as long as it can borrow degrees of freedom from another arm, a door, or other suitably constrained object.

28

The world is full of computational miracles, including those that occur whenever you reach for coffee or throw a baseball. Somehow, you succeed in spite of the enormous mechanical complexity of your arm, with its large number of inertias, frictions, and actuators. Somehow, you get the coffee drunk or the batter out even though there are too many things to model and even though small parameter errors in an otherwise perfect model ensure that motion predictions quickly diverge from the real thing.

In this chapter, Atkeson and Reinkensmeyer argue for an approach to this sort of problem that uses massive amounts of memory. To understand their approach, imagine waving a robot arm around more or less randomly. Every so often, record the instantaneous position, velocities, and acceleration of every arm joint, along with every actuator force, creating a giant table. Then, when you want to move the arm along a prescribed trajectory, break that trajectory up into little pieces, look for table entries with nearby positions, velocities, and accelerations, and interpolate among them to find appropriate forces for the corresponding little piece of trajectory.

You might worry, legitimately, that no table could be sufficiently dense. To combat the density problem, Atkeson and Reinkensmeyer introduce the idea of practice. The first time your robot reaches or throws, it does miserably because its table is sparse. Importantly, however, your robot continues to write into its giant table, so the next time your robot reaches or throws, the giant table contains new entries in the vicinity of the desired positions, velocities, and accelerations. After a few tries, your robot's motion becomes smooth and accurate.

Using Associative Content-Addressable Memories to Control Robots

Christopher G. Atkeson
David J. Reinkensmeyer

For many robot systems, good models are hard to formulate, difficult to identify and calibrate, and computationally expensive to use. This chapter explores a memory-based approach to modeling. In this approach models are learned by storing experiences in a memory, and predictions are made by searching the memory for relevant experience. The memory used is an associative content-addressable memory (ACAM) [Kohonen 1980]. We have implemented an ACAM on a parallel computer, the Connection Machine [Hillis 1985]. In order to explore the feasibility of the approach and identify research issues and problems, we used the ACAM to model and control a simulated planar two-joint arm and a simulated running machine. We found that simply using only the nearest experience to predict new commands produced surprisingly good performance. The results presented in this chapter provide a reference point for more sophisticated schemes under development.

An associative content-addressable memory can be implemented in many ways. There are implementations appropriate for serial computers, parallel computers, dedicated electronic hardware, and model neural networks. We have implemented an associative content-addressable memory on a parallel computer, but the issues raised and experience gained are useful in assessing many proposed memory-based motor control schemes.

Memory-Based Modeling

This section describes how a memory can be used to represent a model. As an example, the dynamics of a one-joint arm are modeled, and the model is used to compute feedforward commands for a robot controller. The robot controller combines these feedforward commands with feedback control to drive the arm along a desired trajectory. The arm dynamics are affected by gravitational, viscous, frictional, and inertial forces. The state of the arm is given by its current joint position and velocity, θ and $\dot{\theta}$. Applying a joint torque, τ, causes a particular joint acceleration, $\ddot{\theta}$. These values can be stored together as a single experience

$$(\theta_i, \dot{\theta}_i, \ddot{\theta}_i, \tau_i) \tag{1}$$

where i designates the ith experience. In this study new experiences are generated by a feedback controller, which refines the feedforward torques according to position and velocity errors.

In order to predict the torques necessary to achieve a desired trajectory, it is useful to have a model of the arm's inverse dynamics, $\hat{R}^{-1}$, which performs the transformation

$$\tau = \hat{R}^{-1}(\theta, \dot{\theta}, \ddot{\theta}). \tag{2}$$

$\hat{R}^{-1}$ can be represented by a memory that contains experiences of particular positions, velocities, torques, and the resulting accelerations. Command torques can be predicted by addressing the memory with the desired performance $(\theta_d, \dot{\theta}_d, \ddot{\theta}_d)$, and finding the stored experience most similar to the desired performance. The appropriate variables of each stored experience are compared with the desired positions, velocities, and accelerations using a distance metric. A simple distance metric is the Euclidean distance between the corresponding values

$$d_i = ((\theta_i - \theta_d)^2 + (\dot{\theta}_i - \dot{\theta}_d)^2 + (\ddot{\theta}_i - \ddot{\theta}_d)^2)^{1/2}. \tag{3}$$

Alternative distance metrics such as the sum of the absolute values of the distances in each dimension could also be used. The torque from the experience with the smallest distance, d_i, is used at each point along the desired trajectory.

This process can be implemented on a standard serial computer. Every time a particular set of positions, velocities, and accelerations is requested, the entire memory can be searched for the closest experience. Viewed as a black box, this process implements an associative content-addressable memory. The memory is content-addressable in that part of the contents of the memory are used to select the rest of the memory; in our example a position, velocity, and acceleration, $(\theta_i, \dot{\theta}_i, \ddot{\theta}_i)$, were used to choose an experience, and the torque from that experience was used, (τ_i). In the case where an exact match is not available this process finds a reasonable answer by finding the most similar experience in the memory. In this way the process acts as an associative memory.

With large computer memories now available, the limiting factor for this simple implementation of an ACAM is the time required to search the memory. The time required to find the closest experience increases linearly

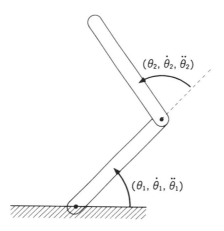

Figure 1. Simulated planar two-joint arm.

with the number of experiences in the memory. Other more efficient ways to implement an ACAM are reviewed in a later section.

We have used a parallel computer to implement an ACAM. In our ACAM implementation each experience is stored in a processor of the Connection Machine, a massively-parallel computer [Hillis 1985]. The Connection Machine can have up to 2^{16} (65536) processors, and can simulate a parallel computer with many more processors. Each experience can be compared to the desired experience simultaneously in each processor, and then a hardwired global-OR bus can be used to find the closest match in constant time independent of the number of stored experiences. This approach is similar to many Connection Machine algorithms that find a best match [Waltz 1987].

Trajectory Following

The feasibility of the ACAM was tested on two simulations, the first of which involved a simulated robot arm following a trajectory. The ACAM was used to learn a model of the robot inverse dynamics and helped improve performance of a single trajectory and a similar trajectory by predicting appropriate feedforward commands.

The arm used in the simulation was a two-joint robot arm (see figure 0) with dynamics given by

$$\ddot{\theta} = R(\theta, \dot{\theta}, \tau) \tag{4}$$

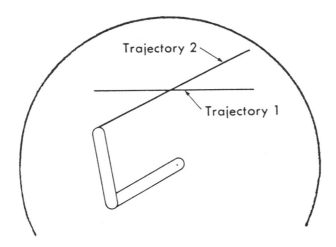

Figure 2. Test trajectories.

where $\ddot{\theta}$ is the joint acceleration vector produced by application of the torque vector τ to the current state of the arm as given by the joint angle and joint velocity vectors θ and $\dot{\theta}$. As the arm is servoed along a trajectory, a model of the inverse dynamics is built by storing values of the vectors $\theta, \dot{\theta}, \ddot{\theta}$, and τ.

In order to use the model to calculate feedforward torques, the memory is searched using $\theta_{\mathbf{d}}$, $\dot{\theta}_{\mathbf{d}}$, and $\ddot{\theta}_{\mathbf{d}}$ as indices, where the subscript $\mathbf{d}$ denotes desired values as supplied by a trajectory planner. This search is done before each attempt at the trajectory, and an array is filled with the feed-forward torques ($\tau_{\mathbf{ff}}$) which are to be added to the output of a feedback controller

$$\tau = -\mathbf{K}(\theta - \theta_{\mathbf{d}}) - \mathbf{B}(\dot{\theta} - \dot{\theta}_{\mathbf{d}}) + \tau_{\mathbf{ff}} \,, \tag{5}$$

$\mathbf{K}$ and $\mathbf{B}$ are constant position and velocity feedback gain matrices. The combination of feedback terms and feedforward terms drives the robot. If $\tau_{\mathbf{ff}}$ is poorly modeled, the feedback terms are responsible for moving the arm in a reasonable way. This is the situation when the memory has not stored many experiences: the feedback terms act as a teacher in generating the initial commands that enable the ACAM to store appropriate experiences. As the model becomes more accurate, the contribution of the feedback terms to the controller becomes smaller. Miller and colleagues [1987] use a similar training paradigm in their learning algorithm.

The two test trajectories shown in figure 2 were planned using a straight line path and a fifth-order polynomial position function which started and ended at rest and had a duration of one second. The movements were in a vertical plane so gravity points downward in this figure.

The links of the arm were modeled as thin uniform rods each with a mass of $1kg$. The feedback controller used decoupled position and velocity gains of $K_{11} = 65.7Nm/rad$, $K_{22} = 13Nm/rad$, $B_{11} = 42Nms/rad$, and $B_{22} = 8Nms/rad$, and applied torques at a rate of 100 Hz. The equations describing the arm dynamics were integrated using Euler's method with a time step of 0.001 seconds.

The ACAM improved trajectory following for a single trajectory. Figure 3 shows the performance of trajectory 1 with the feedback controller alone. After storing these experiences in the ACAM, feedforward torques were computed using the memory.

Figure 3. Trajectory 1—feedback only.

Figure 4. Trajectory 1—first attempt.

Figure 4 shows that on the first attempt using the ACAM there was a performance improvement.

Figure 5 compares the feedforward torques on the first attempt with the ideal feedforward torques for the desired movement. In this and other graphs of feedforward torques the smooth solid lines are the correct feedforward torques.

After three cycles of storing the previous movement's data in the ACAM and computing a new feedforward command, the performance improved further. Figure 6 shows this tracking performance.

Figure 7 shows that the feedforward torques corresponded more closely to the ideal feedforward torques. The ACAM built a better model of the arm dynamics.

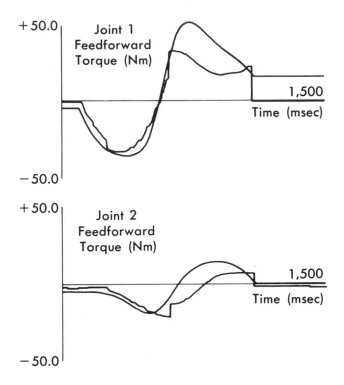

Figure 5. Trajectory 1—feedforward torques for first attempt.

Figure 6. Trajectory 1—third attempt.

The accuracy of trajectory following for trajectory 1 stopped improving after about six attempts. The feedforward torques for attempt ten are shown in figure 8, and show the best performance the memory was able to achieve. We call this phenomena a "stuck state." The problem of stuck states is discussed in a later section.

The model stored in the ACAM after eight attempts at trajectory 1

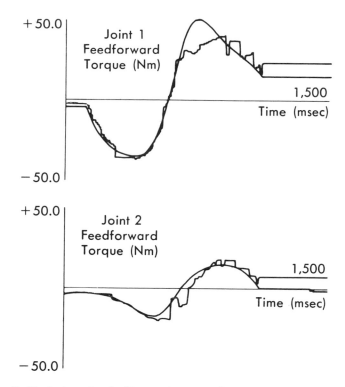

Figure 7. Trajectory 1—feedforward torques for third attempt.

generalized to a similar trajectory, trajectory 2 (see figure 2). The ACAM used only the experiences stored during the attempts at trajectory 1 to calculate the feedforward torques for trajectory 2. Figure 9 shows the trajectory following performance on trajectory 2 with the feedback controller alone.

Figure 10 shows the improved performance on trajectory 2 using the model learned during performance of trajectory 1.

Figure 11 shows how well the feedforward torques generalized from the experiences of trajectory 1. The similarity of these feedforward torques with the ideal feedforward torques suggests that the ACAM can act as a local model by generalizing from limited experience, but it should be noted that the modeling error is large for some parts of the trajectory.

The improved single-trajectory following and the generalization to a similar trajectory seen in these and other experiments demonstrate that an ACAM can build a useful model of the arm dynamics. The simple distance metric was effective in retrieving stored experiences, and reasonable generalization was obtained by using the closest experience. Stuck states present a problem deserving future attention.

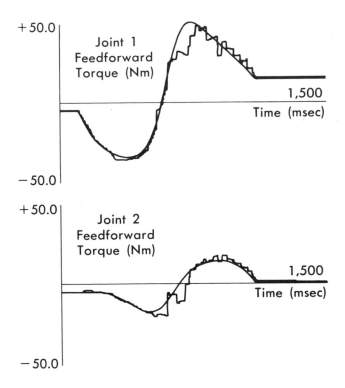

Figure 8. Trajectory 1—feedforward torques for tenth attempt (stuck state).

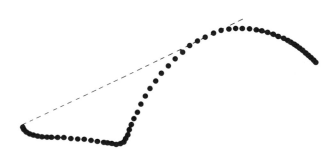

Figure 9. Trajectory 2—feedback only.

Figure 10. Trajectory 2—using trajectory 1 experiences.

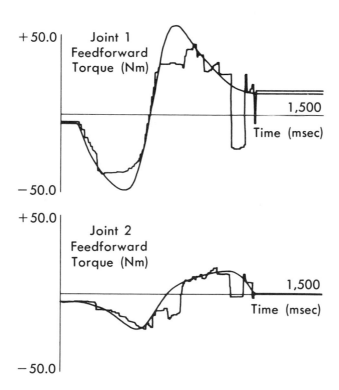

Figure 11. Trajectory 2—feedforward torques using trajectory 1 experiences.

Control of Running

The second simulation involved control of running. Memory-based techniques are well-suited for control of a dynamically-stable, legged robot [Raibert & Wimberly 1984]. Such a legged system is difficult to model, contains a large number of variables, and encounters only a small number of experiences (hops). In this simulation an ACAM was used to build a *correction* to a model of legged running. This learning proved useful in improving control of the simulated robot beyond the performance with the original model alone.

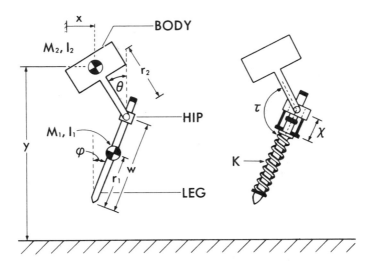

Figure 12. Simulated planar one-legged hopper from Raibert and Wimberly [1984].

Figure 12 shows a simulated legged, hopping machine originally developed by Raibert. It has a body, a springy leg, a leg actuator, and a hip actuator. Control of the hopper is partitioned into three algorithms [Raibert 1984]. In order to control hopping height, the amount of energy contained in the system is adjusted by changing the length of the leg spring during stance. In order to control body angle, the hip actuator servos the body to the appropriate position during the stance portion of a hop. The hip actuator also controls balance and running speed by servoing the foot during flight to an appropriate placement. If the foot is placed at a point called the neutral point, the machine runs with constant velocity. If the foot is placed behind the neutral point, the machine accelerates. If the foot is placed ahead of the neutral point, the machine decelerates.

The ACAM was used to improve the algorithm controlling balance and running speed. The memory acted as a correction to an analytical model of foot placement which is made by predicting the projection that the center of gravity will sweep out during stance. The projection is called a CG-print [Raibert 1984], and is approximated by $T_s\dot{x}$ where T_s is a stance duration predicted from the characteristics of the springy leg, and $\dot{x}$ is the average velocity of the machine during stance, and is approximated by the velocity at takeoff. If on landing the foot has been servoed to the center of a perfect model of the CG-print, the machine experiences no net acceleration. Thus the center of a perfect model of the CG-print is the neutral point. In order to accelerate the machine, the foot can be displaced from the center of the CG-print. The amount of displacement is dictated by a servo which uses the current and desired velocity of the machine

$$fp_{cg}(\dot{x}_d, state) = \frac{1}{2}T_s\dot{x} + K(\dot{x} - \dot{x}_d) \qquad (6)$$

where fp_{cg} is the foot placement calculated by the CG-print model, and K is a gain.

In order to improve the CG-print model, the ACAM builds a corrective model. Corrections to the modeled foot placement are calculated in the following way. Each time the hopper leaves the ground, an appropriate foot placement for the next landing is calculated using the CG-print model and a correction from the ACAM

$$fp(\dot{x}_d, state) = fp_{cg}(\dot{x}_d, state) - A(\dot{x}_d, state) \qquad (7)$$

where fp_{cg} represents an evaluation of the CG-print model, A represents an ACAM lookup, and *state* is the state of the machine as defined by the variables $\dot{x}$, y, $\dot{y}$, θ, $\dot{\theta}$, ϕ, $\dot{\phi}$, w, and $\dot{w}$ (see figure 13). The leg is servoed to this foot placement during flight, and the machine accelerates when it lands, resulting in a new takeoff velocity $\dot{x}_{new}$. The resulting knowledge of the actual physical transformation for this particular foot placement is used to store a correction to the CG-print model. First, a foot placement is calculated using the CG-print model, given the output of the actual transformation, $\dot{x}_{new}$

$$\widehat{fp} = fp_{cg}(\dot{x}_{new}, state). \qquad (8)$$

The difference between what actually happened and what the model predicted, $\widehat{fp} - fp$, is then stored in the ACAM so that it can be accessed by $A(\dot{x}_{new}, state)$.

Results

The ACAM learned how to correct the CG-print model and improved running performance in simulation.

Figure 14 shows an attempt at a series of desired flight velocities using the CG-print model with the parameters and controller gains described in [Raibert 1984]. The flat parts of the plot of the actual center-of-mass

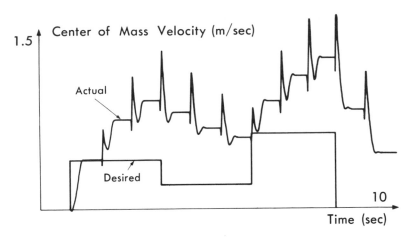

Figure 13. Controlling hopping flight velocity—without ACAM.

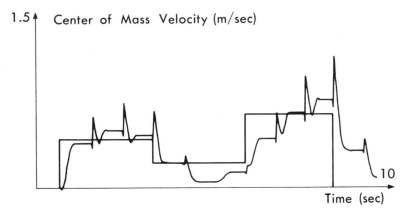

Figure 14. Controlling hopping flight velocity—first attempt with ACAM (100 Hops Previously Stored).

velocities are the flight velocities. Figure 15 shows the first attempt at the series of running velocities using the ACAM for corrections after having stored 100 hops whose desired velocities changed every three hops and varied randomly from -1.0 m/s to 1.0 m/s.

Figure 15 shows the second attempt at the same series after having stored the results of the first series. Steady state errors and response time were reduced. The model that the ACAM learned enhanced the legged

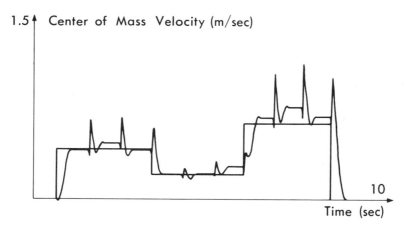

Figure 15. Controlling hopping flight velocity—second attempt with ACAM.

machine's performance. Stuck states were encountered in this simulation also, and limited the performance to a level only slightly better than that shown in figure 15.

Comparison with a table-based approach

Raibert has experimented with table-based control of running [Raibert & Wimberly 1984]. There are several differences between his table-based approach and this implementation of an ACAM.

The first difference involves keeping the table size manageable. With the intent of reducing table size, Raibert partitioned the state variables into 2 groups: a group that varies from hop to hop $(\dot{x}, \phi, \dot{\phi}, \theta)$ and a group that varies periodically $(y, \dot{y}, \dot{\theta}, w, \dot{w})$. Because the periodic variables should be about the same value at takeoff for any given hop, it is not essential to use them as table indices, and thus table size can be substantially reduced. The ACAM allows retention of the periodic variables without taxing memory size because the size grows only linearly with the number of variables or fields in a data point. The benefit of retaining the periodic variables is that they might become more important in certain situations. For example, the vertical takeoff velocity $(\dot{y})$ might be more important for runs where hopping height is varied.

The second difference between the table-based and ACAM approaches is that this implementation used as simple a distance metric as possible. The distance metric considered all variables equally important. The running velocity was the only variable controlled. Raibert's table controlled running velocity, body angle, and body angular velocity and weighed each variable differently depending on which was deemed more important to control. His distance metric took into account weighting factors which assigned the relative importance of different types of errors.

The third difference between the table-based approach and the ACAM implementation is that the table used interpolation in order to compensate for its coarse quantization. Because we wanted to investigate the simplest generalization scheme possible (nearest neighbor), the ACAM was implemented without interpolation. This strategy was not unreasonable because the ACAM quantization depends only on the similarity of the experiences collected, and thus can be arbitrarily small. An interesting point to note is that tabular interpolation becomes computationally expensive as the number of dimensions increases because the number of neighboring table entries grows exponentially with the number of dimensions. Raibert also explored using polynomial surfaces to fit the tabulated data.

Finally, Raibert filled the table by running many simulations before using the table to control the robot. The table replaced the CG-print model. In this implementation, the ACAM was used to correct the CG-print model, experiences were stored during the actual control of the robot, and corrections to the CG-print model were used as soon as the memory had stored a small number of experiences (100). This model correction scheme allows better performance in areas of the state space for which the ACAM has not stored many experiences.

Discussion

These feasibility studies demonstrate that useful models of robots can be learned by storing experiences in a memory. There are several issues that needed to be addressed in this exploration of memory-based modeling, such as the source of the experiences, how to measure similarity, and how to generalize.

The source of the experiences is usually referred to as the "teacher." The experiences can be generated in a variety of ways. For example, random torques can be applied, or a feedback controller can be relied on as a source of torques. In this work the feedback controller served as the teacher.

A simple distance metric is used to measure the similarity between experiences: the Euclidean distance between the experiences represented as points in a vector space. Even with this distance metric it was not clear how to weight or scale the different dimensions, which often had different units of measurement. How should a position be compared to an acceleration, for example? In this study the dimensions were not scaled. Other alternatives would be to scale the dimensions so that the range of values in each dimension are the same, or so that a given change in each dimension had the same effect on the outputs. Designing a perfect distance metric is difficult, but the examples in this chapter show that a simple distance metric can be effective in retrieving stored experiences.

In the version of ACAM presented in this chapter, only the closest experience is used, although a weighted sum of the closest experiences, or an approximation based on a surface which is fit to the closest experiences could be computed. More complex generalization schemes will allow interpolation and extrapolation from the stored data, and may also help in dealing with noisy data, an issue not addressed in this chapter.

In our version of ACAM, every experience is stored. At some point memory-size limitations will be reached. To use memory space more sparingly, only the experiences which are sufficiently different from previous experiences could be stored. Memory size could also be reduced by "forgetting" certain experiences, perhaps those that have not been referenced for a long time. We have not needed to implement any form of "forgetting" or memory consolidation process.

With a poor teacher, such as a low-gain feedback controller, the performance in both feasibility studies improved, but errors were not reduced to zero. We refer to this phenomena as a stuck state, and expect it to be an issue in many ACAM based approaches to control [Miller *et al.* 1987]. The teacher, in our case the feedback controller, is no longer generating improved performance over the stored performance, and only old data is used in generating new commands. Possible solutions include changing the teacher, deliberately adding random noise or other perturbations to the commands, and improving generalization and the distance metric. Preliminary experiments using a generalization function that fits a hyperplane to a set of similar experiences have eliminated the stuck states. Model-based approaches to learning may also prove useful [Atkeson, Aboaf, McIntyre, & Reinkensmeyer 1988].

Related Work

Two forms of modeling previous experience are those approaches that represent the experiences directly, as in this study, and those that represent the experiences using parameters or weights, such as in many table-based schemes, perceptrons and multi-layer connectionist or model neural networks. For a more extensive review of related work see Atkeson [1989].

Direct storage of experience

Memory-based modeling has a long history. Approaches which represent previous experiences directly and use a similar experience or similar experiences to form a local model are often referred to as nearest neighbor or k-nearest neighbor approaches. Local models (often polynomials) have been used for many years to smooth time series [Whittaker & Robinson 1924; Macauley 1931] and interpolate and extrapolate from limited data. Barnhill [1977] and Sabin [1980] survey the use of nearest neighbor interpolators to fit surfaces to arbitrarily spaced points. Eubank [1988] surveys the use of nearest neighbor estimators in nonparametric regression. Lancaster and Šalkauskas [1986] refer to nearest neighbor approaches as "moving least squares" and survey their use in fitting surfaces to data. Farmer and Sidorowich [1988] survey the use of nearest neighbor and local model approaches in modeling chaotic dynamic systems.

An early use of direct storage of experience was in pattern recognition. Fix and Hodges [1951] suggested that a new pattern could be classified by searching for similar patterns among a set of stored patterns, and using the categories of the similar patterns to classify the new pattern. Steinbuch proposed a neural network implementation of the direct storage of experience and nearest-neighbor search process for pattern recognition, and pointed out that this approach could be used for control [Steinbuch & Piske 1963]. Lorenz [1969] explored the use of nearest neighbors to predict the weather. Stanfill and Waltz [1986] proposed using directly stored experience to learn pronunciation, using a Connection Machine and parallel search to find relevant experience. They have also applied their approach to medical diagnosis [Waltz 1987] and protein structure prediction.

Loftsgaarden and Quesenberry [1965] proposed using a nearest neighbor approach to estimate probability density functions.

Nearest neighbor approaches have also been used in nonparametric regression and fitting surfaces to data. Often, a group of similar experiences, or nearest neighbors, is used to form a local model, and then that model is used to predict the desired value for a new point. Local models are formed for each new access to the memory. Watson [1964], Royall [1966], Crain and Bhattacharyya [1967], Cover [1968], and Shepard [1968] proposed using a weighted average of a set of nearest neighbors. Gordon and Wixom [1978] analyze such weighted average schemes. Crain and Bhattacharyya [1967], Pelto, Elkins, and Boyd [1968], Palmer [1969], Lodwick and Whittle [1970], Falconer [1971], and McLain [1974] suggested using a weighted regression to fit a local polynomial model at each point a function evaluation was desired. All of the available data points were used. Each data point was weighted by a function of its distance to the desired point in the regression. Stone [1975] and Franke and Nielson [1980] suggested fitting a polynomial surface to the nearest neighbors, also using distance weighted regression. Stone scaled the values in each dimension when the experiences were stored. The standard deviations of each dimension of previous experiences were used as the scaling factors, so that the range of values in each dimension were approximately equal. This affects the distance metric used to measure closeness of points. Cleveland [1979] proposed using robust regression procedures to eliminate outlying or erroneous points in the regression process. Stone [1977, 1982], Devroye [1981], Lancaster and Šalkauskas [1981], Cheng [1984], Li [1984], Farwig [1987], and, Müller [1987] provide analyses of nearest neighbor approaches. Franke [1982] compares the performance of nearest neighbor approaches with other methods for fitting surfaces to data.

Devroye [1978] has explored nearest neighbor approaches to function optimization.

Several direct implementations of associative content-addressable memories have been proposed. As mentioned previously, a standard serial computer searching experiences sequentially can be used to simulate an ACAM. The problem with this approach is that the search time increases as more experiences are added to the memory. The search time is proportional to the number of experiences. One way to reduce the search time is to use a table. The values of the desired experience are used to compute an address in the table, and all experiences that fall into a particular table entry are stored there. In order to find the nearest neighbor, all experiences in that entry and all neighboring entries must be examined. The dimensions of such a table must match the dimensions of the data, and therefore the number of entries in the table grows exponentially with the number of dimensions of an experience, as does the number of table entries that must be searched on each access.

A benefit of the approach we have used to implement an ACAM is that memory requirements are much less than those of tabular memories. We only store experiences that have actually occurred, rather than allocate storage for all possible experiences. Memory size is proportional to the number of experiences encountered. It is also proportional to the size of each experience, and therefore the number of dimensions stored. The memory required grows only linearly with the number of experiences and the number of dimensions, rather than exponentially. However, the memory used is substantially more complex than a table memory. This type of ACAM is particularly well-suited for systems with a large number of dimensions and a relatively small amount of experience.

Another approach to implementing an ACAM that represents the data directly is to use k-d trees [Friedman, Bentley & Finkel 1977]. This approach uses a tree data structure to speed up the search for the best match. However, the number of data points that must be examined to find the best match grows exponentially with the number of dimensions in the data. Omohundro [1987] proposed that the first experience found in the k-d tree search should be used instead, as it is probably close enough. Using this first match greatly reduces the search time. K-d trees are especially appropriate for ACAM implementations on serial computers. Farmer and Sidorowich [1988] used k-d trees and a variety of generalization functions to model chaotic dynamic systems.

An early implementation of a direct ACAM used a local representation in a network similar to many current neural network models [Steinbuch & Piske 1963]. There is a single layer of neurons, often referred to as "hidden units," which each compute an inner product of the weights on their input connections with the corresponding inputs to the network. This layer is followed by a maximum detection or winner-take-all network. The representation is local because only one "hidden unit" is active at any one time. This type of network can find nearest neighbors or best matches using a Euclidean distance metric [Kazmierczak & Steinbuch 1963]. Steinbuch and Widrow [1965] provide a useful comparison between network models using a local and a distributed representation. Baum and colleagues [1988] provide a more recent analysis of binary networks that use a local representation. Scalettar and Zee [1988] demonstrate that with the appropriate conditions a binary network learns a local rather than distributed representation using the backpropagation algorithm.

It is important to keep in mind that all of the forms of direct data representation will give the same outputs if the design choices for the teacher, distance metric, and generalization function are the same. How a direct ACAM should be implemented is a function of the hardware available. The direct implementation of an ACAM permits experimentation with distance metrics and generalization methods.

Global parametric models

Parametric models whose structure matches the structure of the system being modeled are often used to fit an entire training data set (see An *et al.* [1988] for further references from robotics, and Kawato, Furukawa and Suzuki [1987] for an approximate parametric model of robot arm rigid body dynamics using a connectionist network). These models are often referred to as global models. If the structure of a global model is correct, the model is capable of wide generalization. However, it is often difficult to find the appropriate model structure for a system. Most of the other approaches to modeling described in this chapter are motivated by a desire to avoid having to know an appropriate model structure prior to fitting the data.

Tabular models

We have previously described how a table can speed access to directly represented experiences sorted into the table entries. The experiences assigned to each table entry can also be averaged or combined in some way to form a set of parameters or weights. In this case the directly stored experiences do not need to be examined when the table is used. Raibert and Wimberly's [1984] table was of this form. Michie and Chambers [1968] implemented an early table-based controller to balance an inverted pendulum on a moving cart. Connectionist network representations (described below) with a local representation can be used to implement a table of weights [Barto, Sutton & Anderson 1983]. Albus used a hashing algorithm and a fixed overlap of tabular weights to reduce problems of table size and generalization [Albus 1975ab; Miller, Glanz & Kraft 1987].

Connectionist network representations

An alternative way to implement an associative content-addressable memory is in a distributed connectionist network [Rumelhart *et al.* 1986]. The desired experience is presented to the network as a set of activations to the input nodes. The output is represented as a set of activations on the output nodes. There may be several intermediate layers of nodes. Each node computes a weighted sum of the activations of the nodes connected to it, and some function of that weighted sum of the inputs becomes its activation. The weights are the parameters modified to make the network represent a particular function. Single experiences are represented in a distributed fashion by the weights, and each new experience may modify all the weights. Single layer connectionist networks were used early on to solve control problems [Widrow & Smith 1964]. An example of a recent distributed connectionist approach to modeling robot dynamics is provided by Goldberg and Pearlmutter [1988].

Computing the output is straightforward for connectionist networks, as each node computes in parallel a simple function of its inputs. The appeal of these networks is that they can be implemented using simple and relatively slow computing elements. However, finding the appropriate set of weights for the network is a difficult problem and usually involves some form of iterative gradient descent search, and additional hardware to implement the weight finding algorithm. In contrast, in the direct forms of data representation representing the data is straightforward; the data is simply stored without any conversion or change in representation. Finding the appropriate output, however, usually involves a substantial amount of computation with relatively complex computing elements. Stanfill and Waltz [1986] provide a comparison of a direct data representation (MBRtalk) and a connectionist network representation (NETtalk) in solving a pronunciation task. Farmer and Sidorowich [1988] provide a comparison of a direct data representation system with a connectionist network representation for modeling chaotic dynamic systems.

Representing data in terms of distributed weights has several implications. The need to find the appropriate set of weights to represent a given set of experiences adds an additional learning problem to that of generating useful experiences. If an iterative gradient descent search algorithm is used to find the appropriate set of weights, previous experiences must be presented several times to the network or new experiences collected during the iterative search. Learning new experiences may degrade the representation of older experiences, unless the older experiences are stored in another form of memory and presented again during all learning. It is not certain that the search for appropriate weights will converge to a useful set of values due to the presence of locally optimum weights, and it is not certain that a useful set of weight values exists. It is difficult to detect when there are no close experiences and the best match is too dissimilar to be useful. The original distribution of experiences is not represented in the weights of the network.

Although the algorithms connectionist networks use to compute outputs are easily specified, they are difficult to analyze. It is not clear how to design networks to represent a particular function: How many nodes and layers are required, for example? Although successful network learning procedures have been demonstrated it is not yet clear how well they will scale up to realistically sized problems, how effectively they use data to learn, and how quickly they can learn [Hinton 1986]. The generalization function is implicit in the network design, rather than explicitly chosen. The choice of teaching algorithm is independent of the network design, and the teaching issues are similar for ACAMs implemented using direct data representations and distributed representations.

Direct implementations of ACAMs raise their own set of implementation issues. For example, while the question of how to find the appropriate weights or parameters for a representation is avoided, the distance metric and generalization algorithm must be explicitly provided by the implementor. We should not only explore different neural network designs, but also explore the full range of methods available to implement associative content-addressable memories. The question of whether an ACAM is useful for control should be separated from the question of how best to implement an ACAM.

Conclusion

This initial feasibility study demonstrates that it is possible to learn a useful model by storing experiences in a memory. The use of parallel search in the implementation of an associative content-addressable memory allowed quick searching of stored experiences, and reasonable retrieval was obtained using a simple distance metric and a simple generalization scheme. The memory was able to generalize after storing only a small number of relevant experiences. The use of search by parallel processors also allowed us to avoid many of the problems of previous memory-based or tabular approaches to modeling such as search speed and memory requirements.

Further experimentation and development is required to solve problems such as stuck states.

References

Albus, J. S. [1975a], "A New Approach to Manipulator Control: The Cerebellar Model Articulation Controller (CMAC)," *ASME J. Dynamic Systems, Meas., Control*, pp. 220-227.

Albus, J. S. [1975b] "Data Storage in the Cerebellar Model Articulation Controller (CMAC)," *ASME J. Dynamic Systems, Meas., Control*, pp. 228-233.

An, C. H., C. G. Atkeson, and J. M. Hollerbach [1988], *Model-Based Control of a Robot Manipulator*, MIT Press, Cambridge, MA.

Atkeson, C. G. [1989], "Learning Arm Kinematics And Dynamics," *Annual Review of Neuroscience*, vol. 12, pp. 157-183.

Atkeson, C. G., E. W. Aboaf, J. McIntyre, and D. J. Reinkensmeyer [1988], "Model-Based Robot Learning," *Robotics Research: The Fourth International Symposium*, edited by Robert C. Bolles and Bernard Roth, MIT Press, Cambridge, MA, pp. 103-110.

Barnhill, R. E. [1977], "Representation And Approximation of Surfaces," in *Mathematical Software III*, edited by J. R. Rice, Academic Press, New York, pp. 69-120.

Barto, A. G., R. S. Sutton, and C. W. Anderson [1983], "Neuronlike Adaptive Elements That Can Solve Difficult Learning Control Problems," *IEEE Transactions on Systems, Man, and Cybernetics*, vol. SMC-13, no. 5, pp. 834-845.

Baum, E. B., J. Moody, and F. Wilczek [1988], "Internal Representations for Associative Memory," *Biological Cybernetics*, vol. 59, pp. 217-228.

Cheng, P. E. [1984], "Strong Consistency of Nearest Neighbor Regression Function Estimators," *Journal of Multivariate Analysis*, vol. 15, pp. 63-72.

B. Widrow made the authors aware of early work on neural network implementations of direct associative content addressable memory [Steinbuch & Widrow 1965].

This chapter describes research done at the Whitaker College, Department of Brain and Cognitive Sciences, and the Artificial Intelligence Laboratory of the Massachusetts Institute of Technology. Support was provided under Office of Naval Research contract N00014-88-K-0321, and Air Force Office of Scientific Research contract N00014-88-K-0321. Support for the Artificial Intelligence Laboratory's research is provided in part by the Advanced Research Projects Agency of the Department of Defense under Office of Naval Research contract N00014-85-K-0124, and the Office of Naval Research University Research Initiative Program under Office of Naval Research contract N00014-86-K-0685. Support for CGA was provided by a National Science Foundation Engineering Initiation Award and Presidential Young Investigator Award and a Whitaker Health Sciences Fund MIT Faculty Research Grant.

Cleveland, W. S. [1979], "Robust Locally Weighted Regression and Smoothing Scatterplots," *Journal of the American Statistical Association*, vol. 74, pp. 829-836.

Cover, T. M. [1968], "Estimation by the Nearest Neighbor Rule," *IEEE Transactions on Information Theory*, vol. IT-14, pp. 50-55.

Crain, I. K., and B. K. Bhattacharyya [1967], "Treatment of nonequispaced two dimensional data with a digital computer," *Geoexploration*, vol. 5, pp. 173-194.

Devroye, L. P. [1978], "The Uniform Convergence of Nearest Neighbor Regression Function Estimators and Their Application in Optimization," *IEEE Transactions on Information Theory*, vol. IT-24, pp. 142-151.

Devroye, L. P. [1981], "On the Almost Everywhere Convergence of Nonparametric Regression Function Estimates," *The Annals of Statistics*, vol. 9, no. 6, pp. 1310-1319.

Eubank, R. L. [1988], *Spline Smoothing and Nonparametric Regression*, Marcel Dekker, New York, pp. 384-387.

Falconer, K. J. [1971], "A general purpose algorithm for contouring over scattered data points," *Nat. Phys. Lab.*, Report NAC 6.

Farmer, J. D., and J. J. Sidorowich [1988], "Exploiting Chaos to Predict the Future and Reduce Noise," Technical Report LA-UR-88-901, Los Alamos National Laboratory, Los Alamos, New Mexico.

Farwig, R. [1987], "Multivariate Interpolation of Scattered Data by Moving Least Squares Methods," in *Algorithms for Approximation,* edited by J. C. Mason and M. G. Cox, Clarendon Press, Oxford, pp. 193-211.

Fix, E., and J. L. Hodges, Jr. [1951], "Discriminatory analysis, Nonparametric regression: consistency properties," Project 21-49-004, Report No. 4. USAF School of Aviation Medicine Randolph Field, Texas. Contract AF-41-(128)-31.

Fix, E., and J. L. Hodges, Jr. [1952], "Discriminatory analysis: small sample performance," Project 21-49-004, Rep. 11 USAF School of Aviation Medicine Randolph Field, Texas.

Franke, R. [1952], "Scattered Data Interpolation: Tests of Some Methods," *Mathematics of Computation*, vol. 38, no. 157, pp. 181-200.

Franke, R. and G. Nielson [1980], "Smooth Interpolation of Large Sets of Scattered Data," *International Journal Numerical Methods Engineering*, vol. 15, pp. 1691-1704.

Friedman, J. H., J. L. Bentley, and R. A. Finkel [1977], "An Algorithm for Finding Best Matches in Logarithmic Expected Time," *ACM Trans. on Mathematical Software*, vol. 3, no. 3, pp. 209-226.

Goldberg, K. Y., and B. Pearlmutter [1988], "Using a Neural Network to Learn the Dynamics of the CMU Direct-Drive Arm II," Technical Report CMU-CS-88-160, Carnegie-Mellon University.

Gordon, W. J., and J. A. Wixom [1978], "Shepard's Method of Metric Interpolation to Bivariate and Multivariate Interpolation," *Mathematics of Computation*, vol. 32, no. 141, pp. 253-264.

Hillis, D. [1985], *The Connection Machine*, MIT Press, Cambridge, MA.

Hinton, G. E. [1986], "Learning in massively parallel nets," *Proceedings: AAAI-86: 5th National Conference on Artificial Intelligence*, Philadelphia, PA, p. 1149.

Kawato, M., K. Furukawa, and R. Suzuki [1987], "A Hierarchical Neural-Network Model for Control and Learning of Voluntary Movement," Biol. Cybern. vol 57, pp. 169-185.

Kazmierczak, H., and K. Steinbuch [1963], "Adaptive Systems in Pattern Recognition," *IEEE Trans. on Electronic Computers*, EC-12, pp. 822-835.

Kohonen, T. [1980], *Content-Addressable Memories*, Springer-Verlag, New York, NY.

Lancaster, P., and K. Šalkauskas [1981], "Surfaces Generated by Moving Least Squares Methods", *Mathematics of Computation*, 37(155):141-158.

Lancaster, P., and K. Šalkauskas [1986], *Curve And Surface Fitting*, Academic Press, New York.

Li, K. C. [1984], "Consistency for Cross-Validated Nearest Neighbor Estimates in Nonparametric Regression," *The Annals of Statistics*, vol. 12, pp. 230-240.

Lodwick, G. D., and J. Whittle [1970], "A technique for automatic contouring field survey data," *Australian Computer Journal*, vol 2, pp. 104-109.

Loftsgaarden, D. O., and C. P. Quesenberry [1965], "A Nonparametric Estimate of a Multivariate Density Function," *Annals of Mathematical Statistics*, vol. 36, pp. 1049-1051.

Lorenz, E. N. [1969], "Atmospheric Predictability as Revealed by Naturally Occurring Analogues", *Journal of the Atmospheric Sciences*, vol. 26, pp. 636-646.

Macauley, F. R. [1931], *The Smoothing of Time Series*, National Bureau of Economic Research, New York.

McLain, D. H. [1974], "Drawing Contours From Arbitrary Data Points", *The Computer Journal*, vol. 17, no. 4, pp. 318-324.

Michie, D., and R. A. Chambers [1968], "Boxes: An Experiment in Adaptive Control," *Machine Intelligence 2*, Oliver and Boyd, London, pp. 137-152.

Miller, W. T., F. H. Glanz, and L. G. Kraft [1987], "Application of a general learning algorithm to the control of robotic manipulators," *International Journal of Robotics Research*, vol. 6, pp. 84-98.

Müller, H. G. [1987], "Weighted Local Regression and Kernel Methods for Nonparametric Curve Fitting," *Journal of the American Statistical Association*, vol 82, pp. 231-238.

Omohundro, S. M. [1987], "Efficient Algorithms with Neural Network Behavior," *J. Complex Systems*, vol. 1, no. 2, pp. 273-347.

Palmer, J. A. B. [1969], "Automated mapping," *Proc. 4th Australian Computer Conference,* vol. 6, pp. 463-466.

Pelto, C. R., T. A. Elkins, and H. A. Boyd [1968], "Automatic contouring of irregularly spaced data," *Geophysics,* vol. 33, pp. 424-430.

Raibert, M. H. [1984], "Hopping in Legged Systems—Modeling and Simulation for the Two-Dimensional One-Legged Case," *IEEE Transactions on Systems, Man, and Cybernetics,* vol. SMC-14, no. 3, pp. 451-463.

Raibert, M. H., and F. C. Wimberly [1984], "Tabular Control of Balance in a Dynamics Legged System," *IEEE Transactions on Systems, Man, and Cybernetics,* vol. SMC-14, no. 2, pp. 334-339.

Royall, R. M. [1966], "A class of nonparametric estimators of a smooth regression function," PhD. dissertation and Tech Report No. 14, Public Health Service Grant USPHS-5T1 GM 25-09, Department of Statistics, Stanford University, 1966.

Rumelhart, D. E., J. L. McClelland [1986], and the PDP Research Group, *Parallel Distributed Processing: Explorations in the Microstructure of Cognition, Volume 1: Foundations,* MIT Press, Cambridge, MA.

Sabin, M. A. [1980], "Contouring – A Review of Methods for Scattered Data," in *Mathematical Methods in Computer Graphics and Design,* edited by K. W. Brodlie, Academic Press, New York, pp. 63-86.

Scalettar, R., and A. Zee [1988], "Emergence of Grandmother Memory in Feed Forward Networks: Learning With Noise and Forgetfulness," in *Connectionist Models and Their Implications: Readings From Cognitive Science,* edited by D. Waltz and J. A. Feldman, Ablex Publishing, Norwood, NJ, pp. 309-327.

Shepard, D. [1968], "A two-dimensional function for irregularly spaced data," *Proceedings of 23rd ACM National Conference,* pp. 517-524.

Stanfill, C., and D Waltz [1986], "Toward Memory-Based Reasoning," *Communications of the ACM,* vol. 29 no. 12, pp. 1213-1228.

Steinbuch, K. and U. A. W. Piske [1963], "Learning Matrices and Their Applications," *IEEE Trans. on Electronic Computers,* vol. EC-12, pp. 846-862.

Steinbuch, K. and B. Widrow [1965], "A Critical Comparison of Two Kinds of Adaptive Classification Networks," *IEEE Trans. on Electronic Computers,* vol. EC-14, pp. 737-740.

Stone, C. J. [1975], "Nearest Neighbor Estimators of a Nonlinear Regression Function," *Proc. of Computer Science and Statistics: 8th Annual Symposium on the Interface,* pp. 413-418.

Stone, C. J. [1977], "Consistent Nonparametric Regression," *The Annals of Statistics,* vol. 5, pp. 595-645.

Stone, C. J. [1982], "Optimal Global Rates of Convergence for Nonparametric Regression," *The Annals of Statistics,* vol. 10, no. 4, pp. 1040-1053.

Waltz, D. L. [1987], "Applications of the Connection Machine", *Computer,* vol. 20, no. 1, pp. 85-97.

Watson, G. S. [1964], "Smooth Regression Analysis," *Sankhyā: The Indian Journal of Statistics, Series A,* vol. 26, pp. 359-372.

Whittaker, E., and G. Robinson [1924], *The Calculus of Observations,* Blackie and Son, London.

Widrow, B., and F. W. Smith [1964], "Pattern recognizing control systems," *Computer and Information Sciences,* edited by J. T. Tou and R. H. Wilcox, Clever Hume Press.

29

Most industrial robots are built like football linemen, not because they have to be, but because using lots of muscle and bone is one way to minimize control and vibration problems. Unfortunately, the muscle-and-bone approach produces robots that carry too much heavy, energy-consuming, nonpayload weight.

This chapter is about the vibration half of the problem, which Singer and Seering study using an experimental contraption that looks a little like a giant pinball-machine flipper. Imagine a thin, horizontal steel beam, about the size and shape of a yardstick, attached on one end to a heavy vertical post. Add a weight, about the size of a small cannon ball, to the free end of the steel beam.

When you visit their laboratory, Singer and Seering hand you a joy stick so that you can rotate the post to move the weight. Every time you try, the beam bends back and forth and the weight overshoots and undershoots, vibrating wildly.

Next, the authors flip a switch, putting a few lines of procedure between your joy stick and the post. Now the vibration is gone. You can swing the beam around with abandon, trying to produce some vibration, but you cannot. It is as if the beam had become incredibly stiff. The few lines of weightless procedure have done a job that would otherwise require a lot of heavy, energy-consuming nonpayload metal. Simulations with the Space Shuttle Remote Manipulator show that the approach leads to a 25-fold reduction in end-point residual vibration.

Preshaping Command Inputs to Reduce System Vibration

Neil C. Singer
Warren P. Seering

Input command shaping and closed-loop feedback for vibration control are two distinct approaches toward vibration reduction of flexible systems. Many researchers have examined closed-loop feedback techniques for reducing endpoint vibration, see for example, Hollars and Cannon [1985], Kotnik and Yurkovich [1988], and Pfeiffer and Gebler [1988]. These techniques differ from input shaping in that they use measurements of the system's states to reduce vibration. Command shaping involves altering the shape of either actuator commands or setpoints so that system oscillations are reduced [Meckl & Seering 1988; Smith 1958]. This technique is often dismissed because it is mistakenly considered to be useful only for open loop systems. However, if the input shaping accounts for the dynamic characteristics of the closed loop plant, then shaped input commands can be given to the closed loop plant as well. Thus, any of the preshaping techniques may be readily used as a closed loop technique [Meckl & Seering 1988; Smith 1958].

The earliest form of command preshaping was the use of high-speed cam profiles as motion templates. These input shapes were generated so as to be continuous throughout one cycle (such as, the cycloidal cam profile). Their smoothness (continuous derivatives) reduces unwanted dynamics by not putting high frequency inputs into the system [Sehitoglu & Aristizabal 1986], however, these profiles have limited success.

Another early form of setpoint shaping was the use of posicast control by Smith [1958]. This technique involves breaking a step of a certain magnitude into two smaller steps, one of which is delayed in time. This results in a response with a reduced settling time. In effect, superposition of the responses leads to vibration cancellation. However, this is not generally used because of problems with robustness. The system that is to be commanded must have only one resonance, be known exactly, and be very linear for this technique to work.

Optimal control approaches have been used to generate input profiles for commanding vibratory systems. Chun et al. [1985], Juang et al. [1985], and Junkins and Turner [1986], have made considerable progress toward practical solutions of the optimal control formulation for flexible systems Typically, a penalty function is selected (for example integral squared error plus some control penalty). The resulting "optimal" trajectory is obtained in the form of the solution to the system equations (a model). This input is then given to the system.

Farrenkopf [1979] and Swigert [1980] demonstrated that velocity and torque shaping can be implemented on systems which modally decompose into second order harmonic oscillators. They showed that inputs in the form of the solutions for the decoupled modes can be added so as not to excite vibration while moving the system. Their technique solves for parameters in a template function, therefore, inputs are limited to the form of the template. These parameters that define the control input are obtained by minimizing some cost function using an optimal formulation. The drawback of this approach is that the inputs are difficult to compute and they must be calculated for each move of the system.

Gupta [1980] and Junkins and Turner [1986] also included some frequency shaping terms in the optimal formulation. The derivative of the control input is included in the penalty function so that, as with cam profiles, the resulting functions are smooth.

Several papers also address the closed loop "optimal" feedback gains which are used in conjunction with the "optimal" open-loop input [Junkins & Turner 1986; Juang et al. 1986; Chun et al. 1985].

There are four drawbacks to these "optimal" approaches. First, computation is difficult. Each motion of the system requires recomputation of the control. Though the papers cited above have made major advances toward simplifying this step, it continues to be extremely difficult or impossible to solve for complex systems.

Second, the penalty function does not explicitly include a direct measure of the unwanted dynamics (often vibration). Tracking error is used in the penalty function, therefore, all forms of error are essentially lumped together—the issue of unwanted dynamics is not addressed directly. One side effect is that these approaches penalize residual vibration but allow the system to vibrate during the move. This leads to a lack of robustness under system uncertainties. In addition, vibration during a move may be undesirable.

Third, the solutions are limited to the domain of continuous functions. This is an arbitrary constraint which enables the solution of the problem. Fourth, the value of optimal input strategies depend on move time. Different moves will have different vibration excitation levels.

Another technique is based on the concept of the computed torque approach. The system is first modeled in detail. This model is then inverted— the desired output trajectory is specified and the required input needed to generate that trajectory is computed. For linear systems, this might involve dividing the frequency spectrum of the trajectory by the transfer function of the system, thus obtaining the frequency spectrum of the input. For nonlinear systems this technique involves inverting the equations for the model [Asada *et al.* 1987].

Techniques that invert the plant have four problems. First, a trajectory must be selected. If the trajectory is impossible to follow, the plant inversion fails to give a usable result. Often a poor trajectory is selected to guarantee that the system can follow it, thus defeating the purpose of the input [Bayo 1988]. Second, a detailed model of the system is required. This is a difficult step for machines which are not simple. Third, the plant inversion is not robust to variations in the system parameters because no robustness criterion has been included in the calculation. Fourth, this technique results in large move time penalties because the plant inversion process results in an acausal input (an input which exists before zero time). In order to use this input, it must be shifted in time thus increasing the move time.

Another approach to command shaping is the work of Meckl and Seering [1985, 1985, 1986, 1987, 1988] and Meckl [1988]. They investigated several forms of feedforward command shaping. One approach they examined is the construction of input functions from either ramped sinusoids or versine functions. This approach involves adding up harmonics of one of these template functions. If all harmonics were included, the input would be a time optimal rectangular (bang-bang) input function. The harmonics that have significant spectral energy at the natural frequencies of the system are discarded. The resulting input which is given to the system approaches the rectangular shape, but does not significantly excite the resonances. This technique essentially constructs an input function prior to a move. The approach presented in this chapter does not require continuous functions and the processing can be performed in real-time.

Aspinwall [1980] proposed a similar approach which involves creating input functions by adding harmonics of a sine series. The coefficients of the series are chosen to minimize the frequency content of the input over a band of frequencies. Unlike Meckl, the coefficients were not selected to make the sine series approach a rectangular function, therefore, a large time penalty was incurred.

Wang, Hsia, and Wiederrich [1986] proposed yet another approach for creating a command input that moves a flexible system while reducing the residual vibrations. They modeled the system in software and designed a PID controller for the plant that gave a desired response. They then examined the actual input that the controller gave to the software plant and used this for the real system. Next, they refined this input (the reference) with an iteration scheme that adds the error signal to the reference in order to get better tracking of the trajectory. This technique requires accurate modeling of the system and is not robust to parameter uncertainty. In addition, the method assumes that a good response can be achieved with a PID controller, In fact, systems with flexibility cannot, in general, be given sufficient damping and a reasonable response time by adding a PID controller.

Often, a notch filter is proposed for input signal conditioning. This approach gives poor results for several reasons. First, a causal (real time) filter distorts the phase of the resulting signal. This effect is aggravated by lengthening the filter sequence of digital filters or by increasing the order of analog or recursive filters. Therefore, efforts to improve the frequency characteristics of a filter result in increased phase distortion. Also, penalties, such as filter ringing or long move times often result.

Singer and Seering [1988] investigated an alternative approach of shaping a time optimal input by acausally filtering out the frequency components near the resonances. This has an advantage over notch filtering in that phase distortion and ringing no longer pose a problem. The drawbacks of this approach are the tradeoffs that must be made between fidelity in frequency and reduction of the move time.

Shaping Inputs

Most researchers have examined the transient vibration of manipulators in terms of frequency content of the system inputs and outputs. This approach inherently assumes that the system inputs are not actually transient, but are one cycle of a repeating waveform. The approach taken in this chapter is fourfold: first, the transient residual vibration amplitude of a system will be directly expressed as a function of its transient input. Second, the input will be specified so that the system's natural tendency to vibrate is used to cancel residual vibration. Third, the input will be modified to include robustness to uncertainties. Fourth, the case of arbitrary system inputs will be examined.

Generating a vibration-free output

The derivation of the new technique will be based on linear system theory. The results obtained will then be demonstrated on a more complicated system. The first step toward generating a system input which results in a vibration-free system output is to specify the system response to an impulse input. An uncoupled, linear, vibratory system of any order can be specified as a cascaded set of second-order poles with the decaying sinusoidal response [Bolz & Tuve 1973]

$$y(t) = \left[A \frac{\omega_0}{\sqrt{1.0 - \zeta^2}} e^{-\zeta\omega_0(t-t_0)} \right] \sin\left(\omega_0 \sqrt{1.0 - \zeta^2}(t - t_0) \right), \qquad (1)$$

where A is the amplitude of the impulse, ω_0 is the undamped natural frequency of the plant, ζ is the damping ratio of the plant, t is time, and t_0 is the time of the impulse input. The impulse is usually a torque or velocity command to an actuator. Equation (1) specifies the acceleration or velocity response, $y(t)$, at some point of interest in the system.

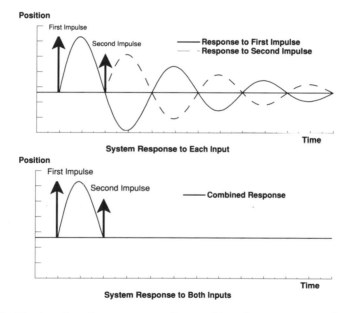

Figure 1. The two impulse responses shown add to form an output that shows a net positive motion with no vibration after the input has ended at the time of the second impulse.

In this section, only one mode is assumed (the general case is treated later). Figure 1 demonstrates that two impulse responses can be superposed so that the system moves forward without vibration after the input has ended. In this case, the input consists of two impulses; the "end" or duration of the input is the time of the last (second) impulse. The same result can be obtained mathematically by adding two impulse responses (each described by equation (1)), and expressing the result for all times greater than the duration of the input. Using the trigonometric relation (from Gieck [1983])

$$B_1 \sin(\alpha t + \phi_1) + B_2 \sin(\alpha t + \phi_2) = A_{amp} \sin(\alpha t + \psi), \qquad (2)$$

where

$$A_{amp} = \sqrt{(B_1 \cos \phi_1 + B_2 \cos \phi_2)^2 + (B_1 \sin \phi_1 + B_2 \sin \phi_2)^2}$$

$$\psi = \tan^{-1} \left(\frac{B_1 \cos \phi_1 + B_2 \cos \phi_2}{B_1 \sin \phi_1 + B_2 \sin \phi_2} \right),$$

The amplitude of vibration for a multi-impulse input is given by

$$A_{amp} = \sqrt{\left(\sum_{j=1}^{N} B_j \cos \phi_j \right)^2 + \left(\sum_{j=1}^{N} B_j \sin \phi_j \right)^2} \qquad (3)$$

$$\phi_j = \omega_0 \sqrt{(1 - \zeta^2)} t_j .$$

The B_j are the coefficients of the sine term in equation (1) for each of the N impulse inputs, and the t_j are the times at which the impulses occur. Elimination of vibration after the input has ended requires that the expression for A_{amp} equal zero at the time at which the input ends, t_N. This is true if both squared terms in equation (3) are independently zero, yielding

$$B_1 \cos \phi_1 + B_2 \cos \phi_2 + \cdots + B_N \cos \phi_N = 0 \qquad (4)$$
$$B_1 \sin \phi_1 + B_2 \sin \phi_2 + \cdots + B_N \sin \phi_N = 0, \qquad (5)$$

with

$$B_j = \frac{A_j \omega_0}{\sqrt{(1 - \zeta^2)}} e^{-\zeta \omega_0 (t_N - t_j)},$$

where A_j is the amplitude of the Nth impulse, t_j is the time of the Nth impulse, and t_N is the time at which the sequence ends (time of the last impulse). Equations (4) and (5) can be simplified further yielding

$$\sum_{j=1}^{N} A_j e^{-\zeta \omega (t_N - t_j)} \sin \left(t_j \omega \sqrt{1 - \zeta^2} \right) = 0$$

$$\qquad (6)$$

$$\sum_{j=1}^{N} A_j e^{-\zeta \omega (t_N - t_j)} \cos \left(t_j \omega \sqrt{1 - \zeta^2} \right) = 0.$$

If the input is chosen so that there are N impulses, N terms must be included in equation (6).

For the two-impulse case, only the first two terms exist in equation (6). By selecting 0 for the time of the first impulse (t_1), and 1 for its amplitude (A_1), two equations (6) with two unknowns (A_2 and t_2) result. A_2 scales linearly for other values of A_1. The solution of these two equations produces the input sequence shown in figure 2. The detailed derivation of this result is long and can be found in Singer and Seering [1988].

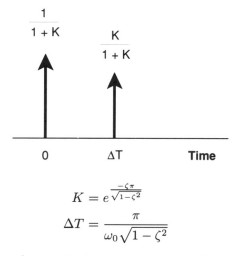

$$K = e^{\frac{-\zeta \pi}{\sqrt{1-\zeta^2}}}$$

$$\Delta T = \frac{\pi}{\omega_0 \sqrt{1-\zeta^2}}$$

Figure 2. Two-impulse input—designed to have a vibration-error expression which is zero at the expected system natural frequency, ω_0. ζ is the expected damping ratio. Note that K happens to be the expression for the step response overshoot of a 2-pole linear system with no numerator dynamics, and ΔT is the time of the first overshoot.

Robustness

$\Diamond$ Robustness to errors in natural frequency

The two-impulse input, however, cancels vibration only if the system natural frequency and damping ratio are exact. In order to quantify the residual vibration level for a system, a vibration-error expression must be defined in this case as the maximum amplitude of the residual vibration during a move as a percentage of the amplitude of the rigid body motion. This definition is expressed mathematically for a simple harmonic oscillation system with equation (3) divided by the sum of all the A_j. Figure 3 shows a plot of the vibration error as a function of the system's actual natural frequency. The input was designed for a system with a natural frequency of ω_0. Acceptable response is arbitrarily defined as less than 5% residual vibration [Ogata 1970]. Figure 3 shows that the two-impulse input is robust for a frequency variation of less than $\approx \pm 5\%$.

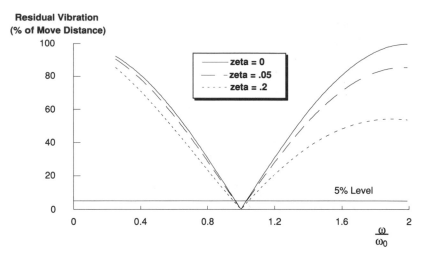

Figure 3. Vibration error versus system natural frequency for three systems with different values of damping ratio excited by the two-impulse sequence in the previous figure.

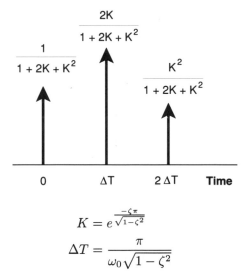

$$K = e^{\frac{-\zeta\pi}{\sqrt{1-\zeta^2}}}$$

$$\Delta T = \frac{\pi}{\omega_0\sqrt{1-\zeta^2}}$$

Figure 4. Three-impulse input—designed to have a vibration-error expression which is both zero and tangent at the expected system natural frequency, ω_0. (ζ) is the expected damping ratio.

In order to increase the robustness of the input under variations of the system natural frequency, a new constraint may be added. The derivatives of equation (6) with respect to *frequency* (ω_0) can be set equal to zero—the mathematical equivalent of setting a goal of small changes in vibration error for changes in natural frequency. The two equations for these derivatives,

$$\sum_{j=1}^{N} A_j t_j e^{-\zeta\omega(t_N-t_j)} \sin\left(t_j\omega\sqrt{1-\zeta^2}\right) = 0$$

$$\sum_{j=1}^{N} A_j t_j e^{-\zeta\omega(t_N-t_j)} \cos\left(t_j\omega\sqrt{1-\zeta^2}\right) = 0\,, \qquad (7)$$

are added to the system; therefore, two more unknowns must be added by increasing the input from two to three impulses (added unknowns: A_3 and t_3). The details of the derivation of this result are given in Singer [1988]. The corresponding input and vibration error curves that result from solving the four equations are shown in figures (4) and (5). In this case, the input is robust for system frequency variations of $\approx \pm 20\%$.

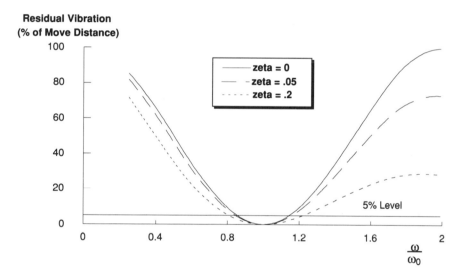

Figure 5. Vibration error versus system natural frequency for three systems with different values of damping ratio excited by the three-impulse sequence in the previous figure.

The process of adding robustness can be further extended to include the second derivatives of equation (6) with respect to ω_0. The general form of the qth derivative of equation (6) with respect to ω is given by

$$\sum_{j=1}^{N} A_j(t_j)^q e^{-\zeta\omega(t_N-t_j)} \sin\left(t_j\omega\sqrt{1-\zeta^2}\right) = 0$$

$$\sum_{j=1}^{N} A_j(t_j)^q e^{-\zeta\omega(t_N-t_j)} \cos\left(t_j\omega\sqrt{1-\zeta^2}\right) = 0\,. \qquad (8)$$

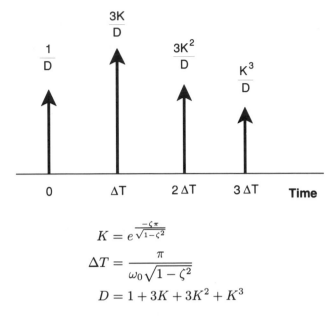

$$K = e^{\frac{-\zeta\pi}{\sqrt{1-\zeta^2}}}$$

$$\Delta T = \frac{\pi}{\omega_0\sqrt{1-\zeta^2}}$$

$$D = 1 + 3K + 3K^2 + K^3$$

Figure 6. Four-impulse input—designed to have a vibration-error expression which is zero, tangent, and flat at the expected system natural frequency, ω_0. (ζ) is the expected damping ratio.

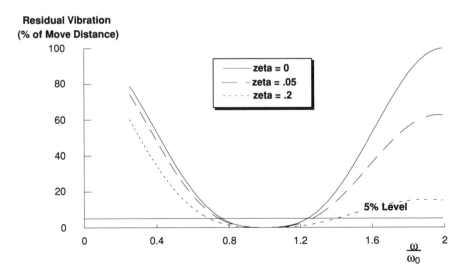

Figure 7. Vibration error versus system natural frequency for three systems with different values of damping ratio excited by the four-impulse sequence in the previous figure.

Setting the second derivatives (equation (8) when $q = 2$) to 0 requires that the vibration error be flat around the intended natural frequency. Two more constraint equations are added, therefore, the impulse sequence is increased by one to a total of four impulses. The corresponding input and vibration error curves are shown in figures 6 and 7. In this case, the input is robust for system frequency variations of $\approx {}^{-30\%}_{+40\%}$.

◇ Robustness to errors in damping

In order for these system inputs to be insensitive to system parameter variation, uncertainty in damping ratio must also be considered. As with respect to natural frequency in the previous section, the derivative of the amplitude of vibration with respect to damping ratio (ζ) can be computed. It can be shown [Singer 1988] that the same expressions that guarantee zero derivatives with respect to frequency also guarantee zero derivatives with respect to damping ratio. Therefore, robustness to errors in damping has already been achieved by the addition of robustness to errors in frequency. Figure 8 shows the vibration-error expression for the same three sequences as were generated previously. Note that extremely large variations in damping are tolerated.

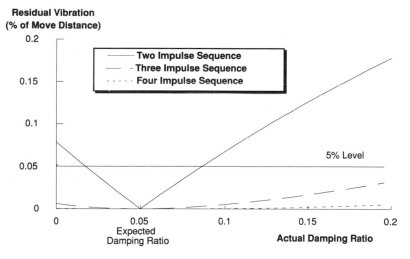

Figure 8. Vibration error versus damping ratio for the two-, three-, and four-impulse inputs calculated for a system with a damping ratio of 0.05.

Including higher modes

The previous sections have assumed only one vibrational mode present in the system. However, the impulse sequence can easily be generalized to handle higher modes. If an impulse or pulse sequence is designed for each of the first two modes of a system independently, they can be convolved to form a sequence which moves a two-mode system without vibration. Figure 9 demonstrates this on two sequences.

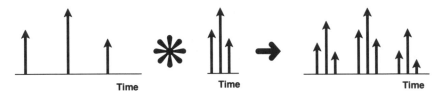

Figure 9. Vibration reduction for several modes. An example of convolving two three-impulse sequences together to form a single sequence that reduces vibration in two separate modes.

The length of the resulting sequence is the sum of the lengths of the individual sequences. The sum, however, is an upper bound on the length of the two-mode sequence which can be generated directly by simultaneously solving together the same equations that generated the two individual sequences. For example, if the four equations used to generate the sequence in figure 4 were repeated for a different frequency, a system of eight equations would result and could be solved for four unknown impulse amplitudes and times (plus the first, arbitrary impulse), yielding a five-impulse sequence. The resulting sequence has four fewer impulses than the result of convolving the two independent sequences, and is always shorter in time. An arbitrary number of such sequences can be combined (either by convolution or by direct solution) to generate an input that will not cause vibration in any of the modes that have been included in the derivation.

Using impulse input sequences to shape inputs

We have presented a method for obtaining a system impulse input sequence which simultaneously eliminates vibration at the natural frequencies of interest and includes robustness to system variability. The impulse sequences shown in figures 2, 4 and 6 are the shortest sequences constructed of only positive impulses which satisfy the constraints in equation (6) and the appropriate derivative constraints. In this sense the sequences are "time-optimal"—no shorter input can be constructed that simultaneously meets the same constraints.

This section presents a method for using the sequences derived above to generate arbitrary inputs with the same vibration-reducing properties. Once the appropriate impulse sequence has been developed, it represents the shortest input that meets the desired design criteria. Therefore, if the system is commanded to make an extremely short move, the best that

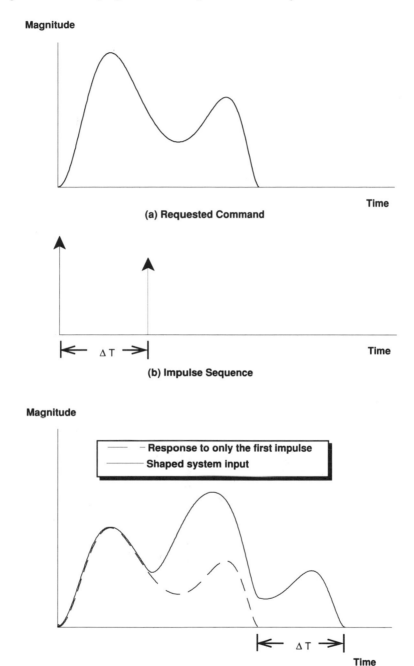

Figure 10. Convolution of a command in (a) with a Two-Impulse Sequence shown in (b) yields the system input shown in (c).

can be commanded in reality is the multiple-impulse sequence that was generated for the system. Just as the single impulse is the building block from which any arbitrary function can be formed, this impulse sequence can be used as a building block for arbitrary vibration-reducing inputs. The vibration reduction can be accomplished by convolving any arbitrary desired input to the system together with the impulse sequence in order to yield the shortest actual system input that makes the same motion without vibration. The sequence, therefore, becomes a prefilter for any input to be given to the system. The time penalty resulting from prefiltering the input equals the length of the impulse sequence (on the order of one cycle of vibration for the sequences shown earlier). Figure 10 shows the convolution of an input (for example, the signal from a joystick in a teleoperated system) with a non-robust, two-impulse sequence.

The impulse sequences described earlier have been normalized to sum to one. This normalization guarantees that the convolved motor input never exceeds the maximum value of the commanded input. If the commanded input is completely known in advance for a particular move, the convolved motor input can be rescaled so that the maximum value of the function is the actuator limit of the system.

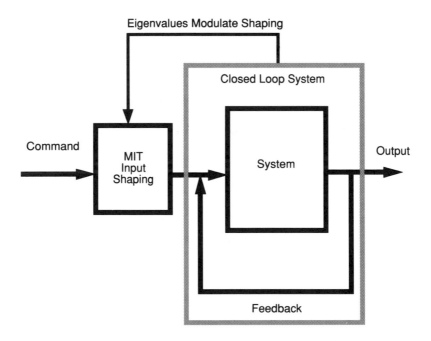

Figure 11. Schematic diagram for implementation of the new technique.

The new technique consists of selecting an impulse sequence that has the desired robustness for the system that is to be controlled. The sequence is designed for the natural frequency and damping ratio of the closed-loop system. This input sequence is then convolved with any inputs that are sent to the closed-loop plant. Figure 11 shows a schematic diagram of the implementation of the new technique. Because the input shaping is for the closed-loop system, any controller may be used.

It is important to note that convolution of a physically-realizable requested input and an impulse sequence *always* results in a physically-realizable shaped command input to the system. The convolution process merely superposes time-shifted copies of the original command. Unachievable impulse inputs are never sent to the system.

For historical reference, the result of convolving a non-robust two-impulse sequence with a step input yields the Posicast input developed by Smith [1958]. The robustness plot of figure 3 demonstrates why Posicast is not generally used. For small changes or uncertainties in the system natural frequency, a considerable amount of residual vibration is incurred.

Application to nonlinear systems

No general statement can be made regarding the application of the new technique to nonlinear systems because each nonlinearity poses unique problems. Nonlinearities that tend to appear as shifts in natural frequency do not seem to interfere with the vibration-reducing effects of the new shaping technique because of the robustness to frequency uncertainty that was included in the derivation. Many simulations of geometrically non-linear systems have been performed. An example of such a simulation is provided below. As long as the system is varying slowly, the new shaping technique tends to work (at least on the nonlinear, manipulator systems that were considered). A more detailed discussion of nonlinear systems is presented in Singer [1988].

Results

The shaped commands are tested on a computer model of the Space Shuttle Remote Manipulator System. The computer simulation was developed by Draper Laboratories for use by NASA to verify and to test payload operations. The Draper shuttle model includes many of the nonlinear complicating features of the hardware Shuttle manipulator such as stiction/friction in the joints; nonlinear gearbox stiffness; asynchronous communication timing; joint freeplay; saturation; digitization effects; and the nonlinear spatial

frequency shifts of the three-dimensional Space Shuttle Remote Manipulator System. The simulation was verified with actual space-shuttle flight
data. Excellent agreement was obtained both for steady-state and for transient behavior.

Figure 12 shows the response of the Draper shuttle model to a 4 second
pulse velocity command from the astronaut operator and response to the
same command shaped by the three-impulse sequence described above.
The residual vibration for this move is reduced by a factor of 25 for the
unloaded shuttle arm. Comparable results were obtained for a variety
of moves tested. The fact that this simulation model is highly nonlinear
demonstrates that this method can work even in the presence of certain
system nonlinearities.

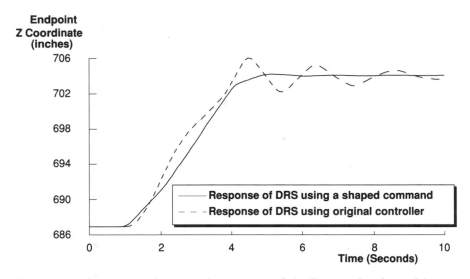

Figure 12. Comparison between the response of the Draper shuttle model using the original Space Shuttle Remote Manipulator System controller (shown as
dotted) and the response generated by shaping the same command with a three-
impulse sequence (shown as solid). The reduced vibration of the solid curve over
the dotted curve is a direct result of preshaping of the input command.

Conclusion

The use of shaped inputs for commanding computer-controlled machines
shows that significant vibration reduction can be achieved. The cost in
extended move time is small (on the order of one cycle of vibration), especially when compared to the time saved in waiting for settling of the
machine's vibrations. A straightforward design approach for implementing

this preshaping technique has been presented along with some results from Draper Laboratory's Space Shuttle manipulator model.

References

Asada, Haruhiko, Zeng-Dong Ma, and Hidekats Tokumaru [1987], "Inverse Dynamics of Flexible Robot Arms for Trajectory Control," *Modeling and Control of Robotic Manipulators,* ASME Winter Annual Meeting, pp. 329–336.

Aspinwall, D. M. [1980], "Acceleration Profiles for Minimizing Residual Response," *Journal of Dynamic Systems, Measurement, and Control,* vol. 102, no. 1, pp. 3–6.

Bayo, E. [1988], "Computed Torque for the Position Control of Open-Chain Flexible Robots," *Proceedings of the 1988 IEEE International Conference on Robotics and Automation,* pp. 316–321, Philadelphia, PA.

Bolz, Ray E., and George L. Tuve [1973], "CRC Handbook of Tables for Applied Engineering Science," CRC Press, Inc., p. 1071, Boca Raton, FA.

Chun, Hon M., James D. Turner, and Jer-Nan Juang [1985], "Disturbance-Accommodating Tracking Maneuvers of Flexible Spacecraft," *Journal of the Astronautical Sciences,* vol. 33, no. 2, pp. 197-216.

Farrenkopf, R. L. [1979], "Optimal Open-Loop Maneuver Profiles for Flexible Spacecraft," *Journal of Guidance and Control,* vol. 2, no. 6, pp. 491–498.

Gieck, Kurt [1983], "Engineering Formulas," McGraw-Hill Book Company, Inc., New York, pp. E4.

Gupta, Narendra K. [1980], "Frequency-Shaped Cost Functionals: Extension of Linear-Quadratic-Gaussian Design Methods," *Journal of Guidance and Control,* vol. 3, no. 6, pp. 529–35.

Hollars, Michael G. and Robert H. Cannon [1985], "Initial Experiments on the End-Point Control of a Two Link Manipulator with Flexible Tendons," *ASME Winter Annual Meeting,*.

Junkins, John L., James D. Turner [1986], *Optimal Spacecraft Rotational Maneuvers,* Elsevier Science Publishers, New York.

The research described in this chapter was performed at the Massachusetts Institute of Technology Artificial Intelligence Laboratory. The laboratory's research is funded in part by the University Research Initiative under ONR contract N00014-86-K-685 and in part by the Defense Advanced Research Projects Agency of the United States Department of Defense under ONR contract N00014-85-K-0124. Neil Singer has been supported by the Office of Naval Research Fellowship Program, and by C. S. Draper Laboratory's Internal Research and Development Program.

Juang, Jer-Nan, James D. Turner, and Hon M Chun [1985], "Closed-Form Solutions for Feedback Control with Terminal Constraints," *Journal of Guidance and Control,* vol. 8, no. 1, pp. 39–43.

Kotnik, P. T., S. Yurkovich, and U. Ozguner [1988], "Acceleration Feedback for control of a flexible Manipulator Arm," *Journal of Robotic Systems,* vol. 5, no 3.

Meckl, P., and W. Seering [1985], "Minimizing Residual Vibration for Point-to-point Motion," *ASME Journal of Vibration, Acoustics, Stress, and Reliability in Design,* vol. 107, no. 4, pp. 378-382.

Meckl, P., and W. Seering [1985], "Active Damping in a Three-Axis Robotic Manipulator," *Journal of Vibration, Acoustics, Stress, and Reliability in Design,* vol. 107, no. 1, pp. 38-46.

Meckl, Peter H., and Warren P. Seering [1986], "Feedforward Control Techniques To Achieve Fast Settling Time in Robots," *Proceedings of The American Controls Conference,* Seattle, WA.

Meckl, Peter H., and Warren P. Seering [1987], "Reducing Residual Vibration in Systems with Time Varying Resonances," *Proceedings of the 1987 IEEE International Conference on Robotics and Automation,* pp. 1690-1695, Raleigh, NC.

Meckl, Peter H., and Warren P. Seering [1988], "Controlling Velocity–Limited Systems to Reduce Residual Vibration," *Proceedings of the 1988 IEEE International Conference on Robotics and Automation,* Philadelphia, PA.

Meckl, Peter H. [1988], "Control of Vibration in Mechanical Systems Using Shaped Reference Inputs," *Ph.D. Thesis, Department of Mechanical Engineering, MIT,.* Also Report AI-TR-1018, Artificial Intelligence Laboratory, Massachusetts Institute of Technology, Cambridge, MA, 1988.

Ogata, Katsuhiko [1970], *Modern Control Engineering,* Prentice-Hall, Inc., Englewood Cliffs, NJ, p. 234.

Pfeiffer, F., and B. Gebler [1988], *Proceedings of the 1988 IEEE International Conference on Robotics and Automation,* Philadelphia, PA, pp. 2–8.

Sehitoglu, H., and J. H. Aristizabal [1986], "Design of a Trajectory Controller for Industrial Robots Using Bang-Bang and Cycloidal Motion Profiles," *Robotics: Theory and Applications,* ASME Winter Annual Meeting, Anaheim, CA, pp. 169–175.

Singer, Neil C., and Warren P. Seering [1988], "Using Acausal Shaping Techniques to Reduce Robot Vibration," *Proceedings of the 1988 IEEE International Conference on Robotics and Automation,* Philadelphia, PA.

Singer, Neil C. [1988], "Residual Vibration Reduction in Computer Controlled Machines," *Ph.D. Thesis, Department of Mechanical Engineering, Massachusetts Institute of Technology,.* Also Report AI-TR-1030, Artificial Intelligence Laboratory, Massachusetts Institute of Technology, Cambridge, MA, 1988.

Smith, O. J. M. [1958], *Feedback Control Systems,* McGraw-Hill Book Company, Inc., NY, p. 338.

Swigert, C. J. [1980], "Shaped Torque Techniques," *Journal of Guidance and Control,* vol. 3, no. 5, pp. 460–467.

Wang, S., T. C. Hsia, and J. L. Wiederrich [1986], "Open-Loop Control of a Flexible Robot Manipulator," *International Journal of Robotics and Automation* vol. 1, no. 2, pp. 54–57.

30

What principles enable us bipeds to hop, skip, and jump?
Are they the same as the principles that enable quadrupeds
to bound, pace, and trot? To answer these questions, Raibert decided to build a series of robots, starting with a one
leg hopping machine. He expected that the lessons learned
would be relevant to understanding robots with more legs.

Raibert's expectation has been realized. To hop about
with one leg, you need three cooperating procedures: one
to control height, one to control body posture, and one
to control forward motion. To run with two legs, all you
need are the same three cooperating procedures duplicated
for each leg. Because only one leg is in contact with the
ground at any time, the legs do not interfere with each
other. Thus biped locomotion reduces to monoped locomotion. To bound, pace, or trot, you treat pairs of legs as
if they were one virtual leg. Thus quadruped locomotion
reduces to biped locomotion.

The results are not just of academic interest. Some
estimates indicate that 40% of the earth's land surface is
inaccessible to wheeled and tracked vehicles. Accordingly,
Raibert has begun to think about taking the fuel directly to
the actuators by embedding single-cylinder internal combus-
tion engines inside them. He expects that this will eliminate
the need for power-supplying tethers.

Much of the work described in this chapter was carried out
while the author was located at Carnegie Mellon University,

Legged Robots

Marc H. Raibert

Why Study Legged Machines?

Aside from the sheer thrill of creating machines that actually run, there are two serious reasons for exploring legged machines. One reason is mobility: There is a need for vehicles that can travel in difficult terrain, where existing vehicles cannot go. Wheels excel on prepared surfaces such as rails and roads, but perform poorly where the terrain is soft or uneven. Because of these limitations only about half the earth's landmass is accessible to existing wheeled and tracked vehicles, whereas a much greater area can be reached by animals on foot. It should be possible to build legged vehicles that can go to the places that only animals can now reach.

One reason legs provide better mobility in rough terrain is that they can use isolated footholds that optimize support and traction, whereas a wheel requires a continuous path of support. As a consequence, a legged system is free to choose among the best footholds in the reachable terrain whereas a wheel is forced to negotiate the worst terrain. A ladder illustrates this point: Rungs provide footholds that enable legged systems to climb, but the spaces between the rungs prevent the wheeled system from making progress.

Another advantage of legs is that they provide an active suspension that decouples the path of the body from the paths of the feet. The payload is free to travel smoothly despite pronounced variations in the terrain. A legged system can also step over obstacles. The performance of legged vehicles can, to a great extent, be independent of the detailed roughness of the ground.

The construction of useful legged vehicles depends on progress in several areas of engineering and science. Legged vehicles will need systems that control joint motions, sequence the use of legs, monitor and manipulate balance, generate motions to use known footholds, sense the terrain to find good footholds, and calculate negotiable foothold sequences. Most of these tasks are not well understood yet, but research is under way. If this research is successful, it will lead to the development of legged vehicles that travel efficiently and quickly in terrain where softness, grade, or obstacles make existing vehicles ineffective. Such vehicles may be useful in industrial, agricultural, and military applications.

A second reason for exploring legged machines is to understand how humans and animals use their legs for locomotion. A few instant replays on television will reveal the large variety and complexity of ways athletes can carry, swing, toss, glide, and otherwise propel their bodies through space, maintaining orientation, balance, and speed as they go. Such performance is not limited to professional athletes; behavior at the local playground is equally impressive from a mechanical engineering, sensory-motor integration, or computational point of view. Animals also demonstrate great mobility and agility. They use their legs to move quickly and reliably through forest, swamp, marsh, and jungle, and from tree to tree. They move with great speed and efficiency.

Despite the skill we apply in using our own legs for locomotion, we are still at a primitive stage in understanding the principles that underlie walking and running. What control mechanisms do animals use? The development of legged machines will lead to new ideas about animal locomotion. To the extent that an animal and a machine perform similar locomotion tasks, their control systems and mechanical structures must solve similar problems. Of course, results in biology will also help us to make progress with legged robots. This sort of interdisciplinary approach has already become effective in other areas where biology and robotics have a common ground, such as vision, speech, and manipulation.

Research on Legged Machines

The scientific study of legged locomotion began just over a century ago when Leland Stanford, then Governor of California, commissioned Eadweard Muybridge to find out whether or not a trotting horse left the ground with all four feet at the same time. Stanford had wagered that it never did. After Muybridge proved him wrong with a set of stop-motion photographs that appeared in *Scientific American* in 1878, Muybridge went on to document the walking and running behavior of over forty mammals, including human [Muybridge 1955, 1957]. Even after 100 years, his photographic data are of considerable value and beauty, and survive as a landmark in locomotion research.

The study of machines that walk also had its origin in Muybridge's time. An early walking model appeared in about 1870 [Lucas 1894]. It used a linkage to move the body along a straight horizontal path while the feet moved up and down to exchange support during stepping (see figure 1).

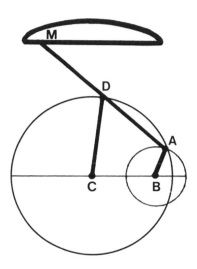

Figure 1. Linkage used in an early walking machine. When the input crank AB rotates, the output point M moves along a straight path during part of the cycle and an arched path during the other part of the cycle. Two identical linkages are arranged to operate out of phase so at least one provides a straight motion at all times. The body is always supported by the feet connected to the straight-moving linkage. After Lucas [1894].

The linkage was originally designed by the famous Russian mathematician Chebyshev some years earlier. During the eighty or ninety years that followed, workers viewed the task of building walking machines as the task of designing linkages that would generate suitable stepping motions when driven by a source of power. Many designs were proposed (for example, Ehrlich [1928], Snell [1947], Urschel [1949], Shigley [1957], Corson [1958], and Morrison [1968]) but the performance of such machines was limited by their fixed patterns of motion. They could not adjust to variations in the terrain by placing the feet on the best footholds (see figure 2).

By the late 1950s it had become clear that linkages providing fixed motion would not do the trick and that useful walking machines would need *control* [Liston 1970].

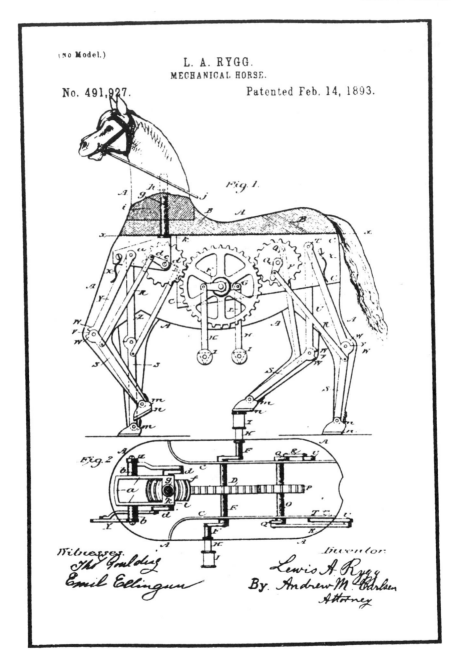

Figure 2. Mechanical horse patented by Lewis A. Rygg in 1893. The stirrups double as pedals so the rider can power the stepping motions. The reins move the head and forelegs from side to side for steering. Apparently the machine was never built.

One approach to control was to harness a human. Ralph Mosher used this approach in building a four-legged walking truck at General Electric in the mid-1960s [Liston & Mosher 1968]. The project was part of a decade-long campaign to build advanced teleoperators, capable of providing better dexterity through high-fidelity force feedback. The walking machine Mosher built stood 11 feet tall, weighed 3000 pounds, and was powered hydraulically. It is shown in figure 3.

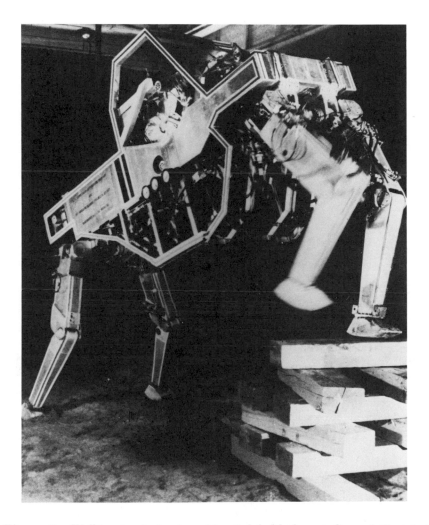

Figure 3. Walking truck developed by Ralph Mosher at General Electric in about 1968. The human driver controlled the machine with four handles and pedals that were connected to the four legs hydraulically. Photograph courtesy of General Electric Research and Development Center.

Each of the driver's limbs was connected to a handle or pedal that controlled one of the truck's four legs. Whenever the driver caused a truck leg to push against an obstacle, force feedback let the driver feel the obstacle as though it were his or her own arm or leg doing the pushing.

After about twenty hours of training Mosher was able to handle the machine with surprising agility. Films of the machine operating under his control show it ambling along at about 5 mph, climbing a stack of railroad ties, pushing a foundered jeep out of the mud, and maneuvering a large drum onto some hooks. Despite its dependence on a well-trained human for control, the GE Walking Truck was a milestone in legged technology.

An alternative to human control became feasible in the 1970s: use of a digital computer. Robert McGhee's group at the Ohio State University was the first to use this approach successfully [McGhee 1983]. In 1977 they built an insectlike hexapod that would walk with a number of gaits, turn, walk sideways, and negotiate simple obstacles. The computer's primary task was to solve kinematic equations in order to coordinate the eighteen electric motors driving the legs. This coordination ensured that the machine's center of mass stayed over the polygon of support provided by the feet while allowing the legs to sequence through a gait (see figure 4).

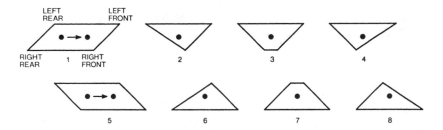

Figure 4. Statically stable gait. The diagram shows the sequence of support patterns provided by the feet of a quadruped walking with a crawling gait. The body and legs move to keep the projection of the center of mass within the polygon defined by the feet. A supporting foot is located at each vertex. The dot indicates the projection of the center of mass. Adapted from McGhee and Frank [1968].

The machine traveled quite slowly, covering several yards per minute. Force and visual sensing provided a measure of terrain accommodation in later developments. The hexapod provided McGhee with an experimental means of pursuing his earlier theoretical findings on the combinatorics and selection of gait [McGhee 1968; McGhee & Jain 1972; Koozekanani & McGhee 1973].

Gurfinkel and his co-workers in the USSR built a machine with characteristics and performance quite similar to McGhee's at about the same time [Gurfinkel *et al.* 1981]. It used a hybrid computer for control, with analog computation aiding in kinematic calculations.

The group at Ohio State has recently built a much larger hexapod (see figure 5) which was designed for self-contained operation on rough terrain [Waldron *et al.* 1984]. It carries a gasoline engine for power, several computers and a human operator for control, and a laser range sensor for terrain preview. At the time of this writing this machine has walked at about 5 mph and negotiated simple obstacles.

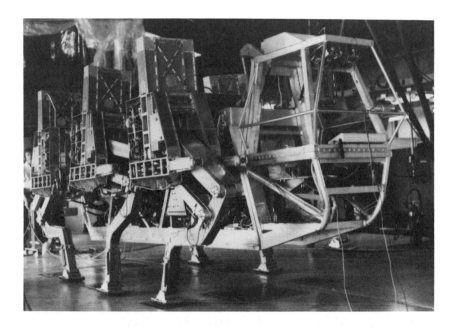

Figure 5. The hexapod walking machine developed at Ohio State University. It stands about 10 feet tall, 15 feet long, and weighs 3 tons. A 90 horsepower motorcycle engine provides power to 18 variable displacement hydraulic pumps that drive the joints. The legs use pantograph linkages to improve energy efficiency. The operator normally provides steering and speed commands while computers control the stepping motions of the legs.

Hirose realized that linkage design and computer control were not mutually exclusive. His experience with clever and unusual mechanisms—he had built seven kinds of mechanical snake—led to his design of a special leg that simplified the control of locomotion and could improve efficiency [Hirose & Umetani 1980; Hirose *et al.* 1984]. The leg was a three-dimensional pantograph that translated the motion of each actuator into a pure Cartesian translation of the foot. With the ability to generate x, y, and z translations of each foot by merely choosing an actuator, the control computer was freed from the arduous task of performing kinematic solutions. The mechanical linkage was helping to perform the calculations needed for locomotion. The linkage was efficient because the actuators performed only positive work in moving the body forward.

Hirose used this leg design to build a small quadruped, about 1 yard long. It was equipped with touch sensors on each foot and an oil-damped pendulum attached to the body. Simple algorithms used the sensors to control the actions of the feet. For instance, if a touch sensor indicated contact while the foot was moving forward, the leg would move backward a little bit, move upward a little bit, then resume its forward motion. If the foot had not yet cleared the obstacle, the cycle would repeat. The use of several simple algorithms like this one permitted Hirose's machine to climb up and down stairs and to negotiate other obstacles without human intervention [Hirose 1984].

These three walking machines, McGhee's, Gurfinkel's, and Hirose's, represent a class called *static crawlers*. Each differs in the details of construction and in the computing technology used for control, but shares a common approach to balance and stability. They all keep enough feet on the ground to guarantee a broad base of support at all times, and the body and legs move to keep the center of mass over this broad support base. The forward velocity is kept low enough so that stored kinetic energy can be ignored in the stability calculation. Each of these machines has been used to study rough terrain locomotion in the laboratory through experiments on terrain sensing, gait selection, and selection of foothold sequences. Several other machines that fall into this class have been studied in the intervening years, for example, see Russell [1983] and Sutherland and Ullner [1984].

Dynamics and Balance Improve Mobility

We now consider the study of dynamic legged machines that balance actively. These systems operate in a regime where the velocities and kinetic energies of the masses are important to the behavior. In order to predict and influence the behavior of a dynamic system, we must consider the energy stored in each mass and spring as well as the geometric structure and configuration of the mechanism. Geometry and configuration taken alone are not adequate to model a system that moves with substantial speed or has large mass. Consider, for example, a fast-moving vehicle that would tip over if it stopped suddenly with its center of mass too close to the front feet.

The exchange of energy among its various forms is also important in dynamic legged locomotion. For example, there is a cycle of activity in running that changes the form of the system's energy several times: the body's potential energy of elevation changes into kinetic energy during falling, then into strain energy when parts of the leg deform elastically during rebound with the ground, then into kinetic energy again as the body accelerates upward, and finally back into potential energy of elevation. This sort of dynamic exchange is central to an understanding of legged locomotion.

Dynamics also plays a role in giving legged systems the ability to balance actively. A statically balanced system avoids tipping and the ensuing horizontal accelerations by keeping its center of mass over the polygon of support formed by the feet. Animals sometimes use this sort of balance when they move slowly, but usually they balance actively.

A legged system that balances actively can tolerate departures from static equilibrium, tipping and accelerating for short periods of time. The control system manipulates body and leg motions to ensure that each tipping interval is brief and that each tipping motion in one direction is compensated by a tipping motion in the opposite direction. An effective base of support is thus maintained over time.

The ability of an actively balanced system to depart from static equilibrium relaxes the rules governing how legs can be used for support, which in turn leads to improved mobility. For example, if a legged system can tolerate tipping, then it can position its feet far from the center of mass in order to use footholds that are widely separated or erratically placed. If it can remain upright with a small base of support, then an actively balanced system can travel where there are closely spaced obstructions or where there is a narrow path of support. The ability to tolerate intermittent support also contributes to mobility. Intermittent support allows a system to move all its legs to new footholds at one time, to jump onto or over obstacles, and to use short periods of ballistic flight for increased speed. These abilities to use narrow base and intermittent support generally increase the types of terrain a legged system can negotiate. Animals routinely exploit active balance to travel quickly on difficult terrain; legged vehicles will have to balance actively, too, if they are to move with animal-like mobility and speed.

Research on Active Balance

The first machines that balanced actively were automatically controlled inverted pendulums. Everyone knows that a human can balance a broom on his finger with relative ease. Why not use automatic control to build a broom that can balance itself? Claude Shannon was probably the first to do so. In 1951 he used the parts from an erector set to build a machine that balanced an inverted pendulum atop a small powered truck. The truck drove back and forth in response to the tipping movements of the pendulum, as sensed by a pair of switches at its base. In order to move from one place to another, the truck first had to drive away from the destination to unbalance the pendulum, then proceeds toward the destination. In order to balance again at the destination, the truck moved past the destination until the pendulum was again upright with no forward velocity, then moved back to the destination.

At Shannon's urging Robert Cannon and two of his students at Stanford University set about demonstrating controllers that balanced two pendulums at once. In one case the pendulums were mounted side by side on the cart, and in the other they were mounted one on top of the other (see figure 6).

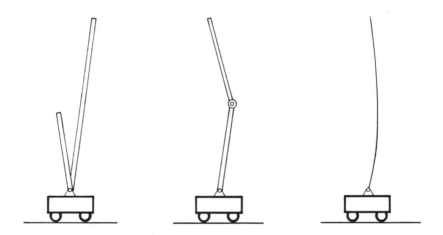

Figure 6. Cannon and his students built machines that balanced inverted pendulums on a moving cart. They balanced two pendulums side by side, one pendulum on top of another, and a long limber inverted pendulum. Only one input, the force driving the cart horizontally, was available for control. Adapted from Schaefer and Cannon [1966].

Cannon's group was interested in the single-input multiple-output problem and in the limitations of achievable balance: how could they use the single force that drove the cart's motion to control the angles of two pendulums as well as the position of the cart? How far from balance could the system deviate before it was impossible to return to equilibrium, given such parameters of the mechanical system as the cart motor's strength and the pendulum's lengths?

Using analysis based on normal coordinates and optimal switching curves, Cannon's group expressed regions of controllability as explicit functions of the physical parameters of the system. Once these regions were found, their boundaries were used to find switching functions that provided control [Higdon & Cannon 1963]. Later, they extended these techniques to provide balance for a flexible inverted pendulum [Schaefer & Cannon 1966]. These studies of balance for inverted pendulums were important precursors to later work on locomotion and the inverted pendulum model for walking would become the primary tool for studying balance in legged systems (for example, see Vukobratovic and Stepaneko [1972], Hemami and Golliday [1977], Kato et al. [1983], and Miura and Shimoyama [1984]). It is unfortunate that no one has yet extended Cannon's elegant analytical results to the more complicated legged case.

The importance of active balance in legged locomotion had been recognized for some years (for example, McGhee and Kuhner [1969], and Frank [1970]) but progress in building physical legged systems that employ such principles was retarded by the perceived difficulty of the task. It was not until the late 1970s that experimental work on balance in legged systems got underway.

Kato and his co-workers built a biped that walked with a *quasi-dynamic* gait [Kato et al. 1983]. The machine had ten hydraulically powered degrees of freedom and two large feet. This machine was usually a static crawler, moving along a preplanned trajectory to keep the center of mass over the base of support provided by the large supporting foot. Once during each step, however, the machine temporarily destabilized itself to tip forward so that support would be transferred quickly from one foot to the other. Before the transfer took place on each step, the *catching* foot was positioned to return the machine to equilibrium passively. No active response was required. A modified inverted pendulum model was used to plan the tipping motion. In 1984 this machine walked with a quasi-dynamic gait, taking about a dozen 0.5 m steps per minute. The use of a dynamic transfer phase makes an important point: A legged system can exhibit complicated dynamic behavior without requiring a very complicated control system.

Miura and Shimoyama [1984] built the first walking machine that balanced itself actively. Their *stilt biped* was patterned after a human walking on stilts. Each foot provided only a point of support, and the machine had three actuators: one for each leg that moved the leg sideways and a third that separated the legs fore and aft. Because the legs did not change length, the hips were used to pick up the feet. This gave the machine a pronounced shuffling gait reminiscent of Charlie Chaplin's stiff-kneed walk.

Control for the stilt biped relied, once again, on the inverted pendulum model of its behavior. Each time a foot was placed on the floor, its position was chosen according to the tipping behavior expected from an inverted pendulum. Actually, the problem was broken down as though there were two planar pendulums, one in the pitching plane and one in the rolling plane. The choice of foot position along each axis took the current

and desired state of the system into account. The control system used tabulated descriptions of planned leg motions together with linear feedback to
perform the necessary calculations. Unlike Kato's machine, which came to
static equilibrium before and after each dynamic transfer, the stilt biped
tipped all the time.

Dynamic bipeds that balance are now being studied in several laboratories around the world. Miura [1986] has edited a videotape that reports
recent work, including new machines by Kato, Arimoto, Masubuchi, and
Furusho.

Matsuoka [1979] was the first to build a machine that ran, where running is defined by periods when all feet are off the ground at one time.
Matsuoka's goal was to model repetitive hopping in humans. He formulated a model with a body and one massless leg, and he simplified the
problem by assuming that the duration of the support phase was short
compared with the ballistic flight phase. This extreme form of running,
in which nearly the entire cycle is spent in flight, minimizes the influence
of tipping during support. This model permitted Matsuoka to derive a
time-optimal state feedback controller that provided stability for hopping
in place and for low speed translations.

To test his method for control, Matsuoka built a planar one-legged
hopping machine. The machine operated at low gravity by rolling on ball
bearings on a table that was inclined 10 degrees from the horizontal in an
effective gravity field of $0.17g$. An electric solenoid provided a rapid thrust
at the foot, so the support period was short. The machine hopped in place
at about 1 hop per second and traveled back and forth on the table.

Running Machines

Running is a form of legged locomotion that uses ballistic flight phases to
obtain high speed. To study running, my co-workers and I have explored
a variety of legged systems and implemented some of them in the form
of physical machines. To study running in its simplest form, we built a
machine that ran on just one leg. The machine hopped like a kangaroo,
using a series of leaps. A machine on one leg allowed us to concentrate on
active balance and dynamics while avoiding the difficult task of coordinat-
ing many legs. We wanted to know if there were algorithms for walking
and running that are independent of gait and that work correctly for any
number of legs. Perhaps a machine capable of just one gait could suggest
answers to this question.

The first machine we built had two main parts: a body and a leg. The
body carried the actuators and instrumentation needed for the machine's
operation. The leg could telescope to change length and could pivot with
respect to the body at a simple hip. The leg was springy along the tele-

1850	Chebyshev	Designs linkage in early walking mechanism.
1872	Muybridge	Uses stop-motion photography to document running animals.
1893	Rygg	Patents human-powered mechanical horse.
1945	Wallace	Patents hopping tank with reaction wheels that provide stability.
1961	Space General	Eight-legged kinematic machine walks in outdoor terrain [Morrison 1968].
1963	Cannon, Higdon, and Schaefer	Control system balances single, double, and limber inverted pendulums.
1968	Frank and McGhee	Simple digital logic controls walking of Phony Pony.
1968	Mosher	GE quadruped truck climbs railroad ties under control of a human driver.
1969	Bucyrus-Erie Co.	Big Muskie—15,000 ton walking dragline. It moves at 900 ft/hr [Sitek 1976].
1977	McGhee	Digital computer coordinates leg motions of hexapod walking machine.
1977	Gurfinkel	Hybrid computer controls hexapod walker in USSR.
1977	McMahon and Greene	Human runners set new speed records on a *tuned track*.
1980	Hirose and Umetani	Quadruped machine climbs stairs and climbs over obstacles using simple sensors.
1980	Kato	Hydraulic biped walks with quasidynamic gait.
1980	Matsuoka	Mechanism balances in the plane while hopping on one leg.
1981	Miura and Shimoyama	Walking biped balances actively in three dimensional space.
1983	Sutherland	Hexapod carries a human rider.
1983	Odetics	Self-contained hexapod lifts and moves to back end of pickup truck [Russell 1983].
1987	OSU	Three ton hexapod carrying human driver, travels at 5 mph and climbs over obstacle.
1988	SFU	McGeer shows passive dynamic walking.

Table 1. Milestones in the development of legged robots.

scoping axis. Sensors measured the pitch angle of the body, the angle of the hip, the length of the leg, the tension in the leg spring, and contact with the ground. This first machine was constrained to operate in a plane, so it could move only up and down and fore and aft and rotate in the plane. An umbilical cable connected the machine to power and a control computer.

The only way this one-legged machine can run is to hop. The running cycle has two phases. During one phase, called *stance* or *support*, the leg supports the weight of the body and the foot stays in a fixed location on the ground. During stance, the system tips like an inverted pendulum. During the other phase, called *flight*, the center of mass moves ballistically, with the leg unloaded and free to move.

Control of running was decomposed into three parts

We found that a simple set of algorithms can control the planar one-legged hopping machine, allowing it to run without tipping over. Our approach was to consider the hopping motion, forward travel, and posture of the body separately. This decomposition lead to a control system with three parts:

- **Hopping.** One part of the control system excites the cyclic hopping motion that underlies running, and regulates the height to which the machine hops. The hopping motion is an oscillation governed by the mass of the body, the springiness of the leg, and gravity. During support, the body bounces on the springy leg, and during flight, the system travels a ballistic trajectory. The control system delivers a vertical thrust with the leg during each support period to sustain the oscillation and to regulate its amplitude. Some of the energy needed for each hop is recovered by the leg spring from the previous hop.

- **Forward Speed.** A second part of the control system regulates the forward running speed. This is done by moving the leg to a specified forward position with respect to the body during the flight portion of each cycle. The position of the foot with respect to the body when landing has a strong influence on tipping and acceleration behavior during the support period that follows. The body will either continue to travel with the same forward speed, accelerate to go faster, or slow down, depending on where the control system places the foot. To calculate a suitable forward position for the foot, the control system takes account of the actual forward speed, the desired speed, and a simple model of the system's dynamics. The algorithm works correctly when the machine is hopping in place, accelerating to a run, running at a constant speed, and slowing to a stationary hop.

    The rule for placing and positioning the foot is based on a kind of symmetry found in running. In order to run at constant forward

speed, the instantaneous forward accelerations that occur during a
stride must integrate to zero. One way to satisfy this requirement is
to shape the running motion so that forward acceleration has an odd
symmetry throughout each stride—functions with odd symmetry integrate to zero over symmetric limits[1]. A symmetric motion is produced
by choosing an appropriate forward position for the foot on each step.
In principle, symmetry of this sort can be used to simplify locomotion
in systems with any number of legs and for a wide range of gaits.

- **Posture.** The third part of the control system stabilizes the pitch
angle of the body to keep the body upright. Torques exerted between
the body and leg about the hip accelerate the body about its pitch
axis, provided that there is good traction between the foot and the
ground. During the support period there is traction because the leg
supports the load of the body. Linear feedback control operates on
the hip actuator during each support period to restore the body to an
upright posture.

Breaking running down into the control of these three functions simplifies
locomotion. Each part of the control system acts as though it influences
just one component of the behavior, and the interactions that result from
imperfect decoupling are treated as disturbances. The algorithms implemented to perform each part of the control task are themselves quite simple,
although the details of the individual control algorithms are probably not
so important as the framework provided by the decomposition.

Using the three-part control system, the planar one-legged machine
hops in place, travels at a specified rate, maintains balance when disturbed,
and jumps over small obstacles. Top running speed is about 2.6 mph.

Locomotion in three dimensions

The one-legged machine just described was mechanically constrained to
operate in the plane, but useful legged systems must balance themselves in
three-dimensional space. Can the control algorithms used for hopping in
the plane be generalized for hopping in three dimensions? A key to answering this question was the recognition that animal locomotion is primarily a
planar activity, even though animals are three-dimensional systems. Films
of a kangaroo hopping on a treadmill first suggested this point. The legs
sweep fore and aft through large angles, the tail sweeps in counteroscilla-
tion to the legs, and the body bounces up and down. These motions all
occur in the sagittal plane, with little or no motion normal to the plane.

Sesh Murthy realized that the plane in which all this activity occurs
can generally be defined by the forward velocity vector and the gravity

---

[1]If $x(t)$ is an odd function of time, then $x(t) = -x(-t)$. If $x(t)$ is even, then
$x(t) = x(-t)$.

vector. He called this the *plane of motion* [Murthy 1983]. For a legged
system without a preferred direction of travel, the plane of motion might
vary from stride to stride, but it would be defined in the same way. We
found that the three-part decomposition could be used to control activity
within the plane of motion.

Figure 7. Three-dimensional hopping machine used for experiments. The control system operates to regulate hopping height, forward velocity, and body posture. Top recorded running speed was about 2.2 m/s (4.8 mph).

We also found that the mechanisms needed to control the remaining *extra-
planar* degrees of freedom could be cast in a form that fit into the original
three-part framework. For instance, the algorithm for placing the foot to
control forward speed became a vector calculation. One component of foot
placement determined forward speed in the plane of motion, whereas the
other component caused the plane to rotate about a vertical axis, per-
mitting the control system to steer. A similar extension applied to body

posture. The result was a three-dimensional three-part control system that was derived directly from the one used for the planar case.

To explore these ideas, we built a second hopping machine which is shown in figure 7. This machine has an additional joint at the hip to permit the leg to move sideways as well as fore and aft. It travels on an open floor without mechanical support. It balances itself as it hops along simple paths in the laboratory, traveling at a top speed of 4.8 mph.

Running on several legs

Experiments on machines with one leg were not motivated by an interest in one-legged vehicles. Although such vehicles might very well turn out to have merit[2] our interest was in getting at the basics of active balance and dynamics in the context of a simplified locomotion problem. In principle, results from machines with one leg could have value for understanding all sorts of legged systems, perhaps with any number of legs.

Our study of locomotion on several legs has progressed in two stages. For a biped that runs like a human, with strictly alternating periods of support and flight, the one-leg control algorithms apply directly. Because the legs are used in alternation, only one leg is active at a time. One leg is placed on the ground at a time, one leg thrusts on the ground at a time, and one leg exerts a torque on the body at a time. We call this sort of running a *one-foot gait*. Assuming that the behavior of the other leg does not interfere, the one-leg algorithms for hopping, forward travel, and posture can each be used to control the active leg. Of course, to make this workable, some bookkeeping is required to keep track of which leg is active, which leg is idle, and it is required to keep the idle leg "out of the way".

Jessica Hodgins and Jeff Koechling demonstrated the effectiveness of this approach by using the one-leg algorithms to control each leg of a planar biped. The machine can run with an alternating gait, run by hopping on one leg, it can switch back and forth between gaits, and it can run fast. Top recorded speed is 13.1 mph. The biped has also climbed stairs and done forward flips and aerials [Hodgins 1989; Hodgins & Raibert 1987] as shown in figure 8. More recently we have built a three-dimensional biped, that has just begun to run.

In principle, this approach could be used to control running on any number of legs, so long as just one touches the ground at a time. Unfortunately, when there are several legs this approach runs into difficulties. There is a conflict between the need to provide balance and the need to

---

[2]Wallace and Seifert saw merit in vehicles with one leg. Wallace [1942] patented a one-legged hopping tank that was supposed to be hard to hit because of its erratic movements. Seifert [1967] proposed the *Lunar Pogo*, as a means of efficient travel on the moon.

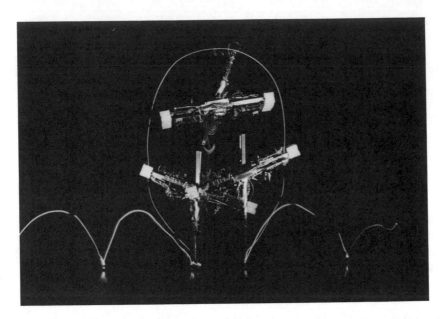

Figure 8. Planar biped doing a flip. The three images were made at the touch-down before the flip, the halfway point of the flip, and the lift-off after the flip.

move the legs without collisions. For the legs to provide balance the feet must be positioned so as to sweep under the center of mass during support. This argues for attaching all the legs to the body directly at or below the center of mass. However, the legs must be able to swing without colliding with one another, suggesting separation between the hips (shoulders). In principle, it is not impossible for a quadruped to run using this approach, however they rarely do [Hildebrand, private communication].

An alternative is to use the legs in pairs. Suppose that we introduce a new control mechanism that coordinates the legs of a pair to act like a single equivalent leg—what Ivan Sutherland called a *virtual leg*. Such coordination requires that the two legs of a pair exert equal forces on the ground, that they exert equal torques on the body, and that the position of each leg's foot with respect to its hip be equal. To control locomotion, the three-part control algorithms described previously specify the behavior of each virtual leg, while the control system ensures that the physical legs move so as to obey the rules required for virtual leg behavior.

Using this approach there are three quadruped gaits to consider: the *trot* which uses diagonal legs in a pair, the *pace* which uses lateral legs in a pair, and the *bound*, which uses the front legs as a pair and the rear legs as a pair.

We argue that the quadruped is like a virtual biped, that a biped is like a one-legged machine, and we already know how to control one-legged machines. A control system for quadruped running consists of a controller that coordinates each pair of legs to act like one virtual leg, a three-part control system that acts on the virtual legs, and a bookkeeping mechanism that keeps track. Figure 9 shows a four-legged machine that trots, paces, and bounds with this sort of control system.

Figure 9. Quadruped machine that runs by trotting. *Virtual legs* are used to make trotting like biped running, which in turn is controlled with one-leg algorithms.

Computer programs for running

The behavior of the running machines just described was controlled by a set of computer programs that ran on our laboratory computer. These computer programs performed several functions including:

- Sampling and filtering data from the sensors.
- Transforming kinematic data between coordinate systems.
- Executing the three-part locomotion algorithms for hopping, forward speed, and body attitude.
- Controlling the actuators.
- Reading operator instructions from the console.
- Recording running behavior.

State	Trigger Event	Action
1 LOADING A	A touches ground	Zero hip torque A Shorten B Don't move hip B
2 COMPRESSION A	A air spring shortened	Erect body with hip A Shorten B Position B for landing
3 THRUST A	A air springs lengthening	Extend A Erect body with hip A Keep B short Position B for landing
4 UNLOADING A	A air spring near full length	Shorten A Zero hip torque A Keep B short Position B for landing
5 FLIGHT A	A not touching touching ground	Shorten A Don't move hip A Lengthen B for landing Position B for landing

States 6–10 repeat states 1–5, with A and B reversed.

Table 2. Details of State Machine for Biped and Quadruped. The state shown in the left column is entered when the event listed in the center column occurs. During normal running states advance sequentially. During states 1–5, leg A is in support and leg B is in recovery. During states 6–10, these roles are reversed. For biped running A refers to leg 1 and B refers to leg 2. For quadruped trotting each letter designates a pair of physical legs.

The control computer was a VAX-11/780 running the UNIX operating system. In order to provide real-time service with short latency and high bandwidth feedback, the real-time control programs were implemented as a device driver that resided within the UNIX kernel. The device driver responded with short latency to a hardware clock that interrupted through the UNIBUS every 8 milliseconds. All sensors and actuators were also accessed through interfaces that connected to the UNIBUS. Each time the

1982	Planar one-legged machine hops in place, travels at a specified rate, keeps its balance when disturbed, and jumps over small obstacles.
1983	Three-dimensional one-legged machine runs and balances on an open floor.
1983	Simulations reveal passively stabilized bounding gait for quadruped-like model.
1984	Data from cat and human runners exhibit symmetries like those used to control running machines.
1984	Quadruped running machine runs with trotting gait. The one-leg algorithms are extended to control this machine.
1985	Planar biped runs with one- and two-legged gaits and changes between gaits.
1986	Planar biped does flips and aerials.
1986	Planar biped sets new speed record of 11.5 mph.
1987	Quadruped runs with pacing, and bounding gaits.
1988	Planar biped uses selected footholds and climbs short stairway. Quadruped switches between gaits while running. Reentrant trajectories found for simulated passive dynamic running.
1989	Planar biped jumps through hoop and runs with top speed of 13.1 mph, and gallops in simulation. Hoof added to monopod improves performance of leafspring foot. Three-dimensional biped does simple running.

Table 3. Summary of research in the Leg Laboratory. (The leg Laboratory was located at CMU from 1981–1986 and at the MIT Artificial Intelligence Laboratory from 1987–present.)

clock ticked the running machine driver programs sampled and scaled data from the sensors, estimated joint and body velocities to determine the state of the running machine, executed the three-part locomotion algorithms, and calculated a new output for each actuator.

The programs performing these tasks were written in a mixture of C and assembly language. Assembly language was used where speed was of primary concern, such as in performing the kinematic transformations used to convert between coordinate systems. In some cases tabulated data were used to further increase the speed of a transformation. For instance, trigonometric functions, square roots, and higher order kinematic operations were evaluated with linear interpolation among precomputed tabulated data. The kinematic relationship between the quadruped's fore/aft hip actuator length and the forward position of the foot in body coordinates is an example of a function that was evaluated with a table.

The control programs were synchronized to the behavior of the running machine by a software finite state machine. The state machine made transitions from one state to another when sensory data from the running machine satisfied the specified conditions. For instance, the state machine made a transition from COMPRESSION to THRUST when the derivative of the support leg's length changed from negative to positive (see figure 10). Table 2 gives some detail for the state machine that was used for the biped and quadruped running machines. We found that using a state machine along with properly designed transition conditions aided the interpretation of sensory data by providing noise immunity and hysteresis.

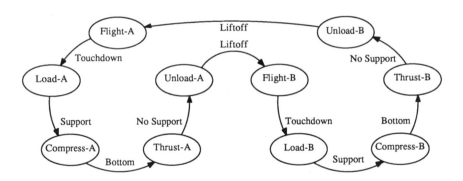

Figure 10. Simplified diagram of a state machine that synchronizes the control programs to the behavior of the running machine. This state machine is for the biped and quadruped machines, but the one-legged state machines are similar. State transitions are determined by sensory events related to the hopping motion. A different set of control actions are put into effect in each state, as indicated in table 2.

Whereas sensory data determine when the state machine makes transitions, the resulting states determine which control algorithms operate to provide control. For instance, when the biped is in the THRUST A state, the control programs extend leg A, exert torque on hip A, shorten leg B, and position foot B.

In addition to the real-time programs that control the running machines, a top-level program was used to control the real-time programs. The top-level program permitted the user to initiate a running experiment, select among control modes, examine or modify the variables and parameters used by the control programs, specify sensor calibration data, mark variables for recording, and save recorded real-time data for later analysis and debugging. Each of these functions was accomplished by one or more system calls to the driver. The top-level program had no particular time constraints, so it was implemented as a time-sharing job that was scheduled by the normal UNIX scheduler.

Experiments in Animal Locomotion

Earlier in this chapter I said that studying legged machines could help us to understand more about locomotion in animals. Detailed knowledge of concrete locomotion algorithms with well understood behavior might help us formulate experiments that elucidate the mechanisms used by humans and animals for locomotion. For instance, one might ask if animals control their forward speed as each of the running machines do, by choosing a forward position for the leg during each flight phase, with no adjustments during stance. Is there any decomposition of control? Examples of such questions are summarized in the following list. Each is based on observations or ideas that arose in the course of studying legged machines.

Animal experiments motivated by robot experiments

Algorithms for Balance.   The legged machines and computer simulations we have studied all use a specific algorithm for determining the landing position of the foot with respect to the body's center of mass. The foot is advanced a distance $x_f = T_s \dot{x}/2 + k_{\dot{x}}(\dot{x} - \dot{x}_d)$. This calculation is based on the expected symmetric tipping behavior of an inverted pendulum.

Do animals use this algorithm to position their feet? To find out, one must measure small changes in the forward running speed, in the angular momentum of the body during the flight phase, and in the placement of the feet. Rather than look at average behavior across many steps, as is done in studies of energetics and neural control, we must look at error terms within each step.

Symmetry in balance.   Symmetry plays a central role in simplifying the control of the dynamic legged robots described earlier. The symmetry of interest specifies that motion of the body in space, and of the feet with respect to the body, are even and odd functions of time during each support period (see figure 11).

These are interesting motions because they leave the forward and angular motion of the body unaccelerated over a stride, and therefore lead to steady state travel. Do animals run with this sort of symmetry? To find out we are examining film data for several quadrupedal animals. Preliminary measurements show that the galloping and trotting cat sometimes

Figure 11. Symmetry in animal locomotion. Animals shown in symmetric configuration halfway through the stance phase for several gaits: rotary gallop (top), transverse gallop (second), canter (third), and amble (bottom). In each case the body is at minimum altitude, the center of support is located below the center of mass, the rearmost leg was recently lifted, and the frontmost leg is about to be placed. Photographs from Muybridge [1957]; reprinted with permission from Dover Press.

runs with symmetric motions [Raibert 1986b; Raibert 1986c]. We would like to know:

- How universal is the use of symmetric running by animals, both in terms of different gaits and different animals?
- What is the precision of the observed symmetry?
- Does the symmetry extend to angular motion of the body, as the theory predicts?
- How do asymmetries in the mechanical structure of the body and legs influence motion symmetry?

Virtual legs. To control the quadruped running machine the control system synchronizes the behavior of pairs of legs that provides support during stance. The synchronization has three parts, requiring that the legs of a pair exert equal vertical forces on the ground, exert equal hip torque on the body, and displace their feet equal distances from the hip or shoulder. The result of such synchronization is called a *virtual leg* [Sutherland & Ullner 1984] because it makes two legs act like one equivalent leg located half way between the pair. The virtue of virtual legs is that they simplify the control algorithms for balance and dynamic control.

Do animals use virtual legs? To answer this question one must examine the horizontal and vertical forces exerted on the ground by both legs during double support in trotting or pacing. From these measurements one can find the differential force or impulse. One would expect the differential force to be zero if the system were using a control strategy based on virtual legs. An important manipulation will be to disturb one or both of the feet during stance, and to measure the active force response of the legs. Asymmetries in the distribution of mass in the system may require a somewhat generalized version of the virtual leg, in which a fixed ratio of forces, torques and displacements prevails.

Distribution of body mass. The distribution of mass in the body can have a fundamental influence on the behavior of a running system. In earlier work we defined the dimensionless group representing the normalized moment of inertia of the body, $j = J/(md^2)$ where J is the moment of inertia of the body, m is the mass of the body, and d is half the hip spacing [Murphy & Raibert 1985]. As shown in figure 12 when $j = 1$ the hips are located at the centers of percussion of the body. Through computer simulations of a simplified model we found that when $j < 1$ the attitude of the body in the sagittal plane can be passively stabilized when running with a bounding gait. However, when $j > 1$ stabilization was not passively obtained.

This finding has implications for the interaction between the mechanical structure of an animal and the control provided by the nervous system. Could it be that bounding animals do not actively control pitching

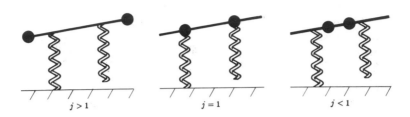

Figure 12. The dimensionless moment of inertia, $j = J/(md^2)$, predicts passive stability of the body's pitching motion for a simple simulated model. (Left) For $j > 1$, a vertical force on the left foot causes the right hip to accelerate upward. The model has no passive pitch stability. (Center) For $j = 1$, the system acts as two separate oscillators, with neutral stability. (Right) When $j < 1$, an upward force on the left leg causes the right hip to accelerate downward. The model has passive pitch stability. From Murphy and Raibert [1985].

of their bodies, but control only forward running speed and direction? A first step toward answering this question is to measure values of j for a variety of quadrupedal animals, and to relate the measurements to their preferred modes of running, trotting or pacing (no pitching) vs. bounding or galloping (pitching). Does the value of j for a quadruped vary with its trot-to-gallop transition speed? Anatomical measurements like those of Fedak, Heglund, and Taylor [1982] will provide much of the data needed to answer this question.

Yaw Control. How do human runners keep themselves from rotating about the yaw axis? Control of this degree of freedom in the one-legged hopping machine is difficult because it does not have a foot that can exert a torsional torque on the ground. But humans have long feet that might be used to develop substantial torsional traction on the ground about the yaw axis. A first step in exploring this question would be to measure the torsional torque humans exert on the ground during running and to relate the measurements to yaw motions and yaw disturbances of the body.

Philosophy of interaction between robotics and biology

It is interesting to combine the study of animals with the study of machines. Biological systems provide both great motivation by virtue of their striking performance, and guidance with the details of their actions. They are existence proofs that give us a lower bound on what is possible. Unfortunately, biological systems are often too complicated to study—there are many variables, precise measurement is difficult, there are limitations on the experimenter's ability to manipulate the preparation, and perhaps, an inherent difficulty in focusing on the information-level of a problem.

On the other hand, laboratory robots are relatively easy to build. Precisely controlled experiments are possible, as are careful measurements and manipulations, and the "subject" can be redesigned when necessary. However, the behavior of these experimental robot systems is impoverished when compared with the biological counterpart. They are easy to study, but they do not do much.

Analysis of living systems and synthesis of laboratory systems are complementary activities, each with strengths and weaknesses. Together, these activities can strengthen one another, leading to fundamental principles that elucidate the domain of both problems, independent of the particular implementation. Because machines face the same physical laws and environmental constraints that biological systems face when they perform similar tasks, the solutions they use may embrace similar principles. In solving the problem for the machine, we generate a set of plausible algorithms for the biological system. In observing the biological behavior, we explore plausible behaviors for the machine. In its grandest form, this approach lets the study of robotics contribute to both robotics and biology and lets the study of biology contribute to both biology and robotics.

The Development of Useful Legged Robots

The running machines described in the previous section are not useful vehicles nor even prototypes for such vehicles. They are experimental apparatus used in the laboratory to explore ideas about legged locomotion. Each was designed to isolate and examine a specific locomotion problem, while postponing or ignoring many other problems. Let us now step back and ask what problems remain to be solved before legged robots are transformed into practical machines that do useful work.

Terrain sensing

Perhaps the deepest problem limiting current walking machines as well as other forms of autonomous vehicle, is their inability to perceive the shape and structure of their immediate surroundings. Humans and animals use their eyes to locate good footholds, to avoid obstacles, to measure their own rate and direction of progress, and to navigate with respect to visible landmarks. The problem of giving machines the ability to see has received intensive and consistent attention for the past twenty-five or thirty years. There has been steady progress during that period. Current machines can see well enough to operate in well structured and partially structured environments, but it is difficult to predict when machines will be able to see well enough to operate autonomously in rough outdoor terrain. I do not expect to see such autonomous machine behavior for at least ten years.

Sensors simpler than vision may be able to provide solutions to certain parts of the problem under certain circumstances. For instance, sonar and laser range data may be used to detect and avoid nearby obstacles. Motion data may be used for measuring speed and direction of travel with techniques that are substantially simpler than those needed to perceive shape in three dimensions.

Travel on rough terrain

Complete knowledge of the geometry of the terrain, as might be supplied by vision or these other senses would not in itself solve the problem of walking or running on rough terrain. A system traveling over rough terrain needs to know or figure out what terrain shapes provide good footholds, which sequence of footholds would permit traversal of the terrain, and how to move so as to place the feet on the available footholds. It will be necessary to coordinate the dynamics of the vehicle with the dynamics of the terrain.

There are several ways that terrain becomes rough and therefore difficult to negotiate:

- Not level.
- Limited traction (slippery).
- Areas of poor or nonexistent support (holes).

Vertical variations:

- Minor vertical variations in available footholds (less than about one-half the of leg length).
- Major vertical variations in available footholds (footholds separated vertically by distances comparable to the dimensions of the whole leg).
- Large obstacles between footholds (poles).
- Intricate footholds (for example, rungs of a ladder).

The techniques that will allow legged systems to operate in these sorts of terrain will involve the mechanics of locomotion, kinematics, dynamics, geometric representation, spatial reasoning, and planning. Although course- and medium-grain knowledge of the terrain will be important, I expect techniques that make legged systems inherently insensitive to fine-grain terrain variations to play an important role too. Ignoring the hard sensing issues mentioned earlier, I believe the perception and control mechanisms required for legged systems to travel on rough terrain will require a substantial research effort, but the important problems can be solved within the next ten years if they are pursued vigorously.

Mechanical design and system integration

When these sensing and control problems are solved, it will remain to develop mechanical designs that function with efficiency and reliability. Useful vehicles must carry their own power, control computers, and a payload. A host of interesting problems present themselves including such matters as energy efficiency, structural design, strength and weight of materials, and efficient control. For instance, the development of materials and structures for efficient storage and recovery of elastic energy will be particularly important for legged vehicles. I expect that early useful legged vehicles can be built with existing mechanical and aerospace technique, but performance will improve rapidly as designs are refined, embellished, and improved.

References

Ehrlich, A. [1928], "Vehicle Propelled by Steppers," Patent Number 1-691-233.

Frank, A. A. [1970], "An approach to the dynamic analysis and synthesis of biped locomotion machines," *Medical and Biological Engineering*, vol. 8, pp. 465–476.

Gurfinkel, V. S., E. V. Gurfinkel, A. Yu. Shneider, E. A. Devjanin, A. V. Lensky, and L. G. Shitilman [1981], "Walking robot with supervisory control," *Mechanism and Machine Theory*, vol. 16, pp. 31–36.

Hemami, H., and C. L. Golliday Jr. [1977], "The inverted pendulum and biped stability," *Mathematical Biosciences*, vol. 34, pp. 95–110.

Higdon, D. T., and R. H. Cannon Jr. [1963], "On the control of unstable multiple-output mechanical systems," *ASME Winter Annual Meeting*.

Hirose, S. [1984], "A study of design and control of a quadruped walking vehicle", *International J. Robotics Research*, vol. 3, pp. 113–133.

Hirose, S., and Y. Umetani [1980], "The basic motion regulation system for a quadruped walking vehicle," *ASME Conference on Mechanisms*.

Hodgins, J. K. [1989], "Legged Robots on Rough Terrain: Experiments in Adjusting Step Length," Ph.D. Thesis, Computer Science Department, Carnegie Mellon University.

Hodgins, J. K., and M. H. Raibert [1987], "Planar Biped Goes Head Over Heels," *ASME Winter Annual Meeting*, Boston.

Hodgins, J. K., J. Koechling, and M. H. Raibert [1985], "Running experiments with a planar biped," *Third International Symposium on Robotics Research*, MIT Press, Cambridge, MA.

Kato, T., A. Takanishi, H. Jishikawa, and I. Kato [1983], "The realization of the quasi-dynamic walking by the biped walking machine," *Fourth Symposium*

This research in this chapter was supported by a grant from the System Development Foundation and a contract from the Defense Advanced Research Projects Agency.

on Theory and Practice of Robots and Manipulators, edited by A. Morecki, G. Bianchi, and K. Kedzior, Polish Scientific Publishers, Warsaw, pp. 341–351.

Koozekanani, S. H., and R. B. McGhee [1973], "Occupancy problems with pairwise exclusion constraints—an aspect of gait enumeration," *J. Cybernetics*, vol. 2 pp. 14–26.

Liston, R. A. [1970], "Increasing vehicle agility by legs: The quadruped transporter," *38th National Meeting of the Operations Research Society of America*.

Liston, R. A., and R. S. Mosher [1968], "A versatile walking truck," *Proceedings of the Transportation Engineering Conference*, Institution of Civil Engineers, London.

Lucas, E. [1984], "Huitieme recreation—la machine a marcher," *Recreations Mathematiques*, vol. 4 pp. 198–204.

Matsuoka, K. [1980], "A mechanical model of repetitive hopping movements," *Biomechanisms*, vol. 5, pp. 251–258.

McGhee, R. B. [1968], "Some finite state aspects of legged locomotion," *Mathematical Biosciences*, vol. 2 pp. 67–84.

McGhee, R. B. [1983], "Vehicular legged locomotion," *Advances in Automation and Robotics*, edited by G. N. Saridis, JAI Press.

McGhee, R. B., and A. A. Frank [1968], "On the stability properties of quadruped creeping gaits," *Mathematical Biosciences*, vol. 3, pp. 331–351.

McGhee, R. B., and A. K. Jain [1972], "Some properties of regularly realizable gait matrices," *Mathematical Biosciences*, vol. 13 pp. 179–193.

McGhee, R. B., and M. B. Kuhner [1968], "On the dynamic stability of legged locomotion systems," *Advances in External Control of Human Extremities*, M. M. Gavrilovic, A. B. Wilson, Jr., (editors), Jugoslav Committee for Electronics and Automation, Belgrade, pp. 431–442.

Miura, H. [1986], "Biped Locomotion Robots," Unpublished videotape.

Miura, H., and I. Shimoyama [1984], "Dynamic walk of a biped," *International J. Robotics Research*, vol. 3 pp. 60–74.

Morrison, R. A. [1968], "Iron mule train," *Proceedings of Off-Road Mobility Research Symposium*, International Society for Terrain Vehicle Systems, WA, pp. 381–400.

Murphy, K. N., and M. H. Raibert [1985], "Trotting and bounding in a planar two-legged model," *Fifth Symposium on Theory and Practice of Robots and Manipulators*, edited by A. Morecki, G. Bianchi, and K. Kedzior, MIT Press, Cambridge, MA, pp. 411–420.

Murthy, S. S., and M. H. Raibert [1983], "3D balance in legged locomotion: modeling and simulation for the one-legged case," *Inter-Disciplinary Workshop on Motion: Representation and Perception*, ACM.

Muybridge, E. [1901], *The Human Figure in Motion*, Dover Publications, NY, 1955; First edition, Chapman and Hall, Ltd., London.

Muybridge, E. [1899], *Animals in Motion*, Dover Publications, NY, 1957; First edition, Chapman and Hall, Ltd., London.

Raibert, M. H. [1986], *Legged Robots That Balance*, MIT Press, Cambridge, MA.

Raibert, M. H. [1986], "Symmetry in running," *Science*, vol. 231 pp. 1292–1294.

Raibert, M. H., and H. B. Brown, Jr. [1984], "Experiments in balance with a 2D one-legged hopping machine," *ASME J. Dynamic Systems, Measurement, and Control*, vol. 106 pp. 75–81.

Raibert, M. H., H. B. Brown Jr., and M. Chepponis [1984], "Experiments in balance with a 3D one-legged hopping machine," *International J. Robotics Research*, vol. 3 pp. 75–92.

Raibert, M. H., M. Chepponis, and H. B. Brown Jr. [1986], "Running on four legs as though they were one," *IEEE J. Robotics and Automation*, vol. 2.

Russell, M., Jr. [1983], and I. Odex, "The first functionoid," *Robotics Age* vol. 5 pp. 12–18.

Schaefer, J. F., and R. H. Cannon Jr. [1966], "On the control of unstable mechanical systems," *International Federation of Automatic Control*, London, vol. 6c, pp. 1–13.

Seifert, H. S. [1967], "The lunar pogo stick," *J. Spacecraft and Rockets*, vol. 4 pp. 941–943.

Shigley, R. [1957], *The Mechanics of Walking Vehicles*, Land Locomotion Laboratory, Report 7, Detroit, MI.

Sitek, G. [1976], "Big Muskie," *Heavy Duty Equipment Maintenance*, vo. 4, pp. 16–23.

Snell, E. [1974], "Reciprocating Load Carrier," Patent Number 2-430-537.

Sutherland, I. E., and M. K. Ullner [1984], "Footprints in the asphalt," *International J. Robotics Research*, vol. 3, pp. 29–36.

Urschel, W. E. [1949], "Walking Tractor," Patent Number 2-491-064.

Vukobratovic, M., and Y. Stepaneko [1972], "On the stability of anthropomorphic systems," *Mathematical Biosciences*, vol. 14, pp. 1–38.

Waldron, K. J., V. J. Vohnout, A. Pery, and R. B. McGhee [1984], Configuration design of the adaptive suspension vehicle, *International J. Robotics Research*, vol. 3, pp. 37–48.

Wallace, H. W. [1942], "Jumping Tank Vehicle", Patent Number 2-371-368.

31

Researchers often joke about doing metaphorical flips for sponsors. In this chapter, Hodgins and Raibert describe how they actually arranged for a biped robot to do a physical forward flip, not only to amaze sponsors, but also to determine if it is possible to perform such gymnastic feats by driving the actuators in fixed sequences, as if from a multiple-channel tape recorder. Evidently, the answer is yes, as long as the fixed flip-producing jump, pitch, tuck, untuck, and land movements operate in concert with the feedback-driven height, posture, and forward motion procedures explained in the previous chapter.

Much of the work described in this chapter was carried out while the authors were located at Carnegie Mellon University.

Biped Gymnastics

Jessica K. Hodgins
Marc H. Raibert

The forward somersault or flip is a gymnastic maneuver in which the performer runs forward, springs off the ground with both feet, rotates the body forward through 360 degrees, and lands in a balanced posture on one or both feet (see figure 1). Human gymnasts can do a forward flip as an isolated maneuver, or as part of a floor routine in which the flip is preceded and followed by other maneuvers. The average teenager can learn to do a forward flip in a few weeks with proper coaching and practice. In the 1988 Summer Olympics, Vladimir Gogoladze of the USSR did triple back flips in the floor exercise.

Rather than study humans doing flips, we programmed a planar biped running machine to do a flip in the laboratory. To perform the flip the bi-

Figure 1. Forward flip as performed by a human gymnast. Drawings reprinted from Tonry [1983].

ped machine runs forward, thrusts with both legs to jump while pitching the body forward, shortens the legs to tuck once airborne, untucks in time to land on the feet, and then continues running. To develop this program of action, we modified three steps in an otherwise normal sequence of steps. At particular points during the three steps the control system initiated the actions required for the maneuver, such as bringing the legs together, tucking the legs, etc. The timing and pattern of some actions, like accelerating the body about the pitch axis, were provided by prespecified parameters. In most cases, the algorithms normally used to control running speed, balance, and body attitude remained in effect, provided they did not interfere with producing the maneuver. Figure 2 is a photograph of the biped taken during a successful flip.

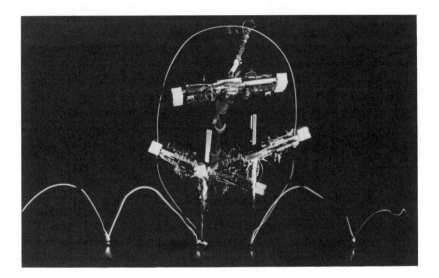

Figure 2. Photograph of planar biped doing a flip. Lines indicate the path of a foot and the flashes are synchronized with liftoff, the highest altitude of the body during flight, and touchdown. The machine was running from right to left.

We studied the flip because it exemplifies a class of maneuvers that have significant dynamic content and incorporate extended ballistic phases. The high jump and baseball pitch are additional examples. The control system responsible for such maneuvers must take action in anticipation of the ballistic phase, because linear and angular momentum cannot be manipulated once the ballistic phase begins. This situation increases the need for an overall plan or strategy for producing the maneuver. A strategy can establish initial conditions for the ballistic phase that will result in the desired ballistic behavior by arranging the events that lead up to the ballistic phase.

In implementing the flip we have begun to test the *motor tape model*, a concept of how animals might produce, store, and modify patterned movement. The motor tape model likens the issuing of neural commands to the playing of a multi-channel tape recorder, with output signals connected directly to actuators [Evarts *et al.* 1971]. We wanted to develop the motor tape model and to see if such a mechanism could be used to produce maneuvers. Although we did not use a pure implementation of the motor tape model, we found that prespecified patterns of actuator output signals could be used to produce flips with a good degree of reliability, when used in conjunction with more conventional algorithms that provided attitude control and balance. Finally, we found working on flips to be lots of fun.

Mechanics of the Flip

The planar biped running machine used for the project is shown in figure 3. It has two telescoping legs connected to a body by pivot joints that form hips. Each hip has a hydraulic actuator that positions the leg fore and aft. A hydraulic actuator within each leg acts along the leg axis to change the length of the leg, while an air spring makes the leg compliant in the axial direction. The overall motion of the biped is constrained to a plane by a tether mechanism that allows it to move fore and aft, up and down, and to rotate about the pitch axis. The biped running machine is described more fully in Hodgins, Koechling, and Raibert [1986].

A flip is a maneuver in which the body and legs rotate through one or more full rotations during the flight phase. The control must ensure that the system neither over-rotates nor under-rotates. A basic equation governing the behavior of the body during the flight phase of a flip is

$$n\pi = \frac{\dot{\phi}\dot{z}}{g} , \tag{1}$$

where

n is the number of full pitch rotations of the body,
$\dot{\phi}$ is the pitch rate of the body,
$\dot{z}$ is the vertical velocity of the body at the beginning of the flight phase, and
g is the acceleration of gravity.

Equation (1) relates the vertical velocity of the body to its angular velocity. For n full rotations of the body during the flight phase, the rate of body pitch rotation $\dot{\phi}$, times the duration of the flight phase $2\dot{z}/g$, equals the angular displacement of the body $2n\pi$.

Equation (1) relies on several simplifying assumptions. We assume that the legs do not swing with respect to the body during the flight phase, so $\dot{\phi}$ represents the angular rates of both the body and the legs. We further assume that the pitch angle of the body is zero at both liftoff and

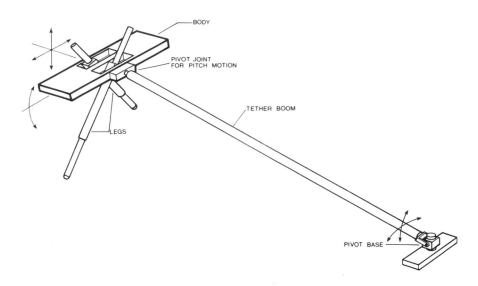

Figure 3. Diagram of planar biped used for experiments. The machine travels by running on a 2.5 m radius circle on the laboratory floor. The body is an aluminum frame on which are mounted actuators, hydraulic accumulators, and computer interface electronics. The hip is driven fore and aft by two low-friction hydraulic actuators. Actuators within the legs change the leg lengths and air springs make the legs springy in the axial direction. Onboard accumulators on the hydraulic supply and return lines increase the instantaneous actuator rate. Sensors on the machine measure the lengths of the legs and air springs, the positions and velocities of the hydraulic hip actuators, and contact between each foot and the floor. A tether mechanism constrains the body to move with three degrees of freedom—fore and aft, up and down, and pitch rotation. Sensors on the tether mechanism measure vertical displacement of the body, forward displacement, and pitch rotation. The tether also supports an umbilical cable that carries hydraulic connections, electrical power, and a connection to the control computer. See Hodgins, Koechling, and Raibert [1986] for more details.

touchdown, that the altitude of the body is the same at liftoff as it is at touchdown, and that there is negligible rotational friction from the pivot at the end of the boom or wind resistance and, therefore, constant angular momentum during flight.

We also assume the pitch rate of the system is constant during the flip. Actually, angular rate may change even though angular momentum is constant. For instance, humans reduce their moment of inertia to increase their rotation rate by tucking the arms and legs in close to their bodies. Tucking reduces the moment of inertia by concentrating the masses nearer to the center of mass of the system than when untucked. The ice skater's spin is a dramatic demonstration of this phenomena.

If the angular rate and moment of inertia of the system in the untucked configuration are $\dot{\phi}_1$ and J_1, and the moment of inertia in the tucked configuration is J_2, then conservation of angular momentum requires the angular rate in the tucked configuration to be $\dot{\phi}_2 = (J_1/J_2)\dot{\phi}_1$. The planar biped tucks[1] by shortening its legs to minimum length during the flight phase. To justify the assumption of constant angular rate during the flip, we further assume that the system tucks instantaneously just after the feet leave the ground, liftoff, and that it untucks instantaneously just before the feet touch the ground, touchdown. This simplification results in constant pitch rate during the flight phase of a flip. Later in the chapter we relax this assumption by considering the case of slower tucking and untucking.

Frohlich [1979, 1980] points out in his elegant papers on the physics of diving, that a system with several masses can change orientation and angular rate without any angular momentum. This is done by windmilling the arms, peddling the legs, or folding the joints of the body in one sequence and unfolding the body in another sequence. Such configuration effects are not considered here.

Flip strategies

Equation (1) shows a direct trade-off between the pitch rate and vertical rate of the body at liftoff. If the control system increases the vertical rate at liftoff, then a lower pitch rate is needed to rotate the body around in time for landing, and vice versa. The values at liftoff are important, because the ballistic nature of the task makes liftoff the last moment the control system can affect either the linear or angular momentum until the next landing. The vertical velocity of the body determines the altitude and the duration of the flight phase, whereas the angular rate determines how far around the body will rotate during that time. The control system must ensure that the system does not over-rotate or under-rotate if it is to continue balanced running. This trade-off between vertical velocity and angular velocity suggests three strategies for producing a flip.

One strategy is to maximize the vertical velocity while adjusting the body pitch rate to provide the correct amount of rotation in the available time. Gymnastics coaches seem to teach this strategy to humans learning

---

[1] In describing the actions of the biped running machine we use the terminology of gymnastics. When the biped *tucks*, it reduces its moment of inertia by shortening its legs. When it *throws* the body, a hip torque is applied that increases the body's rotation rate. In using gymnastic terminology we do not mean to suggest too strong an analogy between the planar biped and a human. The human versions of each of these actions and the human's physical system itself are substantially richer and more elaborate than the planar biped versions we describe here. Moreover, we may find that the suggested functional analogies are not correct.

the forward flip. The second strategy is to maximize the body pitch rate while adjusting the vertical velocity to produce a flight phase that takes the correct amount of time. The third strategy is to compromise on both angular and vertical rates, perhaps by introducing an additional constraint on the maneuver or an optimization criterion. The control system we implemented uses the first of these three strategies—maximize flight duration and adjust pitch rate accordingly.

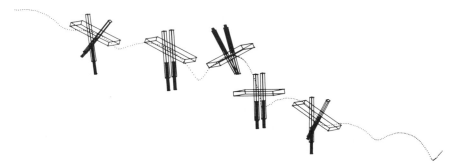

Figure 4. Drawing of planar biped doing a forward flip. The machine was running from left to right. 1) Approach with normal alternating gait, 2) hurdle step to gain altitude and bring the legs together for double support, 3) the body has accelerated forward to initiate the flip and the legs have shortened to increase pitch rate, 4) landing step reduces pitch rate and vertical rate, and 5) resume normal alternating gait. The body configurations are from data recorded from the physical biped during a flip. The dots indicate the path of the center of mass at 12 ms intervals.

Angular rate during flip

Because a system doing a flip can have nonzero body pitch angle at both the beginning and end of the flight phase, the total required rotation of the body may deviate from the nominal one revolution that was used in (1). When the liftoff and touchdown pitch angles have the right sign— nose down at liftoff and nose up at touchdown—the distance the body must rotate is reduced. Equation (1) can be modified to incorporate this reduction in the required rotation angle, $\Delta\phi$. Another correction to (1) is required because the legs do not maintain a fixed orientation with respect to the body during flight. At liftoff the body has rotated into a nose down orientation, so the legs are near their extreme forward position with respect to the body (see figure 4). During the flip the legs are rotated forward over the top to place them near the back end of their travel. This rotation of the legs and conservation of angular momentum causes backward rotation of the body. We use the notation that when a leg is of length r its moment of inertia is given by $J_l(r)$. If we assume the legs reorient through an angle $\Delta\theta$ with respect to the body, that reorientation takes place when each leg has minimum length r_{min}, and that the body has moment of inertia J_b, then reorientation adds $2\Delta\theta J_l(r_{min})/J_b$ to the required rotation of the body. Modifying (1) to account for these factors, the basic flip equation becomes

$$\frac{\Delta\phi_{total}}{2} = n\pi + \frac{\phi_{td} - \phi_{lo}}{2} + \frac{\Delta\theta J_l(r_{min})}{J_b} = \frac{\dot{\phi}\dot{z}}{g}. \tag{2}$$

where ϕ_{lo} and ϕ_{td} are the body pitch angles at liftoff and touchdown, assuming positive values for nose down body pitch angle.

To compute the angular rate during the flip, we need to know the angular momentum of the system. The angular momentum of the system is the sum of the angular momenta of the body and legs. To simplify the analysis we make the approximation that the center of mass of the system remains located at the hip throughout all maneuvers.

The angular momentum of the legs at liftoff is a function of the configuration at liftoff and the forward and vertical speeds. During normal running the net angular momentum of the legs is small because the legs sweep out of phase—one moves forward while the other moves backward. In a flip, however, the legs move together as they sweep backward during stance, giving them substantial angular momentum. The planar biped has telescoping legs as shown in figure 4. Calculation of angular momentum for such legs is simple because the orientation and angular rate for all parts of the leg are determined by the hip-foot axis. The angular velocity of the stance leg is

$$\dot{\theta} = \frac{\dot{z}_f x_f - \dot{x}_f z_f}{x_f^2 + z_f^2}, \tag{3}$$

where x_f is the forward position of the foot with respect to the center of mass and z_f is the altitude of the foot with respect to the center of mass. The forward and vertical position of the center of mass are x and z. During stance when the foot is stationary on the ground $\dot{x}_f = -\dot{x}$ and $\dot{z}_f = -\dot{z}$. The kinematics of the planar biped are given in figure 5. The angular momentum of each leg at liftoff is

$$H_l = \dot{\theta} J_l(r), \tag{4}$$

where the moment of inertia of each leg about the hip is

$$J_l(r) = J_{l1} + m_{l1}r_1^2 + J_{l2} + m_{l2}(r - r_2)^2. \tag{5}$$

J_{l1}, J_{l2}, m_{l1}, m_{l2}, r_1, and r_2 are physical parameters of the leg and are given in table 1. The angular momentum of the body is just $\dot{\phi}J_b$.

The pitch rate of the system once airborne can be found by equating the angular momentum just before liftoff and just after the tuck. If the legs have length r_{lo} just before liftoff, then the angular momentum of the system is

$$\dot{\phi}(J_b + 2J_l(r_{min})) = \dot{\phi}_{lo}J_b + 2\dot{\theta}_{lo}J_l(r_{lo}). \tag{6}$$

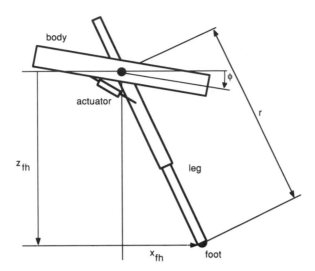

Figure 5. Kinematics of planar two-legged running machine. The length of the leg is r, the angle between the leg and vertical is θ and the pitch angle of the body is ϕ. $\theta = \gamma - \phi - 90$. The foot position relative to the hip, $x_{fh} = r \sin \theta$. The kinematics for the second leg are similar except that the hip actuator is attached to the other side of the body.

If the legs shorten immediately after liftoff to length r_{min} and do not swing with respect to the body, then the pitch rate after the tuck is

$$\dot{\phi} = \frac{\dot{\phi}_{lo} J_b + 2\dot{\theta}_{lo} J_l(r_{lo})}{J_b + 2J_l(r_{min})} . \tag{7}$$

Equation (7) provides a means of predicting the angular rate of the body during the flight phase, given the state of the system just before liftoff.

Control

To control flips we start with normal biped running and the control algorithms described in Hodgins, Koechling, and Raibert [1986]. Briefly, the control system used for normal biped running positions the legs during flight to regulate the forward running speed, thrusts axially with the stance leg to drive the up-and-down bouncing motion of the body, and exerts hip torque between the stance leg and the body to keep the body level. Using these algorithms the machine runs with an alternating gait that uses each leg for support, one at a time, with a flight phase separating each stance phase. The control actions needed for the flip are superimposed on the normal running behavior produced by this set of control algorithms.

Parameter	Symbol	Value
Body mass	m_b	11.45 kg
Body moment of inertia	J_b	0.40 kg-m^2
Upper leg mass	m_{l1}	1.055 kg
Upper leg moment of inertia at COM	J_{l1}	0.0204 kg-m^2
Distance from hip to upper leg COM	r_1	0.0838 m
Lower leg mass	m_{l2}	0.608 kg
Lower leg moment of inertia at COM	J_{l2}	0.0237 kg-m^2
Distance from foot to lower leg COM	r_2	0.317 m
Min leg length	r_{min}	0.44 m
Max leg length	r_{max}	0.67 m
Min leg moment of inertia about hip	$J_l(r_{min})$	0.062 kg-m^2
Max leg moment of inertia about hip	$J_l(r_{max})$	0.126 kg-m^2

Table 1. Physical parameters of planar biped.

Three steps of the normal running sequence are modified to perform
a flip. The three modified steps are the *hurdle step*, *flip step*, and *landing
step*. The hurdle step is used to prepare for the maneuver by developing
extra hopping height and by making a transition from the normal running
gait that uses the legs in alternation, to the double support needed for
the flip. The flip step uses both legs together to power the jump, and
accelerates the body about the pitch axis for the actual rotating maneuver.
The landing step dissipates the high angular and vertical rates and returns
the system to the alternating gait. The activities that take place in these
three steps are summarized in table 1, with additional detail given in the
appendix. We now describe these three steps and how the control system
uses them to generate a flip.

Maximum jump altitude

Earlier we suggested three possible strategies for establishing the trade-off
between pitch velocity and vertical velocity. We decided to control the
flip using the first strategy, which attempts to achieve a maximum vertical
velocity and an intermediate pitch rate. The rationale for this decision was
that it would be easier to remove excess vertical energy with a hard landing
than it would be to remove excess angular energy. The large hip torque
needed to remove angular energy might demand more traction than would
be available, and we were unsure of the ability of the pitch control servo to

Step	Action
Approach	Run forward at 2.5 m/s with alternating gait
Hurdle	Hop with maximum thrust Prepare to land on two legs Extend legs further forward than normal
Flip	Jump with maximum thrust Pitch body forward with large hip torque Shorten legs once airborne Lengthen and position both legs for landing
Landing	Hop with small or negative thrust Return pitch rate to zero and restore posture
Following	Resume running with alternating gait

Table 2. Summary of actions taken by the planar biped to do a flip.

correct large rate errors.

To get maximum altitude during the flip the control program does three things. It jumps high on the hurdle step to increase the vertical energy in the system, it converts forward speed into vertical speed by placing the foot further forward than normal on the landing just before the flip, and it delivers maximum thrust during the flip step.

The control system delivers maximum thrust to the leg on the hurdle step to increase the altitude that will be reached during the next flight phase. Because the legs are springy, they absorb a portion of the system's vertical energy on landing and then return the absorbed energy to help power the next flight. A hurdle step with increased altitude will result in a flip step with increased altitude as well. Gymnastics coaches for humans generally do not recommend a high hurdle step [George 1980].

Maximum thrust is developed during the hurdle step by setting the hydraulic servovalve that extends the leg to its maximum value as soon as the stance phase begins. On a normal step thrust is delayed to the middle of stance, but thrusting throughout all of stance provides more time for the leg actuator to compress the leg spring and accelerate the body upward.

The second thing the control program does to maximize altitude is to convert some of the forward kinetic energy into vertical kinetic energy. This is done by extending the legs further forward than normal just before the stance phase of the flip step. In normal running, the control system positions the foot to leave the forward and vertical speeds of the body unchanged from one step to the next. The foot position that achieves this result is called the *neutral point* [Raibert 1986a]. When the control system places the foot forward of the neutral point, the forward speed declines and the vertical speed increases as shown in figure 6.

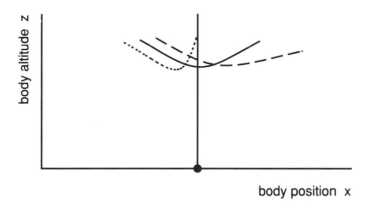

Figure 6. Trajectory of body for various foot positions. During normal running the foot is positioned so that the forward velocity of the body is the same at the end of the stance phase as it was at the beginning of the stance phase (solid line). During a flip the foot is extended forward to transfer some of the forward kinetic energy into vertical kinetic energy, thereby increasing the altitude of the flip and the time available to rotate the body (dotted line). It is also possible to convert vertical velocity into forward velocity, a procedure that can be used upon landing after the flip (dashed line). For each trajectory shown in the plot, the foot is located at the solid circle (●). Adapted from Stentz [1983].

If the foot were positioned to change the forward speed from $\dot{x}_a$ to $\dot{x}_b$ and if there were no mechanical losses in the leg, then the vertical velocity would increase from $\dot{z}_a$ to $\dot{z}_b = \sqrt{\dot{x}_a^2 - \dot{x}_b^2 + \dot{z}_a^2}$ and the duration of flight would increase by $2(\sqrt{\dot{x}_a^2 - \dot{x}_b^2 + \dot{z}_a^2} - \dot{z}_a)/g$. On a typical flip, $\dot{x}_a = 2.5$ m/s and $\dot{x}_b = 1.5$ m/s, so the flight phase could increase by 0.2 seconds if the leg were lossless. We have not measured how much this actually increases flight duration.

The third method of increasing altitude for the flip is to deliver maximum thrust on the flip step itself. During this step there are two legs in support, both of which thrust with maximum hydraulic servovalve settings from the beginning of the stance phase to the end.

Figure 7 shows data recorded from the sensors and actuators of the planar biped as it performed a forward flip. Examining these data, we find that an approach at 2.5 m/s, a hurdle step, and a two-legged jump resulted in a vertical velocity at liftoff of 3.4 m/s, an altitude of 1.04 m, and a flight time of about 0.67 s.

The description so far has centered on maximizing the duration of flight. Assuming this method produces a consistent duration of flight from one flip to the next, the task that remains is to provide one full rotation of the body in the time available. The next section addresses this task.

Desired body rotation

We implemented a simple control program for providing the correct amount of pitch rotation. The human operator chooses a running speed that gives the legs a certain angular momentum, the hip actuator throws the body to give it angular momentum, and once airborne the legs shorten into a tuck to increase the angular pitch rate.

The angular momentum of the body is $\dot{\phi}J_b$. The body is given angular momentum by exerting a large nose-down pitch torque about the hip during the final part of the stance phase, just before the flip. This is called throwing the body. When a gymnast throws, he or she typically uses the arms, head, and trunk. The planar biped has no head or arms, so it is restricted to throwing the body. The control system uses two parameters to regulate how much throw the body is given. One parameter is the magnitude of pitch torque. The other parameter is a threshold for the pitch rate; when the pitch rate exceeds this value, the control system turns off the pitch torque. The actual pitch rate exceeds the threshold value by some amount, which we have found to be repeatable.

It is undesirable for the body to over-travel the limited motion of the hip joint during the period of throw. If the body runs out of travel and hits the mechanical stop before liftoff, the collision and resulting ground forces dissipate the angular momentum of the body. To avoid this the control system initiates the throw early enough so that the pitch rate reaches the threshold value at approximately the same time the feet leave the ground at the end of stance. The control system uses a third parameter to specify this delay.

Acceptable values for these three parameters—the delay for initiation of pitch torque, the magnitude of pitch torque, and the threshold pitch rate to terminate pitch torque—were determined empirically through a series of attempted flips. We started with zero delay, maximum pitch torque, and a very large pitch rate threshold. After about 20 attempts with manual adjustment after each, we arrived at values that provided acceptable rotational behavior for a flip.

When the body reaches its peak altitude during the flight phase of the flip, the control system swings the legs part way forward to center the hip joints. As the body approaches the floor, the control system lengthens the legs to untuck for landing and orients the legs to position the feet. The vertical altitude of the body at which the control system begins to lengthen and orient the legs is specified by another parameter, which was adjusted manually throughout the course of attempting several flips. The leg orientation on landing is calculated as in normal running, where the goal is to provide balance and to control forward running speed.

For the flip shown in figure 7, the biped approaches with a forward running speed of about 2.5 m/s. After 36 ms of the stance phase of the flip step

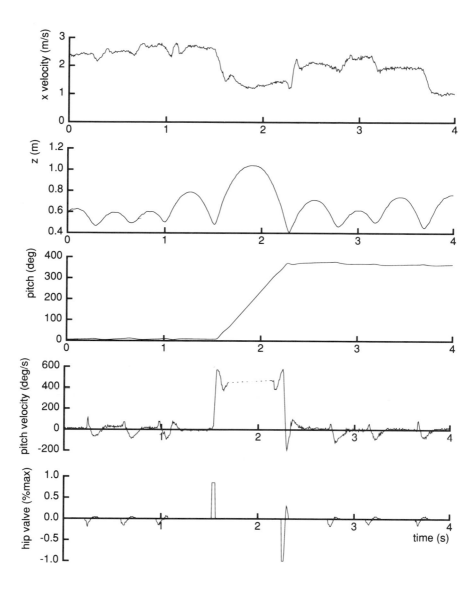

Figure 7. Data recorded during a biped flip. The top two curves show that forward speed is converted into vertical motion. The second graph shows that the flip step is the highest in the sequence. The bottom curves of pitch velocity and hip torque illustrate the inherent symmetry in the flip. Data recorded at 6 ms, the cycle time of the control system.

the control system sets the hip servovalve output signals to 85% of max-imum. The hip servovalve is turned off when $\dot{\phi} = 7.85$ rad/s (450 deg/s). At liftoff the body has developed angular momentum $H_b = 3.9$ kg-m^2/s and each of the two legs has angular momentum $H_l = 0.42$ kg-m^2/s. The total angular momentum at liftoff is $H = 4.7$ kg-m^2/s. Once the system tucks, the total moment of inertia is $J = 0.52$ kg-m^2 and the rotation rate is $\dot{\phi} = 9.97$ rad/s (571 deg/s). Equation (2) suggests a pitch rate of 9.92 rad/s for the measured values $\phi_{lo} = -0.40$ rad, $\phi_{td} = 0.10$ rad, and $\Delta\theta = 0.33$ rad.

Once the system lands after the flip, the control system must eliminate the large vertical and angular energies that were needed for the flip. The control system reduces the vertical energy in two ways. It returns the desired forward running speed to the value used before the flip, converting some of the vertical kinetic energy back into forward kinetic energy. This accelerates the system forward while reducing the height of the next hop. The control program also specifies a smaller than usual leg thrust to absorb some of the vertical energy.

To return the body pitch angle and pitch rate to their normal values, the control program exerts hip torques between both legs and the body using a linear PD servo:

$$\tau = -k_p(\phi - \phi_d) - k_v(\dot{\phi}), \quad (8)$$

where

τ	is the hip torque and
ϕ	is the pitch angle of the body,
ϕ_d	is the desired pitch angle of the body (level),
$\dot{\phi}$	is the pitch rate of the body, and
k_p, k_v	are gains.

This servo is the same mechanism that is used to maintain the body posture in normal running. After the landing step, the control program switches back to an alternating gait with the control algorithms for normal running.

Aerials

The front aerial is a variant of the flip. It differs from the flip in that the performer takes off from one leg rather than two, the legs are spread during the pitch rotation rather than kept together, and the landing takes place on one leg (see figure 8). For humans, an aerial is a variant of the cartwheel, in which the hands do not touch the ground. The aerial is considerably easier than a flip for humans, because humans can spread the legs a large amount to reduce the amount of body rotation needed during the flight phase.

For the biped, the aerial is more difficult than the flip. Just one leg is used to power the flight phase, so the duration of flight for an aerial is about 80% of that for a flip, 0.55 s vs. 0.67 s. The reduced flight time makes it difficult to get adequate rotation during the time available in the flight phase. On the other hand, there is no need to swing the legs forward during the flight phase, because the angles between the legs and the body at liftoff are already correct for landing. This reduces the amount the system has to rotate during flight by about 0.10 rad as compared to a flip.

Figure 8. Aerial as performed by a human gymnast. Drawings reprinted from Tonry [1983].

The planar biped control program for aerials differs from that for the flip in only one important characteristic; both the body and the swing leg are thrown to develop angular momentum about the pitch axis. Because the legs move in opposite directions during the approach for an aerial, the net angular momentum of the legs is small. The stance leg sweeps backward while the swing leg sweeps forward. The control program throws the swing leg along with the body to increase the contribution of the legs to the angular momentum of the system (see figure 9). The procedure for throwing the body is the same as for the flip, but with just one hip actuator exerting torque. Examining the data shown in figure 10, we find that the leg thrown has angular momentum just before liftoff of $H_l = 0.6$ kg-m^2. At that time the angular momentum for the stance leg is $H_l = 0.2$ kg-m^2, for the body is $H_b = 3.7$ kg-m^2, and for the total system is $H_{aerial} = 4.5$ kg-m^2. The total is slightly less than for the flip $H_{flip} = 4.7$ kg-m^2.

The planar biped executes aerials using the control sequence outlined in table 3. Data for one aerial are shown in figure 10. The machine has performed aerials successfully many times. In every case, however, the time available for rotation was so short that the control system could not orient the landing leg to properly position the foot for best stability on landing. The system kept its balance on landing, but with a noticeable reduction in forward running speed after the maneuver, as can be seen in the top curve of figure 10.

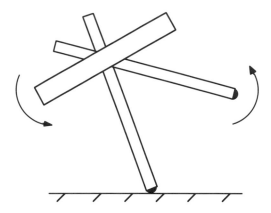

Figure 9. To develop angular momentum in the aerial the control system accelerates both the body and the swing leg in the same direction during the final part of the stance phase.

Step	Action
Approach	Run forward at 2.5 m/s with alternating gait
Hurdle	Hop with maximum thrust Extend leg further forward than normal
Aerial	Hop with maximum thrust Swing free leg backward Pitch body forward with large hip torque Shorten legs once airborne Lengthen and position forward leg for landing
Landing	Hop with small or negative thrust Return pitch rate to zero and restore posture
Following	Resume running with normal alternating gait

Table 3. Summary of actions taken by the planar biped to do an aerial.

Adjusting pitch rate during flight

The control system we implemented for the biped flip makes no attempt to adjust pitch rate once the system is airborne. It keeps the legs tucked during most of the flight phase, resulting in constant moment of inertia and constant angular rate. The amount of rotation during the flight phase is a function of the system's state at liftoff.

It should be possible to control a flip more precisely by manipulating the rate of rotation during the flight phase. Because angular momentum

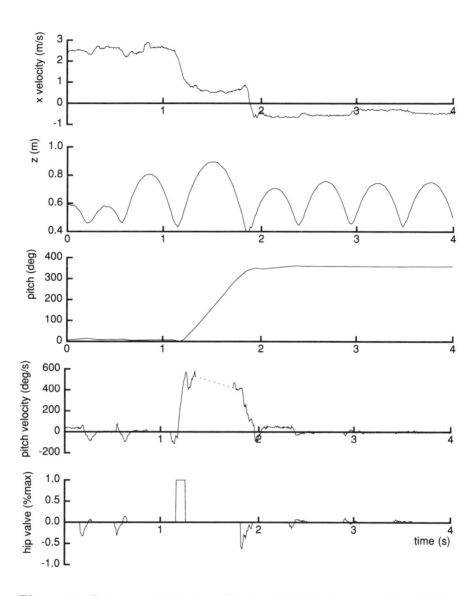

Figure 10. Data recorded during a biped aerial. The top curve of x velocity shows how the forward speed is converted to vertical motion, and how after the aerial the foot is not positioned well enough for the machine to continue traveling forward although it does continue running. The second graph shows that the aerial step is the highest in the sequence, although the difference between the hurdle step and the aerial step is not as dramatic as it was for the flip.

must be conserved during the flight phase, the control system could manipulate the rate of rotation by changing the length and moment of inertia of the legs. To synchronize foot contact with full body rotation, the control system could measure the vertical position and rate of the body and rotational progress of the flip to determine the moment to untuck the legs.

A simplified model assumes that the legs lengthen instantaneously, resulting in just two rates of rotation. If $2J_l(r_{min}) + J_b$ is the moment of inertia of the system with the legs short and $2J_l(r_{max}) + J_b$ is the moment of inertia with the legs long, then to synchronize full rotation with the moment of landing the legs should lengthen when

$$\Delta\phi = \dot{\phi}\left(\frac{2J_l(r_{min}) + J_b}{2J_l(r_{max}) + J_b}\right)\left(\frac{\dot{z} + \sqrt{\dot{z}^2 + 2g(z - z_{td})}}{g}\right) \tag{9}$$

where

$\Delta\phi$ is the remaining rotation required before landing,
$\dot{\phi}$ is the angular rate of the body with the legs short,
z is the vertical position of the body,
z_{td} is the expected vertical position of the body at
         touch-down, and
$\dot{z}$ is the vertical velocity.

The control system could evaluate equation (9) throughout the flight phase of the flip to determine when the legs should lengthen to reduce the rotation rate.

Equation (9) depends on the ability to lengthen the legs in zero time. For the planar biped, the maximum rate at which the legs can lengthen is determined by the maximum rate at which oil can flow through the hydraulic servovalves, which is a system constant. Equation (9) can be modified to accommodate such a fixed rate of leg lengthening.

We start by determining how far the body rotates when the legs are lengthened at a fixed rate. Suppose the legs change length from r_a to r_b at a fixed rate $\dot{r}_k$. Define t_a and t_b so that $r(t_a) = r_a$ and $r(t_b) = r_b$. If the pitch rate is initially $\dot{\phi}_a = \dot{\phi}(t_a)$, then the angular rate during leg lengthening is a function of leg length

$$\dot{\phi}(t) = \dot{\phi}_a\left(\frac{2J_l(r_a) + J_b}{2J_l(r) + J_b}\right). \tag{10}$$

Substituting for $r = r_a + (t - t_a)\dot{r}_k$ and integrating we determine how much ϕ changes during lengthening

$$\Delta\phi' = \int_{t_a}^{t_b} \frac{\dot{\phi}_{lo}(2J_l(r_b) + J_b)}{2J_l(r_a + (t - t_a)\dot{r}_k) + J_b}dt$$

$$= \frac{a}{\dot{r}_k b}\left\{\arctan\left(\frac{r_b - r_2}{b}\right) - \arctan\left(\frac{r_a - r_2}{b}\right)\right\}, \tag{11}$$

where $J_l(r)$ is defined in (5), r_2 and m_{l2} are constants defined in table 3, and

$$a = -\frac{\dot{\phi}_{lo}(J_b + 2J_l(r_b))}{2m_{l2}}$$

$$b = \sqrt{(r_b - r_2)^2 - \frac{J_b + 2J_l(r_b)}{2m_{l2}}}.$$

We can now solve for the state of the system to begin untucking at constant rate. If the legs are length r_a during the tucked part of a flip, then they should lengthen to r_b at rate $\dot{r}_k$ when

$$
\Delta\phi = \dot{\phi}\left(\frac{2J_l(r_a) + J_b}{2J_l(r_b) + J_b}\right)\left(\frac{\dot{z} + \sqrt{\dot{z}^2 + 2g(z - z_{td})}}{g} - t_b + t_a\right)
$$
$$
+ \frac{a}{\dot{r}_k b}\left\{\arctan\left(\frac{r_b - r_2}{b}\right) - \arctan\left(\frac{r_a - r_2}{b}\right)\right\}. \tag{12}
$$

Discussion

Symmetry of the flip

The locomotion algorithms that are normally used to generate running in the planar biped are based on a principle of control called *running symmetry* [Raibert 1986b]. This principle was useful in the design phase of the biped flip. The basic idea of symmetry is that a legged system will travel in steady state when the accelerations it experiences have odd symmetry during each stride. Odd functions integrate to zero over appropriate limits, resulting in no net change in running speed or in posture. For a legged system to run with symmetry throughout a series of steps, the vertical and angular velocities of the body must be coordinated during the flight phases. In normal running the constraint is

$$\frac{\phi}{\dot{\phi}} = \frac{\dot{z}}{g} \tag{13}$$

assuming constant angular rate during flight. An implication of (13) is that the pitch angle of the body at the end of the flight phase is equal and opposite to the pitch angle at the beginning of the flight phase $\phi_{td} = -\phi_{lo}$. Despite temporary but radical departures from the steady state, the flip and aerial conform to these symmetries.

For flips and aerials equation (13) becomes

$$\frac{\phi + n\pi}{\dot{\phi}} = \frac{\dot{z}}{g}, \tag{14}$$

which is related to (1) and (2). Equation (14) implies the same constraint as does equation (13), but with n additional full rotations of the body during flight (see figure 11). Reorientation of the legs with respect to the body during flight is ignored here, but the nonzero pitch angles at liftoff and touchdown are included. The torque exerted at the hip to accelerate the body about the pitch axis to start the flip forms a symmetric pair with the torque exerted at the hip to decelerate the body upon landing— they exhibit the odd actuator symmetry characterized in the theory. The bottom curves in figures 6 and 9 illustrate this symmetry.

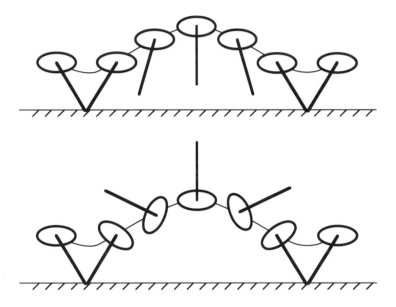

Figure 11. Diagram of symmetric behavior during the flight phase for a normal step and for a flip. In both cases the forward displacement and pitch angle of the body are described by odd functions of time, and the altitude of the body is described by an even function of time.

Recognition that flips, too, should conform to symmetry helped us to reason through the design of the flip control programs and to generalize our understanding of symmetry. For instance, at first we worried about getting adequate traction after the flip to dissipate the large angular momentum. Symmetry considerations permitted us to see if traction at liftoff was adequate to generate the angular momentum in the first place, then there would be adequate traction at touchdown to dissipate the angular momentum. A similar consideration was useful in reasoning about the vertical motion.

Open-loop control

The flip and aerial belong to a class of movements that are dynamic and ballistic. Other members of the class are those that occur in tumbling, diving, and high jumping. These movements are dynamic in that speed and kinetic energy are significant factors in their production. The movements are ballistic in that there are intervals during which the actuators cease to have any direct influence on the key variables of the task. For instance, during the flight phase of a flip no actuator can change the altitude, vertical rate, or angular momentum of the system. In contrast, for the task of making a manipulator move along a trajectory, there is a separate motor to drive the motion of each joint directly and continuously.

Another attribute of these tasks is that outside disturbance plays a relatively minor role. The environment for the movement is essentially unchanging during and between movements, changing only slightly from one repetition to the next. If the initial conditions are precisely established and if the same forces are exerted by each actuator on each repetition, then the behavior repeats in nearly identical form time after time. Sensing and feedback are important in executing such tasks, but in a less direct role than the inner loop of a high bandwidth servomechanism. At the same time, prespecified feedforward control signals can play a more important role in such behavior.

The approach we have taken to control flips and aerials relies on the repeatability of the system, on constancy of the environment, and on repeatably establishing the initial conditions for the movement. These features allow the use of a rather inflexible open-loop actuation pattern to produce the behavior. For instance, to accelerate the pitch rotation of the body the control system waits 36 ms after the start of the flip step, sets the output signal for the hip servovalves to 85% of maximum, waits until the pitch rate reaches 7.85 rad/s, and then turns the hip servovalves off. This control is not devoid of feedback, however, feedback is used sparingly. It uses the pitch rate to determine when to stop throwing the body, and it uses the underlying running pattern to synchronize each flip action to the behavior of the machine.

The control system we implemented for flips is somewhat like a multi-channel tape recorder, with the output signal from each channel wired directly to one actuator. To begin a movement the control system establishes the initial conditions for the movement and "it presses the play button" on the tape recorder. In the biological context, this model of motor control has been called the *motor tape* [Evarts *et al.* 1971]. It is thought that under certain circumstances the nervous system may produce patterned behavior, not through sensors and high-gain feedback loops, but by issuing sequences of open-loop commands that go directly to the muscles. In the pure form of the model, commands would be issued independent of progress in executing the movement. One can also imagine learning complicated patterns of motion by editing short segments of motor tape together. It is not known whether the motor tape accurately models biological motor mechanisms.

The flip implementation described in this chapter does not embody a pure form of the motor tape model. The implementation is like the motor tape in that it uses sequences of motor commands that are issued directly to the actuators, without a local servo. The magnitude of actuator signals for thrust in the hurdle and flip steps and the throw delay and magnitude are specified in this manner. The flip control system is unlike the motor tape in that the timing of control actions is synchronized to events in the loco-motion cycle, and thereby, to the progress of the movement. For example, the maximum vertical thrust does not begin until the normal locomotion control algorithm has entered stance. The starting time and magnitude of hip torque for pitch acceleration are determined with a fixed sequence like the motor tape, but hip torque is terminated when pitch rate reaches a desired value. One could obtain a more systematic study of the motor tape model by comparing maneuvers produced by several implementations: a pure motor tape implementation of a maneuver, a trajectory servoed im-plementation, and an intermediate implementation like the one described here.

The use of feedforward without high bandwidth feedback is not new. It is used to send spacecraft to the moon, Mars, and beyond. At a prede-termined moment the engines ignite for a predetermined period to take the craft out of Earth orbit and send it toward the remote rendezvous. In space travel there is no attempt to adjust thrust continuously throughout the trip to stay exactly on course with precisely the desired speed, because such an approach would require far too much energy. Occasional adjustments are made instead.

There are two characteristics of space travel that make this approach feasible. First, unexpected external disturbances are minimal. Second, variability in the actuators and internal mechanism is small. These con-ditions imply that for the same initial conditions and the same actuator output signals, the actual behavior of the system is very nearly the ex-pected behavior and that behavior of the system will reliably repeat on successive executions. These conditions apply to the maneuvers described in this chapter.

Where do the feedforward control signals come from?

Given a task and strategy, the feedforward signal needed to accomplish the task must be found. The feedforward signal can be found using analytical or empirical techniques. The analytical technique is to calculate the feed-forward signal from models of the mechanism and the task. For instance, to calculate the feedforward signals for the biped flip described earlier, one might:

- Model the running machine, including its springy legs, hydraulic actuators, and hydraulic power supply, to calculate the maximum attainable vertical velocity of the body.

- Find the appropriate pitch rate using equation (2).

- Calculate the forward running speed and the pitch rate of the body required before liftoff using a model of the body and legs.

- Calculate the hip torque needed during stance to develop the desired pitch rate using a model of the body and legs.

- Calculate the output signal that will provide the desired torque using a model of the actuator.

Once again, this approach clearly depends on an *a priori* specification of the general strategy. In the case of a flip, the strategy includes the decision to maximize flight time and to adjust body pitch rate accordingly, as well as many other details.

The empirical approach to finding the feedforward signals uses data obtained by attempting to perform the task. Rather than use a model of the system to determine the maximum attainable vertical velocity, the physical system itself is used to make the measurement. Output is applied, the behavior is measured, and the output is adjusted accordingly. The nature of such adjustment and the effectiveness of the results is a long-standing problem in motor learning.

For both of these approaches, the analytic and the empirical, there is the separate question of what role humans or other outside agents play in the process, as opposed to an automated process. A human could go through the steps described to calculate the control signal from the model, or the control system itself could incorporate these calculations for control. For the empirical approach, a human can look at the results of attempts to do a maneuver and adjust the output for the next try, as we did for the flip and aerial, or the control system could make the adjustment. In the experiments reported in this chapter the empirical approach was used and all adjustments were made by humans.

Formulating strategies

We have described the specific control used to make the biped running machine do forward flips and aerials. The essential features of the approach are a strategy for executing the flip and a set of low-level actions and parameters that implement the strategy. The strategy we chose is based on several decisions:

- Maximize time of flight, with pitch rate adjusted accordingly.
- Extend the legs forward on the flip step to convert forward speed into vertical speed.
- Adjust the start of pitching torque to synchronize the end of hip travel with liftoff.
- Shorten the legs during flight to increase pitch rate.
- Reduce thrust to absorb vertical energy on landing.
- Use normal attitude control algorithm to absorb angular energy on landing.

Each of these decisions was made by humans based on knowledge of the mechanics of the problem and intuition. It is not difficult to imagine that future control systems may be able to formulate strategies such as these automatically. Such systems will embody a model of the mechanical system to be controlled, a working knowledge of the physics that govern behavior of the model, and an ability to reason. Heuristics and optimizations may be important. The need for techniques that bridge the gap between the task level of a motor act and the actuator control level is a deep and important problem.

If strategies for performance of a task were found automatically, optimal behavior might be easier to find. A given strategy for performing a particular task may not be the only or the best strategy, and it may be difficult to know if a better strategy exists. Richard Fosbury demonstrated this point in 1968 when he introduced a previously unknown form for doing the high jump, the *Fosbury Flop*, in which the jumper goes over face-up rather than face down. Fosbury won an Olympic gold medal in 1968, and Dwight Stones used the Fosbury Flop to set a new high jump world record of $7'7\frac{1}{4}''$ in 1974 [Doherty 1976]. Strategy design is crucial for executing maneuvers. Automated techniques may some day permit us to find all possible strategies for a task, and to identify the best possible solution.

References

Doherty, J. K. [1976], *Track and Field Omnibook*, Tafnews Press, Los Altos, CA.

Evarts, E. V., E. Bizzi, R. E. Burk, M. Delong, W. T. Thach, Jr. [1971], "Central control of movement," *Neurosciences Research Progress Bulletin* vol. 9 PP. 1-169.

Frohlich, C. [1979], "Do springboard divers violate angular momentum conservation?" *American Journal of Physics* vol. 47 pp. 583–592.

Frohlich, C. [1980], "The physics of somersaulting and twisting," *Scientific American* vol. 242, pp. 154–164.

The work in this chapter was supported by the Defense Advanced Research Projects Agency and by a grant from the System Development Foundation.

George, G. S. [1980], *Biomechanics of Women's Gymnastics* Prentice-Hall Inc., Englewood Cliffs, NJ.

Hodgins, J., J. Koechling, M. H. Raibert [1986], "Running experiments with a planar biped," *Third International Symposium on Robotics Research*, MIT Press, Cambridge, MA.

Raibert, M. H. [1986a], *Legged Robots That Balance*, MIT Press, Cambridge, MA.

Raibert, M. H. [1986b], "Running with symmetry," *Int. J. of Robotics Research*, vol. 5, no. 4.

Stentz, A. [1983], "Behavior during stance," in *Dynamically Stable Legged Locomotion—Third Annual Report*, M. H. Raibert *et al.*, Robotics Institute, Carnegie-Mellon University, CMU-RI-TR-83-20, pp. 106–110.

Tonry, D. [1983], *Tumbling*, Harper and Row, New York.

Appendix A: Details of Control Sequence for Flip

State	Trigger Event	Action
Approach LOADING 110	Leg 1 touches ground	Hold leg 1 at landing length Zero hip torque leg 1 Keep leg 2 short Don't move hip 2
COMPRESSION 120	Leg 1 air spring shortened	Hold leg 1 at landing length Erect body with hip 1 Keep leg 2 short Position leg 2 for landing
THRUST 130	Leg 1 air spring lengthening	Extend leg 1 Erect body with hip 1 Keep leg 2 short Position leg 2 for landing
UNLOADING 140	Leg 1 air spring near full length	Shorten leg 1 Zero hip torque leg 1 Keep leg 2 short Position leg 2 for landing
FLIGHT 150	Leg 1 not touching ground	**Shorten leg 1** **Don't move hip 1** Lengthen leg 2 for landing Position leg 2 for landing
Hurdle Step LOADING 1210	Leg 2 touches ground	Keep leg 1 short Don't move hip 1 Hold leg 2 at landing length Zero hip torque leg 2
COMPRESSION 1220	Leg 2 air spring shortened	Keep leg 1 short Position leg 1 for landing † **Reduce desired speed** **Max thrust: leg 2** Erect body with hip 2
THRUST 1230	Leg 2 air spring lengthening	Keep leg 1 short Position leg 1 for landing **Max thrust: leg 2** Erect body with hip 2
UNLOADING 1240	Leg 2 air spring near full length	Keep leg 1 short Position leg 1 for landing Shorten leg 2 Zero hip torque leg 2
FLIGHT 1250	Leg 2 not touching ground	Lengthen both legs for landing Position both legs for landing

---

†Expected T_s is adjusted by a factor of $1/\sqrt{2}$ to account for two legs in support during the flip step.

State	Trigger Event	Action
Flip Step LOADING 2110	Both legs touch ground	Hold both legs at landing length **Zero both hip torques**
COMPRESSION 2120	Both air springs shortened	**Max thrust: both legs** Zero both hip torques
THRUST 2130	Compression + delay (36 ms)	**Max thrust: both legs** **Exert large pitch torque: both legs (85% of max)**
THRUST 2131	Pitch velocity > desired pitch velocity (7.85 rad/s)	**Max thrust: both legs** **Zero both hip torques**
UNLOADING 2140	Both air springs near full length	Shorten both legs Zero both hip torques
FLIGHT A 2150	Both legs not touching ground	**Shorten both legs** **Don't move either hip**
FLIGHT B 2151	Vertical velocity zero	**Keep both legs short** **Center both hips**
FLIGHT C 2152	Body altitude < threshold (0.7 m)	Lengthen both legs for landing Position both legs for landing [†]
Landing Step LOADING 3210	Both legs touch ground	Hold both legs at landing length Zero both hip torques
COMPRESSION 3220	Both air springs shortened	Keep both legs at landing length Erect body: both hips
THRUST 3230	Both air springs lengthening	**Reduced thrust: both legs** Erect body: both hips
UNLOADING 3240	Both air springs near full length	Shorten both legs Zero both hip torques
Resume normal running		

[†]Expected T_s is adjusted by a factor of $1/\sqrt{2}$ to account for two legs in support during the flip step.

Appendix B: Details of Control Sequence for Aerial

State	Trigger Event	Action
Approach LOADING 110	Leg 1 touches ground	Hold leg 1 at landing length Zero hip torque leg 1 Keep leg 2 short Don't move hip 2
COMPRESSION 120	Leg 1 air spring shortened	Hold leg 1 at landing length Erect body with hip 1 Keep leg 2 short Position leg 2 for landing
THRUST 130	Leg 1 air spring lengthening	Extend leg 1 Erect body with hip 1 Keep leg 2 short Position leg 2 for landing
UNLOADING 140	Leg 1 air spring near full length	Shorten leg 1 Zero hip torque leg 1 Keep leg 2 short Position leg 2 for landing
FLIGHT 150	Leg 1 not touching ground	Shorten leg 1 Don't move hip 1 Lengthen leg 2 for landing Position leg 2 for landing
Hurdle Step LOADING 1210	Leg 2 touches ground	Keep leg 1 short Don't move hip 1 Hold leg 2 at landing length Zero hip torque leg 2
COMPRESSION 1220	Leg 2 air spring shortened	Keep leg 1 short Position leg 1 for landing **Reduce desired speed** **Maximum thrust: leg 2** Erect body with hip 2
THRUST 1230	Leg 2 air spring lengthening	Keep leg 1 short Position leg 1 for landing **Maximum thrust: leg 2** Erect body with hip 2
UNLOADING 1240	Leg 2 air spring near full length	Keep leg 1 short Position leg 1 for landing Shorten leg 2 Zero hip torque leg 2
FLIGHT 1250	Leg 2 not touching ground	Lengthen both legs for landing Position both legs for landing

–Continued–

State	Trigger Event	Action
Aerial Step LOADING 2110	Leg 1 touches ground	Hold leg 1 at landing length Zero hip torque leg 1 Keep leg 2 short Don't move hip 2
COMPRESSION 2120	Leg 1 air spring shortened	**Maximum thrust: leg 1** **Zero hip torque leg 1** Keep leg 2 short **Don't move hip 2**
THRUST 2130	Compression + delay (36 ms)	**Maximum thrust: leg 1** **Exert large pitch torque:** leg 1 **(85% of maximum)** Keep leg 2 short **Swing leg 2 backward**
THRUST 2131	Pitch velocity > desired pitch velocity (7.85 rad/s)	**Maximum thrust: leg 1** **Zero hip torque: leg 1** Keep leg 2 short **Swing leg 2 backward**
UNLOADING 2140	Leg 1 air spring near full length	Shorten leg 1 Zero hip torque leg 1 Keep leg 2 short **Swing leg 2 backwards**
FLIGHT A 2150	Leg 1 not touching ground	Shorten leg 1 Don't move hip 1 Lengthen leg 2 for landing Position leg 2 for landing
FLIGHT B 2151	Body altitude < threshold (.7 m)	Keep leg 1 short Don't move hip 1 Lengthen leg 2 for landing Position leg 2 for landing
Landing Step LOADING 3210	Leg 2 touches ground	Keep leg 1 short Don't move hip 1 Hold leg 2 at landing length Zero hip torque leg 2
COMPRESSION 3220	Leg 2 air spring shortened	Keep leg 1 short Position leg 1 for landing Erect body with hip 2 Hold leg 2 at landing length
THRUST 3230	Leg 2 air spring lengthening	Keep leg 1 short Position leg 1 for landing **Reduced thrust: leg 2** Erect body with hip 2
UNLOADING 3240	Leg 2 air spring near full length	Keep leg 1 short Position leg 1 for landing Shorten leg 2 Zero hip torque leg 2
Resume		

32

Aside from our brains, it is our hands and the way we use them that sets us apart from other animals and challenges our ability to create machines as flexible and functional as we are.

Such challenges invite innovation and hard work. Ten years ago, most mechanical hands hardly deserved the name for they were really just two-fingered, parallel-jaw grippers. Today, visionary mechanical engineers have designed and built highly articulated, tendon-driven, multi-fingered, fast-moving mechanical hands of amazing complexity and potential.

Creating a beautiful physical hand solves only half of the dexterity problem, however. Solving the other half, the control half, is the subject of this chapter. Working with the three-fingered Salisbury hand, the authors have developed the control ideas required to support all sorts of sophisticated capabilities, many of which require force control. When demonstrated, the hand can hold and orient an egg or crush a can. It can hold a rubber ball stiffly along one axis and limply along the orthogonal axis, with neither axis aligned with any particular hand part. It can run a finger over a surface to determine shape and texture. And most recently, it has begun to exhibit controlled slip, the sort of thing that we do when we adjust our grip on a pencil or pen.

Using an Articulated Hand to Manipulate Objects

Kenneth Salisbury

David Brock

Patrick O'Donnell

With the advent of sophisticated computer systems we are now able to assume a degree of intelligent control over much more complicated mechanical systems than ever before. Concurrently, we have begun to see new and more complex types of hand mechanisms with the potential for performing highly dexterous manipulation. The marriage of high performance computational systems with sophisticated mechanical hand systems promises to provide increased dexterity in prosthetic, robotic, and teleoperation applications. In addition, the experience we gain in trying to understand and achieve machine dexterity may give us insight into some of the mysteries of human dexterity. It is important to observe that, despite the current availability of relatively sophisticated mechanical hands (most notably the Salisbury hand and the Utah/MIT hand), we have not yet seen application of these devices outside the laboratory. One reason is that mechanical sophistication must be complemented by sophistication in the control, sensory, and perceptual components of manipulation. Adding more fingers and motion freedoms to a robot does not free us from having to address the problems of planning and perception in the face of uncertainty; if anything, it forces us to face them more directly. The very nature of manipulation with cooperating fingers implies a degree of unpredictable behavior that requires more sophisticated sensing, feedback, and planning than found in existing robots.

In this chapter we will present our view of the steps that must be taken to achieve dexterity with a robot hand. Some of these, such as mechanical design, low level control, and simple languages have already begun. Others, such as comprehensive sensory integration and high level planning are still in their formative stages. Our experience primarily has been with the Salisbury hand experimental environment at MIT and this will be used to illustrate our perspective.

Hand Functions

The functions which hands are required to perform can be divided into several areas: prehensile, manipulative, and sensory functions. In human experience they often occur in combination with each other in a mixture of exploratory and purposeful motions. In performing complex tasks humans simultaneously employ all three functions to verify, guide, and plan the sequence of operations performed. In the robotic world we are not yet able to smoothly integrate these complex functions into coherent actions; current robotic systems employ a rather loose coupling of their prehensile, manipulative, and sensory functions, both structurally and operationally.

Prehensile capability implies the capacity to hold an object in some controlled state relative to the hand. This requires that the grasp allow exertion of sufficient restoring forces on an object to hold it against disturbance forces. Secure grasping requires that there be sufficient dimension to the collective effect of forces acting through all the contact points to span the space of disturbance forces which may act on the object. For spatial motion of rigid objects this corresponds to six dimensions. The constraints imposed by contacts can be divided into structural constraint and frictional constraint. A grasp which employs more structural constraints will be more secure against large disturbance forces; frictional constraints will cease to be active if disturbance forces become too large in certain directions. The dimension of net forces acting on the grasped object can be no greater than six, therefore the extra freedoms in force exertion by the hand result in the freedom to adjust the internal forces. These internal forces may be varied without changing the net force acting on the body. They permit, within certain limits, changing the direction and magnitude of forces acting through individual contact points. This freedom in allocation of grasp forces permits a degree of optimization of grasp force distribution. It also raises the possibility for modulating the frictional restraints so as to introduce partial freedom of motion within the hand (controlled slipping).

Manipulation of objects with a hand can take several forms. It may simply hold an object securely relative to the wrist and rely on the rest of the arm for imparting motion. This is typical of most robots and of humans moving relatively large objects. Motion of smaller objects can be achieved with the fingers alone. Objects held in the fingertips can be moved and rotated short distances without sliding or breaking finger contact. Larger motions within the hand require controlled slipping and repositioning of fingers. In manipulating very large objects the hand may recursively act as a large fingertip in concert with other cooperating hands.

Sensing includes a number of functions: simple measurement of the mechanism's position, velocity, acceleration, force states, detection of the characteristics of contacts with objects, for example, location and force distribution to the measurement of manipulated object characteristics such as curvature, texture, and temperature. Other sensory modes, such as visual and auditory may provide higher level feedback.

Dexterity

Dexterity is the integration of all of the above and other capacities into a higher level of competence. It is a quality of manipulative capability which implies a degree of skill and deftness of operation. These in turn, depend on the quality of motion, sensing, and control. If we look at examples of increasingly dexterous motion, the distinction between prehension, manipulation, and sensing becomes less obvious. Sensing the shape of an object may require manipulation of it to detect its contours. Holding an object may require adjusting to a more favorable grasp, and moving an object may require a sequence of regrasping. Humans easily integrate these functions to perform complex human dexterity: a high degree of mechanical functionality, rich sensory input, and intellectual capacity. By comparison, dexterity in the machine sense is still in its infancy and suffers from limited functionality in all the above areas.

True *machine dexterity* necessitates that a high degree of mechanical functionality be available. In the same way that the quality of sound from a stereo radio can be no greater than that allowed by the speakers, the net dexterity of a robot hand can be no greater than that allowed by the mechanical and sensory performance of the system. Yet, even with the best possible mechanism, the dexterity of the hand will be limited by the quality of commands or intelligence used to control the system.

From a mechanical point view, the potential dexterity of a hand is dependent upon a number of elements including its kinematic, dynamic, and sensory qualities. The obvious kinematic description of a hand refers to the number of joints and links composing the hand, their placement relative to each other and the ranges of motion possible. The more subtle aspects of a hand's kinematics deal with the shapes of the finger links and their ability to present suitable working surfaces to grasped objects for constraining and manipulating them. The dynamic performance of a hand is affected by the distribution of mass and compliance within the hand, the forces which may be exerted and the speeds and accelerations which may be obtained. In addition the resolution of force and motion affect the precision with which actions may be performed. Finally, the type, accuracy, sensitivity, and resolution of sensing must be able to provide the required perception of hand states and object interactions. The kinematics and dynamics of a hand limit the controllability of states of the manipulated objects. The sensory system limits the observability of task states. A mechanism lacking certain degrees of freedom may not be able to effect certain motions of a manipulated object; a mechanism lacking certain state information may not be able to detect particular motions. Thus, the controllable and observable states permitted by a hand must overlap in the dimensions in which we want to achieve closed loop control. Perhaps the most difficult aspects of machine dexterity are the closely coupled intellectual and perceptual components. It is in performing complex tasks which require a high degree of dexterity that the demand for high level understanding of task goals and progress is greatest. In prosthetic or teleoperation modes these high level functions can be subsumed by the human. In the autonomous system they must be either explicitly encoded in the program, or embodied in a more comprehensive world model from which motions are planned. This is one area where experience and experimentation with hand mechanisms will be of significant value in inspiring and guiding our thinking.

It is important to realize that the skills we observe when several fingers cooperate to manipulate an object are but one example of a more general capacity to understand motions of objects subjected to forces and constraints. These same skills come into play when we clutch an object to our side with an elbow, or when several hands cooperate to move a large object. Thus our research into dexterous hands is really a metaphor for a much broader class of manipulative skill that we hope to employ in robotic systems, including multi-arm and multi-robot operation.

In this chapter we describe research with the three-finger Salisbury hand at MIT. The work is aimed at gaining experience with articulated hand operation and developing strategies for bringing this type of hand into useful application. In addition, we are interested in determining what the minimal sensor/hand mechanism requirements are for performing reasonable and reliable grasping and manipulation with an articulated gripper. Our approach has been to develop an experimental environment, integrating an articulated hand with a variety of control systems, sensors, and command language constructs.

Control System

The Salisbury hand (which was originally called the Stanford/JPL hand) is comprised of three fingers, each with three degrees of freedom (see figure 1). This particular choice of kinematics was made because it is the minimal configuration capable of imparting arbitrarily directed forces (including torques) and small motions (including rotations) to objects held in the

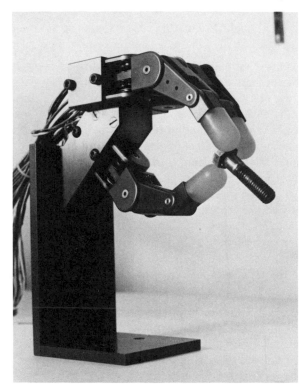

Figure 1. The Salisbury three-finger hand. (Photo courtesy of David Lampe, MIT.)

fingertips. At the same time it permits the imposing of internal forces required for stable grasping with friction contacts [Mason & Salisbury 1985]. In order to actuate the fingers, flexible teflon coated steel cables (seven by seven construction) are routed through teflon lined flexible conduits to each finger. Tension to each cable is provided by a samarium-cobolt D.C. brush-type motor acting through a two-stage 25:1 gear reducer. This ratio was chosen as a compromise between torque/power efficiency and the back drive inertia of the fingers. The flexible conduit permits passing the actuator cables around a robot wrist and placement of the actuator package on the robot forearm. Although the conduit/cable sliding interface introduces some friction into the system, it is significantly less than the reflected brush friction in the motors. Because the cables slide over a teflon interface, the friction is primarily Coulomb in nature and can be minimized by limiting the amount of bend allowed in the conduit. While initial experimentation with the hand at MIT has focused on hand operation alone and has been performed with the hand located on a manually repositionable support, the device has been successfully mounted on a number of PUMA 560 robots at other laboratories. Loucks *et al.* [1987] have demonstrated coordinated control of this hand and an arm in the grasping of moving objects.

The initial control system implemented on this hand (actually one finger) was at Stanford University and is described in Salisbury and Craig [1982]. The system consisted of a hierarchy of controllers (implemented on one PDP 11/45) with a tendon tension controller at the lowest level. Corrections to errors in desired tendon tensions were made by altering the torque (current) command applied to the corresponding motor (through appropriate compensation). Position control with this system was achieved by computing the Cartesian position error at the fingertip, and using a Cartesian stiffness and damping matrix to control the endpoint impedance. Corrective forces to fingertip displacement were then mapped into joint space, and then into tendon space to establish the tendon tension controller setpoints. Because each three degree-of-freedom finger is actuated by four tendons (the minimum possible), the extra freedom in tension selection was used to minimize the tensions required subject to the constraint that they all be positive.

While the original Stanford implementation worked, it suffered from a number of problems. The Cartesian nature of the controller prevented explicit positioning of joints. This allowed multiple configurations of the fingertip to satisfy a given position command (that is, knuckle up or knuckle down). The configuration to which the finger settled was dependent upon the path of the finger; and when attempting to move the finger to singularities (such as fully straightening it), the finger would exhibit large position errors. At these positions the small joint friction torques overwhelmed the small corrective torques mapped from the Cartesian corrective forces through a nearly singular Jacobian. Finally, the force control was not particularly robust to large disturbance forces. The motor brush friction effectively introduced hysteresis into the transmission of force from the motor to the tension sensor, resulting in limit cycles for only moderate gains.

The second control system which was implemented at MIT is described in detail in Salisbury, Brock and Chiu [1986]. This much improved system (called HAND) eliminated the motor brush friction problem by closing a high gain velocity servo around each motor and by using a shaft mounted encoder for feedback and a microprocessor operating at servo rate of 1000 Hz. This allows us to assume velocity control over the proximal end of each tendon, and provides a stable platform from which force control may be effected. In its basic form the force control servo commands tendon velocities are proportional to tendon tension error and the closed loop behavior approximates a first order system response up to about 5 Hz. The behavior of this type of force controller in the presence Coulomb friction and stiction has been analyzed in detail by Townsend and Salisbury [1987] and is stabilizable in the presence of Coulomb friction. Stiction does introduce limit cycles, the amplitude of which can be minimized by keeping the transmission stiffness high between the actuator and source of stiction.

The HAND system closes the force control loop at 50 Hz servo rate using a VAX-750 to command motor velocities and process tension sensor readings. As described in Salisbury, Brock and Chiu [1985] the controller running on the VAX specifies motions of the hand expressed in joint space. A joint space stiffness specification can be utilized to modify the local compliant behavior of the fingers. Trajectories in joint space can be flexibly constructed through a simple editor and used to command the hand motions. While being simple and computationally efficient, the joint space stiffness formulation permits a wide variety of compliant behaviors to be constructed including controlled stiffness in Cartesian space, as well as the simple grasping reflexes. It is also possible to command motions strictly in position control mode. The resulting maximum stiffness in this mode is dominated by the tendon stiffness and is roughly twice that of the maximum stable stiffness attainable under active stiffness control. This is the most precise mode of positioning and it is often used for commanding motion of the fingers when they are not expected to contact an object. With control loop closure in joint space there are no problems with moving the fingers through singularities in the work space. The upper limit on actively controlled stiffness is due to a combination of limited servo rate and unmodeled dynamic modes in the system.

At the highest level, a Symbolics 3600 Lisp Machine communicates with the joint space controller to provide a flexible user interface for commanding motions, reacting to events, and constructing programs. The OOLAH system developed by Chiu [1985] permits the user to construct Cartesian based finger and object motions with the option of superimposing controlled stiffnesses and bias forces. It provides a means for reacting to user-defined force conditions. It also provides a common interface for coupling the hand to higher level sensory, grasp, and trajectory planning modules currently under development.

Object Manipulation

When we wish to move an object with a traditional manipulator we must grasp it firmly with the (simple) gripper and command the necessary arm joint motions to effect the movement. Even a simple reorientation may require large motions of massive links to achieve it. The involvement of the whole arm in even small motions is one of the fundamental limitations we find in current manipulation practice. The power and complex control required to move massive links quickly and precisely place severe constraints on the quality of manipulation achievable. Precise control of forces is limited even more by these massive links. It is these shortcomings that provide one of the prime motivations for developing articulated hands. By placing low mass, high speed links (fingers) near the object to be manipulated, we provide for a whole new range of manipulation modes. Instead of using articulated hand-like mechanisms, we could simply place multi-degree-of-freedom small motion devices between the gripper and wrist to gain some of the benefits of local small motion control. However, it is only by using a number of multiple-degree-of-freedom fingers that we gain the additional benefits of reconfigurable and adaptable grasping.

Humans employ a wide range of grasps which permit varying degrees of dexterity and security in hand based manipulation. Most of our experience with the Salisbury hand has been in the mode of grasping called *fingertip prehension*. In this mode an object is held in the fingertips only and the fingers are commanded to move simultaneously so as to impart the desired net motion or force to the object. If we make the simplifying assumption that each fingertip contacts the object at a single point, fixed in the object, with three degrees of freedom (that is, a point contact with friction which is instantaneously equivalent to a ball and socket joint) then the kinematic and force relationships are easy to compute; given such a grasp defines a rigid grasping triangle. To achieve a desired motion of the the object we simply compute the corresponding rigid body displacement of the triangle and the corresponding fingertip motions necessary to keep them in contact with the corners of the triangle. The two subtle aspects to this process which must be dealt with are explained below.

Quasi-static force relationships

The first is control of the internal forces. Because there are more than six degrees of freedom in the hand motion we must impose additional constraints to completely define the finger motions. Specifying that the grasping triangle shall not deform implicitly imposes these constraints but does not address the need to control the internal or grasping forces. With the three-finger Salisbury hand there are three such grasping forces which may be controlled. These forces must be imposed so as to present sufficient normal force at each contact to keep the tangential frictional forces large enough to constrain the object. The easiest way to do this is to rely on the inherent compliance of the mechanism (servo, transmission, and finger covering) to maintain sufficient internal forces after a grasp has been achieved. This has been repeatedly demonstrated to work well for a wide range of objects in our experimentation. More fragile objects, and delicate operations, require that we be able to assume more precise control over the force interaction between the hand and grasped objects.

Using active force and stiffness control [Chiu 1985] we can specify more precisely the internal grasping forces. This mode is particularly useful for handling fragile objects where grasping as hard as you can is not appropriate. The transformation required for determining the fingertip forces necessary to achieve a desired set of internal and external forces on a grasped object is called the *grip transform, G* [Mason & Salisbury 1985]. Because forces are applied by several contacts acting in parallel, we cannot compute this transform directly from the grasp geometry. We compute the grip transform by first constructing a matrix relating forces applied at the fingertips to the net force and torque on the object. We define a (6×9) $\mathcal{W}$ matrix to have each of its 9 columns correspond to a component of net force which may be exerted upon the grasped object by finger action. This matrix will have rank six unless we have a degenerate grasp (three colinear or two coincident grasp points). The first three columns will correspond to forces exertable by finger one, the second three columns to those exertable by finger two, and the last three to forces exertable by finger three. If we also define a 9-vector of finger force intensities $\underline{F} = [c_1, \ldots, c_9]^T$, then the net (external) force acting on the body is

$$\mathcal{W}\underline{F}. \tag{1}$$

In order to parameterize and assume control over the internal forces on a grasped object, we first define a net generalized force acting on the object,

$$\underline{\mathcal{F}} = [f_x, f_y, f_z, m_x, m_y, m_z, \lambda_1, \lambda_2, \lambda_3]^T. \tag{2}$$

The first six components are the familiar external forces on the object and the last three are the intensities of the internal forces (in a coordinate system yet to be chosen). We next form the (9×9) matrix

$$G^{-T} = \begin{bmatrix} \mathcal{W} \\ \text{-------} \\ \underline{c}_{1,h}^T \\ \vdots \\ \underline{c}_{3,h}^T \end{bmatrix} \tag{3}$$

by augmenting the $\mathcal{W}$ matrix with three linearly independent row vectors which are orthogonal to the rows of $\mathcal{W}$ (that is, in its null space). The product

$$\underline{\mathcal{F}} = G^{-T}\underline{F}. \tag{4}$$

gives the net generalized forces acting on a grasped object when a given set of fingertip forces are exerted. The equation's inverse,

$$\underline{F} = G^T\underline{\mathcal{F}}, \tag{5}$$

indicates which forces the fingers must be commanded to exert in order to apply a desired set of external and internal forces to an object. This equation is fundamental in hand control and, as will be shown later, it can be used to construct a fairly general stiffness specification. Note that the parameterization of the null space is not specified here. The choice of the best set of basis vectors for the null space $(c_{i,h}s)$ is an open research topic; we suggest one useful choice below. Also note that having $\text{rank}(\mathcal{W}) = 6$

is not sufficient alone for achieving a stable grasp. The orientation of the uni-sense contact forces (that is, normal contact forces) must be such that their forces can always be kept positive (and in contact) by readjustment of internal forces.

Via energy conservation principles we can also derive the grip velocity relationships. First we must clarify the meaning of input and output power in grip systems. We define $\underline{V}$ to be a vector of contact velocities occurring at the fingertips, expressed in the same coordinate systems as the contact forces, $\underline{F}$

$$\underline{V} = [d_1, \ldots, d_9]^T . \tag{6}$$

Because the elements of $\underline{V}$ are the intensities of motion along the axes of the corresponding contact forces

$$\underline{F}^T \underline{V} = \sum_{i=1}^{n} c_i d_i \tag{7}$$

is the power being input to the object. It is the sum of the power being input at the contact points as a result of motion along each axis of force application.

We define $\underline{\mathcal{V}}$ to be a 6-vector, the first six components of which represent the body's linear and angular velocity, and the remaining three γ_is are the body's (virtual) velocities resulting from deformation of the body (grasp triangle). Thus,

$$\underline{\mathcal{V}} = [v_x, v_y, v_z, \omega_x, \omega_y, \omega_z, \gamma_1, \ldots, \gamma_3]^T \tag{8}$$

and

$$\underline{\mathcal{F}}^T \underline{\mathcal{V}} = f_x v_x + f_y v_y + f_z v_z + m_x \omega_x + m_y \omega_y + m_z \omega_z + \lambda_1 \gamma_1 + \cdots + \lambda_3 \gamma_3 \tag{9}$$

is the sum of power that is used to do work on the environment, and to store energy as the object deforms. However, because we consider objects rigid and massless no energy can be stored. The internal forces λ_i, may be non-zero but they can do no work without violating our assumptions. Thus, we expect the γ_is to be zero and if we do encounter non-zero values for these internal displacements it will mean that our grip has slipped, and/or our assumptions about contact constraints have been violated.

Equating power input with power output and rate of storage (equations (7) and (9)), and using equation (4), we have

$$\underline{F}^T \underline{V} = \underline{\mathcal{F}}^T \underline{\mathcal{V}} = (\underline{F}^T G^{-1}) \underline{\mathcal{V}}, \tag{10}$$

from which it follows that if $\underline{F} \neq 0$

$$\underline{V} = G^{-1} \underline{\mathcal{V}} \tag{11}$$

and finally, by inversion,

$$\underline{\mathcal{V}} = G \underline{V} . \tag{12}$$

Equation (11) allows us to take a desired set of body velocities (with the γ_is = 0) and determine which set of finger velocities are required. Equation (12) permits us to determine the body's velocity (as well as check for a slipping grip) from a set of finger velocity measurements.

The grip transform G is an integral part of the stiffness control strategy which we have implemented in the HAND and OOLAH systems. For example, it can be used to take a Cartesian stiffness matrix K_C, which represents the desired local compliant behavior of a grasped object, and transform it to an efficient joint space representation

$$K = \mathcal{J}^T G^T K_C G \mathcal{J}, \tag{13}$$

where $\mathcal{J}$ is a block diagonal matrix composed of the three (3×3) finger Jacobian matrices. The stiffness control system was originally designed to impart controlled stiffness to grasped objects, as might be required to place a peg in a hole, or push an object into alignment. We have found that it also permits construction of stiffnesses useful in the acquisition of objects. One particularly useful and simple construct we have employed to build joint space stiffness matrices makes use of the fact that a matrix of rank n may be spectrally decomposed into a weighted sum of n unitary matrices. For example, if K is a matrix of rank 9 with nine linearly independent unit eigenvectors k_i, and eigenvalues λ_i, then

$$K = \sum k_i * k_i^T * \lambda_i. \tag{14}$$

If K is our joint space stiffness matrix then the elements of K represent the rate at which the torque increases on the ith joint with deflection of the jth joint. The principal stiffness directions are defined by each k_i. In this case the direction may be simply the motion of a particular joint (k_i has a non-zero element only in the ith position) or it may be a combination of simultaneous joint motions. By choosing directions along which we wish to resist motion k_i, and magnitudes of stiffness along those directions λ_i, we can construct K from the above relationship. If a set of directions is chosen which do not span the full space of motion, there will be no resistance to motion in the unspanned directions.

It is also possible to use the reverse of this process to remove certain stiffnesses from a grasp. For example, to permit the two fingers to balance the forces on them against the thumb, we would want to remove stiffness for differential motion of the fingers (moving finger one up while finger two moves down). By taking a nominal joint space stiffness k, of full rank (for example, a diagonal matrix) and subtracting the matrix $kx_1x_1^t$ from it, we reduce the rank of k by one. (This is strictly true only if x_1 is an eigenvector of k, but it is often close enough). If x_1 is a vector representing the desired differential motion of the fingers, then the reduction of k's rank corresponds to the freedom introduced between finger one and finger two. In general, we can construct a new reduced rank stiffness matrix by removing the stiffnesses from the directions in which we require compliance

$$K_{\text{new}} = K - Kx_1x_1^T - Kx_2x_2^T - \cdots. \tag{15}$$

Other types of contact

A second subtle aspect of moving and exerting forces upon objects held in fingertip prehension stems from the fact that the contact points with the object are not really fixed on its surface. While the ball and socket contact assumption is reasonably accurate for small motions of large objects, it is not precise for very small objects, or for very large displacements. Clearly, when rolling a pea in our fingertips consideration must be made for the change in contact location on both the finger and the pea as the motion proceeds. While it seems possible to actually derive kinematic relationships for this type of rolling contact, it is not clear that they would be of much use. Slipping in both the contact plane and about the contact normal will introduce inaccuracies which will be impossible to model and predict. Thus, as we press our hand to extreme operating conditions it appears that we will have to rely upon more novel manipulation, sensing, and feedback strategies.

Controlled slip manipulation is one class of manipulation which we have begun to explore at MIT. Brock [1987] has analyzed a broad class of controlled slip manipulation and demonstrated a number of specific examples with the Salisbury hand. When humans manipulate objects our fingers are not always fixed securely to the object's surface. Many times we allow objects to slide or rotate on our fingertips, consciously controlling the motion of the object rather than the motion of our fingers. This controlled slipping technique of manipulation may be the dominant form of dexterous human manipulation. For example, if you try putting a lid on a jar, but start with the lid top down on a table; without thinking, you pick up the lid, spin it around between our two fingers using the edge of the jar or another finger, and screw it on the jar. The use of a pencil eraser is another example of controlled slipping. We stop writing, flip the pencil over, push the pencil through our finger to gain leverage, and erase. In both these motions, and in may others, objects are allowed to slide and rotate at the points of contact with the fingers.

To fully employ this type of manipulation we need to understand a whole new class of *grasps* which do not fully constrain the object. While the design of the Salisbury hand was aimed at obtaining secure (force closure) grasps, it is possible to modify the internal grasping forces to permit some freedom of motion within the grasp. Secure constraint is really a matter of degree. While a given grasp may completely restrain an object for small disturbance forces, it may allow the object to slip for large disturbance forces. Thus, by carefully modulating the constraint state and applying disturbance forces, we may cause the object to slip controllably. The direction of slip will depend upon the grasps constraint state and the direction of applied forces. These intentionally applied disturbance forces may arise from a number of sources including gravity, acceleration, and contact with external objects or other fingers. An obvious and familiar example can be demonstrated by holding one end of a pencil horizontally between two fingers. If you then slightly relax the grip and/or accelerate your hand, the orientation of the pencil in the grasp can be altered.

To actually plan this type of motion for a robot hand we can construct a *constraint state map* by identifying the range of motions permitted for each combination of internal forces that may be imposed. For each point in this three dimensional space of grasp forces there is an associated set of permissible motions (or twists). The goal then, is to find the set of internal forces (if any) which will permit freedom of motion in the desired direction (with no more freedom than necessary), and then apply a disturbance force which will tend to move the object in the desired direction. To simplify this process we have parameterized the three-space of internal forces in a geometrically appealing manner.

We first choose a grasping force focus point (which lies in the plane of the three contacts). This requires two parameters and defines the direction and relative magnitudes of the internal components of the forces applied at the fingertips. The third parameter is the magnitude or intensity of the grasping force. The map of permissible motions can then be constructed by examining each of the possible constraint states and determining the associated freedom of motion. The choice of the grasp forces is made by finding the set of permissible motions which most closely align with the desired motion, and using the associated grasp forces. Finally, we apply the required disturbance force to make the object move.

Obviously, controlled slip manipulation requires a degree a indeterminacy in many case and will require more sophisticated touch or visual feedback to make it useful. There are, however, many cases where the motion is quite well determined. Brock [1987] has demonstrated repeated reorientation of a rectangular solid by a two step process. First, the block is held in two fingers and pressed against a fixed surface. As the block stops against and aligns with the surface, the fingers slip down the block to its end. This brings the fingers to a known position on the block and the block to a known orientation. Then the fingers squeeze more tightly, lift the block away from the surface, and loosen the grip slightly to allow the block to rotate nearly 180 degrees due to the action of gravity, but not fall. This places the block back in the original state (though rotated) and the whole process can be repeated again.

Sensing

In anticipation of harsh operating environments and to reduce complexity we have only employed as many sensors as can be justified by anticipated control and manipulation strategies. High bandwidth control of the motors required direct measure of motor shaft position and this was achieved with incremental encoders. Given the need to control forces in the presence of some mechanism friction, force sensing elements were also required. Strain gauge tendon tension sensors were used on each tendon to minimize the transformations required in the servo loop. The sensors were located at the base of the fingers as a compromise between putting them at the motors (where higher bandwidth might be attainable) and putting them on the joints or fingertips (where maximum accuracy would be attainable). The resulting design is sturdy and unencumbered by excessive wiring. Although direct measurement of finger joint positions and velocities could improve positioning accuracy and bandwidth with a higher order controller, the additional complexity and mechanical vulnerability was not considered warranted.

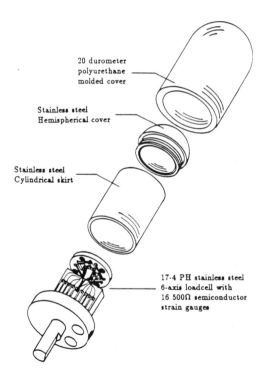

20 durometer
polyurethane
molded cover

Stainless steel
Hemispherical cover

Stainless steel
Cylindrical skirt

17-4 PH stainless steel
6-axis loadcell with
16 500Ω semiconductor
strain gauges

Figure 2. The contact resolving fingertip.

It is less obvious what type of contact or tactile sensor is required to perform dexterous manipulation. Because many motions of objects in the hand are unobservable with traditional position and force measurements, some type of touch information is required. While humans make good use of tactile sensing (measurement of pressure distribution) in manipulation, it is not yet clear how to implement, let alone use, this capability in a robot hand (despite vigorous research into tactile sensor design). Our approach has been to develop a simple sensor which can locate and track the effective point of contact with the finger tip. This has been achieved by building a finger tip which is supported on a miniature 6-axis force sensor. As described in Salisbury [1984] and Brock [1984] (see figure 2), these six measurements permit determination of the location of contact with the fingertip, orientation of the contact plane, and resolution of the contact forces into normal and tangential components.

Though object features such as texture and local curvature are not statically observable with this type of contact resolving sensor, by tracking the frequency content and time histories of the contact forces during exploratory motion, we may be able to observe texture and curvature. To date, this sensor has only been used to probe unknown object shapes for contact location and orientation, but has demonstrated good accuracy and tolerance to abuse. Two clear advantages of this type of sensor are the minimal wiring required (compared to tactile sensors) and the ability to measure tangential forces. The ability to measure normal and tangential contact forces at the contacts permits anticipating incipient slip and should guide us in readjusting the grasp to prevent slip.

Conclusions

This chapter has been aimed at giving our view of how to use an articulated hand to manipulate objects. It may be pretentious to say that we have achieved dexterous manipulation, but it is clear that we have extended the vocabulary of primitive manipulation and sensing elements required for truly dexterous manipulation. The boundary between simple preprogrammed motions and real dexterity is just as fuzzy as the boundary between simply clever and really intelligent programs.

There are a number of hard problems which must be addressed before dexterous articulated hands will be practical and useful to us. Some of the unsolved problems are listed below.

- **Hand Mechanics.** How should we really design a hand to perform useful manipulation? Do we want more fingers and degrees of freedom? Do we want the fingers to spin and gyrate in ways that would make humans cringe? Why not? No person ever thought of rolling himself as a means of locomotion but it is certainly useful in a car. The debate over the choice of anthropomorphic and non-anthropomorphic designs will probably go on forever and there will probably always be an appropriate niche for each approach. Because of the difficulty in building, packaging, maintaining, and controlling these complex mechanisms, it is always important to rationalize the complexity in terms of potential performance. And yet we must not get stuck building hands for single applications and should keep sight of the benefits of designing a single device for many different operations.

- **Actuators and Transmissions.** Actuation and transmission of motion and force have been large stumbling blocks for hand designers. It is hard to build small, efficient actuators and transmit their actions through the robot arm. The headache of passing tendons around or through complex wrist has plagued every hand designer. Until we develop very powerful and compact actuators we will probably be compelled to locate the actuators some distance from the hand, and the problem of efficient, stiff transmission of forces must be addressed.

- **Hand/Arm Integration.** It is wrong to consider the hand as an add on accessory to the arm. Both from the design and control points of view we must begin to consider these as components of a single larger system, so that we may synergistically integrate their capabilities.

- **Manipulation Modes.** There exists a whole range of manipulation modes which do not yet employ with robots. The familiar deterministic modes of robot manipulation do not take advantage of most of the surface area on a robot. Can we extend our ideas of controlled slip to include all the links of the hand and all the surfaces of the arm? Are there novel dynamic modes of operation which humans are too slow or insensitive to employ?

- **Sensing modalities.** What do we really need to know in order to manipulate an object reliably? Obviously force, position, and touch sensing are required, but until we have a clear plan of how to integrate and use the information, it is hard to specify appropriate sensor performance. Determining what the useful bandwidth and sensitivity of these sensors should be would help focus the design efforts. Other sensory modes such as proximity, thermal, acoustic, and just about any part of the electromagnetic spectrum should be considered as candidates for augmenting the manipulative process.

Achieving dexterity with autonomous robots will ultimately depend upon integrating the ability to move and sense with the ability to recognize and plan. To close the high level control loops needed for intelligent robot behavior will require a much broader and coherent understanding of the mechanics of object motion and interaction than we have yet achieved. Our work with robot hands has moved forward in this direction but a garden of delights is yet to be discovered.

The authors would like to acknowledge the financial support of the System Development Foundation.

References

Brock, D. L. [1984], "Strain Gage Based Force and Tactile Sensors," B.S. Thesis, Department of Mechanical Engineering, Massachusetts Institute of Technology, Cambridge, MA.

Brock, D. L. [1987], "Enhancing the Dexterity of a Multi-Fingered Hand Through Controlled Slip Manipulation," M.S. Thesis, Department of Mechanical Engineering, Massachusetts Institute of Technology, Cambridge, MA.

Childress, D. S. [1972], "Artificial Hand Mechanisms," *ASME Mechanisms Conference and International Symposium on Gearing and Transmissions*, San Francisco.

Chiu, S. L. [1985], "Generating Compliant Motion of Objects with an Articulated Hand," M.S. Thesis, Department of Mechanical Engineering, Massachusetts Institute of Technology, Cambridge, MA.

Loucks, C. S., *et al.* [1987], "Modeling and Control of the Stanford/JPL Hand," *Proceedings IEEE International Conference on Robotics and Automation*, Raleigh, NC.

Mason, M. T., and J. K. Salisbury [1985], *Robot Hands and the Mechanics of Manipulation*, MIT Press, Cambridge, MA.

Salisbury, J. K., and J. J. Craig [1982], "Articulated Hands: Force Control and Kinematic Issues," *International Journal of Robotics Research,* vol. 1, no. 1, MIT Press, Cambridge, MA.

Salisbury, K., D. L. Brock, and S. L. Chiu [1985], "Integration of Language, Sensing and Control for a Robot Hand", *Proceedings 3rd ISRR*, Gouvieux France, MIT Press, Cambridge, MA, 1986.

Salisbury, J. K [1984], "Interpretation of Contact Geometries From Force Measurements," *Proceedings 1st ISRR Bretton Woods*, NH, MIT Press, Cambridge, MA.

Townsend, W. T., and J. K. Salisbury [1987], "The Effect of Coulomb Friction and Stiction of Force Control," *Proceedings IEEE International Conference on Robotics and Automation*, Raleigh, NC.

33

Usually we think of robot arms as if their only purpose were to put robot hands where we want them. But if you keep track of what you do with your arms for a day, you will have a list that includes things like pushing, shoving, cradling, cushioning, grasping, and even striking.

This chapter is about principles of design, control, and use of robot arms with these extra manipulation capabilities. In particular, the authors focus their discussion on a high-performance robot arm designed and built in conformance with geometry and drive principles developed by Townsend in his PhD thesis. One immediately striking characteristic of the arm is that power is delivered via a novel, efficient, backlash-free cable transmission, which enables force control, light weight, high stiffness, and rapid movement. When demonstrated, the arm moves incredibly fast, yet with extraordinary grace and precision, going through demonstration sequences as if choreographed, rather than programmed.

An Experimental Whole-Arm Manipulator

Kenneth Salisbury   Michael Levin
Brian Eberman   William Townsend

As the result of an informal collaboration between the Massachusetts Institute of Technology's Artificial Intelligence Laboratory and Woods Hole Oceanographic Institute, two new prototype manipulators have been developed. Both arms employ efficient, stiff cable transmissions, and brushless motors to permit them to be intrinsically force controllable. Both arms are designed to be capable of traditional endpoint manipulation as well as a broader class of operations known as whole-arm manipulation. The arms currently serve as test beds for a variety of concepts in manipulator control and utilization. The four degree-of-freedom arm (upon which we will focus) developed at the MIT Artificial Intelligence Laboratory [Townsend 1988] has been designed to be lightweight and fast, and to operate in terrestrial as well as zero-g environments. A second three degree-of-freedom arm developed at Woods Hole [DiPietro 1988] has been designed and operated at full ocean depths. It was used in the summer of 1989 as part of the JASON/ARGO system to recover artifacts from the floor of the Mediterranean Sea.

Despite intended operation in vastly different contexts, these arms share the common capability of being intrinsically force controllable [Salisbury *et al.* 1988]. While many useful operations can be performed with simple endpoint position control, a much broader class of operations can be performed with an arm (or arms) that can controllably exert forces. Many tasks have inherent kinematic constraints imposed by the geometry of the operation. These constraints can be exploited to make the task easier to perform and robust to errors. Turning a valve or a nut has only one freedom of motion; sliding a rod in a hole has two freedoms; moving a block across a plane has three and so on. To perform such tasks the manipulator must be able to comply to the constrained motions while controllably causing motion in the unconstrained directions [Mason 1981]. While force control and force reflecting operations have long been recognized as useful by both the robotic and teleoperator communities, it is still an expensive and diffi-cult technology to implement. In an effort to make intrinsically non-force controllable arms force controllable, numerous robotics researchers have in-vestigated the use of endpoint (for example, wrist mounted) force sensing devices in the arm's control system. Such systems tend to be limited by either poor mechanical performance of the arm, or the inherent dynamic stability problems of non-collocated sensors. Thus, one of our aims has been to develop mechanical systems which are inherently able to control forces.

A more subtle design goal behind our work was the desire to develop practical arms which are capable of whole-arm manipulation [Salisbury 1987]. Many tasks in the unstructured environment of the real world can be performed without explicit use of the end-effector. Pushing and shov-ing [Mason & Salisbury 1985] as well as striking, cradling, and interlink grasping are examples of such operations. People frequently use their arms to grasp a bundle of logs, grasp a barrel, snag a loop, cushion a blow, and push off from a constraint. To get the maximum utility from expensive manipulators in critical and unstructured situations, we should strive to include such operations in the arm's repertoire. This implies a more global view of manipulators in which all their surfaces are made available for doing work on the environment. With this perspective, the distinction be-tween fingers, arms, and multiple co-operating robots begins to blur. This concept presents a formidable challenge to the operation of autonomous robots and even requires a new vocabulary to describe such operations. It also presents a formidable challenge to the arm designer in attaining the required performance. Our progress on both fronts is addressed in what follows.

Task Framework for Whole-Arm Manipulation

Whole-arm manipulation tasks can be grouped into four main categories: pushing, searching, enclosure, and exclusion. Although this taxonomy is neither complete nor mutually exclusive, it does encompass a variety of useful tasks. For many of these tasks we have found it useful to describe the manipulators' motions by the trajectories of the lines which form the link axes (as opposed to the more traditional endpoint trajectories).

We define *Pushing* as acting on an object with a force or set of forces to cause the object to move, and is distinguished from grasping in that the object may not be fully constrained by the manipulator contact forces.

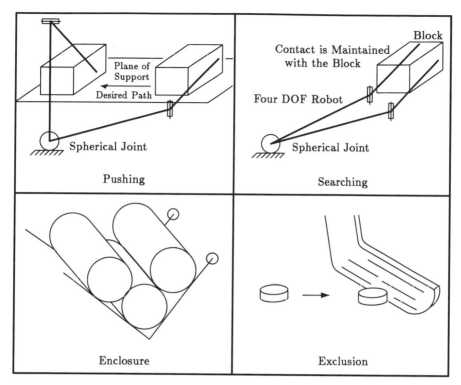

Figure 1. Categories of whole arm manipulation.

Rather, it takes advantage of kinematic constraints inherent in the task geometry and employs less than six degree-of-freedom constraint contact between the arm and the task. Package sorting and handling, moving heavy blocks, and door closing are all accomplished through pushing. In order to stably push on an object on a plane, we need at least two contacts at all times to impose sufficient constraints to determine its motion. A line or planar contact between the robot and the object can accomplish this; line contact is well suited to properly designed link geometries.

The motion of the robot for a pushing operation may be described conveniently by the motion of the line along the axis of links being used to operate on the object. For objects with a plane surface of sufficient size, pushing with a line on this surface will be inherently stable and the object can be guided by controlling the line's motion perpendicular to its axis. Because the entire length of a link is being translated to effect a pushing operation, the process is robust to errors in calibrating the location of the robot and the object. For a number of tasks, pushing has inherent advantages over grasping and lifting. Objects that are too heavy to lift can often be moved by pushing with the links at points nearer to the joints. By using kinematic constraints in the task environment, objects can be aligned and uncertainty in their orientation can be reduced [Mason & Salisbury 1985].

Search is defined here as moving a compliant kinematic structure through the workspace in order to detect objects by contacting them. In searching, as opposed to pushing, the manipulator must not cause the object to move when the contact is made or while the object is being explored.

In order to perform a search, the manipulator must have a way to detect collisions and an efficient procedure for splitting the workspace into regions containing and not containing objects. In addition to finding the geometry of the workspace, the manipulator can be used to identify the apparent stiffness and frictional properties of the objects. As will be shown later, the location of contact between the robot and the object often can be determined from measurement of only the joint torque and positions. This extends the utility of the robot by using it directly as a sensor. Here again we note that the motion of the manipulator may be conveniently specified by the motion of the lines defining the robot's link axes. By moving a line instead of a point through a region of interest, the dimension of the search space is significantly reduced.

Enclosure is defined here as the creation of a kinematic structure around an object such that the object is at rest in a stable equilibrium. Grasping and enclosure are effectively equivalent, where we extend grasping to include grasps using robot links.

There are two methods for forming an enclosure. A stiff kinematic structure can be formed by the manipulator's links which is then used to scoop up the desired objects. In this case, the objects settle under the force of gravity into the constraining shape defined by the manipulator's links. Alternatively for a power grasp, a compliant kinematic structure formed from the manipulator's links can be placed around the object, and then the stiffness of the structure can be increased while keeping the structure in contact with the objects. In this type of grasp, the manipulator conforms to the object. For both types of grasps there are a large number of possible contact points and geometries which will form a stable grasp. Therefore, to generate an enclosure, the final contact location need not be specified; rather, we may generate a set of line motions such that the object is guaranteed to lie within a stable contact region.

Exclusion is defined here as the creation of a kinematic structure that tends to prevent objects from entering a defined region. Exclusion includes catching and blocking objects. Although this structure will push on objects which attempt to enter the region, exclusion is different from pushing because the robot is not trying to move any particular object at a given instant. The structure must be stable under impulse loadings and the holes in the structure must be sufficiently small. The structure can be described by the location and compliance of the lines that define the structure.

Arm Design for Whole-Arm Manipulation

To provide a test-bed for whole arm manipulation concepts, the four degree-of-freedom arm (known as WAM-1, or WAM) shown in figure 2 was designed and built at MIT's AI Laboratory. The arm's geometry and drive mechanics are based upon principles developed in Townsend [1988], and are described in brief here.

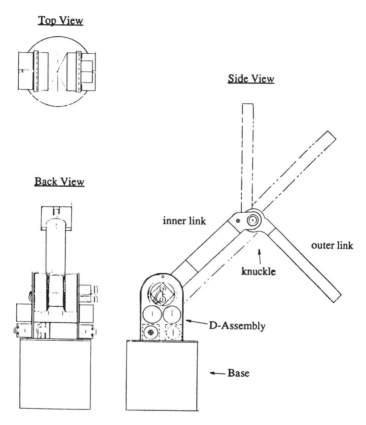

Figure 2. WAM-1 manipulator.

Arm geometry

In anticipation of performing line-based manipulation we required that the arm have at least four degrees-of-freedom. This is the minimum necessary to place the line defined by the last link arbitrarily in space (within the limits of its workspace). While it is desirable to maximize the workspace of a manipulator, it is not yet precisely clear how to define the workspace of a line based manipulator, let alone how to attach a meaningful metric. The kinematics shown in figure 3 permit the last link to be placed on the ensemble of lines defined by all lines passing through the spherical surface traced by the elbow (subject to joint range limits). This geometry was chosen because it exhibited a sufficient workspace for the planned experiments.

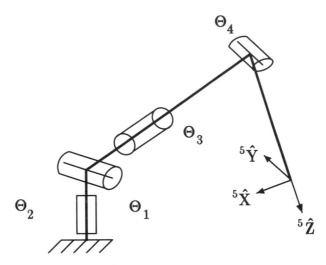

Figure 3. WAM-1 kinematics.

To maximize the range of object sizes which can be grasped between adjacent links or arms, it can be shown that maximizing the links' aspect ratios is of value. By making the links long and slender, their own volume occupies less of the workspace available for enclosing objects. One consequence of this observation requires that the motors be removed to the base of the manipulator to keep their volume from interfering with and confusing the workspace. We also require that the exterior of the arm to be smooth and free of protrusions or dangling cables which might otherwise interfere with tasks. Cylindrical link cross-sections were chosen to avoid the discontinuous contact changes which occur with rectangular cross-sections. Finally a compliant high friction covering was added to both links to provide friction for constraining objects and cushioning of impacts. This not only increases the range of objects which may be grasped between links, but also reduces the magnitude of impact forces encountered.

Arm drive mechanics

The demands of whole-arm manipulation require the arm to be inherently force-controllable. This implies that the arm be easily backdriveable by external forces so that it may respond quickly and naturally to environmental contacts. That it be backdriveable both in the inertia and friction senses, requires that we eliminate friction forces (that is, transmission inefficiency) in the system and that we minimize its mass (including reflected motor inertia) as much as possible. In an ideal system we would generate clean, predictable forces at the actuators and transmit them without attenuation to the contact point.

By actuating with brushless electric motors, the inherent friction of bushes or hydraulic piston seals is eliminated. Current brushless motor technologies do suffer from a fair degree of torque ripple but this can be minimized by proper commutation compensation [Paul 1987; Eberman 1988]. The severity of this ripple torque is expected to diminish with advances in the design of motor magnetic and drive circuits. For underwater applications, brushless electric motors may be cooled by the surrounding water and thus safely driven at maximum output.

While direct connection of the motors to the joints (direct drive) was considered, we felt that in order to keep the volume and mass of the links as small as possible it was desirable to mount the motors remotely from the joints. The use of an efficient reducer between the motor can always make a good motor better by increasing the effective motor constant (torque/square root of power). This is desirable so long as we do not employ such a large reduction ratio that the reflected motor inertia becomes dominant and interferes with the inertial backdriveability of the system. In retrospect, we may find that it is appropriate, from a complexity point of view, to use large direct drive motors on the base joints. For modularity, we chose to employ the same motors for each of the joints.

We considered a number of transmissions to act as a reducer and conduct power to the joints while keeping in mind the need for high efficiency. Cable transmissions have been used widely in mechanisms because of their efficiency and the flexibility they afford the designer. When properly designed, cable drives have high material strength, low weight, low velocity and torque ripple, no backlash, and low friction. Furthermore, they do not leak, do not require surface lubrication, and can be guided over long distances around pulleys, through complex and twisting geometries. Cables and all other tension-element drives, such as tapes and belts, do not transfer power through compression or shear, and so avoid added compliance and strength limitations from bending moments or buckling. When designed for reliability, cable drives have a history of dependability in such demanding applications as aerial trams, ski lifts, cable cars, light-aircraft control surfaces, cranes, and elevators.

For similar torque requirements, cabled reducers, which can spread the high-tension load over a large portion of each pulley circumference, may be built with much thinner pulley walls (1.5 mm aluminum in the WAM-1 design) than gears which must have a heavy wall supporting each cantilevered tooth against the full transmitted load and high tooth surface hardness.

In order to build high-performance tension-element drives it is important to understand that their fundamental performance characteristics allow very efficient transmission when correctly designed with stiff elements. If one considers simple control volumes surrounding the drive and driven pulleys of a multi-stage tension-element transmission, application of the principle of conservation of mass and the first *and* second laws of thermodynamics leads to the conclusion that these drives have an upper-bound efficiency which can never be improved mechanically [Townsend & Salisbury 1988]. This efficiency is quantified as:

$$\eta = \left[1 - \frac{T_2 - T_1}{EA} \right]^{\mathrm{n}},$$
(1)

where

η is the efficiency measured as the ratio of output/input transmission power.

T_2 and T_1 are the high and low element tensions in the drive circuit.

EA is the stiffness of a unit length of tension element.

n is the number of independent stages in the drive.

Clearly, it is necessary to minimize the number of independent stages, maximize the element stiffness, and minimize the tension difference or torque load. In the WAM-1 arm, the worst-case upper-bound efficiency is 96% in each axis (under full torque loading). An estimate of other sources of friction lowers this figure to about 93%. Under no- or low-torque conditions, when force fidelity is most critical, the upper-bound efficiency of equation 1 approaches 100%. The actual measured no-load efficiency for WAM-1 is 99% which compares to about 90% for the PUMA-560 robot based on data reported in Armstrong [1988].

Cabled arms traditionally suffer from a lack of stiffness which can in turn lead to low bandwidth of the system and a lack of kinesthetic fidelity. It is possible to increase the stiffness of the transmission shown in figure 4 by locating the reducer/idler pulleys as close to the output link as possible. For equally stressed high- and low-tension circuits it is possible to increase the overall motor-to-joint stiffness by a factor N (where N is portion of the overall reduction ratio contributed by the reducer/idler pulley) simply by placing the reducer at the output joint rather than at the motor. (This should not be confused with the stiffness increase introduced by the reduction ratio in the first place.) The use of a distantly located reducer results in most of the transmission distance being spanned by the low-tension cable circuit with an attendant reduction in compressive stress in the link structure.

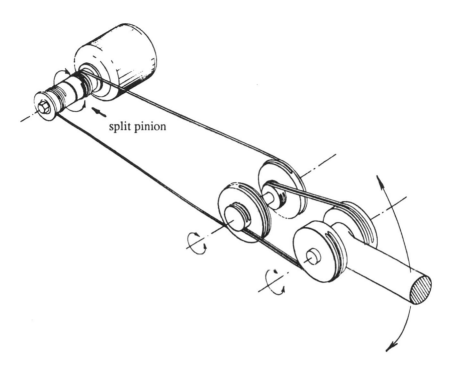

split pinion

Figure 4. Distal reduction mechanism.

WAM-1 design

The WAM-1 arm was built to take advantage of the above considerations. It has an overall reach of 1 meter and has been designed to be light-weight and fast. While no wrist/end-effector system has yet been specified, it has sufficient strength to permit the addition of one. The transmission ratios are sized so that the mechanical advantage is large but so that the backdriven motor inertia is negligible compared to a 0.1 kg payload. Special split-pulley designs allow single-point pretensioning with a pretensioning-propagation scheme which automatically sets the correct pretension in all stages. A novel cabled differential allows the actuators to be placed closer to the base while maintaining backlash free, efficient, and stiff mechanical-power transmission. Figure 5 illustrates the over-all cable scheme used to drive the arm.

The links themselves are long and slender and are covered with a 3 mm thick dense foam to provide it with reasonable friction and impact

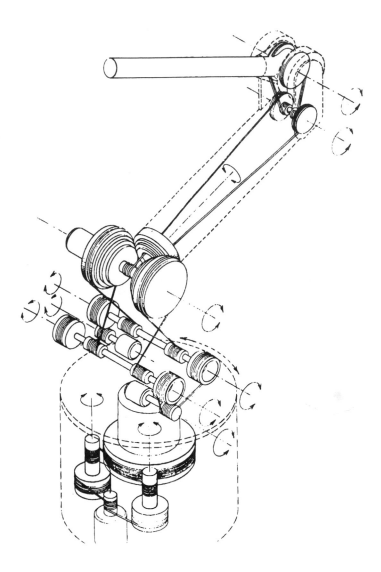

Figure 5. WAM-1 cable details.

characteristics. The inner aluminum link is 76 mm in diameter with a 5 mm wall thickness and is designed to tolerate large local impacts on its surface. The outer carbon-fiber/epoxy link is 50 mm in diameter with a 2 mm wall thickness and is designed for minimum mass while retaining high impact toughness.

Control System

The computational hardware and architecture for the MIT-WAM arm is an extensible and powerful multiprocessing engine. In order to accommodate the demands of the computational task, we have based our system on five 68020 single board computers acting in parallel and on the Condor software development environment developed by the UTAH-MIT hand research group [Narasimhan *et al.* 1988].

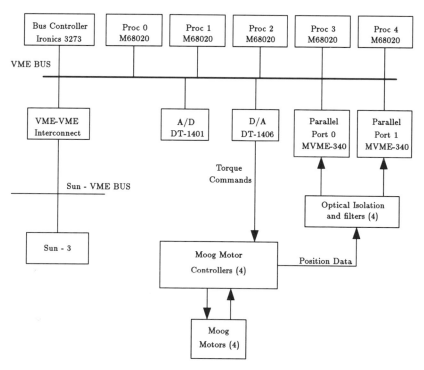

Figure 6. MIT-WAM control hardware block diagram.

Each microprocessor has a separate control function and program. The control program is broken into an input processor, an output processor, a servo controller, a trajectory generator, and a task program/user interface. The first three processors act in concert to perform servo control. The control includes compensation for the torque ripple in the motors, and compensation for the friction and dead zone in the controllers and manipulator. Stiffness control is implemented on the servo processor for both line motion of the last link and for cartesian point motion of the tip.

The two remaining processors are used to generate compliant motions in both line and cartesian space. Motion are created by planning a sequence of joint via points that satisfy a "closeness" constraint by using a recursive bounded deviation algorithm to refine the required path. The trajectory generator then interpolates between the via points using either a cubic or quintic spline interpolation scheme. For compliant and guarded motions, the trajectory processor calculates a contact force metric to determine if the manipulator is in contact with the environment and updates the Jacobian used in the stiffness control algorithm.

Manipulator Performance Tests

Manipulator speed

The theoretical maximum speed for the first three joints is 26 rad/sec, and 39.3 rad/sec for joint 4, neglecting friction and inertial effects. To date, speeds as high as 9, 6, 11.5, and 13 rad/sec have been achieved for joints 1-4 respectively, in a common trajectory. The maximum speed for joint 4 operating alone was observed to be 24 rad/sec. The corresponding joint accelerations were as high as 300 rad/sec^2. Maximum endtip speeds have been estimated to be greater than 10.8 meters/sec, with accelerations of more than 134 meters/sec^2 (13.7 g) [Niemeyer 1989].

Linkage stiffness

To first order, the stiffness of the WAM transmission is inversely proportional to the cable free length. Therefore, the fourth joint should be the most compliant. This stiffness was measured by locking the joint and applying known torques to the motor shaft. The resulting motor rotation was recorded from the resolver. Up to the cable strength limit, a rotational stiffness at the motor shaft of 40.3 in-lb/rad was measured. Seen from the joint with the motor fixed, this corresponds to a rotational stiffness of 16,000 in-lb/rad.

The transmission stiffness is the theoretical upper bound for controllable stiffness using a simple proportional-derivative scheme. We have achieved controlled stiffness values of 1000 in-lb/rad at this joint. Instability at higher gain values is probably due to the phase lag in the servo controller filters and the R/D converter. The base transmission is significantly stiffer than the last joint (due to its shorter free length of cable) and controlled stiffnesses up to 5000 in-lb/rad have been achieved.

Bandwidth

The natural frequencies of the robot are important in determining the controllable bandwidth that can be achieved without detailed dynamic modeling. The natural frequencies are configuration dependent because of the changing inertia of the robot. Bounds on the frequencies can be found by examining the fourth joint, which has the highest frequency, and the first joint, which has the lowest frequency.

The natural frequencies of the fourth joint/transmission/motor system were measured by rigidly constraining all links but the fourth. Square wave drive commands were then applied to the motor at varying frequencies while the velocity of the motor was measured using the R/D converter. Both the input and velocity output were measured with a Hewlett-Packard spectrum analyzer. The resulting bode plot indicated that the transfer function from motor commands to motor velocity had a complex pair of poles at 56 Hz (the natural frequency) and a complex pair of zeros at 32 Hz. This is the frequency of the interaction between the motor and the link mass through the transmission stiffness. The damping ratio on both the poles and zeros is about 0.3.

The natural frequency of the base joint was measured in several configurations. The lowest frequency occurs with the arm horizontal and fully extended. In this configuration, a complex pair of poles was observed at 44 Hz. The damping ratio on the poles is a well-damped 0.6.

The control system should be able to achieve closed-loop bandwidths of 5 Hz without the phase lag from the manipulator dynamics affecting the controller. By measuring the response of the manipulator in the horizontal configuration to a step disturbance in θ_1, we found a closed-loop natural frequency of 2 Hz and a damping ratio of 0.5 for position gains of (4000, 3500, 300, 500) in-lb/rad in each of the joints.

Range and accuracy of open-loop forces

Our approach to force control is to apply forces open-loop at desired locations. The range of forces that the manipulator can apply is direction and configuration dependent. The force accuracy of the manipulator was tested in the fully extended horizontal position. In this configuration, the manipulator can exert a steady-state force of 18 lb in vertical direction at the endtip.

Figures 7 and 8 show the arms ability to exert force in the $^5\hat{x}$ and $^5\hat{y}$ direction at the last link's tip frame of reference, as defined in figure 3. In both directions the measured output force correlates closely with a linear function of the commanded torque. The ratio of the commanded force to actual force in the $^5\hat{x}$ direction, in this configuration, is 1.03 and in the $^5\hat{y}$ direction it is 1.16. The $^5\hat{x}$ graph has a commanded force intercept of 0.25 lb and the $^5\hat{y}$ graph has an intercept of 0.5 lb.

There are a number of possible factors contributing to the deviations from the desired relationship. First, there is some vibration in the robot which causes the force measurement to fluctuate by ±0.5 lb. The torque

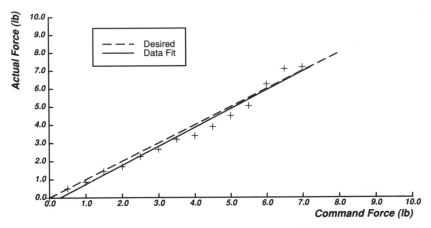

Figure 7. Actual force versus commanded force in the $^5\hat{x}$ direction. Force was applied at the endpoint with joint angles of $(0, -\pi/2, 0, 0)$.

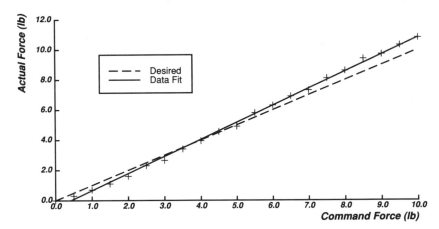

Figure 8. Actual force versus commanded force in the $^5\hat{y}$ direction. Force was applied at the endpoint with joint angles of $(0, -\pi/2, 0, 0)$.

ripple remaining after the application of feedforward compensation can cause variations in the force magnitude of about ±0.2 lb. Lastly, the motor torque-voltage curve could be in error by a few percent from calibration errors or thermal drift.

Repeatability

Manipulator repeatability was measured by determining the maximum deviation that occurred when the endtip was successively commanded to a desired position. For joint angles of (0.0, -1.57, 0.0, 0.0) with active stiffness control, the endpoint deviated by $\pm 1/2$ in. With integral control, the deviation was $\pm 1/32$ in. There was no increase in the error with each successive motion from zero to this position. The repeatability is primarily a function of the joint gains, friction, and dead zone.

Cable fatigue and lifetime

Reliability and maintenance are critical issues for all robotic devices, and the WAM's cable transmission is no exception. Because published analyses [Costello 1978; Costello & Butson 1982] and fatigue life charts [CWRP 1981] only treat the case of cables under static loading, a test fixture was developed to study the factors affecting cable fatigue in a dynamically changing environment. The WAM predecessor, a single link arm with a 2-stage cable reducer, serves as the dynamic load. An analog proportional-derivative control loop ensures that the arm follows a sine input of prescribed frequency and amplitude. Because the arm travels through an identical trajectory on every cycle, stressing the same section of cable, this is a worst-case scenario. The gravity and inertia of the single link arm were representative of the WAM's fourth link supporting a 2 kg mass at its tip.

In all tests, the cables eventually failed at the motor drive pinion, due to its tight bending radius. A series of tests were performed with the only variable being the drive pinion diameter. As the diameters were increased, the cable life went up drastically. An increase of as little as 15% yielded a lifetime improvement of up to 220%. Still larger pinions showed improved results, though not as dramatic.

Another method for reducing cable fatigue is to cut a helical groove in the drive pinion for the cable to lie in. A properly cut groove will support the cable over almost half of its circumference, preventing the cable from flattening out on the shaft and greatly reducing the bending stresses. The helix will also force successive wraps of the cable to be separated, reducing friction and abrasion. In tests pitting a smooth pinion against a grooved one of the same diameter, the pinion with the helix resisted failure approximately 125% longer.

The amount of pretension in the cable has a significant effect on fatigue. In otherwise identical tests, a 25% reduction in pretension yielded a lifetime increase of up to 80%. Unfortunately, due to the nonlinear stiffness characteristics of the cables, a lower pretension will decrease the transmission stiffness, and hence the system bandwidth. The trade-off between performance and reliability should therefore be considered for specific applications.

The actual cable loading is a composite of the various load factors, the most significant of which are pretension, gravity, and inertia terms. One observation worth noting here: A cable undergoing large variations

in loading about a relatively low mean will fatigue more quickly than a
cable with smaller variations about a much higher mean. For example, the
composite loading of one cable ranges from 7 to 23 pounds on every cycle
and fails after 6300 cycles. For another cable the loading varies from 28.9
to 30.5 pounds, yet lasts almost 8000 cycles. The *mean* loading on the
second cable is 30% higher than the *peak* loading of the first, yet lasts 25%
longer.

The next generation drive pinion will most likely have a modestly increased diameter, to 0.7 in. This will lead to a decrease in the transmission
ratio from 30:1 to 26:1 in the first three joints, and from 20:1 to 17:1 in the
last joint. A helical groove will also be cut into the shaft to prevent rub-
bing and provide support over more of the cable's circumference. Although
there will be a decrease in joint torques of about 15%, cable lifetime may
improve by up to 400%.

Actual WAM mean time between failures is impossible to estimate due
to its wide dynamic range and work envelope. Recently the first two cables
to show signs of fatigue were replaced, after approximately 100 hours of
operation. This number is only a guess, and a large percentage of that
time was spent in two or three specific configurations, while the arm was
undergoing performance testing. We expect this lifetime would increase if
the WAM were to operate throughout more of its envelope, stressing the
entire length of the cable more evenly.

Contact Sensing

One mode of sensing which we anticipated for this arm uses joint torque
information to infer contact location and forces. This is an extension to a
previously developed contact resolving force sensor [Salisbury 1984]. That
sensor employs a six-axis force sensing support for a robot fingertip to permit identifying the contact location and force components. Application of
this approach to contact sensing with an articulated arm structure involves
taking measurements of the joint torques and solving for contact locations
and force components that are consistent with the measurements. We assume that the arm's configuration is known from joint angle measurements
taken at the instant of force measurement.

In the case of the four degree-of-freedom WAM-1 arm, we consider single contacts occurring along the last link and, as a simplifying assumption,
treat the last link as a line. If we then assume that the contact transmits
only forces, we seek to solve for five variables—four give the coordinates of
the contact force's line of action and one gives the magnitude of the force
directed along that line. In theory then, we can write five independent
equations in these five unknowns. Four equations define the magnitude of
the torque measured at each joint (corrected for gravity loading) and the

last expresses the constraint that the force line of action must intersect the last link. The assumption that the last link is a line rather than a cylinder will introduce errors to the extent that the contact force's line of action does not pass through the last links central axis. Because the arm can assume a wide variety of configurations, it is possible to find arm postures where the equations are not independent (or at least poorly conditioned) and solving for accurate contact information is impossible.

In our experiments we write the equations in a form that permits us to solve for F, a three-vector of contact force components and L, the scalar distance of the contact from the fourth joint. Thus,

$$\tau = (A + BL)F, \qquad (2)$$

where, A is a 3×3 matrix and B is a 3×1 vector (and $A + BL$ is the Jacobian at the contact point), both dependent upon arm geometry and configuration. In our experiments we have used an iterative Newton-Euler approach to solving equation (2). (See Eberman and Salisbury [1989] for a closed form solution to this problem). For the WAM-1, if the rank of the Jacobian is two, a line of action exists which will cause no net torque on the manipulator. We find two conditions under which this occurs. First, if $\theta_3 = \pm\pi/2$ and $\theta_2 = 0$, a force anywhere along the fourth link whose line of action passes through the origin of the fourth joint will produce no net torque on the manipulator. However, this configuration is outside of the normal working range of the manipulator.

A second condition is found for a single location along the link given by:

$$L = \frac{A_3 A_4 S_4 - A_4 L_3 C_4}{L_3 S_4 + A_3 C_4}, \qquad (3)$$

where L is the location of the contact, A_3 and A_4 are joint offsets, and L_3 is the length of the third link. A force applied at this point along the fourth link, with a line of action which passes through the origins of both axis four and the base will produce no torques about the joints. Both these conditions result in unobservable forces.

If $\theta_2 = 0$, $\theta_3 = 0$, or $\theta_3 = \pi/2$, the ${}^5\hat{x}$ and ${}^5\hat{z}$ forces affect only two torques. For the first two cases, torques are produced about joints 2 and 4, and in the second case torques are produced about joints 1 and 4. If the ${}^5\hat{y}$ force is zero two of the torque measurements will be zero. We can determine from these zero torques that this ${}^5\hat{y}$ force is zero but we cannot infer the contact location. Therefore, the two remaining torque measurements are insufficient to determine the ${}^5\hat{x}$ and ${}^5\hat{z}$ forces and the contact location in this configuration.

With this procedure, we can use the manipulator as a sensor and can apply it to sensing collisions during a search. The algorithm can detect contact with an object and detect the motion of the contact along the link as the search proceeds. However, the procedure will not be able to resolve contacts at more than one location or contacts along the inner link. Both of these types of contacts will be incorrectly resolved by the algorithm as contacts along the last link. More sophisticated exploratory techniques and/or sensors would be required in this case.

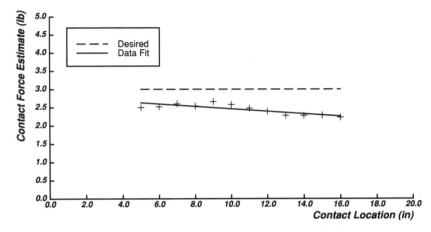

Figure 9. Contact force estimate versus contact location—Y force.

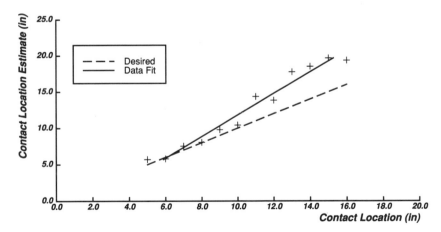

Figure 10. Contact position estimate versus contact location—Y force.

Figures 9 and 10 illustrate the results of a set of contact resolving experiments. In both cases the arm's joints were located at $(0, -\pi/2, 0, -1)$ radians and external forces were applied to the last link in the $^5\hat{y}$ direction. Figure 9 illustrates the method's estimate of the magnitude of a 3 lb force applied at various locations along the link. Figure 10 illustrates the method's perception of the location of the point where the 3 lb force is applied. Further examples may be found in Eberman [1989].

The method is able to determine contact forces and locations with accuracy of approximately 30%. Some error may be due to the accuracy of the forward problem of force exertion described in the previous section. Additional error could be caused by the remaining torque ripple, friction in the system and gravity bias forces. In either direction, the contact estimate is configuration and gain dependent, and is sensitive to errors in calibration and nonlinearities in the system. Nonetheless, without additional hardware investment, it is clear that it is possible to make reasonable contact information estimates from joint torque and position information alone, in some cases.

Conclusions

This work has been focused on a number of developments required to expand the application of robots into the whole-arm domain of tasks. Conceptually we have begun to develop a framework for describing these tasks and a line-based approach to manipulator control for executing some of the tasks. Our investigation of the arm mechanism requirements for such tasks has lead to the development of a very high performance, intrinsically force controllable manipulator. The arm employs a geometry that is well-suited for interacting with the environment in a rich variety of ways. A novel technique for sensing contacts with the last link has been demonstrated.

Future developments will focus in a number of areas. The utility of line-based manipulation needs to be clarified and quantified; both to aid in the kinematic design of whole arm manipulators and to articulate the elements of this style of manipulation for use by planning systems. We feel that the quality of mechanical transmission that we have achieved is sufficient that we now must re-focus on actuator performance in order to improve our arm's intrinsic force controllability. While acceptable contact sensing has been demonstrated, its configuration dependent accuracy suggests that we introduce additional force sensing elements to provide well conditioned solutions throughout the workspace.

References

Armstrong, Brian [1988], "Dynamics for Robot Control: Friction Modeling and Ensuring Excitation During Parameter Identification," Ph.D. Thesis, Department of Electrical Engineering, Stanford University, Stanford, CA.

The authors would like to gratefully acknowledge the financial assistance of the Office of Naval Research for support in this research under ONR contracts N00014-86-K-0685 and N00015-85-K-0124.

Costello, G. A. [1978], "Analytical Investigation of Wire Rope," Applied Mechanics Reviews, vol. 31, no. 7.

Costello, G. A., and G. J. Butson [1982], "Simplified Bending Theory for Wire Rope," Proceedings of the American Society of Civil Engineers, vol. 108, no. EM2.

CWRP [1981], Committee of Wire Rope Producers, Wire Rope Users Manual, American Iron and Steel Institute, Washington, DC.

DiPietro, D. M. [1988]," Development of an Actively Compliant Underwater Manipulator," M.S. Thesis, Woods Hole Oceanographic Institution Joint Program in Oceanography and Oceanographic Engineering.

Eberman, B. S. [1989], "Whole Arm Manipulation: Kinematics and Control," Master's Thesis, Department of Mechanical Engineering, Massachusetts Institute of Technology, Cambridge, MA.

Eberman, B. S., and J. K. Salisbury [1989], "Determination of Manipulator Contact Information from Joint Torque Measurements", Proceedings of the First International Symposium on Experimental Robotics, Montréal, Canada.

Mason, M. T. [1981], "Compliance and Force Control of Computer Controlled Manipulators," IEEE Trans. on Systems, Man, and Cybernetics, vol. SMC-11, no. 6.

Mason, M. T., and J. K. Salisbury [1985], Robot hands and the Mechanics of Manipulation, MIT Press, Cambridge, MA.

Narasimhan, S., D. M. Siegel, and J. M. Hollerbach [1988], "Condor: A Revised Architecture for Controlling the UTAH-MIT hand," Proceedings of the 1988 IEEE International Conference on Robotics and Automation, Philadelphia, PA.

Niemeyer, G., and J. J. Slotine [1989], "Performance in Adaptive Manipulator Control," Submitted to 1989 IEEE International Conf. on Robotics and Automation, Scottsdale, AZ.

Paul, B. J. [1987], "A Systems Approach to the Torque Control of a Permanent Magnet Brushless Motor," M.S. Thesis, Department of Mechanical Engineering, Massachusetts Institute of Technology, Cambridge MA.

Salisbury, J. K. [1984], "Interpretation of Contact Geometries from Force Measurements," Proceedings of the 1st International Symposium on Robotics Research, Bretton Woods, NH, MIT Press, Cambridge, MA.

Salisbury, J. K. [1987], "Whole-Arm Manipulation," Proceedings of the 4th International Symposium on Robotics Research, Santa Cruz, CA, MIT Press, Cambridge MA.

Salisbury, J. K., W. T. Townsend, B. S. Eberman, and D. M. DiPietro [1988], "Preliminary Design of a Whole-Arm Manipulation System (WAMS)," Proceedings of the 1988 IEEE International Conf. on Robotics and Automation, Philadelphia, PA.

Townsend, W. T. [1988], "The Effect of Transmission Design on Force-Controlled Manipulator Performance," Ph.D. Thesis, Department of Mechanical Engineering, Massachusetts Institute of Technology, Cambridge MA, also Report AI-TR-1054, Artificial Intelligence Laboratory, MIT.

Townsend, W. T., and J. K. Salisbury [1988], "The Efficiency Limit of Belt and Cable Drives," *ASME Journal of Mechanisms, Transmissions, and Automation in Design*, vol. 110, no. 3.

34

The position of the end of your arm, relative to you, is determined by joint angles and by a large number of limb-length
and angle-offset parameters. If you know where you want
your arm to be, you have to decide what joint angles get it
there and you have to know the values of the limb and angle
parameters.

Of course, calibrating the parameter values for a robot
arm by direct measurement, using the equivalent of measuring tapes and protractors, is tedious beyond description. If
there are more than six joints, however, no measurements
have to be made. Astonishingly, Bennett and Hollerbach
show that such a robot arm can be calibrated by moving it
to various configurations while keeping its end firmly fixed to
an object at a known location. Each configuration provides
an equation that relates the known end point to the known
joint angles and the unknown parameters. With enough
configurations, hence enough equations, the equations can
be solved by iterative methods.

Curiously, two arms can be calibrated together by having them hold hands while they move about. With this
arrangement, the two manipulators are viewed as one manipulator and the base of one of the two manipulators is
viewed as the object at a known location.

Calibrating Closed Kinematic Chains

David J. Bennett
John M. Hollerbach

Redundant manipulators have become of increasing interest because of the various advantages that they offer over standard six-degree-of-freedom (6-DOF) manipulators. Advantages studied in the past have included singularity avoidance [Hollerbach 1985], workspace enlargement [Burdick 1988], torque optimization [Hollerbach & Suh 1985], and secondary task performance [Nakamura & Hanafasu 1985]. It is the intent of this chapter to investigate a further advantage: namely, the potential for redundant manipulators to self-calibrate their kinematic models.

Automatically determining kinematic models is an important aspect of any model based robot control scheme [An, Atkeson & Hollerbach 1988]. To this end we [Hollerbach & Bennett 1988] and many other authors (see review paper Hollerbach [1988]) have developed techniques for automatically calibrating the kinematics of open chain manipulators (that is, determining the geometric and static non-geometric model parameters). These 'open-loop' kinematic calibration methods rely on special purpose pre-calibrated endpoint sensing systems. It is the goal of this chapter to investigate an alternative approach which eliminates the need for endpoint tracking devices. Specifically, it will be demonstrated that if a manipulator(s) is formed into a mobile closed kinematic chain then its joint angle readings alone are enough to identify the kinematic parameters. We shall refer to this method as 'closed-loop' kinematic calibration.

Actually, there is a precedent for identifying closed linkages in the classical mechanism synthesis literature [Hartenberg & Denavit 1964]. In fact, it will be found that, because serial manipulators typically have joint angle sensors on all degrees of freedom, the problem posed here is considerably easier than mechanism synthesis.

The critical ingredient for such a closed-loop calibration method to work is that the manipulator must be able to form a mobile closed-loop kinematic chain. This is where redundant manipulators are involved: if a manipulator is redundant with respect to the task that it is performing then it forms a mobile closed loop kinematic chain. For the purposes of this chapter we will only consider the 6-DOF task of positioning and orienting the end effector at a single location (that is, fixing the end effector to the ground) while executing internal joint movements. Thus, we will study manipulators with seven or more degrees of freedom. Such manipulators are said to be redundant with respect to the 6-DOF positioning task.

Although the discussion will be confined to redundant manipulators with their end effectors rigidly attached to the ground (a 6-DOF positioning task), the development is equally applicable to identifying two manipulators (with a combined total of seven or more degrees of freedom) attached together at their endpoints. These two situations are equivalent as the last link of the second manipulator may be defined as the base, and the entire closed kinematic chain viewed as a single equivalent manipulator.

The reader may wish to refer to Appendix A for a simplified planar version of the identification problem discussed. This example is meant to motivate the more general treatment, but is not necessary for continuity. Finally, note that portions of this work have been previously reported in Bennett and Hollerbach [1988].

The Kinematic Model

Manipulator kinematics

◇ Geometric parameters

Consider a redundant manipulator with n_f degrees of freedom. Let the 4×4 homogeneous transformation $\mathbf{A}_j$ from link j to link $(j-1)$ be defined by the Denavit-Hartenberg (D-H) convention [Denavit & Hartenberg 1955] given in figure 2 and symbolically as

$$\mathbf{A}_j = \mathbf{Rot}(z, \theta'_j)\mathbf{Trans}(z, s_j)\mathbf{Trans}(x, a_j)\mathbf{Rot}(x, \alpha_j), \qquad (1)$$

where the notation $\mathbf{Rot}(x, \phi)$ indicates a rotation about an axis x by ϕ and $\mathbf{Trans}(x, a)$ indicates a translation along an axis x by a. The position of the last link is computed by a sequence of D-H transformations defining the kinematic model

$$\mathbf{T}_c = \mathbf{A}_1\mathbf{A}_2...\mathbf{A}_{n_f}. \qquad (2)$$

The goal of kinematic calibration is to identify the geometric parameters s_j, α_j, and a_j, and also any non-geometric parameters that may be included in the kinematic model.

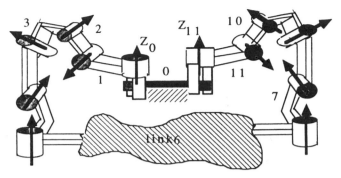

Figure 1. A single loop kinematic chain formed by a redundant manipulator or by dual manipulators.

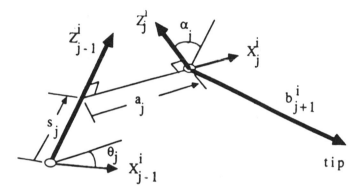

Figure 2. Denavit-Hartenberg coordinates and tip vector $\mathbf{b}_j^i$.

◇ Non-geometric parameters

The non-geometric effects on the kinematic model include backlash, gear eccentricity, joint compliance, and joint angle sensor error. While parametric models of each of these processes may be included in the foregoing scheme, we choose to only model joint angle sensor error. In particular, the D-H joint angle is presumed to be related to the sensor reading as

$$\theta_j' = \theta_j + \theta_j^{off} . \tag{3}$$

Thus, we also wish to identify the constant joint angle offset θ_j^{off}.

Finally, all of the unknown kinematic parameters are placed into a single vector

$$\varphi = (\theta_{off}^T, \mathbf{s}^T, \mathbf{a}^T, \alpha^T)^T , \tag{4}$$

where $\mathbf{s} = (s_1, s_2, ...)^T$ etc.

Base coordinate assignment and endpoint location

Because the endpoint is fixed to a single location on the ground it may be considered to have zero orientation and position. This may be made precise as follows: define the base coordinates so that the actual location of the last D-H coordinate frame (referred to as the endpoint) coincides with the base coordinates. The combined manipulator tool and ground may be viewed as a single effective link that connects the last joint of the manipulator to the first joint of the manipulator.

It should be emphasized that the location at which the endpoint grasps the environment is unknown and may be chosen arbitrarily. In addition to the robot kinematic parameters, we will also identify the D-H parameters of the effective link that closes the loop and defines where the endpoint is relative to the manipulator's first joint axis.

Endpoint location error calculation

Although the endpoint position and orientation error may be calculated directly we observe that in many cases the endpoint location computed by the model, $\mathbf{T}_c$, may be assumed to differ from the base coordinates (the 'actual' location) by only a small amount. The computations can therefore be simplified as follows. Let the computed position be $(dx_c, dy_c, dz_c)^T$. This is simply the fourth column of $\mathbf{T}_c$. Similarly, let the calculated orientation $\mathbf{R}_c$ (that is, the upper left 3×3 matrix of $\mathbf{T}_c$) be represented by infinitesimal xyz-Euler rotations

$$\mathbf{R}_x(\partial x_c)\mathbf{R}_y(\partial y_c)\mathbf{R}_z(\partial z_c) \approx \begin{bmatrix} 1 & -\partial z_c & \partial y_c \\ \partial z_c & 1 & -\partial x_c \\ -\partial y_c & \partial x_c & 1 \end{bmatrix}, \quad (5)$$

where the right hand side of (5) is computed by directly expanding the left hand side and ignoring second order differential terms. Thus, the modeled endpoint location, evaluated at the ith joint configuration θ^i, may be represented as a six vector

$$\mathbf{x}_c^i = \mathbf{x}_c^i(\theta^i, \varphi) = (dx_c, dy_c, dz_c, \partial x_c, \partial y_c, \partial z_c)^T \quad (6)$$

directly computed from $\mathbf{T}_c$. As stated in the previous section, the actual position and orientation of the endpoint are taken to be zero

$$\mathbf{x}_a^i = (0, 0, 0, 0, 0, 0)^T. \quad (7)$$

Thus, the endpoint error is

$$\Delta \mathbf{x}^i = \mathbf{x}_a^i - \mathbf{x}_c^i = -\mathbf{x}_c^i. \quad (8)$$

The loop closure equations

The six kinematic loop closure equations are therefore given by

$$0 = \mathbf{x}_c^i(\theta^i, \varphi) + \mathbf{n}^i. \quad (9)$$

The error term $\mathbf{n}^i$ has been added to indicate that there is modeling and measurement noise.

Iterative Identification

In order to solve for the kinematic parameters equation (9) is linearized and iteratively identified.

Differential kinematics and Jacobian calculation

At the *ith* joint configuration θ^i the first differential of (9) is

$$\Delta\mathbf{x}^i = \frac{\partial\mathbf{x}_c^i}{\partial\theta}\Delta\theta + \frac{\partial\mathbf{x}_c^i}{\partial\mathbf{s}}\Delta\mathbf{s} + \frac{\partial\mathbf{x}_c^i}{\partial\mathbf{a}}\Delta\mathbf{a} + \frac{\partial\mathbf{x}_c^i}{\partial\alpha}\Delta\alpha + \mathbf{n}'^i, \qquad (10)$$

where again $\Delta\mathbf{x}^i = 0 - \mathbf{x}_c^i$ and $\Delta\mathbf{s} = \mathbf{s} - \mathbf{s}^0$ etc. By denoting the combined Jacobian

$$\mathbf{C}^i = \frac{\partial\mathbf{x}_c^i}{\partial\varphi} = \left[\frac{\partial\mathbf{x}_c^i}{\partial\theta} \ \frac{\partial\mathbf{x}_c^i}{\partial\mathbf{s}} \ \frac{\partial\mathbf{x}_c^i}{\partial\mathbf{a}} \ \frac{\partial\mathbf{x}_c^i}{\partial\alpha}\right], \qquad (11)$$

equation (10) may be expressed more concisely as

$$\Delta\mathbf{x}^i = \mathbf{C}^i\Delta\varphi + \mathbf{n}'^i. \qquad (12)$$

Each of the matrices in (10) are Jacobians with respect to the particular parameters. For example, $\partial\mathbf{x}_c^i/\partial\theta$ is the familiar Jacobian which relates infinitesimal joint movements to end effector movements. Although the derivation of the Jacobians may be performed in a variety of ways, the following procedure [Whitney 1972; Sugimoto 1985] reveals that the columns of the Jacobian may be interpreted as *screw coordinates*.

Imagine the end effector variation $\Delta\mathbf{x}^i$ to be an instantaneous screw displacement composed of linear and angular velocity components. The combined variation in all the parameters is presumed to cause this end point variation. Specifically, a variation of the D-H parameter s_j along the local link z axis, $\mathbf{z}_{j-1}^i$, causes a contribution to the end effector linear velocity of $\Delta s_j\mathbf{z}_{j-1}^i$. The parameter variation $\Delta\alpha_j$ about the local link x axis, $\mathbf{x}_j^i$, causes a contribution to the endpoint's angular velocity of $(\Delta\alpha_j)\mathbf{x}_j^i = \mathbf{w}_{\alpha_j}$, and a linear velocity contribution of $\mathbf{w}_{\alpha_j} \times \mathbf{b}_{j+1}^i$, where $\mathbf{b}_{j+1}^i$ is a vector from the *jth* coordinate system to the endpoint (see figure 2). The θ_j and a_j parameters are treated analogously. In total, the endpoint translation due to all of the parameter variations is given by

$$\sum_{j=1}^{n}\mathbf{z}_{j-1}^i \times \mathbf{b}_j^i\Delta\theta_j + \mathbf{z}_{j-1}^i\Delta s_j + \mathbf{x}_j^i \times \mathbf{b}_{j+1}^i\Delta\alpha_j + \mathbf{x}_j^i\Delta a_j, \qquad (13)$$

and angular variation given by

$$\sum_{j=1}^{n}\mathbf{z}_{j-1}^i\Delta\theta_j + \mathbf{x}_j^i\Delta\alpha_j. \qquad (14)$$

Comparing these to (10) it is seen that the columns of each of the four Jacobians are

$$\text{col}_j \frac{\partial \mathbf{x}_c^i}{\partial \mathbf{a}} = \begin{bmatrix} \mathbf{x}_j^i \\ \mathbf{0} \end{bmatrix}, \quad \text{col}_j \frac{\partial \mathbf{x}_c^i}{\partial \mathbf{s}} = \begin{bmatrix} \mathbf{z}_{j-1}^i \\ \mathbf{0} \end{bmatrix}, \tag{15}$$

and

$$\text{col}_j \frac{\partial \mathbf{x}_c^i}{\partial \theta} = \begin{bmatrix} \mathbf{z}_{j-1}^i \times \mathbf{b}_j^i \\ \mathbf{z}_{j-1}^i \end{bmatrix}, \quad \text{col}_j \frac{\partial \mathbf{x}_c^i}{\partial \alpha} = \begin{bmatrix} \mathbf{x}_j^i \times \mathbf{b}_{j+1}^i \\ \mathbf{x}_j^i \end{bmatrix}. \tag{16}$$

Data collection and parameter estimation

A series of n configurations of the actual mechanism provides n sets of joint angle measurements θ^i, and n equations of the form (12). Compactly, the equations may be written

$$\Delta \mathbf{X} = \mathbf{C} \Delta \varphi + \mathbf{n}', \tag{17}$$

where

$$\mathbf{C} = \begin{bmatrix} \mathbf{C}^1 \\ \cdot \\ \mathbf{C}^n \end{bmatrix}, \quad \Delta \mathbf{X} = \begin{bmatrix} \Delta \mathbf{x}^1 \\ \cdot \\ \Delta \mathbf{x}^n \end{bmatrix}. \tag{18}$$

An estimate of the parameter errors is provided by minimizing

$$LS = (\Delta \mathbf{X} - \mathbf{C}\varphi)^T (\Delta \mathbf{X} - \mathbf{C}\varphi), \tag{19}$$

which yields

$$\Delta \varphi = (\mathbf{C}^T \mathbf{C})^{-1} \mathbf{C}^T \Delta \mathbf{X}. \tag{20}$$

Finally, the guess at the parameters is updated as

$$\varphi = \varphi_0 + \Delta \varphi, \tag{21}$$

and the iteration continues until $\Delta \mathbf{X} \to 0$.

Identifiability

The goal of kinematic calibration is to determine the φ that satisfies the loop closure equation (9) for all configurations. These equations may be combined into one vector equation

$$\mathbf{X} = \mathbf{f}(\varphi). \tag{22}$$

It is desirable to answer the question of whether or not there is a unique solution to (22), and if not how many solutions there are. For the purposes of this chapter we will not answer this global question, but restrict our attention to determining the local uniqueness of an obtained solution φ'. We draw on some results from differential topology [Guilleman & Pollack 1974; Spivak 1965].

First a definition is needed: a smooth[1] function $\mathbf{f}(\varphi')$ is defined to be (locally) *identifiable* at φ' if:

---

[1]A smooth function has continuous partial derivatives of all orders.

1   The solution φ' given by $\mathbf{f}^{-1}(\mathbf{X})$ is unique within a small neighborhood of φ' (locally unique), and

2   There exists a *smooth* identification function $\mathbf{f}^{-1}$ which maps the image of $\mathbf{f}$ back onto the parameter space (that is, the space of $\varphi's$).

The motivation for the first part of the definition is clear. The second part, is included to ensure that any identification algorithm used to find the parameters φ is numerically well behaved.

Though not relevant to the flow of the argument, it is noted that if we are to collect just enough equations to equal the number of unknown parameters then the above condition of identifiability is equivalent to requiring that $\mathbf{f}$ is a *local diffeomorphism* [Guilleman & Pollack 1974]. It is established in Guilleman and Pollack [1974] that the square Jacobian matrix $\mathbf{C}$ of $\mathbf{f}$ being non-singular is a necessary and sufficient condition for a local diffeomorphism. This motivates the following results for when $\mathbf{C}$ is not necessarily a square matrix.

Claim: If the columns of the Jacobian $\mathbf{C}$ are linearly independent (that is, it does not have a non-zero nullspace) then the kinematics $\mathbf{f}$ are identifiable. This claim may be proven by expanding the kinematics with a Taylor series expansion. In a sufficiently small neighborhood of φ' the higher order terms may be neglected with respect to the first differential term (which is non-zero by hypothesis). Thus, in this neighborhood the solution φ' to the truncated expansion $\mathbf{f}(\varphi) = \mathbf{f}(\varphi') + \mathbf{C}(\varphi - \varphi')$ is unique, because $\mathbf{C}$ does not have a nullspace. Furthermore, there exists a smooth inverse function $\mathbf{f}^{-1}$, for example, equation (20) suffices.

The converse is also true: If the Jacobian $\mathbf{C}$ has dependent columns (that is, it has a non-zero nullspace) then the kinematics are unidentifiable. This is true because if $\mathbf{C}$ has a non-zero nullspace then part two of the identifiability definition is violated. Namely, any inverse function $\mathbf{f}^{-1}$ does not have a continuous first derivative. This may be seen by a modification of a result in Spivak [1965, p. 39]. *Assume* that $\mathbf{f}^{-1}$ is differentiable. Now, note that by definition $\mathbf{f}^{-1}(\mathbf{f}(\varphi)) = \varphi$. Differentiating with the chain rule gives the following matrix product, $[\partial \mathbf{f}^{-1}/\partial \mathbf{X}][\partial \mathbf{f}/\partial \varphi] = I$. But post multiplying both sides of the previous equation by any non-zero element of the nullspace of $\mathbf{C} = [\partial \mathbf{f}/\partial \varphi]$, say $\mathbf{n}$, gives a contradiction, $0 = \mathbf{n}$. Thus, $\mathbf{f}^{-1}$ is not differentiable.

Finally, note that if Jacobian $\mathbf{C}$ has dependent columns then we may *not* necessarily conclude that the solution to (22) is not locally unique (that is, part one of the identifiability definition) because higher order terms of the Taylor series expansion of $\mathbf{f}$ may be non-zero. Part two of the identifiability condition is needed.

In summary, we have shown that the linear independence of the columns of $\mathbf{C}$ provides a necessary and sufficient condition for identifiability. Physically, if the columns of $\mathbf{C}$ are linearly dependent (unidentifiable) then the corresponding kinematic parameters may vary arbitrarily (these variations only satisfying the linear dependence). Also, a dependence of the columns of the matrix $\mathbf{C}$ causes $\mathbf{C}^T\mathbf{C}$ to become singular and the algorithm fails. We now attempt to derive a simple test for identifiability.

An identifiability test

According to definition (18) the columns of $\mathbf{C}$ are a concatenation of the screw coordinates (15) and (16) for all configurations of the mechanism. Therefore, the columns of $\mathbf{C}$ will be linearly dependent and thus *the mechanism unidentifiable if and only if there is a constant linear relation among the screw coordinates for all configurations of the mechanism.* This condition can be made more useful by inspecting the form of the D-H screw coordinates; specifically, *the necessary and sufficient condition for identification is that there exist no constant linear relation among the local link x and z axes; that is,*

$$\sum_{j=1}^{n_f} k_j \mathbf{x}_j^i + c_j \mathbf{z}_j^i = 0 \ \ \forall_{i \in [1..n]} \Rightarrow k_j = c_j = 0. \tag{23}$$

This is proven simply as follows: A violation of (23) implies that *at least* the screw coordinates of the form (15) have a constant linear dependence. Conversely, a constant linear dependence of any of the screw coordinates, (equations (15) and (16)) implies that (23) is violated.

The sources of singularities (violations of (23)) will now be enumerated. The first three sources of singularities are particular to closed mechanisms, while the remainder are singularities that also arise in open-loop kinematic calibration. Bear in mind that although not expressly discussed in each category the real problem is associated with near singular situations. These situations cause intractable numerical sensitivity problems while solving for the parameters.

1 Parameters that enter linearly: A first source of parameter ambiguity becomes apparent by writing out the kinematic closure equation (9) (for revolute manipulators) to explicitly show the linear dependence of the length parameters [Mooring & Tang 1984].

$$\sum_{j=1}^{n_f} s_j \mathbf{z}_{j-1}^i + a_j \mathbf{x}_j^i = \mathbf{0}. \tag{24}$$

Clearly, equation (24) violates condition (23). The natural solution to this problem is to define one non-zero link length as unity; this particular parameter determines the units of length.

2 Inherent singularities in the mechanism: Certain mechanisms have particular symmetries which allow the kinematics to be described in less than four parameters per joint. It is difficult to provide a general rule for when this will happen, but it is usually restricted to mechanisms of mobility one. As a very simple example consider trying to calibrate the 3-DOF planar manipulator discussed in Appendix A. If the closed loop four-bar linkage happens to be a parallelogram then the opposite x axes are always parallel

$$\mathbf{x}_1 + \mathbf{x}_3 = 0. \tag{25}$$

This contradicts condition (23), and thus the lengths of the opposite sides, a_1, and a_3, are not identifiable (except as a sum). Clearly, this problem may be eliminated by having the manipulator change its endpoint location so that a parallelogram is no longer formed.

3   Structural immobility: If a particular joint i is immobile then two consecutive joint coordinates are fixed relative to one another. This implies that $\mathbf{x}_i, \mathbf{z}_i, \mathbf{x}_{i+1}$, and $\mathbf{z}_{i+1}$ have a constant linear relation (violating equation (23) because these four vectors span a three dimensional space). Of course, it is not surprising that the parameters of the links connected by the immobile joint are unidentifiable. Conceivably a fictitious link which combined the two links could be defined and the rest of the mechanism identified.

In order to properly deal with the problem of immobile joints it is necessary to predict the immobility by condition (35) in Appendix B, and perhaps re-design the constraint imposed at the endpoint in order to make the joint mobile.

As an example consider the mechanism formed by rigidly fixing the hand of an anthropomorphic arm [Hollerbach 1985] relative to its shoulder (that is, imagine holding onto the desk in front of you). Nominally, this mechanism has a classical mobility [Hartenberg & Denavit 1964] of 1 (7–6), but we observe that the elbow joint is immobile. To see that this is indeed the case consider the upper arm to be the base link and form the screw coordinates for the mechanism, $\$_0$ .. $\$_6$ (see figure 3).

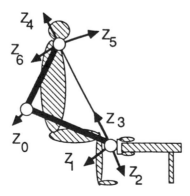

Figure 3. Anthropomorphic arm screw coordinate assignment.

Without loss of generality one of the three wrist joint axes may be defined to intersect the shoulder joint. It is then found that because the three shoulder joints and the one wrist joint intersect their four respective joint screws are linearly dependent. Thus, the joint screws numbered 1 to 6 only span a space of dimension five $(K(span\,[\$_6...\$_1]) = 5)$, whereas all seven screws span the full six dimensional space $(K(span\,[\$_6...\$_0]) = 6)$. Therefore, (35) implies that the elbow joint is immobile. The solution to this problem is to relax the end point constraint so that the elbow is mobile (for example, only maintain a point contact with the ground, allowing arbitrary orientation of the hand). This solution requires a reformulation of the identification equations.

4   Singularities related to the coordinate description: In other instances mechanisms have arbitrary parameters as a result of a poor choice of coordinate description. For example, if there are two consecutive parallel joint axes when using the D-H convention then there is not a unique common normal in figure 2. Parallel axes imply

$$\mathbf{z}_i - \mathbf{z}_{i-1} = 0\,. \tag{26}$$

Thus, (23) is violated and the corresponding s_i and s_{i+1} may not be identified alone. Note that the difference $s_i - s_{i+1}$ *can* be identified. The real solution to this problem, though, is to change the coordinate description of the parallel axes to a convention such as Hayati's [1983]. This alternate convention may not be used exclusively because it too suffers from a parameter ambiguity, in this case occurring when two consecutive joint axes are perpendicular.

Any coordinate description of a revolute mechanism with greater than four parameters per link is *always* singular (unless extra constraints are imposed). This can be seen by forming the screw coordinates for any five (or greater) parameter system. The five screws for a given joint must belong to a vector space of dimension four or less, because they locate the *line vector* of the next coordinate axis. Thus, these five screws are linearly dependent and only four of the associated parameters are identifiable.

Similarly, a prismatic (linear) joint axis is a *free vector* defined by only two orientation parameters. Thus, coordinate descriptions with any more than two parameters are singular.

5   Not sufficient excitation: Another source of singularity arises from not moving the mechanism into a sufficient number of configurations. Otherwise stated, the data is not *sufficiently exciting* [Armstrong 1987]. A good way of understanding this problem is to consider all of the unknown geometric parameters, φ, as variables; then ask the question: What displacements of the end effector would be caused by small variations in these parameters? The optimal data set would maximize the model error over variations in all of the parameters [Sinha & Kuszta 1983]. An impoverished data set would not be able to distinguish changes in particular parameters, thereby allowing those parameters to change arbitrarily. A trivial example would be to not move a particular joint (say joint i) at all. In this case the axes $\mathbf{x}_i, \mathbf{z}_i, \mathbf{x}_{i-1}, \mathbf{z}_{i-1}$ would always be linearly dependent.

6   Transient singularities: In general, the real mechanism may not have singularities (such as consecutive parallel joint axes), but during the course of the iterative search for its parameter set an *intermediate* parameter set may be found which is singular (or near singular). Simulations show that this situation is surprisingly common when the initial guess at the parameters, φ^0, is not close to the true solution. Because this singularity is associated with the algorithm it may be avoided by modifying the minimization criteria LS as follows

$$LS' = LS + \lambda \Delta \varphi^T \Delta \varphi. \tag{27}$$

Thus, in addition to minimizing the end effector tracking error, LS' minimizes the variation in parameters, such that at a potential singularity the arbitrary parameters tend to remain fixed. Minimizing LS' now yields

$$\Delta \varphi = (\mathbf{C}^T \mathbf{C} + \lambda I)^{-1} \mathbf{C}^T \Delta \mathbf{X}. \tag{28}$$

Iteratively applying equation (28) results in the Levenberg-Marquardt algorithm [Norton 1986]. The free parameter λ determines the trade-off between a straight Newton iteration and a much slower gradient descent.

Simulations

A 7-DOF manipulator self-calibrating

Joint	s (m)	a (m)	α (rad)	θ_{off} (rad)
1	1.694	0.837	3.774	1.100
2	1.622	-0.627	-0.553	0.080
3	1.000	-0.100	0.930	0.090
4	-0.430	-0.430	2.040	0.900
5	0.540	-0.600	-0.150	0.050
6	-0.560	-0.550	1.350	0.040
7	-1.693	0.711	-1.859	0.000

Table 1. 7 DOF mechanism. Initial parameters.

A 7-DOF manipulator formed into a closed 7-DOF mechanism (by having the end effector grasp the ground at a fixed arbitrary position) is given by the parameters in table 2. This mechanism was simulated in 40 distinct configurations. Starting with the initial guesses in table 1 and with

Joint	s (m)	a (m)	α (rad)	θ_{off} (rad)
1	1.594	0.737	3.604	0.000
2	1.722	-0.527	-0.503	0.000
3	1.000	0.000	0.530	0.000
4	-0.330	-0.330	2.300	0.000
5	0.440	-0.440	-0.900	0.000
6	-0.660	-0.550	1.200	0.000
7	-1.793	0.911	-1.459	1.825

Table 2. 7 DOF mechanism. Calibrated parameters.

the definition $s_3 = 1$, the simulated joint angles were fed into the iterative Levenberg-Marquardt algorithm, and the parameters in table 2 were recovered to within four decimal places.

Two 6-DOF manipulators self-calibrating

Consider two arbitrary 6-DOF manipulators. When their end effectors are rigidly grasping together the 12-DOF closed mechanism formed is given in table 4. These parameters were used to simulate the movements of this mechanism into 40 different configurations. With the initial parameters given in table 3 and the simulated joint angles the calibration was performed (also $s_3 = 1$ fixed). The parameters in table 4 were recovered to within four decimal places.

Summary

A novel approach to identifying the kinematic models of redundant or dual manipulators without endpoint sensing has been presented. Starting from the observation that such manipulators may be made to form mobile closed kinematic chains, it was shown that these closed loops can be identified by an iterative least squares algorithm similar to that used in calibrating open chain manipulators. Simulations demonstrated that this technique is indeed viable.

The issue of identifiability of the kinematic parameters of the closed loop was reduced to inspecting the rank of the matrix $\mathbf{C}$. Rank degeneracies were in turn studied with the screw coordinate interpretation of the columns of the Jacobians $\mathbf{C}^i$. Specifically, a requirement that there be no constant linear relation among the local link x and z axes accounts for all

Joint	s (m)	a (m)	α (rad)	$\Delta\theta$ (rad)
1	-1.694	-0.837	3.504	0.100
2	-1.822	0.627	-0.553	0.050
3	1.000	0.100	0.580	0.070
4	0.430	0.430	2.380	1.070
5	-0.540	0.540	-0.980	0.080
6	0.760	0.650	1.280	0.050
7	1.200	0.760	-1.390	0.100
8	1.200	1.500	3.800	0.100
9	0.600	-1.400	1.5500	0.200
10	0.300	1.100	-1.380	0.300
11	1.300	0.600	0.880	0.900
12	-1.982	-1.839	1.772	0.400

Table 3. 12 DOF mechanism. Initial parameters.

Joint	s (m)	a (m)	α (rad)	$\Delta\theta$ (rad)
1	-1.594	-0.737	3.604	0.000
2	-1.722	0.527	-0.503	0.000
3	1.000	0.000	0.530	0.000
4	0.330	0.330	2.300	0.000
5	-0.440	0.440	-0.900	0.000
6	0.660	0.550	1.200	0.000
7	1.100	0.660	-1.300	0.000
8	1.100	1.400	3.900	0.000
9	0.500	-1.300	1.400	0.000
10	0.200	1.000	-1.300	0.000
11	1.200	0.500	0.800	0.000
12	-1.882	-1.939	1.722	0.000

Table 4. 12 DOF mechanism. Calibrated parameters.

singularities. These singularities were classified into six categories relating to:

1   The linear occurrence of the length parameters.
2   The mechanism's special geometries.
3   Mobility.
4   The coordinate description.
5   The set of configurations used to provide the joint angle data input
6   The iterative search algorithm employed.

References

Hollerbach, J. M. [1985], "Optimum kinematic design for a seven degree of free-dom manipulator," *Robotics Research: The Second International Symposium*, edited by H. Hanafusa and H. Inoue, MIT Press, Cambridge, MA, pp. 349-356.

Burdick, J. W. [1988], *Kinematic analysis and design of redundant manipulators*, Ph.D. Thesis, Stanford University.

Hollerbach, J. M., and K. C. Suh [1985], "Redundancy resolution of manipulators through torque optimization," *IEEE Int. Conf. Robotics and Automation*, St. Louis, pp. 1016-1021.

Nakamura, Y., and H. Hanafasu [1985], "Task priority based redundancy control of robot manipulators," *Robotics Research: The Second International Symposium*, edited by H. Hanafusa and H. Inoue, MIT Press, Cambridge, MA, pp. 155-162.

An, C. H., C. G. Atkeson, and J. M. Hollerbach [1988], *Model-based Control of a Robot Manipulator*, MIT Press, Cambridge, MA.

Hollerbach, J. M., and D. J. Bennett [1988], "Automatic kinematic calibration using a motion tracking system," *Robotics Research: the Fourth International Symposium*, edited by R. Bolles and B. Roth, MIT Press, Cambridge, MA, pp. 191-198.

Hollerbach, J. M. [1988], "A survey of kinematic calibration," *Robotics Review*, edited by O. Khatib, J. J. Craig, and T. Lozano-Perez, MIT Press, Cambridge, MA.

This chapter describes research done at the Artificial Intelligence Laboratory of the Massachusetts Institute of Technology. Support for the laboratory's artificial intelligence research is provided in part by the University Research Initiatives under Office of Naval Research contract N00014-86-K-0180 and in part by the Advanced Research Projects Agency of the Department of Defense under Office of Naval Research contract N00014-85-K-0124. Personal support for JMH was also provided by an NSF Presidential Young Investigator Award, and for DJB by a Fairchild fellowship and a scholarship from the Natural Sciences and Engineering Research Council of Canada.

Hartenberg, R. S., and J. Denavit [1964], *Kinematic Synthesis of Linkages*, McGraw-Hill Book Co., New York, NY.

Denavit, J., and R. S. Hartenberg [1955], "A kinematic notation for lower pair mechanisms based on matrices," *J. Applied Mechanics*, vol. 22, pp. 215-221.

Bennett, D. J., and J. M. Hollerbach [1988], "Self-calibration of single-loop, closed kinematic chains formed by dual or redundant manipulators," *Proc. 27th IEEE Conf. Decision and Control*, Austin, Texas,

Whitney, D. E. [1972], "The mathematics of coordinated control of prosthetic arms and manipulators," *ASME Journal of Dynamic Systems, Measurement, Control*, pp. 303-309.

Sugimoto, K., and T. Okada [1985], "Compensation of positioning errors caused by geometric deviations in robot system," *Robotics Research: The Second International Symposium*, edited by H. Hanafusa and H. Inoue, MIT Press, Cambridge, MA, pp. 231-236.

Guilleman, V., and A. Pollack [1974], *Differential Topology*, Prentice Hall, Inc., Englewood Cliffs, NJ.

Spivak, M. [1965], *Calculus on Manifolds*, W. A. Benjamin, Inc., New York.

Mooring, B. W., and G. R. Tang [1984], "An improved method for identifying the kinematic parameters in a six-axis robot," *ASME Proc. Int. Computers in Engineering Conf.*, Las Vegas, pp. 79-84.

Hayati, S. A. [1983], "Robot arm geometric link parameter estimation," *Proc. 22nd IEEE Conf. Decision and Control*, San Antonio, pp. 1477-1483.

Armstrong, B. [1987], "On finding 'exciting' trajectories for identification involving systems with non-linear dynamics," *Proc. IEEE Int. Conf. Robotics and Automation*, Raleigh, NC, pp. 1131-39.

Sinha, N. K., and B. Kuszta [1983], *Modeling and Identification of Dynamic Systems*, Van Nostrand Reinhold Co., New York, NY,

Norton, J. P. [1986] *An Introduction to Identification*, Academic Press, Orlando, FL.

Sugimoto, K., and J. Duffy [1982], "Applications of linear algebra to screw systems," *Mechanisms and Machine Theory*, vol. 17, no. 1, pp. 73-83.

Appendix A: Simplified Example

Consider a 3-DOF planar manipulator making a point contact with the ground—a 2-DOF task. This manipulator is redundant with respect to the point contact constraint, and thus forms a mobile 4-bar closed linkage (see figure 4). The ground is considered to be the fourth link with a length of a_4. The kinematic parameters of the manipulator a_1, a_2, and a_3, and the distance a_4 are to be determined from the joint angle readings θ_1, θ_2, and θ_3. The three kinematic loop closure equations (at the *ith* configuration) may be written as

$$a_1 cos(\theta_1^i) + a_2 cos(\theta_1^i + \theta_2^i) + a_3 cos(\theta_1^i + \theta_2^i + \theta_3^i) + a_4 = 0 \qquad (29)$$

$$a_1 sin(\theta_1^i) + a_2 sin(\theta_1^i + \theta_2^i) + a_3 sin(\theta_1^i + \theta_2^i + \theta_3^i) = 0 \qquad (30)$$

$$\sum_{j=1}^{4} \theta_j^i = 0. \qquad (31)$$

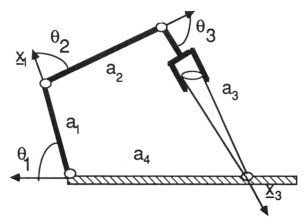

Figure 4. A three degree of freedom planar manipulator making a point fixed point contact with the ground.

Evidently, the length parameters may be scaled arbitrarily and still satisfy equations (29) and (30). For this reason one link length must be defined as unity (or measured). Let $a_4 = 1$. To continue, each additional configuration of the mechanism provides two additional position equations. Placing the equations from two configurations into matrix form we have

$$0 = C\varphi + \mathbf{y}, \qquad (32)$$

where $\varphi = (a_1 \; a_2 \; a_3)^T$, $\mathbf{y} = (1 \; 0 \; 1 \; 0)^T$, $\phi_j^i = \sum_{k=1}^{j} \theta_j^i$, and

$$C = \begin{bmatrix} cos(\phi_1^1) & cos(\phi_2^1) & cos(\phi_3^1) \\ sin(\phi_1^1) & sin(\phi_2^1) & sin(\phi_3^1) \\ cos(\phi_1^2) & cos(\phi_2^2) & cos(\phi_3^2) \\ sin(\phi_1^2) & sin(\phi_2^2) & sin(\phi_3^2) \end{bmatrix}. \qquad (33)$$

The least squares solution is $\varphi = (\mathbf{C}^T C)^{-1} \mathbf{C}^T (-\mathbf{y})$. A unique solution is guaranteed provided that the columns of C are independent. Observe that the columns of C will only be dependent if the mechanism happens to be a parallelogram (that is, $\phi_1^i = \phi_3^i$).

Appendix B: Joint Mobility

When calibrating closed kinematic chains it is necessary to be able to determine if any or all of the joints of the closed mechanism are immobile. This is most easily achieved by following the approach of Sugimoto and

Duffy [1982]. First, consider determining whether a general single-loop mechanism with n_f degrees of freedom is totally immobile. The classical mobility definition [Hartenberg & Denavit 1964] does not suffice for special mechanisms so the following condition is derived:

A single loop closed kinematic chain is mobile (at the configuration θ^i) iff the columns of the Jacobian $\partial \mathbf{x}_c^i / \partial \theta$ (that is, the joint screw coordinates) are dependent.

This result is proven by using the first differential of the closure equations with respect to θ^i (given by (10)) $0 = [\partial \mathbf{x}_c^i / \partial \theta] \dot{\theta}^i$. Denoting the columns of the Jacobian as screws gives

$$0 = \$_1 \dot{\theta}_1^i + \dots + \$_{n_f} \dot{\theta}_{n_f}^i . \tag{34}$$

By the definition of linear independence all of $\dot{\theta}_j^i$ will be identically zero if the joint screws are independent and visa versa. Thus, the proof is complete.

   A more difficult problem is determining whether or not a single joint is immobile. Consider first the movement of link one relative to the base link zero (also link n_f). Its instantaneous movement is given by $\dot{\theta}_1 \$_1$ (the super-scripts i will be suppressed for convenience) and also by $-\dot{\theta}_{n_f} \$_{n_f} - \dot{\theta}_{n_f-1} \$_{n_f-1} - \dots - \dot{\theta}_2 \$_2$ (see (34)). Thus, for link one to move $\$_1$ must lie in the span of the other screws $\$_{n_f}, \dots, \$_2$ (that is, it must be a linear combination of the other screws). Stated otherwise, the space spanned by $\$_1$ must intersect the space spanned by $\$_{n_f}, \dots, \$_2$ (abbreviated *span* $[\$_{n_f}, \dots, \$_2]$). To establish if these two spaces intersect we invoke the following theorem from linear algebra [Sugimoto & Duffy 1982]:

Let a vector space V have a dimension of $K(V)$, and also let two vector spaces A and B be subspaces of V with dimensions $K(A)$ and $K(B)$ respectively. Further, let $V = A + B$ (where $+$ is defined as $A + B = [v \mid v = a + b, \, a\epsilon A, \, b\epsilon B]$). Under these conditions the dimension of the intersection is $K(A \cap B) = K(A) + K(B) - K(V)$.

Thus, identifying A with *span* $[\$_1]$ and B with *span* $[\$_{n_f} \dots \$_2]$ then we see that: the two spaces will intersect, or equivalently, *joint one will be mobile if and only if*

$$1 + K(span\,[\$_{n_f} \dots \$_2]) - K(span\,[\$_{n_f} \dots \$_1]) > 0 . \tag{35}$$

Moreover, any joint's mobility may be ascertained by (35) with the appropriate re-numbering of the links.

35

In the previous chapter, Bennett and Hollerbach show how to calibrate robot arms, given arms that have more than six degrees of freedom, usually realized as joint angles. Frequently, however, arms have exactly six degrees of freedom because that is the minimum number that permits an arm to hold an object at an arbitrary position and at an arbitrary orientation. And even more frequently, especially in industrial settings, arms have fewer than six joint angles because fewer happen to be adequate for the intended purpose.

Nevertheless, Bennett and Hollerbach show that their calibration technique still applies as long as the arm's environment can provide extra degrees of freedom. To understand how this works, imagine grabbing a door handle and swinging the door open and closed. The hinges provide one additional joint angle, and if the arm's connection to the handle is flexible, that connection provides one or two more. Thus the door can be viewed as an extension of the arm, with the end of the combination fixed at the hinges. Now the calibration technique produces not only the length and offset parameters of the arm, but also those of the door itself.

Identifying the Kinematics of Robots

David J. Bennett
John M. Hollerbach

While modeling of robot manipulators for the purpose of model-based control has received considerable attention (for instance, see An, Atkeson and Hollerbach [1988]), modeling of the environments with which robots interact has been given less consideration. With respect to manipulator calibration many investigators (see review in Hollerbach [1988]) have developed techniques for automatically determining the kinematics of open-loop serial chain manipulators through the use of endpoint measurement systems. In contrast, analogous methods have not been developed for identifying passive environment kinematics. Thus, one purpose of this chapter is to extend open-loop kinematic calibration methods to include the identification of the geometry (kinematics) of a task being performed by a manipulator. For instance, we are interested in identifying the kinematics of such tasks as opening a door or screwing in a bolt. As we shall see, the solution that we propose also satisfies a second objective: namely, it provides a means of self-calibrating non-redundant manipulators by a closed-loop approach—thus, generalizing the work of Bennett and Hollerbach [1989a]. Effectively, the environment degrees of freedom augment those of the manipulator to make the whole system redundant. Thus, the manipulator and environment may form a mobile closed-loop kinematic chain which may self-calibrate. By self-calibration it is meant that the kinematics are identified by only using the manipulator's joint angle sensors.

Of course, the automatic calibration of a robot could be achieved with the usual techniques [Hollerbach 1988] which employ endpoint tracking systems. In contrast, the automatic calibration of the environment kinematics cannot be likewise achieved. This is so because the environment kinematics is properly viewed as an un-actuated (passive) manipulator without sensors on the various degrees of freedom. For example, a door with a handle may be viewed as a two degree of freedom passive manipulator with perpendicular non-intersecting axes. Thus, the environment must be *moved* in order to be identified. This may obviously be achieved with the manipulator, for example, by actually opening the door. Coincidentally, this movement may also be the desired task.

Because a manipulator interacting with an environment (see figure 1) generally forms a single loop closed kinematic chain, there are six kinematic constraint equations which define the closed loop: three position and three orientation equations. These equations have as variables only the degrees of freedom in the loop, that is, the joint angles. The goal of any calibration procedure is to generate enough equations, by moving the kinematic chain, to identify the fixed kinematic parameters (link lengths, axis skew angles, etc.) which occur in the kinematic equations. If all of the degrees of freedom have sensors on them, there are six equations generated for each configuration of the mechanism. Fortunately, most manipulators have sensors on all joints, so the only unsensed degrees of freedom are the degrees of freedom occurring in the task kinematics. Because there are six useful equations for a spatial mechanism, up to five unsensed degrees of freedom may be eliminated, and there still remains at least one equation for the identification procedure. This means that the closed loop kinematic parameters may be identified for arbitrary (up to 5-DOF) task kinematics, merely by using the manipulator joint angle readings.

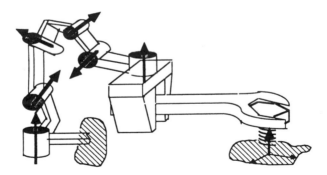

Figure 1. A manipulator forming a single-loop closed kinematic chain by interacting with the environment.

As the whole closed-loop kinematic chain may be identified, it is clear that the manipulator may not have to be calibrated before hand. In fact, *the most general scenario is to imagine an uncalibrated manipulator moving an unknown environment.* Provided that the number of degrees of freedom of the environment are known, then the manipulator and the environment kinematics may be determined simultaneously from a series of movement data (joint angle readings). We develop this most general scenario. Known parameters may easily be incorporated into the calibration scheme. The main technical problem thus amounts to developing a method of identifying closed kinematic chains. We shall refer to this technique as *closed single-loop kinematic calibration.*

To summarize, we observed that:

- The environment kinematics must be moved to be identified.

- If the manipulator is used to move the environment then the manipulator's joint sensors alone are enough to identify arbitrary environment geometries.

- The kinematics of the manipulator may be identified simultaneously with the identification of the environment.

This last point is important because it provides a means of calibrating non-redundant manipulators. For example, a 6-DOF manipulator interacting with a 1-DOF hinge form a mobile 7-DOF spatial mechanism. In general, the environment kinematics may serve to augment the manipulator degrees of freedom, so that the closed manipulator/environment loop is mobile.

In order to make the discussion concrete we focus on two specific examples. The first is a six degree of freedom (6-DOF) manipulator performing the task of opening a door, which is a 1-DOF task geometry (see figure 1). In addition to determining the manipulator's kinematics, our goal is to determine the location and orientation of the line of action of the hinge with respect to the manipulator. The second example is to study a manipulator with at least four degrees of freedom making a fixed point contact with the ground—much as you would do while holding a pencil tip at fixed location. The manipulator and the location of the point contact is identified. In this second example the environment kinematics (effectively a spherical joint) provide three extra degrees of freedom. Thus, a manipulator with as few as four degrees of freedom forms a mobile closed kinematic loop when interacting with this environment. What makes these two examples different from the calibration of redundant manipulators discussed in Bennett and Hollerbach [1989a] is that the task degrees of freedom (for example, orientation of the door, or pencil) must be eliminated from the kinematic equations. While we find that for these two examples the elimination of the unknown environment degrees of freedom is simple, it is more difficult for arbitrary task kinematics. In the discussion section we indicate how the method described may be generalized to arbitrary kinematic constraints.

Historical perspective

Recently, there has been a tremendous amount of robot calibration research based on endpoint tracking systems (both manual and automatic). A comprehensive review may be found in Hollerbach [1988]. Our approach has roots in the class of iterative open-loop kinematic calibration techniques typified by Hollerbach and Bennett [1988], Sugimoto and Okada [1985], and Veitschegger and Wu [1987]. More directly, the work presented here was influenced by our recent efforts to develop a method for self-calibration of redundant manipulators [Bennett & Hollerbach 1988, 1989a, 1989b]. In Bennett and Hollerbach [1989a] we introduced the idea that a mobile closed kinematic chain formed by one or two manipulator(s) may be calibrated with only internal joint angle readings. In the present investigation we extend this closed-loop calibration approach to include the calibration of the task kinematics, and manipulators with less than seven degrees of freedom. Portions of the present work have been previously reported in Bennett and Hollerbach [1989c].

Kinematic Model

Coordinate convention

Following the notation of Bennett and Hollerbach [1989], consider a manipulator with six degrees of freedom. Let the 4×4 homogeneous transformation $\mathbf{A}_j$ from link j to link $(j-1)$ be defined by the Denavit-Hartenberg (D-H) convention [Denavit & Hartenberg 1955] given in figure 2 and symbolically as

$$\mathbf{A}_j = \mathbf{Rot}(z, \theta'_j)\mathbf{Trans}(z, s_j)\mathbf{Trans}(x, a_j)\mathbf{Rot}(x, \alpha_j), \qquad (1)$$

where the notation $\mathbf{Rot}(x, \phi)$ indicates a rotation about an axis x by ϕ and $\mathbf{Trans}(x, a)$ indicates a translation along an axis x by a.

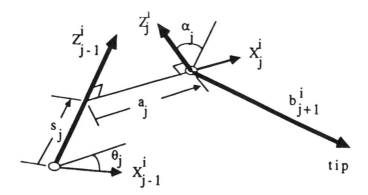

Figure 2. Denavit-Hartenberg coordinates and tip vector $\mathbf{b}^i_j$.

The position of the manipulator's endpoint is computed by a sequence of D-H transformations defining the kinematic model

$$\mathbf{T}_c = \mathbf{A}_0\mathbf{A}_1...\mathbf{A}_6 . \tag{2}$$

The transformation $\mathbf{A}_0$ is a fixed transformation which locates the first axis of the robot with respect to the base coordinate frame.

In addition to the geometric parameters (s_j, α_j and a_j), there are non-geometric parameters relating the θ'_j to the joint angle measurements. In particular, it is assumed that the only joint angle error is the offset θ_j^{off}. That is, let $\theta'_j = \theta_j + \theta_j^{off}$.

For convenience, all of the *unknown* parameters are also placed into a single vector $\varphi = (\theta_{off}^T, \mathbf{s}^T, \mathbf{a}^T, \alpha^T)^T$, where $\mathbf{s} = (s_1, s_2, ...)^T$ etc.

Door opening task

◇ Task geometry

So far, only the manipulator kinematics have been modeled. The task geometry of a manipulator gripping onto a door is defined as follows. Observe that in the D-H convention the endpoint z axis (given by $\mathbf{A}_6$) is arbitrary. Thus, it is convenient to define this axis to coincide with the axis of the door hinge (figure 3). Further, define the z axis of the base coordinates to also align with the door hinge. Finally, define the origins of the endpoint and base frames to be identical.

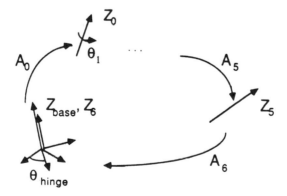

Figure 3. The coordinate description of a manipulator connected to a hinge joint.

◇ Closed-loop model

Given the above definitions, the endpoint coincides with the base coordinate axes with the exception of an unknown rotation about the base z axis. The modeled endpoint is assumed to differ only slightly from the actual endpoint (presumably as a result of parameter errors). Thus, let the position *computed* by $\mathbf{T}_c$ be represented by an infinitesimal displacement, $(dx_c, dy_c, dz_c)^T$. Similarly, let the *computed* orientation $\mathbf{R}_c$ (the upper left 3×3 matrix of $\mathbf{T}_c$) be represented by the three xyz-Euler rotations $\mathbf{Rot}(x, (\partial x_c))\mathbf{Rot}(y, (\partial y_c))\mathbf{Rot}(z, (\theta_z))$

$$
\begin{bmatrix} 1 & 0 & 0 \\ 0 & 1 & -\partial x_c \\ 0 & \partial x_c & 1 \end{bmatrix}
\begin{bmatrix} 1 & 0 & \partial y_c \\ 0 & 1 & 0 \\ -\partial y_c & 0 & 1 \end{bmatrix}
\begin{bmatrix} cos(\theta_z) & -sin(\theta_z) & 0 \\ sin(\theta_z) & cos(\theta_z) & 0 \\ 0 & 0 & 1 \end{bmatrix}, \quad (3)
$$

where ∂x_c and ∂y_c are infinitesimal, and θ_z is finite. Expanding the first column of (3) and neglecting the second order terms it can be seen that the modeled door hinge angle is $\theta_z = atan2([\mathbf{R}_c]_{(2,1)}/[\mathbf{R}_c]_{(1,1)})$, where the indices denote the elements of the rotation matrix $\mathbf{R}_c$. The desired variations ∂x_c and ∂y_c are extracted from

$$
\begin{bmatrix} 1 & 0 & \partial y_c \\ 0 & 1 & -\partial x_c \\ -\partial y_c & \partial x_c & 1 \end{bmatrix} = [\mathbf{R}_c]
\begin{bmatrix} cos(\theta_z) & sin(\theta_z) & 0 \\ -sin(\theta_z) & cos(\theta_z) & 0 \\ 0 & 0 & 1 \end{bmatrix}. \quad (4)
$$

Thus, the modeled endpoint location, evaluated at the *ith* joint configuration θ^i, may be represented as a five vector

$$
\mathbf{x}_c^i = (dx_c, dy_c, dz_c, \partial x_c, \partial y_c)^T \quad (5)
$$

and the five kinematic loop closure equations given by

$$
\mathbf{0} = \mathbf{x}_c^i(\theta^i + \theta_{off}, \mathbf{s}, \mathbf{a}, \alpha). \quad (6)
$$

The kinematic parameters are explicitly shown in the above equation by the vectors $\mathbf{s}$, $\mathbf{a}$ etc. Note that we have used up one kinematic equation in order to eliminate the unmeasured door hinge angle.

Point contact task

◇ Task geometry

The point contact task may be treated in an analogous manner. The manipulator has its endpoint constrained to a fixed position in base coordinates. Thus, it is convenient to define the base origin to coincide with the endpoint location (see figure 4). In this manner, $\mathbf{T}_c$ defines the closed-loop *position* completely. Of course, the orientation of the endpoint relative to the base is variable from configuration to configuration. Thus, the base coordinate's relative orientation is arbitrary. In particular, the three orientation parameters θ_0, α_0 and α_{n_f} are taken as arbitrary fixed values.

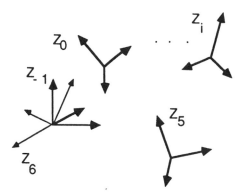

Figure 4. The coordinate description of a manipulator connected to the ground by a point contact. A '-1' denotes the base coordinates.

◇ Closed-loop model

The modeled endpoint is assumed to differ only slightly from the actual endpoint (presumably as a result of parameter errors). Thus, because the actual endpoint position coincides with the base origin, let the position *computed* (from $\mathbf{T}_c$) at *ith* joint configuration θ_i be represented by an infinitesimal displacement

$$\mathbf{x}_c^i = (dx_c, dy_c, dz_c)^T \, . \tag{7}$$

The three kinematic loop closure equations are then given by

$$0 = \mathbf{x}_c^i(\theta^i + \theta_{off}, \mathbf{s}, \mathbf{a}, \alpha) \, . \tag{8}$$

It is important to note that none of the arbitrary parameters defined in the previous section should be included in φ.

Note that we have used up three kinematic equation in order to eliminate the unmeasured orientation degrees of freedom of the endpoint.

Differential kinematics

Because the kinematic equations are non-linear, it is necessary for both analysis and solution purposes to linearize the equations about a nominal guess at the parameters φ^0. Proceed by augmenting $\mathbf{x}_c^i$ (either (5) or (7)) to be a full six vector of position and orientation. For the door opening task this gives $\tilde{\mathbf{x}}_c^i = (dx_c, dy_c, dz_c, \partial x_c, \partial y_c, \theta_z)^T$, where θ_z is the unmeasured door hinge angle. For the point contact task we have $\tilde{\mathbf{x}}_c^i = (dx_c, dy_c, dz_c, *, *, *)^T$ instead, where the $*$'s represent the unmeasured endpoint orientation. At the *ith* joint configuration θ^i the first differential of the augmented closure equations is [Bennett & Hollerbach 1989]

$$\Delta \tilde{\mathbf{x}}^i = \frac{\partial \tilde{\mathbf{x}}_c^i}{\partial \theta} \Delta \theta + \frac{\partial \tilde{\mathbf{x}}_c^i}{\partial \mathbf{s}} \Delta \mathbf{s} + \frac{\partial \tilde{\mathbf{x}}_c^i}{\partial \mathbf{a}} \Delta \mathbf{a} + \frac{\partial \tilde{\mathbf{x}}_c^i}{\partial \alpha} \Delta \alpha \qquad (9)$$

where $\Delta \tilde{\mathbf{x}}^i = (0,0,0,0,0,*) - \tilde{\mathbf{x}}_c^i$ for the door opening task, and $\Delta \tilde{\mathbf{x}}^i = (0,0,0,*,*,*) - \tilde{\mathbf{x}}_c^i$ for the point contact task. Here again a $*$ indicates an undetermined quantity. Also, $\Delta \mathbf{s} = \mathbf{s} - \mathbf{s}^0$, $\Delta \varphi = \varphi - \varphi^0$ etc. Denoting the combined Jacobian

$$\tilde{\mathbf{C}}^i = \frac{\partial \tilde{\mathbf{x}}_c^i}{\partial \varphi} = \left[\frac{\partial \tilde{\mathbf{x}}_c^i}{\partial \theta} \ \frac{\partial \tilde{\mathbf{x}}_c^i}{\partial \mathbf{s}} \ \frac{\partial \tilde{\mathbf{x}}_c^i}{\partial \mathbf{a}} \ \frac{\partial \tilde{\mathbf{x}}_c^i}{\partial \alpha} \right] \qquad (10)$$

equation (9) may be expressed more concisely as

$$\Delta \tilde{\mathbf{x}}^i = \tilde{\mathbf{C}}^i \Delta \varphi . \qquad (11)$$

◇ Differential kinematics: Door opening task

The un-augmented first differential of (6) is now found to be

$$\Delta \mathbf{x}^i = \mathbf{C}^i \Delta \varphi , \qquad (12)$$

where $\Delta \mathbf{x}^i = (0,0,0,0,0)^T - \mathbf{x}_c^i$, $\mathbf{x}_c^i$ is given by (5), and $\mathbf{C}^i$ contains all but the last row of $\tilde{\mathbf{C}}^i$.

◇ Differential kinematics: Point contact task

Likewise the un-augmented first differential of (8) is found to be

$$\Delta \mathbf{x}^i = \mathbf{C}^i \Delta \varphi . \qquad (13)$$

where $\Delta \mathbf{x}^i = (0,0,0)^T - \mathbf{x}_c^i$, $\mathbf{x}_c^i$ is given by (7), and the matrix $\mathbf{C}^i$ now only contains all but the last three rows of $\tilde{\mathbf{C}}^i$.

Note that the columns of $\mathbf{C}^i$ in this case may be interpreted as *partial velocity* vectors with respect to the parameters.

◇ The Jacobian

Each of the matrices in (9) are Jacobians with respect to the particular parameters. For example, $\partial \tilde{\mathbf{x}}_c^i / \partial \theta$ is the familiar Jacobian which relates infinitesimal joint movements to end effector movements. As derived in Bennett and Hollerbach [1989a] the *jth* columns of each of the four Jacobians composing $\tilde{\mathbf{C}}^i$ are

$$\mathrm{col}_j \frac{\partial \tilde{\mathbf{x}}_c^i}{\partial \mathbf{a}} = \begin{bmatrix} \mathbf{x}_j^i \\ \mathbf{0} \end{bmatrix} , \quad \mathrm{col}_j \frac{\partial \tilde{\mathbf{x}}_c^i}{\partial \mathbf{s}} = \begin{bmatrix} \mathbf{z}_{j-1}^i \\ \mathbf{0} \end{bmatrix} . \qquad (14)$$

and

$$\mathrm{col}_j \frac{\partial \tilde{\mathbf{x}}_c^i}{\partial \theta} = \begin{bmatrix} \mathbf{z}_{j-1}^i \times \mathbf{b}_j^i , \\ \mathbf{z}_{j-1}^i \end{bmatrix} \quad \mathrm{col}_j \frac{\partial \tilde{\mathbf{x}}_c^i}{\partial \alpha} = \begin{bmatrix} \mathbf{x}_j^i \times \mathbf{b}_{j+1}^i \\ \mathbf{x}_j^i \end{bmatrix} , \qquad (15)$$

where $\mathbf{z}_j^i$ and $\mathbf{x}_j^i$ represent are the local z and x axes of the jth coordinate frame at the ith configuration of the manipulator. Also, $\mathbf{b}_{j+1}^i$ is a vector from the jth coordinate system to the endpoint (see figure 2).

Iterative Parameter Identification

Data collection

In both examples a series of m configurations of the actual manipulator provides m sets of joint angle measurements θ^i, and m equations of the form (12) or (13). Compactly, the equations may be written as

$$\Delta \mathbf{X} = \mathbf{C} \Delta \varphi, \tag{16}$$

where

$$\mathbf{C} = \begin{bmatrix} \mathbf{C}^1 \\ . \\ \mathbf{C}^m \end{bmatrix}, \quad \Delta \mathbf{X} = \begin{bmatrix} \Delta \mathbf{x}^1 \\ . \\ \Delta \mathbf{x}^m \end{bmatrix}. \tag{17}$$

The $\mathbf{C}^i$ may be for either the door opening task (12) or the point contact task (13).

Minimization

An estimate of the parameter errors is provided by minimizing the modified least squares criterion [Bennett & Hollerbach 1989a]

$$LM = (\Delta \mathbf{X} - \mathbf{C} \Delta \varphi)^T (\Delta \mathbf{X} - \mathbf{C} \Delta \varphi) + \lambda \Delta \varphi^T \Delta \varphi. \tag{18}$$

Minimizing LM yields

$$\Delta \varphi = (\mathbf{C}^T \mathbf{C} + \lambda I)^{-1} \mathbf{C}^T \Delta \mathbf{X}. \tag{19}$$

Iteratively applying equation (19) results in the Levenberg-Marquardt algorithm [Norton 1986]. The free parameter λ determines the trade-off between a straight Newton iteration and a much slower gradient descent. The guess at the parameters is updated at each iteration as

$$\varphi = \varphi_0 + \Delta \varphi. \tag{20}$$

The iteration continues until the model forms a closed loop to within the desired tolerance $(\Delta \mathbf{X} \to 0)$.

Identifiability

As in Bennett and Hollerbach [1989a] there may be situations in which the parameters are not determined uniquely by the kinematic equations collected during movement of the mechanism. All sources of parameter ambiguity may be linked to the rank of the matrix $\mathbf{C}$. If the columns of $\mathbf{C}$ are linearly dependent (that is, $\mathbf{C}$ is not full rank) then the corresponding kinematic parameters may vary arbitrarily, these variations only satisfying the linear dependence. A linear dependence of the columns of the matrix $\mathbf{C}$ (evaluated at the actual parameters) thus indicates that certain parameters are unidentifiable.

In order to derive an identifiability condition we first study the following augmented Jacobian

$$\tilde{\mathbf{C}} = \begin{bmatrix} \tilde{\mathbf{C}}^1 \\ \cdot \\ \tilde{\mathbf{C}}^m \end{bmatrix}. \tag{21}$$

The columns of $\tilde{\mathbf{C}}$ are a concatenation of the screw coordinates (14) and (15) for all i configurations of the mechanism. Therefore, the columns of $\tilde{\mathbf{C}}$ will be linearly dependent *if and only if there is a constant linear relation among one or more of the screw coordinates for all configurations of the mechanism.* As proven in Bennett and Hollerbach [1989a] this condition is equivalent to the following statement: *The necessary and sufficient condition for the columns of $\tilde{\mathbf{C}}$ to be independent is that there exist no constant linear relation among the local link x and z axes; that is*

$$\sum_{j=0}^{6} k_j \mathbf{x}_j^i + c_j \mathbf{z}_j^i = 0 \, \forall_{i \epsilon [1..m]} \Rightarrow k_j = c_j = 0. \tag{22}$$

General identifiability for both tasks

Observe that if the columns of $\tilde{\mathbf{C}}$ are linearly dependent, so too will the columns of $\mathbf{C}$ (in either the point contact or the door opening tasks) be linearly dependent. Thus, a violation of (22) provides a *sufficient* condition for $\mathbf{C}$ to be rank deficient and for the mechanism to be unidentifiable.

The various sources of parameter unidentifiabilty were discussed in Bennett and Hollerbach [1989a]. In particular, it is important to recall that the length parameters were found to enter linearly into the kinematics and thus scale arbitrarily. We therefore must define one link length as unity—determining the units of scale. Also, it should be remembered that the specific closed mechanism being calibrated should be tested for full joint mobility [Bennett & Hollerbach 1989a].

Point contact task identifiability

In the case of the point contact task we may derive a stronger result than (22). Note that by definition (17) the columns of $\mathbf{C}$ in the point contact example are a concatenation of the upper vectors in (14) and (15) (that is, the partial velocity vectors) for all configurations of the mechanism. Therefore, the columns of $\mathbf{C}$ will be linearly dependent *if and only if there* *is a constant linear relation among the partial velocity vectors for all configurations of the mechanism. Thus, the necessary and sufficient condition for the mechanism to be identifiable is that there exist no constant linear relation among the local link x axes, z axes, and their associated moments. That is,*

$$\sum_{j=0}^{n_f} c_j^1[\mathbf{x}_j^i] + c_j^2[\mathbf{z}_j^i] + c_j^3[\mathbf{z}_{j-1}^i \times \mathbf{b}_j^i] + c_j^4[\mathbf{x}_j^i \times \mathbf{b}_{j+1}^i] = 0 \ \forall_{i \in [1..m]} \tag{23}$$

$$\Rightarrow c_j^k = 0 \forall_{k,j} \, .$$

It is instructive to re-assess the section under "Task Geometry" in light of condition (23). Consider trying to determine all of the D-H parameters without first noticing that certain orientation parameters were arbitrary. Proceed by forming the partial velocity vectors which are fixed in the base coordinates (except $[\mathbf{x}_{n_f} \times \mathbf{b}_0]$). These are: $[\mathbf{z}_{-1}]$, $[\mathbf{z}_{-1} \times \mathbf{b}_0]$, $[\mathbf{x}_{n_f} \times \mathbf{b}_0]$, $[\mathbf{z}_0]$, $[\mathbf{z}_0 \times \mathbf{b}_1]$, and $[\mathbf{x}_0 \times \mathbf{b}_1]$ (the base axes are subscripted with a '−1' and the tip axes are subscripted with an 'n_f'). There is no partial velocity vector $[\mathbf{x}_{-1}]$ because the loop is only closed in orientation. Instead there is a $[\mathbf{x}_{n_f}]$, but it is not relevant here. Now, since $\mathbf{b}_0$ is zero the partial velocity vectors $[\mathbf{z}_{-1} \times \mathbf{b}_0]$ and $[\mathbf{x}_{n_f} \times \mathbf{b}_0]$ are identically zero, and their associated parameters θ_0 and α_{n_f} are unidentifiable (by (23)). Of course, we noted that these parameters were arbitrary and defined them to be fixed and not included in φ. Further, note that the remaining four fixed partial velocity vectors $[\mathbf{z}_{-1}]$, $[\mathbf{z}_0]$, $[\mathbf{z}_0 \times \mathbf{b}_1]$, and $[\mathbf{x}_0 \times \mathbf{b}_1]$ must be linearly dependent because they only span a three dimensional space. Again, recall that we observed that α_0 is arbitrary and did not compute its partial velocity. That leaves $[\mathbf{z}_{-1}]$, $[\mathbf{z}_0]$, and $[\mathbf{z}_0 \times \mathbf{b}_1]$, which are in general not linearly dependent, and condition (23) is satisfied.

Simulations

Door opening task

A 6-DOF manipulator grasping a door with a hinge joint forms a closed 7-DOF mechanism defined by the D-H parameters in table 2 (see also figure 3). The hinge joint axis and the base axis (joint 0) align, and thus, no joint 0 offset is defined. This offset is taken to be zero (marked with a * in tables 1 and 2). The angle θ_0^i is also arbitrary and defined as zero. The parameters labeled 'joint 0' transform the base coordinates to the first joint of the manipulator. The transformation from the first joint of the manipulator to the second is given by the parameters labeled as 'joint 1' etc. Finally, the transformation from the sixth joint to the door hinge is given by the parameters labeled 'joint 6'. This entire mechanism was simulated in 40 distinct configurations. Then, starting with the initial

Joint	s (m)	a (m)	α (rad)	θ_{off} (rad)
0	1.694	0.837	3.774	*
1	1.622	-0.627	-0.553	0.080
2	1.000	-0.100	0.930	0.090
3	-0.430	-0.430	2.040	0.900
4	0.540	-0.600	-0.150	0.050
5	-0.560	-0.550	1.350	0.040
6	-1.693	0.711	-1.859	1.400

Table 1. The initial D-H parameters of a 6-DOF manipulator performing a door opening task. A * indicates an undefined parameter.

guesses in table 1 and with the definition $s_3 = 1$, the simulated robot joint angles were fed into the iterative Levenberg-Marquardt algorithm using (12) (17) (19) and (20), and the parameters in table 2 were recovered to within four decimal places.

Joint	s (m)	a (m)	α (rad)	θ_{off} (rad)
0	1.594	0.737	3.604	*
1	1.722	-0.527	-0.503	0.000
2	1.000	0.000	0.530	0.000
3	-0.330	-0.330	2.300	0.000
4	0.440	-0.440	-0.900	0.000
5	-0.660	-0.550	1.200	0.000
6	-1.793	0.911	-1.459	1.825

Table 2. The actual/calibrated D-H parameters of a 6-DOF manipulator performing a door opening task. A * indicates an undefined parameter.

Point contact task

The actual parameters of a 6-DOF manipulator making a point contact with the ground are given in table 4 (see also figure 4). As discussed in the section under "Task geometry" a number of parameters are arbitrary and fixed. These are marked with a * in tables 3 and 4. Their values were randomly assigned.

This entire mechanism was simulated in 30 distinct configurations. Then, starting with the initial guesses in table 1, the 30 sets of six sim-

Joint	s (m)	a (m)	α (rad)	θ_{off} (rad)
0	1.694	0.837	3.600*	0.000*
1	1.622	-0.627	-0.553	0.100
2	1.000*	-0.100	0.930	0.090
3	-0.430	-0.430	2.040	0.100
4	0.540	-0.600	-0.150	0.050
5	-0.560	-0.550	1.350	0.040
6	-1.693	0.711	-1.860*	1.700

Table 3. The initial D-H parameters of a 6-DOF manipulator performing a point contact task. A * indicates an undefined parameter.

ulated robot joint angles were fed into the iterative Levenberg-Marquardt algorithm (using (13), (17), (19), and (20), and the parameters in table 2 were recovered to within four decimal places.

Joint	s (m)	a (m)	α (rad)	θ_{off} (rad)
0	1.594	0.737	3.600*	0.000*
1	1.722	-0.527	-0.503	0.120
2	1.000*	0.000	0.530	0.000
3	-0.330	-0.330	2.300	0.000
4	0.440	-0.440	-0.900	0.000
5	-0.660	-0.550	1.200	0.000
6	-1.793	0.911	-1.860*	1.825

Table 4. The actual/calibrated D-H parameters of a 6-DOF manipulator performing a point contact task. A * indicates an undefined parameter.

Discussion: Identifying Arbitrary Task Kinematics

We now discuss how the algorithm presented for closed-loop kinematic calibration readily generalizes to identifying arbitrary task kinematics. As mentioned earlier, the chief difficulty is eliminating the unknown degrees of freedom from the environment kinematics. This may be achieved by determining the unknown degrees of freedom in terms of the known ones (and the kinematic parameters). For instance, in calibrating a system comprised of a robot opening a door with a handle, both the door hinge angle and the handle angle may be determined in terms of the known manipulator joint angles. Once all of the degrees of freedom are determined the iterative identification algorithm presented above is directly applicable to identifying the kinematic parameters. In particular, the over-determined system of equation (11) may be solved by the iterative Levenberg-Marquardt algorithm.

Determining the unknown degrees of freedom may proceed as follows:

1 Using the nominal model of the robot, compute the position of the endpoint at a specific configuration.
2 Note that this endpoint also locates the endpoint of the environment kinematic chain.
3 Using the nominal kinematics of the environment calculate the inverse kinematic solution of the endpoint position given in step 1.

The resulting joint angles are the unknown degrees of freedom. The inverse kinematics of step 3 may be performed analytically in very special cases, but in general it must be performed iteratively (for example, with standard iterative inverse Jacobian methods). Note that a nominal model of the kinematics is required. Each iteration of kinematic calibration algorithm presented in the section under "Iterative Parameter Identification" improves the nominal model. Thus, the above determination of joint angles must be performed anew for each step of the kinematic calibration iteration.

In an example of a door with a handle the two unknown degrees of freedom must be determined at each step of the calibration iteration. This is done by calculating the position of the manipulator endpoint $\mathbf{x}$ in terms of the manipulator joint angles, and solving the six kinematic equations $\mathbf{x} = \mathbf{f}(\theta_{hinge}, \theta_{handle})$ for the two joint angles. Here $\mathbf{f}$ models the endpoint of the door/handle kinematic chain shown in figure 5. Note that only two of the six equations are necessary to solve for the two angles.

Of course, there is the issue of identifiability of the task kinematic parameters. This issue can only be addressed on an example by example basis. A simple instance where not all of the parameters are identifiable would be if the task kinematic chain was such that its endpoint was constrained to move on the surface of a sphere. There would be no way of distinguishing this kinematic chain from a spherical joint or any other kinematic chain that implemented a spherical joint. This is not a problem when we realize that we are building the model of the environment to assist in the task of effectively interacting with the environment, and not for knowing its exact structure.

Summary

A new approach to identifying the kinematic models of manipulators and their task geometry has been presented. Starting with the observation

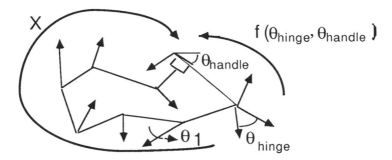

Figure 5. Determining the unknown degrees of freedom in identifying arbitrary task kinematics.

that in many tasks manipulators naturally form mobile closed kinematic chains, we have shown that these closed loops can be identified by an iterative least squares algorithm similar to that used in calibrating open chain manipulators. While only the tasks of a manipulator opening and a manipulator maintaining a point contact were studied in detail, the method readily generalizes to a large class of robot tasks (refer to the discussion in the previous section).

In the development of the closed-loop kinematic calibration technique a number of problems were solved. The issue of identifiability of the kinematic parameters of the closed loop was reduced to inspecting the rank of the Jacobian matrix $\mathbf{C}$. Rank degeneracies were in turn studied with the screw coordinate interpretation of the columns of the Jacobians $\tilde{\mathbf{C}}_i$. Specifically, a requirement that there be no constant linear relation among the local x and z axes accounts for many singularities. These singularities were previously [Bennett & Hollerbach 1989a] classified into six categories relating to:

1   The linear occurrence of the length parameters.

2   The mechanism's mobility.

3   Special geometries.

4   Coordinate description.

5   The number of configurations used to provide the joint angle data.

6   The iterative search algorithm employed.

In the present chapter a further development relevant to the identifiability of the task kinematics was provided.

Of course, there is no reason why the full kinematics of the robot must be calibrated for each new task; only the unknown task related parameters need be included in φ. On the other hand, the closed-loop kinematic calibration method provides an opportunity to calibrate a manipulator without endpoint sensing. This in itself is a novel result.

In general, the 'closed-loop' approach to kinematic calibration represents a departure from the typical dichotomy found in robotics between model building and task performance. We feel that this is a point worth stressing because the removal of this dichotomy may generalize to other problem areas in robotics. In the situation discussed in this chapter the models of the task and the manipulator are improved *while* performing the task. The benefits of this technique are numerous. First, the manipulator calibration and registration is truly autonomous: no special endpoint measurement device, or external 'teacher,' is needed. Further, the identification of the environment kinematics is made possible. Finally, a more subtle benefit is related to the identifiability of the kinematic parameters. As discussed, certain closed-loop chains have kinematic parameters that are unidentifiable. While it is nice to know all the kinematic parameters (for other tasks), note that the identification of the parameters is specifically to improve the performance on the task that forms the closed-loop in question. Thus, unidentifiable parameters are immaterial from the point of view of the task, and may be set arbitrarily (by definition unidentifiable parameters may vary arbitrarily and not effect the configurations of the closed chain).

References

An, C. H., C. G. Atkeson, and J. M. Hollerbach [1988], *Model-based Control of a Robot Manipulator*, MIT Press, Cambridge, MA.

Bennett, D. J., and J. M. Hollerbach [1988], "Self-calibration of single-loop, closed kinematic chains formed by dual or redundant manipulators," *Proc. 27th IEEE Conf. Decision and Control*, Austin, TX.

Bennett, D. J., and J. M. Hollerbach [1989a], "Self-calibration of single-loop, closed kinematic chains formed by dual or redundant manipulators," *IEEE Journal of Robotics and Automation*,

This chapter describes research done at the Artificial Intelligence Laboratory of the Massachusetts Institute of Technology. Support for the laboratory's artificial intelligence research is provided in part by the University Research Initiatives under Office of Naval Research contract N00014-86-K-0180 and in part by the Advanced Research Projects Agency of the Department of Defense under Office of Naval Research contract N00014-85-K-0124. Personal support for JMH was also provided by an NSF Presidential Young Investigator Award, and for DJB by a Fairchild fellowship and a scholarship from the Natural Sciences and Engineering Research Council of Canada.

Bennett, D. J., and J. M. Hollerbach [1989b], "Identifying the kinematics of non-redundant serial chain manipulators by a closed-loop approach," *Proc. Fourth International Conference on Advanced Robotics*, Columbus, OH.

Bennett, D. J., and J. M. Hollerbach [1989c], "Identifying the kinematics of robots and their tasks," *Proc. IEEE Int. Conf. Robotics and Automation*, Scottsdale, AZ.

Denavit, J., and R. S. Hartenberg [1955], "A kinematic notation for lower pair mechanisms based on matrices," *J. Applied Mechanics*, vol. 22, pp. 215-221.

Duffy J. [1980], *Analysis of Mechanisms and Robot Manipulators*, Edward Arnold Ltd., London.

Hartenberg, R. S., and J. Denavit [1964], *Kinematic Synthesis of Linkages*, McGraw-Hill Book Co., New York, NY.

Hollerbach, J. M. [1988], "A survey of kinematic calibration," *The Robotics Review 1988*, edited by O. Khatib, J. J. Craig, and T. Lozano-Perez, MIT Press, Cambridge, MA.

Hollerbach, J. M., and D. J. Bennett [1988], "Automatic kinematic calibration using a motion tracking system," *Robotics Research: the Fourth International Symposium*, edited by R. Bolles and B. Roth, MIT Press, Cambridge, MA, pp. 191-198.

Norton, J. P. [1986], *An Introduction to Identification*, Academic Press, Orlando, FL.

Roth, B. [1984], "Screws, motors, and wrenches that cannot be bought in a hardware store," *Robotics Research: The First International Symposium*, edited by M. Brady, and R. Paul, MIT Press, Cambridge, MA, pp. 679-693.

Sugimoto, K., and T. Okada [1985], "Compensation of positioning errors caused by geometric deviations in robot system," *Robotics Research: The Second International Symposium*, edited by H. Hanafusa and H. Inoue, MIT Press, Cambridge, MA, pp. 231-236.

Veitschegger, W. K., and C-H. Wu [1987], "A method for calibrating and compensating robot kinematic errors," *Proc. IEEE Int. Conf. Robotics and Automation*, Raleigh, NC, pp. 39-44.

Whitney, D. E. [1972], "The mathematics of coordinated control of prosthetic arms and manipulators," *ASME J. Dynamic Systems, Meas., Control*, pp. 303-309.

Part VI

Recognizing Objects and
Understanding Images

Image understanding is more satisfying, as a science, than most of the
other disciplines within Artificial Intelligence because many image understanding problems yield to traditional mathematical analysis, as amply
demonstrated in Part VI, which focuses on object recognition, navigation,
theoretical unification, system integration, and VLSI implementations:

- Grimson describes how to recognize manufactured objects by performing a consistency-constrained match between a few image points and
  surface models.

- Grimson goes on to show how his technique can recognize objects
  like scissors and shears in spite of scaling, stretching, or the relative
  rotation of their parts.

- Ullman explains a radically new approach to recognition in which sub-
  tly different objects, such as look-alike cars, are recognized by bringing
  their images into congruence with model images.

- Ullman then explains a program that determines the relative positions
  of corresponding points in a sequence of images under the assumption
  that shape varies slowly, if at all, as the sequence evolves.

- Horn and Weldon show how you can keep track of where you are,
  relative to some coordinate system, given only that you have an eye
  or a camera to look through, and that your motion is pure rotation,
  pure translation, or arbitrary motion when the rotation is known.

- Poggio et al. explain how image understanding procedures can be
  brought together via the mathematics of regularization, thus providing
  theoretical insight and facilitating practical implementation.

- Poggio et al. describe the MIT Vision Machine, a testbed for system
  integration which includes modules for the real-time computation of
  edges, stereo disparity, motion, texture, and color information.

- And finally, Horn demonstrates that many image-understanding operations are understood well enough to be implemented by way of VLSI
  chips.

36

How can you recognize objects ranging from industrial parts
to highway vehicles? Twenty years ago, there was no answer, and many researchers assumed there was no answer
because not enough was known about transforming images
into matchable symbolic descriptions.

Today, the conventional assumptions have been pushed
aside as new approaches to recognition emerge. Ullman, in a
subsequent chapter, pursues a biologically-plausible image-
alignment approach. In this chapter, Grimson pursues an
approach that is wildly implausible biologically, but is enormously effective nevertheless.

Grimson's key idea is that objects can be recognized
by performing a consistency-constrained match between a
few image points and the object's surfaces. Importantly,
Grimson buttresses the idea with a whole stock of research
tools: he does complexity analysis to study how performance
depends on object characteristics, he runs a simulation program to validate his analytic assumptions, and he experiments with real data to validate his simulation assumptions.

The results are impressive. You can walk into the
recognition laboratory, pick a random part from a collection
of similar-looking parts, camouflage your part by nearly covering it completely with the others, and still the recognition
system finds your part for you and tells you its precise location and orientation, even when you have trouble finding
the part yourself.

Object Recognition by Constrained Search

W. Eric L. Grimson

A ubiquitous problem in computer vision is determining the identity and pose (position and orientation) of objects in a scene, that is, an intelligent system must know *what* objects are and *where* they are in its environment. Examples of this problem arise in tasks involving hand-eye coordination, such as for assembly or sorting, in inspection tasks, in gaging operations, and in navigation and localization of mobile robots.

In this chapter, we consider one aspect of this problem: how to locate a known object from sensory data, especially when that object may be occluded by other (possibly unknown) objects. We present one approach to the problem, by describing a recognition system called Recognition and Attitude Finder (RAF) that identifies and locates objects from noisy, occluded data [Grimson & Lozano-Pérez 1984, 1987]. Of course, there are many other possible approaches, good examples of which include: Ayache and Faugeras [1986], Baird [1986], Bolles and Cain [1982], Bolles and Horaud [1986], Faugeras and Hebert [1983], Goad [1983], Huttenlocher and Ullman [1987], Huttenlocher [1988], Lowe [1987], Schwartz, and Sharir [1987], Lamdan, Schwartz, and Wolfson [1987], Stockman [1987], and Thompson and Mundy [1987].

Definition of the problem

The specific problem is to identify an object from among a set of known objects and to locate it relative to a sensor. The object sensed is initially assumed to be a single, possibly nonconvex, polyhedral object, for which we have an accurate geometric model, although extensions to broader classes of objects are possible [Grimson 1989b]. The object may have up to six degrees of freedom relative to the sensor (three translational and three rotational). The sensor is assumed to be capable of providing three-dimensional information about the position and local surface orientation of a small set of surface patches on the object. These patches could be point-like, in the case of tactile sensing, or extended, in the case of range sensing. Each sensory datum is processed to obtain an estimate of the position of the patch relative to the sensor, determined up to some volume of uncertainty, and to obtain an estimate of the surface normal to the object's surface, up to some cone of uncertainty. Note that we concentrate on planar patches of surface, or approximations thereto. Also note that reductions to two dimensional recognition problems are straightforward.

Our goal is to use local information about sensed features to determine the set of positions and orientations of an object that are consistent with the sensed data. If there are no consistent poses, the object can be excluded from the set of possible objects. Each such consistent pose of the object constitutes an hypothesized solution to the problem of where the object is.

In this chapter, we do not discuss how surface points and normals may be obtained from actual sensor data because this process is sensor dependent. Our aim is to show, instead, how such data may be used in conjunction with object models to recognize and localize objects. Indeed, the approach we describe does not depend critically on a specific sensory modality, and is applicable to a wide range of methods. Possible sources of data include edge based stereo systems (for example, Grimson [1981], Baker [1982], Mayhew and Frisby [1981], and Pollard, Mayhew and Frisby [1985]), laser range-finding (for example, Nitzan, Brain and Duda [1977], and Lewis and Johnston [1977]), structured light systems (for example Shirai and Suwa [1971]), photometric stereo (for example, Woodham [1980], and Ikeuchi [1981]), and tactile sensors (for example, Hillis [1982], Overton and Williams [1981], and Raibert and Tanner [1982]).

Recognition as Constrained Search

Definition of a solution

Suppose we are given some data features, obtained from the boundary of an object or objects, and measured in a coordinate system centered about the sensor. Suppose we are also given a set of object models, specified by a set of features measured in a local coordinate frame specific to the model. A solution to the recognition problem consists of identifying an object from the library, an association of data features to model features from that object, and a transformation that maps the model from its local coordinate frame into the sensor coordinate frame in such a manner that each data fragment correctly lies on its assigned model feature. In other words, a solution consists of identifying which object, where it is, and what data it accounts for.

As has been described elsewhere [Grimson & Lozano-Pérez 1984, 1987], we approach the recognition problem as one of search. Thus, we first focus on finding legitimate pairings of data and model fragments, for some subset of the sensory data. We chose to structure this search process as a constrained depth first search, using an *interpretation tree* (IT), described below.

Suppose we order the data features in some arbitrary fashion. We select the first data feature, and hypothesize that it is in correspondence with the first model feature. We can represent this choice as a node in a tree. We can consider all the other possible assignments of model features to this first data feature as well. We represent this set of alternatives as other nodes at the same level of the tree (see figure 1).

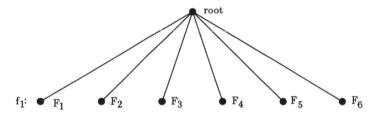

Figure 1. Interpretation Tree—Level 1. We can build a tree of possible interpretations, by first considering all the ways of matching the first data feature, f_1, to each of the model features, $F_j, j = 1, \ldots, m$.

Given each one of these hypothesized assignments of data feature f_1 to a model feature, $F_j, j = 1, \ldots, m$, we turn to the second data feature. Again, we can consider all possible assignments of the second data feature f_2 to model features, relative to the assignment of the first data feature. This is shown in figure 2.

We can continue in this manner, adding new levels to the tree, one for each data feature. A node at level n of the interpretation tree describes a partial n-interpretation, in that the nodes lying directly between the current node and the root of the tree identify an assignment of model features to the first n data features. Any leaf of the tree defines a complete s-interpretation, where s is the number of sensor features. A simple-minded method would examine each leaf of the tree, testing to see if there exists a rigid transformation mapping each model feature into its associated data feature. This is clearly too expensive, as it simply reverts to an exploration of the entire, exponential-size, search space. The key is to find constraints that will allow us to exclude entire subtrees, and hence entire subspaces of

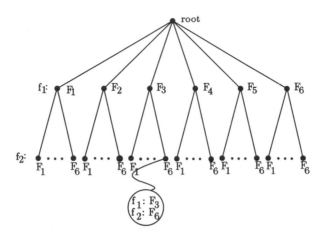

Figure 2. Interpretation Tree—Level 2. For each pairing of the first data feature with a model feature, we can consider matchings for the second data feature with each of the model features. Each node in the second level of the tree defines a pairing for the first two data features, found by tracing up the tree to the nodes. An example is shown.

the search space, without having explicitly to explore them. The advantage of using a tree of interpretations is that we can focus our search of the space in a coherent manner. In particular, we can explore the interpretation tree in a depth-first, backtracking manner, by starting at its root, and testing interpretations as we move downward in the tree. As soon as we find a node that is not consistent, that is, for which no rigid transform will correctly align model and data feature, we can terminate any further downward search below that node, as adding new data-model pairings to the interpretation defined at that node will not turn an inconsistent interpretation into a consistent one.

In testing for consistency at a node, we have two choices. We could explicitly solve for the best rigid transformation, and test that all of the model features do in fact get mapped into agreement with their corresponding data features. This approach has two drawbacks. First, computing such a transformation is generally computationally expensive, and we would like to avoid any unnecessary use of such a computation. Second, in order to compute such a transformation, we will need an interpretation of at least k data-model pairs, where k depends on the characteristics of the features. This means we must wait until we are at least k levels deep in the tree, before we can apply our consistency test, and this increases the amount of work that must be done.

Our second choice is to look for less complete methods for testing consistency. We can seek constraints that can be applied at any interpretation tree node, with the property that while no single constraint can uniquely guarantee the consistency of an interpretation, each constraint can rule out some interpretations. The hope is that if enough independent constraints can be combined together, their aggregation will prove powerful in determining consistency, while at a lower cost than full consistency constraints.

In our system, we use unary and binary constraints. Unary constraints apply to single pairings of a data feature and a model feature. If a unary constraint, applied to such a pairing, is true, then this implies that that data-model pairing may be part of a consistent interpretation. If it is false, however, then that pairing cannot possibly be part of such an interpretation. Binary constraints apply to pairs of data-model pairings, with the same logic. The advantages of these kinds of constraints are that they can be computationally quite simple, while retaining considerable power to separate consistent from inconsistent interpretations, and that they can be applied at virtually any node in the interpretation tree.

The constraints reduce the search

To employ these constraints, we must now specify the manner in which we explore the interpretation tree. Our general approach to exploring this tree is to use backtracking depth-first search. That is, we begin at the root of the tree, and explore downwards along the first branch. At the first node, we check the consistency of that node by examining the truth value of the unary constraints associated with the data-model pairing defined by that node. For notational purposes, we let

- **unary-constraints** (i, p) = True iff the pairing of the ith data feature to the pth model feature is locally consistent.

If the pairing is consistent, we continue downwards along the first branch from this node. At the new node, we again check the unary consistency of the data-model pairing defined by that node.

We also check any available binary constraints. In particular, each node at the second level of the tree defines a 2-interpretation, that is, an assignment of two data elements to model elements, so we can apply our binary constraints to these pairings. For notational purposes, we let

- **binary-constraints** (i, j, p, q) = True iff the pairing of the ith data feature to the pth model feature and the pairing of the jth data feature to the qth model feature are mutually locally consistent.

Again, if all the constraints are satisfied, we continue downward in the tree. Note that at each new node, there is a new data-model pairing that must be subjected to the unary constraints. There are also several new binary constraints, because each new node at the nth level of the tree allows for $n - 1$ new pairs of data-model pairings that can be checked for constraint consistency. Thus, the lower we go in the tree, the more constraints we have that must hold true, and hence the stronger the likelihood that the interpretation is in fact globally consistent. If we reach a leaf of the tree, we have a possible interpretation of the data relative to the model.

If we reach a node at which a constraint does not hold, we abandon the remaining subtree below that node, and backtrack to the previous node. We then explore the next branch of that node. If there are no more branches, we backtrack another level, and so on. Even if we do reach a leaf of the tree, we do not abandon the search. Rather, we accumulate that possible interpretation, backtrack and continue, until the entire tree has been explored, and all possible interpretations have been found.

Dealing with Spurious Data

As described in the previous sections, the tree search method only works when all of the sensory data is known to have come from a single object. This is clearly an overly restrictive assumption. It either requires that the scene being observed by the sensor can be guaranteed to contain only a single object, or it requires that some other mechanism has partitioned the data from a cluttered scene into subsets that are known to correspond to single objects. The first solution is possible in situations in which one has some control over the environment, for example, in some manufacturing environments. But it still excludes a wide range of sensing situations. The second solution allows for more general scenarios, but rather than expecting some other mechanism to provide the partitioned data, we should be able to perform the partitioning ourselves.

We can extend our search method to exclude data features that are inconsistent with the current interpretation, while preserving the constrained search paradigm. We do this by adding a mechanism for null-character matches, as explained below. Unfortunately, while this allows our method to find correct interpretations of the data in the presence of spurious features, it does so at an unacceptable computational cost. To limit the search process in the presence of spurious data, we can consider several additional methods. The first uses information about the best interpretations previously obtained to terminate further downward search when it cannot possibly lead to a better interpretation. The second extends this idea to terminate all search as soon as an interpretation that is "good enough" is found. The third explores the idea of preselecting "good" subspaces of the search space on which to initially concentrate our efforts.

Extending the tree search method

Our first attack on the problem of selecting relevant sensory data relies on extending our search method, while preserving its advantages. The diffi-

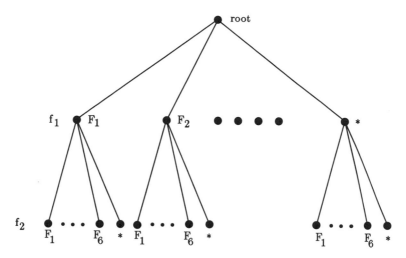

Figure 3. Interpretation Tree—With Null Character. The interpretation tree can be extended by adding the null character '∗' as a final branch for each node of the tree. A match of a data feature and this character indicates that the data feature is not part of the current interpretation. In the example shown, the simple tree of figure 2 has been extended to include the null character.

culty is that if some of the sensory data does not arise from the object of interest, then no leaf of the tree can correspond to a consistent interpretation. As a consequence, our constrained search method is likely to terminate its downward search along each path before reaching a leaf, and no interpretation will be hypothesized as a possible solution. How can we extend our search method to allow for spurious data, while preserving the backtracking constraint satisfaction properties?

One easy solution is to introduce into our matching vocabulary a new model feature, called a *null character* feature. At each node of the interpretation tree, we add as a last resort an extra branch corresponding to this feature (see figure 3). This feature (denoted by a '∗' to distinguish it from actual model features F_j) indicates that the data feature to which it is matched is to be excluded from the interpretation, and treated as spurious data. To complete this addition to our matching scheme, we must define the consistency relationships between data-model pairings involving a null character match. Because the data feature is to be excluded, it cannot affect the current interpretation, and hence any constraint involving a data feature matched to the null character is deemed to be consistent.

The constraints still reduce the search

With the addition of the null character, we can now find interpretations that include spurious data. We describe the actual process formally below.

◇ **Definition of the tree search method, with null character**

(0) D ← 0 ; *initialize at root of tree, d denotes depth in tree*
       Mode ← search ; *start in search mode*
       I_0 ← {} ; *initial interpretation is empty*
       Status ← consistent ; *initial interpretation is consistent*

(1) If mode = search & status = consistent ; *still okay*
       Then d ← d +1 ; *increment depth*
         j_d ← 1 ; *start with first model feature*
       (1.1) I_d ← $I_{d-1} \cup \{(f_d, F_{j_d})\}$
       ; *add new pairing to interpretation*
       (1.2) If $j_d = m + 1$; *null match, automatically consistent*
       Then if d = s, save I_d ; *save interpretation as possible solution*
               and set mode ← backtrack
               Go to (3)
               ; *back track to look for next one*
       Else go to (1)
       ; *continue with downward search*

       If $j_d \neq m + 1$; *real model feature*
       Then if **unary-constraints**(d, j_d) = True
       ; *new pairing satisfies unary constraints*
           & $\forall i = 1, \ldots, d - 1$
          binary-constraints(i, d, j_i, j_d) = True
          ; *all new binary constraints are satisfied*
          ; *so new interpretation is still consistent*
          Then if d = s, save I_d ; *save possible solution*
             and set mode ← backtrack
             Go to (3)
             ; *back track to look for next one*
             Else go to (1)
             ; *still have more features to consider*
             ; *so continue with downward search*
          Else status ← inconsistent, go to (2)
          ; *some constraint is invalid,*
          ; *so interpretation inconsistent*

(2) If mode = search & status = inconsistent
       Then if $j_d = m$; *no more choices at this d*
          set mode ← backtrack,
          go to (3)

           else $j_d \leftarrow j_d + 1$
             ; select next model feature at this depth
                go to (1.1) *; try next choice of model feature*

(3) If mode $=$ backtrack *; backtracking to find next alternative*
        then if $j_d \neq$ m+1 *; still have choices at this depth*
            set $j_d \leftarrow j_d + 1$ *; increment*
                mode $\leftarrow$ search
                go to (1.1)
      else d $\leftarrow$ d - 1 *; decrement depth*
           $I_d \leftarrow I_{d+1}/\{(f_{d+1}, F_{j_{d+1}})\}$ *; remove most recent pairing*
           go to (3)*; continue backtracking*

Note that the only real changes to the search process are to include constraints involving the null character, which are automatically consistent, and to add a final branch at each node of the tree, corresponding to the null character.

Model tests to verify hypothesized interpretations

Once the search process reaches a leaf of the interpretation tree, we have accounted for all of the data features, and it would seem that we therefore have a solution to the recognition problem. The entire interpretation defined by this node need not be a globally consistent one, however. The reason is that our means of reaching this node was through unary and binary constraints, and this only implies that any two of the data-model pairings of the interpretation are consistent.

We must therefore check each leaf of the tree reached by the constrained search process to verify that the interpretation at that leaf is in fact globally valid. To do this, we solve for a rigid transformation mapping points $\mathbf{V}$ in model coordinates into points $\mathbf{v}$ in sensor coordinates. In the general case, this is given by

$$\mathbf{v} = sR\mathbf{V} + \mathbf{v}_0$$

where R is a rotation matrix, $\mathbf{v}_0$ is a translation vector, and s is a scale factor (if this is one of the free parameters). An example in which the scale factor is fixed is shown in figure 4.

Typically, we will use a least-squares method to find this transformation from the data-model pairings of the interpretation. This will find the transformation that minimizes the amount of error between the transformed model features and the data features. To ensure that this transformation really is correct, we must test that the application of the transform

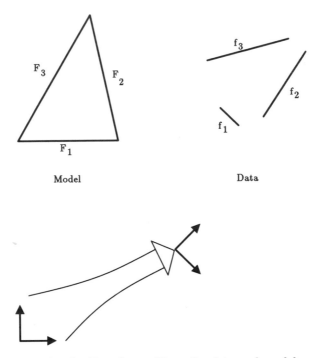

Figure 4. Solving for the Transform. Given the data and model segments, one feasible interpretation associates $f_1 : F_1$, $f_2 : F_2$, $f_3 : F_3$. This is a consistent interpretation because there exists a rigid coordinate frame transformation that maps each model segment into agreement with its corresponding data segment.

to each model feature causes it to be mapped to a position in the sensor coordinate frame that is in agreement (to within the bounds of error) with the corresponding data feature. Note that we exclude any pairings involving the null character from this computation.

Using Branch-and-bound to reduce the search

If the above method is applied to data including spurious features it will find all feasible interpretations of the data. Unfortunately, as it stands it will also do some redundant work. Suppose we have s sensory data features, c $(c \leq s)$ of which actually come from the object of interest. Our modified constrained search method will find the interpretation in which the c data features are correctly assigned to their corresponding model features. It will also find all c interpretations involving only $c - 1$ of the features, with the other feature assigned to the null character, as well as all $\binom{c}{2}$ interpretations involving $c - 2$ of the features and so on. After all, by our definition, all of these are feasible interpretations, but at the same time, they are redundant, because the c-length interpretation implicitly contains within it all the remaining interpretations. Not only is it redundant to determine those remaining $2^c - 1$ different interpretations, but spending time in the search process deducing them is clearly inefficient. We could benefit from a method for avoiding that extra search.

A straightforward way to do this is to use information about previously found interpretations to terminate fruitless search. In particular, consider the following variation. Suppose that whenever the search process reaches a leaf of the interpretation tree, a model test is applied immediately to verify that the hypothesized interpretation is correct. If the interpretation is accepted as feasible, we can measure the size of that interpretation. Possible measures include the number of data features assigned to an actual model feature, defined by

$$\sum_{i=1}^{s} \delta(i)$$

where

$$\delta(i) = \begin{cases} 1 & \text{if } F_{j_i} \neq * \\ 0 & \text{otherwise} \end{cases},$$

or the total extent of the matched data features, defined in two dimensions, for example, by

$$\sum_{i=1,\ldots,s} \delta(i) A_i$$

where A_i is the area of the ith patch. Similar definitions for measures of the size of an interpretation can be obtained in the two dimensional case.

Given such a measure, which we denote $\mu((f_1, F_{j_1}), \ldots (f_k, F_{j_k}))$, we can modify our search process to remove fruitless paths. In particular, we keep track of the best measure obtained in the search, by means of a global variable BEST. If we reach a point in the search at which further exploration down the tree would not result in an improvement in this best score, we immediately backtrack without exploring further down that path in the tree. This simple change will still allow our method to find correct answers, it simply attempts to reduce the amount of wasted search invested in finding them.

The use of the global variable BEST allows us to terminate a downward search in the interpretation tree, when it is impossible for any interpretation below the current node to exceed the current best interpretation. Note that we can use an initialization value other than 0 for BEST, if we are only interested in interpretations better than some amount. Also note that we can be more conservative about the effects of noise in the process by saving any interpretation that has a measure of quality of match no more than ϵ less than the current BEST interpretation, for some value of ϵ.

With these simple changes to our search method, we now have a system that can be applied to cluttered scenes, in which many of the sensory data features are spurious, arising from objects other than the one to be identified. Unfortunately, adding the null character, while enabling us to deal with spurious data, also causes the system to slow down considerably. The problem is that the null character is always consistent, and hence much more time is spent exploring portions of the search space in which very few pairings are actually made with real model features. To regain efficiency, we need additional methods for dealing with spurious data.

Selecting search subspaces

While the interpretation tree search technique described above will succeed in finding all consistent interpretations of the sensory data for a given object model, it is not particularly computationally efficient. This is mostly due to the problem of segmenting the data to determine subsets that belong to a single object. In order to improve the efficiency of the method when dealing with spurious data, we add two additional methods to our search process.

◇ Searching the pose space with Hough transforms

We need some means of keeping our search method from thrashing in fruitless portions of the search space. One way to do this is to first select subspaces of the full search space that are more likely to contain solutions and explore those first.

In particular, we can use the Hough transform (for example, Hough [1962], Merlin and Farber [1975], Sklansky [1978], Ballard [1981], and Davis [1982]) as a method for selecting likely subspaces. The Hough transform or related parameter hashing techniques can in principle be used on its own to solve the recognition and localization problem (for example, Thompson and Mundy [1987], Stockman [1987], Silberberg, Harwood and Davis [1986], Silberberg, Davis and Harwood [1984], Lamdan, Schwartz and Wolfson [1987], Turney, Mudge and Volz [1985]). Our experience in using the Hough transform, however, suggests that it is best suited as a preprocessor to restrict our attention to small portions of the search space [Grimson & Huttenlocher 1989a].

To use the Hough transform as a preprocessor, we consider all pairings of data and model features. For each one, we compute the complete set of transformations that would map the model feature into a consistent relationship with the data feature, where the consistency allows for error in the measurements and partial occlusion of the feature. For each such transformation, we enter the data-model pairing into a hash table, indexed by the parameters of the transformation. Once we have hashed all data-model feature pairings, we sort the hash table based on the size of the entries. Starting with the largest entry, we use the contents of the hash bucket to define an interpretation tree, and apply our earlier method. This interpretation tree is much smaller than the full one, and leads to much more efficient exploration of the search space. If a consistent interpretation is found, we accept it. If not, we move on to the next best bucket, and so on.

◇ **Early termination**

We can add a second heuristic to our interpretation tree search method, which also drastically reduces the effort involved. Suppose we have reached a leaf in one of our interpretation trees, and the interpretation associated with it is consistent. Because many of the data fragments in the interpretation are likely to have been assigned the null character, our search method would proceed to backtrack, attempting to find another interpretation that accounted for more of the data. In many cases, this is a fruitless task [Grimson & Lozano-Pérez 1987]. We can truncate this search, at the possible risk of occasionally misinterpreting the data. In particular, we can apply a measure of goodness of match to each consistent interpretation. If that measure exceeds some predefined threshold, then we can accept the interpretation, and terminate the search in that particular interpretation tree. This method of terminating search may be applied at any leaf of the interpretation tree, or can be generalized to apply to any node of the interpretation tree, further reducing excess search. This idea of early termination once an interpretation that is "good enough" is found has been used by other authors (for example, Ayache and Faugeras [1986], and Lowe [1987]). Techniques for determining what constitutes "good enough" are possible [Grimson & Huttenlocher 1989b].

These two techniques can be combined to produce a very efficient recognition system. We can search through the sorted Hough buckets, applying our constrained search method to the interpretation tree defined by the bucket contents. If we find an interpretation that exceeds our predefined measure of match, we can remove the data fragments that have been accounted for, adjust our Hough buckets accordingly, and continue the process, looking for more objects, until we have either identified all of the edges in the data, or all of the Hough buckets have been exhausted. Note that if we use an early cutoff, the threshold can be used to remove many of the smaller Hough buckets, thereby increasing efficiency. As well, because we halt the search once an interpretation that is good enough is found, this allows us to reduce the size of the search problem by removing the data features associated with the interpretation from further consideration, without having to fully explore the interpretation tree.

Deriving Constraints

To complete the description of our approach, we must provide a method
for computing actual constraints. These are described in detail elsewhere
[Grimson & Lozano-Pérez 1984, 1987; Grimson 1989]. For illustrative purposes, we indicate appropriate constraints for recognizing objects from 3D
edges. We assume that the object can be modeled as a wire-frame polyhedron, defined in a coordinate frame fixed with respect to the model. We
also assume that sensory input of a scene can be processed to obtain a
similar set of linear fragments from the objects in the scene.

Because we are dealing with the case of linear fragments, the ith data
fragment can be represented by

$$\texttt{linear}_i = (\hat{\mathbf{n}}_i, (\mathbf{b}_i, \mathbf{e}_i))$$

where $\hat{\mathbf{n}}_i$ is a unit vector normal to the edge, and $\mathbf{b}_i, \mathbf{e}_i$ are the endpoints of
the edge, measured in the three-dimensional sensor coordinate frame (see
figure 5). We can also define a unit tangent vector for the edge, by letting
$\hat{\mathbf{t}}_i$ be the unit vector pointing from $\mathbf{b}_i$ to $\mathbf{e}_i$. Note that to uniquely define
the unit normal, we require that it lie in the plane that bisects the planes
of the two intersecting faces that define the edge.

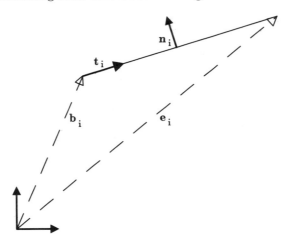

Figure 5. The representation of an edge. An edge is given by the pair

$$\hat{\mathbf{n}}_i \qquad \text{and} \qquad \mathbf{b}_i + \alpha_i \hat{\mathbf{t}}_i, \quad \alpha_i \in [0, \ell_i]$$

where $\hat{\mathbf{n}}_i$ is a unit normal vector, $\hat{\mathbf{t}}_i$ is a unit tangent vector, oriented so that it
points from $\mathbf{b}$ to $\mathbf{e}$, $\mathbf{b}_i$ is a vector to the base point of the edge, and α_i can vary
from 0 to the length of the edge ℓ_i.

Similarly, we can represent each model edge by

$$\texttt{LINEAR}_p = (\hat{\mathbf{N}}_p, (\mathbf{B}_p, \mathbf{E}_p))$$

where these vectors are measured in the model coordinate frame.

As we suggested earlier, given a model with m such edges, and an image with s sensory data edges, we need to find an interpretation of the data edges consistent with the model. Recall that by an *interpretation*, we mean an assignment of a model edge to each data edge. By *consistent*, we mean that there exists a rigid coordinate frame transformation, which, when applied to the model, will cause each model edge to take on a position in the transformed coordinate system that agrees with the position of the corresponding data edge (see figure 4).

◇ Constraints for 2-D edges

Given a partial interpretation (for example, some node in an interpretation tree), we need to find ways of determining that a node in that tree is inconsistent, meaning that there does not exist a rigid transformation that would map the model into the sensor coordinate frame in such a manner as to ensure that the transformed model features would align with their associated image features. Of course, we could do this by solving for the transform that best attains this alignment, and then measuring the deviation from an exact alignment. This, however, is likely to be computationally expensive, and so we seek simpler constraints. (Note, however, that Ayache and Faugeras [1986] provide an interesting approach along these lines that uses the Kalman filter to dramatically reduce the computational overhead.)

Because we are dealing with geometric features, and because the transformation from model coordinates to sensor coordinates is one of the things to be determined, we focus on finding constraints that can compare coordinate frame independent measurements from sensory and model fragments.

◇ Unary constraints

We begin with unary constraints. We let ℓ_i denote the length of the ith data fragment, and L_p denote the length of the pth model fragment

$$\ell_i = \|\mathbf{e}_i - \mathbf{b}_i\|$$
$$L_p = \|\mathbf{E}_p - \mathbf{B}_p\|.$$

In the ideal case, with no noise and no occlusion, we can derive a simple length constraint on our matching process, namely that for LINEAR$_p$ to match linear$_i$, we must have $L_p = \ell_i$ (where we are excluding any variation in scale). Of course, in general, there will be noise and occlusion, so we select a more general, but less precise constraint.

We let ϵ_L denote a predefined upper bound on the amount of error inherent in measuring the length of an edge. Then we have the following constraint

length-constraint (i, p) = True iff $\ell_i \leq L_p + \epsilon_L$.

In other words, this constraint says that if the length of the ith image edge is less than the length of the pth model edge, subject to error in the measurement, then it is possible to assign this model edge to this data edge. If not, then such an assignment is inconsistent. Note that the constraint explicitly allows for error in the measurements (the use of the ϵ_L term), and explicitly allows for occlusion of the edges (the use of an inequality, rather than an equality). Hence, the constraint may be satisfied even in cases which are not, in fact, correct, due to our allowance for occlusion and noise. While each individual constraint is therefore weaker than in the case of ideal data, we will see that the aggregation of the constraints still maintains considerable power.

Such a constraint can be applied at any node in the interpretation tree. That is, for any possible pairing of a data element and a model element, we can partially determine the consistency of such a pairing by applying this constraint to the respective geometric parameters. If this constraint is found to hold true, then we know that an interpretation involving this pairing of data and model fragments is still possibly consistent, and we can continue exploration of this portion of the search space. If the constraint is found not to hold true, then the entire subtree below that node is known to be inconsistent, because the node itself is inconsistent.

◇ Binary constraints

Now consider two linear data fragments,
$$\text{linear}_i = (\hat{\mathbf{n}}_i, (\mathbf{b}_i, \mathbf{e}_i)) \qquad \text{linear}_j = (\hat{\mathbf{n}}_j, (\mathbf{b}_j, \mathbf{e}_j))$$
and two possible matching model fragments
$$\text{LINEAR}_p = \left(\hat{\mathbf{N}}_p, (\mathbf{B}_p, \mathbf{E}_p)\right) \qquad \text{LINEAR}_q = \left(\hat{\mathbf{N}}_q, (\mathbf{B}_q, \mathbf{E}_q)\right).$$
Again we need to derive a set of constraints that will help measure the consistency of assigning the data fragments to lie on the model ones. Because one of our goals is to determine the pose of the object, the constraints we derive should be independent of the specific pose involved. This argues that we want measurements that are coordinate frame independent, and this argues that we need measurements that describe aspects of the relative shape of fragments of an object. We derive such a set of constraints below.

◇ Angle constraint

Let θ_{ij} denote the angle between $\hat{\mathbf{n}}_i$ and $\hat{\mathbf{n}}_j$, and let Θ_{pq} denote the angle between $\hat{\mathbf{N}}_p$ and $\hat{\mathbf{N}}_q$. We let
$$\textbf{angle-constraint } (i, j, p, q) = \text{True iff } \theta_{ij} \in [\Theta_{pq} - 2\epsilon_a, \Theta_{pq} + 2\epsilon_a]$$

where all arithmetic comparisons are performed modulo 2π and where ϵ_a is an upper bound on the amount of error inherent in determining the direction of a normal.

This says that if the angle between the data normals agrees with the angle between the model normals, within some error, then it is possible to consistently assign these data fragments to lie on these model ones.

$\Diamond$ Distance constraint

Given two data fragments, there is a range of distances associated with the family of vectors having tails on one edge and heads on the other.

The range of such distances, denoted by $[d_{\ell,ij}, d_{h,ij}]$, can be computed easily. If $i = j$, then the minimum distance is 0 and the maximum distance is the length of the edge. In the more general case, let $\rho\,(\mathbf{v}, \mathbf{u})$ denote the distance between two points. Then the maximum distance is given by

$$d_{h,ij} = \max\{\rho\,(\mathbf{b}_i, \mathbf{b}_j), \rho\,(\mathbf{b}_i, \mathbf{e}_j), \rho\,(\mathbf{e}_i, \mathbf{b}_j), \rho\,(\mathbf{e}_i, \mathbf{e}_j)\}$$

that is, the maximum distance can be found by looking at all possible vectors between extreme points of the edge. For the minimum distance, we must consider both the smallest distance between endpoints of the edge, and also the possibility that the projection from an endpoint of one edge in the direction of the normal of the second edge intersects that edge (the cases are shown in figure 6). Hence, the minimum distance will be denoted by $d_{\ell,ij}$ and is given by

$$\min\{\rho\,(\mathbf{b}_i, \mathbf{b}_j), \rho\,(\mathbf{b}_i, \mathbf{e}_j), \rho\,(\mathbf{e}_i, \mathbf{b}_j), \rho\,(\mathbf{e}_i, \mathbf{e}_j),$$

$$\rho\,(\mathbf{b}_j, \mathbf{b}_i + \langle \mathbf{b}_j - \mathbf{b}_i, \hat{\mathbf{t}}_i \rangle \hat{\mathbf{t}}_i) \qquad \text{if} \ \ \langle \mathbf{b}_j - \mathbf{b}_i, \hat{\mathbf{t}}_i \rangle \in [0, \ell_i]$$

$$\rho\,(\mathbf{e}_j, \mathbf{b}_i + \langle \mathbf{e}_j - \mathbf{b}_i, \hat{\mathbf{t}}_i \rangle \hat{\mathbf{t}}_i) \qquad \text{if} \ \ \langle \mathbf{e}_j - \mathbf{b}_i, \hat{\mathbf{t}}_i \rangle \in [0, \ell_i]$$

$$\rho\,(\mathbf{b}_i, \mathbf{b}_j + \langle \mathbf{b}_i - \mathbf{b}_j, \hat{\mathbf{t}}_j \rangle \hat{\mathbf{t}}_j) \qquad \text{if} \ \ \langle \mathbf{b}_i - \mathbf{b}_j, \hat{\mathbf{t}}_j \rangle \in [0, \ell_j]$$

$$\rho\,(\mathbf{e}_i, \mathbf{b}_j + \langle \mathbf{e}_i - \mathbf{b}_j, \hat{\mathbf{t}}_j \rangle \hat{\mathbf{t}}_j) \qquad \text{if} \ \ \langle \mathbf{e}_i - \mathbf{b}_j, \hat{\mathbf{t}}_j \rangle \in [0, \ell_j]\}$$

where we let $< .,. >$ denote the dot (or inner) product of two vectors, and where the terms followed by the if clauses are included in the set only if the if clause holds true.

For the model fragments, we can compute similar ranges, which we denote by $D_{\ell,pq}, D_{h,pq}$. We let

distance-constraint $(i, j, p, q) = $ True

$$\text{iff} \ [\, d_{\ell,ij}, d_{h,ij}] \subseteq [\, D_{\ell,pq} - 2\epsilon_p, D_{h,pq} + 2\epsilon_p]$$

where we assume that the position of an edge point is known to within an error bound ϵ_p.

This says that if the range of distances between the data edges is contained within the range of distances between the model edges, subject to some error, then it is possible to consistently assign the data fragments to

a   b

Figure 6. Cases in the computation of the distance constraint. (a) The maximum distance is found by considering the four vectors between the endpoints of the edges. (b) The minimum distance is found by considering the vectors between the endpoints of the edges (shown as hatched lines), and by considering the perpendicular projection of each endpoint onto the infinite extension of the other edge (shown as solid lines). Only those projections that actually intersect the other edge are considered.

lie on the model ones. Note that such a constraint allows for the possibility that only part of the model edge is visible in the image, and allows for the inclusion of bounded amounts of noise in the measurements.

◇ Component constraint

The third constraint basically corresponds to decomposing a family of vectors between two edges into components defined by a local coordinate frame, namely that defined by the normals to the two edges. Because this coordinate frame is defined by the edges themselves, measurements made relative to it are independent of the particular pose of the object, and hence can be used to determine the consistency of pairs of model edges and pairs of data edges.

Algebraically, this consistency is expressed by the dot product

$$\left\langle \mathbf{b}_i + \alpha_i \hat{\mathbf{t}}_i - \mathbf{b}_j - \alpha_j \hat{\mathbf{t}}_j,\ \hat{\mathbf{n}}_i \right\rangle$$

where $\hat{\mathbf{t}}_i$ is the unit tangent vector pointing from $\mathbf{b}_i$ to $\mathbf{e}_i$. This dot product reduces to

$$\left\langle \mathbf{b}_i - \mathbf{b}_j,\ \hat{\mathbf{n}}_i \right\rangle - \alpha_j \left\langle \hat{\mathbf{t}}_j,\ \hat{\mathbf{n}}_i \right\rangle \qquad \alpha_j \in [0,\ \ell_j]$$

Of course, there is an equivalent constraint for components in the direction of $\hat{\mathbf{n}}_j$. Note that this expression actually determines a range of values, with extrema when $\alpha_j = 0, \ell_j$. We denote this by

$$d^{\perp}_{\ell,\,ij} = \min \left\{ \left\langle \mathbf{b}_i - \mathbf{b}_j,\ \hat{\mathbf{n}}_i \right\rangle - \ell_j \left\langle \hat{\mathbf{t}}_j,\ \hat{\mathbf{n}}_i \right\rangle, \left\langle \mathbf{b}_i - \mathbf{b}_j,\ \hat{\mathbf{n}}_i \right\rangle \right\}$$

$$d^{\perp}_{h,\,ij} = \max \left\{ \left\langle \mathbf{b}_i - \mathbf{b}_j,\ \hat{\mathbf{n}}_i \right\rangle - \ell_j \left\langle \hat{\mathbf{t}}_j,\ \hat{\mathbf{n}}_i \right\rangle, \left\langle \mathbf{b}_i - \mathbf{b}_j,\ \hat{\mathbf{n}}_i \right\rangle \right\}$$

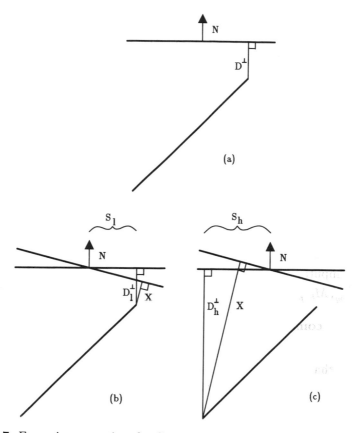

Figure 7. Errors in computing the direction constraint.
(a) The component of a vector from one endpoint in the direction of the other edge's normal is given by the perpendicular distance **d** to the extended edge.
(b) Because the actual normal is only accurate to within ϵ_a, one extreme case is given by rotating the extended edge about its midpoint by that amount and finding the new perpendicular distance.
(c) The other extreme is obtained by considering the other endpoint.

These ranges can be computed both for pairs of data edges and pairs of model edges. In the ideal case, consistency will hold only if the data range is contained within the model range (because the data edges may correspond to only parts of the model edges). As in the case of the other constraints, we also need to account for error in the measurements. We derive a simple method for doing this below.

Consider the base case, shown in figure 7. The perpendicular distance from the endpoint of one edge to the other edge is shown as $D^\perp$. In figure 7, the edge is rotated by ϵ_a about its midpoint, and the new perpendicular distance X is shown. We need to relate X to measurable values. We already have $D^\perp$. We can also measure S, the distance from the midpoint of the edge to the perpendicular dropped from the endpoint of the other edge, as shown. Standard trigonometry then yields the new distance

$$X = D^\perp \cos \epsilon_a - S \sin \epsilon_a \, .$$

Because the position of the second edge is not known exactly, we must adjust this expression, to yield one limit on the range of possible measurements

$$D^\perp_{\ell, pq} = D^\perp \cos \epsilon_a - S \sin \epsilon_a - \epsilon_p \, .$$

The other extreme is shown in figure 7. Trigonometric manipulation yields the following upper bound

$$D^\perp_{h, pq} = D^\perp \cos \epsilon_a + S \sin \epsilon_a + \epsilon_p.$$

Thus, given two model edges indexed by p, q, we can compute a range of possible measurements (modulo known error bounds), by using $D^\perp_{\ell, pq}$ and $D^\perp_{h, pq}$ computed over all the endpoints of the edges. We denote this range by $[M^\perp_{\ell, pq}, M^\perp_{h, pq}]$.

We let

$$\textbf{component-constraint}(i, j, p, q) = \text{True}$$

$$\text{iff } [d^\perp_{\ell, ij}, d^\perp_{h, ij}] \subseteq [M^\perp_{\ell, pq}, M^\perp_{h, pq}]$$

This says that if the range of distance components between the data edges is contained within the corresponding range between the model edges, subject to some error, then it is possible to consistently assign these data fragments to lie on these model ones.

Empirical Testing

The method has been extensively tested on a variety of sensory data including grey-level images, tactile data, stereo data, laser range data, and sonar data. Examples are given in Grimson and Lozano-Pérez [1984, 1987], and Grimson [1989]. Our experience was that when the data came from a single object, the method was quite fast. When spurious data was included, the method slowed down considerably, but this loss of efficiency could be recovered by using the Hough transform as a preprocessor, and using early termination of search once an acceptable interpretation was found.

Formal Combinatorics

We have verified these empirical observations by a formal combinatorial analysis of the method, the highlights of which are as follows [Grimson 1989c, 1989d].

- When all of the data features are known to have come from a single object, the number of interpretations is asymptotic to 1.

- When only c of the s data features come from an object with m model features, the number of interpretations n_s^*, with null character matches allowed, is bounded above by an expression of order

$$O\left(n_s^*\right) = 2^c + [1 + \alpha]^s + 2ms\,[1 + p_2]^c$$

  where p_2 is the probability of a pair of random data-model pairings satisfying binary consistency, and α is a small (< 1) constant that depends on the object characteristics and the amount of noise in the measurements. The number of interpretations is bounded below by an expression of order

$$o\left(n_s^*\right) = 2^c + [1 + \beta\,]^s + 2ms\,[1 + p_2]^c\,.$$

- The expected probability of two random data-model pairings being consistent p_2 is given by

$$p_2 = \left[\frac{\kappa}{m}\right]^2$$

  where κ is a constant (usually less than 1) that can be derived from properties of the object and noise characteristics.

- If all s sensory measurements are known to lie on a single object with m equal sized features, the sensory data is distributed uniformly, and if the noise is small enough, then the expected amount of search needed to find the interpretation is bounded by

$$m^2 \le N_s \le m^2 + ams$$

  where a is a constant that depends on the object characteristics and the amount of noise in the sensory measurements.

- If c of the s sensory measurements lie on an object with m equal sized features, the sensory data is distributed uniformly, and if the noise is small enough, then the expected amount of search needed to find the interpretations, is bounded by an expression of order

$$O\left(N_s^*\right) = m[1 + \gamma]^s + ms2^c + \delta m^6 + m^2 s^2[1 + \mu]^c$$

  and is bounded below by an expression of order

$$o\left(N_s^*\right) = m2^c + ms$$

  where γ, δ are constants that depend on the object characteristics and the amount of sensor noise, $\gamma < 1$.

- If the scene clutter and the noise in the data is such that

$$\frac{s}{m} < \frac{2}{\kappa^2}$$

where κ is a constant derived from characteristics of the object and the noise in the measurements, then early termination has an expected search that is of order

$$O\left(W(s)\right) = amts\frac{s}{c}$$

and

$$o\left(W(s)\right) = ms\frac{s}{c}.$$

Summary

Both the empirical testing and the formal analyses imply that constrained search methods can be quite effective at finding instances of objects in cluttered noisy data. As a consequence, the RAF system has been used as an integral part of a hand-eye system [Lozano-Pérez et al. 1987], as part of a robot navigation system Drumheller [1987], and as part of an industrial parts inspection system [Lozano-Pérez, Grimson & White 1987].

References

Ayache, N., and O. D. Faugeras [1986], "HYPER: A new approach for the recognition and positioning of two-dimensional objects," *IEEE Trans. Pat. Anal. Mach. Intel.*, vol. 8, no. 1 pp. 44–54.

Baird H. [1986], *Model-Based Image Matching Using Location*, MIT Press, Cambridge, MA.

Baker H. H. [1982], "Depth from edge and intensity based stereo," Stanford University Technical Report STAN-CS-82-930.

Ballard, D. H. [1981], "Generalizing the Hough transform to detect arbitrary patterns," *Pattern Recogn.*, vol. 13, no. 2, pp. 111–122.

Bolles, R. C., and R. A. Cain [1982], "Recognizing and locating partially visible objects: The Local-Feature-Focus method," *Int. J. Robotics Res.*, vol. 1, no. 3, pp. 57–82.

Bolles, R. C., and P. Horaud [1986], "3DPO: A three-dimensional part orientation system," *Int. J. Robotics Res.*, vol. 5, no. 3, pp. 3–26.

This chapter describes research done at the Artificial Intelligence Laboratory of the Massachusetts Institute of Technology. Support for the laboratory's artificial intelligence research is provided in part by an Office of Naval Research University Research Initiative grant under contract N00014-86-K-0685, in part by the Advanced Research Projects Agency of the Department of Defense under Army contract number DACA76-85-C-0010 and in part by DARPA under Office of Naval Research contract N00014-85-K-0124. The author is also supported by the Matsushita Chair of Electrical Engineering.

Davis L. S. [1982], "Hierarchical generalized Hough transforms and line-segment based generalized Hough transforms," *Pattern Recognition*, vol. 15, pp. 277.

Drumheller, M. [1987], "Mobile robot localization using sonar," *IEEE Trans. Pat. Anal. Mach. Intel.*, vol. 9, no. 2, pp. 325–332.

Faugeras, O. D., and M. Hebert [1983], "A 3-D recognition and positioning algorithm using geometrical matching between primitive surfaces," *Proc. Eighth Int. Joint Conf. Artificial Intell.*, Karlsruhe, W. Germany, pp. 996–1002.

Goad, C. [1983], "Special purpose automatic programming for 3d model-based vision," *Proceedings of DARPA Image Understanding Workshop.*

Grimson, W. E. L. [1981], *From Images to Surfaces: A Computational Study of the Human Early Visual System*, MIT Press, Cambridge, MA.

Grimson, W. E. L., and T. Lozano-Pérez [1984], "Model-based recognition and localization from sparse range or tactile data," *Int. J. Robotics Res.*, vol. 3, no. 3, pp. 3–35.

Grimson, W. E. L., and T. Lozano-Pérez [1987], "Localizing overlapping parts by searching the interpretation tree," *IEEE Trans. Patt. Anal. and Mach. Intel.*, vol. 9, no. 4, pp. 469–482.

Grimson, W. E. L. [1989a], "On the recognition of curved objects in two dimensions," *IEEE Trans. Pat. Anal. Mach. Intel.*, vol. 11, no. 6, pp. 632–643.

Grimson, W. E. L. [1989b], "On the recognition of parameterized 2d objects," *International Journal of Computer Vision*, vol. 3, pp. 353–372.

Grimson, W. E. L. [1989c], "The combinatorics of object recognition in cluttered environments using constrained search," *Artificial Intelligence*, to appear. See also Report AIM-1019, Artificial Intelligence Laboratory, Massachusetts Institute of Technology, Cambridge, MA.

Grimson, W. E. L. [1989d], "The combinatorics of heuristic search termination for object recognition in cluttered environments," Report AIM-1111, Artificial Intelligence Laboratory, Massachusetts Institute of Technology, Cambridge, MA.

Grimson, W. E. L., and D. P. Huttenlocher [1989a], *On the sensitivity of the Hough transform for object recognition*, IEEE Pattern Analysis and Machine Intelligence, (to appear).

Grimson, W. E. L., and D. P. Huttenlocher [1989b], "On the Verification of Hypothesized Matches in Model-Based Recognition," Report AIM-1110, Artificial Intelligence Laboratory, Massachusetts Institute of Technology, Cambridge, MA.

Hillis, W. D. [1982], "A high resolution image touch sensor," *Int. Journ. Robotics Research*, vol. 1, no. 2, pp. 33–44.

Hough, P. V. C. [1962], "Methods and means for recognizing complex patterns," U.S. Patent 3069654.

Huttenlocher D. P. [1988], "Three-dimensional recognition of solid objects from a two-dimensional image," Report AI-TR-1045, Artificial Intelligence Laboratory, Massachusetts Institute of Technology, Cambridge, MA.

Huttenlocher, D. P., and S. Ullman [1987], "Object recognition using alignment," *Proc. First International Conference on Computer Vision*, London, pp. 478–484.

Ikeuchi K. [1981], "Determining surface orientations of specular surfaces by using the photometric stereo method," *IEEE Trans. Pattern Analysis and Machine Intelligence*, vol. 3, no. 6, pp. 661–669.

Lamdan, Y., J. T. Schwartz, and H. J. Wolfson [1988], "Object recognition by affine invariant matching," *Proc. Comp. Vision and Patt. Recog.*, pp. 335–344.

Lewis, R. A., and A. R. Johnston [1977], "A scanning laser range finder for a robotic vehicle," *Fifth Intl. Joint Conf. on Artificial Intell.*, pp. 762–768.

Lowe, D. G. [1987], "Three-dimensional object recognition from single two-dimensional images," *Artificial Intelligence*, vol. 31, pp. 355–395.

Lozano-Pérez, T., W. E. L. Grimson, and S. J. White [1987], "Finding cylinders in range data," *IEEE Computer Society Int. Conf. on Robotics and Automation*, Raleigh, NC, pp. 202–207.

Lozano-Pérez, T., J. L. Jones, E. Mazer, P. A. O'Donnell, W. E. L. Grimson, P. Tournassoud, and A. Lanusse [1987], "Handey: A robot system that recognizes, plans, and manipulates," *IEEE Computer Society Int. Conf. on Robotics and Automation*, Raleigh, NC, pp. 843–849.

Mayhew, J. E. W., and J. P. Frisby [1981], "Psychophysical and computational studies towards a theory of human stereopsis," *Artificial Intelligence*, vol. 17, pp. 349-386.

Merlin, P. M., and D. J. Farber [1975], "A parallel mechanism for detecting curves in picture," *IEEE Trans. Comput.*, vol. 24, pp. 96–98.

Nitzan, D., A. E. Brain, and R. O. Duda [1977], "The measurement and use of reflectance and range data in scene analysis," *Proc. of IEEE*, vol. 65, pp. 206–220.

Overton, K. J., and T. Williams [1981], "Tactile sensation for robots," *Proc. IJCAI*, Vancouver, Canada, pp. 791–795.

Pollard S. B., J. E. W. Mayhew, and J. P. Frisby [1985], "PMF: A stereo correspondence algorithm using a disparity gradient limit," *Perception*, vol. 14, pp. 449–470.

Raibert, M. H., and J. E. Tanner [1982], "Design and implementation of a VLSI tactile sensing computer," *Int. Journ. Robotics Research.*, vol. 1, no. 3, pp. 3–18.

Schwartz, J. T., and M. Sharir [1987], "Identification of partially obscured objects in two and three dimensions by matching noisy characteristic curves," *Int. Journ. Robotics Research*, vol. 6, no. 2, pp. 29–44.

Shirai, Y., and M. Suwa [1971], "Recognition of polyhedrons with a range finder," *Second Intl. Joint Conf. on Artificial Intell..*

Silberberg, T. M., L. S. Davis, and D. A. Harwood [1984], "An iterative Hough procedure for three-dimensional object recognition," *Pattern Recognition*, vol. 17, no. 6, pp. 612–629.

Silberberg, T. M., D. A. Harwood, and L. S. Davis [1986], "Object recognition using oriented model points," *Computer Vision, Graphics, and Image Processing*, vol. 35, pp. 47–71.

Sklansky, J. [1978], "On the Hough Technique for curve detection," *IEEE Trans. Comput.*, vol. 27, pp. 923–926.

Stockman, G. [1987], "Object recognition and localization via pose clustering," *Comp. Vision, Graphics, and Image Proc.*, vol. 40, pp. 361–387.

Thompson, D. W., and J. L. Mundy [1987], "Three-dimensional model matching from an unconstrained viewpoint," *Proceedings of the International Conference on Robotics and Automation*, Raleigh, NC, pp. 208–220.

Turney, J. L., T. N. Mudge, and R. A. Volz [1985], "Recognizing partially occluded parts," *IEEE Trans. Pat. Anal. Mach. Intel.*, vol. 7, no. 4, pp. 410–421.

Woodham, R. J. [1980], "Photometric method for determining surface orientation from multiple images," *Optical Engineering*, vol. 19, no. 1, pp. 139–144.

37

In the previous chapter, Grimson shows how to use local measurements of position and surface orientation to recognize two-dimensional and three-dimensional objects by way of an elegant constrained search. Only objects with known sizes and shapes can be recognized, however.

In this chapter Grimson shows how to generalize his approach such that knowledge about size and shape need not be so procrustean. His revised program recognizes objects in spite of scaling, stretching, or the relative rotation of their parts. Thus, once Grimson's generalized program has seen one washer, or bolt, or pair of scissors, or Sequoia tree, it has seen them all.

On the Recognition of Parameterized 2D Objects

W. Eric L. Grimson

The general problem considered in this chapter is how to locate a known object from sensory data, when that object may be occluded by other (possibly unknown) objects. In previous work [Grimson & Lozano-Pérez 1984, 1987] we described a recognition system, called Recognition and Attitude Finder (RAF), that identifies and locates objects from noisy, occluded data. In that work, we concentrated on a particular subclass of rigid models. If the sensory data provided two-dimensional geometric data, for example intensity edges from a visual image, we considered the recognition of objects that consisted of sets of linear segments, or equivalently, polygonal objects in which some edges are not included. If the sensory data was three-dimensional, we considered the recognition of objects that consisted of sets of planar fragments, or equivalently, polyhedral objects in which some of the faces are not included.

Of course, we cannot guarantee that the system will be confronted only with rigid polyhedral objects of known size. The Recognition and Attitude Finder has been extended to deal with curved objects, in the two-dimensional case [Grimson 1987]. In this chapter, we consider extensions of our method to deal with families of objects that are characterized by sets of free parameters. We do the extension for the case of two-dimensional objects, similar methods apply to the three-dimensional case.

Recognition as Constrained Search

Before dealing with the problem of parameterized parts, we briefly review the recognition method used [Grimson & Lozano Pérez 1984, 1987].

Definition of a solution

Suppose we are given a set of data fragments, obtained from the boundary of an object or objects, and measured in a coordinate system centered about the sensor. Suppose we are also given a set of object models, specified by a set of faces (whose definition we will make formal shortly) measured in a local coordinate frame specific to the model. A solution to the recognition problem consists of a three-tuple

$$\langle \texttt{object}_i, \{(d_{i_1}, m_{j_1}), (d_{i_2}, m_{j_2}), \ldots (d_{i_k}, m_{j_k})\}, (R, \mathbf{v}_0) \rangle \,,$$

where $\texttt{object}_i$ identifies which object from a library of known objects, the d, m pairings are associations of a subset of the sensory data d with model faces m from $\texttt{object}_i$ and R is a rotation matrix, and $\mathbf{v}_0$ is a translation vector such that a vector $\mathbf{v}_m$ in model coordinates is transformed into a vector $\mathbf{v}_d$ in sensor coordinates by

$$\dot{\mathbf{v}}_d = R\mathbf{v}_m + \mathbf{v}_0 \,,$$

and where this coordinate frame transformation maps the model from its local coordinate frame into the sensor coordinate frame in such a manner that each data fragment correctly lies on its assigned model face.

As has been described in the previous chapter we approach the recognition problem as one of search. Thus, we first focus on finding legitimate pairings of data and model fragments, for some subset of the sensory data. We chose to structure this search process as a constrained depth first search, using an *interpretation tree* (IT). Each node of the tree describes a partial interpretation of the data, and implicitly contains a set of pairings of data fragments and model faces. Nodes at the first level of the tree define assignments for the first data fragment, nodes at the second level define assignments for the first and second data fragments, and so on. Each node branches at the next level in up to $n + 1$ ways, where n is the number of model faces in the object. The last branch is a *wild card* or *null* branch and has the effect of excluding the data fragment corresponding to the current level of the tree from part of the interpretation.

Given s data fragments, any leaf of the tree specifies an interpretation

$$\{(d_1, m_{j_1}), (d_2, m_{j_2}), \ldots (d_s, m_{j_s})\} \,,$$

where some of the m_{j_h} may be the wild card character. By excluding such matches, the leaf yields a partial interpretation

$$\left\{(d_{i_1}, m_{j_{i_1}}), (d_{i_2}, m_{j_{i_2}}), \ldots (d_{i_k}, m_{j_{i_k}})\right\} \,,$$

where $1 \leq i_1 < i_2 < \ldots < i_k$ but these indices may not include the entire set from 1 to s. This interpretation may then be used to solve for a rigid, scaled transformation that maps model faces into corresponding data fragments, if such a transformation exists. Thus, by searching for leaves of the tree and testing that the interpretation there yields a legal

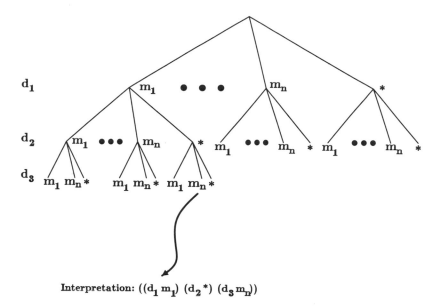

Interpretation: $((d_1\, m_1)\ (d_2\, *)\ (d_3\, m_n))$

Figure 1. An interpretation tree. Each node of the tree defines a partial interpretation, where the level of each ancestor defines a sensory data point, and the branch leading to each such node defines the corresponding model face. An example of a partial interpretation is shown, where d_i denotes the ith data point and m_k denotes the kth model face.

transformation, we can find possible instances of object models in the data (see figure 1).

Because this search process is inherently an exponential problem, the key to an efficient solution is to use constraints to remove large subtrees from consideration without having explicitly to explore them. In this chapter, the object models and the sensory data consist of linear edge or face fragments. The constraints include the following:

- The length of a data fragment must be smaller than the length of a corresponding model fragment, up to some bounded measurement error.
- The angle between the normals to a pair of data fragments must differ from the angle between the normals of the corresponding model fragments by no more than a bounded measurement error.
- The range of distances between two data fragments must lie within the range of distances of the corresponding model fragments, where the model range has been expanded to account for measurement errors.
- The range of components of a vector spanning the two data fragments in the direction of each of the fragment's normal must lie within the corresponding range of components for vectors spanning the model fragments, modulo measurement error.

In Grimson [1988] we extended these constraints to include curved objects in two dimensions.

The constraints reduce the search

Given these unary and binary constraints, the constrained search process can be straightforwardly specified. Suppose the search process is currently at some node at level k in the interpretation tree and with a consistent partial interpretation given by

$$\{(d_1, m_{j_1}), (d_2, m_{j_2}), \ldots (d_k, m_{j_k})\}.$$

We now consider the next data fragment d_{k+1}, and its possible assignment to model face $m_{j_{k+1}}$, where j_{k+1} varies from 1 to $n+1$.

The following rules hold:

- If $m_{j_{k+1}}$ is the wild card match, then the new interpretation

$$\{(d_1, m_{j_1}), (d_2, m_{j_2}), \ldots (d_{k+1}, m_{j_{k+1}})\}$$

   is consistent, and we continue downward in our search.

- If $m_{j_{k+1}}$ is a real model edge segment, we must verify that the length constraint holds for matching d_{k+1} to $m_{j_{k+1}}$, and that the angle, distance and component constraints hold for $(d_{k+1}, m_{j_{k+1}})$ and (d_i, m_{j_i}), for $1 \leq i \leq k$.

- If all of these constraints are true, then

$$\{(d_1, m_{j_1}), (d_2, m_{j_2}), \ldots (d_{k+1}, m_{j_{k+1}})\}$$

   is a consistent partial interpretation, and we continue our depth first search. If one of them is false, then the partial interpretation is inconsistent. In this case, we increment the model face index j_{k+1} by 1 and try again, until $j_{k+1} = n+1$.

If the search process is currently at some node at level k in the interpretation tree, and has an inconsistent partial interpretation given by

$$\{(d_1, m_{j_1}), (d_2, m_{j_2}), \ldots (d_k, m_{j_k})\}$$

then it is in the process of backtracking. If $j_k = n+1$ (the wild card) we backtrack up another level, otherwise we increment j_k and continue.

Model tests

Once the search process reaches a leaf of the interpretation tree, we have accounted for all of the data points. We are now ready to determine if the interpretation is in fact globally valid. To do this, we solve for a rigid transformation mapping points $\mathbf{v}_m$ in model coordinates into points $\mathbf{v}_d$ in sensor coordinates,

$$\mathbf{v}_d = R\mathbf{v}_m + \mathbf{v}_0$$

where R is a rotation matrix, and $\mathbf{v}_0$ is a translation vector. We can solve for this transformation in a number of ways as shown in Grimson and Lozano-Pérez [1984, 1987] and Ayache and Faugeras [1986].

Given such a transformation, which is usually found using some type of least squares fit, we must then ensure that the interpretation actually satisfies it. We do this by considering each of the data fragments associated with a real model fragment in the interpretation, and transforming the associated model fragment by the computed transform. For each such fragment, we then verify that the transformed fragment differs in position and orientation from its associated data fragment by amounts that are less than some acceptable error bounds. These bounds on transform error can be obtained from the predefined bounds on the sensor error [Grimson 1986b]. Any interpretation that passes such a model test is a consistent interpretation of the data.

Additional search reductions

While the constrained search technique described above will succeed in finding all consistent interpretations of the sensory data, for a given object model, it is not particularly computationally efficient. This is mostly due to the problem of segmenting the data to determine subsets that belong to a single object. Indeed, if all of the sensory data do belong to one object, the described method is known to be quite efficient, as has been verified both empirically [Grimson & Lozano-Pérez 1984, 1987] and theoretically [Grimson 1986, 1988]. In order to improve the efficiency of the method, we can add two additional methods to our search process, both previously discussed for the case of linear fragments in Grimson and Lozano-Pérez [1987], and extended to circular segments in Grimson [1987].

The first is to use a parameter hashing scheme, such as a Hough transform, to hypothesize small subspaces of the entire search space that are likely to contain an interpretation. The second is to use a measure of matching, such as the portion of the object perimeter correctly accounted for by the matched sensory data, to prematurely terminate the search process. In this chapter, we use only the second heuristic.

Parameterized Families

In dealing with parameterized families, we restrict our attention to two dimensional objects, composed of sets of linear edge fragments. Each *linear edge fragment* consists of two endpoints, and a unit vector normal to the line between them and pointing away from the interior of the object. Formally, this is given by
$$\text{linear}_i = (\hat{\mathbf{n}}_i, (\mathbf{b}_i, \mathbf{e}_i)).$$

Note that a point on the edge can be represented by

$$\hat{\mathbf{n}}_i \qquad \text{and} \qquad \mathbf{b}_i + \alpha_i \hat{\mathbf{t}}_i, \quad \alpha_i \in [0, \ell_i]$$

where $\hat{\mathbf{n}}_i$ is the unit normal vector, $\hat{\mathbf{t}}_i$ is a unit tangent vector, oriented so that it points from $\mathbf{b}$ to $\mathbf{e}$, and α_i can vary from 0 to the length of the edge ℓ_i (see figure 2).

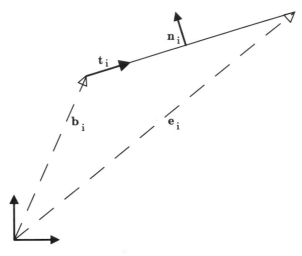

Figure 2. The representation of an edge. An edge is given by the pair

$$\hat{\mathbf{n}}_i \qquad \text{and} \qquad \mathbf{b}_i + \alpha_i \hat{\mathbf{t}}_i, \quad \alpha_i \in [0, \ell_i]$$

where $\hat{\mathbf{n}}_i$ is a unit normal vector, $\hat{\mathbf{t}}_i$ is a unit tangent vector, oriented so that it points from $\mathbf{b}$ to $\mathbf{e}$, $\mathbf{b}_i$ is a vector to the base point of the edge, and α_i can vary from 0 to the length of the edge ℓ_i.

Examples of parameterized objects

While our previous chapter has illustrated the utility of our approach to the problem of rigid objects, we are interested here in extending the method to deal with parameterized objects. We consider a number of different possibilities.

◇ Scale

Perhaps the simplest example of a parameterized family is that defined by a rigid object that can undertake a range of possible sizes, that is, the shape of the object is fixed, but the overall scale factor can vary. Many techniques for object recognition and localization can easily deal with this case, because the scale factor can simply be considered part of the coordinate frame transformation required to map the model patches into their corresponding sensed patches.

◇ Coordinate-frame transformations

A more interesting class of parameterized objects are those that involve a limited number of moving parts. A good example is a pair of scissors, which has a single degree of freedom, namely the rotation of the two blades relative to a common joint. We would like to be able to recognize the scissors, independent of the relative orientation of the blades, and without requiring a different model to represent each orientation. This class could further be extended to include scissors of different sizes.

◇ Stretching deformations

A third class of parameterized objects are those in which subparts can stretch along an axis. An example would be a family of hammers, for which there is a generic handle shape, but which can stretch along the axis of the handle, as indicated in figure 3.

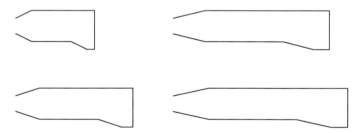

Figure 3. A set of parameterized subparts, in which the generic shape in the upper left is stretched along the axis of the shape.

Possible approaches

A large number of methods have been explored in the literature for recognizing rigid objects, both in two dimensions and in three. When considering parameterized objects, like those just described, far fewer methods have been considered. In particular, while a number of schemes have been suggested for representing parameterized objects, such as generalized cylinders and superquadrics, at this point very few actual recognition engines based on such parameterized representations have been demonstrated. The best known such system is probably ACRONYM [Brooks 1981]. Within the context of our approach to recognition, there are two distinct alternatives for extending the method to handle parameterized parts, both related in a global sense to the approach taken by Brooks [1981].

The first approach is to extend our geometric constraints to directly incorporate the free parameters. In essence, the approach taken in the Recognition and Attitude Finder relies on finding coordinate-frame independent measurements, applicable either to single elements from the model or data, or to pairs of model or data elements. Because they are independent of the particular coordinate frame, these measurements capture aspects of the relative shape of an object. As a consequence, by taking the same measures on elements for the data and elements of the model, we can determine the consistency of matching data elements to model elements, simply by determining whether the set of measurements are consistent, modulo error in the data. As such, the Recognition and Attitude Finder is basically a constraint satisfaction system. To extend the system to deal with parameterized parts, we need to extend our constraint system to determine ranges of consistent parameters, rather than simply determining consistency. In this case, the search process would become a constraint propagation technique, in which the current range of possible values for each of the parameters would be passed from a parent node of the IT to each of its children. At each new node, the constraints imposed by matching the new data patch to its assigned model patch would be used to refine the range of free parameters, which would then be passed to that node's children. If any parameter is reduced to an empty range of values, the interpretation is inconsistent and the search along that subtree can be terminated.

The main difficulty with this approach is finding a clean way of representing the parameterized constraints, especially in a manner that will easily allow the computing and updating of feasible ranges for each of the parameters. Consider a pair of scissors, where the parameter to be determined is the angle between the two blades. If two data fragments are being considered as belonging to two model fragments that are part of the same rigid subpart, then the constraints are the same as in our earlier approach. They either indicate consistency, in which case the range of possible values for the rotation parameter remains the same as it was before considering this pairing, or they indicate inconsistency, in which case the search must backtrack. On the other hand, suppose two data fragments are being considered as belonging to model fragments on different rigid subparts. In this case, we need a means of expressing the range of possible values for the rotation parameter as an explicit function of the relative geometry of the two model fragments and the two data fragments. This may prove difficult to obtain.

The second approach is to break the object model into rigid subparts, all of which are connected to a global model-based coordinate frame through a series of coordinate frame transformations. Each subpart can then be recognized by application of our earlier technique, including a free scale parameter. Once the subparts have been recognized and located, we must check that they are consistent by confirming that the parts satisfy a set of predetermined global coordinate-frame constraints.

Consider the earlier example of a pair of scissors, with a free overall scale factor. In this approach, we treat each blade of the scissors as a rigid subpart. Thus, we attempt to locate instances of the right and left blade in the sensory data. Once we have done this, we then confirm that the subparts are parts of a consistent whole. In the case of the scissors, this would involve checking two things:

1   The scale factor associated with each blade is roughly the same, and

2   The transformations from model coordinates to sensory coordinates associated with each blade are such that the position, in sensor coordinates, of the pin joining the two blades is roughly the same (that is, the located instances of the blades in the data are rotated about the expected common axis).

The advantage of this second method is that the geometric constraints remain simple, yet combinatorially powerful.

Note that we can apply our search for rigid subparts in several ways. The simplest is to search the data independently for each rigid subpart, then test all possible combinations of subparts for consistent wholes. A more efficient method would be to first search the data for one subpart (for example, the largest). For each candidate solution found in the data, we can then use limits on the ranges of the parameters to restrict the possible positions of the other subparts in the sensory data. Using this reduced data set, we can then search for instances of the other subparts, testing each instance for global consistency. If no instance of the initial seed subpart is found, (for example, it is occluded in the data) we can then consider the next seed subpart (for example, the next largest) and proceed as before.

In this chapter, we explore both options. We first derive the set of geometric constraints on interpretations, and then illustrate the search process on some simple examples.

Scale factors

Perhaps the simplest family of objects to consider are those in which a single, rigid object of known shape can undergo an arbitrary global scaling, within some limits. We need to consider how to adjust the recognition process, so that it can not only recognize where an object is in the data, but also its overall size.

We assume that the scale factor is applied to the data, so that the transformation from a point in model coordinates, $\mathbf{v}_m$, to sensor coordinates, $\mathbf{v}_d$, is given by

$$s\mathbf{v}_d = R_\theta \mathbf{v}_m + \mathbf{v}_0$$

where s is a scale factor, θ is an angle, R_θ is a rotation matrix of angle θ and $\mathbf{v}_0$ is a translation vector.

◇ Length constraint

If we are matching data edge d_i, given by

$$(\hat{\mathbf{n}}_i, (\mathbf{b}_i, \mathbf{e}_i))$$

to model edge m_p, given by

$$\left(\hat{\mathbf{N}}_p, (\mathbf{B}_p, \mathbf{E}_p)\right)$$

then the length of the data edge must be less than the length of the corresponding model edge, modulo measurement error. We let ℓ_i denote the length of the data fragment, and L_p denote the corresponding length of the model fragment, where these lengths are given by

$$\ell_i = |\mathbf{b}_i - \mathbf{e}_i|, \qquad L_p = |\mathbf{B}_p - \mathbf{E}_p|.$$

Then we must have

$$s\ell_i \le L_p + \epsilon_l \qquad \forall s$$

where ϵ_L is a predefined upper bound on the amount of error inherent in measuring the length of an edge.

We can define

$$\textbf{scaled-length-constraint}(i, p) = \left[0, \frac{L_p + \epsilon_L}{\ell_i}\right]$$

that is, the range of scales consistent with this assignment. This constraint returns a (possibly empty) range of values.

◇ Angle constraint

Let θ_{ij} denote the angle between $\hat{\mathbf{n}}_i$ and $\hat{\mathbf{n}}_j$, and let Θ_{pq} denote the angle between $\hat{\mathbf{N}}_p$ and $\hat{\mathbf{N}}_q$. We let

binary-angle-constraint(i, j, p, q) = True iff $\theta_{ij} \in [\Theta_{pq} - 2\epsilon_a, \Theta_{pq} + 2\epsilon_a]$

where all arithmetic comparisons are performed modulo 2π and where ϵ_a is an upper bound on the amount of error inherent in determining the direction of a normal.

◇ Component constraint

The third constraint concerns the separation of the two edge fragments. In particular, we consider the range of components of a vector between the two edge fragments, in the direction of each of the edge normals. Algebraically, this is expressed by the dot product

$$\langle \mathbf{b}_i + \alpha_i \hat{\mathbf{t}}_i - \mathbf{b}_j - \alpha_j \hat{\mathbf{t}}_j, \hat{\mathbf{n}}_i \rangle$$

which reduces to

$$\langle \mathbf{b}_i - \mathbf{b}_j, \hat{\mathbf{n}}_i \rangle - \alpha_j \langle \hat{\mathbf{t}}_j, \hat{\mathbf{n}}_i \rangle \qquad \alpha_j \in [0, \ell_j].$$

Of course, there is an equivalent constraint for components in the direction of $\hat{\mathbf{n}}_j$. Note that this expression actually determines a range of values, with extrema when $\alpha_j = 0, \ell_j$. We denote this by

$$d^\perp_{\ell,ij} = \min\{\langle \mathbf{b}_i - \mathbf{b}_j, \hat{\mathbf{n}}_i \rangle, \langle \mathbf{b}_i - \mathbf{b}_j, \hat{\mathbf{n}}_i \rangle - \ell_j \langle \hat{\mathbf{t}}_j, \hat{\mathbf{n}}_i \rangle\}$$
$$d^\perp_{h,ij} = \max\{\langle \mathbf{b}_i - \mathbf{b}_j, \hat{\mathbf{n}}_i \rangle, \langle \mathbf{b}_i - \mathbf{b}_j, \hat{\mathbf{n}}_i \rangle - \ell_j \langle \hat{\mathbf{t}}_j, \hat{\mathbf{n}}_i \rangle\}$$

These ranges can be computed both for pairs of data edges and pairs of model edges. In the ideal case, consistency will hold only if the data range is contained within the model range (because the data edges may correspond to only parts of the model edges). As in the case of the other constraints, we also need to account for error in the measurements. We derive a simple method for doing this below.

Consider the base case, shown in figure 4a. The perpendicular distance from the endpoint of one edge to the other edge is shown as $D^\perp$. In figure 4b, the edge is rotated by ϵ_a about its midpoint, and the new perpendicular distance X is shown. We need to relate X to measurable values. We already have $D^\perp$. We can also measure S_ℓ, the distance from the midpoint of the edge to the perpendicular dropped from the endpoint of the other edge, as shown. Straightforward trigonometry then yields the new distance

$$X = \left(D_\ell^\perp \cos \epsilon_a - S_\ell \sin \epsilon_a \right).$$

Because the position of the second edge is not known exactly, we must adjust this expression, to yield one limit on the range of possible measurements:

$$D^\perp_{\ell,pq} = D_\ell^\perp \cos \epsilon_a - S_\ell \sin \epsilon_a - \epsilon_p.$$

The other extreme is shown in figure 4c. Trigonometric manipulation yields the following upper bound

$$D^\perp_{h,pq} = D_h^\perp \cos \epsilon_a + S_h \sin \epsilon_a + \epsilon_p.$$

Thus, given two model edges indexed by p, q, we can compute a range of possible measurements (modulo known error bounds), by using $D^\perp_{\ell,pq}$ and $D^\perp_{h,pq}$ computed over all the endpoints of the edges. We denote this range by $[M^\perp_{\ell,pq}, M^\perp_{h,pq}]$.

Given a range of projections of data edge i onto edge j, and a corresponding range of projections for model edge p onto model edge q, we need to determine bounds on s such that

$$[sd^\perp_{\ell,ij}, sd^\perp_{h,ij}] \subseteq [M^\perp_{\ell,pq}, M^\perp_{h,pq}].$$

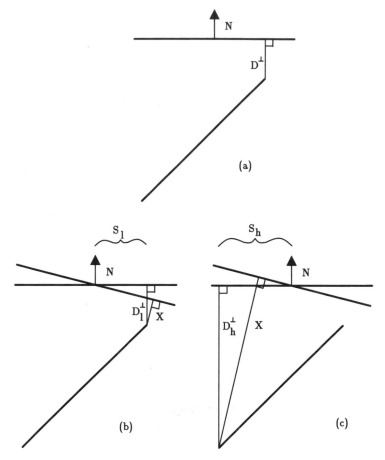

Figure 4. Errors in computing the direction constraint. (a) The component of a vector from one endpoint in the direction of the other edge's normal is given by the perpendicular distance $\mathbf{D}^{\perp}$ to the extended edge. (b) Because the actual normal is only accurate to within ϵ_a, one extreme case is given by rotating the extended edge about its midpoint by that amount and finding the new perpendicular distance. (c) The other extreme is obtained by considering the other endpoint.

The following cases hold:

$$
s_\ell \geq \begin{cases}
\dfrac{M_{h,pq}^{\perp}}{\langle \mathbf{b}_j - \mathbf{b}_i, \hat{\mathbf{n}}_j \rangle} & \text{if } \langle \hat{\mathbf{t}}_i, \hat{\mathbf{n}}_j \rangle > 0 \text{ and } \langle \mathbf{b}_j - \mathbf{b}_i, \hat{\mathbf{n}}_j \rangle < 0 \\[3.5ex]
\dfrac{M_{\ell,pq}^{\perp}}{\langle \mathbf{b}_j - \mathbf{b}_i, \hat{\mathbf{n}}_j \rangle - \ell_i \langle \hat{\mathbf{t}}_i, \hat{\mathbf{n}}_j \rangle} & \text{if } \langle \hat{\mathbf{t}}_i, \hat{\mathbf{n}}_j \rangle > 0 \text{ and } \langle \mathbf{b}_j - \mathbf{b}_i, \hat{\mathbf{n}}_j \rangle - \ell_i \langle \hat{\mathbf{t}}_i, \hat{\mathbf{n}}_j \rangle > 0 \\[3.5ex]
\dfrac{M_{\ell,pq}^{\perp}}{\langle \mathbf{b}_j - \mathbf{b}_i, \hat{\mathbf{n}}_j \rangle} & \text{if } \langle \hat{\mathbf{t}}_i, \hat{\mathbf{n}}_j \rangle < 0 \text{ and } \quad \langle \mathbf{b}_j - \mathbf{b}_i, \hat{\mathbf{n}}_j \rangle > 0 \\[3.5ex]
\dfrac{M_{h,pq}^{\perp}}{\langle \mathbf{b}_j - \mathbf{b}_i, \hat{\mathbf{n}}_j \rangle - \ell_i \langle \hat{\mathbf{t}}_i, \hat{\mathbf{n}}_j \rangle} & \text{if } \langle \hat{\mathbf{t}}_i, \hat{\mathbf{n}}_j \rangle < 0 \text{ and } \langle \mathbf{b}_j - \mathbf{b}_i, \hat{\mathbf{n}}_j \rangle - \ell_i \langle \hat{\mathbf{t}}_i, \hat{\mathbf{n}}_j \rangle < 0
\end{cases}
$$

$$s_h \leq \begin{cases} \dfrac{M_{h,pq}^{\perp}}{\langle \mathbf{b}_j - \mathbf{b}_i, \hat{\mathbf{n}}_j \rangle} & \text{if } \langle \hat{\mathbf{t}}_i, \hat{\mathbf{n}}_j \rangle > 0 \text{ and } \langle \mathbf{b}_j - \mathbf{b}_i, \hat{\mathbf{n}}_j \rangle > 0 \\[3mm] \dfrac{M_{\ell,pq}^{\perp}}{\langle \mathbf{b}_j - \mathbf{b}_i, \hat{\mathbf{n}}_j \rangle - \ell_i \langle \hat{\mathbf{t}}_i, \hat{\mathbf{n}}_j \rangle} & \text{if } \langle \hat{\mathbf{t}}_i, \hat{\mathbf{n}}_j \rangle > 0 \text{ and } \langle \mathbf{b}_j - \mathbf{b}_i, \hat{\mathbf{n}}_j \rangle - \ell_i \langle \hat{\mathbf{t}}_i, \hat{\mathbf{n}}_j \rangle < 0 \\[3mm] \dfrac{M_{\ell,pq}^{\perp}}{\langle \mathbf{b}_j - \mathbf{b}_i, \hat{\mathbf{n}}_j \rangle} & \text{if } \langle \hat{\mathbf{t}}_i, \hat{\mathbf{n}}_j \rangle < 0 \text{ and } \qquad \langle \mathbf{b}_j - \mathbf{b}_i, \hat{\mathbf{n}}_j \rangle < 0 \\[3mm] \dfrac{M_{h,pq}^{\perp}}{\langle \mathbf{b}_j - \mathbf{b}_i, \hat{\mathbf{n}}_j \rangle - \ell_i \langle \hat{\mathbf{t}}_i, \hat{\mathbf{n}}_j \rangle} & \text{if } \langle \hat{\mathbf{t}}_i, \hat{\mathbf{n}}_j \rangle < 0 \text{ and } \langle \mathbf{b}_j - \mathbf{b}_i, \hat{\mathbf{n}}_j \rangle - \ell_i \langle \hat{\mathbf{t}}_i, \hat{\mathbf{n}}_j \rangle > 0 \end{cases}$$

Thus, based on the measured and model constraint ranges, we can compute a range of scale factors $[s_{\ell,i,j,p,q}, s_{h,i,j,p,q}]$ for which the assignment of data edges to model edges is consistent. We let

scaled-component-constraint$(i, j, p, q) = [s_{\ell,i,j,p,q}, s_{h,i,j,p,q}]$.

Given these unary and binary constraints, we can now modify our constrained search process. With each node of the search tree, we associate a range of consistent values for the scale parameter, which we will denote $[s_\ell^{(k)}, s_h^{(k)}]$, where k indicates the level of the node in the tree. Suppose the search process is currently at some node at level k in the interpretation tree and with a consistent partial interpretation given by

$$\{(d_1, m_{j_1}), (d_2, m_{j_2}), \ldots (d_k, m_{j_k})\}.$$

We now consider the next data fragment d_{k+1}, and its possible assignment to model fragment $m_{j_{k+1}}$, where j_{k+1} varies from 1 to $n+1$. The following rules hold:

- If $m_{j_{k+1}}$ is the wild card match, then the new interpretation

$$\{(d_1, m_{j_1}), (d_2, m_{j_2}), \ldots (d_{k+1}, m_{j_{k+1}})\}$$

is consistent, and we continue downward in our search, setting

$$[s_\ell^{(k+1)}, s_h^{(k+1)}] = [s_\ell^{(k)}, s_h^{(k)}].$$

- If $m_{j_{k+1}}$ is a linear edge segment, we let

$$[s_\ell^{(k+1)}, s_h^{(k+1)}] = [s_\ell^{(k)}, s_h^{(k)}] \bigcap \textbf{scaled-length-constraint}(k+1, j_{k+1}).$$

If this new range is non-empty, then for all $i \in \{1, \ldots, k\}$ such that d_i is a linear edge fragment, we verify that

$$\textbf{binary-angle-constraint}(i, k+1, j_i, j_{k+1}) = \text{True}$$

and we set

$$[s_\ell^{(k+1)}, s_h^{(k+1)}] = [s_\ell^{(k+1)}, s_h^{(k+1)}]$$

$$\bigcap \textbf{scaled-component-constraint}(i, k+1, j_i, j_{k+1})$$

$$\bigcap \textbf{scaled-component-constraint}(k+1, i, j_{k+1}, j_i).$$

- If $[s_\ell^{(k+1)}, s_h^{(k+1)}]$ is non-empty, then

$$\{(d_1, m_{j_1}), (d_2, m_{j_2}), \ldots (d_{k+1}, m_{j_{k+1}})\}$$

is a consistent partial interpretation, and we continue our depth first search. Otherwise, the partial interpretation is inconsistent. In this case, we increment the model fragment index j_{k+1} by 1 and try again, until $j_{k+1} = n + 1$.

If the search process is currently at some node at level k in the interpretation tree, and has an inconsistent partial interpretation given by

$$\{(d_1, m_{j_1}), (d_2, m_{j_2}), \ldots (d_k, m_{j_k})\}$$

then it is in the process of backtracking. If $j_k = n + 1$ (the wild card) we backtrack up another level, otherwise we increment j_k and continue.

In this manner, we can naturally extend our constrained search method to recognize objects from families in which the free parameter is overall scale. An example is shown in figure 5. In this figure, the two elongated pieces (the largest of which is recognized by the system) have been scaled by factors of roughly 1.5 and 2. from the basic model. The system is able to correctly isolate the data corresponding to the larger of the two objects, and determine its position, orientation, and overall scale.

Rotating subparts

More interesting classes of parameterized families include those in which parts of the object are allowed to move with respect to one another. A good example of such a family is a pair of scissors. A fixed size pair of scissors has a single degree of freedom, namely the rotation of the two blades relative to a common joint. We would like to be able to recognize the scissors, independent of the relative orientation of the blades, and without requiring a different model to represent each orientation. This class could further be extended to include scissors of different sizes.

As we suggested earlier, this could be done by generalizing the constraints to directly take the free parameters into account. However, an easier approach is to break the object up into rigid subparts, and deal with each separately. We illustrate this with our scissors example.

Suppose we treat each blade assembly as a separate part. We choose the location of the common pin as the origin of the model coordinate frame. Using this coordinate frame, we then construct a model of each of the two blades. Now suppose that we run our recognition system on each part. In other words, we first find an instance of the left blade, treated as a separate model, and yielding a transformation $\theta_L, s_L, \mathbf{v}_{0,L}$. We then solve independently for the right blade, yielding a transformation $\theta_R, s_R, \mathbf{v}_{0,R}$. This can proceed in a manner identical to that described previously. To ensure that the two subparts are actually part of a common whole, we need to test that their interpretations are globally consistent. This can be done by means of a simple set of geometric constraints on their respective

Figure 5. Examples of recognition when the free parameter is overall scale. The first part shows a set of linear edges segments, the second shows the overlay of the located object, and the third shows the located object in isolation. The identified object is scaled by roughly a factor of 2 from the actual model.

transformations. In this case, we require

$$s_L \approx s_R$$

$$\mathbf{v}_{0,L} \approx \mathbf{v}_{0,R},$$

that is, the centers of the left and right blade must roughly overlap, and the scale factors of the two blades must be roughly the same. Note that θ_L and θ_R could in principle take on any values. In practice, there is a limited range of orientations that the scissors can take on, so that a third constraint would be

$$\|\theta_L - \theta_R\| \leq C$$

where C is some threshold on the range of rotations, and the arithmetic is done modulo 2π. An example is shown in figure 6, in which the system uses models of a left and a right scissors blade, plus constraints on their

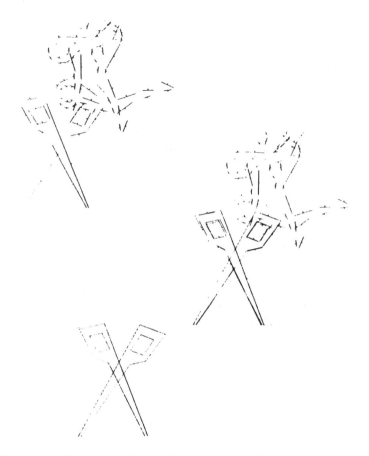

Figure 6. Examples of recognition when the free parameters are overall scale and rotation about a common axis. The first part shows a set of linear edges segments, the second shows the overlay of the located object, and the third shows the located object in isolation. The model consists of a set of rigid subparts, each of which is separately identified, together with constraints on the relationship between the subparts.

relationship to each other, to correctly identify the object.

Note that although the search can be done independently for each part, we can also solve for the location of one of the subparts and then use that position to restrict the possible positions of the second part, thereby directly removing some portions of the sensory data from consideration. We can also use the solution for the first subpart to restrict the values of the free parameters, for example, limiting the range of acceptable scale factors before beginning the search for the second subpart.

When using objects that consist of sets of subparts, we must add another level of backtracking search to our system. To see this, suppose we have found a candidate for the first rigid subpart, but we cannot find an acceptable candidate for the second one. This could be because the second part is not visible, but it is more likely that our candidate solution for the first subpart is incorrect. In this case, we must backtrack to the point in the search for the first subpart at which we found the first candidate, and continue that search. If a second candidate for the first subpart can be found, then we can initialize a new search for the second subpart, and so on.

Subparts that stretch

As a third example, consider a family of tools, say a set of hammers with identical heads, but different handles. Again, we would like to extend our method to recognize both the identity and location of the hammer, and to determine which handle is attached. To model the handles, we assume that a generic shape (such as that shown in the left of figure 3) can stretch by some variable amount along an axis (in the case of the handle in figure 3 this is the axis of symmetry). The problem is to extend the search method to deal with constraints that are themselves parameterized. We do this as follows.

Without loss of generality, we assume that the model part has been oriented so that the axis of stretching is the x-axis in model coordinates. We let α denote the amount of stretching along that axis, with $\alpha = 1$ designating the base case. Note that α is likely to be restricted to some range of values, which may be specified beforehand.

Consider first the constraints on the surface normals. In the case of rigid models, our constraint was that the angle between two data normals must be the same as the angle between the corresponding model normals, to within some error. In the case of stretching parts, the normals will vary relative to one another as a function of the stretching parameter α. Suppose we let θ_{ij} denote the measured angular difference, we let ϵ denote the allowed error range in measuring the angles, and we let Φ_p, Φ_q denote the corresponding model angles, in model coordinates, for the base case $\alpha = 1$ (see figure 7). By appropriate algebraic manipulation, the following cases hold:

- $\Phi_p, \Phi_q \in \{0, \pi, \frac{\pi}{2}, -\frac{\pi}{2}\}$. In this case, we need only check that $\theta_{ij} \in [\Phi_p - \Phi_q - \epsilon, \Phi_p - \Phi_q + \epsilon]$.

- $\Phi_p \in \{0, \pi\}$. $\Phi_q \notin \{0, \pi, \frac{\pi}{2}, -\frac{\pi}{2}\}$. In this case, the stretching factor is given by

$$\alpha = \frac{-\tan \theta_{ij}}{\tan \Phi_q}.$$

A similar case holds when the roles of i and j are reversed.

- $\Phi_p \in \{\frac{\pi}{2}, -\frac{\pi}{2}\}$. $\Phi_q \notin \{0, \pi, \frac{\pi}{2}, -\frac{\pi}{2}\}$. In this case, the stretching factor is given by

$$\alpha = \frac{1}{\tan \theta_{ij} \tan \Phi_q}.$$

  A similar case holds when the roles of i and j are reversed.

- $\tan \Phi_p \neq 0, \tan \Phi_q \neq 0, \tan \theta_{ij} = 0$ In this case, $\alpha = 0$ which indicates an inconsistency.

- All other cases. The stretching factor is given by

$$\alpha = \frac{\tan \Phi_p - \tan \Phi_q}{2 \tan \Phi_p \tan \Phi_q \tan \theta_{ij}} \left[1 + \sqrt{1 - \frac{4 \tan^2 \theta_{ij} \tan \Phi_p \tan \Phi_q}{(\tan \Phi_p - \tan \Phi_q)^2}} \right].$$

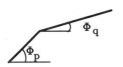 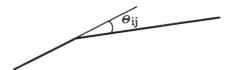

| Base Case Model: $a = 1$ | Measured edges, (stretched by 2) |

Figure 7. The stretch angle constraint. α determines the amount of stretching along the axis. The angles Φ_p and Φ_q denote the edge angles in the model base case, Θ_{ij} the measured angular difference in the data edges, (shown here with a stretch factor of $\alpha = 2$).

Note that the measurement θ_{ij} is actually a range of measurements, due to error in sensory data. Thus, by applying the above computation over a sampling of values for θ_{ij} within this range, we can obtain a range of consistent values for the stretch factor, which we represent by

$$[\alpha_{\ell,i,j,p,q}, \alpha_{h,i,j,p,q}]$$

and we define

$$\mathbf{stretch\text{-}angle\text{-}constraint}(i, j, p, q) = [\alpha_{\ell,i,j,p,q}, \alpha_{h,i,j,p,q}].$$

For the component constraint, we can perform a similar analysis. Suppose we are given two non-parallel data edges, each of which is designated by a base point $\mathbf{b}_i$ and an end point $\mathbf{e}_i$. These are chosen so that the tangent vector pointing from the base point to the end point is 90 deg clockwise from the normal vector $\hat{\mathbf{n}}_i$ to the edge. For these two edges, we can compute the component of the vector $\mathbf{b}_j - \mathbf{b}_i$ in the direction of the normal vector $\hat{\mathbf{n}}_i$, which we call

$$d^{\perp}_{\ell,ij} = \langle \mathbf{b}_j - \mathbf{b}_i, \hat{\mathbf{n}}_i \rangle$$

and the component

$$d^{\perp}_{h,ij} = \langle \mathbf{e}_j - \mathbf{b}_i, \hat{\mathbf{n}}_i \rangle.$$

Then given a corresponding pair of model edges, we can compute similar components

$$M_{\ell,pq}^{\perp} = \left\langle \mathbf{B}_q - \mathbf{B}_p, \hat{\mathbf{N}}_p \right\rangle$$

and

$$M_{h,pq}^{\perp} = \left\langle \mathbf{E}_q - \mathbf{B}_p, \hat{\mathbf{N}}_p \right\rangle.$$

We also let

$$\sigma = \text{signum}\left\{ \left\langle (\mathbf{e}_i - \mathbf{b}_i)^{\perp}, (\mathbf{e}_j - \mathbf{b}_j) \right\rangle \right\}$$

and we let Δx_i and Δy_i denote the x and y components respectively of the vector $\mathbf{e}_i - \mathbf{b}_i$. Then the range of values of the stretch factor α is given by the range spanned by

$$\alpha = \frac{\sigma d_{\ell,ij}^{\perp} |\Delta y_i|}{\sqrt{(M_{\ell,pq}^{\perp})^2 - (d_{\ell,ij}^{\perp})^2 (\Delta x_i)^2}}$$

and

$$\alpha = \frac{\sigma d_{h,ij}^{\perp} |\Delta y_i|}{\sqrt{(M_{h,pq}^{\perp})^2 - (d_{h,ij}^{\perp})^2 (\Delta x_i)^2}}.$$

In fact, one must also allow for error in the measurements, which will yield a range of values for $d_{\ell,ij}^{\perp}$ and $d_{h,ij}^{\perp}$, leading to a larger range of values for the stretching factor α, again denoted

$$[\alpha_{\ell,i,j,p,q}, \alpha_{h,i,j,p,q}].$$

We define

stretch-component-constraint$(i,j,p,q) = [\alpha_{\ell,i,j,p,q}, \alpha_{h,i,j,p,q}].$

Finally, we can also alter the length constraint, which in this case is given by

$$\textbf{stretch-length-constraint}(i,p) = \left[\sqrt{\frac{(L_p - \epsilon_L)^2 - (\Delta x_i)^2}{(\Delta y_i)^2}}, \infty \right].$$

Given these unary and binary constraints, we can now modify our constrained search process. With each node of the search tree, we associate a range of consistent values for the stretch parameter, which we will denote $[\alpha_{\ell}^{(k)}, \alpha_{h}^{(k)}]$, where k indicates the level of the node in the tree. Suppose the search process is currently at some node at level k in the interpretation tree and with a consistent partial interpretation given by

$$\{(d_1, m_{j_1}), (d_2, m_{j_2}), \ldots (d_k, m_{j_k})\}.$$

We now consider the next data fragment d_{k+1}, and its possible assignment to model fragment $m_{j_{k+1}}$, where j_{k+1} varies from 1 to $n+1$.

The following rules hold:

- If $m_{j_{k+1}}$ is the wild card match, then the new interpretation
$$\{(d_1, m_{j_1}), (d_2, m_{j_2}), \ldots (d_{k+1}, m_{j_{k+1}})\}$$
is consistent, and we continue downward in our search, setting
$$[\alpha_\ell^{(k+1)}, \alpha_h^{(k+1)}] = [\alpha_\ell^{(k)}, \alpha_h^{(k)}].$$

- If $m_{j_{k+1}}$ is a linear edge segment, we let
$$[\alpha_\ell^{(k+1)}, \alpha_h^{(k+1)}] = [\alpha_\ell^{(k)}, \alpha_h^{(k)}] \bigcap \textbf{stretch-length-constraint}(k+1, j_{k+1}).$$

  If this new range is non-empty, then for all $i \in \{1, \ldots, k\}$ such that d_i is a linear edge fragment, we let
$$[\alpha_\ell^{(k+1)}, \alpha_h^{(k+1)}] = [\alpha_\ell^{(k+1)}, \alpha_h^{(k+1)}]$$

$$\bigcap \textbf{stretch-component-constraint}(i, k+1, j_i, j_{k+1})$$

$$\bigcap \textbf{stretch-component-constraint}(k+1, i, j_{k+1}, j_i)$$

$$\bigcap \textbf{binary-angle-constraint}(i, k+1, j_i, j_{k+1}).$$

- If
$$[\alpha_\ell^{(k+1)}, \alpha_h^{(k+1)}]$$
is non-empty, then $\{(d_1, m_{j_1}), (d_2, m_{j_2}), \ldots\ldots (d_{k+1}, m_{j_{k+1}})\}$ is a consistent partial interpretation, and we continue our depth first search. Otherwise, the partial interpretation is inconsistent. In this case, we increment the model fragment index j_{k+1} by 1 and try again, until $j_{k+1} = n + 1$.

If the search process is currently at some node at level k in the interpretation tree, and has an inconsistent partial interpretation given by
$$\{(d_1, m_{j_1}), (d_2, m_{j_2}), \ldots (d_k, m_{j_k})\}$$
then it is in the process of backtracking. If $j_k = n + 1$ (the wild card) we backtrack up another level, otherwise we increment j_k and continue.

Figure 8 shows an example of a set of overlapping handles (taken from the family illustrated in figure 3). Each instance of one of the handles is identified and located, including determining the actual value of the stretching parameter.

Combining parameterizations

It is useful to be able to recognize objects that combine different types of parameterizations. For example, consider a pair of shears, that have both a rotational freedom between the two blades, and a stretching freedom along the axis of each blade. We can combine the methods described earlier to deal with this more general problem. An example is shown in figures 9–12.

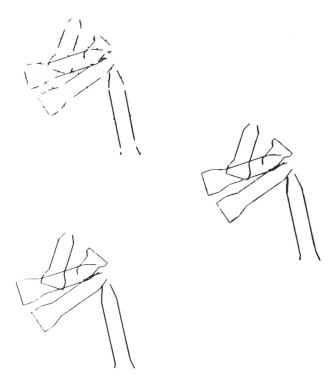

Figure 8. Examples of recognition when the free parameter is stretching along an axis. The first part shows a set of linear edges segments, the second shows the overlay of the located objects, and the third shows the located objects in isolation.

Here, the system correctly solves for the position and orientation of the object, the angle of rotation between the blades and the stretching factor of the blades.

One could also combine stretching and scaling parameters in a single family of objects. This is equivalent to allowing independent stretching in two orthogonal directions. In this case, there are two parameters for which to solve, so that each constraint only specifies a relationship between the parameters. We can define a two-dimensional parameter space, spanned by the stretching parameter in the x and y directions. Initially, this space will contain a region of feasibility, defined by any limits on the range of parameters. As we add each constraint in our search process, a new region of the space will be defined, and the intersection of the two will determine the range of feasible parameter values consistent with the current interpretation. As in the earlier cases, if the region of feasibility becomes empty, the interpretation is inconsistent.

Determining the region of feasibility defined by the constraints is some-

Figure 9. Example of recognition with different types of parameterizations. The object has a rotational free parameter and a stretching free parameter. The figure shows the original image.

what delicate. The length constraint, for example, yields an ellipse centered at the origin of the parameter space, whose complement demarks the feasible region. The angle constraint yields a feasible region that consists of a contiguous family of rays passing through the origin of the parameter space. In principle, one could use such constraints, together with procedures for intersecting regions in the plane to implement a recognition system for parts that stretch, scale and rotate at the same time. We have not yet done so.

Conclusions

This chapter has reported on an extension to an earlier system that uses constrained search to recognize and locate occluded objects from noisy data. The extension handles some classes of parameterized objects, rather than just rigid objects.

The motivation behind this extension was to explore means of extending an existing, well tested recognition system to the task of recognizing

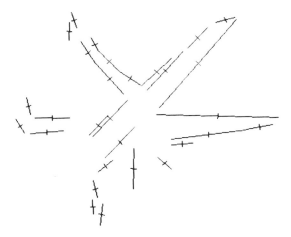

Figure 10. Example of recognition with different types of parameterizations. The edge fragments extracted from the image in figure 9 are shown.

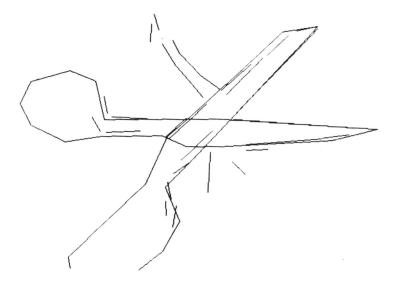

Figure 11. Example of recognition with different types of parameterizations. The solution is overlaid on the edge fragments extracted from the image in figure 9.

objects from libraries of similar objects, and to the task of recognizing objects that can undergo complex, but qualitatively shape preserving, deformations. The hope was that because the basic method worked well in

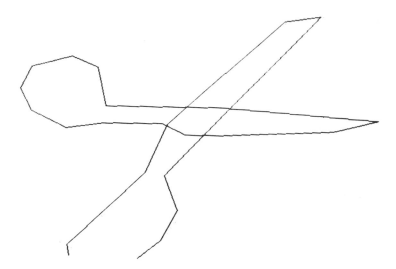

Figure 12. Example of recognition with different types of parameterizations. The solution for the image in figure 9 is shown in isolation.

dealing with rigid objects, there was some chance that extensions to deformable objects would also be successful.

While the demonstrations here show that the extension is possible, in our experience, there are some drawbacks to the methods developed here. The first is that the analysis of how to parameterize an object model is done by hand, rather than automatically determining the parameterization for a model [Brooks 1981]. To be practical, a parameterized object recognition system should be able to automatically build models of objects, correctly determining the appropriate free parameters. We have not addressed this important issue.

The second drawback of the parameterized object recognition system described here is the amount of search performed by the system in order to find instances of parameterized objects. We know from our previous experience that the Recognition and Attitude Finder constrained search method is particularly effective when using rigid objects, and when the sensory data is known to have come from a single object. In this case, a formal analysis shows that the expected amount of search required is linear in the product of the number of model edges and the number of data edges [Grimson 1988]. When spurious sensory data must be excluded from the interpretation, the constrained search method used by Recognition and Attitude Finder slows down considerably. Formally, the expected amount of search now becomes exponential in the size of the correct interpretation [Grimson 1988]. This effect is observed in empirical trials, and has led us to consider other techniques, such as the Hough preprocessing as a means of preselecting subspaces of the full search space within which to search for a solution. The increase in the complexity of the search is further exacerbated by the inclusion of free parameters. While the system still finds correct solutions, it tends to spend considerably more time thrashing in the search space, due to the additional flexibility of adjusting free parameters, in order to bring random assortments of data fragments into consistency with model fragments. In order to make the method described here reasonably efficient, we feel it is necessary to consider additional techniques for selecting subsets of the input data that are likely to have come from a single object, on which the recognition method can be run. Some early work on first-principles grouping [Jacobs 1988] suggests that precomputing subspaces of the search space can dramatically reduce the search required.

The third drawback is that all of the development given here deals only with the two dimensional case. While extensions to three dimensions are in principle straightforward, it is unclear whether the likely explosion in the combinatorics will make such extensions useful.

Relation to Previous Work

The literature on object recognition stretches over a period of at least twenty years. An extensive (70 page) review of much of this literature for 3D objects can be found in Besl and Jain [1985]. A survey of model-based image analysis systems can be found in Binford [1982].

In terms of the approach to be described here, a number of authors have taken a similar view to ours that recognition can be structured as an explicit search for a match between data elements and model elements [Ayache & Faugeras 1985; Baird 1986; Bolles & Cain 1982; Bolles & Horaud 1986; Faugeras & Hebert 1983; Goad 1983; Ikeuchi 1987; Lowe 1987; Stockman & Esteva 1984]. Of these, the work of Bolles and his colleagues [1982, 1986], Faugeras and his colleagues [Ayache & Faugeras 1986; Faugeras & Hebert 1983], and that of Baird [1986] are closest to the approach presented here.

The interpretation tree approach is an instance of the consistent labeling problem that has been studied extensively in computer vision and artificial intelligence [Waltz 1975; Montanari 1974; Mackworth 1977; Freuder 1978, 1982; Harlick & Elliott 1980; Harlick & Shapiro 1979; Mackworth & Freuder 1985]. This chapter can be viewed as suggesting a particular consistency relation (the constraints on distances and angles) and exploring its performance in a wide variety of circumstances. An alternative approach to the solution of consistent labeling problems is the use of relaxation. A number of authors have investigated this approach to object recognition

[Davis 1979; Bhanu & Faugeras 1984; Ayache & Faugeras 1982]. These techniques are more suitable for implementation on parallel machines.

The literature on recognition of parameterized objects is much smaller. The best known system is probably ACRONYM [Brooks 1981], which also attacks the recognition problem by means of constraints to reduce ranges of parameterized variables. One of the main differences is that Brooks' system dealt with both rigid subparts and constraints that incorporated free parameters at runtime. In the approach presented here, we are compiling special cases of parameterization by hand in advance, so that the runtime portion of the problem is much simpler, and uses stronger constraints. This makes our system somewhat less general than Brooks', although it does benefit from a simpler recognition engine. An approach similar to that taken here has also been reported in Tomita and Kanade [1985].

Recently, a number of researchers have considered scale parameterization in the context of matching three-dimensional object models into two-dimensional affine projections [Lowe 1987; Thompson & Mundy 1987; Lamdan *et al.* 1987; Huttenlocher 1988; Huttenlocher & Ullman 1987]. Such methods in principle can be extended to deal with other parameterizations, although to this point, only Huttenlocher [1988] has been demonstrated on non-rigid or parameterized parts. Because many of these methods rely on alignment to drive the recognition process, they are likely to have better combinatorial behavior than the method described here, provided they can be extended to deal with the same class of parameterized objects.

References

Ayache, N. J., and O. D. Faugeras [1982], "Recognition of partially visible planar shapes," *Proc. 6th Intl. Conf. Pattern Recognition*, Munich.

Ayache, N. J., and O. D. Faugeras [1986], "HYPER: A new approach for the recognition and positioning of two-dimensional objects," *IEEE Trans. Pattern Anal. Machine Intell.* PAMI, vol. 8 no. 1, pp. 44–54.

Baird, H. [1986], *Model-Based Image Matching Using Location*, MIT Press, Cambridge, MA.

The author would like to thank R. Bolles, R. Brooks, O. Faugeras, B. Horn, T. Lozano-Pérez and the referees for useful comments and suggestions on this chapter.

This chapter describes research done at the Artificial Intelligence Laboratory of the Massachusetts Institute of Technology. Support for the laboratory's artificial intelligence research is provided in part by an Office of Naval Research University Research Initiative grant under contract N00014-86-K-0180, in part by the Advanced Research Projects Agency of the Department of Defense under Army contract number DACA76-85-C-0010 and in part by DARPA under Office of Naval Research contract N00014-85-K-0124.

Besl, P. J., and R. C. Jain [1985], "Three-dimensional object recognition," *ACM Computing Surveys* vol. 17, no. 1, pp. 75–145.

Bhanu, B., and O. D. Faugeras [1984], "Shape matching of two-dimensional objects," *IEEE Trans. Pattern Anal. Machine Intell.*, PAMI, vol. 6, no. 3.

Binford, T. O. [1982], "Survey of model-based image analysis systems," *Int. Journ. of Robotics Research*, vol. 1, no. 1, pp. 18–64.

Bolles, R. C., and R. A. Cain [1982], "Recognizing and locating partially visible objects: The Local-Feature-Focus method," *Int. J. Robotics Res.*, vol. 1, no. 3, pp. 57–82.

Bolles, R. C., and P. Horaud [1986], "3DPO: A three-dimensional part orientation system," *Int. J. Robotics Res.*, vol. 5, no. 3, pp. 3–26.

Brooks, R. [1981], "Symbolic reasoning among 3-dimensional models and 2-dimensional images," *Artificial Intel.*, vol. 17, pp. 285–349.

Davis, L. [1979], "Shape matching using relaxation techniques," *IEEE Trans. Pattern Anal. Machine Intell.*, PAMI, vol. 1, no. 1, pp. 60–72.

Faugeras, O. D., and M. Hebert [1983], "A 3-D recognition and positioning algorithm using geometrical matching between primitive surfaces," in *Proc. Eighth Int. Joint Conf. Artificial Intell.*, Karlsruhe, W. Germany, pp. 996–1002.

Freuder, E. C. [1978], "Synthesizing constraint expressions," *Comm. of the ACM*, vol. 21, no. 11, pp. 958–966.

Freuder, E. C. [1982], "A sufficient condition for backtrack-free search," *J. ACM*, vol. 29, no. 1, pp. 24–32.

Goad, C. [1983], "Special purpose automatic programming for 3d model-based vision," in *Proceedings of DARPA Image Understanding Workshop*.

Grimson, W. E. L., [1986a], "The combinatorics of local constraints in model-based recognition and localization from sparse data," *J. ACM* vol. 33, no. 4, pp. 658–686.

Grimson, W. E. L., [1986b], "Sensing Strategies for Disambiguating Among Multiple Objects in Known Poses", *IEEE Journal of Robotics and Automation*, vol. 2, pp. 196–213.

Grimson, W. E. L. [1987], "On the recognition of curved objects," Report AIM-983, Artificial Intelligence Laboratory, Massachusetts Institute of Technology, Cambridge, MA; also to appear in *IEEE Trans. Pattern Anal. Machine Intell.*.

Grimson, W. E. L. [1988], "The Combinatorics of Object Recognition in Cluttered Environments using Constrained Search", Report AIM-1019, Artificial Intelligence Laboratory, Massachusetts Institute of Technology, Cambridge, MA.

Grimson, W. E. L., and T. Lozano-Pérez [1984], "Model-based recognition and localization from sparse range or tactile data," *Int. J. Robotics Res.*, vol. 3, no. 3, pp. 3–35.

Grimson, W. E. L., and T. Lozano-Pérez [1987], "Localizing overlapping parts by searching the interpretation tree," *IEEE Trans. Patt. Anal. and Mach. Intel.*, PAMI, vol. 9, no. 4, pp. 469–482.

Haralick, R. M., and G. Elliott [1980], "Increasing tree search efficiency for constraint satisfaction problems," *Artificial Intelligence*, vol. 14, pp. 263–313.

Haralick, R. M., and L. G. Shapiro [1979], "The consistent labeling problem: Part I," *IEEE Trans. Pattern Anal. Machine Intell.*, PAMI, vol. 1, no. 4, pp. 173–184.

Huttenlocher, D. P. [1988], "Three-dimensional recognition of solid objects from a two-dimensional image", PhD. Thesis, Department of Electrical Engineering and Computer Science, Massachusetts Institute of Technology, Cambridge, MA.

Huttenlocher, D. P., and S. Ullman [1987], "Object recognition using alignment," *Proc. First International Conference on Computer Vision*, London, pp. 478–484.

Ikeuchi, K. [1987], "Generating an interpretation tree from a CAD model for 3d-object recognition in bin-picking tasks," *Int. Journ. Computer Vision*, vol. 1, no. 2, pp. 145–166.

Jacobs, D. [1988], *The Use of Grouping in Visual Object Recognition,* MS. Thesis, Department of Electrical Engineering and Computer Science, Massachusetts Institute of Technology.

Lamdan, Y., J. T. Schwartz, and H. J. Wolfson [1987], "On recognition of 3-d objects from 2-d images," New York University, Courant Institute Robotics Report, no. 122.

Lowe, D. G. [1987], "Three-dimensional object recognition from single two-dimensional images," *Artificial Intelligence*, vol. 31, pp. 355–395.

Mackworth, A. K. [1977], "Consistency in networks of constraints," *Artificial Intelligence*, vol. 8, pp. 99–118.

Mackworth, A. K., and E. C. Freuder [1985], "The complexity of some polynomial network consistency algorithms for constraint satisfaction problems," *Artificial Intelligence*, vol. 25, pp. 65–74.

Montanari, U. [1974], "Networks of constraints: Fundamental properties and applications to picture processing," *Inform. Sci.*, vol. 7, pp. 95–132.

Stockman, G., and J. C. Esteva [1984], "Use of geometrical constraints and clustering to determine 3D object pose.", TR84-002, East Lansing, Michigan State University, Department of Computer Science.

Thompson, D. W., and J. L. Mundy [1987], "Three-dimensional model matching from an unconstrained viewpoint," *Proc. IEEE International Conference on Robotics and Automation*, Raleigh, N.C., pp. 208–220.

Tomita, F., and T. Kanade [1985], "A 3D vision system: Generating and matching shape description in range images," in *Robotics Research 2*, edited by H. Hanafusa and H. Inoue, MIT Press, Cambridge, pp. 35–42.

Waltz, D. [1975], "Understanding line drawings of scenes with shadows," in *The Psychology of Computer Vision*, edited by P. H. Winston, McGraw-Hill, New York, pp. 19–91.

38

Many years ago, SAAB automobiles looked very much like Volkeswagon beetles. Its hard to imagine how any image recognition system could distinguish between them, even with powerful modules for image description, surface description, space-occupancy description, and symbolic matching.

In this chapter, Ullman explains a radically new approach to recognition in which objects are recognized by bringing their images into congruence with images of models, rather than by matching their symbolic descriptions with symbolic models. With Ullman's approach, distinguishing old-style SAABs from old-style Volkswagons is easy.

More specifically, Ullman shows how to find the image transformation that makes the object to be recognized look as much as possible like a standard-viewpoint image of a model. Repeating this for each model produces a set of object-model image pairs. At this point, recognition is usually easy because one of the pairs is nearly congruent and the rest consist of images that are plainly not congruent. Because image comparisons occur after the best possible transformations are applied, there is just one image comparison for each model, not one image comparison for every possible view of each model. Because recognition is done on images, not on coarse symbolic descriptions, fine discriminations are possible.

Aligning Pictorial Descriptions

Shimon Ullman

The Problem of Shape-Based Recognition

Object recognition is one of the most important, yet least understood, aspects of visual perception. Objects such as the ones depicted in figure 1 (taken from a children's coloring book) can be recognized immediately and effortlessly by young children, but not by any recognition scheme proposed so far. The difficulties involved in this problem do not seem to result from the lack of sufficient progress in our understanding of the early processing stages. That is, it does not seem that further improvements in processes such as edge detection or stereo computation would be of fundamental importance for making progress in the area of visual object recognition. (In figure 1, for example, the edges are already clearly marked, and stereoscopic information is not available). What appears more important is a better understanding of the underlying issues: Why is object recognition difficult? Are there different types of object recognition processes? Can the overall task be broken down into more manageable problems?

Two goals of the chapter

This chapter has two related goals. The first is a succinct classification of past approaches to object recognition. The goal is not to give a comprehensive survey of the large number of different methods proposed in the literature, but to classify the approaches into a small number of major classes. (For general overviews of psychological aspects of recognition see

Figure 1. Objects that can be recognized readily on the basis of the shape of their contours. *Courtesy of Barron's Educational Series, Inc.*

Uhr [1966], Zunse [1970], Corcoran [1971], Reed [1973], Lindsay and Norman [1977], Leeuwenberg and Buffart [1978], Palmer [1983], and Pinker [1984]. For reviews of computational methods see Uhr [1973], Binford [1982], Besl and Jain [1985]).

The different approaches are classified into three main classes: recognition by invariant properties, recognition by object decomposition into parts, and alignment methods. Various combinations of the first two have been used extensively in the past, while the third, with a few exceptions, has not been used for object recognition.

The second goal of the chapter is to present an approach that appears to offer a promising general strategy for a variety of object recognition problems. This approach belongs primarily to the class of alignment methods (although it uses some of the ideas of the other classes), and is termed the *alignment of pictorial descriptions*.

Scope of the problem: Shape-based recognition

Visual object recognition is not a single problem. One reason for the diversity of approaches to the problem is that there are several different paths leading to visual object recognition.

We often recognize an object (a car, a familiar face, a printed character) visually on the basis of its characteristic shape. We may also use visual but non-shape cues, such as color and texture. The recognition of a tree of a given type is based in some cases more on its texture properties, branching pattern, and color, than on precise shape. Similarly, various material types, and different scene types such as a "lake scenery" or "mountainous terrain" can be recognized visually, without relying on precise shape. Certain animals such as a tiger or a giraffe can sometimes be identified on the basis of texture and color pattern rather than shape.

Objects can also be recognized visually primarily on the basis of their location relative to other objects. For example, a door knob may have a non-standard shape, and still be recognized immediately as a door knob mainly on the basis of its location relative to the door. Yet another possibility is to recognize objects visually on the basis of their characteristic motion, rather than specific shape [Johansson 1973; Cutting 1977]. For example, a fly in the room may be perceived as a small dark blob, and still be recognized as a fly, on the basis of its characteristic erratic motion.

In all of the above examples, recognition can be said to be primarily visual, that is, the recognition process proceeds primarily on the basis of the visual data. There are also situations in which the recognition process uses sources that are better classified as not primarily visual in nature. One example has to do with the use of prior knowledge, expectations, and temporal continuity [Morton 1969; Palmer 1975; Potter 1975]. For example, one may recognize a white object on one's desk as being a telephone even when the visual image does not contain enough detail for clear object recognition (because the viewing was too brief, or the illumination level too low, etc.). Finally, in some cases, visual recognition employs processes that may be described as reasoning. For example, recognizing the object on the table as last week's New York Times.

This chapter is concerned with the problem of shape-based recognition. Most common objects can be recognized in isolation, without the use of context or expectations. For many objects color, texture, and motion, play only a secondary role. In these cases, the objects are recognized by their shape properties. This is probably the most common and important aspect of visual recognition and therefore "object recognition" is often taken to mean the visual recognition of objects based on their shape properties. There are some difficulties in defining the term "shape" unequivocally, but such a precise definition will not be required in the ensuing discussion. The main point is that certain types of visual object recognition, for example, on the basis of color or motion alone, will not be considered here.

Difficulties with the definition of "object recognition"

Although we are constantly engaged in the process of object recognition, it is not easy to define the term "object recognition" in a simple, precise and uncontroversial manner. This problem is raised here briefly not to suggest a general definition of the term, but to delineate the scope of the problem as examined in this chapter.

In recognizing an object, we wish sometimes to identify an individual object, or a specific "token" (such as: "my car"), while in other cases recognition means identifying the object as a member of a certain class, or a type, ("a truck"). Furthermore, an object may belong to a number of classes or categories simultaneously (for example, my cat, a Siamese cat, a cat, an animal). Recognition would require in such cases a classification at the appropriate level, and what is considered appropriate may depend on the circumstances.

An image often contains multiple objects, and each object may contain a number of recognizable parts. Again, the problem of appropriateness arises. In a cat-image, one may also recognize an eye, a whisker, or a tail. If the question is, "what's in the image," different answers may be appropriate under different circumstances.

These and related issues pose important problems for the general theory of object recognition, but they will not be considered in this chapter. For the purpose of the present discussion we will focus on the recognition of individual objects (although the methods discussed are often applicable to classes of objects as well). We will assume initially that there exists a collection of individual objects that can change their location and orientation in space with respect to the viewer, as well as their sizes. (We will deal later with objects that can change in more complex manners.) We are then given an image of a single object, or a region in the image containing a single object or a partial view of it. That is, we will not confront directly the segmentation problem. (The recognition scheme must take into account, however, the possibility that parts of the object may be occluded.) Given such a region (that will be called the "image of the object," or a "viewed object") the problem is to identify (that is, to name) the object that gave rise to the image in question.

The basis for classifying past approaches: The problem of regularity across views

The process of object recognition requires the inversion of a complicated one-to-many mapping. The image cast by a single object will change when the object translates or rotates in space. It will also change with the illumination conditions: the level of illumination, the positions and distribution of the light sources, their spectral composition, etc. Formally, one can think of a mapping M that maps a given object 0_i to one of a large set of possible views $(V_{i_1}, \ldots, V_{i_{k_i}})$. Given a single view of the object, the problem is in a sense to invert M and recover the original object O_i (a problem sometimes referred to as "stimulus equivalence"). This problem is not limited to recognition based on visual sensory information. Objects can be recognized from, for example, their radar or infra-red images. In these cases, the mapping M depends on such properties as the object's density and temperature. As in vision, object recognition from such images involves the inversion of a one-to-many mapping.

The recognition problem is difficult because the set of possible views of a given object is often large, and because different views of the same object can be widely dissimilar.

The direct approach

One extreme approach to the problem of object recognition would be to store a sufficiently large number of different views associated with each object, and then compare the image of the currently viewed object with all the views stored in memory [Abu-Mostafa & Psaltis 1987]. Several mechanisms, known as associative memories, have been proposed for implementing this "direct" approach. These mechanisms, usually embodied in neuron-like networks, can store a large set of patterns $(P_1, P_2 \ldots P_n)$, and then, given an input pattern Q, they can retrieve the pattern P_i which is most similar to Q [Willshaw *et al.* 1969; Kohonen 1978; Hopfield 1982; Huberman & Hogg 1984].

Have associative memories of this type solved the problem of object recognition? Discussions of associative memories sometimes suggest that they have. When the system has stored a representative view, or a few views, of each object, a new view would automatically retrieve the stored representation which most closely resembles it.

The problem is that the notion of similarity used in associative memories (at least the ones for which a simple parallel implementation has been demonstrated) is a restricted one. The typical similarity measure used is the so-called "Hamming distance." (This measure is defined for two binary vectors. Suppose that **u** and **v** are two binary vectors, that is, strings of 1's and 0's. The Hamming distance between **u** and **v** is simply the number of coordinates in which they differ.)

Such a simple similarity measure may be appropriate for some special applications and for certain non-visual domains, such as olfaction [Freeman 1979]. For the general problem of visual object recognition this direct approach is implausible for two reasons. First, the space of all possible views of all the objects to be recognized is likely to be prohibitively large. Second, objects can be recognized from novel views (induced by effects of context, illumination conditions, viewing position, geometrical changes and distortions, etc.), whereas in the direct approach, generalization to substantially new views would be severely limited.

The situation, then, is that certain similarity measures between input images, such as the Hamming distance and some variations of it, can be implemented directly by known mechanisms. In terms of these similarity measures, however, different views of the same object can be widely dissimilar. The problem remains, therefore, to find the processes by which the disparate views can be identified as representing the same object.

It will be possible to outperform the direct approach significantly when the set of views belonging to a given object is not arbitrary, but contains certain regularities. To recognize, for instance, triangles of any shape, position, and size, it is clearly not necessary to store in memory a large number of representative shapes. All of the shapes in this set have certain properties in common, and these regularities can be used to overcome the two limitations of the direct approach mentioned above. That is, it will become possible to limit the number of stored representations, and it will be possible to recognize novel shapes that are not similar in any simple direct measure to triangles seen before.

The conclusion is that finding regularities in the set of views that belong to a single object (or class or objects) is the key to visual object recognition. I will refer to this problem below as the problem of regularity across views, or just the "regularity problem." As we shall see, different approaches to object recognition can be classified into a small number of major classes according to their proposed solution to the regularity problem.

The problem of defining these regularities becomes difficult when we consider natural objects under various possible viewing conditions. For simple geometrical shapes, such as triangles, the set of transformations that a member in the family of views may undergo is well defined and straightforward to characterize. For the family of views representing a three-dimensional object, the set of "allowable transformations" that the views may undergo cannot be defined easily, especially when the object can undergo non-rigid transformations. For example, what would be, the regularities in the transformations linking the different possible views of a rabbit?

Different approaches to visual object recognition differ in the type of regularities they propose to exploit. The proposal is not always made explicit, but any theory of object recognition that goes beyond the direct approach must make some assumptions regarding the expected regularities within a family of views that belong to the same object.

In the following sections, prevailing theories of object recognition are classified on the basis of their approach to the regularity problem. Three main classes of theories are distinguished:

1   Invariant properties methods.

2   Parts decomposition methods.

3   Alignment methods.

Theories in the first class assume that certain simple properties remain invariant under the transformations that an object is allowed to make. This approach leads to the notions of invariances, feature spaces, clustering, and separation techniques. The second class relies on the decomposition of objects into parts. This leads into the notions of symbolic structural descriptions, feature hierarchies, and syntactic pattern recognition. By and large, the first of these general approaches was the dominant one in the earlier days of pattern recognition and the second approach has become more popular in recent years. It will be argued that both of these approaches are insufficient by themselves for the general problem of shape-based visual recognition. A third approach, called the alignment method, will be presented and compared with the previous two.

The classification into invariant properties, part decomposition, and alignment methods, is a taxonomy of the underlying ideas, not of existing schemes. That is, a given scheme is not required to belong strictly to one of these classes, but may employ one or more of these ideas. A successful recognition scheme is likely in fact to benefit from incorporating key ideas from all three classes. The main point of Part I is that the variety of methods used seem to rely on a small number of basic ideas for dealing with the regularity problem, and these ideas fall under the three mentioned categories.

The plan of the remainder of the chapter is as follows. Part I describes the invariant properties, decomposition, and alignment approaches. Part II discusses the recognition of objects using the alignment of pictorial descriptions.

PART I: APPROACHES TO OBJECT RECOGNITION

Invariant Properties and Feature Spaces

A common approach to object recognition has been to assume that objects have certain invariant properties that are common to all of their views [Pitts & McCulloch 1947]. For example, in identifying different types of biological cells a "compactness measure," defined as the ratio between the cell's apparent area and its perimeter length squared, has been used as a useful characteristic. Cells that tend to be round and compact will have a high score on this measure, whereas long and narrow objects will have a low score. Furthermore, the measure will be unaffected by rotation, translation, and scaling in the image plane. Certain Fourier descriptors (coefficient in the Fourier transform) and object moments are additional examples of invariant measures that have been proposed. The idea is to define a number of such measures, and collectively they will then serve to identify each object unambiguously. This approach is quite different from a direct approach based on a similarity measure such as the Hamming distance. In the domain of binary vectors discussed above, an invariant property may be defined, for example, as the number of 1's in the string. Two strings may clearly have similar (global) invariant properties while being separated by a large Hamming distance.

Formally, a property of this type can be defined as a function from the set of object-views to the real numbers. It is important that these functions be relatively simple to compute. Otherwise, in recognizing, for example, different instances of the letter "A," one may define a function whose value is 1 if the viewed object is the letter "A," and 0 otherwise. This function would be an invariant of the letter A, but the problem of computing this invariance would be, of course, equivalent to the original problem of recognizing the letter. The invariant properties approach must therefore prescribe, together with the set of invariant properties proposed, effective procedures for extracting these properties.

In an invariant properties scheme the overall recognition process is thus broken down into the extraction of a number of different properties followed by a final decision based on these properties, where each of these stages is relatively simple to compute.

Feature spaces and separating functions

In some approaches, a property defined for a given object (or class of objects) is not expected to remain entirely invariant, only to lie within a restricted range. Properties of different objects may have partially overlapping ranges, but the hope is that by defining a number of different properties, it will become possible to define each object (or class) uniquely. This leads naturally to the concept of "feature spaces" which have been used extensively in pattern recognition. (A better term would have been "property spaces" but "feature spaces" is the accepted terminology.) If n different properties are measured, each viewed object is characterized by a vector of n real numbers. It then becomes possible to represent a given view by a point in an n-dimensional space, R^n. The set of all the views induced by a given object define in this manner is a subspace of R^n (for example, Tou and Gonzalez [1974]). This representation could become useful for identifying and classifying objects, provided that the subspaces have simple shapes. For example, suppose that each class to be recognized is contained within a sphere in R^n, and the spheres for the different classes are non-overlapping. Each class can then be represented simply by the center point and the radius of its sphere. A viewed object, including a novel view, would then be classified by determining the sphere in which the point lies in R^n.

Another common method of carving up the space R^n is by a set of linear separating functions. In the case of $n = 3$, for example, the three dimensional feature space is divided into subspaces using a set of two-dimensional planes. The main reason for using planar separating functions is to keep the computations involved manageable. When the shape of the subspaces does not permit the use of simple separation functions, the space can sometimes be "corrected" by, for example, re-scaling different axes.

A well-known psychological theory that does not use such feature spaces, yet belongs to the general category of invariant-properties theories, is Gibson's theory of high-order invariances [Gibson 1950, 1979]. Gibson postulated that invariant properties of objects may be reflected in so-called "higher order" invariances in the optic array. Such invariances may be based on, for example, spatial and temporal gradients of texture density. A set of invariances may be "picked up," according to this theory, by the visual system, and may be used to characterize objects and object classes.

How useful have invariant-properties methods been for approaching the problem of visual object recognition? The invariant properties approach, including the construction of feature spaces and their separation into sub-spaces, have probably been studied more extensively than any other method for object recognition. It has met with some success within certain limited domains: a number of industrial vision systems perform simple recognition of industrial parts based on the measurement of global properties such as area, elongation, perimeter length, and different moments (see a review in Bolles and Cain [1982]). For the general problem of visual object recognition, however, this approach on its own is not very promising. In limited domains, such as the recognition of flat unoccluded parts lying parallel to the image plane, well-defined invariant properties may be sufficient to reliably characterize different objects. In more general visual recognition problems, the usefulness of simple invariant properties appears doubtful. What simple invariances would distinguish, for example, a fox from a dog? To make such distinctions, it appears that a more precise description of shape, rather than a restricted set of basic invariances, would be necessary. Even with simpler, man-made objects, it is not clear how a set of invariances would suffice to capture the regularities in the different views of an object or a class of objects. For example, it would be difficult to recognize the set of all motorcycles using primarily global invariant properties such as apparent area, perimeter length, different moments, and the like.

In summary, the invariant properties approach offers one possible solution to the regularity problem of object recognition. The required many-to-one mapping is performed in an efficient manner (compared with the direct approach) by computing invariant properties rather than storing a comprehensive set of views. In some special cases simple invariant properties may indeed be common to all the members of a given class. In other cases such invariances may not exist. The weakness of this approach is that in visual object recognition there is no particular reason to assume the existence of relatively simple properties (particularly global ones) that are preserved across the transformations that an object may undergo. It is not surprising, therefore, that, despite considerable effort, invariant properties of general applicability for visual object recognition proved difficult to find.

Recognition Using Object Decomposition

A second general approach to object recognition relies on the decomposition of objects into constituent parts. This approach clearly has some intuitive appeal. Many objects seem to contain natural parts: a face, for example, contains the eyes, nose, and mouth as distinct parts that can often be recognized on their own. These parts could be found first, and then the recognition of the entire object could use the identified parts.

The approach assumes that each object can be decomposed into a small set of generic components. The components are "generic" in the sense that all objects can be described as different combinations of these components. The decomposition must also be stable, that is, preserved across views. The recognition process locates the parts, classifies them into the different types of generic components and then describes the objects in terms of their constituent parts. In this approach, the many-to-one mapping implied by object recognition begins at the part level. This can result in substantial savings compared with the direct approach.

Two comments are noteworthy regarding this use of parts. First, its usefulness depends of the structure of the domain in question: some sets of patterns may admit useful part structures, others may not. Second, part decomposition and the use of invariant properties are not mutually exclusive, but can be combined. We may use, for example, a description such as "a bushy tail" in the recognition of a squirrel ("tail" being a part, and "bushy" a global property describing it). The idea behind such descriptions is to combine the advantages of part-decomposition with the use of invariant properties for classifying the constituent parts.

Following the initial classification of the individual components, there remains the problem of recognizing the object itself on the basis of the constituent components. Different methods within the part decomposition approach differ in the manner they handle this second stage.

Feature hierarchies and syntactic pattern recognition

There have been two main approaches to this second classification stage. One approach is to try to repeat the decomposition process: certain part subgroups, containing two or more parts, can be identified as new substructures, or higher-order parts. As in the process of parts identification, the assumption is that certain configurations can be classified independent of other parts and configurations, and that the internal structure of a configuration is immaterial as far as the recognition process is concerned.

An example of a simple part-hierarchy is to detect straight line segments as the most basic parts and then detect higher-level parts such as corners and vertices, based on the already-detected line segments. These parts can be combined in turn into higher-level structures. For example, certain configurations of lines and vertices can be combined to define triangles. Such approaches are known as "feature hierarchies." The simple basic level parts are termed "features" (a term also used in many other contexts) and higher level structures are constructed hierarchically [Selfridge 1959; Sutherland 1959; Barlow 1972; Milner 1974]. This approach has been motivated in part by physiological findings [Hubel & Wiesel 1962, 1968] in the cat and monkey, that can be interpreted as the extraction by the visual cortex of elementary features such as oriented edge fragments and line segments.

A close relative of the feature-hierarchy approach is the syntactic pattern recognition method [Fu 1974]. Here, too, the first stage consists of identifying simple parts in the input image, followed by the grouping of elementary parts into higher-order ones. The emphasis in the syntactic approach is on the construction of higher order parts using methods borrowed from the syntactic analysis of formal languages.

Structural descriptions

The underlying assumption is that it would be easier to capture object invariances at the level where parts have been identified. For example, the total number of parts of a given type may be an invariant of the object. A triangle, for instance, always has three lines, three vertices, and no free line terminators. This is in fact how perceptrons, which are simple parallel pattern recognition devices, have been used to recognize triangles independent of shape, location and size [Minsky & Papert 1969]. Such schemes combine feature extraction with simple invariants (the existence and lack of certain features) without attempting to describe inter-part relationships. Similarly, in the "pandemonium" scheme [Selfridge 1959] a shape is classified based on the existence of certain parts, or features, without describing spatial relations among different parts.

In other schemes, relations between constituent parts are used to capture invariant that are common to all the object's views. In the capital letter "A," for example, two of the line-segment parts meet at a vertex, and this property holds for most variations of the letter. Here, again, part decomposition is obtained first, and in the next stage simple invariances are defined in terms of the constituent parts. The invariances are expressed in terms of relations between two or more parts, such as "above," "to the left of," "longer than," "containing," etc. [Barlow et al. 1972]. For two-dimensional applications, in which objects are restricted to move parallel to the image plane, simple relations such as distances and angles measured in the image would remain invariant [Bolles & Cain 1982; Grimson & Lozano-Perez 1984; Faugeras 1984]. In the more general three-dimensional case, part decomposition schemes often try to employ relations that would remain invariant over a wide range of different viewing positions [Marr & Nishihara 1978; Biederman 1985; Lowe 1985].

The use of spatial relations among parts and features allows the system to distinguish between configurations that have similar parts, but in different arrangements. The capacity to make such distinctions is fundamental to the human visual system, but apparently it is only rudimentary is some other visual systems. For example, pigeons have been shown to recognize successfully pictures containing, for example, people, a particular person, trees, pigeons, fish, and letters in the alphabet. They fail to distinguish, however, a given figure from a scrambled version of it [Herrnstein 1984; Cerella 1986]. This behavior is more consistent with recognition on the basis of a collection of local parts and features, rather than a direct comparison (for example by correlation) of complete figures. It also suggests that, in contrast to the human visual system, simpler systems may not possess developed mechanisms for extracting spatial relations among features and parts.

When augmented with descriptions of relations among parts, the object decomposition approach leads to the notion of structural descriptions. Recognition using such structural descriptions has become in recent years a popular approach to visual object recognition.

Early computational examples of this approach include Grimsdale *et al.* [1959], Clowes [1967], and Winston [1970]. As psychological models, early examples of structural descriptions theories applied to human vision are Sutherland's [1968] theory, and Milner's [1974] model of visual shape recognition. The main basic-level parts used in these two theories are edges and line segments. In a second level, invariant properties and relations are defined using, for example, the total number of parts (such as the number of line segments of a given orientation) and length ratios of line pairs.

A number of psychological experiments, involving primarily the recognition of two-dimensional characters at different orientations [Corbalis *et al.* 1978; White 1980] have been interpreted as supporting this general approach to recognition.

A recent example of a structural description recognition scheme applied to three-dimensional objects is Biederman's [1985] theory of recognition by components (RBC). According to this scheme, objects are described in terms of a small set of primitive parts called "geons." These primitives are similar to the generalized cylinders used by Binford [1971], Marr and Nishihara [1978], and Brooks [1981]. They include simple three-dimensional shapes such as boxes, cylinders, and wedges. More complex objects are described by decomposing them into their constituent geons, together with a description of the spatial relations between components. The number of primitive geons is assumed to be small (less than 50), and objects are typically composed of a small number of parts (less than 10).

In any scheme that relies on decomposition into parts it is crucial to devise a reliable and stable procedure for identifying part boundaries. Otherwise, the same object may give, under slightly different viewing conditions, different descriptions in terms of its constituent parts. In Biederman's scheme certain "non accidental" relationships between contours in the image are used to determine the part decomposition. These relations include, for example, the collinearity of points or lines, symmetry and skew symmetry, and parallelism of curve segments.

Another recent scheme employing part-decomposition is the "codon" scheme proposed by Hoffman and Richards [1986] for the description and recognition of contours. Contours are segmented at curvature minima (the "transversality rule"). The resulting parts are then described in terms of a small "vocabulary" of shape primitives termed "codons."

The RBC and the codon schemes are complementary in that they emphasize different aspects of the problem. The codon scheme concentrates on the initial stages of analyzing image contours. Biederman's RBC scheme assumes that certain analysis of image contours has already been performed and then goes on to consider the description of complete objects.

Attempts have been made recently at combining these two levels of analysis into working systems that would actually recognize three-dimensional objects from their projections. An example is a recent scheme developed by Connell [1985]. This scheme starts at the level of analyzing image contours. It first describes the contours in terms of constituent parts and their properties, using a representation scheme developed by Brady and his co-workers [Asada & Brady 1986]. It then proceeds to generate higher-level constructs that eventually correspond to entire objects. The resulting description can become quite elaborate. Formally, it has a graph structure in which the nodes represent components and labeled arcs represent relations between parts. Recognition can proceed later by matching such graphs generated from the image with similar graph structures stored in memory.

Figure 2(a) shows an example of a contour image of an airplane, 2(b) shows the description generated by the system for a part of this figure (the right elevator). In schemes of this type that use simple parts the graph typically contains a large number of nodes, and the matching stage faces combinatorial problems (sub-graph isomorphism is NP-complete, [Garey & Johnson 1979] see Grimson and Lozano-Perez [1984, 1987] for a discussion of the computational complexity involved in the matching).

The schemes mentioned above use primarily 1-D contour segments and three-dimensional volumes as their primitive shape parts. Other schemes use two-dimensional surface patches as their primitives [Dane & Bajcsy 1982; Potmesil 1983; Faugeras 1984; Brady *et al.* 1985; Faugeras & Hebert 1986]. There are significant differences between the various structural description schemes that have been proposed, but they all share a basic underlying idea: regularities in the families of views corresponding to an object (or class of objects) can be best captured by part-decomposition. Different schemes differ in the type of parts they use (contours, surface patches, primitive volumes, etc.), but they all attempt to employ simple parts, so that the identification of a part would be significantly simpler than the recognition of a complex object. The entire object is then recognized in a second stage in terms of the already classified parts.

For a variety of objects, the notion of part decomposition appears to be natural. A table, for instance, is often composed of a flat surface supported from below by four legs. Such a description appears much more natural than trying to characterize table-images in terms of simple properties such as total area, perimeter length, etc., as used in the invariant properties approach. It is also true that, as argued by Palmer [1977], Hoffman [1983], and Biederman [1985], human observers sometimes find it easy to identify the parts of an object even when the object is unfamiliar.

The identification of object parts, when parts are clearly distinguishable, has some clear advantages. At the same time, it appears that for the

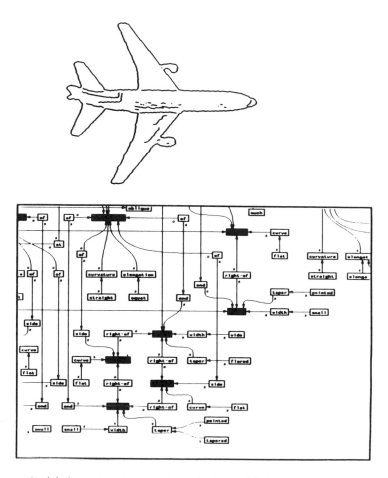

Figure 2. (a) A contour image of an airplane. (b) A structural description of a part of this image (the right elevator). *From Connell [1985].*

purpose of visual object recognition the use of structural descriptions has at least two severe limitations. The first problem is that the decomposition into generic parts often falls considerably short of characterizing the object in question. For example, a dog, a fox, and a cat, (as well as several other animals) probably have similar and perhaps identical decompositions into main parts. This may be useful at some level, for example, as an intermediate level in the recognition process. Eventually, however, these animals are distinguishable not because each one has a different arrangement of parts, but because of differences in the detailed shape at particular locations (such as the snout). It may be argued, perhaps, that these animals are indistinguishable at some "basic level" or "entry level" category [Rosch *et al.* 1976;

Biederman 1985]: they are first recognized perhaps as four-legged animals, and only a second recognition stage distinguishes among them. This possibility cannot be dismissed on the basis of current evidence, but at the same time, it is not clear that two such separate stages actually operate in this example. Moreover, the separation into two stages does not, by itself, solve the problem; an explanation of how the objects are eventually recognized (which is the problem addressed here) is still required.

A second limitation of the structural description approach is that many objects (for example, the shoe, loaf of bread, or rabbit shown in figure 1) are difficult to decompose into parts that are sufficient to characterize the objects, and at the same time generic, that is, common to many other objects as well. A possible approach, illustrated by the aircraft example in figure 2, is to include in the description very simple generic parts, such as edges and line segments. The use of such parts, however, causes the resulting structural descriptions to be highly complex.

In conclusion, it seems that for many objects the attempt to construct a structural description results in making strong commitments too early in the recognition process. The approach forces a categorization of shapes and relations into a small set of classes, and assumes that, as far as recognition is concerned, the internal structure (that is, the details of the shapes and relations not captured by the structural descriptions) are immaterial.

The approach presented next (the alignment method) attempts to avoid these limitations. It preserves details of the viewed shape without enforcing a classification into predetermined categories of parts and spatial relations.

The alignment approach is not incompatible with the notion of part decomposition. Aspects of both approaches can, in fact, be usefully incorporated in a single scheme. (As will be seen, the alignment method can incorporate the use of parts, but spatial relations are represented "pictorially" rather than by structural descriptions.) However, to keep the distinction between the approaches clear, the alignment approach will be presented first in a simple and "pure" form. Combinations with other schemes will be considered in a subsequent section.

The Alignment Approach To Object Recognition

To introduce the alignment approach, it is convenient to view visual recognition as a problem involving search in a large space: given a viewed object, a best match is sought in the space of all stored object-models and all of their possible views. If V denotes the viewed object, (M_i) are the different object-models stored in memory, and (T_{ij}) is the set of allowed transformations that can be applied to object-model M_i, then the goal of the search is to find a particular model and a particular transformation that will maximize some measure of fit F between the object and a model. That is, the search is for a maximum in $F(V, (M_i, T_{ij}))$ over all possible object-models M_i and their transformations T_{ij}.

The basic idea of the alignment approach is to decompose this search into two stages. First, determine the transformation between the viewed object and the object model, for all candidate models. This is the *alignment* stage. Second, determine the object-model that best matches the viewed object. At this stage, the search is over all the possible object-models, but not over their possible views, because the transformation has already been determined uniquely in the alignment stage.

In terms of the maximization problem stated above, the idea is to determine for each potential object-model M_i a unique transformation T_{ij} that aligns M_i and V optimally. (It is also possible to transform the viewed object V rather than the model M_i.) The search for a best match is now reduced to finding the maximum in $F(V, M_i)$ only; that is, a search over the set of objects, but not over their different views.

A simple example may help to clarify the approach. The example is taken from the domain of character recognition. This is one of the few domains in which a rudimentary version of an alignment method has been attempted [Neisser 1967, Chapter 3], and it can be used to illustrate the differences between the alignment method and alternative approaches. It is, however, a somewhat special domain. Learning to recognize the letters in an alphabet is a difficult task that requires considerable training. It may require the use of some specialized skills that are not necessarily representative of object recognition in general. Later the application of a more general alignment approach to other objects will be considered.

Suppose that a character recognition system is required to recognize characters in the alphabet regardless of position, size, and orientation. A simple alignment scheme would proceed in the following manner. For each character, a single instance of the character would be stored in memory. Given an input character, the system will first go through an alignment phase. The goal of this stage is to "undo" the shift, scale, and rotation transformations. This may be accomplished by applying compensating transformations to the character. For example, to "undo" a possible shift, the center of mass of the input can be computed, and the character is then shifted, so that its center of mass always coincides with a fixed predetermined location. In this manner, characters that differ in their position in the input image are "transformed back" to a canonical location. Similarly, scale can be compensated for by computing, for instance, the area of the character's convex hull. (The convex hull is the smallest convex envelope surrounding the character; [Preparata & Shamos 1985]).

Orientation changes are more complicated to compensate for. (They are often more problematic in human perception as well [Neisser 1967; Rock 1973; Wiser 1981; Shwartz 1981; Jolicoeur & Landau 1984; Jolicoeur

1985]). Orientation can be determined for some letters on the basis of bilateral symmetry. Many characters have a line segment that, in the proper orientation, is oriented either vertically or horizontally, and these can be used to determine a small number of likely orientations. The detection of bilateral symmetry and the orientation of the component line segments, together with the computation of center of mass and the convex hull area, would be performed during the alignment stage. (A "top" direction may also be identified to distinguish between 180° rotations). After the shift, scale, and orientation have been compensated for, the "normalized" input is matched (possibly in parallel) against the stored representations of the different characters. Because the transformations have already been removed, the matching stage itself is expected to be relatively straightforward. At this stage, an associative memory-like mechanism may suffice to compare the transformed input in parallel with the stored models. It should be noted, however, that even following the alignment the final matching cannot be as simple as, for example, two-dimensional correlation between the contours. The difference between different characters, such as O and Q, may be a small but crucial contour element. Some parts of the model may therefore contribute more to the overall quality of the match than other parts.

The process of compensating for the transformations prior to comparing the viewed object with potential models is often referred to as a *normalization* stage. The use of such a normalization stage has been limited in the past to restricted applications, such as the domain of character recognition mentioned above. In this domain, the normalization scheme would perform well provided that the set of allowable transformations is indeed limited to changes in position, scale, and orientation. If the input characters are allowed to change in a less restricted manner, so that additional distortions, changes in style, etc., are also permitted, these additional transformations should also be compensated for, as much as possible, during the alignment stage.

The use of a normalization-like stage for more general object recognition suffers from two main shortcomings. First, normalization as used in the past has been usually restricted to changes in position, orientation, scale, and sometimes inversion [Foster & Mason 1979; Palmer 1983] in the two-dimensional image plane. In contrast, the set of transformations that must be compensated for in three-dimensional object recognition is not limited to these transformations. When an object moves and rotates in three-dimensional space the transformations induced in the image are considerably more complicated. The second reason is that the methods used for normalization usually relied on global properties such as the object's apparent area, perimeter length, or center of mass. Such measures do not perform well in the face of occlusion, when only a part of the object is visible. A number of schemes [Fischler & Bolles 1981; Hinton 1981; Ballard

& Tanaka 1985; Lowe 1985; Ballard 1986; Faugeras & Hebert 1986] have attempted recently to extend the normalization stage to meet these limitations. Of these, the scheme that comes closest to the alignment approach is Lowe's SCERPRO system [Lowe 1985, 1986], discussed later.

The alignment approach described in the next three sections can be viewed as an extension of the simple notion of normalization. It has the same main goal, namely, compensating for the transformations separating the viewed object and potential object models prior to the matching stage. The main differences, detailed in the next two sections, are that:

- The alignment process can compensate for a larger set of transformations, including rigid rotation in space as well as non-rigid transformations.
- The proposed alignment method includes the use of abstract descriptions that are not usually incorporated in normalization schemes.
- The alignment process does not rely on global measures such as area or center of mass.

The remainder of the chapter, elaborates the alignment method presented above, first it illustrates the application of the method to the shape-based recognition of simple rigid objects, and then to more general non-rigid objects. Finally it extends the "pure" alignment method to include pictorial descriptions, and summarizes the overall structure of the recognition process.

PART II: THE ALIGNMENT OF PICTORIAL DESCRIPTIONS

The Alignment Approach Applied To Simple Objects

This section illustrates the application of the alignment approach to the recognition of simple objects. It discusses the problem of aligning objects in three-dimensional space using examples from a computer implementation by D. Huttenlocher [Huttenlocher & Ullman 1987].

The system uses an alignment approach to recognize objects of the type shown in figure 3. These objects are flat rigid machine parts that were allowed to translate, rotate in space, and change scale (as their distance from the camera changed).

Goal and restrictions

The goal of the recognition system is to demonstrate, in a restricted and simplified application, how the alignment approach described above in general terms may be used for the recognition of objects. The domain of application of the current example is simplified in three respects. First, the

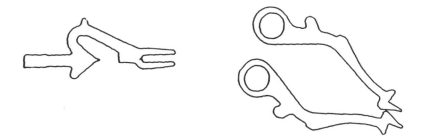

Figure 3. Machine parts that were used in the recognition example.

objects considered are flat. It should be noted, however, that this is not a two-dimensional problem, because the objects are not restricted to move in the plane, but are allowed to move and rotate in three-dimensional space. The second restriction is that the transformations applied to the objects are limited to the class of rigid transformations, combined with changes of scale. Many real objects can undergo more complicated transformations, such as bending, stretching and other types of distortions. The class of allowable transformations is, however, less restrictive than many examples considered in the past. In various discussions of object recognition [Milner 1972; Baird 1984] the transformations that the recognition system is required to cope with are limited to changes in position, orientation, and scale. These are relatively simple transformations, that preserve the similarity of shapes. The transformations considered here are not similarity-preserving, because the objects are allowed to rotate in three-dimensional space.

The third simplification in these examples is that only a "pure alignment" approach is used. This means that the recognition scheme will not be combined with invariant properties or part decomposition methods. The method described in this section uses the boundary and internal contours of objects as object models, without describing them further, or extracting invariant properties of objects or objects' parts. Such a simple description would be insufficient in more complicated situations, for example, when the objects contain parts that can move with respect to one another in a constrained manner. Useful combinations of the "pure" alignment scheme with certain aspects of other methods are possible, and are discussed later.

The information needed for alignment: Three points suffice

Earlier we examined the problem of defining regularities, or lawfulness, in the set of views that belong to the same object. Given two views, V_1 and V_2, that at the input level may be quite dissimilar (using simple distance metrics) the problem is to find methods for deciding whether or not the two views belong to the same object without necessarily storing both V_1 and V_2 separately in memory. The alignment method approaches this problem by noting that objects do not change in an arbitrary manner: the set of transformations applied to them is often restricted. The key point about these restrictions is that the transformation can be determined uniquely on the basis of very limited information.

Three-point alignment

To illustrate this concept, assume for the present that three dots, a red one, a green one, and a blue one, have been painted on every object in the collection the system is required to recognize. The exact location of the points on the object's surface is immaterial. They must only be visible (that is, not occluded), and must not be colinear. We will call these points, which are used in the alignment stage, the "anchor points" of the object.

For each object 0_i in the collection, the system stores an internal model, M_i, which is simply a picture of the object in a frontal view. This picture is an orthographic projection of the object on the image plane. It includes the projection of the object's boundary, as well as the position of the three anchor points (see figure 4). The real projection of objects on the retina or a camera's image plane is, of course, perspective rather than orthographic, but an orthographic projection combined with an admissible scale change provides a good approximation unless the projection center is very close to the viewed object. The deviation of perspective projection from its approximation by the combination of orthographic projection and scale change will be treated as any other distortion of the object (see also Appendix 1).

We are now given a view of an unknown object, and the problem is to decide, for a given model M_i, whether or not V matches M_i (that is whether V is a possible view of M_i). To reach a decision, we can at first ignore the entire image of the object, and examine only the position of the three anchor points. Let (P_1, P_2, P_3) be the (three-dimensional) coordinates of the three points in the model, and (p_1, p_2, p_3) their two-dimensional image coordinates.

The crucial point is that the model M_i and the view V can be aligned in a unique manner given only the coordinates (P_1, P_2, P_3) (known in the model) and p_1, p_2, p_3 (recovered from the image). In other words, the displacement D, the rotation in space R, and the scaling S, possibly relating M_i to V, are uniquely determined on the basis of the three corresponding points. These transformations are now applied to M_i. Following the transformations, M_i and V should be in complete registration (figure 4). Unlike the original situation, M_i and V following the transformations are very similar in the Hamming or similar distance metrics. If V is not an instance of M_i, then M_i and V following the compensating transformations would still be out of register (figure 5). The recognition process is decomposed in this manner into two stages: an initial alignment followed by a matching stage. Following the alignment, the similarity between the object and model increases significantly, and a relatively straightforward matching metric can determine the appropriate model.

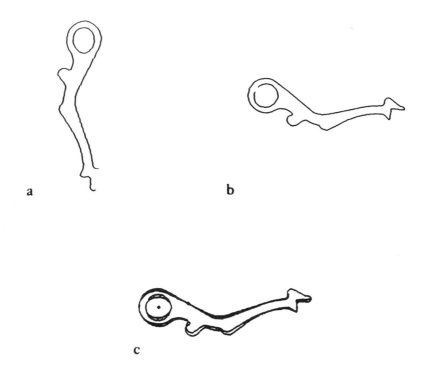

a   b

c

Figure 4. Matching an object with the correct model using alignment. (a) A part-image. (b) A part-model. The image is both larger and slanted. (c) The aligned model superimposed on the image. The points used for alignment are marked by black dots. Following the alignment, the model and image are in close agreement.

The fact that three corresponding points are sufficient to "undo" the rotation, translation, and scale is shown in Appendix 1. These transformations can be specified by six parameters: three for the rotation, two for the translation (under orthographic projection, absolute depth remains undetermined), and one for the scaling. Three points supply six equations (two for each point) and therefore the number of constraints matches the number of unknowns. This counting argument by itself is insufficient (the

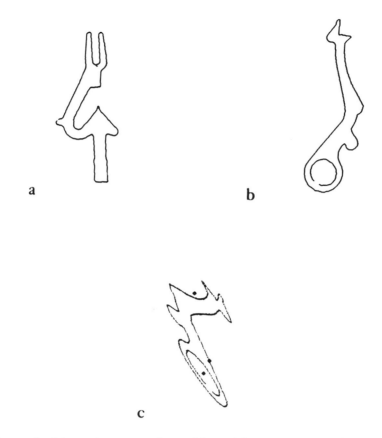

a

b

c

Figure 5. Attempting to match an object with an incorrect model using alignment. (a) A part-image. (b) A part-model. (c) The model transformed in an attempt to align it with the image. The points used in the alignment are marked by black dots. Following the alignment, the model and object are still in disagreement.

two-dimensional projection of three known lines which also provide six parameters, does not guarantee in general a unique transformation), but it suggests why such a small number of points may be sufficient for recovering the transformation uniquely. A proof of the existence and uniqueness of three point alignment is given in the Appendix. As noted in the Appendix, it is also possible to replace some or all of the points by straight lines, and use, for example, two lines and a point instead of three points.

It is worth noting that, as shown in Appendix 1, the alignment stage does not require the extraction of three-dimensional information from the image: the two-dimensional coordinates of the points are sufficient. Three-dimensional information could be used, when available, to simplify the alignment stage somewhat, but the process can proceed in the absence of precise three-dimensional data.

The recognition system illustrated in this section did not in fact use colored points painted on the object. Instead, it identified a small number of salient and stable points defined by the object's boundary. Such points included deep concavities, strong maxima in curvature, and the centers of closed or almost closed blobs. The anchor points identified and used by the recognition program are marked in figures 4 and 5. (For more discussion on the extraction of alignment anchor points see Huttenlocher and Ullman [1987]).

Instead of the color of the points, the scheme uses simple labels to determine uniquely the correspondence between image-points and points in the model without the need for search. A label of a point includes a point-type, such as blob-center, concavity, or a sharp curvature maximum, and may include a rough description of location. It is desirable, although not strictly necessary, to obtain a unique correspondence between object and model anchor points based on their associated labels. If this correspondence is not unique, a number of transformations will have to be evaluated, for the different possible pairings of the anchor points.

Following the alignment, a simple matching measure (similar to the Hamming distance) was sufficient in this domain to unambiguously select the appropriate model. For more general recognition problems such a matching criterion may not be sufficient. More general considerations regarding the final matching and model selection are discussed in the final section.

An alignment scheme somewhat similar to the three-point method has been used in Lowe's SCERPO system [Lowe 1985, 1986]. SCERPO is one of the few systems in existence that attempts to use an alignment process for recognizing objects in three-dimensional space, and it is applicable mainly to polyhedral objects. Starting with a candidate model and an initial guess regarding its position and orientation, the scheme evaluates new image features, and updates its estimate of the object's three-dimensional parameters. The alignment is not performed in a separate stage, it is intertwined with the recognition process (see also Faugeras and Hebert [1986]). The alignment procedure used in the system relies on perspective rather than orthographic projection. This is implemented as an iterative scheme, based on Newton's method. Another difference between the two alignment procedures is that SCERPO does not attempt to "label" the alignment features in a manner that will eliminate the required search between corresponding image and model features. Finally, the scheme uses object contours only, and not the pictorial descriptions discussed in the final section.

Another scheme that has certain properties in common with the alignment approach is the shape recognition networks proposed by Hinton [1981] and by Ballard [Ballard & Tanaka 1985; Ballard 1986]. In this scheme a rigid transformation that could align a stored model with (three-dimensional) image data is sought. The alignment is combined with a matching process in a network performing a Hough transform. Essentially, a histogram of all possible pairings of image and model features and their associated transformations is computed in parallel, and possible matches are identified as peaks in this histogram.

Alignment using simple image transformations

For the flat objects considered in this section, the alignment phase can be decomposed into a sequence of simple operations acting on the image. These operations include translation and rotation of the image, scaling along one axis, and a "shear" transformation: scaling along one axis by an amount that varies linearly with the distance from an orthogonal axis. The order of these operations and how they are used to bring the viewed object and model into correspondence is described in Appendix 2.

Orientation alignment

Unique object-to-model alignment can be performed (for rigid transformations accompanied by scale changes) using three identifiable anchor points. Such points can be defined by distinguished locations such as inflections and cusps on the object's boundary, small salient blobs, etc, or locations defined more globally, such as the endpoints of elongated parts, the centers of large blobs, or places where large parts join together. The three-point scheme is only an example, other types of alignment schemes are also possible. In particular, if the object has a well-defined orientation, then this orientation can be used for alignment instead of the anchor points.

A number of properties can be used to define an overall orientation for an object, including overall elongation, bilateral symmetry or skew symmetry, oriented texture on the object surface, the existence of a flat or nearly flat side, the distribution of mass, and the existence of salient protrusions or nicks. The process of alignment by orientation is illustrated schematically in figure 6, and described in more detail in Appendix 3. The viewed object (or the model) is first rotated to align their orientations. Let this common orientation denote the y-direction. The object is next scaled along the x-direction so that the viewed object and the model match. A final scaling and shear (in the y direction) completes the alignment. (In figure 6 the final y-transformation is pure scaling, no shear was necessary.) The amount of scaling and shear can be deduced from any three locations along the object's boundary (for details, see Appendix 3).

Orientation alignment is simpler than the three-point scheme, because orientation is often easier to extract in a reliable and consistent manner,

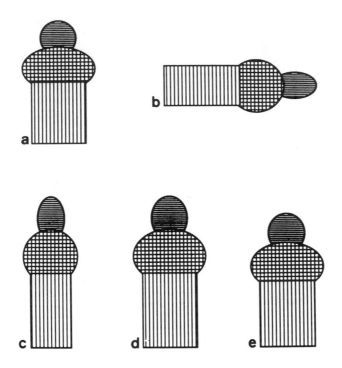

Figure 6. Orientation alignment. (a) An object, and (b) its model. (c) The model is rotated, (d) scaled in x, and (e) in y. In this case no y-shear was necessary.

compared with the extraction of discrete identifiable points. The main disadvantage of the orientation scheme is in the case that the object or its image does not have a clearly defined orientation. There are indications that such cases can also cause difficulties for recognition by humans. That is, in the absence of a well-defined orientation, human observers are more likely to fail to recognize shapes that are, in fact, identical [Rock 1973], (see also review in Jolicoeur and Landau [1984]). This suggests that the extraction of dominant orientation may play an important role in the recognition process used by the human visual system. It also appears that when the object lacks (perceptually) a preferred orientation, the human visual system may use instead an externally defined orientation (such as the direction of gravity, or the orientation of the page, in the case of printed pictures) to define orientation for alignment. If orientation is indeed used by the human visual system for alignment purposes, there are some limitations on its use. In particular, complicated figures such as faces, are difficult to recognize when their orientation differs substantially from the familiar one. This appears to be a general limitation, not specific to faces alone

[Diamond & Carey 1986].

Regardless of the exact form of the alignment scheme, the important point is that alignment can be performed using only very limited information. I shall refer to the information extracted from the image to align the viewed object with a candidate model as its "alignment key." We have seen above examples of two such alignment keys. One consists of a small set of identifiable anchor points (three, for the case of rigid motion and scale changes). The second consists of a dominant orientation, together with fragments of the object's boundary (Appendix 3).

The kind of information required for the alignment keys can, in principle, be extracted from the image in a bottom–up manner. The reason is that the alignment keys are defined by the object's bounding contour, a small number of salient points, dominant orientation, etc. This kind of information can usually be extracted by processes that do not require object–specific knowledge. Using such processes the alignment key can be extracted first, and the object can be aligned with a potential model, before the object's identity has been determined. After alignment has been performed, the viewed object and the model should be in close agreement (under ideal conditions they should match exactly) and therefore the task of determining the closest match becomes relatively straightforward. At this stage, a comparison (potentially in parallel) of the aligned object with all of the candidate models using a simple comparison method (analogous to the Hamming distance) becomes feasible.

The Alignment of Flexible Objects

Recognition by alignment was presented above in the simplified domain of flat rigid objects. In more general cases, the recognition process will still proceed using the same two stages: alignment followed by matching. The main difference is that when the objects are not flat, and the transformations are less restricted, additional information will be required to perform the alignment and "undo" the transformations. That is, the object's model will contain more information than the flat silhouette used above, and more than three anchor points (or their equivalents) will be required.

From the point of view of compensating for the allowed transformations, cases of increasing complexity include the following:

- Three dimensional objects (rather than flat) in rigid transformations. This case can be further subdivided according to whether the visible contours are "sharp," such as the edges of a cube (figure 7(a)), or smooth, such as the projected silhouette of a sphere or a cylinder (figure 7(b)). Contours of the second type are usually more difficult to represent and align. Alignment scheme for identifying the objects

in figure 7 and similar objects have been developed recently and will
be described elsewhere.

- Articulated objects, that is, objects containing movable parts, such as
  a pair of scissors or the human body. In this case the model must
  include these movements in the set of allowable transformations.

- Flexible objects, that are allowed to stretch, bend, and deform in complicated manners.

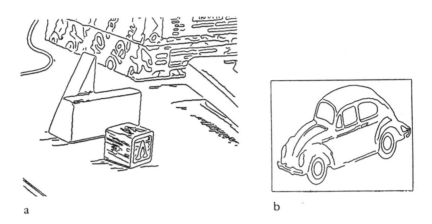

a   b

Figure 7. The edges in (a) correspond to sharp boundaries, (b) contains many
smooth boundaries.

In this section, the alignment scheme applied to flat objects transforming
rigidly is extended to deal with non-flat objects that are allowed to transform in a non-rigid manner. The goal is not to discuss the problem of
recognizing such objects in detail, but mainly to support the claim that
alignment schemes can play a useful role in the recognition of large classes
of objects.

Dealing with flexible objects is important for the purpose of object
recognition for two reasons. First, many objects such as animals and faces
can change in a non-rigid manner. Second, the differences between individual members of the same class of objects, such as two apples, can often
be viewed as small non-rigid distortions. Dealing with flexible distortions
may therefore provide a tool for handling classes of similar objects.

It also appears that for recognition by the human visual system strict
rigidity is not crucial. Objects can be recognized easily in a distorting
mirror provided that the distortions are not too extreme. Object models
can be constructed (for example, from playdough) and distorted without
affecting recognition severely. For animals such as the pigeon, rigid transformations play an even lesser role in recognition. Pigeons can learn to

recognize a large variety of objects from different views and in different contexts. In recognizing objects, they apparently do not, however, distinguish small non-rigid distortions from rigid transformations of simple three-dimensional objects [Herrnstein 1984].

Treating flexible objects as locally rigid and planar

A straightforward generalization of the simple alignment scheme is to treat regions of the object as locally planar and rigid. This generalization can be accomplished using two extensions of the simple scheme:

1   Use more than the minimum set of three anchor points.

2   Treat local regions of the object as semi-rigid.

The second of these extensions can be implemented by a simple variation of the three-point alignment scheme outlined above. It is obtained by imposing a triangulation on the set of anchor points. The rationale for the triangulation is that it divides the object into regions within which the alignment method discussed above can be applied directly. Suppose, for example, that five anchor points have been selected for alignment. As in the previous section, these points may be curvature extrema, the extreme points of elongated parts, etc. The spatial arrangement of the points themselves (without the contours to which they belong) is shown in figure 8(a). In figure 8(b), a triangulation has been applied to the points. (A triangulation of a set of points means that the points are connected by non—intersecting lines in such a way that every region internal to the convex hull of the points is a triangle, see for example, Preparata and Shamos [1985]. The triangulation is non-unique, but this does not affect the scheme.)

Each triangle is now aligned exactly as before, using its three vertices. This alignment induces a transformation to all the contours internal to the triangle. (Different triangles may undergo different transformations, but neighboring triangles coincide in the transformation assigned to their common edge.) In this manner, the alignment of the anchor points defines a transformation for the entire object. (If the anchor points are all internal to the object, some pieces of its bounding contour will fall outside the triangulated area. These pieces can be transformed as well, but this issue will not be discussed here.) As before, the final stage consists of comparing the transformed object with each candidate model.

Other extensions of the basic alignment method are also possible. The main goal behind the suggestion above is to support the point that the alignment method can be extended to cover ill-defined and complex non rigid transformations. Two examples of this alignment procedure applied non-rigidly are shown in figures 9 and 10.

Figure 9(a) and (b) shows two rabbits that are initially quite different. Shown also are a number of anchor points that were selected; they

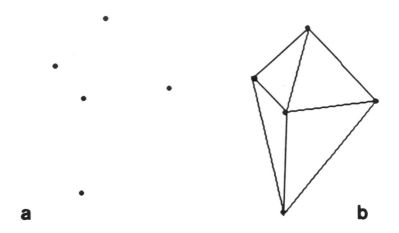

Figure 8. Triangulating a set of points. (a) The original set. (b) The set triangulated.

are primarily sharp curvature extrema and inflection points. Figure 9(c) shows the first rabbit with a subset of the anchor points that were used for alignment and their triangulation. Seven internal points have been used (Also a number of external points that were used by the algorithm but are not directly relevant here.) Figure 9(d) shows the superposition of the two rabbits following the alignment. It can be seen that the alignment, which was initially very poor, is sufficient to bring the two figures into close agreement.

Figure 10(a) and (b) shows a similar sequence applied to two different objects, a car and a rocking-horse. Anchor points were selected manually on the two figures in an attempt to bring them to the closest possible match. Figure 10(c) shows the rocking horse following the alignment; it has been transformed to approximate the car figure as much as possible. Figure 10(d) shows the aligned figures superimposed. Clearly, the agreement between the two figures is still poor.

The use of multiple models

The alignment of a flat object can be accomplished using a single model, (or sometimes two, one for each side of the surface). In the case of three-dimensional objects, in either rigid or non-rigid transformations, two possible approaches are possible. One is to maintain a single three-dimensional model for each object, and use the three-dimensional transformations recovered in the alignment stage to transform the model into alignment with the viewed object. The required transformation will be complicated from

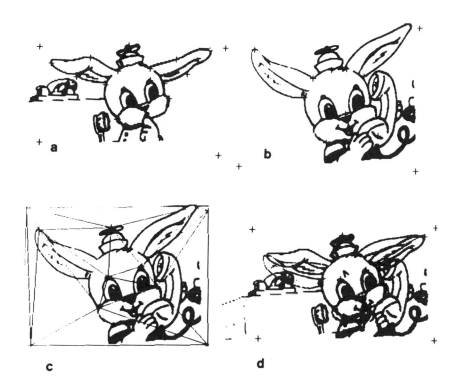

Figure 9. Matching an object to a model using flexible alignment. (a) A rabbit-image. (b) A rabbit-model. (c) The model triangulated. (d) The transformed model and the rabbit-image superimposed. Initially, the image and model are quite different. Following the alignment they are in close agreement.

a computational standpoint. The computation will require, for instance, a process of "hidden line elimination," that is, the computation of which object features are visible from a given viewing position [Lowe 1985, 1986]. In addition, a problem arises because the "alignment key" visible from some viewing angles may be occluded from others, making it difficult to use a single model to represent the object from all viewing directions.

   An alternative possibility is to store a number of models corresponding to sufficiently different viewing positions (refer to Koenderink and van Doorn [1979]. The required computations will be simplified, but at the expense of storing more models. For a system such as the brain, that appears to have a capacity to store a large number of patterns and retrieve them in a parallel manner [Willshaw *et al.* 1969; Kohonen 1978; Hopfield 1982], this is probably a useful tradeoff.

   In the first of these alternatives the model is truly object centered and view independent [Marr & Nishihara 1978]. In the second, the repre-

Figure 10. An attempt to match an object with an incorrect model using flexible alignment. (a) A car-image. (b) A horse-model. (c) The model transformed to align it with the image. (d) The transformed model and image superimposed. Because the model is an incorrect one, the agreement between the two figures following the alignment remains poor.

sentation is view dependent, because a number of different models of the same object from different viewing positions will be used [Rock *et al.* 1981; Perrett *et al.* 1985; Rock & DiVita 1987]. It is, however, expected to be view insensitive, because the differences between views are partially compensated by the alignment process.

As far as the human visual system is concerned, there are indications that observers can identify under certain situations views that correspond to the same three-dimensional object from new and widely disparate viewing positions. A number of studies have suggested the possible existence of a relatively slow process that allows the "mental rotation" of an internal model over large angles. This may be taken as evidence in support of the single model hypothesis. However, some of these studies have investigated the comparison of two objects viewed simultaneously [Shepard & Metzler 1971; Shepard & Cooper 1982], and their relation to object recognition is not entirely clear (see Palmer [1978] on the large differences between recognition and simultaneous comparison). Other studies Cooper [1976], Jolicoeur and Landau [1984], Jolicoeur [1985], and Maki 1986] have reported orientation effects consistent with an alignment approach. In these studies the time to identify shapes or recognition performance showed a dependence on the orientation difference of the shapes in the training and test presentations, or between the tested and the upright orientation. The fact that these effects diminished with increased exposure to different orientations [Corbalis *et al.* 1978; Jolicoeur 1985] is consistent with the notion of multiple models, rather than a single model view.

Additional complications regarding the internal model arise in the case of articulated objects containing parts that can move with respect to one another in a constrained manner. Examples include objects with hinges and joints, such as a pair of scissors, a hand, a limb, etc. An object of this type has associated with it a set of allowable transformations that are less restricted than the rigid transformations discussed in the previous section, but more constrained than the non-rigid transformations discussed above. The problem of representing and matching such objects is a difficult one, and it will not be examined here. It appears, however, that the notion of an alignment scheme will be applicable to such objects as well. The transformations separating a model of an articulated object of this type and a particular view of it can still be determined on the basis of partial information. This information can be used, as before, to compensate for the transformations, and bring the viewed object and the model into alignment.

The discussion in this and the previous section suggests that if the alignment stage is performed properly, then, for both rigid and non-rigid objects, the match with the correct model would stand out as significantly better than with all other models. The alignment stage itself, however, raises a number of difficulties. For example, the anchor points, or other alignment keys, such as the orientation of the object or of its parts, must be extracted reliably from the viewed object and these points must be matched against the corresponding locations in the model. These and related difficulties are examined in the next section.

Two main requirements from the alignment approach

Each of the approaches to visual object recognition makes a number of critical assumptions that give rise to certain difficulties when the approach is applied to large classes of natural objects. The invariant properties approach assumes that simple invariant properties would be sufficient to characterize the different objects. But finding properties that are feasible to compute and at the same time powerful enough to characterize uniquely a large variety of objects did not prove successful, and the approach has been applied to limited domains only.

The structural description approach assumes the existence of categories for both parts and spatial relations that are sufficiently sensitive and stable [Marr & Nishihara 1978]. They should be sufficiently sensitive to be able to make the required distinctions between objects, and at the same time stable enough to produce the same description for different instances of the same object (or class of objects). This proved to be difficult, especially for the categories of spatial relations. The structural description approach also faces some difficult computational problems—such as the reliable segmentation into parts and the computation of their spatial relations.

The alignment approaches uses the constraint that the transformations involved in object recognition are usually "low dimensional" in the sense that given the effect of the transformation on restricted parts of the image (for example three points in the case of rigid objects) it is possible to approximate its effect everywhere. This constraint often holds even in cases when global invariants and natural parts are difficult to define.

The use of alignment in the course of object recognition raises two main problems. The first is performing consistent alignment in a bottom-up manner. The second is a computational problem of transforming a large number of models.

Consistent bottom-up alignment

For alignment to be successful, the information required (the alignment key) must be extracted reliably from the image. This stage is performed early in the recognition process, and therefore it must depend only on general image properties such as the saliency of some special points rather than on properties associated with specific objects. If alignment is performed, for example, on the basis of three points, then a small number of points, ideally always including the same three, must be extracted from the image in a reliable and consistent manner.

At least two factors can help this alignment process. The first is the use of object orientation. As mentioned in the previous section, when a dominant orientation for the object can be computed, it can substantially facilitate the alignment process. The alignment process can also be facilitated by using a number of different models for the same object. If the views become too disparate so that the use of the same alignment key becomes difficult, a new model can be added to the library of models.

It remains to be seen to what extent alignment keys can be extracted reliably from object images. The task, however, appears considerably less demanding than the problem of decomposing an object in a consistent and reliable manner into all of its constituent parts. Alignment requires less information, and relatively stable prominent properties can be used for the task, such as the most salient points associated with a given object, or its dominant orientation.

It is also possible that in the recognition of a specific object, alignment may sometimes be obtained in more than a single stage. A matching may first be obtained with a general category, such as a face. This match may trigger routines for extracting features that can serve as useful additional anchor points, such as the eyes, even in cases where these features were not particularly salient in the original image.

Transforming the models

In matching a viewed object to a potential model using the alignment method, one of them (at least) must be transformed to compensate for the transformations between the two. It is possible to transform either the viewed object, or the stored model, (or both).

Applying the alignment transformations to the viewed object only has one important advantage: the transformation is applied only once. All the models remain unchanged. This can be accomplished provided that the various models are stored in memory in a common "canonical" form. Consider, for example, the case in which the viewed object is aligned to the model on the basis of three anchor points. For simplicity assume that each model has exactly three anchor points. An alignment transformation applied to the viewed object must bring the three points into alignment with the corresponding points in all of the potentially relevant models simultaneously. This can be accomplished in a single step if the models are stored in a canonical form, in which the three anchor points are already in register.

A canonical form may be defined in an analogous manner also for alignment based on dominant orientation rather than anchor points. In either case, however, the use of canonical forms for the models also has its drawbacks. One complication arises if it is desired to recognize the same object using different alignment keys. Such a redundancy is, for example, useful for dealing with occlusion. In a canonical form scheme, each model will have to be represented by multiple copies, one for each different alignment key.

An alternative would be to apply an alignment transformation separately to each of the potentially relevant models. In this case, the models need not be stored in any canonical form, because each one is transformed individually to align it with the viewed object. This also has the advantage that different transformations may be applied to different models. For example, the model of an object may include three-dimensional information that is not available from a single view of the object. This three-dimensional information could be used in transforming the model and predicting how it will appear from a different viewpoint. The model may also specify, for instance, that a certain point in the object can serve as a joint, where parts can change their relative orientation. For this model, but not for other ones, an attempt to align the model with the object may include bending around this known point. Such individual transformations add flexibility to the matching process, but at the cost of increased computational effort.

It is not clear at this stage which approach (transforming the viewed object or transforming the models) should be preferred. Two additional considerations are relevant in this regard. First, it is not necessary to adopt an extreme approach, a combination of the two is also possible. For example, oriented objects may be stored in a canonical orientation. The viewed object is then rotated once to bring its own orientation into alignment with the canonical orientation of the models. Following this common stage, an additional transformation, such as change of scale, may be applied to each model individually. More generally, the mixed approach is to apply to the viewed object all the alignment transformations that are common to all of the relevant models, yet allow the application of additional transformations to the different models. The second comment is that it may be possible to keep the transformations applied individually to the different models simple in nature, for example, some scaling or stretching along one direction (as discussed in Appendix 2). When the discrepancy between a particular view of an object and its models already stored in memory becomes too large to be overcome using these restricted transformations, an additional model of the object can be added to the model library. The transformations that are applied individually to the different models may therefore be kept sufficiently restricted, so that the computational load required for applying the transformations to many objects in parallel may be kept within reasonable bounds. The resulting computational load is likely to be less prohibitive than some alternative schemes, for example, the matching of graph-like structures required in the structural description approach.

Aligning Pictorial Descriptions

Adding abstract descriptions

The last few sections have discussed the alignment approach in its "pure" form. The examples used unarticulated object contours as models, without defining parts in the object, and without using abstract descriptions, as done in the object decomposition approach.

It is also possible, however, to combine the main advantages of the part-decomposition approach with an alignment approach. The resulting

Figure 11. The use of an abstract label in a pictorial description.

scheme appears to be more suitable for dealing with the recognition of various objects that cannot be handled easily by either method alone.

Consider for instance the rooster sketch in figure 11. An internal model for this figure in a structural description method will contain a number of parts with their associated shape descriptions, and a symbolic description of the spatial relations among the various parts. A pure alignment method would keep a replica of the figure as an internal model. In evaluating the match between this model and a new viewed object, which is another possible instance of a rooster figure, the method will first try to align the model and the viewed object as precisely as possible. Clearly, the details of the rooster's crown have no particular importance in the normal process of recognizing such a figure. The part decomposition method seems to offer a more appropriate approach in this case. As mentioned under "Recognition using object decomposition," the main step in this method is to start the many-to-one reduction at the part level. The details of the part depicting the crown will be ignored and replaced by a more abstract description, perhaps a "wiggly contour" of a certain type. The same kind of abstraction can be used in the alignment approach as well. One can imagine a "label" stating "wiggly line" being overlaid over the crown contour. This more abstract label is associated with a given location in the figure and it is shifted along with it in the course of the alignment process. When the aligned figure is then matched against the rooster model, the detailed internal contours of the crown in the aligned object and the model may not be in good agreement, but they will both have the same label in corresponding locations. Labels of this type may describe properties of two-dimensional contours, but may also be three-dimensional in nature, such as locally convex or concave surface patches, etc.

There are two differences in the manner that abstract descriptions are used in the alignment scheme compared with the structural description approach. The most important difference is that in the alignment method the description may be called "pictorial." It is much closer to the image compared with structural descriptions. In structural descriptions, spatial relations, like part shapes, are described using a limited set of categories such as "above," "in between," "near," etc. The position of part A may be described as "above B and near it, and to the left of C." This description is abstract in the sense that many different configurations in the input would fit a given category such as "above" or "left of." In contrast, in the alignment approach spatial relations are not categorized. Instead, the actual position of parts and labels is preserved. The resulting description consequently has an image-like structure in which labels are associated with particular locations. Unlike part-decomposition schemes, descriptive labels are associated with specific locations, without requiring a precise delineation of part boundaries. In such a scheme it is natural to associate descriptions for example with locations such as the cheeks or forehead in a face image. These are well-defined locations, but not precisely delineated parts in the sense used in part-decomposition schemes.

The second difference is that in the alignment method abstract descriptions do not replace lower-level descriptions—they are added to them. A match may eventually occur at a low level (the actual contours may be in close agreement), or it may occur at a higher level (the corresponding abstract descriptions may match without a good match at the lower level). In the pure structural description method, without alignment, the low-level components such as boundary contours cannot be expected to match. The scheme must rely instead entirely on the correct categorization of parts; that is, that different views of the same part will end up with the same abstract description. Unlike the part decomposition scheme, in the alignment scheme the part decomposition is therefore not required to be complete. Abstract labels may be associated with some locations, while other pieces of the object may remain unarticulated, not broken into parts, and not assigned to any category, or described by any abstract descriptors. Because of the alignment stage, which is not used in the structural description approach, these unarticulated parts are expected to produce (following the alignment) a good match with the stored model.

The use of pictorial labels of this general type is not entirely new. In fact, one can view edge detection and representation as a simple example of pictorial descriptions. At the raw input level the light intensity distribution around an object boundary would change, for example, with the illumination conditions. The operation of edge detection replaces the intensity distribution around an intensity edge with a more abstract label (the presence of an edge). The label is pictorial: it is associated with a location, and transforms with it during alignment.

The combined scheme, using alignment as well as abstract descriptions, can be described as the *"alignment of pictorial descriptions."* This name implies three components. First, it is an alignment method. Second, it also uses (unlike the examples in the previous two sections) abstract descriptions. Third, these descriptions are used pictorially: they are associated with specific locations, rather than being described by spatial relation categories. Such descriptions can be rotated, scaled, stretched, etc. prior to the matching stage.

The entire object recognition process is, in the alignment approach, less symbolic, more pictorial, and closer to the lower-level visual processes, than the structural description approach.

Steps in the recognition process

The alignment of pictorial descriptions is a general approach to the regularity problem in object recognition. This approach does not specify directly the processing stages that must take place in extracting the information from the image prior to the alignment stage, or the matching that takes place following it. These processing stages are required not only in the alignment scheme, but also in most other recognition schemes that have been proposed.

To put the alignment scheme in perspective, this final section will list briefly some of the major steps that are involved in the recognition process, and describe the problems that they raise.

◇ Selection

By "selection" I mean identifying in the image a location that is likely to contain an object of interest. A human observer rarely scans the entire scene in a systematic manner. Very often, objects of interest somehow attract our attention, and subsequent processing seems to be concentrated at these locations. Lowe [1986] has proposed a scheme in which feature configurations that have the least probability of arising by coincidence are examined first. (A similar notion has been suggested by Witkin and Tenenbaum [1983]). In human vision the initial selection appears to be based on simpler criteria. The human visual system seems unable to extract relational properties among features in the early, pre-attentive, parallel stage [Treisman & Gelade 1980]. Selection may be based instead on some measure of saliency defined by local differences in contrast, color, size, orientation, etc. [Engel 1974; Sagi & Julesz 1985; Mahoney 1986].

◇ Segmentation

By "segmentation" in this context I mean the delineation of a sub-part of the image to which subsequent recognition processes will be applied. Segmentation schemes have been investigated extensively in the field of image processing, but their goals are usually more ambitious than what is required for recognition by alignment. For example, they often attempt to segment the entire image, as opposed to just the region of interest. Segmentation for recognition, applied to the region of interest only, can therefore be obtained by universal routines [Ullman 1984] that are spatially focused, rather than as a part of the base representations, where the computation is spatially uniform. For recognition by alignment, the main requirement from the segmentation stage is that the alignment key will be selected from a region that is likely to correspond to a single object. For example, if alignment is performed on the basis of a small number of salient points, then the alignment process would not be successful if the points belong in fact to different objects. However, the exact delineation of the entire object is not of major importance at this stage.

◇ **Description**

The next stage involves the extraction from the region of interest the information that will be used for matching the viewed object with stored object-models. Most recognition schemes propose that the viewed object is described for this purpose in some fashion, using one-dimensional contours [Baker 1977], two-dimensional surface patches [Dane & Bajcsy 1982; Potmesil 1983; Faugeras 1984; Brady *et al.* 1985], or three-dimensional volumetric descriptions [Marr & Nishihara 1978; Biederman 1985].

An important decision at this stage is to what extent the description of the viewed object should rely on detailed three-dimensional information. Some recognition schemes (see Besl and Jain [1985]) assume the availability of a detailed and precise depth map of the visible surfaces. Such information is not always available in the image, and from human vision it appears that recognition can usually proceed in the absence of detailed three-dimensional information. It is desirable, therefore, for the recognition process not to depend critically on detailed three-dimensional information, although such information may be used when available.

If detailed three-dimensional information is not required, it appears that descriptions based on object contours are better suited for the recognition task than surface based and volumetric descriptions. At the same time, it is important not to identify object contours with intensity edges. Many intensity edges in the image are irrelevant for the purpose of recognition, and recognition can proceed in the lack of intensity edges altogether. For example, some objects can be recognized in random dot stereograms. In this case object contours are defined, for example, by discontinuities in depth and surface orientation, but not by intensity changes.

◇ **Alignment key extraction**

The alignment key is used to bring the viewed object and internal models into alignment. As discussed under "The Alignment approach applied to simple objects," a number of different alignment procedures may be used, depending on some properties of the viewed object. For example, if it has a clearly defined orientation, then this orientation may be used for alignment. If the object is unoriented, the alignment key may be composed of salient points.

◇ Alignment

This stage brings the object into register with potentially matching objects. As suggested in the previous section, it may be possible to break down the alignment stage into two successive steps. In the first, which may be called "common alignment," the viewed object is brought into correspondence with a large number of models stored in memory in some canonical form. The second stage is composed of individual alignments: different models align themselves individually to the viewed object. A number of problems remain regarding the parallel execution of this stage. Can a large number of models be aligned simultaneously? If not, how can the load required by individual alignments be reduced?

◇ Model filtering

Following alignment, the degree of match between the viewed object and different models must be assessed, and the best match selected. A number of different recognition schemes precede the final match with a process of model filtering. The goal of this stage is to use some simple criteria to "filter out" unlikely models, and obtain a smaller set of likely candidates [Lowe 1985]. In other schemes this stage also includes rank-ordering of the models, so that matching with the more likely ones is attempted first.

It is not clear, however, that model filtering of this type can lead to significant savings in the required computations. If we start with a large number of models, it is unreasonable to expect that a simple filtering scheme would be sufficient to select a small number of candidates, because this will place the burden of the recognition process on the filtering stage. Furthermore, it may be dangerous to eliminate a potential match on the basis of partial evidence. For example, the presence of eyes is likely to eliminate in a filtering stage the object "telephone" (along with many others) from the list of viable candidates. We have no major difficulties, however, in trying to recognize for example a telephone with eyes painted on it. It seems, for the above reasons, that the viewed object will have to be matched, perhaps in parallel, against a large number of object models.

Similarly, rank-ordering the models is not likely to result in substantial savings. In many instances the matching process will not result in a perfect match. We still wish to retrieve in these cases the best matching model.

This means that the matching process will have to be fairly exhaustive, unless a perfect match is encountered. It seems, in conclusion, that filtering and rank-ordering may help to limit the search in some specific sequential implementations, but in the more general case matching against a large number of object models is probably unavoidable.

◇ Matching

Following the alignment stage, the correct model and the viewed object are expected to be in better agreement, but usually differences between them will still exist. A measure of the degree of match is therefore required to decide which of the models resembles the viewed object most closely. I will not attempt to define such a measure, but only define three general requirements for this measure.

First, as mentioned in under "The alignment approach to object recognition," the contributions of different parts of the object to the match quality may carry different weights. Some parts may be small in size, but still be crucial for defining the object. Other parts may carry little weight and even no weight at all. In some cases it is also expected that the distinction between highly similar objects may require an additional separate stage. Two objects that differ only in small details would not be distinguished immediately, but would trigger a specialized routine [Ullman 1984] to distinguish between them.

Second, in aligning pictorial descriptions a match may be obtained at different levels, such as the underlying object contours, or the level of more abstract descriptors. The contributions of the different levels will have to be combined in an appropriate manner. The matching score is likely to increase with the set of features (contours and labels) in common to the object and model, and decrease as a function of the features that appear in one but not in the other (see Tversky [1977]).

Finally, the decision regarding the best matching model will be affected by factors other than similarity of shape. The degree of match may have to take into account, for instance, the amount of distortion that was required to bring the viewed object and model into registration. As discussed in the first section, the selection of the appropriate model may also be biased, for example, by prior expectation and by proximity to other objects in the scene.

Empirical evidence related to alignment in human vision

A number of psychological studies have reported effects supporting the notion that viewed objects are aligned with stored models prior to recognition. There is also some evidence relating to two other aspects of the alignment method: the storage of multiple views (as opposed, for example, to a single structural description), and the storage and use of pictorial information (at least as one possible avenue in recognition). Evidence related to these three areas is listed briefly below. In reviewing these empirical findings, it should be noted that the currently available psychological and physiological evidence is insufficient for deciding between competing theories of visual object recognition. Some experiments (for example White [1980], Ely [1982], and Biederman [1985]) have been interpreted as supporting a structural description approach, while others, such as the ones listed below, appear to agree more with an alignment approach. For many of the reported experiments, competing interpretations are possible. Additional work will be required to allow more precise and unambiguous distinctions between competing theories.

◇ **Aligning transformations**

The empirical evidence related to the possible role of an alignment stage in human object recognition has focused primarily on the effects of orientation and scale on the recognition process. A number of studies have suggested that during recognition the orientation of viewed objects is brought into alignment with their corresponding stored models [Cooper 1976; Shwartz 1981; Wiser 1981; Jolicoeur & Landau 1984; Jolicoeur 1985; Maki 1986]. The main finding in these studies was that recognition latencies depended on the angle separating the orientation of a previously learned model and the subsequently viewed version of it. Similar effects of orientations were also found in related perceptual tasks, such as the comparison of two simultaneously presented shapes (for example, Shepard and Metzler [1971], and Shepard and Cooper [1982]). It appears, however, that the mechanisms used in simultaneous comparison tasks may be different from those used in visual recognition, (see for example, Palmer [1978] on the large differences between recognition and simultaneous viewing) and therefore it may not be possible to generalize directly from one set of experiments to the other.

Although the evidence for orientation alignment in human visual recognition appears fairly compelling, there is no universal agreement on this point. For example, several studies using character recognition [Corballis & Nagourney 1978; White 1980; Eley 1982] have not found appreciable orientation effects on recognition latencies. However, as noted for example by Shwartz [1981], these studies tend to fall under one of two categories:

1   Objects that have some special distinguishing features.

2   Objects that have been learned in many different orientations (a point that was tested by Taar and Pinker, see below).

In experiments that used natural objects rather than letters and digits (for example, Shwartz [1981] and Jolicoeur [1985]), the orientation effects were usually pronounced. Even in the case of alphanumeric characters, it appears that, when examined at a finer time resolution using a masking technique, effects indicative of orientation normalization emerge [Jolicoeur & Landau 1984].

As for scale, a number of studies have suggested the existence of a size normalization operation in human recognition prior to the matching process. This is based primarily on experiments showing that recognition latencies increase with the discrepancy in size between stored and viewed shapes (for example, Sekuler and Nash [1972], Larsen and Bundesen [1978], Jolicoeur [1987], and Jolicoeur and Besner [1987]), with some evidence for model rather than image scaling [Larsen & Bundesen 1978]. Again, similar results were obtained in experiments using simultaneous presentations (for example, Bundesen and Larsen [1975], and Larsen [1985]). In some studies (for example, Besner and Coltheart [1975] and Besner [1983]) a monotonic size discrepancy was observed for "same" but not for "different" trials. A possible explanation for this was proposed and tested by Jolicoeur and Besner [1987], who concluded that a scaling operation probably precedes the matching in recognition for both "same" and "different" conditions.

In conclusion, it appears that a considerable body of psychophysical evidence supports the possible use of aligning transformations for both orientation and scale in human object recognition. With respect to orientation alignment, it should be noted that past studies have focused on orientation changes in the image plane (that is, rotation about the line of sight). To allow a more detailed comparison with the alignment process described in this chapter, it would be of considerable interest to test the effect on recognition latencies of rotations in three-dimensional space.

◇ The use of multiple views

The alignment method discussed above suggested the use of a number of models for each objects. Multiple models are required in the alignment scheme when the discrepancy between different views of the same object become too large to be compensated by the aligning transformations.

There is only limited empirical evidence regarding the storage of multiple views, but the existing evidence tends to support this notion. For example, several studies that examined the effect of orientation on recognition latencies have found that the initial latencies depended on the angular deviation of the image from the learned model. The effect often diminished, however, after the image has been presented repeatedly at several different orientations, suggesting the possibility that a number of new models, at different orientations, have been added to the internal store of models (for example Corballis et al. [1978], and Jolicoeur [1985]). This possibility has been tested directly recently by Taar and Pinker [1988]. In their experiments, the same target object was learned by the subjects at four different orientations. Subsequent recognition times depended on the angular separation of the test image from the closest learned target, suggesting that all four views have been stored and used in the alignment process.

The use of multiple views is also supported by the studies of Rock *et al.* [1981] and Rock and DiVita [1987]. These experiments have shown that recognition is severely impaired when the spatial rotation separating the learned model from the viewed object becomes too large. There is also some physiological evidence [Perret *et al.* 1986] that is consistent with this notion. Recording from face-sensitive neurons in the macaque's STS, Perret *et al.*'s conclusion was that memory representations for faces are viewer-centered rather than object-centered, and that each representation is usually view-insensitive, covering a rather wide range of orientations in space. These characteristics agree well with the alignment scheme.

◇ Pictorial matching

In the alignment scheme the matching is performed pictorially, comparing contours and abstract labels at corresponding locations in the aligned image and model. Again, the relevant empirical evidence is limited, but pictorial comparisons appear to be at least one possible avenue in the process of object recognition. In one experiment, Palmer [1978] used figures that had different amounts of pictorial overlap, and different degree of structural similarity (number of parts, closure, etc.). The experiments showed that structural similarity had a strong effect on similarity judgments and on simultaneous comparisons, whereas in sequential presentation, which is essentially a recognition task, the main determinant was the degree of pictorial overlap. Similarly, Larsen and Bundesen [1978] conclude from their set of experiments on the recognition of shapes of different sizes that "[the results]... tend to support the initial supposition that visual pattern recognition is based on point-wise comparison of stimulus patterns with memory representations" (p. 19).

It appears, in conclusion, that there are significant points of agreement between empirical findings regarding human visual object recognition and several aspects of the alignment process, such as the use of aligning transformations prior to the matching, the use of several view-insensitive models to represent a given object, and the employment of pictorial representations. As mentioned above, however, the available evidence should be considered preliminary, and additional testing would be necessary to reveal in more detail the processes subserving object recognition in human vision.

Summary

Figure 12 summarizes schematically the main general approaches to visual object recognition as discussed in this chapter. At the top level classification there are three broad classes of theories: invariant properties, object decomposition into parts, and alignment methods.

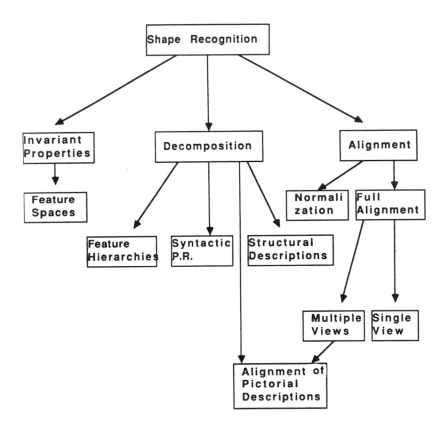

Figure 12. Classification of the main approaches to visual object recognition.

In the invariant properties method the main approaches have been associated with the use of multidimensional feature spaces. Object decomposition theories can be further subdivided into generic *versus* non-generic ones. In schemes using generic parts objects are described exclusively in terms of a small number of prototypical parts. Once a part has been found, its internal structure becomes immaterial for the purpose of classification. For example, after a part has been approximated by a particular generalized cylinder [Binford 1971; Marr & Nishihara 1978], or a geon [Biederman 1985], classification proceeds on the basis of the part type rather than its detailed shape. Most of the decomposition schemes that have been proposed (feature hierarchies, syntactic pattern recognition, structural descriptions) belong to this category. In contrast, the use of labels as described under "The alignment of flexible objects" is non-generic: a label is added to the low level description rather than replacing it, and a match to the model may occur at either level.

Alignment methods are divided in the diagram into normalization and full alignment methods. Normalization schemes are more restricted: they compensate for similarity transformations (displacement, scaling, rotation in the image plane), using primarily global measures (such as center of mass, convex hull, etc.) Full alignment methods attempt to compensate for a larger set of transformations, such as rotation in space and non-rigid transformations. A further distinction can be made between object-centered alignment schemes, using a single model, and a more viewer-centered approach using multiple views.

The alignment of pictorial descriptions described in the final three sections combines a full alignment approach with decomposition using non-generic parts, and it uses multiple views rather than a single object-centered description.

Theoretical consideration and preliminary tests suggest that this approach is likely to prove useful for the general problem of visual object recognition. Additional work will be required to extend the scheme to more complicated domains and to compare it with shape based object recognition by the human visual system.

References

Abu-Mostafa, Y. S., and D. Praltis [1987], "Optical neural computing," *Scientific American*, vol. 256, no. 3, pp. 66–73.

Albert, A. E. [1972], "Regression and the Moore-Penrose pseudoinverse," Academic Press, New York.

Alt, F. Z. [1962], "Digital pattern recognition by moments," in *Optical Character Recognition*, edited by G. L. Fischer, D. K. Pollock, B. Raddack, and M. E. Stevens, McGregor & Werner Inc., Washington.

Asada, H., and M. Brady [1985], "The curvature primal sketch," *IEEE PAMI* vol. 8, no. 1, pp. 2-14.

Figure 1 by J. Schick is reproduced from "All Around the House," [1985], by W. H. Hooks, B. D. Boegehold, B. Brenner, J. Oppenheim, S. V. Reit, and J. Schick with the kind permission of Barron's Educational Series, Inc.

I thank W. Richards, E. Hildreth, S. Kosslyn, E. Grimson, D. Huttenlocher, and J. Mahoney for valuable discussions and comments, and J. and T. Ullman for insightful comments on figure 1.

Baird, H. S. [1984], *Model-Based Image Matching Using Locations,* MIT Press, Cambridge, MA.

Ballard, D. H. [1986], "Cortical connections and parallel processing: Structure and function," *Behavioral & Brain Sciences,* vol. 9, pp. 67-120.

Ballard, D. H., and H. Tanaka [1985], "Transformational form perception in 3D: Constraints, algorithms, implementation," *Proc. 9th Joint. Int. Conf. Art. Intel.,* pp. 964-968.

Barlow, H. B. [1972], "Single units and sensation: A neuron doctrine for perceptual psychology?" *Perception, I.,* pp. 371-394.

Barlow, H. B., R. Narasimhan, and A. Rosenfeld [1972], "Visual pattern analysis in machines and animals," *Science,* vol. 177, pp. 567-575.

Besl, P. J., and R. C. Jain [1985], "Three–dimensional object recognition," *Computing surveys,* vol. 17, no. 1, pp. 75-145.

Besner, D. [1978], "Pattern recognition: Are size and orientation additive factors?" *Perception & Psychophysics,* vol. 23, p. 93.

Besner, D. [1983], 'Visual pattern recognition: Size preprocessing reexamined," *Quat. J. Exp. Psychol.,* vol. 35A, pp. 209-216.

Besner, D., and M. Coltheart [1975], "Same-different judgments with words and nonwords: The differential effect of relative size," *Memory & Cognition,* vol. 3, pp. 673-677.

Biederman, I. [1985], "Human image understanding: Recent research and a theory," *Comp. Vis. Graph. Im. Proc.,* vol. 32, pp. 29-73.

Binford, T. O. [1971], "Visual perception by computer. Presented to the IEEE Conference on Systems and Control," Miami.

Binford, T. O. [1982], "Survey of model-based image analysis systems," *Int. J. Robotics Research,* vol. 1, no. 1, pp. 18-64.

Bolles, R. C., and R. A. Cain [1982], "Recognizing and locating partially visible objects: The local-feature-focus method," *Int. J. Robotics Research,* vol. 1, no. 3, pp. 57-82.

Brady M., J. Ponce, A. Yuille, and H. Asada [1985], "Describing surfaces," Report AIM-882, Artificial Intelligence Laboratory , Massachusetts Institute of Technology, Cambridge, MA.

Brooks, R. [1981], "Symbolic reasoning among 3-dimensional models and 2-dimensional images," *Artificial Intelligence,* vol. 17, pp. 285-349.

Bundesen, C., and A. Larsen [1975], "Visual transformation of size," *J. Exp. Psychol., HP&P,* vol. 1, pp. 214-220.

Cerella, J. [1986], "Pigeons and perceptrons," *Pattern Recognition,* vol. 19, no. 6, pp. 431–438.

Clowes, M. B. [1967], "Perception, picture processing, and computers," in *Machine Intelligence,* edited by N. L. Collins, and D. Michie, vol. 1, pp. 181–197, Oliver & Boyd, Edinburgh.

Connell, J. H. [1985], "Learning shape descriptions: Generating and generalizing models of visual objects," Report AIM-853, Artificial Intelligence Laboratory , Massachusetts Institute of Technology, Cambridge, MA.

Cooper, L. A. [1976], "Demonstration of a mental analog of an external rotation," *Perception & Psychophysics*, vol. 1, pp. 20–43.

Corballis, M. C., and B. A. Nagourney [1978], "Latencies to categorize disoriented alphanumeric characters as letters or digits," *Canad. J. Psychol.,* vol. 32, pp. 186-188.

Corballis, M. C., N. J. Zbrodoff, L. I. Schetzer, and P. B. Butler, [1978], "Decisions about identity and orientation of rotated letters and digits," *Memory & cognition*, vol. 6, pp. 98–107.

Corcoran, D. W. J. [1971], *Pattern Recognition*, Penguin Books.

Cutting, J. E., and L. T. Kozlowski [1977], "Recognizing Friends by Their Walk: Gait Perception Without Familiarity Cues," *Bull. Psychonometric Soc.,* vol. 9, no. 5, pp. 353-356.

Dane, C., and R. Bajcsy [1982], "An object-centered three-dimensional model builder," *Proc. 6th Int. Conf. Pat. Recog.*, Munich, West Germany, pp. 348-350.

Diamond, R., and S. Carey [1986], "Why faces are and are not special: an effect of expertise," *Journal of Experimental Psychology; General* vol. 115, no. 2, pp. 107–117.

Eley, M. G. [1982], "Identifying rotated letter-like symbols," *Memory & Cognition,* vol. 10, pp. 25-32.

Engel, F. L. [1974], "Visual conspecuity and selective background interference in eccentric vision," *Vision Research* vol. 14, pp. 459–471.

Faugeras, O. D. [1984], "New steps towards a flexible 3 D vision system for robotics," *Proc. 7th Int. Conf. Pat. Recog.*, Montreal, Canada, pp. 796-805.

Faugeras, O. D., and M. Hebert [1986], "The representation, recognition, and location of 3-D objects," *Int. J. Robotics Research* vol. 5, no. 3, pp. 27–52.

Fischler, M. A., and R. C. Bolles [1981], "Random sample consensus: a paradigm for model fitting with application to image analysis and automated cartograph," *Communication of the ACM* vol. 24, no. 6, pp. 381-395.

Foster, D. H., and R. j. Mason [1979], "Transformation and relational-structure schemes for visual pattern recognition," *Biol. Cyber.* vol. 32, pp. 85-93.

Freeman, W. J. [1979], "EEG Analysis gives model of neuronal template matching mechanism for sensory search with olfactory bulb," *Biological Cybernetics* vol. 35, pp. 221–234.

Fu, K. S. [1974], *Syntactic Methods in Pattern Recognition* Academic Press, New York.

Garey, M. R., and D. S. Johnson [1979], *Computers and Intractability*, Freeman, San Francisco.

Gibson, J. J. [1950], *The perception of the visual world.* Houghton Mifflin, Boston.

Gibson, J. J. [1979], *The ecological approach to visual perception,* Houghton Mifflin, Boston.

Grimsdale, R. L., F. H. Sumner, C. J. Tunis, and T. Kilburn [1959], "A system for the automatic recognition of patterns," *Proc. Inst. Elec. Eng.*, vol. 106, no. 26, pp. 210–221.

Grimson, W. E. L., and T. Lozano-Perez [1984], "Model-based recognition and localization from sparse data," *Int. J. Robotics. Research*, vol. 3, no. 3, pp. 3-35.

Grimson, W. E. L., and T. Lozano-Perez [1987], "Localizing overlapping parts by searching the interpretation tree," *PAMI* vol. 9, no. 4, pp. 469–482.

Herrnstein, R. J. [1984], "Objects, categories, and discriminative stimuli," in *Animal Cognition*, edited by H. L. Roitblat, T. G. Bever, and H. S. Terrace, Lawrence Erlbaum Assoc., Hillsdale NJ.

Hinton, G. F. [1981], "Shape representation in parallel systems," *Proc. 7th Joint. Int. Conf. Art. Intel.*, pp. 964-968.

Hoffman, D. [1983], "The interpretation of visual illusions," *Scien. Am*, vol. 249, no. 6, pp. 154-162.

Hoffman, D., and W. Richards [1986], "Parts of Recognition," in *From Pixels to Predicates*, edited by A. P. Pentland, Ablex Publishing Corp., Norwood NJ.

Hopfield, J. J. [1982], "Neural networks and physical systems with emergent collective computational abilities," *Proc. Nat. Acad. Sci. USA 79,* pp. 2554-2558.

Hubel, D. G., and T. N. Wiesel [1962], "Receptive fields, binocular interaction, and functional architecture in the cat's visual cortex," *Journal of Physiology (London)*, vol. 160, pp. 106-154.

Hubel, D. H., and T. N. Wiesel [1968], "Receptive fields and functional architecture of monkey striate cortex," *Journal of Physiology (London)*, vol. 195, pp. 215-243.

Huberman, B. A., and T. Hogg [1984], "Adaptation and self-repair in parallel computing structures," *Phys. Rev. Let.* vol. 52, no. 12, pp. 1048-1051.

Huttenlocher, D. P., and S. Ullman [1987], "Object recognition using alignment," Report AIM-937, Artificial Intelligence Laboratory , Massachusetts Institute of Technology, Cambridge, MA.

Johansson, G. [1973], "Visual Perception of Biological Motion and a Model for Its Analysis," *Perception and Psychophysics,* vol. 14, no. 2, pp. 201-211.

Jolicoeur, P. [1985], "The time to name disoriented natural objects," *Memory & Cognition*, vol. 13, no. 4, pp. 289-303.

Jolicoeur, P. [1987], "A size-congruency effect in memory for visual shape," *Mem. & Cog.,* vol. 15, no. 6, pp. 531-543.

Jolicoeur, P., and D. Besner [1987], "Additivity and interaction between size ratio and response category in the comparison of size-discrepant shapes," *J. Exp. Psychol., HP&P,* vol. 13, no. 3, pp. 478-487.

Jolicoeur, P., and M. Landau [1984], "Effects of orientation on the identification of simple visual patterns," *Canad. J. Psychol.* vol. 38 no. 1, pp. 80-93.

Kanade, T., and J. R. Kender [1983], "Mapping image properties into shape constraints: Skewed symmetry, affine-transformable patterns and the shape from texture paradigm," in *Human and Machine vision* edited by J. Beck, B. Hope, and A. Rozenfeld, Academic Press, New York.

Koenderink, J. J., and A. J. van Doorn [1979], "The internal representation of solid shape with respect to vision," *biol. Cybernetics,* vol. 32, pp. 211–216.

Kohonen, T. [1978], *Associative Memory: A System Theoretic Approach,* Springer Verlag, Berlin.

Lamdan, Y., J. T. Schwartz, and H. Wolfson [1987], "On recognition of 3-D objects from 2-D images," Report 122, Courant Inst. of Math. Sciences, Robotics Tech.

Larsenv, A. [1985], "Pattern matching: Effects of size ratio, angular difference in orientation, and familiarity," *Perception & Psychophysics,* vol. 38, pp. 63-68.

Larsen, A., and C. Bundesen [1978], "Size scaling in visual pattern recognition," *J. Exp. Psychol., HP&P,* vol. 4, no. 1, pp. 1-20.

Leeuwenberg, E. L. J., and H. f. J. M. Buffart [1978], (eds) *Formal Theories of Visual Perception,* J. Wiley & Sons, Chichester.

Lindsay, P. H., and D. A. Norman [1977], "Human Information Processing," (2nd edition) Academic Press, New york.

Lowe, D. G. [1985], *Perceptual Organization and Visual Recognition.* Kluwer Academic Publishers, Boston.

Lowe, D. G. [1986], "Three-dimensional object recognition from single two-dimensional images," *Robotics Research Technical Report 202,* Courant Institute of Math. Sciences, New York University.

Mahoney, J. V. [1986], "Image chunking: defining spatial building blocks for scene analysis," M.S. Thesis, Department of Electrical Engineering and Computer Science, Massachusetts Institute of Technology, Cambridge, MA.

Maki, R. [1986], "Naming and locating the tops of rotated pictures," *Canad. J. Psychol.,* vol. 40, no. 4, pp. 368-387.

Marr, D., and H. K. Nishihara [1978], "Representation and recognition of the spatial organization of three-dimensional shapes," *Proc. Roy. Soc. B., 200,* pp. 269-291.

Milner, P. M. [1974], "A model for visual shape recognition," *Psychol. Rev.,* vol. 81, no. 6, pp. 521-535.

Minsky, M., and S. Papert [1969] *Perceptrons*, The MIT Press, Cambridge, MA and London.

Morton, J. [1969], "Interaction of information in word recognition," *Psychological Review*, vol. 76, pp. 165–178.

Neisser, U. [1966], *Cognitive Psychology*, Appelton-Century-Crofts, New York.

Palmer, S. E. [1975], "The effects of contextual scenes on the identification of objects," *Memory & Cognition*, vol. 3, no. 5, pp. 519–526.

Palmer, S. E. [1977], "Hierarchical structure in perceptual representation," *Cognitive Psychology*, vol. 9, pp. 441–474.

Palmer, S. E. [1978], "Structural aspects of visual similarity," *Memory & Cognition*, vol. 6, no. 2, pp. 91–97.

Palmer, S. E. [1983], "The psychology of perceptual organization: A transformational approach," in *Human and Machine Vision*, edited by J. Beck, B. Hope, and A. Rosenfeld, Academic Press, New York.

Perrett, D. I., P. A. J. Smith, D. D. Potter, A. J. Mistlin, A. S. Head, A. D. Milner, and M. A. Jeeves [1985], "Visual cells in the temporal cortex sensitive to face view and gaze direction," *Proc. Roy. Soc. B,* vol. 223, pp. 293-317.

Pinker, S. [1984], "Visual cognition: an introduction," *Cognition,* vol. 18, pp. 1-63.

Pitts, W., and W. S. McCulloch [1947], "How we know universals: The perception of auditory and visual forms," *Bulletin of Math. Biophysics* vol. 9, pp. 127–147.

Potmesil, M. [1983], "Generating models of solid objects by matching 3D surface segments," *Proc. 8th Int. Joint Conf. Art. Intell.*, Karlsruhe, West Germany, pp. 1089-1093.

Potter, M. C. [1975], "Meaning in visual search," *Science*, vol. 187, pp. 965-966.

Preparata, F. P, and M. I. Shamos [1985], *Computational Geometry* Springer–Verlag, New York.

Reed, S. K. [1973], *Psychological Processes in Pattern Recognition*, Academic Press, New York.

Rock, I.[1973], *Orientation and Form*, Academic Press, New York.

Rock, I., J. DiVita, and R. Barbeito [1981], "The effect on form perception of change of orientation in the third dimension" *J. Exp. Psychol. H.P.& P.*, vol. 7, no. 4, pp. 719–733.

Rock, I., J. DiVita [1987], "A case of viewer-centered object perception," *Cog. Psychol.*, vol. 19, pp. 280–293.

Rosch, E., C. B. Mervis, W. D. Gray, D. M. Johnson, and P. Boyes-Braem [1976], "Basic objects in natural categories," *Cog. Psychol.*, vol. 8, pp. 382–439.

Sagi, D., and B. Julesz [1985], ""Where" and "what" in vision," *Science*, vol. 228, pp. 1217–1219.

Sekuler, R., and D. Nash [1972], "Speed of size scaling in human vision," *Psychonomic Sci.,* vol. 27, pp. 93-94.

Selfridge, O. G., [1959], "Pandemonium: A paradigm for learning," in, *The Mechanization of Thought Processes,* H.M. Stationary Office, London.

Shepard, R. N., and L. A. Cooper [1982], *Mental Images and Their Transformations,* MIT Press/Bradford Books, Cambridge, MA.

Shepard, R. N., and J. Metzler [1971], "Mental rotation of three-dimensional objects," *Science,* vol. 171, pp. 701-703.

Shwartz, S. P. [1981], "The perception of disoriented complex objects." *Proc. 3rd Conf. Cog. Sci.,* Berkeley, pp. 181-183.

Suen, C. Y., M. Berthod, and S. Mori [1980], "Automatic recognition of handprinted & characters—the state of the art," *Proc. IEEE* vol. 68, no. 4, pp. 469–487.

Sutherland, N. S. [1959], "Stimulus analyzing mechanisms," in *The Mechanization of Thought Processes,* H.M. Stationary Office, London.

Sutherland, N. S. [1968], "Outline of a theory of visual pattern recognition in animal and man," *Proc. Royal Society, B,* vol. 171, pp. 297–317.

Taar, M. J., and S. A. Pinker [1988], "Viewer-centered and object-centered representations for visual object recognition," submitted for publication.

Thompson, D. W., and J. L. Mundy [1987], "Three dimensional model matching from an unconstrained viewpoint," *Proc. IEEE Int. Conf. on Robotics and Automation,* Raleigh, N.C., pp. 208–220.

Tou, J. T., and R. C. Gonzalez [1974], *Pattern Recognition Principles,* Addison-Wesley, Reading, MA.

Treisman, A., and G. Gelade [1980], "A feature integration theory of attention," *Cog. Psychol.,* vol. 12, pp. 97-136.

Ullman, S. [1984], "Visual routines," *Cognition,* vol. 18, pp. 97-159.

Uhr, L. (ed) [1966], "Pattern Recognition," Wiley, NY.

Uhr, L. [1973] *Pattern Recognition, Learning, and Thought,* Englewood Cliffs, Prentice-Hall, NJ.

White, M. J. [1980], "Naming and categorization of tilted alphanumeric characters do not require mental rotation," *Bulletin of the Psychonomic Society,* vol. 15 no. 3, pp. 153–156.

Willshaw, D. J., O. P. Buneman, and H. C. Longuet-Higgins [1969], "Nonholographic associative memory," *Nature,* vol. 222, pp. 960–962.

Winston, P. H. [1970], "Learning structural descriptions from examples," Ph.D. Thesis, Massachusetts Institute of Technology, Cambridge, MA. Also in *The Psychology of Computer Vision* 1975, edited by P. H. Winston [1975], McGraw-Hill, New York.

Wiser, M. [1981], "The role of intrinsic axes in shape recognition," *Proc. 3rd Conf. Cog. Sci.,* Berkeley, pp. 184-186.

Witkin, A. P., and J. M. Tenenbaum [1983], "On the role of structure in vision," in *Human and Machine Vision* , edited by J. Beck, B. Hope, and A. Rosenfeld, Academic Press, New York, pp. 481-543.

Zunse, L. [1970], *Visual Perception of Form*, Academic Press, New York.

APPENDIX 1

Three-Point Alignment: Existence and Uniqueness

In this Appendix we show that alignment can be performed uniquely (up to sign) on the basis of three corresponding model and image points.

This result concerning three-point alignment will follow from the proposition below that relates affine transformations of the plane and similarity transformations in space. Roughly, it says that each affine transformation of the plane is the projection of a unique similarity transformation in space.

Proposition 1: *Any affine transformation of the image plane can be produced by the orthographic projection of a three-dimensional similarity transformation of the plane. The three-dimensional transformation is unique, up to a reflection about the image plane, and translation in depth.*

Comments: The image plane P is the plane $z = 0$. An affine transformation A of P is $L(P) + d$, where $L(P)$ is linear and d a translation. A similarity transformation T of P is composed of a translation in space D, rotation in space R, and scaling by a factor s $(s > 0)$. The orthographic projection π of a point (x, y, z) in space is (x, y) in the image plane. Given A, we are looking for T such that $\pi T = A$. Without loss of generality we can assume that $d = 0$ (no translation in the image plane). The reason is that under orthographic projection $\pi D = d$ (translation in space and the image plane coincide, translation in depth remains undetermined), and therefore the translation component is immediately recoverable. The problem is therefore to determine, given $L(P)$, s, R such that $\pi(sR) = L(P)$. (That is, expressing a linear transformation of the plane as the orthographic projection of a rotation in space accompanied by scaling). We will show that s, R always exist and are unique, up to reflection of the transformed plane about the image plane (which is an inherent ambiguity of orthographic projection).

Proof: Given a linear transformation L of the plane we can determine its effect on a pair of perpendicular unit vectors ϵ_1, ϵ_2. That is, $\|\epsilon_1\| = \|\epsilon_2\| = 1$, $\epsilon_1 \cdot \epsilon_2 = 0$, $L(\epsilon_1) = \epsilon'_1$, $L(\epsilon_2) = \epsilon'_2$. We seek a rotation in space R, and scaling s, such that $\pi s R(\epsilon_1) = \epsilon'_1$, $\pi s R(\epsilon_2) = \epsilon'_2$. Let $sR(\epsilon_1)$ be v_1, $sR(\epsilon_2)$ be v_2. $v_1 = \epsilon'_1 + c_1\hat{z}$, $v_2 = \epsilon'_2 + c_2\hat{z}$ where c_1, c_2 are the unknown depth coordinates of v_1 and v_2 respectively. Because rotation and scaling preserve orthogonality

$$v_1 \cdot v_2 = 0 \qquad (A1.1)$$

therefore

$$(\epsilon'_1 + c_1\hat{z}) \cdot (\epsilon'_2 + c_2\hat{z}) = 0 \qquad (A1.2)$$

$$c_1 c_2 = -\epsilon'_1 \cdot \epsilon'_2. \qquad (A1.3)$$

Let us denote $-\epsilon'_1 \cdot \epsilon'_2 = c_{12}$, which is measurable in the image. Following uniform scaling $\|v_1\| = \|v_2\|$, therefore

$$c_1^2 - c_2^2 = \|\epsilon'_2\|^2 - \|\epsilon'_1\|^2 \qquad (A1.4)$$

or $c_1^2 - c_2^2 = k_{12}$, where k_{12} is measurable in the image. The two equations

$$c_1 c_2 = c_{12}$$

$$c_1^2 - c_2^2 = k_{12}.$$

always have exactly two real solutions for c_1, c_2, that differ only in sign.

One way of verifying this is to define a complex number $z = c_1 + ic_2$. Then $z^2 = k_{12} + ic_{12}$. Therefore z^2 is known, and c_1, c_2 are simply determined by the square roots of z. There are exactly two solutions, for z, of the form $c_1 + ic_2$ and $-c_1 - ic_2$.

This shows that the transformation sR of the plane always exists and is unique, up to a reflection about the image plane. That is, one transformation takes $\epsilon_1 \to \epsilon'_1 + c_1\hat{z}$, $\epsilon_2 \to \epsilon'_2 + c_2\hat{z}$, the other takes $\epsilon_1 \to \epsilon'_1 - c_1\hat{z}$, $\epsilon_2 \to \epsilon'_2 - c_2\hat{z}$.

The fact that sR transforms ϵ_1 to v_1 and ϵ_2 to v_2 determines sR completely. It is also clear that a solution always exists for any choice of ϵ'_1 and ϵ'_2. (See Appendix 2 for an explicit calculation of s, R.)

Proposition 1 above has been formulated in terms of an affine transformation of the plane. Because an affine transformation is uniquely determined by three non colinear points, we immediately obtain:

Proposition 2: *Let* (P_1, P_2, P_3) *and* (P'_1, P'_2, P'_3) *be two sets of three non-colinear points in the plane. Then there exists a transformation T in space, composed of rotation, translation, and scaling, such that $\pi T P_i = P'_i$, $i = 1, 2, 3$. The transformation is unique, up to reflection of the points $T P_i$ about the image plane and translation in depth.*

Comments: A proposition similar to the above has been proposed, without a complete proof, by Kanade and Kender [1983]. For the perspective rather than orthographic case, Fischler and Bolles [1981] suggested, without a complete proof, that six corresponding points may be required for alignment. Finding six corresponding points in the image and model may be difficult. In addition, perspective effects are often small, leading to instability in the computation. It appears, therefore, that the use of orthographic projection accompanied by scale change provide a useful approximation for performing alignment.

Instead of three points, it is possible to use combinations of lines and points lying in the same plane. Except for certain degenerate configurations, three straight lines, or two lines and a point, can be used to define the affine transformation, and hence the inducing spatial transformation as well (two points and a line are not entirely sufficient).

APPENDIX 2

Three-Point Alignment—Computation

In this Appendix we show briefly how the proof above can be used for actually performing the alignment based on three corresponding points in the model and in the image.

The problem is the following. We are given the three-dimensional coordinates of three non colinear points. Without loss of generality we can assume that the points lie initially in the image plane $z = 0$. We are next given the image of the same points (with known correspondence) following a transformation T. The image is an orthographic projection on the image plane, and T is composed of rotation R and scaling s. The objective is to determine R and s. As discussed above, the translation component can be ignored, and we assume that the object is fixed at one point. With this point as the origin, T transforms the other two points: $\pi T(P_1) = P'_1$, $\pi T(P_2) = P'_2$. In the image plane, an affine transformation A that maps $P_1 \to P'_1$, $P_2 \to P'_2$ is easy to determine. A is a 2×2 matrix, $AP_1 = P'_1$. $AP_2 = P'_2$. This gives four equations for the components of A. (In fact two sets of equations with two unknowns in each. The equations are independent for non-colinear points.) Having determined A, we can compute its effect on two perpendicular unit vectors $A\hat{x} = (x_1, y_1)$ $A\hat{y} = (x_2, y_2)$.

We now compute c_1, c_2 using the equations

$$c_1 c_2 = c_{12}$$
$$c_1^2 - c_2^2 = k_{12} \qquad (A2.1)$$

where

$$c_{12} = -(x_1 x_2 + y_1 y_2)$$
$$k_{12} = (x_2^2 + y_2^2) - (x_1^2 + y_1^2).$$

From (A2.1) c_1 and c_2 can be recovered

$$c_1^4 - k_{12} c_1^2 - c_{12}^2 = 0. \qquad (A2.2)$$

This is a quadratic equation in c_1^2. There will be one real solution $c_1^2 > 0$, and another $c_1^2 < 0$. (This can be shown directly, or based on the uniqueness result above). c_2 is also determined up to a common sign. That is, the solutions to A2.1 are (c_1, c_2) and $(-c_1, -c_2)$.

To obtain T explicitly, we compute its effect on the vector $\hat{z}$. Let $T(\hat{z}) = (x_3, y_3, c_3)$. The direction of $T\hat{z}$ is along $(x_1, y_1, c_1) \times (x_2, y_2, c_2)$, and because of the scaling its length is given by $x_3^2 + y_3^2 + c_3^2 = x_1^2 + y_1^2 + c_1^2$, hence $T\hat{z}$ is determined uniquely.

T is then given explicitly by the matrix

$$T = \begin{pmatrix} x_1 & x_2 & x_3 \\ y_1 & y_2 & y_3 \\ c_1 & c_2 & c_3 \end{pmatrix}$$

or by

$$T' = \begin{pmatrix} x_1 & x_2 & -x_3 \\ y_1 & y_2 & -y_3 \\ -c_1 & -c_2 & c_3 \end{pmatrix}.$$

As discussed above, the difference between T and T' is a reflection of the points about the image plane. From this it is also easy to factor out s and R $(s^2 = x_1^2 + x_2^2 + x_3^2)$.

Using more than three points

If more than three corresponding points can be identified on a planar object, it is possible to determine the best affine transformation in the least square sense. Let m_i and p_i $i = 1 \ldots k$, $k \geq 3$ be corresponding model and image points. We want $A(m_i)$ to be as close as possible to p_i (where A is an affine transformation), minimizing $\sum_i \|A(m_i) - p_i\|^2$. $A(m)$ can be expressed as $L(m) + d$, where L is a linear transformation and d is displacement. It can be shown that d is the displacement that moves c the center-of-mass of (m_i) to that of (p_i). We then seek to minimize $\|LM - P\|$ where M is the $2 \times k$ model matrix $(m_1, \ldots, m_k)$ and P the image matrix $(p_1, \ldots, p_k)$. The solution to this problem is $L = PM^+$, where M^+ denotes the pseudoinverse of M [Albert 1972]. M^+ in this case can be computed by using the equality $M^+ = M^T(MM^T)^{-1}$. This equality holds whenever MM^T is non-singular, which holds in our case unless all of the points m_i are colinear. $(MM^T)^{-1}$ can be written explicitly as

$$(MM^T)^{-1} = \frac{1}{\Delta} \begin{pmatrix} \sum y_i^2 & -\sum x_i y_i \\ -\sum x_i y_i & \sum x_i^2 \end{pmatrix},$$

where $m_i = (x_i, y_i)$ and Δ is the determinant $\sum x_i^2 \sum y_i^2 - (\sum x_i y_i)^2$. From this, an explicit formula for L can be easily derived. Once the affine transformation has been determined, the computation of the three-dimensional parameters s, R, proceed as in the three point case.

Alignment by image transformations

We have obtained above formulas for solving for the transformation parameters in space. When the model is entirely flat, it is possible to align the model with the viewed object using a sequence of simple image transformations: image rotation, stretch, and shear. This gives the transformed image without deriving explicitly the transformation itself.

Assume first that the transformation is composed of rotation only. As before, the rotation of the model is broken down into a rotation in the image plane (about the z axis), followed by rotations about the x and y axes. The rotation about the x axis simply induces a stretch in the y direction ("y-scaling") by a factor $S_y = (\frac{\bar{y}_2}{y_2})$. The subsequent rotation about the y axis induces a transformation that can be expressed as x-scaling by a factor $S_x = (\frac{\bar{x}_1}{x_1})$, followed by a shear transformation of the form: $x \rightarrow x + \Delta y$. The value of Δ is given by: $\Delta = \frac{x_1 \bar{x}_2 - x_2 \bar{x}_1}{x_1 \bar{y}_2}$

If scaling is added to the rotation, its effect can be subsumed by the y-scaling and x-scaling stages, and exactly the same sequence of image transformations would align the model with the viewed object. Given three model points and the three corresponding image points it is possible to apply in this manner a sequence of image transformations to the model to align it with the viewed object. In summary, the model can be aligned with the viewed object using the following sequence of operations: rotation in the image plane, y-scaling, x-scaling, and shear.

The main difference between the two methods is that image alignment is applicable to planar models only. The first method is applicable to non-planar models as well. Based on three points the transformation (in space) is determined, and this transformation can then be applied to any three-dimensional model to determine its new position in space.

APPENDIX 3

Orientation Alignment

Appendix 1 and 2 have shown how a viewed object can be aligned with a potential model using three corresponding points. This is only one example of an alignment procedure; alternative procedures are also possible. In particular, if the viewed object has a prominent orientation, this orientation can be used for alignment. For a planar region, the orientation together with small pieces of the region's bounding contour are sufficient for alignment, without using any identifiable points in the object and model. This procedure also assumes that the occlusion is not too severe, as specified below.

The use of orientation means that it is possible to identify an orientation **u** in the image, which, following the alignment, should be parallel to a known direction **v** in the model. This information is more restricted than the use of an axis: an axis is a line whose position as well as orientation are known. Oriented texture on the object, for example, may specify an orientation in the image without specifying an axis location.

Given the orientation **u** in the image, the first step in the alignment is to rotate the model (or the image) until the direction of **u** is parallel to the desired direction **v**. The alignment can be completed by applying to the model the following sequence of operations:

x-scaling, that is $(x, y) \rightarrow (\gamma x, y)$
y-scaling, that is $(x, y) \rightarrow (x, \beta y)$
y-shear, that is $(x, y) \rightarrow (x, y + \alpha x)$
translation, that is $(x, y) \rightarrow (x + \Delta x, y + \Delta y)$

The amount of x-scaling can be determined directly. Scaling the model by γ in the x-direction should make the overall width of the model and the viewed object identical. (This assumes limited occlusion: the extrema of the viewed object in the x direction should be in view. If they are not in view, internal contours can be used instead.) The translation in the x direction is also immediately recoverable following this step.

The remaining parameters $(\alpha, \beta, \Delta y)$ can now be recovered from any three points along the object boundary. For each point on the viewed object's boundary, the corresponding point in the model is already known: it is a point with the same x-coordinate (because all of the transformations involving the x dimension have already been performed). Three boundary points will supply three simple linear equations in $(\alpha, \beta, \Delta y)$. The process can be further simplified by the appropriate selection of points. For example, from two points with the same x but different y coordinates the value of β can be recovered directly.

This orientation alignment uses no identifiable "anchor" points that are used in the three-point alignment. It is also possible to use various intermediate approaches. For example, if an axis, rather than a dominant orientation, can be identified in the image, the alignment process can be facilitated, and can become more tolerant to occlusions.

39

We humans have an amazing ability to determine an object's shape by watching it move. If someone paints a few polka dots on an otherwise completely transparent stationary object, the object looks two-dimensional. But if the object starts to tumble around, its three-dimensional shape quickly emerges.

In this chapter, Ullman explains a program that determines the relative positions of corresponding points in a sequence of images. As with human shape perception, the position estimates start out as if the points were on a plane and then get better, albeit nonmonotonically.

The key point of theory behind the program is the assumption that shape varies slowly if at all. To enforce this assumption, which Ullman calls the incremental rigidity assumption, his program determines the distances between each pair of points using their current position estimates. When the next image is available, the program calculates new position estimates that are consistent with the image and that minimize a function that measures changes in point-to-point distances. Experiments demonstrate that the program determines the approximate shape of truly rigid objects and copes with objects whose shape does, in fact, vary with time.

Maximizing Rigidity: Recovery of 3-D Structure from Motion

Shimon Ullman

The Rigidity-Based Recovery of Structure from Motion

The human visual system is capable of extracting three-dimensional (3-D) shape information from two-dimensional (2-D) transformations in the image. Experiments employing shadow projections of moving objects and computer-generated displays have established that the three-dimensional shape of objects in motion can be perceived when their changing projection is observed, when each static view is completely devoid of three-dimensional information.

The perception of structure from motion by human observers

Observations related to this intriguing capacity were reported as early as 1860 by Sinsteden (described in Miles [1931]), who first observed the perception of depth and depth reversals induced by a distant windmill, and then examined this phenomenon in the laboratory using rotating cardboard objects. The early experiments in this area were concerned primarily with the perceived depth-reversals of rotating objects. The fact that the three-dimensional structure of moving objects can be recovered perceptually from their changing projection was noted by Musatti in 1924 (see Johansson [1978]). It was investigated systematically for the first time with the use of shadow projections by Wallach and O'Connell [1953] who coined the term "kinetic depth effect" to describe the perception of three-dimensional structure from motion information. Since then the perception of structure from motion has been investigated extensively under various conditions, including the motion of connected and unconnected elements, and with both perspective and orthographic projections. (In orthographic projection the projecting rays are parallel, and perpendicular to the image plane; in a perspective projection they meet at a common point.) For detailed reviews of the extensive research in this area, (see Braunstein [1976], Johansson [1978], and Ullman [1979a]).

Computational studies of the recovery of structure from motion

In trying to recover three-dimensional structure from the transformations in the image, one is faced with the problem of inherent ambiguity: unless some constraints are imposed, the image transformations are insufficient to determine the three-dimensional structure uniquely. This ambiguity problem has been the focus of a number of computational studies that attempted to discover the conditions under which three-dimensional structure is uniquely determined by the projected transformations in the image.

From the earliest empirical studies of the kinetic depth effect it has been suggested that the rigidity of objects may play a key role in the perception of structure from motion [Wallach & O'Connell 1953; Gibson & Gibson 1957; Green 1961; Johansson 1975]. Computational studies have later established that rigidity is a sufficiently powerful constraint for imposing uniqueness upon the three-dimensional interpretation of the viewed transformations. (Uniqueness is defined up to an overall scaling factor for perspective projections, and up to overall distance and a mirror-reflection about the image plane for orthographic projections.) A two-dimensional transformation can be tested to determine whether or not it is compatible with the projection of a rigid object in motion. If it is, then the inducing object is in general guaranteed to be unique, and its three-dimensional structure can be recovered. (Under orthographic projection the structure is determined uniquely up to a reflection about the image plane. This is an unavoidable ambiguity, because the orthographic projections of a rotating object, and its mirror image rotating in the opposite direction, coincide.)

Uniqueness results have been established under a number of different conditions. Ullman and Fremlin [Ullman 1979b] have shown that under orthographic projection three views of four noncoplanar points are sufficient to guarantee a unique three-dimensional solution. Longuet–Higgins and Prazdny [1980] proved that the instantaneous velocity field and its first and second spatial derivatives at a point admit at most three different three-dimensional interpretations. Recently, Tsai and Huang [1982] in an elegant analysis have show that, with the exception of a few special configurations, two perspective views of seven points are also sufficient to guarantee uniqueness. Additional uniqueness results have been obtained for situations where certain restrictions are imposed upon the objects or their motion, such as planar surfaces in motion [Hay 1966], pure translatory motion [Clocksin 1980], planar or fixed axis motion [Bobick 1983; Hoffman & Flinchbaugh 1982; Webb & Aggarwal 1981], and translation perpendicular to the rotation axis [Longuet–Higgins 1982]. Related studies have shown how certain three-dimensional parameters such as gaussian curvature [Koenderink & van Doorn 1975], time to collision [Lee 1976, 1980], and edge types [Clocksin 1980] can be extracted from the transforming image. A review of these and other computational results obtained to date on the recovery of structure from motion has been presented by Ullman [1983].

In summary, the uniqueness results establish that by exploiting a rigidity constraint the recovery of three-dimensional structure is possible on the basis of motion information alone, and that the recovery is possible in principle on the basis of information that is local in space and time.

Additional requirements for the recovery of structure from motion

There are a number of interesting differences between the mathematical results cited above and the recovery of structure from motion by the human visual system.

◇ Extension in time

Although the recovery of structure from motion is possible in principle from the instantaneous velocity field, the human visual system requires an extended time period to reach an accurate perception of the three-dimensional structure [Wallach & O'Connell 1953; White & Mueser 1960; Green 1961]. This difference is not surprising, especially when the recovery scheme is applied locally to small objects or local surface patches. For surface patches extending about 2° of visual angle, drastically different objects can induce almost identical instantaneous velocity fields. This limitation of the instantaneous velocity field is illustrated in figure 1. The figure shows a cross section of two surfaces, S_1 and S_2, seen from a side view. The surfaces are assumed to be rotationally symmetric around the observer's line of sight, so that S_1, for example, is a part of the surface of a sphere. When the viewing distance is such that the surfaces in figure 1 occupy 2° of visual angle, the difference in their velocity fields within the entire patch does not exceed 6%. The implication is that although the instantaneous velocity field contains sufficient information for the recovery of the three-dimensional shape, the reliable interpretation of local structure from motion requires the integration of information over a more extended time period.

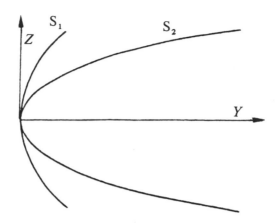

Figure 1. Limitations of the instantaneous velocity field. S_1 and S_2 are two rotationally symmetric surfaces. When the surfaces occupy $2°$ of visual angle, the difference in their velocity fields at each point does not exceed 6%.

◇ Deviations from rigidity

In interpreting structure from motion, the visual system can cope with less than strict rigidity [Johansson 1964, 1978; Jansson & Johansson 1973]. If the viewed object undergoes a rigid transformation combined with some nonrigid distortions, the changing shape of the three-dimensional object can often be perceived. This tolerance for deviations from rigidity also implies that the recovery process enjoys a certain immunity to noise. If the viewed object is in fact rigid, but the measurement of its motion and the computations performed are not entirely accurate, the result would not be a complete breakdown of the recovery process, but a perception of a slightly distorting object [Petersik 1979]. Robustness with respect to errors in the measured velocity field is particularly important, because an accurate measurement of the velocity field is surprisingly difficult to obtain [Fennema & Thompson 1979; Horn & Schunck 1981; Adelson & Movshon 1982; Ullman & Hildreth 1983]. For human observers, kinetic depth displays of rigid objects often give rise to the perception of a somewhat distorting object [Wallach *et al.*1956; White & Mueser 1960; Green 1961; Braunstein 1962].

◇ Successive approximation

For the human visual system, the recovery of structure from motion is not an all-or-none process. Some notion of a coherent three-dimensional structure can be obtained with short presentations [Lappin *et al.* 1980], but an accurate perception of the three-dimensional shape usually requires a longer viewing time [White & Mueser 1960; Green 1961]. For short viewing times, objects often appear flatter than their correct three-dimensional structure. For example, a rotating cylinder [Ullman 1979b] would not appear to have the full depth of the correct three-dimensional object. The perceived shape is qualitatively similar to the correct one, and, as mentioned above, often improves with time.

◇ Integrating sources of 3-D information

The kinetic depth experiments demonstrated the capacity of the human visual system to recover three-dimensional structure on the basis of motion information alone. Wallach and O'Connell, for example, included in their experiments wire-frame objects whose static projection induced no three-dimensional perception. Such objects appear initially as flat and lying in the frontal image plane, but acquire the correct three-dimensional shape when viewed in motion. Under more natural conditions, motion information is seldom dissociated from the other sources of information. In this case, problems related to the integration of different sources of information arise. Wallace *et al.*[1953], for instance, reported a kinetic depth experiment with an object whose static projection was often perceived as a 90° corner (that is, three mutually perpendicular rods). The actual shape of this object was different: the angle between the rods was in fact 110° rather than 90°. Observers who initially saw the 90° corner, often perceived a three-dimensional structure that agreed better with the correct structure of the object after viewing the projection of the moving object for a sufficiently long time. The initially perceived structure is therefore not necessarily flat, and it may be influenced by different sources of three-dimensional information. In the above experiment the structure-from-motion interpretation sometimes eventually dominated over the static cues. There are also cases of conflicting three-dimensional information in which the perceived three-dimensional structure is determined primarily by the static cues rather than the motion information [Ullman 1979a, chapter 5]. The case where the structure-from-motion process is ineffective is not directly relevant to the present discussion, and will not be considered further.

A hypothesis: Maximizing rigidity relative to the current internal model

The above discussion suggests that to be comparable in performance to the human visual system the process of recovering structure from motion should meet the following requirements:

- At each instant there should exist an estimation of the three-dimensional structure of the viewed object; this internal model of the viewed structure may be initially crude and inaccurate, and may be influenced by static sources of three-dimensional information.
- The recovery process should prefer rigid transformations.
- The recovery scheme should tolerate deviations from rigidity.
- It should be able to integrate information from an extended viewing period.
- It should eventually recover the correct three-dimensional structure, or a close approximation to it.

Most of these requirements can be met naturally by the following "incremental rigidity" scheme. Assume that at any given time there is an internal model of the viewed object. Let $M(t)$ denote the internal model at time t. As the object continues to move, its projection would change. If $M(t)$ is not an accurate model of the object at time t, then no rigid transformation of $M(t)$ would be sufficient to account for the observed transformation in the image. The crucial step is that the internal model would then be modified by the minimal change that is still sufficient to account for the observed transformation. In other words, the internal model resists changes as much as possible, and consequently becomes as rigid as possible.

Such a scheme takes into account the use of a current three-dimensional model which initially may be inaccurate (requirement 1), the tendency to perceive rigid transformations when possible (requirement 2), without requiring strict rigidity (requirement 3). It also combines information from extended periods, by incorporating incremental changes into the internal model (requirement 4). It thus has the appealing property of combining information from extended periods, and at the same time using at any instant only the internal model and the incoming image at that instant. It does not require storing and using long sequences of different views of the object as might be used, for example, in a computer implementation of a structure-from-motion process. Unlike Johansson's [1974] trajectory-based scheme, which also integrates information over an extended viewing period, this model of temporal integration is not limited to fixed-axis motion, but can be applied to objects under general motion.

The incremental rigidity scheme therefore meets four of the five requirements listed above. It remains unclear, however, whether such a scheme can cope with the last, and most crucial requirement. That is, if $M(t)$ is initially incorrect, would it eventually converge to the correct three-dimensional structure? The answer is not obvious: if the model is incorrect at time t, it is not clear whether an attempt to transform it as rigidly as possible would bring it any closer to the unknown structure of the viewed object. To assess the feasibility of the incremental rigidity scheme it is therefore necessary to examine whether the incremental changes in $M(t)$

would cause it in the long run to converge to the correct three-dimensional structure of the viewed object. The main problem regarding the incremental rigidity scheme can thus be summarized as follows. If $M(t)$ is updated by transforming it at each instant as rigidly as possible, will it converge eventually to the correct three-dimensional structure under rigid motion, and under deviations from rigidity? This problem is examined in the next two sections. The next describes more precisely the incremental rigidity scheme and how it is applied to recover three-dimensional structure from motion. The section "Recovery of the three-dimensional structure by the incremental rigidity scheme" describes the results of applying this scheme to rigid as well as nonrigid objects. The general conclusion is that the incremental rigidity scheme copes successfully with rigid objects as well as with considerable deviations from rigidity, and that it resembles various aspects of the perceptual recovery of structure from motion.

The Incremental Rigidity Scheme

Analytical treatment of the convergence requirement did not seem tractable; therefore, a computer program was devised to test the convergence of the incremental rigidity scheme to the correct three-dimensional structure under both rigid and nonrigid motion. This section will describe the incremental rigidity scheme that has been employed, it describes the basis scheme, considers possible modifications, and then examines briefly problems of efficiency, including the execution of the scheme in an analog and distributed manner. The next section describes the behavior of the scheme as revealed by the computer simulations, and in particular its convergence to the correct three-dimensional structure under rigid and nonrigid motion.

The basis scheme

For the computer implementation it is convenient to consider the visual input as a sequence of frames, each one depicting a number of identifiable feature points rather than continuous flow. (The temporal discreteness of the input is not a necessary aspect of the scheme: a continuous formulation is also conceivable.) The scheme maintains and updates an internal model $M(t)$ of the viewed object. $M(t)$ consists of a set of three-dimensional coordinates (X_i, Y_i, Z_i). Assuming orthographic projection onto the $X - Z$ image plane, (X_i, Z_i) are the image coordinates of the ith point, and Y_i is its depth as estimated in the current model. ($X - Z$ was chosen as the image plane, with the positive Y direction pointing away from the observer. This notation keeps the coordinate system right-handed.) As will be noted below, a similar scheme can be defined for a perspective rather than orthographic projection. For small objects, or small surface patches of objects, the two projections are in close agreement; consequently the type of projection employed has little effect on the behavior of the scheme. The relation between the two projections is discussed in more detail in the section "Orthographic and perspective projections." Lacking of information about the three-dimensional shape of the viewed object, the initial model $M(t)$ at $t = 0$ is taken to be completely flat, that is, $Y_i = 0$ (or any other constant, because the overall distance to the object remains undetermined) for $i = 1 \dots n$, where n is the number of points considered in the computation.

Next, a frame corresponding to a later time t' is considered, and the problem is then to update $M(t)$ so as to agree with the new frame, while making the transformation from $M(t)$ to $M(t')$ as rigid as possible. The new frame is represented as a set of two-dimensional image coordinates (x_i, z_i). The new depth values y_i are as yet undetermined. It is assumed, however, that the correspondence between points in the two successive frames is known. When the y_i values have been estimated, the set of coordinates (x_i, y_i, z_i) is the estimated structure at time t', denoted by $S(t')$. The notation convention used is that all the parameters that refer to $M(t)$ are denoted by capital letters (X, Y, Z, etc.), and those referring to $S(t)$ by small letters (x, y, z, etc.).

The most rigid transformation of the internal model $M(t)$ is now determined in the following manner. Let L_{ij} denote the distance between points i and j in $M(t)$. That is

$$L_{ij}^2 = (X_i - X_j)^2 + (Y_i - Y_j)^2 + (Z_i - Z_j)^2 \quad . \tag{1}$$

Similarly, ℓ_{ij} is the internal distance in the estimated structure between points i and j at time t'. That is

$$\ell_{ij}^2 = (x_i - x_j)^2 + (y_i - y_j)^2 + (z_i - z_j)^2 \quad . \tag{2}$$

A rigid transformation implies that $L_{ij} = \ell_{ij}$ for all i, j (that is, all the internal distances in the object remain unchanged). To make the transformation as rigid as possible, the unknown depth values y_i should therefore be chosen so as to make the values of ℓ_{ij} and L_{ij} agree as closely as possible. If $D(L_{ij}, \ell_{ij})$ is a measure of the difference between L_{ij} and ℓ_{ij}, then the problem of determining the most rigid transformation of the model can be formulated as determining the values of y_i so as to minimize the overall deviation from rigidity $\sum_{ij} D(L_{ij}, \ell_{ij})$ ($i = 1, \dots, n-1$; $j = i+1, \dots, n$).

This deviation from rigidity can also serve as a useful "confidence" measure: the smaller the deviation, the more likely is the internal model to reflect accurately the correct three-dimensional structure of the observed object.

A reasonable choice of the distance function D should make the contributions from nearby points weigh more than those from distant points. The reason is that the nearest neighbors to a given point are more likely

than distant neighbors to belong to the same object. A point is consequently more likely to move rigidly with its nearest neighbors. A simple
example of a distance measure with such a falloff is

$$D(L_{ij}, \ell_{ij}) = \frac{(L_{ij} - \ell_{ij})^2}{L_{ij}^3} \ . \tag{3}$$

As required, the effect in this measure of, say, a 10% change in L_{ij} decreases
as L_{ij} increases.

After the values of y_i have been determined with the use of the minimization criterion, (x_i, y_i, z_i) becomes the new model $M(t')$. A new frame
is then registered, and the process repeats itself. The change in the model
M between time t and t' corresponds to the perceived change in the object
during this time interval. The motion is given in relative terms, and may
arise from either the object's or the observer's own motion.

In summary, the computation involved at each step in establishing the
most rigid interpretation is the following. Given an internal model $M(t)$
in the form (X_i, Y_i, Z_i), $i = 1, \ldots n$, and the new frame (x_i, z_i), $i = 1, \ldots n$,
find a vector of depth values y_i such that the overall deviation from rigidity
$\sum_{i,j} D(L_{ij}, \ell_{ij})$ for $i = 1, \ldots, n - 1$; $j = i + 1, \ldots, n$ is minimized.

Possible modifications

Some modifications of the basic scheme presented above are possible. For
example, a somewhat different form of the metric D can be used. The
important issue to explore, however, is whether any such scheme converges
successfully to the correct three-dimensional structure. As discussed above,
the incremental rigidity scheme meets requirements 1 through 4, but it
is unclear whether it can also meet the convergence requirement. To be
considered a plausible scheme for the recovery of structure from motion by
the human visual system, the convergence requirement must also be met
for rigid as well as not strictly rigid objects. If a particular version of the
scheme accomplishes the three-dimensional recovery task successfully, then
it provides a certain existence proof that an incremental rigidity scheme
can meet all of the requirements listed in the previous section.

Two modifications of the basic scheme described above were explored.
One was to introduce some changes to the metric D. The other, more
substantial modification, takes into account the fact that $M(t)$, the internal
model at time t, may be inaccurate, and allows it to be corrected.

The basic scheme described in the previous section can be summarized
as minimizing $D\left(M(t), S(t')\right)$, a measure of the overall distortion between
the three-dimensional model at time t and the new computed structure at
time t'. The modified method searches for a modified, corrected model
$M'(t)$, such that the transition from $M(t)$ to $M'(t)$ (the correction to

the internal model) is small, and the transition from $M'(t)$ to $S(t')$ is as rigid as possible. This modified scheme minimizes therefore the sum $D(M(t), M'(t)) + D(M'(t), S(t'))$. Because it allows changes in the internal model $M(t)$, this scheme will be referred to below as the "flexible model" scheme. In general, the modifications explored of the metric D had only small effects on the convergence to the correct three-dimensional structure. The use of the more complicated flexible-model scheme also did not introduce fundamental changes, but usually resulted in an overall improvement of the computed structure. This flexible model also has the advantage that other three-dimensional cues (such as stereo or shading) could influence the transition from $M(t)$ to $M'(t)$. The above observations suggest that the basic incremental rigidity scheme is not sensitive to variations in the exact formulation of the minimization problem. Additional comments regarding the modified scheme are incorporated in the discussion of the results in the next section.

Implementation

The incremental rigidity scheme described above has been implemented as a computer program on a Lisp Machine at the MIT Artificial Intelligence Laboratory. The computation made use of a relatively efficient variable-metric minimization procedure developed by Davidon [1968]. From a quadratic function of n variables, this method is guaranteed to converge to a minimum within at most n iterations. The computational load at each stage is relatively small, estimated by Davidon [1968] to require approximately $\frac{3}{2}n^2$ multiplications. When the objective function (in our case, the overall deviation from rigidity) has more than a single minimum, the minimization process will converge to a local, but not necessarily the global, minimum. The results described in the next section demonstrate that this convergence is sufficient for the recovery of the unknown three-dimensional structure. Some consequences of the convergence to the local minimum are discussed in the section "Convergence to the local minimum."

For the flat initial model, an additional minor step is required to ensure convergence to a local minimum. The flat internal model can change into two equally likely configurations, one being the mirror image reflection of the other about the image plane. The model is therefore perturbed slightly, to cause it to prefer one of the two symmetric minima over the other.

This minimization method is efficient for implementation on a serial digital computer. More parallel distributed implementations are also possible. Such extensions will not be analyzed here mathematically (for a discussion of minimization in distributed networks see Ullman [1979c]). Instead, a mechanical analog that performs essentially the same computation in a parallel distributed manner will be briefly described. This mechanical spring model, which bears some similarity to Julesz's spring-dipole model of stereopsis [Julesz 1971], can help to visualize the computation performed at each step by the incremental rigidity scheme, and can be helpful in suggesting parallel distributed computations for maximizing rigidity.

The mechanical spring model is illustrated in figure 2 for a three-element object. As before, let (x_i, z_i) denote the image coordinates of the ith point, and y_i be the unknown depth coordinates that must be recovered. This situation is modeled in figure 2 by a set of rigid rods, each one connected to one of the viewed points, and extending perpendicularly to the image plane. The ith point is constrained to lie along the ith rod, but its position along this rod (that is, its depth value) is still undermined. The points are now connected by a set of springs. The resting length of the spring connecting points i and j is L_{ij}, their distance in the internal model prior to the introduction of the new frame, and k_{ij} is the spring constant. The points will now slide along the rods, stretching some of the springs and compressing others, until a minimum energy configuration is reached. If l_{ij} denotes the distance between points (i, j) in the final configuration, then the total energy of the system would be $\frac{1}{2} \sum_{i,j} k_{ij}(L_{ij} - \ell_{ij})^2$.

To mimic the computation described in the preceding section, the spring constants k_{ij} should be smaller for longer springs (it can also be assumed that each point is connected only to a number of its neighbors).

The "computation" of the most rigid transformation is performed in this mechanical system in a parallel distributed manner. It can be used, therefore, to illustrate the possibility of maximizing rigidity in the observed transformation with the use of a parallel network of simple interacting computing elements.

This mechanical analog illustrated the computation for the case of orthographic projection. For perspective projection, only a slight modification is required: the rods should converge to a common point rather than be perpendicular to the image plane. Continuous versions of this scheme, in which the rods move continuously and the spring lengths and constants are also modified continuously are possible, but they will not be discussed further here.

Recovery of the 3-D Structure by the Incremental Rigidity Scheme

Rigid motion

Typical results showing the incremental rigidity scheme in operation are illustrated in figure 3. The object in this example is shown in figure 3(a). It contains six points: the vertices of the outlined pentagon, and a sixth

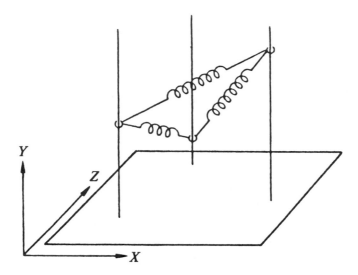

Figure 2. A spring model for the distributed computation of the most rigid transformation. Each of the viewed points (three in this example) is constrained to move along one of the rigid rods, and its position along the rods represents its depth value. The connecting springs represent the distances between points in the current internal model. The points would slide along the rods until a minimum energy configuration is reached. The final configuration represents the modified internal model.

point at the origin (marked by the unfilled circle). The object was three--dimensional, not merely planar. The two-dimensional projection of this object is shown in the figure from a top view, that is, as projected on the $X - Y$ plane. The input to the incremental rigidity program consisted of the projection of the object on the $X - Z$ image plane. That is, only the (x_i, z_i) coordinates for $i = 0, \ldots, 5$ were given. This projection on the $X - Z$ image plane at time $t = 0$ is shown in figure 4. Clearly, such an image conveys no information regarding the correct three-dimensional structure of the object. The unknown depth values y_i were assumed initially to be constant $y_i = 0$ for $i = 0, \ldots 5$. That is, no depth was assumed, and the initial internal model consisted of a planar object, lying parallel to the image plane. (The dashed line in figure 3(a) illustrates the projection of the internal model onto the $X - Y$ plane.)

The object was then rotated by $10°$ at a time, and the internal model was modified according to the scheme described in the previous section. The rotations were around the vertical Z axis. Any other axis in space

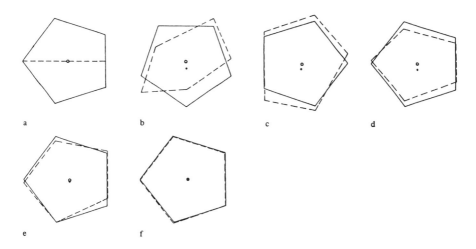

Figure 3. The incremental rigidity scheme applied to a six-point rigid object (the pentagon outlined with the solid line and unfilled dot at the center). The object is three-dimensional, the figure depicts its projections on the $X-Y$ plane (Y is the depth axis). The internal model (dashed curves and filled dot near the center) is compared to the correct structure after a rotation of (a) $0°$, (b) $90°$, (c) $180°$, and (d) $360°$; (e) after two revolutions; (f) after four revolutions.

can be used instead, however, and the axis may also change over time. To illustrate the behavior of the scheme, the error between the internal model and the correct three-dimensional structure of the object was computed at the end of each step. This error was measured by the root-mean-square expression $\left[\sum_{i,j}(d_{ij}-L_{ij})^2\right]^{1/2}$ where d_{ij} is the correct three-dimensional distance between points i and j in the object, and L_{ij} is the corresponding distance in the internal model. When the internal model is completely accurate, $L_{ij}=d_{ij}$ for all i, j and the total error vanishes. The initial error was normalized to 1.0 at $0°$ rotation. Its development as a function of the rotation angle is shown in figure 5 (dotted curve). It declines rapidly to about 0.3 after the first $180°$ of rotation (note in figure 3(c) that this error already yields an approximation to the actual structure), and then continues to decline to about 2–5%. Figure 3 shows the development of the internal model. It starts as entirely flat (figure 3(a)), After $90°$ of rotation is acquires some depth, but it is still too flat, and the shape is inaccurate (figure 3(b)). After the first $190°$ of rotation the internal model is already similar in overall shape to the correct structures (figure 3(c)). The internal model continues to improve (figures 3(d), 3(e)) until it becomes virtually indistinguishable from the correct three-dimensional structure (figure 3(f)).

A more rapid initial approximation to the correct three-dimensional structure can be obtained by using the flexible-model scheme described in the previous section. The continuous curve in figure 5 illustrates the error measure as a function of rotation angle for the flexible-model scheme. It can be seen that the approximation improved rapidly over the first 180° of rotation, but it remains somewhat more oscillatory than the basic scheme.

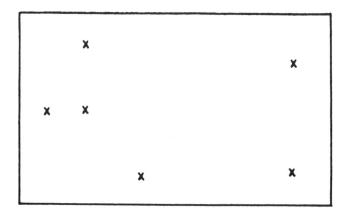

Figure 4. The initial projection of the six-point object on the image $(X - Z)$ plane.

The results of applying the incremental rigidity scheme to various objects in motion show that for most of the rotation time the internal model approximates the actual three-dimensional structure. The model does not converge, however, to the precise solution, but often wobbles somewhat around the correct solution to the three-dimensional structure. In both the basic and the flexible-model schemes the approximation to the correct solution does not improve monotonically as a function of rotation angle. The lack of monotonicity in the overall convergence to the computed three-dimensional structure suggests that an analytic treatment of the convergence properties of the incremental rigidity scheme is probably difficult to obtain.

During these oscillations of the error function, the correct structure is occasionally lost temporarily and then recovered. In the course of such a phase, when the structure is lost and recaptured, a spontaneous depth reversal may occur. That is, the internal model converges not to the original three-dimensional structure, but to its mirror image, reflected about the image plane. The convergence to the reflected rather than to the correct structure is a "legal" solution under orthographic projection, because, as noted in the section "Computational studies of the recovery of structure from motion," the two are indistinguishable under orthographic projection. (This point of depth reversals under orthographic and perspective projections is discussed further in the next section).

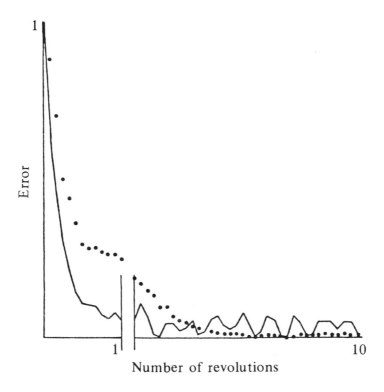

Figure 5. The error of the internal model as a function of rotation angle over ten revolutions. The initial error for the basic scheme (dots) and flexible model (solid curve) is normalized to 1. The error is shown every 30° for the first revolution, and every 90° thereafter.

Such a depth reversal is shown in figure 6, which illustrates the development of the internal model for a five-point object, similar to the six-point object examined before, but without the point at the origin. Figures 6(a), 6(b), and 6(c) compare the internal model (dashed lines) with the actual structure (solid lines) after 0, 90, and 180° rotation, respectively. Towards the end of the second revolution the structure was temporarily lost, and then recovered successfully. During this phase, a depth reversal occurred. That is, the internal model later converged not to the correct three-dimensional structure, but to its mirror image, reflected about the image plane. The approximation to the reflected structure eventually becomes quite accurate. Figure 6(d) shows the correct structure together with the best approximation obtained within the first five revolutions. Figure 6(e) is similar to figure 6(d), but the correct structure has been reflected about the image plane. It can be seen that the internal model provides a good approximation to the reflected structure. The best approximation obtained within the first ten revolutions is compared in figure 6(f) against the correct (but reflected) structure. That the structure is recaptured after a total loss, together with the initial convergence from a totally flat internal model, indicates that almost irrespective of the initial conditions the scheme eventually converges, in the sense that it spends most of its time near the correct solution.

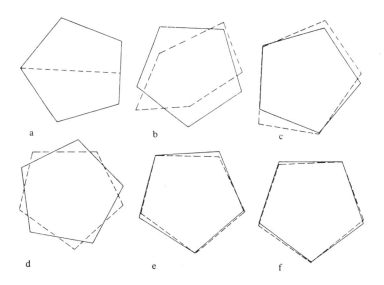

Figure 6. The internal model (dashed figures) is compared to the correct structure (solid-line pentagons) after a rotation of (a) 0°, (b) 90°, and (c) 180°; (d, e) after five revolutions; (f) after ten revolutions. Towards the end of the second revolution, the structure was temporarily lost. During this phase, a depth reversal occurred (d). Figures (e) and (f) compare the internal model to the correct three dimensional structure reflected about the image plane.

In the examples discussed above, the objects have been rotated 10° between successive views. It might have been expected that if a sequence of frames were taken, say, every 5° of rotation, the recovery of the structure would require a smaller overall rotation, because the deviation from rigidity at each step is smaller. In fact, when smaller angular separations between views are used, the convergence becomes somewhat slower. Figure 7 compares the decline of the error function over the first five rotations for 10° (dotted curve) and 5° (discontinuous curve) rotations between successive views. This difference in convergence rate suggests that the incremental rigidity scheme performs better when successive views of the object differ significantly. This preference may be related to the findings of Petersik [1980] who compared the contribution of the short-range and long-range motion processes [Braddick 1974] to the recovery of structure from motion. The long-range process, which operates over relatively large spatial and temporal separations, was found in this study to be the main contributor to the structure-from-motion process.

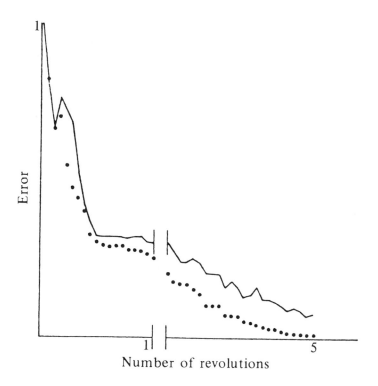

Figure 7. The decline of the error function for a rotating rigid object when successive frames are separated by 5° (solid) and 10° (dots) of rotation. The convergence is faster when successive views of the object are sufficiently distinct.

Comparisons were also made with type of to-and-fro motion used in the original kinetic depth experiments by Wallach and O'Connell [1953]. In the examples examined above, the objects rotated continuously in one direction for several rotations. In contrast, the objects in Wallach and O'Connell's experiments were rotated to-and-fro through a limited angular excursion. Under this condition the observers did not have the benefit of viewing the object from all directions, but they were nevertheless able to recover the correct three-dimensional structure of the moving objects. A simulation of this condition, in which the objects were rotated by only 40° in each direction, revealed that the incremental rigidity scheme manifests a similar capacity. As the object rotated to-and-fro, the internal model continued to improve until the correct three-dimensional structure was recovered, in a manner analogous to the recovery of the three-dimensional structure of continuously rotating objects.

In summary, when applied to rigid objects in motion (the objects described in this section and the next section, and others), the incremental rigidity scheme exhibits the following properties.

- **Veridicality:** for most of the time a reasonable approximation of the correct three-dimensional structure is maintained.

- **Temporal extension:** the time (number of frames) required for an approximation to be obtained is longer than the theoretical minimum required for the recovery of structure from motion [Ullman 1979a, Longuet–Higgins & Prazdny 1980; Tsai & Huang 1982].

- **Residual nonrigidity:** although the changing image was induced by completely rigid objects in motion, the computed three-dimensional structure included residual nonrigidity.

- **Nonmonotonicity:** starting from a flat internal model, the solution generally improves with time. This improvement is however, nonmonotonic. The error often increases and then decreases again.

- **Depth reversals:** occasionally the increased error is associated with a spontaneous depth reversal. The flexible-model scheme is less susceptible to such reversals.

Similar general properties are also manifested in the perception of structure from motion by human observers. The perceived three-dimensional structure is usually similar to the correct three-dimensional structure. It improves with time, but it is usually not entirely accurate [Wallach & O'Connell 1953; White & Mueser 1960]. The perception is often of a stable three-dimensional configuration accompanied by some residual elastic deformations, particularly when the number of participating elements is small.

Nonrigid motion

In this section the capacity of the incremental rigidity scheme to cope with deviations from rigidity will be examined. Unlike in the previous section where the viewed objects were assumed to be entirely rigid, in this section they are allowed to deform while they move.

An example of the scheme applied to nonrigid motion is shown in figure 8. At time $t = 0$ the object was identical in shape to the five-point object examined under rigid motion in the previous section. Again, the object was three-dimensional and not merely planar. The figure depicts the projection of this object from a top view on the $x - y$ plane. A nonrigid transformation was now added to the rotation of the object. The nonrigid distortion was quite significant, as can be seen in figure 8(a). The shape of the object after two revolutions is compared in the figure with its original shape. The incremental rigidity scheme copes successfully with such deviation from rigidity. The internal model by the end of the second revolution is shown in figure 8(b) and compared with the correct structure.

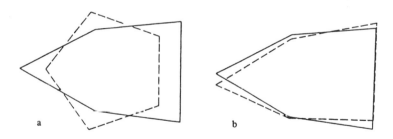

Figure 8. The recovery of nonrigid shape. A pentagon distorts while it moves. (a) Its shape after two revolutions (solid line) is compared with its original shape (dashed line). (b) The internal model by the end of the second revolution (dashed line) is compared with the correct three-dimensional structure seen from a top view (solid line).

Figure 9 illustrates the results of applying the same scheme to an object distorting twice as fast. That is, the distortion of the object after one revolution is identical to the distortion spread in the previous example over two revolutions. The figure compares the actual object with its internal model after (a) 180, (b) 369, (c) 450 (where the error is relatively low), and (d) 720° of rotation (where the error is relatively high again). The internal model becomes less accurate compared to the lower distortion rate, but the three-dimensional structure is still essentially recovered.

When the rate of distortion was doubled again, the incremental rigidity scheme could no longer cope with the rate of deviation from rigidity. Before the end of the second revolution the structure was lost entirely. The distortion was evidently developing too fast to allow the scheme to recover from this loss. This limitation held for both the basic and the flexible-model schemes. In contrast with previous cases, the error measure in this case tended to grow without bounds.

Different objects under different distortions were also examined, with similar results. For moderate distortions the incremental rigidity scheme can cope successfully with nonrigid motion. The amount of distortion that can be tolerated is difficult to quantify, but, as illustrated in figures 8 and 9, it can be substantial.

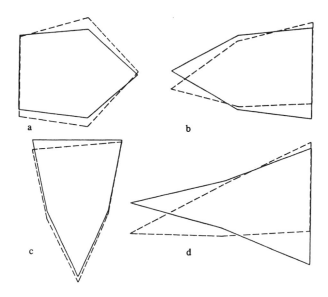

Figure 9. An object distorting twice as fast as that in figure 8. The internal model (dashed line) is compared to the correct structure after a rotation of (a) 180°, (b) 360°, (c) 450°, and (d) 720°. When the amount of distortion increases further, the structure of the object can no longer be recovered by the incremental rigidity scheme.

As noted in the first section, the human visual system can also cope to some degree with kinetic depth effects that are not entirely rigid. Although no systematic studies of this capacity have been reported, the human visual system is probably susceptible to similar difficulties with nonrigid motion.

That is, it is expected to fail under pure kinetic depth conditions (that is, when no other sources of three-dimensional information are available) when the deviation from rigidity becomes excessive. It may be of interest to investigate further the performance of the human visual system under nonrigid conditions and compare the results with the performance of the incremental rigidity scheme.

Additional Properties of the Incremental Rigidity Scheme

Four additional topics pertaining to the incremental rigidity scheme under both rigid and nonrigid motion are discussed here. Within each topic, the scheme is compared to previous mathematical models and to human perception of structure from motion.

Orthographic and perspective projections

The computations described above used orthographic projection. As noted in the section "Implementation," a similar scheme can also be adapted for perspective projection. For small objects (compared to the overall viewing distance) the two projections are similar. It is not surprising, therefore, that although perspective effects can be useful under some conditions (for example, Braunstein [1962, 1976] and Lappin and Fuqua [1983]), the human visual system can recover structure from motion under both perspective and orthographic projections. For the kinetic depth effect, Johansson [1978] reports that for object subtending up to about 15° of visual angle perspectivity has a very limited effect. Under such conditions orthographic projection can be viewed as insensitive to small distortions, it should be able to cope with both types of projection. In fact, the capacity to deal successfully with both types of projection can be used as a test for the scheme's robustness. A scheme that can recover the structure under perspective projection but fails under orthographic projection cannot be robust when applied locally. This comment is relevant in particular to schemes that rely exclusively on the instantaneous velocity field, because such schemes fail under orthographic projection [Ullman 1983].

For larger objects perspective and orthographic projections differ. It is still possible, however, to use a parallel scheme [Ullman 1979a] in which the interpretation is performed locally (and therefore it is immaterial whether orthographic or perspective projections are employed), and the local results are then combined in a second stage. For sufficiently large objects this integration stage will eliminate the ambiguity inherent in orthographic projection regarding direction of rotation and reflection about the image plane. In conclusion, for small objects or surface patches it is immaterial which of the two projection types is employed, and a robust recovery method should be able to cope with both. For larger objects it is still theoretically possible to use either type, and either one can be incorporated in the incremental rigidity scheme.

The effect of number of points

In this section the effect of the number of moving feature points is discussed.

◇ Two points in motion

Mathematically, for two points the three-dimensional structure is not determined uniquely by any number of views. The structure imposed by the incremental rigidity scheme would be of a rigid rod rotating in depth, and the view where the rod's length is maximal would be taken as lying in the frontal plane. This three-dimensional interpretation is in agreement with human perception of two-dot configurations [Johansson & Jansson 1968].

◇ Three points

This configuration has not been analyzed mathematically in the past. It is known that four points in three views determine the three-dimensional structure uniquely if the structure is assumed to be rigid. Three points in three views do not always guarantee uniqueness, but it is still possible that with additional views the three-dimensional structure is determined uniquely by three points alone. The results of applying the incremental rigidity scheme support this possibility, because the three-dimensional structure of three-point configurations can be successfully recovered. (This result holds for orthographic projections. For perspective projections, three points are still insufficient.)

The recovery of the three-dimensional structure of three moving points is shown in figure 10. As before, the initial model was taken as entirely flat. The evolving internal model (dashed line) is compared in the figure with the actual three-dimensional structure after 90, 180, 360, and 720° of rotation. The figure shows that a fast and accurate recovery can be obtained when there are only three points in motion.

◇ Four points

Three views are theoretically sufficient for recovering the structure of four (noncoplanar) points moving rigidly. The incremental rigidity scheme can

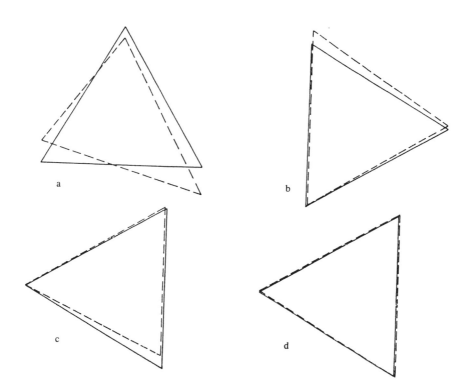

Figure 10. The incremental rigidity scheme applied to a three-point object. The internal model (dashed line) is compared to the correct structure (solid line) as seen from a top view after a rotation of (a) 90°, (b) 180°, (c) 360°, and (d) 720°. Three points are sufficient for the recovery of structure from motion.

recover the structure of four-point objects, but three views are insufficient for an accurate recovery.

The recovery of the three-dimensional structure of four points arranged in a square when seen from a top view is shown in figure 11. The initial model was taken again as entirely flat. The internal model (dashed line) after 90, 180, 260, and 720° of rotation is compared to the actual three-dimensional structure. It can be seen that the model is initially inaccurate, but that the correct three-dimensional structure is eventually recovered and retained with only minor residual deviations from rigidity.

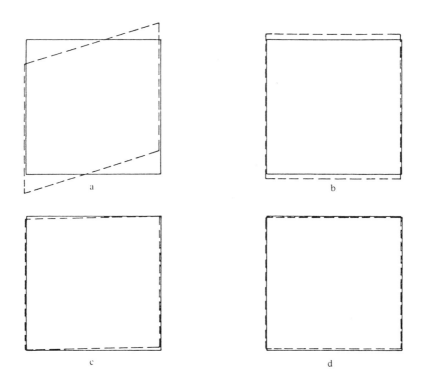

Figure 11. The recovery of the three-dimensional structure of four points arranged in a square when seen from a top view. The initial model was entirely flat. The internal model (dashed line) is compared to the actual structure after a rotation of (a) 90°, (b) 180°, (c) 360°, and (d) 720°. The recovery takes longer than the known minimum of three views, but the correct structure is eventually recovered and maintained.

◇ Additional points

The effect of additional points on the incremental rigidity scheme would depend on the method of applying the scheme to large collections of elements. There are two possible methods of applying the scheme to such large collections. The first is a single-stage scheme, in which the computation described in the section "The incremental rigidity scheme" is simply applied simultaneously to all of the elements in view. The second possibility is a two-stage scheme (similar to the polar-parallel scheme described in Ullman [1979b]). In the first stage the incremental rigidity scheme is applied independently to small subcollections of elements. In the second stage the local results are combined. It is expected that for the two-stage scheme there would be a more noticeable improvement with the number of elements (refer to, Braunstein [1962], and Johansson 1978]).

The effects of numerosity would also depend on the function D, used in measuring the deviation from rigidity. If it falls off rapidly as a function of spatial distance, only the nearest neighbors would make a substantial contribution to the computation, and the effect of numerosity would be more restricted compared to a function that falls off more gradually with distance.

On multiple objects

One possible method of dealing with multiple independently moving objects is to segregate the scene into objects (for example, on the basis of distance, two-dimensional common motion characteristics, *etc.*) before applying the rigidity-based interpretation scheme to each object separately. An interesting alternative is that object segregation may not be required as a separate stage, but may be a by-product of the three-dimensional interpretation process. As in the previous section, two methods for achieving such segregation seem possible. First, the segregation may be accomplished in a single-stage process by the appropriate choice of the deviation measure D. The suggestion is that D would prefer "partial rigidity" in the following sense. Suppose that no rigid transformation of the internal model can account for the incoming input. The model must then be modified nonrigidly. For simplicity, assume that only two different modifications of the model are possible. In the first all the internal distances are changed somewhat. The second maintains partial rigidity: some distances change more than in the first deformation, but others remain completely rigid. We would want the measure of deviation from rigidity to be lower for this second, partially rigid, transformation. For two independently moving objects a scheme that maximizes rigidity would then prefer the solution in which the scene contains two rigid substructures. In this manner the appropriate choice of D may endow the incremental rigidity scheme with the capacity to divide the scene into its rigid components.

A second possibility for dealing with multiple objects is within the framework of the two-stage process mentioned above. The general suggestion is that substructures that share similar motion parameters (for example, same axis of rotation) in the first stage, will be grouped together in the second stage. This method is similar to the one described by Ullman

[1979a] for completely rigid objects, in that it places the burden of the segregation process on the integration stage.

Convergence to the local minimum

The schemes described in "The incremental rigidity scheme" seek the local minimum in the measure of deviation from rigidity. As illustrated by the examples examined in "Recovery of the three-dimensional structure by the incremental rigidity scheme," this convergence to the local minimum is usually sufficient to recover the correct three-dimensional structure. Under certain conditions, however, the incremental rigidity scheme may converge to a local minimum which is not the most rigid structure possible. Similar behavior is also exhibited by the human perception of structure from motion. Under certain conditions human observers perceive nonrigid structure in motion when an entirely rigid solution is also possible. A well known example of this phenomenon is the Mach illusion. (Mach originally described a static version of this illusion. The dynamic version is described by Eden [1962] and Lindsay and Normal [1972].) This illusion can be created by folding a sheet of paper to create a vertical V-shaped figure. Under monocular viewing, this shape is ambiguous and can reverse in depth. To observe the dynamic illusion the observer waits for a depth reversal to occur, and then moves his head in different directions. Under these conditions the object is seen to move whenever the observer's head moves. The illusory motion arises despite the observer's knowledge of the correct three-dimensional configuration, and it often contradicts shading clues, stability criteria, and touch cues [Eden 1962]. When the object is close to the observer's eye, its motion is no longer rigid, but appears to distort considerably while it moves.

The incremental rigidity scheme would also be susceptible to this illusion. The reason lies in the initial internal model. Unlike the pure kinetic depth situation, a three-dimensional structure is perceived from the static view. Because of the depth reversal, the initial internal model resembles the reflection of the three-dimensional structure about the image plane. It subsequently converges not to the correct three-dimensional structure, but to its mirror image which, under perspective projection, can be considerably less rigid than the correct structure.

Sperling *et al.* [1983] have shown that when one face of a rotating wire cube is increased in brightness, the cube is often perceived as nonrigid. This behavior is again consistent with the incremental rigidity scheme. The brighter face is usually perceived as somewhat closer to the observer even when in fact it may be the farther face. This bias of the internal model will cause the incremental rigidity scheme to converge to the reflected structure and miss the correct, entirely rigid, solution.

Summary

A new scheme has been suggested for the recovery of three-dimensional structure from rigid and nonrigid motion. According to this scheme an internal model representing the three-dimensional structure of the viewed object is maintained and modified as the object moves with respect to the viewer, or changes its structure. The transformations in the internal model thus mirror the changes in the environment, in a manner similar to that suggested by Shepard [Shepard & Metzler 1971; Shepard & Cooper 1982]. The internal model resists changes in its shape as much as possible. Consequently, of all the modifications of the model that may account for the observed transformation, the most rigid one is preferred.

This method of recovering three-dimensional structure from motion shares a number of properties with the perception of kinetic depth displays by human observers. The internal model is initially inaccurate and improves with time (successive approximation). In the lack of static three-dimensional information the model prior to the beginning of the motion may initially be entirely flat. As the object starts to move, the model begins to acquire depth, and eventually it reaches a configuration that approximates the actual three-dimensional structure (convergence). If the initial view does convey three-dimensional information, this information may affect the structure of the internal model (integrating sources of information). The recovery process eventually integrates information from different views of the object (temporal extension). The entire history of the process is summarized, however, in the structure of the internal model: the scheme does not operate on long sequences of views or stored trajectories.

The proposed incremental rigidity approach raises two main questions:

1   Its convergence to the correct three-dimensional structure?

2   Its capacity to cope with deviations from rigidity?

The computer simulations have demonstrated that the use of the instantaneous internal model alone, coupled with a principle of maximizing rigidity, is sufficient for the recovery of three-dimensional structure from motion. The resulting scheme has an inherent preference for rigid transformations, but it can also cope with considerable deviations from rigidity.

The simulations also revealed the main advantages and disadvantages of the incremental rigidity scheme. Compared with previous approaches, one limitation of the scheme is that the resulting three-dimensional structure is usually not entirely accurate (although it often approximates the correct structure quite closely). Even for strictly rigid objects, the computed three-dimensional solution usually constrains residual nonrigid distortions. On the other hand, two advantages of the incremental rigidity scheme make it an attractive approach to the recovery of structure from motion. The first is its capacity to cope with nonrigid motion: the three-dimensional structure can be approximated in the face of substantial deviations from rigidity. The second is its robustness: errors in the measured velocity and in the computations employed do not result in complete failure, but in some additional nonrigid distortions superimposed on the correct three-dimensional structure.

A number of problems remain open for further studies. Mathematically, it would be of interest to analyze the convergence properties of the incremental rigidity scheme. As noted in "Rigid Motion," one complicating factor in this analysis is the lack of monotonicity in the decline of the residual error. This error function has been defined above as a root-mean-square measure, using the differences in the internal distances in the correct three-dimensional structure and the internal model. It remains possible that a different error measure would prove more amenable to analytic treatment.

From a psychological point of view, there is a qualitative similarity between the perception of structure from motion by humans, and the behavior of the incremental rigidity scheme. Quantitative data regarding the perception of structure from motion under deviations from rigidity are, however, scant. It would be of interest to investigate further this capacity of the human visual system, and compare the empirical results with the behavior of the incremental rigidity scheme.

References

Adelson, E. H., and J. A. Movshon [1982], "Phenomenal coherence of moving visual patterns," *Nature (London)* vol. 300, pp. 523–525.

Bobick, A. [1983], "A hybrid approach to structure-from motion," in *Proceedings of the ACM Interdisciplinary Workshop on Motion*, Toronto, Canada, pp. 91-109.

Braddick, O. J. [1974], "A short-range process in apparent motion," *Vision Research*, vol. 14, pp. 519-527.

Braunstein, M. L. [1976], *Depth Perception through Motion*, Academic Press, New york.

Clocksin, W. F. [1980], "Perception of surface slant and edge labels from optical flow: a computational approach," *Perception*, vol. 9, pp. 253-269.

Davidon, W. C. [1968], "Variance algorithm for minimization" *The Computer Journal*, vol. 10, pp. 406-413.

I thank Dr. Ellen Hildreth for her valuable comments and Carol Jean Bonomo for her help in preparing this manuscript. This chapter describes research done at the Artificial Intelligence Laboratory of the Massachusetts Institute of Technology. Support was provided by National Science Foundation Grant 79–23110MCS.

Eden, M. [1962], "A three-dimensional optical illusion," *MIT Research Laboratory of Electronics Quarterly Progress Report*, vol. 64, pp. 267-274.

Fennema, C. L., and W. B. Thompson, [1979], "Velocity determination in scenes containing several moving objects," *Computer Graphics and Image Processing*, vol. 9, pp. 301-315.

Gibson, J. J., and E. J. Gibson, [1957] "Continuous perspective transformations and the perception of rigid motion," *Journal of Experimental Psychology*, vol. 54, pp. 129-138.

Green, B. F. [1961], "Figure coherence in the kinetic depth effect," *Journal of Experimental Psychology*, vol. 62, pp. 272-282.

Hay, C. J. [1966], "Optical motions and space perception—an extension of Gibson's analysis," *Psychological Review*, vol. 73, pp. 550-565.

Hoffman, D. D., and B. E. Flinchbaugh [1982], "The interpretation of biological motion," *Biological Cybernetics*, vol. 42, pp. 195-204.

Horn, B. K. P, and B. G. Schunck [1981], "Determining optical flow," *Artificial Intelligence*, vol. 17 pp. 185-203.

Jansson, G., and G. Johansson [1973], "Visual perception of bending motion," *Perception*, vol. 2, pp. 321-326.

Johansson, G. [1964], "Perception of motion and changing form," *Scandinavian Journal of Psychology*, vol. 5, pp. 181-208.

Johansson, G. [1974], "Visual perception of rotary motion as transformation of conic sections—a contribution to the theory of visual space perception," *Psychologia*, vol. 17, pp. 226-237.

Johansson, G. [1978], "Visual event perception," in *Handbook of Sensory Physiology*, edited by R. Held, H. W. Liebowitz, H-L. Teuber, Springer, Berlin.

Johansson, G., and G. Jansson [1968], "Perceived rotary motion from changes in a straight line," *Perception and Psychophysics*, vol. 4, pp. 165-170.

Julesz, B. [1971], *Foundation of Cyclopean Perception*, University of Chicago Press, Chicago.

Koenderink, J. J., and A. J. van Doorn [1975], "Invariant properties of the motion parallax field due to the motion of rigid bodies relative to the observer," *Optica Acta*, vol. 22, pp. 773-791.

Lappin, J. S., J. F. Doner, and B. l. Kottas [1980], "Minimal conditions for the visual detection of structure and motion in three dimensions," *Science*, vol. 209, pp. 717-719.

Lappin, J. S., and M. A. Fuqua [1983], "Accurate visual measurement of three-dimensional moving patterns," *Science*, vol. 221, pp. 480-482.

Lee, D. N. [1976], "A theory of visual control of braking based on information about time to collision," *Perception*, vol. 5, pp. 437-459.

Lee,D. N. [1980], "The optic flow field: the foundation of vision," *Philosophical Transactions of the Royal Society of London, Series B*, vol. 290, pp. 169-179.

Lindsay, P. H., and D. A. Normal [1972], *Human Information Processing*, Academic Press, New York.

Longuet–Higgins, H. C., and K. Prazdny [1980], "The interpretation of a moving retinal image," *Proceedings of the Royal Society of London, Series B*, vol. 208, pp. 385-397.

Miles, W. R. [1931], "Movement interpretations of the silhouette of a revolving fan," *American Journal of Psychology*, vol. 43, pp. 392-405.

Petersik, J. T. [1979], "three-dimensional object constancy: coherence of a simulated rotating sphere in noise," *Perception & Psychophysics*, vol. 15, pp. 328-335.

Petersik, J. T. [1980], "The effect of spatial and temporal factors on the perception of stroboscopic rotation simulations," *Perception*, vol. 9, pp. 271-283.

Shepard, R. N., and L. A. Cooper [1982], *Mental Images and Their Transformations*, MIT Press, Cambridge, MA.

Shepard, R. N.,and J. Metzler [1971], "Mental rotation of three-dimensional objects," *Science*, vol. 171, pp. 701-703.

Sperling, G., M. Pavel, Y. Cohen, M. S. Landy, and B. J. Schwartz [1983] in *Physical and Biological Processing of Images*, edited by O. J. Braddick, and A. C. Sleigh, Springer, Berlin.

Tsai, R. Y, and T. S. Huang [1982], "Uniqueness and estimation of three--dimensional motion parameters of rigid objects with curved surfaces," University of Illinois at Urbana-Champaign Coordinated Science Laboratory Report R-921.

Ullman, S. [1979a], *The Interpretation of Visual Motion*, MIT Press, Cambridge, MA.

Ullman, S. [1979b], "The interpretation of structure from motion," *Proceedings of the Royal Society of London, Series B*,vol. 203, pp. 405-426.

Ullman, S. [1979c], "Relaxation and constrained optimization by local processes," *Computer Graphics and Image Processing*, vol. 9, no. 6, pp. 115-125.

Ullman, S. [1983], "Recent computational results in the interpretation of structure from motion," in *Human and Machine Vision*, edited by A. Rosenfeld, and J. Beck, Academic Press, New york, pp. 459-480.

Ullman, S., and E. Hildreth [1983], "The measurement of visual motion," in *Physical and Biological Processing of Images*, edited by O. J. Braddick, and A. C. Sleigh, Springer,Berlin.

Wallach, H., and D. N. O'Connell [1953], "The kinetic depth effect," *Journal of Experimental Psychology*, vol. 45, pp. 205-217.

Wallach, H., D. N. O'Connell, and U. Neisser[1953], "The memory effect of visual perception of 3-D form," *Journal of Experimental Psychology*, vol. 45, pp. 360-368.

Wallach, H, A. Weisz, and P. A. Adams [1956], "Circles and derived figures in rotation," *American Journal of Psychology*, vol. 69, pp. 48-59.

Webb, J. A., and J. K. Aggarwal [1981], "Visually interpreting the motions of objects in space," *Computer*, vol. 14, no. 8, pp. 40-49.

White, B. W., and G. E. Mueser [1960], "Accuracy in reconstructing the arrangement of elements generating kinetic depth displays," *Journal of Experimental Psychology*, vol. 60, pp. 1-11.

40

Imagine that you are a terrestrial, aquatic, or flying robot and that you want to keep track of where you are, relative to some coordinate system, given only that you have an eye or a camera to look through. You have no gyroscope, no compass, no navigation radio, no form of radar or sonar, and no map.

You might think that the only hope would be to understand what you see at least to the point of identifying some features or objects to keep track of as you move. Perhaps surprisingly, it seems better, in most cases, to work directly with large numbers of image points, noting only their first derivatives of brightness with respect to time and space. Although a general solution is not yet known, Horn and Weldon show how to deal with special cases in which the motion is pure rotation, pure translation, or arbitrary motion when the rotation is known. Their analysis demonstrates the critical importance of sufficient field of view and of adequate, aliasing-avoiding spatial and temporal filtering.

Direct Methods
for Recovering Motion

Berthold K. P. Horn
E. J. Weldon Jr.[†]

In this chapter we consider the problem of determining the motion of a monocular observer moving with respect to a rigid, unknown world. We use a "least squares," as opposed to a discrete method of solving for the motion parameters; our method uses all of the points in a two-image sequence and does not attempt to establish correspondence between the images. Hence the method is relatively robust with respect to quantization error, noise, illumination gradients, and other effects.

So far, we can determine the observer motion in two special cases:

- When the motion is pure rotation.
- When the motion is pure translation or when the rotational component of the motion is known.

At this writing we have not developed a direct method that is applicable to arbitrary motion.

Earlier work

In the continuous or least squares approach to motion vision, motion parameters are found that are consistent with the observed motion of the entire image. Bruss and Horn [1983] use this approach to calculate motion parameters assuming that the optical flow is known at each point. Adiv [1984] uses the approach of Bruss and Horn to segment the scene into independently moving planar objects; he shows that given the optical

[†]Department of Electrical Engineering, University of Hawaii at Manoa, Honolulu, Hawaii 96822.

flow, segmentation can be performed and the motion calculated. Negahdaripour and Horn [1987] eschew the use of optical flow and calculate the
observer's motion directly from the spatial and temporal derivatives of the
image brightness, assuming a planar world. The advantage of this direct
approach, which we also use here, is that certain computational difficulties
inherent in the calculation of optical flow are avoided. In particular, it is
not necessary to make the usual assumption that the optical flow field is
smooth; an assumption that is violated near object boundaries, necessitat-
ing flow segmentation.

Waxman and Ullman [1985] and Waxman and Wohn [1985] also avoid
the discrete approach to motion vision; their techniques make use of first
and second derivatives of the optical flow to compute both the motion
parameters and the structure of the imaged world. In the interests of
developing methods which can be implemented, the techniques presented
in this chapter avoid the use of second and higher-order derivatives.

Summary of the chapter

One of our approaches to the motion vision problem can be summarized
as follows: Given the observer motion and the spatial brightness function
of the image one can predict the time derivative of brightness at each
point in the image. We find the motion that minimizes the integral of the
square of the difference between this predicted value and the observed time
derivative. The integral is taken over the image region of interest, which,
in the discussion here, is usually taken to be the whole image.

We use auxiliary vectors derived from the derivatives of brightness and
the image position that occur in the basic brightness change constraint
equation. Study of the distribution of the directions of these vectors on the
unit sphere suggests specific algorithms and also helps uncover relationships
between accuracy and parameters of the imaging situation.

We have developed a simple robust algorithm for recovering the angular velocity vector in the case of pure rotation. This algorithm involves
solving three linear equations in the three unknown components of the rotation vector. The coefficients of the equations are moments of components
of one of the auxiliary vectors over the given image region. We show that
the accuracy of the recovered component of rotation about the direction
towards the image region is poor relative to the other components, unless
the image region subtends a substantial solid angle.

We have developed several algorithms for recovering the translational
velocity in the case of pure translation. These algorithms exploit the constraint that objects have to be in front of the camera in order to be imaged.
This constraint leads to a non-linear constrained optimization problem.

The performance of these algorithms depends on a number of factors including:

- Angle subtended by the image, that is, the field of view.
- Direction of motion relative to the optical axis.
- Depth range.
- Distribution of brightness gradients.
- Noise in the estimated time derivative of brightness.
- Noise in the estimated spatial gradient of brightness.
- Number of picture cells considered.

We have not yet been able to select a "best" algorithm from the set developed, because one may be more accurate under one set of circumstances while another is better in a different situation. Also, the better algorithms tend to require more computation, and some do not lend themselves to parallel implementation. Further study using real image data will be needed to determine the range of applicability of each algorithm.

We found a strong dependence of the accuracy of recovery of certain components of the motion on the size of the field of view. This is in concert with other reports describing difficulties with small fields of view, such as Adiv [1984] and Waxman and Wohn [1985].

Comments on sampling, filtering, and aliasing

Work with real image data has demonstrated the need to take care in filtering and sampling. The estimates of spatial gradient and time derivatives are sensitive to aliasing effects resulting from inadequate low-pass filtering before sampling. This is easily overlooked, particularly in the time direction. It is usually a mistake, for example, to simply pick every n^{th} frame out of an image sequence. At the very least, n consecutive frames should be averaged before sampling in order to reduce the high frequency components. One may object to the "smearing" introduced by this technique, but a series of widely separated snap-shots typically do not obey the conditions of the sampling theorem, and as a result the estimates of the derivatives may contain large errors.

This, of course, is nothing new, because the same considerations apply when one tries to estimate the optical flow using first derivatives of image brightness [Horn & Schunck 1981]. It is important to remember that the filtering must be applied before sampling—once the data has been sampled, the damage has been done.

The Brightness-Change Constraint Equation

Following Longuet-Higgins and Prazdny [1980] and Bruss and Horn [1983] we use a viewer-based coordinate system. Figure 1 depicts the system under consideration. A world point

$$\mathbf{R} = (X, Y, Z)^T \tag{1}$$

is imaged at

$$\mathbf{r} = (x, y, 1)^T. \tag{2}$$

That is, the image plane has equation $Z = 1$. The origin is at the projection center and the Z-axis runs along the optical axis. The X- and Y-axes are parallel to the x- and y-axes of the image plane. Image coordinates are measured relative to the principal point, the point $(0, 0, 1)^T$ where the optical axis pierces the image plane. The points $\mathbf{r}$ and $\mathbf{R}$ are related by the perspective projection equation

$$\mathbf{r} = (x, y, 1)^T = \left(\frac{X}{Z}, \frac{Y}{Z}, \frac{Z}{Z}\right)^T = \frac{\mathbf{R}}{\mathbf{R} \cdot \hat{\mathbf{z}}}, \tag{3}$$

with

$$Z = \mathbf{R} \cdot \hat{\mathbf{z}}, \tag{4}$$

and where $\hat{\mathbf{z}}$ denotes the unit vector in the Z direction.

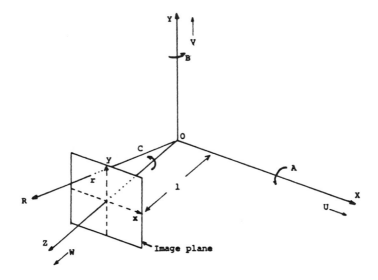

Figure 1. The viewer-centered coordinate system. The translational velocity of the camera is $\mathbf{t} = (U, V, W)^T$, while the rotational component is $\boldsymbol{\omega} = (A, B, C)^T$.

Suppose the observer moves with instantaneous translational velocity $\mathbf{t} = (U, V, W)^T$ and instantaneous rotational velocity $\boldsymbol{\omega} = (A, B, C)^T$ relative to a fixed environment, then the time derivative of the vector $\mathbf{R}$ can be written as

$$\mathbf{R}_t = -\mathbf{t} - \boldsymbol{\omega} \times \mathbf{R}. \tag{5}$$

The motion of the world point $\mathbf{R}$ results in motion of the corresponding image point; the value of this *motion field* is given by

$$\mathbf{r}_t = \frac{d\mathbf{r}}{dt} = \frac{d}{dt}\left(\frac{\mathbf{R}}{\mathbf{R}\cdot\hat{\mathbf{z}}}\right) = \frac{\mathbf{R}_t(\mathbf{R}\cdot\hat{\mathbf{z}}) - (\mathbf{R}_t\cdot\hat{\mathbf{z}})\mathbf{R}}{(\mathbf{R}\cdot\hat{\mathbf{z}})^2}. \tag{6}$$

This can also be expressed as

$$\mathbf{r}_t = \frac{\hat{\mathbf{z}}\times(\mathbf{R}_t\times\mathbf{r})}{\mathbf{R}\cdot\hat{\mathbf{z}}}, \tag{7}$$

since $\mathbf{a}\times(\mathbf{b}\times\mathbf{c}) = (\mathbf{c}\cdot\mathbf{a})\mathbf{b} - (\mathbf{a}\cdot\mathbf{b})\mathbf{c}$. Substituting equation (5) into this result (see Negahdaripour and Horn [1987]) gives:

$$\mathbf{r}_t = -\hat{\mathbf{z}}\times\left(\mathbf{r}\times\left(\mathbf{r}\times\boldsymbol{\omega} - \frac{\mathbf{t}}{\mathbf{R}\cdot\hat{\mathbf{z}}}\right)\right). \tag{8}$$

In component form this can be expressed as

$$\mathbf{r}_t = \begin{pmatrix} x_t \\ y_t \\ 0 \end{pmatrix} = \begin{pmatrix} \frac{-U+xW}{Z} + Axy - B(x^2+1) + Cy \\ \frac{-V+yW}{Z} - Bxy + A(y^2+1) - Cx \\ 0 \end{pmatrix}, \tag{9}$$

a result first obtained by Longuet-Higgins and Prazdny [1980].

This shows how, given the world motion, the motion field can be calculated for every image point. If we assume that the brightness of a small surface patch is not changed by motion, then expansion of the total derivative of brightness E leads to

$$\frac{\partial E}{\partial x}\frac{dx}{dt} + \frac{\partial E}{\partial y}\frac{dy}{dt} + \frac{\partial E}{\partial t} = 0. \tag{10}$$

(The applicability of the constant brightness assumption is discussed in Appendix A.) Denoting the vector $(\partial E/\partial x, \partial E/\partial y, 0)^T$ by $E_{\mathbf{r}}$ and $\partial E/\partial t$ by E_t, permits us to express this result more compactly in the form

$$E_{\mathbf{r}}\cdot\mathbf{r}_t + E_t = 0. \tag{11}$$

Substituting equation (8) into this result and rearranging gives

$$E_t - \left(\left(\left(E_{\mathbf{r}}\times\hat{\mathbf{z}}\right)\times\mathbf{r}\right)\times\mathbf{r}\right)\cdot\boldsymbol{\omega} + \frac{\left(\left(E_{\mathbf{r}}\times\hat{\mathbf{z}}\right)\times\mathbf{r}\right)\cdot\mathbf{t}}{\mathbf{R}\cdot\hat{\mathbf{z}}} = 0. \tag{12}$$

To simplify this expression we let

$$\mathbf{s} = (E_{\mathbf{r}}\times\hat{\mathbf{z}})\times\mathbf{r} \tag{13}$$

and

$$\mathbf{v} = -\mathbf{s}\times\mathbf{r}, \tag{14}$$

so equation (12) reduces to the *brightness change constraint equation* of Negahdaripour and Horn [1987], namely

$$\mathbf{v}\cdot\boldsymbol{\omega} + \frac{\mathbf{s}\cdot\mathbf{t}}{\mathbf{R}\cdot\hat{\mathbf{z}}} = -E_t. \tag{15}$$

The vectors $\mathbf{s}$ and $\mathbf{v}$ can be expressed in component form as

$$\mathbf{s} = \begin{pmatrix} -E_x \\ -E_y \\ xE_x + yE_y \end{pmatrix} \quad \text{and} \quad \mathbf{v} = \begin{pmatrix} +E_y + y(xE_x + yE_y) \\ -E_x - x(xE_x + yE_y) \\ yE_x - xE_y \end{pmatrix}. \tag{16}$$

Note that $\mathbf{s} \cdot \mathbf{r} = 0$, $\mathbf{v} \cdot \mathbf{r} = 0$, and $\mathbf{s} \cdot \mathbf{v} = 0$. These three vectors thus form an orthogonal triad. The vectors $\mathbf{s}$ and $\mathbf{v}$ are inherent properties of the image. Note that the projection of $\mathbf{s}$ into the image plane is just the (negative) gradient of the image. Also, the quantity $\mathbf{s}$ indicates the directions in which translation of a given magnitude will contribute maximally to the temporal brightness change of a given picture cell. The quantity $\mathbf{v}$ plays a similar role for rotation.

Solving the Brightness Change Constraint Equation

Equation (15) relates observer motion $(\mathbf{t}, \boldsymbol{\omega})$, the depth of the world $\mathbf{R} \cdot \hat{\mathbf{z}} = Z(x, y)$, and certain measurable quantities of the image $(\mathbf{s}, \mathbf{v})$. In general, it is not possible to solve for the first two of these given the last. Some interesting special cases are addressed in this chapter and in Negahdaripour and Horn [1987]; these are:[1]

1   **Known depth:**   We show that given Z, $\mathbf{s}$ and $\mathbf{v}$, the quantities, $\mathbf{t}$ and $\boldsymbol{\omega}$ can be calculated in closed form using a least-squares method.

2   **Pure rotation** ($\|\mathbf{t}\| = 0$):   We show that given $\mathbf{v}$, the rotation vector $\boldsymbol{\omega}$ can be calculated in closed form.

3   **Pure translation or known rotation:**   We present a least-squares method for determining $\mathbf{t}$. Once $\mathbf{t}$ is known, the brightness change constraint equation can be used to find the depth at each picture cell:

$$Z = \mathbf{R} \cdot \hat{\mathbf{z}} = -\frac{\mathbf{s} \cdot \mathbf{t}}{E_t + \mathbf{v} \cdot \boldsymbol{\omega}}. \qquad (17)$$

4   **Planar world:**   Negahdaripour and Horn [1987] present a closed form solution for $\mathbf{t}$, $\boldsymbol{\omega}$ and the normal $\mathbf{n}$ of the world plane.

5   **Quadratic patches:**   Negahdaripour [1986] gives a closed-form solution in the case that a portion of the world can be represented as a quadratic form.

In this chapter we consider various integrals over an image region thought to correspond to a single rigid object in motion relative to the viewer. In the simplest case, the observer is moving relative to a static environment and the whole image can be used. The size of the field of view has a strong effect on the accuracy of the determination of the components of motion along the optical axis. When we need to estimate this accuracy, we will, for convenience, assume a circular image of radius r_v. This corresponds to a conical field of view with half angle θ_v, where $r_v = \tan \theta_v$, because we have assumed that the focal length equals one (we assume that $0 < \theta_v < \pi/2$).

We will show that the field of view should be large. Although orthographic projection usually simplifies machine vision problems, this is one case in which we welcome the effects of perspective "distortion"!

---

[1]We do not discuss here related methods using optical flow, such as those of Bruss and Horn [1983].

Depth known

When depth is known, it is straightforward to recover the motion. (Depth may have been obtained using a binocular stereo system or some kind of range finder.) We cannot, in general, find a motion to satisfy the brightness change constraint equation at every picture cell, because of noise in the measurements. Instead we minimize

$$\iint [E_t + \mathbf{v} \cdot \boldsymbol{\omega} + (1/Z)\mathbf{s} \cdot \mathbf{t}]^2 \, dx \, dy \,. \tag{18}$$

Differentiating with respect to $\boldsymbol{\omega}$ and $\mathbf{t}$ and setting the results equal to zero leads to the pair of vector equations

$$\left[\iint (1/Z)^2 \mathbf{s}\mathbf{s}^T \, dx \, dy\right] \mathbf{t} + \left[\iint (1/Z)\mathbf{s}\mathbf{v}^T \, dx \, dy\right] \boldsymbol{\omega}$$

$$= -\iint E_t(1/Z)\mathbf{s} \, dx \, dy$$

$$\left[\iint (1/Z)\mathbf{v}\mathbf{s}^T \, dx \, dy\right] \mathbf{t} + \left[\iint \mathbf{v}\mathbf{v}^T \, dx \, dy\right] \boldsymbol{\omega} = -\iint E_t \mathbf{v} \, dx \, dy \,.$$

$$\tag{19}$$

This is a set of six linear equations in six unknowns with a symmetric coefficient matrix. (The equations can be solved by partitioning in order to reduce the computational effort.) The coefficients are all integrals of products of components of $(1/Z)\mathbf{s}$ and $\mathbf{v}$. It may be useful to note that

$$\text{Trace}(\mathbf{s}\mathbf{v}^T) = \text{Trace}(\mathbf{v}\mathbf{s}^T) = \mathbf{s} \cdot \mathbf{v} = 0 \,. \tag{20}$$

We could have obtained slightly different equations for $\boldsymbol{\omega}$ and $\mathbf{t}$ if we had chosen to weight the integrand in equation (18) differently. We study the special case in which $\|\mathbf{t}\| = 0$ and the special case in which $\|\boldsymbol{\omega}\| = 0$ later.

One application of the above result is to "dynamic stereo." A binocular stereo system can provide disparity estimates from which $1/Z$ can be calculated. The above equations can then be used to solve for the motion, provided estimates of the derivatives of image brightness are also supplied. The correspondence problem of binocular stereo has, unfortunately, been found to be a difficult one. It would represent the major computational burden in a "dynamic stereo" system. We hope that motion vision research will eventually lead to simpler methods for recovering depth than those used for binocular stereo—although they are likely to be relatively inaccurate when based only on instantaneous translational and rotational velocity estimates.

Pure rotation

When $\|\mathbf{t}\| = 0$, the brightness change constraint equation reduces to

$$E_t + \mathbf{v} \cdot \boldsymbol{\omega} = 0 \,. \tag{21}$$

We wish to find the value of $\boldsymbol{\omega}$ that minimizes the sum of the squares of the errors in the time derivative of brightness, that is, we want to minimize

$$\iint [E_t + \mathbf{v} \cdot \boldsymbol{\omega}]^2 \, dx \, dy \,. \tag{22}$$

Differentiating with respect to $\boldsymbol{\omega}$ and setting the result equal to zero gives us

$$2 \iint [E_t + \mathbf{v} \cdot \boldsymbol{\omega}] \mathbf{v} \, dx \, dy = 0 \,. \tag{23}$$

Since $(\mathbf{v} \cdot \boldsymbol{\omega})\mathbf{v} = \mathbf{v}(\mathbf{v} \cdot \boldsymbol{\omega}) = (\mathbf{v}\mathbf{v}^T)\boldsymbol{\omega}$, we can write this in the form

$$\left[\iint \mathbf{v}\mathbf{v}^T \, dx \, dy \right] \boldsymbol{\omega} = - \iint E_t \mathbf{v} \, dx \, dy \,, \tag{24}$$

which is just a special case of equation (19). This is a set of three linear equations in the three unknown components of $\boldsymbol{\omega}$, namely, A, B, and C. The coefficient matrix is symmetric and only the right-hand side depends on the time derivative of brightness.

One can tell whether one is dealing with a case of pure rotation or not. In the presence of a translational component, equation (21) will not be a good approximation and so the integral in formula (22) will not be small. Experiments show that this simple method of determining rotation is robust and easy to implement. Slight variations are possible by weighting the intergrand differently. This method is reminiscent of the optical flow based method of Bruss and Horn [1983] and very similar to a method developed by Aloimonos and Brown [1984], to which our attention was drawn after we wrote this chapter.

Shown in figure 2 is every tenth frame out of a 40 frame sequence taken with a tripod-mounted CCD camera rotated manually about its vertical axis. The vertical component of the computed rotational velocity is shown in figure 3 as a function of the frame number. The units along the vertical axis are picture cells per time step in the center of the image (rather than say radians/second). After the initial acceleration, image components near the center of the image move by about 7 to 8 picture cells between successive frames. Three curves are given for varying amounts of image low-pass filtering and sub-sampling. The lowest curve (A) corresponds to the raw image data, and shows that for this particular scene at least, a motion of 7 to 8 picture cells is too much for accurate recovery of the angular velocity. The computed velocity appears to "saturate" at around 4 picture cells per time step. The next higher curve (B) corresponds to image compression by low-pass filtering and sub-sampling by a factor of two in each direction. In the compressed image sequence, the motion is in effect only about 3 to 4 picture cells per time step. The top curve (C) was obtained using images that were low-pass filtered and sub-sampled a second time to reduce them by a total of a factor of four in each direction. In this doubly compressed sequence, motion in the center of the image amounts to only about 1.5

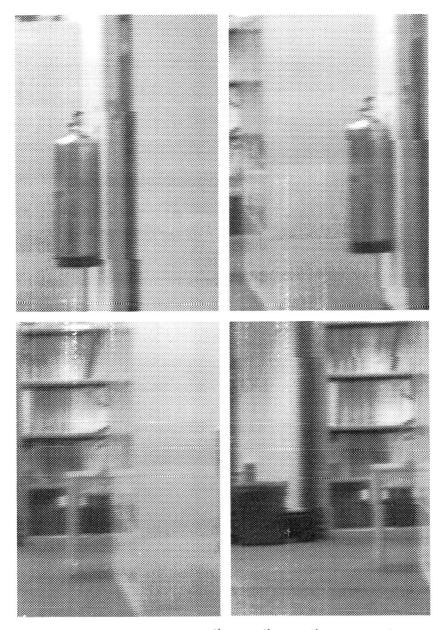

Figure 2. Shown here are the (a)10th, (b)20th, (c)30th, and (d)40th image out of a 40-image sequence obtained when a CCD camera mounted on a tripod was (manually) rotated about its vertical axis. After the initial acceleration, the image motion in the center is between 7 and 8 picture cells between successive frames. Image motion between frames is slightly larger in the corners of the image.

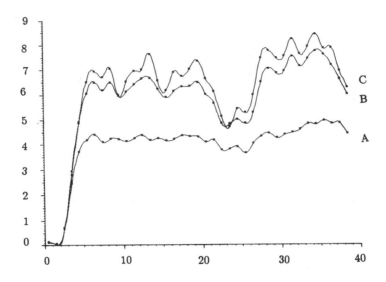

Figure 3. Recovered vertical component of the angular velocity vector as a function of the frame number. The angular velocity is given in picture cells of image displacement at the center of the image per time step. Curve A was obtained using the raw image data, curve B from a low-pass filtered and subsampled image sequence, and curve C from an image sequence that was low-pass filtered and sampled twice. Further low-pass filtering and subsampling produces essentially the same curve.

to 2 picture cells per time step, and the angular velocity is accurately recovered. Further filtering and sub-sampling leads to velocity estimates that are essentially the same as the ones obtained with this sequence.

◇ Distribution of the directions of v

To understand the properties of the algorithm for recovering the instantaneous rotational velocity, one needs to study the matrix obtained by integrating $\mathbf{v}\mathbf{v}^T$. We can think of the direction of $\mathbf{v}$ as identifying a point on the unit sphere and of $\|\mathbf{v}\|$ as the mass of a particle placed there. The collection of vectors corresponding to an image region then can be thought of as a set of particles on the unit sphere. The integral of $\mathbf{v}\mathbf{v}^T$ is the symmetric 3×3 matrix whose elements are integrals of the nine pair-wise products of components of $\mathbf{v}$. This matrix is related to the inertia matrix of this set of particles. If the particles were spread uniformly over the surface of the sphere, this matrix would be the total mass times the identity matrix. As we show next, the particles are confined to a band, so this matrix, while diagonal on average, is not a multiple of the identity matrix.

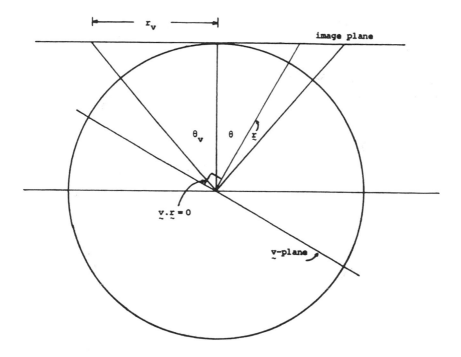

Figure 4. A cross-section through the **v**-sphere defined by the image point **r**.

We know that $\mathbf{v} \cdot \mathbf{r} = 0$ and that the possible directions of **r** lie within a cone defined by the field of view. For a particular value of **r**, the equation $\mathbf{v} \cdot \mathbf{r} = 0$ defines a plane that cuts the unit sphere in a great circle (see figure 4). The vector **v** must point in a direction corresponding to a point on this great circle. Since **r** lies inside a cone of directions with half-angle θ_v, these great circles have axes that lie in this cone also. The collection of great circles lies in a band around the unit sphere of width equal to the total width of the visual field.

We can obtain the same result algebraically as follows: Let $\hat{\mathbf{r}}$, $\hat{\mathbf{v}}$, and $\hat{\mathbf{s}}$ be unit vectors in the directions **r**, **v**, and **s**. Then, because **r**, **s**, and **v** are mutually orthogonal,

$$(\hat{\mathbf{z}} \cdot \hat{\mathbf{r}})^2 + (\hat{\mathbf{z}} \cdot \hat{\mathbf{v}})^2 + (\hat{\mathbf{z}} \cdot \hat{\mathbf{s}})^2 = 1 \,, \tag{25}$$

while

$$(\hat{\mathbf{x}} \cdot \hat{\mathbf{v}})^2 + (\hat{\mathbf{y}} \cdot \hat{\mathbf{v}})^2 + (\hat{\mathbf{z}} \cdot \hat{\mathbf{v}})^2 = 1 \,, \tag{26}$$

where $\hat{\mathbf{x}}$, $\hat{\mathbf{y}}$, and $\hat{\mathbf{z}}$ are unit vectors in the X, Y, and Z directions. Subtracting the two equalities we obtain

$$(\hat{\mathbf{x}} \cdot \hat{\mathbf{v}})^2 + (\hat{\mathbf{y}} \cdot \hat{\mathbf{v}})^2 = (\hat{\mathbf{z}} \cdot \hat{\mathbf{r}})^2 + (\hat{\mathbf{z}} \cdot \hat{\mathbf{s}})^2 \,, \tag{27}$$

which, since

$$(\hat{\mathbf{z}} \cdot \hat{\mathbf{r}})^2 \geq \cos^2 \theta_v \qquad \text{and} \qquad (\hat{\mathbf{z}} \cdot \hat{\mathbf{s}})^2 \geq 0 , \tag{28}$$

tells us that

$$(\hat{\mathbf{x}} \cdot \hat{\mathbf{v}})^2 + (\hat{\mathbf{y}} \cdot \hat{\mathbf{v}})^2 \geq \cos^2 \theta_v . \tag{29}$$

Thus the directions of $\mathbf{v}$ lie within an angle θ_v of the "equator" of the unit sphere. We call this band (shown in figure 5) the *permissible band*.

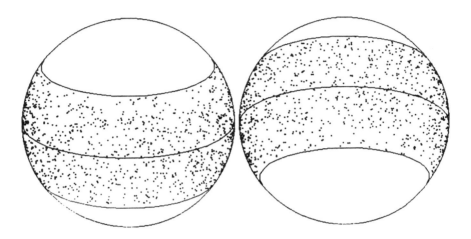

Figure 5. The permissible band on the $\mathbf{v}$-sphere (front and rear views).

◇ Estimate of the condition number

It is important to determine under what circumstances the recovery of the rotational velocity is ill conditioned, and whether the different components of the rotation vector are equally affected by noise in the data. To study these issues, one needs to estimate some of the properties of the coefficient matrix of the equations. We can get a rough idea of what the integral of $\mathbf{v}\mathbf{v}^T$ looks like by assuming that the particles corresponding to $\mathbf{v}$ are spread *uniformly* within the permissible band. In Appendix B we show that the area of this band is

$$K = 4\pi \sin \theta_v . \tag{30}$$

The mixed inertia terms (such as the integral of the product of x and y) are all zero because of the symmetry of the band. The resulting 3×3 matrix is thus diagonal. Furthermore, if we let I_{xx}, I_{yy}, and I_{zz} be the diagonal terms then it can be shown (in Appendix B) that

$$I_{xx} = I_{yy} = (K/3) \left[1 + (1/2) \cos^2 \theta_v \right] , \tag{31}$$

while
$$I_{zz} = (K/3)\sin^2\theta_v .\tag{32}$$
Thus I_{xx}/K and I_{yy}/K vary little with θ_v, while I_{zz}/K changes dramatically. The (L^2) condition number of this matrix—the ratio of the largest to the smallest eigenvalue—is just
$$\frac{I_{xx}}{I_{zz}} = \frac{1 + (1/2)\cos^2\theta_v}{\sin^2\theta_v} = \frac{3/2}{\sin^2\theta_v} - \frac{1}{2} .\tag{33}$$
This is very large when the field of view is small. When the condition number is very large, small errors in the right hand sides of the equations, or in the coefficients of the matrix itself, can lead to large errors in the solution.

In fact, the particles are *not* spread uniformly within the permissible band and do not have mass independent of position, so the above is only an estimate. We obtain the exact result later.

◇ Stability of the solution method

The numerical stability of the solution for $\boldsymbol{\omega}$ is reduced when the condition number is large. In practice, the elements of the matrix of equation (24) will be corrupted by noise in the measurements, as will the right-hand side vector in this equation. The estimate of the third component of $\boldsymbol{\omega}$ will be affected more by these perturbations than the other two. Experiments confirm that the component of rotation about the optical axis is disturbed more by noise than the others. The ratio of the errors grows roughly as the inverse of the size of the field of view. This is not a peculiarity of our method, but applies in general.

It is intuitively obvious why this should be. Rotations about the x- and y-axes produce motion fields that vary but little over the image. A small field of view can be used to estimate these components with almost the same accuracy as can a large field of view (provided the same number of picture cells used.) Rotation about the z-axis, on the other hand, produces a motion field that varies directly with distance from the principal point. Thus the maximum velocity depends on the size of the field of view. With a small field of view, the maximum velocity in the image will be small and relative errors in measurements correspondingly larger.

If an image region is used that is smaller than the whole field of view and perhaps off center, the analysis becomes more complex. In this case, the component of rotation about the direction towards the center of the region is less accurately known; the accuracy again decreasing with the size of the image region. This shows the futility of approaches based on data from small image patches, or higher derivatives of brightness at one point in the image. When working with very small image regions, the best one can do is to estimate the optical flow—there is no point in trying to recover the "rotation" about the center of the region.

◊ Ensemble average of the integral of $\mathbf{vv}^T$

The integral of $\mathbf{vv}^T$ varies from image to image. It has already been suggested, however, that it will be approximately diagonal. We can obtain a more precise answer by averaging over an ensemble of images with all possible directions for the brightness gradient at each image point. We assume that different directions for the brightness gradient are equally likely. The result so obtained can be viewed in another way: it is the integral obtained in the limit from a textured image as the scale of the texture is made smaller and smaller. In this case we can arrange for every direction of the brightness gradient to be found in any small patch of the image. By suitable choice of the texture we can arrange that no directions of the brightness gradient is favored—all directions occur with equal frequency.

If we take into account the distribution of directions of $\mathbf{v}$ and the weights $\|\mathbf{v}\|$, we find (in Appendix B) that

$$\overline{\iint \mathbf{vv}^T \, dx \, dy} = k_v \begin{pmatrix} 1 + r_v^2/2 + r_v^4/6 & 0 & 0 \\ 0 & 1 + r_v^2/2 + r_v^4/6 & 0 \\ 0 & 0 & r_v^2/2 \end{pmatrix}, \quad (34)$$

where r_v is the diameter of the image and the constant k_v depends on the size of the field of view as well as the distribution of magnitudes of the brightness gradient. In practice we can easily find k_v since

$$\text{Trace}\left(\iint \mathbf{vv}^T \, dx \, dy\right) = \iint \text{Trace}(\mathbf{vv}^T) \, dx \, dy = \iint \mathbf{v} \cdot \mathbf{v} \, dx \, dy, \quad (35)$$

so

$$2k_v(1 + 3r_v^2/4 + r_v^4/6) = \overline{\iint \mathbf{v} \cdot \mathbf{v} \, dx \, dy}. \quad (36)$$

Note that the condition number is

$$\frac{1 + r_v^2/2 + r_v^4/6}{r_v^2/2} = \frac{2}{r_v^2} + 1 + \frac{r_v^2}{3}. \quad (37)$$

It attains a minimum of $1 + 2\sqrt{2/3} = 2.633\ldots$ when $r_v = \sqrt{\sqrt{6}} = 1.565\ldots$. Thus the component of rotation about the optical axis is not recovered as accurately as the other two components, no matter how large the field of view. Also, as far as rotation is concerned, there is little advantage to making the field of view wider than a half-angle $\theta_v = \tan^{-1}\sqrt{\sqrt{6}} = 57.42\ldots$ degrees, because the condition number reaches its minimum there.

Some simplifications of the method for recovering the rotational velocity based on the above analysis are discussed by us in Horn and Weldon [1987].

◇ The v-Bar projection

We know that the directions of the vectors **v** lie in the permissible band. But what about the vectors

$$\overline{\mathbf{v}} = -E_t\mathbf{v} \tag{38}$$

occurring in the integral on the right-hand side of equation (24)? We know that in the case of pure rotation $E_t = -\mathbf{v}\cdot\boldsymbol{\omega}$, so $\overline{\mathbf{v}} = (\mathbf{v}\cdot\boldsymbol{\omega})\mathbf{v}$. We conclude that

$$\overline{\mathbf{v}}\cdot\boldsymbol{\omega} = (\mathbf{v}\cdot\boldsymbol{\omega})^2 \geq 0. \tag{39}$$

Thus the directions of the vectors $\overline{\mathbf{v}}$ are confined to a hemisphere with $\boldsymbol{\omega}$ at its pole or "navel." We call this the *compatible hemisphere* for the case of pure rotation.

If the vectors $\overline{\mathbf{v}}$ covered this hemisphere uniformly, we could easily estimate $\boldsymbol{\omega}$ by finding the center of mass of the particles on the unit sphere corresponding to the values of $\overline{\mathbf{v}}$. The center of mass of a hemisphere of uniform density is at a point midway between the center of the sphere and the navel of the hemisphere, so we could use the formula

$$\boldsymbol{\omega} \approx \frac{2\iint \overline{\mathbf{v}}\, dx\, dy}{\iint \|\overline{\mathbf{v}}\|\, dx\, dy}. \tag{40}$$

Unfortunately, the vectors $\overline{\mathbf{v}}$ do not cover the whole compatible hemisphere, because they are confined to the permissible band, in the same way as vectors **v**. In fact, the vectors $\overline{\mathbf{v}}$ lie in the intersection of the permissible band and the compatible hemisphere, as shown in figure 6.

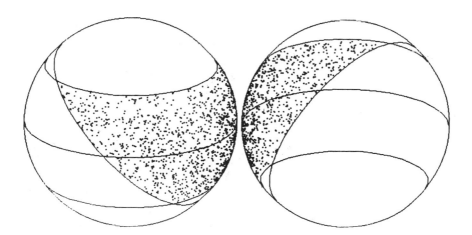

Figure 6. The **v**-sphere showing the intersection of the permissible band and the compatible hemisphere, in the case when the field of view is wide (front and rear views).

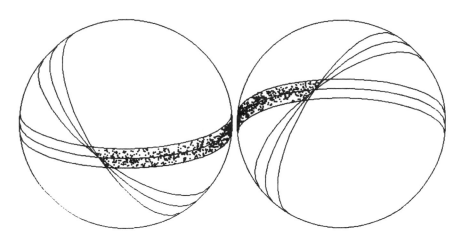

Figure 7. The intersection of the permissible band with three different compatible hemispheres when the field of view is narrow.

We can now see in another way why a small field of view reduces the accuracy with which we can estimate the component of rotation about the optical axis. If the field of view is small, the permissible band will be narrow, a mere ring. Our task is to guess which hemisphere cut the ring in half. This is easy when we are dealing with a band that covers almost the whole sphere—when it is very narrow, however, there is some uncertainty. A hemisphere claimed to provide a solution can easily be rotated about the line connecting the ends of the cut ring without significantly changing the intersection of the hemisphere and the ring as illustrated in figure 7. Thus the z-component of the direction to the navel of the hemisphere is uncertain in the presence of noise, or, when measurements from only a small number of picture cells are available.

We could use the geometric insight that the vectors **v** all lie in the intersection of the permissible band and the compatible hemisphere to construct algorithms for recovering the direction of the vector $\boldsymbol{\omega}$. Some other method would then have to be found to estimate the magnitude of $\boldsymbol{\omega}$. However, we do not need to approach the problem in this way, in light of the least-squares solution presented above. This geometric approach, however, *will* be fruitful in the case of pure translation where we find a similar geometric constraint and have no need to find the magnitude of the motion vector.

If there is a translational component to the motion, the points $\bar{\mathbf{v}}$ will not be confined to a hemisphere. This provides a convenient test to see whether the method presented above can be applied or not.

Rotation known or pure translation

If the rotation is known, perhaps measured by some other instrument, but depth is not, then the general problem reduces to the problem of pure translation. We can write

$$E'_t + (1/Z)\mathbf{s} \cdot \mathbf{t} = 0 \,, \tag{41}$$

where

$$E'_t = E_t + \mathbf{v} \cdot \boldsymbol{\omega} \,. \tag{42}$$

In the remainder of this section we do not distinguish between E_t and E'_t.

Note that equation (41) is not altered if we replace Z by $k\check{Z}$ and $\mathbf{t}$ by $k\mathbf{t}$. Thus we can recover motion and depth only up to a scale factor. In the sequel we will set $\|\mathbf{t}\| = 1$ when convenient.

First, note that unlike the case in which depth is known, we cannot obtain a useful result by simply minimizing

$$\iint [E_t + (1/Z)\mathbf{s} \cdot \mathbf{t}]^2 \, dx \, dy \,, \tag{43}$$

because the integrand can be trivially made equal to zero at each point by the choice

$$Z = -(\mathbf{s} \cdot \mathbf{t})/E_t \,. \tag{44}$$

(However, this may produce negative values for Z, a fact that we exploit later.) Given the correct value of $\mathbf{t}$, the above equation provides a means for recovering depth, as already mentioned.

Equation (44) and the fact that depth must be positive leads to a simple upper bound on the depth at a particular point even when the direction of translational velocity is not known. Because $Z > 0$ we can write

$$Z = |Z| = |\mathbf{s} \cdot \mathbf{t}| \, / \, |E_t| \,, \tag{45}$$

and so

$$Z \leq \|\mathbf{s}\| \, \|\mathbf{t}\| \, / \, |E_t| \,. \tag{46}$$

The right-hand side here is the depth computed on the assumption that $\mathbf{s}$ is parallel to $\mathbf{t}$. Of course this is only an upper bound, because Z will be much smaller if $\mathbf{s}$ happens to be nearly orthogonal to $\mathbf{t}$. The bound is particularly poor, as a result, where $\mathbf{r}$ is nearly parallel to $\mathbf{t}$, that is, near the focus of expansion (or the focus of compression) in the image.

◇ **Depth known—the case of pure translation**

If we know the depth, as earlier, we can minimize the total error in the time derivative of brightness:

$$\iint [E_t + (1/Z)\mathbf{s} \cdot \mathbf{t}]^2 \, dx \, dy \tag{47}$$

by differentiating with respect to **t**. Setting the result equal to zero gives

$$\left[\iint (1/Z)^2 \mathbf{ss}^T\right] \mathbf{t}\, dx\, dy = -\iint (1/Z)E_t \mathbf{s}\, dx\, dy\,, \qquad (48)$$

which is just equation (19) with $\|\boldsymbol{\omega}\| = 0$. This is a set of three linear equations in the three components of **t** (U, V, and W). The coefficient matrix is symmetric and only the right-hand side depends on the time derivative of brightness. Note that in equation (48) we attach less weight to information from points where Z is large.

The method is accurate if the correct values of depth are given. If estimates are used, the quality of the result will depend on the quality of the estimates. The accuracy of the result also depends on the size of the field of view, as we show later.

We get slightly different results if we weight the integrand in equation (47) differently. Multiplying by Z, for example, gives $[ZE_t + \mathbf{s} \cdot \mathbf{t}]$ for the integrand and

$$\left[\iint \mathbf{ss}^T\, dx\, dy\right] \mathbf{t} = -\iint ZE_t \mathbf{s}\, dx\, dy\,, \qquad (49)$$

for the solution. Alternatively multiplying by Z/E_t gives $[Z + (1/E_t)\mathbf{s} \cdot \mathbf{t}]$ for the integrand and

$$\left[\iint (1/E_t)^2 \mathbf{ss}^T\, dx\, dy\right] \mathbf{t} = -\iint (Z/E_t)\mathbf{s}\, dx\, dy\,, \qquad (50)$$

for the solution. In this case we are minimizing the error in depth, rather than the error in the time derivative of brightness, as in equation (48).

The two alternate solutions given in Eqs. (49) and (50) have the advantage that the depth Z does not appear in the integrals on the left-hand side. This means that they are particularly well suited for iterative schemes where Z is re-estimated on each cycle. The solution of equation (49) has the further advantage that neither Z nor E_t appear on the left-hand side. This makes it easy to compute an ensemble average for this integral.

◇ Distribution of the directions of s

To understand the properties of the above algorithms for recovering **t**, we must examine the matrix obtained by integrating multiples of $\mathbf{ss}^T$. Once again, we can think of the direction of **s** as identifying a point on the unit sphere and of a multiple of $\|\mathbf{s}\|$ as the mass of a particle placed there. The integral considered is related to the inertia matrix of the set of particles on the unit sphere.

Now just as the directions of **v** lay in a band of width equal to the width of the field of view, because $\mathbf{v} \cdot \mathbf{r} = 0$, so do the directions of **s**, because $\mathbf{s} \cdot \mathbf{r} = 0$. The distribution of points within the band is not quite the same, but we will ignore such details for now. First, assuming again a uniform distribution within the permissible band, we get the same estimate of the condition number as previously, namely

$$\frac{1 + (1/2)\cos^2\theta_v}{\sin^2\theta_v} = \frac{3/2}{\sin^2\theta_v} - \frac{1}{2}.$$

Accuracy in the determination of W, the Z component of $\mathbf{t}$, will be reduced relative to that of the other two components when the field of view is small. Experiments confirm that for small fields of view, the estimate of the component of translation along the optical axis is disturbed more by noise than the other two. Hence a wide field of view is called for.

The integral of $\mathbf{ss}^T$ varies from image to image. In order to better understand the matrix defined by $\mathbf{ss}^T$, we would like to examine a "typical" image. Because it is difficult to define such an image, instead, we can take an average over an ensemble of images containing all possible directions for the brightness gradient at each image point. If we take into account the distribution of directions of $\mathbf{s}$ and the weights $\|\mathbf{s}\|$, we find (in Appendix B) that

$$\overline{\iint \mathbf{ss}^T \, dx \, dy} = k_s \begin{pmatrix} 1 & 0 & 0 \\ 0 & 1 & 0 \\ 0 & 0 & r_v^2/2 \end{pmatrix}, \tag{51}$$

where r_v is the radius of the image and the constant k_s depends on the size of the field of view as well as the distribution of magnitudes of the brightness gradient. In practice we can find k_s by noting that

$$\text{Trace}\left(\iint \mathbf{ss}^T \, dx \, dy\right) = \iint \text{Trace}(\mathbf{ss}^T) \, dx \, dy = \iint \mathbf{s} \cdot \mathbf{s} \, dx \, dy, \tag{52}$$

so

$$2k_s\left(1 + r_v^2/4\right) = \overline{\iint \mathbf{s} \cdot \mathbf{s} \, dx \, dy}. \tag{53}$$

Note that the condition number is just $\min(r_v^2/2, 2/r_v^2)$ which reaches a minimum of 1 when $r_v = \sqrt{2}$. In the case of pure translation, the component of translation along the optical axis is found with more accuracy than the other two when the field of view has a half-angle wider than $\theta_v = \tan^{-1}\sqrt{2} = 54.74\ldots$ degrees, because $r_v^2/2$ then is larger than one.

Some simplifications of the method for recovering the translational velocity based on the above analysis are discussed by us in Horn and Weldon [1987].

Translation with rotation known

In this section we deal with the problem of determining the direction of translation and depth $Z(x, y)$ given the rotation vector $\boldsymbol{\omega}$.

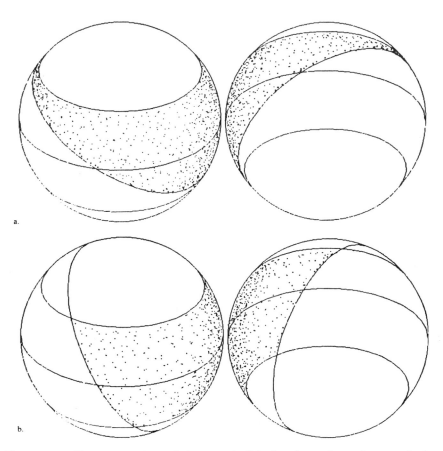

Figure 8. The intersection of the permissible band on the s-shape and the compatible hemisphere for two cases. (a) Focus of expansion within field of view. (b) Focus of expansion outside field of view.

◇ The importance of a wide field of view

In the general case, the need for a wide field of view is very clear. In a small image region near the center of the image, for example, rotation about the y-axis looks the same as translation along the x-axis, while rotation about the x-axis looks the same as translation along the (negative) y-axis. As is well known in stereo-photogrammetry, a large field of view is needed to separate these components of the transformation between two camera positions [Wolf 1983; Gosh 1972].

   If we take note of this ambiguity, and the uncertainty with which the components of rotation and translation along the optical axis can be determined, we see that locally, out of six parameters, only two combinations can be estimated. These two quantities are just the components of the motion field. The same argument can be made for points at some distance from the principal point of the image.

There is a difference between the case when the motion is predominantly along the optical axis and the case where it is predominantly parallel to the image plane. The transition between the two situations occurs when the direction of the vector **t** moves outside the cone of directions of the field of view, that is, when the focus of expansion (or compression) moves outside the image. When the focus of expansion is inside the image, then the great circle defined by $\mathbf{s} \cdot \mathbf{t} = 0$ lies entirely inside the permissible band on the unit sphere (figure 8a). The measured values of **s** then provide constraint all the way around the great circle. Conversely, when the focus of expansion lies outside the image, the great circle cuts the permissible band (see figure 8b).

In this case the known values of **s** provide constraint only along two segments of the great circle. These segments get shorter and shorter as the vector **t** becomes more and more parallel of the image plane. It should be clear that in this case the direction of the vector **t** can be determined with somewhat lower accuracy than when the focus of expansion is near the principal point.

◇ The s-Bar projection

The integrals on the right hand side of the equations for **t** developed earlier contain positive multiples of the vector

$$\bar{\mathbf{s}} = -\text{sign}(E_t)\mathbf{s}\,. \tag{54}$$

(Here we only care about the directions of the vectors, so we ignore scale factors.) Now in the case of translation with known rotation, we have (from equation (41))

$$E_t = -(1/Z)\mathbf{s} \cdot \mathbf{t}\,,$$

and

$$\bar{\mathbf{s}} \cdot \mathbf{t} = (1/Z)\,\text{sign}(\mathbf{s} \cdot \mathbf{t})\,\mathbf{s} \cdot \mathbf{t} = (1/Z)\,|\mathbf{s} \cdot \mathbf{t}| \geq 0\,, \tag{55}$$

because $Z > 0$. We are only interested at this point in the sign of $\bar{\mathbf{s}} \cdot \mathbf{t}$, so we can use any convenient positive multiple of $\bar{\mathbf{s}}$ such as

$$-(1/E_t)\mathbf{s}, \qquad -\text{sign}(E_t)\mathbf{s}, \qquad \text{or} \qquad -E_t\mathbf{s}$$

in the discussion that follows.

Equation (55) states that $\bar{\mathbf{s}}$ can only lie in the hemisphere that has **t** as its navel. We call this the *compatible hemisphere* in the case of translation with known rotation. Because $\bar{\mathbf{s}}$ is a multiple of **s**, it must also lie in the permissible band. Thus $\bar{\mathbf{s}}$ can only lie in the intersection of the permissible band and the compatible hemisphere. We will exploit this geometric insight shortly.

Our task can be viewed as that of finding the hemisphere that contains all of the directions specified by the vectors $\bar{s}$ derived from the image. Note that the solution may not be unique and that there may not be any solution. Later we will modify the problem definition somewhat to deal with these possibilities.

If there is a rotational component to the motion, then the points $\bar{s}$ will not be confined to a hemisphere. This provides a convenient test to see whether the methods presented here can be applied or not.

◇ Motion determination as a linear programming problem

We wish to find a vector $\mathbf{t}$ that makes $\bar{s} \cdot \mathbf{t} \geq 0$ at all image points. We can think of this as a gigantic linear programming problem.[2] There are three unknowns and one inequality for every picture cell. (Actually, because we do not care about the magnitude of $\mathbf{t}$, there are only two degrees of freedom.)

Because we do not have a criterion function to be extremized, we will have an infinite number of solutions—if there are any solutions at all. All of these solutions will lie in a convex polygon on the unit sphere. The sides of this polygon are portions of great circles corresponding to constraints which we will call *critical constraints* (see figure 9). With data from a large number of cells we expect this solution polygon to be small. We may choose its center as the "best" solution.

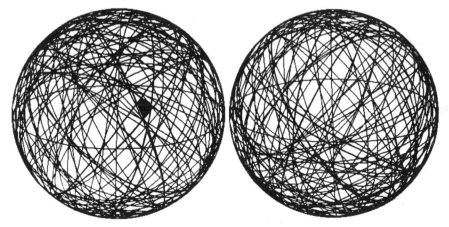

Figure 9. The s-sphere showing great circles for many image points. Circles for critical points (emphasized) constrain location of $\mathbf{t}$.

---

[2]We do not wish to suggest, by the way, that linear programming algorithms could be fruitfully applied to this problem.

Typically, the solution polygon will have relatively few sides. Thus data from a small number of *critical picture cells* fully constrains the solution. First, note that each side of this polygon corresponds to an equality of the form $\bar{\mathbf{s}} \cdot \mathbf{t} = 0$ for some picture cell. From the brightness change constraint equation we know that $E_t = 0$ when $\bar{\mathbf{s}} \cdot \mathbf{t} = 0$. Thus the critical constraints are provided by picture cells where E_t is small (and $\bar{\mathbf{s}}$ is not). This is an important observation, which can be used to reduce the size of the linear programming problem; we simply disregard the inequalities arising from picture cells where E_t is large.

There is a class of points for which $\bar{\mathbf{s}} \cdot \mathbf{t}$ is arbitrary, even though E_t is small and $\bar{\mathbf{s}}$ is not; these are image points for which Z is large. Such points provide "false" constraints on $\mathbf{t}$. For a practical system, some means must be found for identifying these points. One way of doing this, for images with large depth range, is based on the following observation. In a real image, regions for which Z is large, that is, the background, tend to encompass a significant area with *all* points in the area having $E_t \approx 0$. On the other hand, points with $\mathbf{s} \cdot \mathbf{t} = 0$ and $\bar{\mathbf{s}}$ large are usually isolated and surrounded by regions for which $E_t \neq 0$. The above difficulty appears in all of the methods of determining motion; it is harder to determine $\mathbf{t}$ when the depth range is large.

We observe in passing that the points that are most useful in constraining the translational motion vector are the very same points where it is difficult to calculate depth accurately! One may also make the observation that a method for segmenting the scene into foreground and background regions would be very useful in the case of general motion, because the background regions can then be used to recover the rotationally component. The known rotational velocity can then, in turn, be used to recover the translational component from the foreground regions.

The linear programming method of determining $\mathbf{t}$ discussed above uses relatively little of the image data. In fact, only points at the edge of the compatible hemisphere influence the solution at all. While this is a sensible procedure if the data is trustworthy, it will be quite sensitive to noise. For noisy, that is, real images, it may be worthwhile to consider other points, such as those in a band for which E_t is less than a small cutoff value.

◇ The perceptron "learning" algorithm

One way of finding the solution of a large number of homogeneous inequalities is by means of the iterative perceptron "learning" algorithm [Minsky & Papert 1969; Duda & Hart 1973]. Given a set of vectors $\{\bar{\mathbf{s}}_i\}$, this procedure is guaranteed to find a vector $\mathbf{t}$ that satisfies $\bar{\mathbf{s}}_i \cdot \mathbf{t} \geq 0$, *if* such a vector exists. It even does this in a finite number of steps, provided there exists some ϵ such that $\bar{\mathbf{s}}_i \cdot \mathbf{t} > \epsilon$ for all $\bar{\mathbf{s}}_i$ in the given set (which almost always happens when the set is finite).

The idea is to start with some non-zero vector $\mathbf{t}^0$ and to test whether the inequalities are satisfied. (A reasonable choice for $\mathbf{t}^0$ is one of the vectors $\bar{\mathbf{s}}_i$.) If the inequality is not satisfied for a particular vector in the set, then the smallest adjustment is made to make the dot-product zero. (Note that this may disturb inequalities that have passed the test already). Suppose that the present estimate for the direction of the translation vector is the direction of $\mathbf{t}^n$. We now test the dot-product $\bar{\mathbf{s}}_i \cdot \mathbf{t}^n$. If it is negative, we adjust our estimate of the vector $\mathbf{t}$ according to the rule

$$\mathbf{t}^{n+1} = \mathbf{t}^n + \delta\mathbf{t}^n , \tag{56}$$

where

$$\delta\mathbf{t}^n = -\frac{\mathbf{s}_i \cdot \mathbf{t}^n}{\mathbf{s}_i \cdot \mathbf{s}_i}\mathbf{s}_i . \tag{57}$$

Note that $\bar{\mathbf{s}}_i \cdot \mathbf{t}^{n+1} = 0$ and that the magnitude of $\mathbf{s}_i$ does not matter. (Also, the test above can be replaced with a test that checks whether $-\mathbf{s}_i \cdot \mathbf{t}^n$ has the same sign as E_t.)

If the inequalities are inconsistent, that is, if the $\bar{\mathbf{s}}_i$ are not confined to a hemisphere (or nearly so), as will happen in practice due to noise, the algorithm will not converge. Furthermore, there is no guarantee that the guess at any stage is particularly good. We discuss several simple refinements that can help in this case in Horn and Weldon [1987].

The vector $\mathbf{t}^n$ in the perceptron "learning" algorithm is obviously a linear combination of vectors drawn from the set $\{\bar{\mathbf{s}}_i\}$. Vectors in this set have directions that correspond to points in the permissible band. Now suppose that this band is very narrow. Then, to build a vector with a significant z-component one has to add many of these vectors. In order to keep the x- and y-components small, these vectors must almost come in pairs from opposite ends of the narrow band. Not surprisingly, the algorithm performs rather poorly in this situation; it is much happier with vectors sprinkled uniformly in direction over a full hemisphere.

It should also be noted that in a "real-time" application, we do not expect the velocity estimates to change rapidly. Thus the previous value of the velocity is likely to be an excellent first estimate for the current value of $\mathbf{t}$. This means that very few iterations will be needed to get an acceptable new value. A considerable amount of computation can be saved this way, just as it can in the computation of the optical flow [Horn & Schunck 1981]. We discuss a "parallel" perceptron algorithm in Horn and Weldon [1987].

$\Diamond$ Minimizing the integral of Z^2

In this section we assume that the depth range Z_{max}/Z_{min} is finite. This will generally be the case in robotic applications. The method discussed in this section can also be applied to images in which the background has very large Z, if, as discussed earlier, these regions are excised from the image before the motion vector is calculated.

We have seen that we can compute depth when the motion $\mathbf{t}$ is known using equation (44)

$$Z = -(1/E_t)\mathbf{s} \cdot \mathbf{t}.$$

Now if we use the *wrong* value $\mathbf{t}'$ in this formula, we get the wrong depth value:

$$Z' = -(1/E_t)\mathbf{s} \cdot \mathbf{t}' = Z(\mathbf{s} \cdot \mathbf{t}')/(\mathbf{s} \cdot \mathbf{t}). \tag{58}$$

We expect only positive values for Z, but this formula may give us negative values, because $(\mathbf{s} \cdot \mathbf{t}')$ may be negative where $(\mathbf{s} \cdot \mathbf{t})$ is positive and *vice versa*. More interestingly, we may obtain very large values for Z (both positive and negative), because $(\mathbf{s} \cdot \mathbf{t})$ may be almost zero while $(\mathbf{s} \cdot \mathbf{t}')$ is not. That is, the magnitude of Z will often be very large near points where $E_t \approx 0$. We may conclude that we could determine the correct value for $\mathbf{t}$ by minimizing the integral of Z^2 over the image, that is by minimizing the quadratic form

$$\iint (1/E_t)^2 (\mathbf{s} \cdot \mathbf{t})^2 \, dx \, dy = \mathbf{t}^T \left[\iint (1/E_t^2)\mathbf{s}\mathbf{s}^T \, dx \, dy \right] \mathbf{t}, \tag{59}$$

subject to the constraint $\|\mathbf{t}\| = 1$. The solution is the eigenvector of the real symmetric 3×3 matrix

$$M = \iint (1/E_t^2)\mathbf{s}\mathbf{s}^T \, dx \, dy \tag{60}$$

associated with the smallest eigenvalue. We can prove this by minimizing the sum

$$S = \mathbf{t}^T M \mathbf{t} + \lambda(1 - \mathbf{t}^T \mathbf{t}), \tag{61}$$

where λ is a Lagrangian multiplier. Then

$$\frac{\partial S}{\partial \mathbf{t}} = 2M\mathbf{t} - 2\lambda\mathbf{t} = 0, \tag{62}$$

which yields

$$M\mathbf{t} = \lambda\mathbf{t}. \tag{63}$$

Thus λ is an eigenvalue of M, and $\mathbf{t}$ is the corresponding eigenvector. Substituting equation (63) into equation (61) gives the results $S = \lambda$. Thus $\mathbf{t}^T M \mathbf{t}$ is minimized by taking the smallest of the three eigenvalues of M for λ.

To minimize problems due to noise, we can add a small positive constant to E_t^2 commensurate with the expected noise in E_t^2. That is, we take as our solution the eigenvector of

$$M' = \iint \frac{1}{E_t^2 + n^2} \mathbf{s}\mathbf{s}^T \, dx \, dy \tag{64}$$

associated with the smallest eigenvalue.

If $\mathbf{e}$ is an eigenvector, so is $-\mathbf{e}$. But we want Z to be positive. Rather than test this condition at a single point, we compute an average like

$$\bar{\mathbf{s}}_0 = -\iint (1/E_t)\mathbf{s}\,dx\,dy \quad \text{or} \quad \bar{\mathbf{s}}_0 = -\iint \frac{E_t}{E_t^2 + n^2}\mathbf{s}\,dx\,dy \quad (65)$$

and check whether

$$\bar{\mathbf{s}}_0 \cdot \mathbf{t} > 0. \quad (66)$$

If it is not, we simply change the sign of the solution $\mathbf{t}$.

As before, we may choose to weight the integral of equation (59) according to some measure of how trustworthy the data from each picture cell is.

The method presented in this section produces an estimate of the translation vector $\mathbf{t}$ in closed form and with high accuracy. Of course, a cubic must be solved to obtain the eigenvalues—but there is an analytic method for doing that. The corresponding eigenvectors can then be found by taking cross products of two rows of a 3×3 matrix.

The preceding method of calculating $\mathbf{t}$ has another justification that some readers might find more persuasive. From equation (41) we know that $\mathbf{s} \cdot \mathbf{t} \approx 0$ for points with $E_t \approx 0$ (again ignoring background points). Thus we are basically looking for a vector $\mathbf{t}$ that makes $\mathbf{s} \cdot \mathbf{t} \approx 0$ whenever $E_t \approx 0$. The points where the time derivatives are small provide most constraint, as already discussed. We could try to minimize something like

$$\iint_C (\mathbf{s} \cdot \mathbf{t})^2, \quad (67)$$

where C is the set of image points where $E_t \approx 0$. Rather than use a strict cut-off on E_t, we may consider a weighting scheme in an integral like

$$\iint w(\mathbf{s} \cdot \mathbf{t})^2\,dx\,dy, \quad (68)$$

over the whole image where the weighting function w is chosen to emphasize points where $E_t \approx 0$. A reasonable choice, $w = 1/(E_t^2 + n^2)$, leads to integral given in equation (64). The eigenvector corresponding to the smallest eigenvalue is a normal of the plane that best fits the weighted set of points (see figure 10).

If there is a rotational component to the motion then the vectors $\bar{\mathbf{s}}$ where E_t is small will not lie near a great circle. In this case the smallest eigenvalue will not be small. This provides a convenient test. We discuss a method that avoids the need to find eigenvalues and eigenvectors in Horn and Weldon [1987]. Related methods for finding the focus of expansion are discussed in Negahdaripour and Horn [1987].

Figure 11 shows a scatter plot of positions on the unit sphere for $\mathbf{t}$ recovered from noisy synthetic data. Each estimate is based on brightness gradient at 200 picture cells with 1% noise in the derivatives of brightness. Note the elongation of the cluster of points in a direction parallel to the

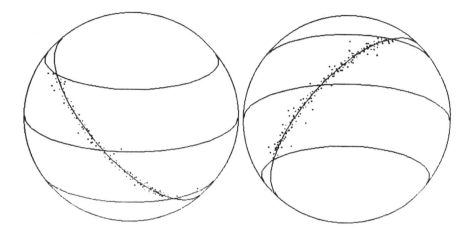

Figure 10. The great circle corresponding to the motion **t** which best fits the points on the s-sphere for which $E_t \approx 0$.

optical axis.   When tens of thousands of picture cells are used, instead of hundreds, the algorithm can tolerate considerably more noise.   While further experimentation is called for, we found that this algorithm behaves at least as well, if not better than the others we have investigated.

Conclusions

We have developed methods for recovering motion directly from the first derivatives of brightness in an image region in the cases of pure rotation and pure translation (and general motion when the rotational component is known).   We have tested these methods on synthetic image data and, to a limited extent, on some kinds of real image sequences.   In the case of pure rotation we give an exact simple solution to the obvious least-squares problem.   In the case of pure translation we give several methods with different trade-offs between accuracy, noise-sensitivity and computational expense. While we have preliminary ideas about the relative merits of these methods, detailed conclusions will have to await further careful experimentation with real images.   Some further results on both synthetic and real image

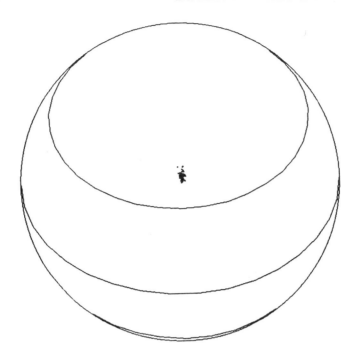

Figure 11. Plot of several noisy estimates of the translation vector **t** on the s-sphere (200 pixels/estimate, 1% noise in brightness measurements).

data are reported in Horn and Weldon [1987] and Negahdaripour and Horn [1987].

We show that it is trivial to recover depth when the motion is known and that it is trivial to recover the motion when depth is known. We emphasize the importance of a large field of view and point out difficulties arising in the pure translation case when there is a very large depth range. We also note that image points where the brightness derivative is small provide most constraint on the translation vector while the depth at these points is hard to recover. We also show that it is difficult to recover the translational motion towards, and rotational motion about, the line connecting the projection center to the image region of interest, when that region is small. We emphasize the need for adequate low-pass filtering in both spatial and time dimension before sampling in order to ensure that estimates of derivatives are accurate.

The discussion is facilitated by introduction of the auxiliary vectors **s** and **v**. The directions of these vectors have been shown to be constrained to lie in the intersection of a "permissible band" and a "compatible hemisphere" on the unit sphere. These geometric concepts help lend intuitive support to the algebraic results.

References

Adiv, G. [1984], "Determining 3-D Motion and Structure from Optical Flow Generated by Several Moving Objects," COINS TR 84-07, Computer and Information Science, University of Massachusetts, Amherst, MA.

Aloimonos, Y., and C. Brown [1984], "Direct Processing of Curvilinear Motion from a Sequence of Perspective Images," *Proceedings of the Workshop on Computer Vision, Representation and Control*, Annapolis, Maryland.

Bruss, A. R., and B. K. P. Horn [1983], "Passive Navigation," *Computer Vision, Graphics, and Image Processing*, vol. 21, pp. 3–20.

Duda, R. O., and P. E. Hart [1973], *Pattern Classification and Scene Analysis*, John Wiley, New York.

Gosh, S. K. [1972], *Theory of Stereophotogrammetry*, Ohio State University Bookstores.

Horn, B. K. P., and B. G. Schunck [1981], "Determining Optical Flow," *Artificial Intelligence*, vol. 17, pp. 185–203.

Horn, B. K. P., and E. J. Weldon Jr. [1987], "Computationally efficient methods of recovering translational motion," *International Conference on Computer Vision*, London, England, pp. 8–11.

Longuet-Higgins, H. C., and K. Prazdny [1980], "The Interpretation of a Moving Retinal Image," *Proc. of Royal Society of London*, Series B, vol. 208, pp. 385–397.

Minsky, M., and S. Papert [1969], *Perceptrons: An Introduction to Computational Geometry*, MIT Press, Cambridge, MA.

Negahdaripour, S. [1986], "Direct Methods for Structure from Motion," Ph.D. Thesis, Mechanical Engineering, Massachusetts Institute of Technology.

Negahdaripour, S., and B. K. P. Horn [1987], "A Direct Method for Locating the Focus of Expansion," Report AIM-939 Artificial Intelligence Laboratory, Massachusetts Institute of Technology, Cambridge.

Negahdaripour, S., and B. K. P. Horn [1987], "Direct Passive Navigation," *IEEE Trans. Pattern Analysis and Machine Intelligence*, vol. 9, no. 1, pp. 168–176.

Waxman, A. M., and K. Wohn [1985], "Contour Evolution, Neighborhood Deformation, and Global Image Flow: Planar Surfaces in Motion," *The International Journal of Robotics Research*, vol. 4, no. 3, pp. 95–108.

Waxman, A. M., and S. Ullman [1985], "Surface Structure and 3-D Motion from Image Flow: A Kinematic Analysis." *The International Journal of Robotics Research*, vol. 4, no. 3, pp. 72–94.

Wolf, P. R. [1983], *Elements of Photogrammetry*, McGraw-Hill, New York.

The authors would like to thank the other members of the Waikiki Surfing and Computer Vision Society, and especially Shahriar Negahdaripour, for their contributions to this chapter.

The research in this chapter was supported by the National Science Foundation under Grant No. DMC85-11966. Additional support was provided by NASA (Grant No. GSFC 5-1162) and by the Veteran's Administration.

Appendix A: The Brightness Change Constraint Equation

The brightness change constraint equation is based on the assumption that the brightness of the image of a patch on the surface does not change as the observer moves relative to the surface. Expansion of the total derivative in the equation $dE/dt = 0$ by means of the chain-rule leads to the constraint equation

$$\frac{\partial E}{\partial x}\frac{dx}{dt} + \frac{\partial E}{\partial y}\frac{dy}{dt} + E_t = 0 \,, \qquad (A1)$$

or

$$uE_x + vE_y + E_t = 0 \,, \qquad (A2)$$

where E_x, E_y, and E_t are the partial derivatives of brightness with respect to x, y, and t, while u and v are the time derivatives of x and y.

In practice, the brightness of a patch rarely remains exactly the same. The brightness change constraint equation is nevertheless a useful approximation, as long as the change in brightness at an image point due to the motion is much larger than the change in brightness due to other effects, such as change in viewing direction or illumination. This will be the case as long as there is good contrast at high spatial frequencies, as will be shown next.

Suppose that the brightness of a patch does in fact change due to changes in viewing direction or changes in illumination. In most cases the rate of change of brightness will be relatively small. Let us say that $dE/dt = \epsilon$, and so

$$E_t = -(uE_x + vE_y) + \epsilon \,. \qquad (A3)$$

Consider now a simple grating pattern in the image that, at a particular time, is described by the equation

$$E = E_0\big(1 + \sin(ax + by)\big) \,. \qquad (A4)$$

Then the components of the brightness gradients are

$$\begin{aligned} E_x &= aE_0 \cos(ax + by) \\ E_y &= bE_0 \cos(ax + by) \,. \end{aligned} \qquad (A5)$$

Consequently

$$uE_x + vE_y = (au + bv)E_0 \cos(ax + by) \,. \qquad (A6)$$

It is clear that the error in E_t, the rate of change of brightness at a point in the image, resulting from changes in the brightness of the surface, is relatively small, as long as $(au + bv)E_0$ is large compared to ϵ. (This term, $(au + bv)E_0$, will be zero when the image motion happens to be parallel to the ridges of the grating. In practice, however, surface markings will contain many spatial frequency components and most of these will not be aligned in this special way). We conclude that the relative error in the rate of change of brightness with time is small, as long as there is significant contrast at the higher spatial frequencies.

The approximation breaks down when the surface markings are weak and the changes of brightness due to changes in viewing direction or illumination are rapid. This happens, for example, in the rare situation where a specular surface momentarily lines up exactly to reflect the light from a point source towards the viewer. It also happens when an object moving relative to a point source enters a cast shadow.

A number of additional factors help keep the relative error in E_t small. First of all, some surfaces have the property that they appear equally bright from all viewing directions. A Lambertian surface is a very special case of this, where the brightness varies as the cosine of the incident angle. The image brightness is not affected at all by the motion of the observer when a surface of this type is fixed relative to the light source. While most real surfaces do not appear equally bright from all viewing directions, brightness typically varies slowly with changes in observer position (slowly enough that we are usually not aware of any such changes).

Brightness variations resulting from changes in surface orientation are most severe when there is a single point source. These variations are reduced when there are multiple sources or an extended source. In the extreme case of a scene illuminated from all sides, for example, image brightness does not depend on surface orientation at all, even if the surface is specular!

Similarly, a lens occupying a large solid angle, as seen from the object, will smooth out changes in brightness resulting from changes in viewer position. One can see this easily in the extreme case of a glossy reflection, which will be seen only over a small range of positions if a small lens or pin-hole is used. A large entrance aperture on the other hand will smear out the highlight effect over a larger range of viewing positions. This is not a big help in many imaging situations, however, because objects are far from the sensor relative to the size of the sensor, except in the case of microscopy.

To summarize: The brightness of the image of a patch may change somewhat as the observer moves relative to the surface. The brightness change constraint equation nevertheless provides a good way of estimating the rate of change of brightness with respect to time at a point in the image. The relative error in this estimate will be small when there is significant contrast in the surface markings at higher spatial frequencies. (There will be no error at all when the surface appears equally bright from all viewing directions and the object does not move relative to the light source).

Appendix B: Ensemble Averages

Some of the integrals that appear in this chapter, while functions of the scene content, tend to lie close to "average" values when evaluated over sufficiently large textured regions. These average values can be useful in two different enterprises:

- Analyzing the relative stability of the components of the solution.
- Developing simplified methods for recovering the solution (as shown in Horn and Weldon [1987]).

In order to compute these averages we have to make some assumptions about the probability distribution of brightness gradients. We assume here that this distribution is rotationally symmetric and independent of image position. That is, on average we see the same brightness gradients at every image point and all directions of the brightness gradient are equally likely. The distribution of magnitude of this gradient is left arbitrary, however, because it does not directly affect the main results.

Moment integrals for the uniform band

Before we start, let us quickly obtain the equivalent results under the assumption that data points ($\mathbf{s}$ or $\mathbf{v}$) are *uniformly* distributed over the permissible band. Let η denote the latitude and ξ the longitude on the unit sphere. We see that the area of the band is just

$$K = \int_{-\pi}^{\pi} \int_{-\theta_v}^{\theta_v} \cos \eta \, d\eta \, d\xi = 4\pi \sin \theta_v \,. \tag{B1}$$

The Cartesian coordinates of a point on the unit sphere are given by $\mathbf{p} = (x, y, z)^T$ where

$$\begin{aligned} x &= \cos \eta \cos \xi \,, \\ y &= \cos \eta \sin \xi \,, \\ z &= \sin \eta \,. \end{aligned} \tag{B2}$$

Let the integral of $\mathbf{p}\mathbf{p}^T$ be

$$\int_{-\pi}^{\pi} \int_{-\theta_v}^{\theta_v} \mathbf{p}\mathbf{p}^T \, d\eta \, d\xi = \begin{pmatrix} I_{xx} & I_{xy} & I_{xz} \\ I_{yx} & I_{yy} & I_{yz} \\ I_{zx} & I_{zy} & I_{zz} \end{pmatrix} \,. \tag{B3}$$

Then

$$I_{xx} = \int_{-\pi}^{\pi} \int_{-\theta_v}^{\theta_v} x^2 \cos \eta \, d\eta \, d\xi = \int_{-\pi}^{\pi} \cos^2 \xi \, d\xi \int_{-\theta_v}^{\theta_v} \cos^3 \eta \, d\eta \,, \tag{B4}$$

that is,

$$I_{xx} = \frac{\pi}{3} \left[3 \sin \theta_v + (1/3) \sin 3\theta_v \right] = \frac{4\pi}{3} \sin \theta_v \left[1 + (1/2) \cos^2 \theta_v \right] \,, \tag{B5}$$

while

$$I_{zz} = \int_{-\pi}^{\pi} \int_{-\theta_v}^{\theta_v} z^2 \cos \eta \, d\eta \, d\xi = \int_{-\pi}^{\pi} d\xi \int_{-\theta_v}^{\theta_v} \sin^2 \eta \cos \eta \, d\eta \,, \tag{B6}$$

that is,

$$I_{zz} = \frac{4\pi}{3} \sin^3 \theta_v . \tag{B6}$$

Also, by symmetry, $I_{yy} = I_{xx}$ and the off-diagonal terms, I_{xy}, I_{yz}, and I_{zx}, are all zero. We have

$$I_{xx} = (K/3) \left[1 + (1/2) \cos^2 \theta_v \right] = I_{yy} , \tag{B7}$$

and

$$I_{zz} = (K/3) \sin^2 \theta_v , \tag{B8}$$

so

$$I_{xx} + I_{yy} + I_{zz} = K . \tag{B9}$$

The moment matrix is diagonal and so I_{xx}, I_{yy} and I_{zz} are the three eigenvalues. The condition number is the ratio of the largest to the smallest or

$$\frac{1 + (1/2) \cos^2 \theta_v}{\sin^2 \theta_v} . \tag{B10}$$

These results give us a quick estimate of the ensemble averages of the integrals if $\mathbf{ss}^T$ and $\mathbf{vv}^T$. To do better, we have to take into account the actual distribution of $\mathbf{s}$ and $\mathbf{v}$ in the permissible band.

Ensemble average of the integral of $\mathbf{ss}^T$

It is convenient to use polar coordinates in the case of a circular image. We have

$$\begin{aligned} x &= r \cos \theta & -\pi \le \theta \le +\pi , \\ y &= r \sin \theta & 0 \le r \le r_v . \end{aligned} \tag{B11}$$

Similarly, we may use polar coordinates for the brightness gradient

$$\begin{aligned} E_x &= \rho \cos \phi & -\pi \le \phi \le +\pi , \\ E_y &= \rho \sin \phi & 0 \le \rho . \end{aligned} \tag{B12}$$

Let the probability of seeing a brightness gradient with magnitude lying between ρ and $\rho + \delta\rho$ be $2\pi\rho\, P(\rho)\, \delta\rho$. Now

$$\mathbf{s} = \begin{pmatrix} -E_x \\ -E_y \\ xE_x + yE_y \end{pmatrix} = \rho \begin{pmatrix} -\cos\phi \\ -\sin\phi \\ r\cos(\theta - \phi) \end{pmatrix} . \tag{B13}$$

Consequently

$$\mathbf{s} \cdot \mathbf{s} = \rho^2 \left(1 + r^2 \cos^2(\theta - \phi) \right) . \tag{B14}$$

Consider first the integral of $\mathbf{s} \cdot \mathbf{s}$:

$$\int_{-\pi}^{\pi} \int_0^{r_v} (\mathbf{s} \cdot \mathbf{s})\, r\, dr\, d\theta . \tag{B15}$$

To obtain the desired ensemble average we integrate over ρ and ϕ as follows:

$$\int_{-\pi}^{\pi} \int_0^{\infty} P(\rho) \left[\int_{-\pi}^{\pi} \int_0^{r_v} (\mathbf{s} \cdot \mathbf{s}) r\, dr\, d\theta \right] \rho\, d\rho\, d\phi . \tag{B16}$$

This integral can be split into two parts:

$$\int_0^\infty \rho^3 P(\rho)\, d\rho \int_{-\pi}^{\pi} d\phi \int_0^{r_v} r\, dr \int_{-\pi}^{\pi} d\theta = 2\pi^2 P_2\, r_v^2, \qquad (B17)$$

and

$$\int_0^\infty \rho^3 P(\rho)\, d\rho \int_{-\pi}^{\pi} d\phi \int_0^{r_v} r^3\, dr \int_{-\pi}^{\pi} \cos^2\theta'\, d\theta' = \frac{\pi^2}{2} P_2\, r_v^4, \qquad (B18)$$

where $\theta' = (\theta - \phi)$ and

$$P_2 = \int_0^\infty \rho^3 P(\rho)\, d\rho. \qquad (B19)$$

We note in passing that P_2 is a measure of the average squared magnitude of the brightness gradient. Combining the two parts above we find that

$$\overline{\iint \mathbf{s} \cdot \mathbf{s}\, dx\, dy} = 2\pi^2 P_2\, r_v^2 (1 + r_v^2/4). \qquad (B20)$$

Similarly we obtain

$$I_{xx} = \int_{-\pi}^{\pi} \int_0^\infty P(\rho) \left[\int_{-\pi}^{\pi} \int_0^{r_v} \rho^2 \cos^2\phi\, r\, dr\, d\theta \right] \rho\, d\rho\, d\phi$$
$$= \int_0^\infty \rho^3 P(\rho)\, d\rho \int_{-\pi}^{\pi} \cos^2\phi\, d\phi \int_0^{r_v} r\, dr \int_{-\pi}^{\pi} d\theta = \pi^2 P_2\, r_v^2, \qquad (B21)$$

and

$$I_{zz} = \int_{-\pi}^{\pi} \int_0^\infty P(\rho) \left[\int_{-\pi}^{\pi} \int_0^{r_v} \rho^2 r^2 \cos^2(\theta - \phi)\, r\, dr\, d\theta \right] \rho\, d\rho\, d\phi$$
$$= \int_0^\infty \rho^3 P(\rho)\, d\rho \int_{-\pi}^{\pi} d\phi \int_0^{r_v} r^3\, dr \int_{-\pi}^{\pi} \cos^2\theta'\, d\theta' = \frac{\pi^2}{4} P_2\, r_v^4, \qquad (22)$$

while $I_{yy} = I_{xx}$.

The moment matrix is diagonal, so I_{xx}, I_{yy} and I_{zz} are the eigenvalues. The condition number is the ratio of the largest to the smallest or

$$\frac{2}{r_v^2} \quad \text{for} \quad r_v^2 \leq 2 \quad \text{and} \quad \frac{r_v^2}{2} \quad \text{for} \quad r_v^2 \geq 2. \qquad (B23)$$

This result does not depend on P_2, as stated earlier.

Ensemble average of the integral of $\mathbf{vv}^T$

Here we proceed much as in the previous section with

$$\mathbf{v} = \begin{pmatrix} +E_y + y(xE_x + yE_y) \\ -E_x - x(xE_x + yE_y) \\ yE_x - xE_y \end{pmatrix} = \rho \begin{pmatrix} +\sin\phi + r^2 \sin\theta \cos(\theta - \phi) \\ -\cos\phi - r^2 \cos\theta \cos(\theta - \phi) \\ r\sin(\theta - \phi) \end{pmatrix}, \qquad (B24)$$

and

$$\mathbf{v} \cdot \mathbf{v} = \rho^2 (1 + r^2)\left(1 + r^2 \cos^2(\theta - \phi)\right), \qquad (B25)$$

which follows from $\mathbf{v} = \mathbf{s} \times \mathbf{r}$, $\mathbf{s} \cdot \mathbf{r} = 0$, $\mathbf{r} \cdot \mathbf{r} = 1 + r^2$ and

$$\mathbf{s} \cdot \mathbf{s} = \rho^2 \left(1 + r^2 \cos^2(\theta - \phi)\right) . \tag{B26}$$

After some tedious manipulations, similar to those in the last section, we find

$$\overline{\iint \mathbf{v} \cdot \mathbf{v} \, dx \, dy} = \frac{\pi^2}{2} P_2 \, r_v^2 \left(1 + 3r_v^2/4 + r_v^4/6\right) . \tag{B27}$$

and

$$I_{xx} = \pi^2 P_2 \, r_v^2 \left(1 + r_v^2/2 + r_v^4/6\right) = I_{yy} , \tag{B28}$$

and

$$I_{zz} = \pi^2 P_2 \left(r_v^4/2\right) . \tag{B29}$$

Again, the matrix is diagonal and so I_{xx}, I_{yy} and I_{zz} are the eigenvalues. The condition number is just

$$\frac{2}{r_v^2} + 1 + \frac{r_v^2}{3} , \tag{B30}$$

which is independent of P_2 once more.

41

At first glance, image understanding competences seem disparate. The problem of edge detection, for example, seems different from the problem of shape from shading, and both seem different from surface construction using sparse stereo knowledge.

On closer inspection, however, many image understanding competences involve ill-posed mathematical problems, as defined by the mathematician Hadamard, because a two-dimensional image does not specify the three-dimensional world that produced it uniquely. Accordingly, if an image is to produce a single three-dimensional interpretation, an additional constraint, such as smoothness, has to be introduced. For example, all sorts of surfaces may pass through or near a sparse set of data points produced by a stereo module, but only one of those surfaces will minimize a suitable cost function that increases with departure from the data points and with surface curvature.

In this chapter, the authors show that many ill-posed image understanding problems are like the surface construction problem, thus enabling access to the powerful mathematical technique called regularization. Importantly, once a problem has been regularized, it often succumbs to solution by either iterative methods or by analog circuitry of a sort that certainly can be implemented in VLSI chips and that may be implemented in biological retinas.

Computational Vision and Regularization Theory

Tomaso Poggio
Vincent Torre[†]
Christof Koch

Computational vision denotes a new field in artificial intelligence, centered on theoretical studies of visual information processing. Its two main goals are: to develop image understanding systems which automatically construct scene descriptions from image input data and to understand human vision.

Early vision is the set of visual modules that aim to extract the physical properties of the surfaces around the viewer, that is, distance, surface orientation, and material properties (reflectance, color, texture). Much current research has analyzed processes in early vision because the inputs and the goals of the computation can be well characterized at this stage (see Marr [1982], Brady [1982], Brady *et al.* [1983], and Brown [1984] for reviews). Several problems have been solved and several specific algorithms have been successfully developed. Examples are stereomatching, the computation of the optical flow, structure from motion, shape from shading, and surface reconstruction.

A new theoretical development has now emerged that unifies many of these results within a single framework. The approach has its roots in the recognition of a common structure of early vision problems. Problems in early vision are *ill-posed*, requiring specific algorithms, and parallel hardware. Here we introduce a specific regularization approach and discuss its implications for computer vision and parallel computer architectures, including parallel hardware that could be used by biological visual systems.

[†]Instituto di Fisica, Universita di Genova, Genova, Italy.

Early Vision Processes

Early vision consists of a set of processes that recover physical properties of the visible three-dimensional surfaces from the two-dimensional intensity arrays. Their combined output roughly corresponds to Marr's [1982] 2-1/2D sketch, and to Barrow and Tennenbaum's [1981] intrinsic images. Recently, it has been customary to assume that these early vision processes are general and do not require domain-dependent knowledge, but only generic constraints about the physical word and the imaging stage (see box). They represent conceptually independent modules that can be studied, to a first approximation, in isolation. Information from the different processes, however, has to be combined. Furthermore, different modules may interact early on. Finally, the processing cannot be purely *bottom-up*: specific knowledge may trickle down to the point of influencing some of the very first steps in visual information processing.

Examples of early vision processes
- Edge detection
- Spatio-temporal interpolation and approximation
- Computation of optical flow
- Computation of lightness and albedo
- Shape and contours
- Shape from texture
- Shape from shading
- Binocular stereo matching
- Structure from motion
- Structure from stereo
- Surface reconstruction
- Computation of surface color

Computational theories of early vision modules typically deal with the dual issues of representation and process. They must specify the form of the input and the desired output (the representation) and provide the algorithms that transform one into the other (the process). Here we focus on the issue of processes and algorithms for which we describe the unifying theoretical framework of regularization theories. We do not consider the equally important problem of the primitive tokens that represent the input of each specific process.

A good definition of early vision is that it is inverse optics. In classical optics or in computer graphics the basic problem is to determine the images of three-dimensional objects, whereas vision is confronted with the inverse problem of recovering surfaces from images. As so much information is lost during the imaging process that projects the three-dimensional world into the two-dimensional images, vision must often rely on natural constraints, that is, assumptions about the physical world, to derive unambiguous output. The identification and use of such constraints is a recurring theme in the analysis of specific vision problems.

Two important problems in early vision are the computation of motion and the detection of sharp changes in image intensity (for detecting physical edges). They illustrate well the difficulty of the problems of early vision. The computation of the two-dimensional field of velocities in the image is a critical step in several schemes for recovering the motion and the three-dimensional structure of objects. Consider the problem of determining the velocity vector V at each point along a smooth contour in the image. following Marr and Ullman [1981], one can assume that the contour corresponds to locations of significant intensity change. Figure 1 shows how the local velocity vector is decomposed into a normal and a tangential component to the curve. Depending on the definition that is used, certain local motion measurements provide only the normal component of velocity. The tangential component remains *invisible* to such local measurements. The problem of estimating the full velocity field is thus, in this case, underdetermined by the measurements that are directly available from the image. The measurement of the optical flow is under these conditions ambiguous. It can be made unique only by adding information or assumptions.

The difficulties involved in edge detection are somewhat different. Edge detection denotes the process of identifying the physical boundaries of three-dimensional surfaces from intensity changes in their image. What is usually intended with edge detection is a first step towards this goal, that is, detecting and localizing sharp changes in image intensity. This is a problem of numerical differentiation of image data, which is plagued by noise—unavoidable during the imaging and the sampling processes. Differentiation amplifies noise and this process is thus inherently unstable. Figure 3 shows an example of an edge profile and its second derivative, where noise is significantly amplified. Most problems in early vision present similar difficulties. They are mostly underconstrained, as in the computation of the optical flow, or not robust against noise, as in edge detection.

Ill-Posed Problems

The common characteristics of most early vision problems (in a sense, their deep structure) can be formalized: most early vision problems are ill-posed problems in the precise sense defined by Hadamard [Bertero, Poggio and Torre 1988; Poggio and Torre 1984]. This claim captures the importance of constraints and reflects the definition of vision as inverse optics.

Hadamard [1923] first introduced the definition of ill-posedness in the field of partial differential equations. Ill-posed problems, typically inverse problems, are of great practical interest (for instance, computer tomography). A problem is well-posed when its solution exists, is unique, and depends continuously on the initial data. Ill-posed problems fail to satisfy one or more of these criteria. Note that the third condition does not imply that the solution is robust against noise in practice. For this, the problem must not only be well-posed but also be well conditioned to ensure numerical stability [Bertero, Poggio & Torre 1988].

It is easy to show formally that several problems in early vision are ill-posed in the sense of Hadamard [Poggio & Torre 1984]: stereo matching, structure from motion, computation of the optical flow, edge detection, shape from shading, the computation of lightness, and surface reconstruction. Computation of the optical flow is ill-posed because the *inverse* problem of recovering the full velocity field from its normal component along a contour fails to satisfy the uniqueness condition. Edge detection, intended as numerical differentiation, is ill-posed because the solution does not depend continuously on the data.

The main idea for *solving* ill-posed problems, that is for restoring *well-posedness*, is to restrict the class of admissible solutions by introducing suitable *a priori* knowledge. *A priori* knowledge can be exploited, for example, under the form of either variational principles that impose constraints on the possible solutions or as statistical properties of the solution space. We will use the general term regularization for any method used to make an ill-posed problem well-posed. Variational regularization will indicate the regularization methods that reformulate an ill-posed problem in terms of a variational principle. We will next outline specific variational methods that we will denote as the standard regularization methods, attributable mainly to Tikhonov [1963] (see also Tikhonov and Arsenin [1977], Bertero [1982], and Nashed [1976]). We will also outline future extensions of the standard theory from the perspective of early vision.

The regularization of the ill-posed problem of finding z from the data y

$$Az = y \tag{1}$$

requires the choice of norms $\| \cdot \|$ and of a stabilizing functional $\|Px\|$. In standard regularization theory, A is a linear operator, the norms are quadratic and P is linear. Two methods that can be applied are [Poggio & Torre 1984; Bertero 1982]:

1 Among z that satisfy $\|Az - y\| \leq \epsilon$ find z that minimizes (ϵ depends on the estimated measurement errors and is zero if the data are noiseless)

$$\|Pz\|^2. \tag{2}$$

2 Find z that minimizes

$$\|Az - y\|^2 + \lambda\|Pz\|^2 \tag{3}$$

where λ is a so-called regularization parameter.

The first method computes the function z that is sufficiently close to the data and is most *regular*, that is minimizes the *criterion* $\|Pz\|^2$. In the second method, λ controls the compromise between the degree of regularization of the solution and its closeness to the data. Standard regularization theory provides techniques for determining the best λ [Tikhonov & Arsenin 1977; Wahba 1980]. Thus, standard regularization methods impose the constraints on the problem by a variational principle, such as the cost functional of equation (3). The cost that is minimized reflects physical constraints about what represents a good solution: it has to be both close to the data and regular by making the quantity $\|Pz\|^2$ small. P embodies the physical constraints of the problem. It can be shown for quadratic variational principles that under mild conditions the solution space is convex and a unique solution exists. It must be pointed out that standard regularization methods have to be applied after a careful analysis of the ill-posed nature of the problem. The choice of the norm $\| \cdot \|$, of the stabilizing functional $\|Pz\|$ and of the functional spaces involved is dictated both by mathematical properties and by physical plausibility. They determine whether the precise conditions for a correct regularization hold for any specific case.

Variational principles are used widely in physics, economics and engineering. In physics, for instance, most of the basic laws have a compact formulation in terms of variational principles that require minimization of a suitable functional, such as the energy or the lagrangian.

Examples

Variational principles of the form of equation (3) have been used in the past in early vision [Horn 1974, 1985; Horn & Schunck 1981; Ikeuchi & Horn 1981; Grimson 1982; Terzopoulos 1983; Hildreth 1984a, 1984b; Horn & Brooks 1985]. Other problems have now been approached in terms of standard regularization methods (see table 1). Most stabilizing functionals used so far in early vision are of the Tikhonov type, being linear combinations of the first p derivatives of the desired solution z (see Tikhonov and Arsenin [1977]). The solutions arising from these stabilizers correspond to either interpolating or approximating splines. We return now to our examples of motion and edge detection, and show how standard regularization techniques can be applied.

Intuitively, the set of measurements of the normal component of velocity over an extended contour should provide considerable constraint on the global motion of the contour. Some additional assumptions about the nature of the real world are needed, however, in order to combine local measurements at different locations. For instance, the assumption of rigid motion on the image plane is sufficient to determine V uniquely [Hildreth

Problem	Regularization Principle
Edge detection	$\int \left[(Sf - i)^2 + \lambda\,(f_{xx})^2 \right] dx$
Optical flow (area based)	$\int \left[i_x u + i_y v + i_t)^2 + \lambda\left(u_x^2 + u_y^2 + v_x^2 + v_y^2 \right) \right] dx\,dy$
Optical flow (contour based)	$\int \left[\left(V \cdot N - V^N \right)^2 + \lambda\,((\partial/\partial_s)\,V)^2 \right] ds$
Surface reconstruction	$\int \left[(S \cdot f - d)^2 + \lambda\left(f_{xx}^2 + 2f_{xy}^2 + f_{yy}^2 \right)^2 \right] dx\,dy$
Spatiotemporal approximation	$\int \left[(S \cdot f - i)^2 + \lambda\,(\nabla f \cdot V + ft)^2 \right] dx\,dy\,dt$
Color	$\|I^\nu - Az\|^2 + \lambda\|Pz\|^2$
Shape from shading	$\int \left[(E - R(f,g))^2 + \lambda\left(f_x^2 + f_y^2 + g_x^2 + g_y^2 \right) \right] dx\,dy$
Stereo	$\int \left\{ \left[\nabla^2 G * (L(x,y) - R(x + d(x,y), y)) \right]^2 + \lambda(\nabla D)^2 \right\} dx\,dy$

Table 1. Regularization in early vision: Some of the early vision problems that have been solved in terms of variational principles. The first five are standard quadratic regularization principles. In edge detection [Poggio *et al.* 1985] the data on image intensity ($i = i(x)$) (for simplicity in one dimension) are given on a discrete lattice: the operator S is the sampling operator on the continuous distribution f to be recovered. A similar functional may be used to approximate time-varying imagery. The spatio-temporal intensity to be recovered from the data $i(x, y, t)$ is $f(x, y, t)$; the stabilizer imposes the constraint of constant velocity V in the image plane (see Fahle and Poggio [1953]). In area-based optical flow [Horn & Schunck 1981], i is the image intensity, u and v are the two components of the velocity field. In surface reconstruction [Grimson 1982; Terzopoulos 1983] the surface $f(x, y)$ is computed from sparse depth data $d(x, y)$. In the case of color [Hildreth 1984a] the brightness is measured on each of three appropriate color coordinates I^ν ($\nu = 1, 2, 3$). The solution vector z contains the illumination and the albedo components separately; it is mapped by A into the ideal data. Minimization of an appropriate stabilizer enforces the constraint of spatially smooth illumination and either constant or sharply varying albedo. For shade from shading [Ikeuchi & Horn 1981] and stereo (T. Poggio and A. Yuille [unpublished]), we show two non-quadratic regularization functionals. R is the reflectance map, f and g are related to the components of the surface gradient, E is the brightness distribution [Ikeuchi & Horn 1981]. The regularization of the disparity field d involves convolution with the laplacian of a gaussian of the left (L) and the right (R) images and a Tikhonov stabilizer corresponding to the disparity gradient.

1984a, 1984b]. In this case, local measurements of the normal component at different locations can be used directly to find the optical flow, which is the same everywhere. The assumption, however, is overly restrictive, because it does not cover the case of motion of a rigid object in three-dimensional space (see figure 1).

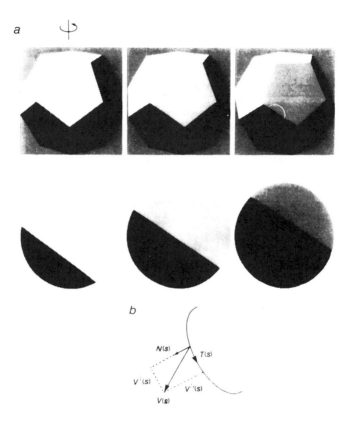

Figure 1. Ambiguity of the velocity field. (a) Local measurements cannot measure the full velocity field in the image plane, originated here by three-dimensional rotation of a solid object (three frames are shown). Any process operating within the aperture (shown as a white circle) can compute only the component of motion perpendicular to the contour. (b) Decomposition of the velocity vector along the contour, parameterized by the arc length s into components normal ($V^N(s)$) and tangential ($V^T(s)$) to the curve. The computer drawing was kindly provided by Karl Sims.

Hildreth [1984a, 1984b] suggested, following Horn and Schunck [1981], a more general smoothness constraint on the velocity field. The underlying physical consideration is that the real world consists of solid objects with smooth surfaces, whose projected velocity field is usually smooth. The specific form of the stabilizer (a Tikhonov stabilizer) was dictated by mathematical considerations, especially uniqueness of the solution. The two regularizing methods correspond to the two algorithms proposed and implemented by Hildreth [1984a]. The first one, which assumes that the measurements of the normal velocity components $V^N(s)$ are exact, minimizes

$$\|PV\|^2 = \int \left(\frac{\partial V}{\partial s}\right) ds \qquad (4)$$

subject to the measurements of the normal component of velocity (where s is arc length). The integral is evaluated along the contour. For non-exact data the second method provides the solution by minimizing

$$\|V \cdot N - V^N\|^2 + \lambda \int \left(\frac{\partial V}{\partial s}\right)^2 ds \qquad (5)$$

where N is the normal unit vector to the contour and λ^{-1} expresses the reliability of the data. Figure 2a shows an example of a successful computation of the optical flow by the first algorithm.

Recently, regularization techniques have been applied to edge detection [Poggio et al. 1985]. The problem of numerical differentiation can be regularized by the second method with a Tikhonov stabilizer that reflects a constraint of smoothness on the image (see table 1). The physical justification is that the image is an analytical function with bounded derivatives, because of the band-limiting properties of the optics that cuts off high spatial frequencies. This regularized solution is equivalent, under mild conditions, to convolving the intensity data with the derivative of a filter similar to the gaussian [Poggio et al. 1985] (see figure 3), proposed earlier [Marr & Poggio 1979; Marr & Hildreth 1980].

Other early vision problems can be solved by standard regularization techniques from a sparse set of depth values by imposing smoothness of the surface [Grimson 1981, 1982; Terzopoulos 1983]. Optical flow can be computed at each point in the image, rather than along a contour, using a constraint of smooth variation, in the form of a Tikhonov stabilizer [Horn 1985]. Variational principles that are not exactly quadratic but have the form of equation (3) can be used for other problems in early vision. The main results of Tikhonov can in fact be extended to the case in which the operators A and P are nonlinear, provided they satisfy certain conditions [Morozov 1984]. The variation of an object's brightness gives clues to its shape: the surface orientation can be computed from an intensity image in terms of the variational principle shown in table 1, which penalizes orientations violating the smoothness constraint and the irradiance constraint [Horn & Schunck 1981]. Stereo matching is the problem of inferring the correct binocular disparity (and therefore depth) from a pair of binocular images, by finding which feature in one image corresponds to

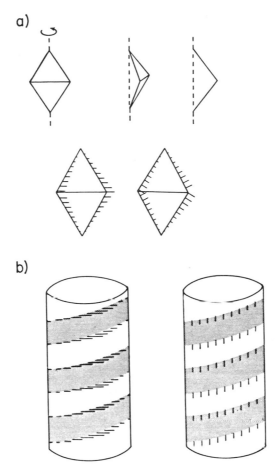

Figure 2. Computing the smoothest velocity field along contours. (a) Three-dimensional stimulus first used by Wallach and Connell [1953] to demonstrate the ability of the human system to derive three-dimensional structure from the projected two-dimensional motion of an object (kinetic depth effect). The top part shows three views of a figure as it is rotated around the vertical axis. The initial measurements of the normal velocity components V_i^N are shown on the lower right. The velocity field computed using equation (4) is shown on the lower left. The final solution corresponds to the physical correct velocity distribution. Recent electrophysiological evidence implicates the middle temporal area of the monkey as a site where a similar motion integration may occur [Movshon *et al.* 1984]. (b) Circular helix on a imaginary three-dimensional cylinder, rotating about its vertical axis (barber pole). The projection of the curve onto the image plane, together with the resulting two-dimensional velocity vectors are drawn on the left. Although the true velocity field V is strictly horizontal (left), the smoothest velocity field (right) is vertical. This example illustrates a case where both the algorithm and the human visual system suffer the same optical illusion. Adapted from Hildreth [1984a].

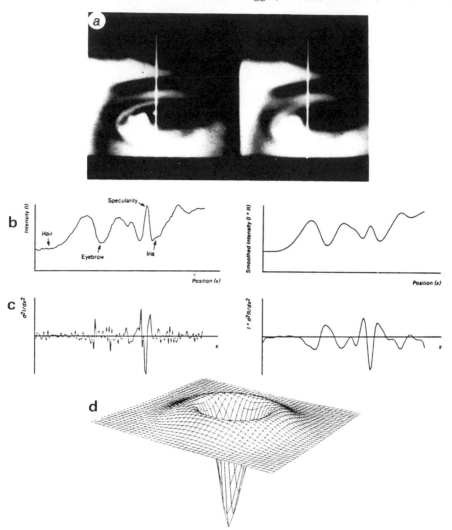

Figure 3. A regularized solution to edge detection. (a) Digital image (256×256 pixels) without any filtering (left) and (right) with the two-dimensional operator provided by standard regularization theory [Poggio *et al.* 1985] shown in *d*. (b) Intensity profile along the scale line indicated in *a* without (left) and with (right) the regularizing operation provided by filtering with the one-dimensional regularized filter [Poggio *et al.* 1985]. (c) Second derivative of the profile shown in *b* without (left) and with (right) the one-dimensional regularizing filtering. (d) Two-dimensional filter obtained by regularizing the ill-posed problem of edge detection [Poggio *et al.* 1985]. It is a quintic spline, very similar to a gaussian distribution. The parameter Λ controls the scale of the filter. Its value depends on the signal-to-noise ratio in the image. The spatial receptive field of most ganglion cells in the vertebrate retina have a very similar structure with a central excitatory region and an inhibitory surround [Barlow 1953; Kuffler 1953]. Drawings kindly provided by Harry Voorhees.

the which feature in the other image. This is an ill-posed problem which, under some restrictive conditions corresponding to the absence of occlusions, can be regularized by a variational principle that contains a term measuring the discrepancy between the feature maps extracted from the two images and a stabilizer that penalizes large disparity gradients (see table 1) and effectively imposes a disparity gradient limit. The algorithm can reduce to an area-based correlation algorithm of the Nishihara [1984] type if the disparity gradient is small. A standard regularization principle has been proposed for solving the problem of separating a material reflectance from a spatially varying illumination of color images [Hurlbert 1985]. The algorithm addresses the problem known in visual psychophysics as color constancy [Land 1984].

Physical Plausibility and Illusions

Physical plausibility of the solution, rather than its uniqueness, is the most important concern in regularization analysis. A physical analysis of the problem, and of its significant constraints, plays the main role [Poggio & Torre 1984]. The *a priori* assumptions required to solve ill-posed problems may be violated in specific instances where the regularized solution does not correspond to the physical solution. The algorithm suffers an optical illusion. A good example is provided by the computation of motion. The smoothness assumption of equation (5) gives correct results under some general conditions (for example, when objects have images consisting of connected straight lines [Yuille 1983]). For some classes of motion and contours, the smoothness principle will not yield the correct velocity field. In several of these cases, however, the human visual system also seems to derive a similar, incorrect velocity field, thereby possibly revealing *a priori* assumptions the brain is making about the world. A striking instance is the barber-pole illusion [Hildreth 1984a] (illustrated in figure 2b).

Analog Networks

One of the mysteries of biological vision is its speed. Parallel processing has often been advocated as the answer to this problem. The model of computation provided by digital processes is, however, unsatisfactory, especially given the increasing evidence that neurons are complex devices, very different from simple digital switches. It is, therefore, interesting to consider whether the regularization approach to early vision may lead to a different type of parallel computation. We have recently suggested that linear, analog networks (either electrical or chemical) are, in fact, a natural way of solving the variational principles dictated by standard regularization theory (see Terzopoulos [1983] and Ullman [1979]).

The fundamental reason for such a mapping between variational principles and electrical or chemical networks is Hamilton's least action principle. The class of variational principles that can be computed by analog networks is given by Kirchhoff's current and voltage laws, which represent conservation and continuity restrictions satisfied by each network component (appropriate variables are usually voltage and current for electrical networks and affinity and turnover rate for chemical systems [Eigen 1974]; see also Oster *et al.* [1971]). There is in general no unique network but possibly many networks implementing the same variational principle. For example, graded networks of the type proposed by Hopfield in the context of associative memory [Hopfield 1984] can solve standard regularization principles [Koch & Yuille 1985].

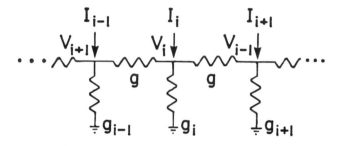

Figure 4. Analog networks. A resistive network computing the smoothest velocity field [Hildreth 1984a]. The network corresponds to the situation where the measurements of the normal velocity component V^N are assumed to be exact. Discretizing the associated variational equation (4) along the contour yields the Euler-Lagrange equations $(2 + k_i^2)V_i^T - V_{i+1}^T - V_{i-1}^T = d_i$, where k_i is the curvature of the contour at location i, d_i is a function of the data V_i^N and the contour and V_i^T is the unknown tangential component of the velocity V at location i along the contour. The equation describing the ith node in the electrical circuit is $(2g + g_i)V_i - gV_{i+1} - g_i = I_i$, where V_i is the voltage corresponding to the unknown V_i^T. A slightly more complicated circuit can be designed for the case when the measurements of V_i^N are not exact [Poggio & Koch to appear] (see equation (5)). Uniqueness of the regularized solution always ensures stability of the corresponding network, even if capacities are introduced. Equivalent analog networks can be implemented by diffusion-reaction systems, where the interaction between neighboring locations are mimicked using diffusion or chemical reactions with first-order kinetics. Hypothetical neuronal implementations may be envisaged. The conductance g may correspond to a small segment of a dendrite, the variable conductance g_i to a synaptic input with a reversal potential close or equal to the resting potential of the dendrite (that is, silent or shunting inhibition) and the current source to a conventional chemical synapse injecting current I_i into the dendrite. The output is sampled at location i by a chemical synapse. Adapted from Poggio and Torre [1984].

From Kirchhoff's law, it can be proved that for every quadratic variational problem with a unique solution (which is usually the case [Poggio & Torre 1984]), there exists a corresponding electrical network consisting of resistances and voltage or current sources having the same solution. In other words, the steady-state current (or voltage) distribution in the network corresponds to the solution, for example to the tangential velocity distribution $V^T(s)$, of the standard regularization problem (prevfigure 5). Furthermore, when capacitances are added to the system, thereby introducing dynamics, the system is stable. The data are supplied by injecting currents or by introducing batteries, that is by constant current or voltage sources.

This analog parallel model of computation is especially interesting from the point of view of the present understanding of the biophysics of neurones, membranes and synapses. Increasing evidence shows that electronic potentials play a primary role in many neurones [Schmitt et al. 1976]. Mechanisms as diverse as dendrodendritic synapses [Graubard & Calvin 1979; Shepherd & Brayton 1979], gap junctions [Bennett 1977], neurotransmitters acting over different times and distances [Marder 1984], voltage-dependent channels that can be modulated by neuropeptides [Schmitt 1984], and interactions between synaptic conductance changes [Koch & Poggio 1982] provide neurones with various different circuit elements. Patches of neural membrane are equivalent to resistances, capacitances, and phenomenological inductances [Cole 1968]. Synapses on dendritic splines mimic voltage sources, whereas synapses on thick dendrites or the soma act as current sources [Jack et al. 1975; Koch & Poggio 1983]. Thus, single neurones or small networks of neurones could implement analog solutions of regularization principles. Hypothetical neuronal implementations of the analog circuits of figure 4 have been devised, involving only one or two separate dendrites.

Beyond Standard Regularization Theory

The new theoretical framework for early vision clearly shows the attractions and the limitations that are intrinsic to the standard Tikhonov form of regularization theory. The main problem is the degree of smoothness required for the unknown function that has to be recovered. For instance, in surface interpolation, the degree of smoothness corresponding to the so-called thin-plate splines smoothes depth discontinuities too much, and often leads to unrealistic results [Grimson 1981] (discontinuities may, however, be detected and then used in a second regularization step [Terzopoulos 1984]).

Standard regularization theory deals with linear problems and is based on quadratic stabilizers. It leads therefore to the minimization of quadratic functionals and to linear Euler–Lagrange equations. Non-quadratic functionals may be needed to enforce the correct physical constraints (table 1 shows the non-quadratic case of shape-from-shading). Even in this case, methods of standard regularization theory can be used [Morozov 1984], but the solution space is no longer convex and many local minima can be found in the process of minimization.

A non-quadratic stabilizer has been proposed for the problem of preserving discontinuities in the reconstruction of the surfaces from depth data [Marroquin 1984]. The stabilizer, in its basic form attributable to Geman and Geman [1984] (a similar principle but without a rigorous justification was proposed by Blake [1983], see also the variational continuity control of Terzopoulos [1985]), embeds prior knowledge about the geometry of the discontinuities (the line process) and, in particular, that they are continuous and often straight contours. In standard regularization principles, the search space has only one local minimum to which suitable algorithms always converge. For non-quadratic functionals, the search space may be similar to a mountain range with many local minima. Stochastic algorithms for solving minimization problems of this type have been proposed recently, to escape from local minima at which simple hill-climbing algorithms would be trapped [Hinton & Sejnowski 1983; Kirkpatrick et al. 1983; Metropolis et al. 1953]. The basic idea is somewhat similar to adding a forcing noise term to the search algorithm. If the non-quadratic variational principle can be represented in a nonlinear analog network (as in Koch et al. [1985]), an appropriate source of gaussian noise could drive the analog network. The dynamics of the system would then be described by a nonlinear stochastic differential equation, representing a diffusion process.

The challenge now for the regularization theory of vision is to extend it beyond standard regularization methods. The universe of computations that can be performed in terms of quadratic functionals is rather restricted. To see this, it is sufficient to realize that minimization of quadratic cost functionals leads to a linear regularization operator, that is, to a linear mapping of the input data into the solution space. In the special case when data are on a regular grid and obey suitable conditions, the linear operator may become a convolution, that is, a simple filtering operation on the data. Similar to linear models in physics, standard regularization theory is an extremely useful approximation in many cases, but cannot deal with the full complexity of vision.

Stochastic Route to Regularization

A different rigorous approach to regularization is based on Bayes estimation and Markov random fields models. In this approach the *a priori* knowledge is represented in terms of appropriate probability distributions, whereas in standard regularization *a priori* knowledge leads to restrictions on the solution space. Consider as an example the case of surface reconstruction. A *priori* knowledge can be formulated in terms of a Markov random field (MRF) model of the surface. In an MRF the value at one discrete location depends only on the values within a given neighborhood. In this approach the best surface maximizes some likelihood criterion such as the maximum *a posteriori* estimate or the *a posteriori* mean of the MRF. It has been pointed out [Marroquin 1984] that the maximum *a posteriori* estimate of a MRF is equivalent to the variational principle of the general form of equation (3); the first term measures the discrepancy between the data and the solution, the second term is now an arbitrary potential function of the solution (defined on a discrete lattice). The overall variational principle, in general not quadratic, reduces to a quadratic functional of the standard regularization type when the noise is additive and gaussian and first-order differences of the field are zero-mean, independent, gaussian random variables. In this case the maximum *a posteriori* estimate (MAP) coincides with all estimates and, in particular, with the *a posteriori* mean. But Marroquin [1985] has shown recently that this is not true in general: in most cases the MAP estimate is not optimal with respect to natural error measures and better estimates such as the *a posteriori* mean can be found. In these cases the problem is not equivalent to finding the global minimum of an energy functional: simulated annealing is not needed, and a Metropolis-type algorithm [Metropolis *et al.* 1953] can be used instead.

In the case of Hildreth's [1984a] motion computation the smoothness assumption corresponds to the hypothesis that the changes in velocity between neighboring points along the contour are zero-mean, independent, gaussian random variables. This connection between the stochastic approach and standard regularization methods gives an interesting perspective on the nature of the constraints and the choice of the stabilizer. The variational principles used to solve the inverse problems of vision correspond to the Markov structure that generates plausible solutions.

A related area of future investigation concerns the problem of learning a regularizing operator. In the case of standard regularization, the corresponding linear operator mapping the data into the solution may be learned by an associative learning scheme [Poggio & Hurlbert 1984], of the type proposed in connection with biological memory [Kohonen 1984].

Towards Symbolic Descriptions

So far, we have restricted our discussion to the early stages of vision that create image-like representations of the physical three-dimensional surfaces around the viewer. The step beyond these representations, also called intrinsic images [Barrow & Tennenbaum 1981], or $2 - 1/2$D sketches [Marr 1982], is a large one. Intrinsic images are still image-like numerical representations, not yet described in terms of objects. They are already sufficient for some of the high-level tasks of a vision system such as manipulation and navigation. They cannot be used directly for the tasks of recognition and description that require the generation and use of more symbolic representations. It seems at first difficult to see how the computation of symbolic representations may fit at all in the perspective of regularizing ill-posed problems.

The basic idea of all regularization methods is to restrict the space of possible solutions. If this space is constrained to have finite dimensions, there is a good chance that an inverse problem will be well-posed. Thus, a representation based on a finite set of discrete symbols regularized a possibly ill-posed problem. From this point of view, the problem of perception (regularizing an otherwise underconstrained problem using generic constraints of the physical world) becomes practically equivalent to the classical artificial intelligence problem of finding ways of solving intractable problems (such as chess) by limiting the search for solutions.

Conclusions

We suggest a classification of vision algorithms that maps naturally into parallel digital computer architectures now under development. Standard regularization, when sufficient, leads to two classes of parallel algorithms. Algorithms for finding minima of a convex functional such as steepest descent or the more efficient multigrid algorithms developed for vision can always be used. They can be replaced by convolution algorithms if the data are given on a regular grid and 'A' in equation (1) is space invariant. In the latter case, the regularized solution is obtained by convolving the data through a precomputed filter.

All these algorithms may be implemented by parallel architecture of many processors with only local connections. Problems that cannot be approached in terms of regularization, and that require symbolic representations and operations on them, may need parallel architectures with a global communication facility; such as the Connection Machine [Hillis 1985].

The concept of ill-posed problems and the associated old and new regularization theories seem to provide a satisfactory theoretical framework for much of early vision. This new perspective also provides a link between the computational (ill-posed) nature of early vision problems, the structure of the algorithms for solving them, and the parallel hardware that can be used for efficient visual information processing. It also shows the intrinsic limitations of the variational principles used so far in early vision, indicating at the same time how to extend regularization analysis beyond the standard theory.

References

Brady, J. M., G. E. Hinton, and T. J. Sejnowski [1983], *Nature*, vol. 306, pp. 21–26.

Barlow, H. B. [1953], *J. Phsiol. Lond.*, vol. 119, pp. 69–88. (1953).

Barrow, H. G., and J. M. Tennenbaum [1981], *Artificial Intelligence*, vol. 17, pp. 75–117.

Bennett, M. V. L. [1977], in *Handbook of Physiology*, pp. 221–250 American Physiological Society, Bethesda.

Bertero, M., C. Del Mol, and E. R. Pike [to appear], *J. inverse Prob.*.

Bertero, M. [1982], in *Problem non ben posti ed inversi*, Istituto di Analisi Globale, Firenze.

Bertero, Mario, Tomaso Poggio, and Vincent Torre [1988], "Ill-Posed Problems in Early Vision," *Proceedings of the IEEE*, vol. 76, pp. 869-889.

Blake, A. [1983], *Pattern Recognition Lett.*, vol. 1, pp. 393–399.

Brown, C. M. [1984], *Science*, vol. 224, pp. 1299–1305.

Cole, K. S. [1968], *Membranes, Ions and Impulses*, University of California Press, Berkeley.

Eigen, M. [1974], in *The Neurosciences: 3rd Study Program*, edited by F. O. Schmitt, and F. G.Worden) xix–xxvii, MIT Press, Cambridge, MA.

Fahle, M., and T. Poggio [1953], *Proc. R. Soc.*, vol. B213, pp. 451–477.

Geman, S., and D. Geman [1984], *IEEE Trans. Pattern Analysis Machine Intelligence*, vol. 6, pp. 721–741.

Graubard, K., and W. H. Calvin [1979], in *The Neurosciences: 4th Study Program*, edited by F. O. Schmitt, and F. G. Worden, pp. 317–332, MIT Press, Cambridge, MA.

Grimson, W. E. L. [1981], *From Images to Surfaces: A Computational Study of the Human Early Visual System*, MIT, Cambridge, MA.

Grimson, W. E. L. [1981], *Phil. Trans. R. Soc.*, vol. B298, pp. 395–427.

We thank E. Hildreth, A. Hurlbert, J. Marroquin, G. Mitchison, D. Terzopoulos, H. Voorhees, and A. Yuille for discussions and suggestions. Mario Bertero first pointed out to us that numerical differentiation is an ill-posed problem. E. Hildreth, L. Ardrey and especially H. Voorhees, K. Sims and M. Drumheller helped with some of the figures.

Support for the Artificial Intelligence Laboratory's research in artificial intelligence is provided in part by the Advanced Research Projects Agency of the Department of Defense under Office of Naval Research contract N00014-80-C-0505. The Center for Biological Information Processing is supported in part by the Sloan Foundation and in part by Whitaker College. C. Koch is supported by a grand from the Office of Naval Research, Engineering Psychology Division.

Hadamard, J. [1923], *Lectures on the Cauchy Problem in Linear Partial Differential Equations*, Yale University Press.

Hildreth, E. C. [1984a], *Proc. R. Soc.*, vol. B221, pp. 189–220.

Hildreth, E. C. [1984b], *The Measurement of Visual Motion*, MIT Press, Cambridge, MA.

Hillis, W. D. [1985], *The Connection Machine*, MIT Press, Cambridge.

Hinton, G. E., and T. J. Sejnowski [1983], *Proc. IEEE 1983 Conf. Computer Vision and Pattern Recognition*, Washington, DC.

Hopfield, J. J. [1984], *Proc. Natn. Acad. Sci. U.S.A.*, vol. 81, pp. 3088–3092.

Horn, B. K. P., and M. J. Brooks [1985], Report AIM-813, Artificial Intelligence Laboratory, Massachusetts Institute of Technology, Cambridge, MA.

Horn, B. K. P. [1974], *Computer Graphics Image Processing*, vol. 3, pp. 111-299.

Horn, B. K. P. [1985], *Robot Vision*, MIT Press and McGraw-Hill, Cambridge and New York.

Horn, B. K. P., and B. G. Schunck [1981], *Artificial Intelligence*, vol. 17, pp. 185–203.

Hurlbert, A. [1985], Report AIM-814, Artificial Intelligence Laboratory, Massachusetts Institute of Technology, Cambridge, MA.

Ikeuchi, K., and B. K. P. Horn [1981], *Artificial Intelligence*, vol. 17, pp. 141–184.

Jack, J. J., D. Nobel, and R. W. Tsien [1975], *Electric Current Flow in Excitable Cells*, Clarendon, Oxford.

Kirkpatrick, S., C. D. Gelatt Jr., and M. P. Vecchi [1983], *Science*, vol. 220, pp. 671–680.

Koch, C. Marroquin, Jr., and A. Yuille [1985], Report AIM-751, Artificial Intelligence Laboratory, Massachusetts Institute of Technology, Cambridge, MA.

Koch, C., and T. Poggio [1983], *Proc. R. Soc.*, vol. B218, pp. 455–477.

Koch, C., T. Poggio [1982], and V. Torre, *Phil. Trans. R. Soc.*, vol. B298, pp. 227–268.

Kohonen, T. [1984], *Self-Organization and Associative Memory*, Springer, Berlin.

Kuffler, S. W. [1953], *J. Neurophysiol.*, vol. 16, pp. 37–68.

Land, E. H. [1984], *Proc. Natn. Acad. Sci. U.S.A.*, vol. 80, pp. 5163–5169.

Marder, E. [1984], *Trends Neurosci.* vol. 7, pp. 48–53.

Marr, D., and S. Ullman [1981], *Proc. R. Soc.*, vol. B211, pp. 151–180.

Marr. D., and E. C. Hildreth, *Proc. R. Soc.*, vol. B207, pp. 187–217.

Marr. D., and T. Poggio [1979], *Proc. R. Soc.*, vol. B204, pp. 301–328.

Marroquin, J. [1984], Report AIM-792, Artificial Intelligence Laboratory, Massachusetts Institute of Technology, Cambridge, 1984.

Marroquin, J. [1985], Report AIM-839, Artificial Intelligence Laboratory, Massachusetts Institute of Technology, Cambridge, MA.

Metropolis, N., A. Rosenbluth, M. Rosenbluth, A. Teller, and E. Teller [1953], *J. chem. Phys.*, vol. 21, no. 6, pp. 1087–1092.

Morozov, V. A. [1984], *Methods for Solving Incorrectly Posed Problems*, Springer, New York.

Movshon, J. A., E. H. Adelson, M. S. Gizzi, and W. T. Newsome [1984], in *Pattern Recognition Mechanisms*, edited by C. Chagas, R. Gattar, and C. G. Gross, pp. 95–107, Vatican, Rome; *Expl. Brain Res.*, to appear.

Nashed, M. Z. [1976], (editor), *Generalized Inverses and Applications*, Academic, New York.

Nishihara, H. K. [1984], Report AIM-780, Artificial Intelligence Laboratory, Massachusetts Institute of Technology, Cambridge, MA.

Oster, G. F., A. Perelson, and A. Katchalsky [1971], *Nature*, vol. 234, pp. 393–399.

Poggio, T., and C. Koch [to appear], *Proc. R. Soc.*, vol. B.

Poggio, T., and A. Hurlbert [1984], Report AIW-264, Artificial Intelligence Laboratory, Massachusetts Institute of Technology, Cambridge, MA.

Poggio, T., and V. Torre [1984], Report AIM-773, Artificial Intelligence Laboratory, Massachusetts Institute of Technology, Cambridge, MA.

Poggio, T., H. Voorhees, and A. Yuille, Report AIM-833, Artificial Intelligence Laboratory, Massachusetts Institute of Technology, Cambridge, MA.

Schmitt, F. D. [1984], *Neuroscience*, vol. 13, pp. 991–1002.

Schmitt, F. O., P. Dev, and B. H. Smith [1976], *Science*, vol. 193, pp. 114–120.

Shepherd, G. M., and R. K. Brayton, *Brain Res.*, vol. 175, pp. 337–383.

Terzopoulos, D. [1983], *Computer Graphics Image Processing*, vol. 24, pp. 52–96.

Terzopoulos, D. [1984], Thesis, Massachusetts Institute of Technology, Cambridge, MA.

Terzopoulos, D. [1985], Report AIM-800, Artificial Intelligence Laboratory, Massachusetts Institute of Technology, Cambridge, MA.

Terzopoulos, D. [to appear], *IEEE Trans. Pattern Analysis Machine Intelligence*.

Tikhonov, A. N., and V. Y. Arsenin [1977], *Solutions of Ill-Posed Problems*, Winston, Washington, DC.

Tikhonov, A. N. [1963], *Sov. Math. Dokl.*, vol. 4, pp. 1035–1038.

Ullman, S. [1979], *Computer Graphics Image Processing*, vol. 9, pp. 115–125.

Wahba, G. [1980], Report TR-595, University of Wisconsin.

Wallach, H., and D. N. O'Connell [1953], *J. exp. Psychol.*, vol. 45, pp. 205–217.

Yuille, A. [1983], Report AIM-724, Artificial Intelligence Laboratory, Massachusetts Institute of Technology, Cambridge, MA; *Advances in Artificial Intelligence*, edited by T. M. M. O'Shea, Elsevier, Amsterdam, (to appear).

42

One reason we see so well is that we see in so many ways. We constantly combine evidence from all sorts of modules, including edge, stereo disparity, motion, texture, and color modules, to name a few of the most conspicuous.

Quite properly, most image-understanding researchers have concentrated historically on single competences, for there is little point in trying to understand how to combine evidence until there is evidence to combine. Today, however, our understanding of individual image-understanding problems, and their mathematical unification, has progressed sufficiently for us to ask how we can benefit from integration.

Accordingly, the authors have built the Vision Machine, a testbed for both integration ideas and for parallel implementations of various early vision procedures. It has a computer-controlled, two-camera head, which provides rich sensory input, and it has a Connection Machine, which provides enormous computing power.

That enormous computing power is essential because one objective is to extract edge, stereo disparity, motion, texture, and color information and to combine that information in real time. Ultimately, the plan is to replace the Connection Machine with VLSI chips that will do the right things at low cost once we have determined what the right things are.

The MIT Vision Machine

T. Poggio	D. Geiger	T. Cass	W. Yang
J. Little	D. Weinshall	H. Bülthoff	A. Hurlbert
E. Gamble	M. Villalba	M. Drumheller	D. Beymer
W. Gillett	N. Larson	P. Oppenheimer	P. O'Donnell

Introduction: The Project and Its Goals

Computer vision has developed algorithms for several early vision processes, such as edge detection, stereopsis, motion, texture, and color, which give separate cues as to the distance from the viewer of three-dimensional surfaces, their shape, and their material properties. Biological vision systems, however, greatly outperform computer vision programs. It is clear that one of the keys to the reliability, flexibility, and robustness of biological vision systems in unconstrained environments is their ability to integrate many different visual cues. For this reason, we continue the development of a *Vision Machine* system to explore the issue of integration of early vision modules. The system also serves the purpose of developing parallel vision algorithms, because its main computational engine is a parallel supercomputer, the Connection Machine.

The idea behind the Vision Machine is that the main goal of the integration stage is to compute a map of the visible discontinuities in the scene, somewhat similar to a cartoon or a line-drawing. There are several reasons for this. First, experience with existing model-based recognition algorithms suggest that the critical problem in this type of recognition is to obtain a reasonably good map of the scene in terms of features such as edges and corners. The map does not need to be perfect (human recognition works with noisy and occluded line drawings) and, of course, it cannot be. But it should be significantly cleaner than the typical map provided by an edge detector. Second, discontinuities of surface properties are the most important locations in a scene. Third, we have argued that discontinuities are ideal for integrating information from different visual cues.

It is also clear that there are several different approaches to the problem of how to integrate visual cues. Let us list some of the obvious possibilities:

1   There is no active integration of visual processes. Their individual outputs are "integrated" at the stage at which they are used, for example by a navigation system. This is the approach advocated by Brooks [1987]. While it makes sense for automatic, insect-like, visuo-motor tasks such as tracking a target or avoiding obstacles (for example, the fly's visuo-motor system [Reichardt & Poggio 1976]), it seems quite unlikely for visual perception in the wider sense.

2   The visual modules are so tightly coupled that it is impossible to consider visual modules as separate, even to a first order approximation. This view is unattractive on epistemological, engineering, and psychophysical grounds.

3   The visual modules are coupled to each other and to the image data in a parallel fashion—each process represented as an array coupled to the arrays associated with the other processes. This point of view is in the tradition of Marr's $2\frac{1}{2}$-D sketch, and especially of the "intrinsic images" of Barrow and Tenenbaum [1978]. Our present scheme is of this type, and exploits the machinery of Markov Random Field (MRF) models.

4   Integration of different vision modalities is taking place in a task-dependent way at specific locations—not over the whole image—and when it is needed—therefore not at all times. This approach is suggested by psychophysical data on visual attention and by the idea of visual routines [Ullman 1984] (see also Hurlbert and Poggio [1986], Mahoney [1987], and Bülthoff and Mallot [1988]).

We are presently exploring the third of these approaches. We believe that the last two approaches are compatible with each other. In particular, visual routines may operate on maps of discontinuities such as those delivered by the present Vision Machine, and therefore be located after a parallel, automatic integration stage. In real life, of course, it may be more a matter of coexistence. We believe, in fact, that a control structure based on specific knowledge about the properties of the various modules, the specific scene and the specific task will be needed in a later version of the Vision Machine to overview and control the MRF integration stage itself and its parameters. It is possible that the integration stage should be much more goal-directed than what our present methods (MRF based) allow. The main goal of our work is to find out whether this is true.

The Vision Machine project has a number of other goals. It provides a focus for developing parallel vision algorithms and for studying how to organize a real-time vision system on a massively parallel supercomputer. It attempts to alter the usual paradigm of computer vision research over the past years: choose a specific problem, for example stereo, find an algorithm, and test it in isolation. The Vision Machine allows us to develop and test an algorithm in the context of the other modules and the requirements of the overall visual task, above all, visual recognition. For this reason, the project is more than an experiment in integration and parallel processing: it is a laboratory for our theories and algorithms.

Finally, the ultimate goal of the Vision Machine project is no less than the ultimate goal of vision research: to build a vision system that achieves human-level performance.

The Vision Machine System

The overall organization of the system is shown in figure 1. The image(s) are processed in parallel through independent algorithms or modules corresponding to different visual cues. Edges are extracted using Canny's edge detector. The stereo module computes disparity from the left and right images. The motion module estimates an approximation of the optical flow from pairs of images in a time sequence. The texture module computes texture attributes (such as density and orientation of textons [Voorhees 1987]). The color algorithm provides an estimate of the spectral albedo of the surfaces, independently of the *effective illumination*, that is, illumination gradients and shading effects, as suggested by Hurlbert and Poggio (see Poggio and Staff [1985]).

The measurements provided by the early vision modules are typically noisy, and possibly sparse (for stereo and motion). They are smoothed and made dense by exploiting known constraints within each process (for instance, that disparity is smooth). This is the stage of *approximation* and *restoration* of data, performed using a Markov Random Field model. Simultaneously, discontinuities are found in each cue. Prior knowledge of the behavior of discontinuities is exploited, for instance, the fact that they are continuous lines, not isolated points. Detection of discontinuities is aided by the information provided by brightness edges. Thus each cue, disparity, optical flow, texture, and color, is coupled to the edges in brightness.

The full scheme involves finding the various types of physical discontinuities in the surfaces, *depth discontinuities* (extremal edges and blades), *orientation discontinuities, specular edges, albedo edges* (or marks), and *shadow edges*, and coupling them with each other and back to the discontinuities in the visual cues, as illustrated in figure 1 (and suggested by Gamble, Geiger, Poggio, and Weinshall [1989]). So far we have implemented only the coupling of brightness edges to each of the cues provided by the early algorithm. As we will discuss later, the technique we use to

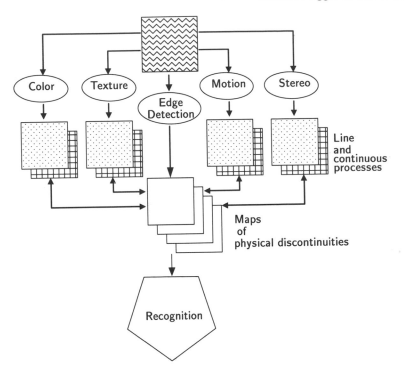

Figure 1. Overall organization of the Vision Machine.

approximate, to simultaneously detect discontinuities, and to couple the different processes, is based on MRF models. The output of the system is a set of labeled discontinuities of the surfaces around the viewer. Thus the scheme—an instance of inverse optics—computes *surface properties*, that is, attributes of the physical world and not anymore of the images. Note that we attempt to find discontinuities in surface properties and therefore qualitative surface properties: the *inverse optics* paradigm does **not** imply that physical properties of the surfaces, such as depth or reflectance, should be extracted *precisely, everywhere*. These discontinuities, taken together, represent a "cartoon" of the original scene which can be used for recognition and navigation (along with, interpolated depth, motion, texture, and color fields). As yet we did not integrate our ongoing work on grouping in the Vision Machine. We expect to use a saliency operation on the output of the edge detection process possibly before the use of intensity edges by the MRF stage. The grouping based on T-junctions [Beymer 1989] should take place on the intensity edges at the same level as the MRF stage. Initial work in recognition has been integrated in the system. The Vision Machine has been demonstrated working form images to recognition through the integration of visual cues.

The plan of this chapter is as follows. We will first review the current hardware of the Vision Machine: the eye-head system and the Connection Machine. We will then describe in some detail each of the early vision algorithms that are presently running and are part of the system. After this, the integration stage will be discussed. We will analyze some results, and illustrate the merits and the pitfalls of our present system. The last section will discuss a real-time visual system, and some ideas on how to put the system into VLSI circuits of analog and digital type.

Hardware

The Eye-Head system

Because of the scope of the Vision Machine project, a general purpose image input device is required. Such a device is the eye-head system. Here we discuss its current and future configurations.

The eye-head system consists of two CCD cameras, which act as eyes, mounted on a variable-attitude platform, which acts as the head. Inspired by biology, the apparatus is configured such that the head moves the eyes as a unit, while allowing the eyes to point independently. Each eye is equipped with a motorized zoom lens ($F1.4$, focal length from 12.5 to 75mm), allowing control of the iris, focus, and focal length by the host computer (currently a Symbolics 3600 Lisp Machine). Other hardware allows for repeatable calibration of the entire apparatus.

Because of the size and weight of the motorized lenses, it would be impractical to achieve eye movement by pointing the camera/lens assemblies directly. Instead, each assembly is mounted rigidly on the head, with eye movement achieved indirectly. In front of each lens is a pair of front surface mirrors, each of which can be pivoted by a galvanometer, providing two degrees of freedom in aiming the cameras. At the expense of a more complicated imaging geometry, we get a simple and fast pointing system for the eyes.

The head is attached to its mount via a spherical joint, allowing head rotation about two orthogonal axes (pan and tilt). Each axis is driven by a stepper motor coupled to its drive shaft through a harmonic drive. The latter provides a large gear ratio in conjunction with very little mechanical backlash. Under control of the stepper motors, the head can be panned 180 degrees from left to right, and tilted 90 degrees (from vertical-down to horizontal). Each of the stepper motors is provided with an optical shaft encoder for shaft position feedback (a closed-loop control scheme is employed for the stepper motors). The shaft encoders also provide an index pulse (one per revolution) which is used for joint calibration in conjunction with mechanical limit switches. The latter also protect the head from damage due to excessive travel.

The overall control system for the eye-head system is distributed over a micro-processor network (UNET) developed at the MIT AI Laboratory for the control of vision/robotics hardware. The UNET is a "multi-drop" network supporting up to 32 micros, under the control of a single host. The micros normally function as network slaves, with the host acting as the master. In this mode the micros only "speak when spoken to," responding to various network operations either by receiving information (command or otherwise) or by transmitting information (such as status or results). Associated with each micro on the UNET is a local 16-bit bus (UBUS), which is totally under the control of the micro. Peripheral devices such as motor drivers, galvanometer drivers, and pulse width modulators (PWMs), to name a few, which can be interfaced at this level.

At present, three micro-processors are installed on the eye-head UNET: one each for the galvanometers, motorized lenses, and stepper motors. The processors currently employed are based on the Intel 8051. Each of these micros has an assortment of UBUS peripherals under its control. By making these peripherals sufficiently powerful, each micro's control task can remain simple and manageable. Code for the micros, written in both assembly language and C, is facilitated by a Lisp-based debugging environment.

Our computational engine: The Connection Machine

The Connection Machine is a powerful fine-grained parallel machine which has proven useful for implementation of vision algorithms. In implementing these algorithms, several different models of using the Connection Machine have emerged, because the machine provides several different communication modes. The Connection Machine implementation of algorithms can take advantage of the underlying architecture of the machine in novel ways. We describe here several common, elementary operations which recur throughout the following discussion of parallel algorithms.

◇ The Connection Machine

The CM-2 version of the Connection Machine [Hillis 1985] is a parallel computing machine with between 16K and 64K processors, operating under a single instruction stream broadcast to all processors. It is a Single Instruction Multiple Data (SIMD) machine; all processors execute the same control stream. Each processor is a simple 1-bit processor, currently with 64K bits of memory, optionally with a floating point arithmetic accelerator, shared among 16 (or 32) processors. There are two modes of communication among the processors: the NEWS network and the *router*. The NEWS network (so-called because the connections are in the four cardinal directions) provides rapid direct communication between neighboring processors in an rectangular grid of arbitrary dimension. For example, 64K processors could be configured into a two-dimensional 256×256 grid, or into a four-dimesional $64 \times 64 \times 4 \times 4$ grid. The second mode of communication is the *router*, which allows messages to be sent from any processor to any other processor in the machine. The processors in the Connection Machine can be envisioned as being the vertices of a 16-dimensional hypercube (in fact, it is a 12-dimensional hypercube; at each vertex of the hypercube resides a chip containing 16 processors). Each processor in the Connection Machine is identified by its hypercube address in the range $0 \ldots 65535$, imposing a linear order on the processors. This address denotes the destination of messages handled by the router. Messages pass along the edges of the hypercube from source processors to destination processors. The Connection Machine also has facilities for returning to the host machine the result of various operations on a field in all processors; it can return the global maximum, minimum, sum, logical AND, and logical OR of the field.

The floating-point arithmetic accelerator, which may optionally be added to the Connection Machine, provides a significant increase in the speed of both single and double precision computations. One floating-point processor chip serves a pair Connection Machine processor chips with 32 total processors in a pipelined fashion, and can produce a speed-up of more than a factor of twenty.

To allow the machine to manipulate data structures with more than 64K elements, the Connection Machine supports *virtual processors*. A single physical processor can operate as a set of multiple virtual processors by serializing operations in time, and by partitioning the memory of each processor. This is otherwise invisible to the user. Connection Machine programs utilize Common Lisp syntax, in a language called *Lisp, and are manipulated in the same fashion as Lisp programs.

◇ Powerful primitive operations

Many vision problems must be solved by a combination of communication modes on the Connection Machine. The design of these algorithms takes advantage of the underlying architecture of the machine in novel ways. There are several common, elementary operations used in this discussion of parallel algorithms: routing operations, scanning, and distance doubling.

Routing.   Memory in the Connection Machine is associated with processors. Local memory can be accessed rapidly. Memory of processors nearby

in the NEWS network can be accessed by passing it through the processors
on the path between the source and the destination. At present, NEWS ac-
cesses in the machine are made in the same direction for all processors. The
router on the Connection Machine provides parallel reads and writes among
processor memory at arbitrary distances and with arbitrary patterns. It
uses a packet-switched message routing scheme to direct messages along the
hypercube connections to their destinations. This powerful communication
mode can be used to reconfigure completely, in one parallel write operation
taking one router cycle, a field of information in the machine. The Connection Machine supplies instructions so that many processors can read
from the same location or write to the same location, but because these
memory references can cause significant delay, we will usually only consider
exclusive read, exclusive write instructions. We will usually not allow more
than one processor to access the memory of another processor at one time.
The Connection Machine can combine messages at a destination by various
operations, such as logical AND, inclusive OR, summation, and maximum
or minimum.

Scanning.   The *scan* operations [Blelloch 1987] can be used to simplify
and speed up many algorithms. They directly take advantage of the hypercube connections underlying the router, and can be used to distribute
values among the processors and to aggregate values using associative operators. Formally, the *scan* operation takes a binary associative operator
$\oplus$, with identity 0, and an ordered set $[a_0, a_1, \ldots, a_{n-1}]$, and returns the
set $[a_0, (a_0 \oplus a_1), \ldots, (a_0 \oplus a_1 \oplus \ldots \oplus a_{n-1})]$. This operation is sometimes
referred to as the *data independent prefix operation* [Kruskal *et al.* 1985].
Binary associative operators include *minimum, maximum,* and *plus.*

The four scan operations *plus-scan, max-scan, min-scan,* and *copy-
scan* are implemented in microcode, and take about the same amount of
time as a routing cycle. The *copy-scan* operation takes a value at the first
processor and distributes it to the other processors. These scan operations
can take *segment bits* that divide the processor ordering into segments.
The beginning of each segment is marked by a processor whose segment
bit is set, and the scan operations start over again at the beginning of each
segment.

The *scan* operations also work using the NEWS addressing scheme,
termed *grid-scans.* These compute the sum, and quickly find the maximum,
copy, or number values along rows or columns of the NEWS grid.

For example, *grid-scans* can be used to find, for each pixel, the sum of a
square region with width $2m+1$ centered at the pixel. This sum is computed
using the following steps. First, a *plus-scan* operation accumulates partial
sums for all pixels along the rows. Each pixel then gets the result of the
scan from the processor m in front of it and m behind it; the difference
of these two values represents the sum, for each pixel, of its neighborhood

along the row. We now execute the same calculation on the columns, resulting in the sum, for each pixel, of the elements in its square. The whole process only requires a few *scans* and routing operations, and runs in time independent of the size of m. The summation operations are generally useful to accumulate local support in many of our algorithms, such as stereo and motion.

Distance Doubling.   Another important primitive operation is *distance doubling* [Wyllie 1979; Lim 1986] which can be used to compute the effect of any binary, associative operation, as in *scan*, on processors linked in a list or a ring. For example, using *max*, *distance doubling* can find the extremum of a field contained in the processors. Using message-passing on the router, *distance doubling* can propagate the extreme value to all processors in the ring of N processors in $O(\log N)$ steps. Each step involves two *send* operations. Typically, the value to be maximized is chosen to be the hypercube address. At termination, each processor in the ring knows the label of the maximum processor in the ring, hereafter termed the *principal processor*. This labels all connected processors uniquely, and nominates a processor as the representative for the entire set of connected processors. At the same time, the distance from the *principal* can be computed in each processor. Each processor initially, at step 0, has the address of the next processor in the ring, and a value which is to be maximized. At the termination of the ith step, a processor knows the addresses of processors $2^i + 1$ away, and the maximum of all values within 2^{i-1} processors away. In the example, the maximum value has been propagated to all 8 processors in $\log 8 = 3$ steps.

Early Vision Algorithms and their Parallel Implementation

Edge detection

Edge detection is a key first step in correctly identifying physical changes. The apparently simple problem of measuring sharp brightness changes in the image has proven to be difficult. It is now clear that edge detection should be intended not simply as finding "edges" in the images, an ill-defined concept in general, but as measuring appropriate derivatives of the brightness data. This involves the task-dependent use of different two-dimensional derivatives. In many cases, it is appropriate to mark locations corresponding to appropriate critical points of the derivative such as maxima or zeroes. In some cases, later algorithms based on these binary features (presence or absence of edges) may be equivalent, or very similar, to algorithms that directly use the continuous value of the derivatives. A case in point is provided by our stereo and motion algorithms, to be described later. As a consequence, one should not always make a sharp distinction between edge-based and intensity based algorithms; the distinction is more blurred, and in some cases it is almost a matter of implementation.

In our current implementation of the Vision Machine, we are using two different kinds of edges. The first consists of zero-crossings in the Laplacian of the image filtered through an appropriate Gaussian. The second consists of the edges found by Canny's edge detector. Zero-crossings can be used by our stereo and motion algorithms (though we have mainly used Canny's edges at fine resolution). Canny's edges (at a coarser resolution) are input to the MRF integration scheme.

◇ Zero-crossings

Because the derivative operation is ill-posed, we need to filter the resultant data through an appropriate low-pass filter [Torre & Poggio 1984]. The filter of choice (but not the only possibility!) is a Gaussian at a suitable spatial scale. An interesting and simple implementation of Gaussian convolution relies on the binomial approximation to the Gaussian distribution. This algorithm requires only integer addition, shifting, and local communication on the 2D mesh, so it can be implemented on a simple 2D mesh architecture (such as the NEWS network on the Connection Machine).

The Laplacian of a Gaussian is often approximated by the difference of Gaussians. The Laplacian of a Gaussian can also be computed by convolution with a Gaussian followed by convolution with a discrete Laplacian; we have implemented both on the Connection Machine. To detect zero-crossings, the computation at each pixel need only examine the sign bits of neighboring pixels.

◇ Canny edge detection

The Canny edge detector is often used in image understanding. It is based on directional derivatives, so it has improved localization. The Canny edge detector on the Connection Machine consists of the following steps:

- Gaussian smoothing
- Directional derivative
- Non-maximum suppression
- Thresholding with hysteresis.

Gaussian filtering, as described above, is a local operation. Computing directional derivatives is also local, using a finite difference approximation referencing only local neighbors in the image grid.

Non-maximum Suppression.   Non-maximum suppression selects as edge candidates those pixels for which the gradient magnitude is maximal in the direction of the gradient. This involves interpolating the gradient magnitude between each of two pairs of adjacent pixels among the eight neighbors of a pixel, one forward in the gradient direction, and one backward. However, it may not be crucial to use interpolation, in which case magnitudes of neighboring values can be directly compared.

Thresholding with Hysteresis.   Thresholding with hysteresis eliminates weak edges due to noise, using the threshold, while connecting extended curves over small gaps using hysteresis. Two thresholds are computed, *low* and *high*, based on an estimate of the noise in the image brightness. The non-maximum suppression step selects those pixels where the gradient magnitude is maximal in the direction of the gradient. In the thresholding step, all selected pixels with gradient magnitude below *low* are eliminated. All pixels with values above *high* are considered as edges. All pixels with values between *low* and *high* are edges if they can be connected to a pixel above *high* through a chain of pixels above *low*. All others are eliminated.

This is a spreading activation operation; it propagates information along a set of connected edge pixels. The algorithm iterates, in each step marking as *edge* pixels any *low* pixels adjacent to *edge* pixels. When no pixels change state, the iteration terminates, taking $O(m)$ steps, a number proportional to the length m of the longest chain of *low* pixels which eventually become *edge* pixels. The running time of this operation can be reduced to $O(\log m)$, using *distance doubling*.

Noise Estimation.   Estimating noise in the image can be done by analyzing a histogram of the gradient magnitudes. Most computational implementations of this step perform a global analysis of the gradient magnitude distribution, which is essentially non-local; we have had success with a Connection Machine implementation using local histograms. The thresholds used in Canny edge detection depend on the final task for which the edges are used. A conservative strategy can use an arbitrary low threshold to eliminate the need for the costly processing required to accumulate a histogram. Where a more precise estimate of noise is needed, it may be possible to find a scheme that uses a coarse estimate of the gradient magnitude distribution, with minimal global communication.

Stereo

The Drumheller-Poggio parallel stereo algorithm [Drumheller & Poggio 1986] runs as part of the Vision Machine. Disparity data produced by the algorithm comprise one of the inputs to the MRF-based integration stage of the Vision Machine. We are exploring various extensions of the algorithm, as well as the possible use of feedback from the integration stage. In this section, we will review the algorithm briefly, then proceed to a discussion of current research.

The stereo algorithm runs on the Connection Machine system with good results on natural scenes in times that are typically on the order of one second. The stereo algorithm is presently being extended in the context of the Vision Machine project.

◇ The Drumheller-Poggio stereo algorithm

Stereo matching is an ill-posed problem (see Bertero *et al.* [1988]) that cannot be solved without taking advantage of natural constraints. The *continuity constraint* (see, for instance, Marr and Poggio [1976]) asserts that the world consists primarily of piecewise smooth surfaces. If the scene contains no transparent objects, then the *uniqueness constraint* applies: there can be only one match along the left or right lines of sight. If there are no narrow occluding objects, the *ordering constraint* [Poggio & Yuille 1984] holds: any two points must be imaged in the same relative order in the left and right eyes.

The specific *a priori* assumption on which the algorithm is based is that the disparity, that is, the depth of the surface, is locally constant in a small region surrounding a pixel. It is a restrictive assumption which, however, may be a satisfactory *local* approximation in many cases (it can be extended to more general surface assumptions in a straightforward way, but at a high computational cost). Let $E_L(x, y)$ and $E_R(x, y)$ represent the left and the right image of a stereo pair, or some transformation of it, such as filtered images or a map of the zero-crossings in the two images (more generally, they can be maps containing a feature vector at each location (x, y) in the image).

We look for a discrete disparity $d(x, y)$ at each location x, y in the image that minimizes

$$\|E_L(x, y) - E_R(x + d(x, y), y)\|_{\text{patch}_i} \tag{1}$$

where the norm is a summation over a local neighborhood centered at each location (x, y); $d(x)$ is assumed constant in the neighborhood. The previous equation implies that we should look at each (x, y) for $d(x, y)$ such that

$$\int_{\text{patch}_i} (E_L(x, y) E_R(x + d(x, y), y))^2 dx dy \tag{2}$$

is maximized.

The algorithm that we have implemented on the Connection Machine is actually somewhat more complicated, because it involves geometric constraints that affect the way the maximum operation is performed (see Drumheller and Poggio [1986]). The implementation currently used in the Vision Machine at the Artificial Intelligence Laboratory uses the maps of Canny edges obtained from each image for E_L and E_R.

In more detail, the algorithm is composed of the following steps:

1   Compute features for matching.

2   Compute potential matches between features.

3   Determine the degree of continuity around each potential match.

4   Choose correct matches based on the constraints of continuity, uniqueness, and ordering.

Potential matches between features are computed in the following way. Assuming that the images are registered so that the epipolar lines are horizontal, the stereo matching problem becomes one-dimensional: an edge in the left image can match any of the edges in the corresponding horizontal scan line in the right image. Sliding the right image over the left image horizontally, we compute a set of *potential match planes*, one for each horizontal disparity. Let $p(x, y, d)$ denote the value of the (x, y) entry of the potential match plane at disparity d. We set $p(x, y, d) = 1$ if there is an edge at location (x, y) in the left image and a compatible edge at location $(x - d, y)$ in the right image; otherwise, set $p(x, y, d) = 0$. In the case of the DOG edge detector, two edges are compatible if the sign of the convolution for each edge is the same.

To determine the degree of continuity around each potential match (x, y, d), we compute a local support score $s(x, y, d) = \sum_{Patch} p(x, y, d)$, where *patch* is a small neighborhood of (x, y, d) within the dth potential match plane. In effect, nearby points in *patch* can "vote" for the disparity d. The score $s(x, y, d)$ will be high if the continuity constraint is satisfied near (x, y, d), that is, if *patch* contains many votes. This step corresponds to the integral over the patch in the last equation.

Finally, we attempt to select the correct matches by applying the uniqueness and ordering constraints (see above). To apply the uniqueness constraint, each match suppresses all other matches along the left and right lines of sight with weaker scores. To enforce the ordering constraint, if two matches are not imaged in the same relative order in left and right views, we discard the match with the smaller support score. In effect, each match suppresses matches with lower scores in its forbidden zone [Yuille & Poggio 1984]. This step corresponds to choosing the disparity value that maximizes the integral of the last equation.

◊ **Improvements**

Using this algorithm as a base, we have explored several of the following topics:

Detection of Depth Discontinuities.   The Marr-Poggio continuity constraint is both a strength and a weakness of the stereo algorithm. Favoring continuous disparity surfaces reduces the solution space tremendously, but also tends to smooth over depth discontinuities present in the scene. Consider what happens near a linear depth discontinuity, say a point near the edge of a table viewed from above. The square local support neighborhood for the point will be divided between points on the table and points on the floor; thus, almost half of the votes will be for the wrong disparity.

One solution to this problem is feedback from the MRF integration stage. We can take the depth discontinuities located by the integration stage (using the results from a first pass of the stereo algorithm, among other inputs) and use them to restrict the local support neighborhoods so that they do not span discontinuities. In the example mentioned above, the support neighborhood would be trimmed to avoid crossing the discontinuity between the table and the floor, and thus would not pick up spurious votes from the floor.

We can also try to locate discontinuities by examining intermediate results of the stereo algorithm. Consider a histogram of votes versus disparity for the table/floor example. For a support region centered near the edge of the table, we expect to see two strong peaks: one at the disparity of the floor, and the other at the disparity of the table. Therefore a bimodal histogram is strong evidence for the presence of a discontinuity.

These two ideas can be used in conjunction. Discontinuity detection within stereo can take advantage of the extra information provided by the vote histograms. By passing better depth data (and perhaps candidate discontinuity locations) to the integration stage, we improve the detection of discontinuities at the higher level.

Improving the Stereo Matcher.   The original Drumheller-Poggio algorithm matched DOG zero-crossings, where the local support score counted the number of zero-crossings in the left image patch matching edges in the right image patch at a given disparity. We have modified the matcher in a variety of ways.

1   Canny edges. The matcher now uses edges derived by a parallel implementation of the Canny edge detector [Canny 1983; Little *et al.* 1987] rather than DOG zero-crossings, for better localization.

2   Gradient direction constraint. We allow two Canny edges to match only if the associated brightness gradient directions are aligned within

a parameterized tolerance. This is analogous to the restriction in the Marr-Poggio-Grimson stereo algorithm [Grimson 1981] where two zero-crossings can match only if the directions of the DOG gradients are approximately equal. Matching gradient orientations is a tighter constraint than matching the sign of the DOG convolution. Furthermore, the DOG sign is numerically unstable for horizontally oriented edges.

3   The scores are now normalized to take into account the number of edges in the left and right image patches eligible to match, so that patches with high edge densities do not generate artificially high scores. We plan to change the matcher so that edges that fail to match would count as negative evidence by reducing the support score, but this has not yet been implemented.

In the near future, we will explore matching brightness values as well as edges, using a cross-correlation approach similar to that of Little, for motion estimation.

Identifying Areas that are Outside of the Matcher's Disparity Range. The stereo algorithm searches a limited disparity range, selected manually. Every potential match in the scene (an edge with a matching edge at some disparity) is assigned the in-range disparity with the highest score, even though the correct disparity may be out of range. How can we tell when an area of the scene is out of range? The most effective approach that we have attempted to date is to look for regions with low matching scores. Two patches that are incorrectly matched will, in general, produce a low matching score.

◊ **Memory-based registration and calibration**

Registration of the image pair for the stereo algorithm is done by presenting to the system a pattern of dots, roughly on a sparse grid, at the distance around which stereo has to operate. The registration is accomplished using a warping computed by matching the dots from the left and right images. The dots are sparse enough that matching is unambiguous. The matching defines a warping vector for each dot; at other points the warping is computed by bilinear interpolation of the two components of warping vectors. The warping necessary for mapping the right image onto the left image is then stored. Prior to stereo-matching, the right image is warped according to the pre-stored addresses by sending each pixel in the right image to the processor specified in the table.

     The warping table corrects for deformations, including those due to vertical disparities and rotations, those due to the image geometry (errors in the alignment of the cameras, perspective projection, errors introduced by the optics, etc.) We plan to store several warping tables for each of a few convergence angles of the two cameras (assuming symmetric convergence). We conjecture that simple interpolation can yield sufficiently accurate warping tables for fixation angles intermediate to the ones stored. Note that these tables are independent of the position of the head. Absolute depth is not the concern here (we are not using it in our present Vision Machine), but it could easily be recovered from knowledge of the convergence angle. Note also that the whole registration scheme has the flavor of a learning process. Convergence angles are inputs and warping tables are the outputs of the modules; the set of angles, together with the associated warping tables, represent the set of input-output examples. The system can "generalize" by interpolating between warping tables and providing the warping corresponding to a vergence angle that does not appear in the set of "examples." Calibration of disparity to depth could be done in a similar way.

Motion

The motion algorithm [Bülthoff *et al.* 1989] computes the optical flow field, a vector field that approximates the projected motion field. The procedure produces sparse or dense output, depending on whether it uses edge features or intensities. The algorithm assumes that image displacements are small, within a range $(\pm\delta, \pm\delta)$. It is also assumed that the optical flow is locally constant in a small region surrounding a point. This assumption is strictly only true for translational motion of 3D planar surface patches parallel to the image plane. It is a restrictive assumption which, however, may be a satisfactory *local* approximation in many cases. Let $E_t(x, y)$ and $E_{t+\Delta t}(x, y)$ represent transformations of two discrete images separated by time interval Δt, such as filtered images, or a map of the brightness changes in the two images (more generally, they can be maps containing a feature vector at each location (x, y) in the image) [Kass 1986; Nishihara 1984].

We look for a discrete motion displacement $\underline{v} = (v_x, v_y)$ at each location x, y in the image that minimizes

$$\|E_t(x, y) - E_{t+\Delta t}(x + v_x\Delta t, y + v_y\Delta t)\|_{\text{patch}_i} = \min \qquad (3)$$

where the norm is a summation over a local neighborhood centered at each location (x, y); $\underline{v}(x, y)$ is assumed constant in the neighborhood. The previous equation implies that we should look at each (x, y) for $\underline{v} = (v_x, v_y)$ such that

$$\int_{\text{patch}_i} (E_t(x, y) - E_{t+\Delta t}(x + v_x\Delta t, y + v_y\Delta t))^2 dx dy \qquad (4)$$

is minimized. Alternatively, one can maximize the negative of the integrated result. The last equation represents the sum of the pointwise squared differences between a patch in the first image centered around the location (x, y) and a patch in the second image centered around the location $(x + v_x \Delta t, y + v_y \Delta t)$.

This algorithm can be translated easily into the following description. Consider a network of processors representing the result of the integrand in the previous expression. Assume for simplicity that this result is either 0 or 1 (this is the case if E_t and $E_{t+\Delta t}$ are binary feature maps). The processors hold the result of differencing (taking the logical "exclusive or") the right and left image map for different values of (x, y) and v_x, v_y. The next stage, corresponding exactly to the integral operation over the patch, is for each processor to summate the total in an (x, y) neighborhood at the same disparity. Note that this summation operation is efficiently implemented on the Connection Machine using *scan* computations. Each processor thus collects a vote indicating support that a patch of surface exists at that displacement. The algorithm iterates over all displacements in the range $(\pm \delta, \pm \delta)$, recording the values of the integral for each displacement. The last stage is to choose $\underline{v}(x, y)$ among the displacements in the allowed range that maximizes the integral. This is done by an operation of "non-maximum suppression" across velocities out of the finite allowed set: at the given (x, y), the processor is found that has the maximum vote. The corresponding $\underline{v}(x, y)$ is the velocity of the surface patch found by the algorithm. The actual implementation of this scheme can be simplified so that the "non-maximum suppression" occurs during iteration over displacements, so that no actual table of summed differences over displacements need be constructed. In practice, the algorithm has been shown to be effective both for synthetic and natural images using different types of features or measurements on the brightness data, including edges (both zero-crossings of the Laplacian of Gaussian and Canny's method), which generate sparse results along brightness edges, or brightness data directly, or the Laplacian of Gaussian, or its sign, which generate dense results. Because the optical flow is computed from quantities integrated over the individual patches, the results are robust against the effects of uncorrelated noise.

The comparison stage employs patchwise cross-correlation, which exploits local constancy of the optical flow (the velocity field is guaranteed to be constant for translations parallel to the image plane of a planar surface patch); it is a cubic polynomial for arbitrary motion of a planar surface (see Waxman [1987], and Little *et al.* [1987]). Experimentally, we have used zero-crossings, the Laplacian of Gaussian filtered image, its sign, and the smoothed brightness values, with similar results. It is interesting that methods *superficially* so different (edge-based and intensity-based) give such similar results. As we mentioned earlier, this is not surprising. There are theoretical arguments that support, for instance, the equivalence of cross-correlating the sign bit of the Laplacian filtered image and the Laplacian filtered image itself. The argument is based on the following theorem, which is a slight reformulation of a well-known theorem.

Theorem. If $f(x, y)$ and $g(x, y)$ are zero mean jointly normal processes, their cross-correlation is determined fully by the correlation of the sign of f and of the sign of g (and determines it). In particular

$$R_{\tilde{f}, \tilde{g}} = \frac{2}{\pi} arcsin(R_{f,g})$$

where $\tilde{f} = sign\ f$ and $\tilde{g} = sign\ g$.

Thus, cross-correlation of the sign bit is exactly equivalent to cross-correlation of the signal itself (for Gaussian processes). Note that from the point of view of information, the sign bit of the signal is completely equivalent to the zero-crossing of the signal. Nishihara [1984] first used patchwise cross-correlation of the sign bit of DOG filtered images, and has implemented it more recently on real-time hardware [Nishihara & Crossley 1988].

The existence of discontinuities can be detected in optical flow, as in stereo, both during computation and by processing the resulting flow field. The latter field is input to the MRF integration stage. During computation, discontinuities in optical flow arising from occlusions are indicated by low normalized scores for the chosen displacement.

Color

The color algorithm that we have implemented is a very preliminary version of a module that should find the boundaries in the surface spectral reflectance function, that is, discontinuities in the surface color. The algorithm relies on the idea of *effective illumination* and on the *single source* assumption, both introduced by Hurlbert and Poggio.

The single source assumption states that the illumination may be separated into two components, one dependent only on wavelength, and one dependent only on spatial coordinates; this generally holds for illumination from a single light source. It allows us to write the image irradiance equation for a Lambertian world as

$$I^\nu = k^\nu E(x, y) \rho^\nu(x, y) \tag{5}$$

where I^ν is the image irradiance in the νth spectral channel ($\nu = red,$ *green, blue*), $\rho^\nu(x, y)$ is the surface spectral reflectance (or albedo), and the effective illumination $E(x, y)$ absorbs the spatial variations of the illumination and the shading due to the 3D shape of surfaces (k^ν is a constant for each channel, and depends only on the luminant). A simple segmentation algorithm is then obtained by considering the equation

$$H(x, y) = \frac{I^r}{I^r + I^g} = \frac{k^r\ \rho^r}{k^r \rho^r\ +\ k^g \rho^g} \tag{6}$$

which changes only when ρ^r, or ρ^g, or both change. Thus H, which is piecewise constant, has discontinuities that mark changes in the surface albedo, independently of changes in the effective illumination.

The quantity $H(x, y)$ is defined almost everywhere, but is typically noisy. To counter the effect of noise, we exploit the prior information that H should be piecewise constant with discontinuities that are themselves continuous, non-intersecting lines. As we will discuss later, this restoration step is achieved by using a MRF model. This algorithm works only under the restrictive assumption that specular reflections can be neglected. Hurlbert [1989] discusses in more detail the scheme outlined here and how it can be extended to more general conditions.

Texture

The texture algorithm is a greatly simplified parallel version of the texture algorithm developed by Voorhees and Poggio [1987]. Texture is a scalar measure computed by summation of texton densities over small regions surrounding every point. Discontinuities in this measure can correspond to occlusion boundaries, or orientation discontinuities, which cause foreshortening. Textons are computed in the image by simple approximation to the methods presented in Voorhees and Poggio [1987]. For this example, the textons are restricted to blob-like regions, without regard to orientation selection.

To compute textons, the image is first filtered by a Laplacian of Gaussian filter at several different scales. The smallest scale selects the textural elements. The Laplacian of Gaussian image is then thresholded at a non-zero value to find the regions which comprise the blobs identified by the textons. The result is a binary image with non-zero values only in the areas of the blobs. A simple summation counts the density of blobs (the portion of the summation region covered by blobs) in a small area surrounding each point. This operation effectively measures the density of blobs at the small scale, while also counting the presence of blobs caused by large occlusion edges at the boundaries of textured regions. Contrast boundaries appear as blobs in the Laplacian of Gaussian image. To remove their effect, we use the Laplacian of Gaussian image at a slightly coarser scale. Blobs caused by the texture at the fine scale do not appear at this coarser scale, while the contrast boundaries, as well as all other blobs at coarser scales, remain. This coarse blob image filters the fine blobs; blobs at the coarser scale are removed from the fine scale image. Then, summation, whether with a simple scan operation, or Gaussian filtering, can determine the blob density at the fine scale only. This is one example where multiple spatial scales are used in the present implementation of the Vision Machine.

The integration stage and MRF

Whereas it is reasonable that combining the evidence provided by multiple cues (for example, edge detection, stereo, and color) should provide a more reliable map of the surfaces than any single cue alone, it is not obvious how this integration can be accomplished. The various physical processes that contribute to image formation, *surface depth, surface orientation, albedo* (Lambertian and specular component), *illumination*, are coupled to the image data, and therefore to each other, through the imaging equation. The coupling is, however, difficult to exploit in a robust way, because it depends critically on the reflectance and imaging models. We argue that the coupling of the image data to the surface and illumination properties is of a more qualitative and robust sort at locations in which image brightness changes sharply and surface properties are discontinuous, in short, at edges. The intuitive reason for this is that at discontinuities, the coupling between different physical processes and the image data is robust and qualitative. For instance, a depth discontinuity usually originates a brightness edge in the image, and a motion boundary often corresponds to a depth discontinuity (and an brightness edge) in the image. This view suggests the following integration scheme for restoring the data provided by early modules. The results provided by stereo, motion, and other visual cues are typically noisy and sparse. We can improve them by exploiting the fact that they should be smooth, or even piecewise constant (as in the case of the albedo), between discontinuities. We can exploit *a priori* information about generic properties of the discontinuities themselves, for instance, that they usually are continuous and non-intersecting.

The idea, is then, to detect discontinuities in each cue, for instance depth, simultaneously with the approximation of the depth data. The detection of discontinuities is helped by information on the presence and type of discontinuities in the surfaces and surface properties (see figure 1), which are coupled to the brightness edges in the image.

Note that reliable detection of discontinuities is critical for a vision system, because discontinuities are often the most important locations in a scene; depth discontinuities, for example, normally correspond to the boundaries of an object or an object part. The idea is thus to couple different cues through their discontinuities and to use information from several cues simultaneously to help refine the initial estimation of discontinuities, which are typically noisy and sparse.

How can this be done? We have chosen to use the machinery of Markov Random Fields (MRFs), initially suggested for image processing by Geman and Geman [1984]. In the following section, we will give a brief, informal outline of the technique and of our integration scheme. More detailed information about MRFs can be found in Geman and Geman [1984] and Marroquin [1987]. Gamble and Poggio [1987] describe an earlier version of our integration scheme and its implementation as outlined in the next section.

◇ MRF models

Consider the prototypical problem of approximating a surface given sparse and noisy data (depth data) on a regular 2D lattice of sites. We first define the prior probability of the class of surfaces we are interested in. The probability of a certain depth at any given site in the lattice depends only upon neighboring sites (the Markov property). Because of the Clifford-Hammersley theorem, the prior probability is guaranteed to have the Gibbs form

$$P(f) = \frac{1}{Z} e^{-\frac{U(f)}{T}} \tag{7}$$

where Z is a normalization constant, T is called temperature, and $U(f) = \sum_C U_C(f)$ is an energy function that can be computed as the sum of local contributions from each neighborhood. The sum of the *potentials*, $U_C(X)$, is over the neighborhood's *cliques*. A clique is either a single lattice site or a set of lattice sites such that any two sites belonging to it are neighbors of one another. Thus $U(f)$ can be considered as the sum over the possible configurations of each neighborhood (see Marroquin [1987]). As a simple example, when the surfaces are expected to be smooth, the prior probability can be given as sums of terms such as

$$U_c(f) = (f_i - f_j)^2 \tag{8}$$

where i and j are neighboring sites (belonging to the same clique).

If a model of the observation process is available (that is, a model of the noise), then one can write the conditional probability $P(g/f)$ of the sparse observation g for any given surface f. Bayes Theorem then allows one to write the posterior distribution

$$P(f/g) = \frac{1}{Z} e^{\frac{-U(f/g)}{T}} \tag{9}$$

In the simple earlier example, we have (for Gaussian noise)

$$U(f/g) = \sum_C \alpha \gamma_i (f_i - g_i)^2 + (f_i - f_j)^2 \tag{10}$$

where $\gamma_i = 1$ only where data are available. More complicated cases can be handled in a similar manner.

The posterior distribution cannot be solved analytically, but sample distributions can be obtained using Monte Carlo techniques such as the Metropolis algorithm. These algorithms sample the space of possible surfaces according to the probability distribution $P(f/g)$ that is determined by the prior knowledge of the allowed class of surfaces, the model of noise, and the observed data. In our implementation, a highly parallel computer generates a sequence of surfaces from which, for instance, the surface corresponding to the maximum of $P(f/g)$ can be found. This corresponds to finding the global minimum of $U(f/g)$ (simulated annealing is one of the possible techniques). Other criteria can be used: Marroquin [1985] has shown that the average surface f under the posterior distribution is often a better estimate, and one which can be obtained more efficiently by simply finding the average value of f at each lattice site.

One of the main attractions of MRFs is that the prior probability distribution can be made to embed more sophisticated assumptions about the world. Geman and Geman [1984] introduced the idea of another process, the line process, located on the dual lattice, and representing explicitly the presence or absence of discontinuities that break the smoothness assumption. The associated prior energy then becomes

$$U_C(f) = (f_i - f_j)^2(1 - l_i^j) + \beta V_C(l_i^j) \tag{11}$$

where l is a binary line element between site i, j. V_C is a term that reflects the fact that certain configurations of the line process are more likely than others to occur. In our world, depth discontinuities are usually themselves continuous, non-intersecting, and rarely isolated joints. These properties of physical discontinuities can be enforced locally by defining an appropriate set of energy values $V_C(l)$ for different configurations of the line process in the neighborhood of the site (note that the assignment of zero energy values to the non-central cliques mentioned in Gamble and Poggio [1987] is wrong, as pointed out to us by Tal Symchony).

◇ Organization of integration

It is possible to extend the energy function of Equation (5) to accommodate the interaction of more processes and their discontinuities. In particular, we have extended the energy function to couple several of the early vision modules (depth, motion, texture, and color) to brightness edges in the image. This is a central point in our integration scheme; brightness edges guide the computation of discontinuities in the physical properties of the surface, thereby coupling surface depth, surface orientation, motion, texture, and color, each to the image brightness data and to each other. The reason for the role of brightness edges is that changes in surface properties usually produce large brightness gradients in the image. It is exactly for this reason that edge detection is so important in both artificial and biological vision.

The coupling to brightness edges may be done by replacing the term $V_C(l_i^j)$ in the last equation with the term

$$V(l, e) = g(e_i^j, V_C(l_i^j)) \tag{12}$$

with e_i^j representing a measure of the presence of an brightness edge between site i, j. The term g has the effect of modifying the probability

of the line process configuration depending on the brightness edge data
($V(l, e) = -log \ p(l/e)$). This term facilitates formation of discontinuities
(that is, l_i^j) at the locations of brightness edges. Ideally, the brightness
edges (and the neighboring image properties) activate, with different prob-
abilities, the different surface discontinuities (see figure 1), which in turn
are coupled to the output of stereo, motion, color, texture, and possibly
other early algorithms.

We have been using the MRF machinery with prior energies like that
shown above (see also figure 1) to integrate edge brightness data with
stereo, motion, and texture information on the MIT Vision Machine System.

We should emphasize that our present implementation represents a
subset of the possible interactions shown in figure 1, itself only a simplified
version of the organization of the likely integration process. The system will
be improved in an incremental fashion, including pathways not shown in
figure 1, such as feedback from the results of integration into the matching
stage of the stereo and motion algorithms. Examples can be found in
Poggio, Gamble and Little [1988] and in Poggio and The Staff [1987].

◇ Algorithms: Deterministic and stochastic

We have chosen to use MRF models because of their generality and theoretical attractiveness. This does not imply that stochastic algorithm must
be used. For instance, in the cases in which the MRF model reduces to
standard regularization [Marroquin 1987] and the data are given on a regular grid, the MRF formulation leads not only to a purely deterministic
algorithm, but also to a convolution filter. Recent work in color [Hurlbert
& Poggio 1989] shows that one can perform integration similar to the MRF-
based scheme using a deterministic update. Geiger and Girosi [1989] have
shown that there is a class of deterministic schemes that are the mean-field
approximations of the MRF models. These schemes have a much higher
speed than the Montecarlo schemes we used so far, while promising similar
performance.

Recognition

The output of the integration stage provides a set of edges labeled in terms
of physical discontinuities of the surface properties. They represent a good
input to a model-based recognition algorithm like the ones described by
Huttenlocher and Cass [1988]. In particular, we have interfaced the Vision
Machine as implemented so far with the Cass algorithm. We have used
only discontinuities for recognition; later we will also use the information
provided by the MRFs on the surface properties *between* discontinuities.

We have more ambitious goals for the recognition stage of the Vision Machine. In an unconstrained environment the library of models that a system with human-level performance requires is in the order of many thousands. Thus, the ability to learn from examples appears to be essential for the achievement of high performance in real-world recognition tasks. Learning the models becomes then a primary concern in developing a recognition system for the Vision Machine. This has not been the case in other approaches of the last few years, mainly motivated by a robotic framework.

Learning in a three-stage recognition scheme

Although some of the existing recognition systems incorporate a module for learning object models from examples (for example Tucker's 2D system [Tucker *et al.* 1988]) no such capability exists yet for the more difficult problems of recognizing 3D objects [Huttenlocher & Ullman 1987] or handwriting [Edelman & Ullman to appear 1990]. We believe that incorporating learning into a general-purpose recognition system may be facilitated by breaking down the task of recognition into three distinct but interacting stages: *selection, indexing,* and *verification.*

Selection.   Selection or segmentation breaks down the image into regions that are likely to correspond to single objects. The utility of an early segmentation of a scene into meaningful entities lies in the great reduction of complexity of scene interpretation. Each of the detected objects can in turn be subjected to separate recognition, by comparing it with object models stored in memory. Without prior segmentation, every possible combination of image primitives such as lines and blobs can in principle constitute an object and must be checked out. The power of early segmentation may be enhanced by integrating all available visual cues, especially if the integration parameters are automatically adjusted to suit the particular scene in question.

Indexing.   By indexing we mean defining a small set of candidate objects that are likely to be present in the image. Although one cannot hope to achieve an ideal segmentation in real-world situations, partial success is sufficient if the indexing process is robust. Assuming that most objects in the real world are redundantly specified by their local features, a good indexing mechanism would use such features to overcome changes in viewpoint and illumination, occlusion and noise.

What kind of feature is good for indexing? Reliably detected lines provided by the integration of several low-level cues in the process of segmentation may suffice in many cases. We conjecture that *simple* viewpoint-invariant combinations of primitive elements, such as two lines forming a corner, parallel lines, and symmetry are also likely to be useful. Ideally, only 2D information should be used for indexing, although it may be augmented sometimes by qualitative 3D cues such as relative depth.

Verification.   In the verification stage each of the candidates screened by the indexing process is tested to find the best match to the image. At this stage, the system can afford to perform complicated tests, because the number of candidate objects is small. We conjecture that hierarchical indexing by a small number (two or three) features that are spatially localized in 2D suffices to achieve useful interpretations of most everyday scenes. In general, however, further verification by model dependent routines (if it is a Mercedes it must have a three joint star in front) or precise shape matching, possibly involving 3D information, is required [Ullman 1884; Lowe 1986; Huttenlocher & Ullman 1987; Bolles *et al.* 1983; Ayache & Faugeras 1986; Tucker *et al.* 1988].

Future Developments

The Vision Machine will evolve in several parallel directions:

- Improvement and extensions of its early modules
- Improvement of the integration and recognition stages (recognition is discussed later)
- Use of the eye-head system in an active mode during recognition task by developing appropriate gaze strategies
- Use of the results of the integration stage in order to improve the operation of early modules such as stereo and motion by feeding back the preliminary computation of the discontinuities

Two goals will occupy most of our attention. The first one is the development of the overall organization of the Vision Machine. The system can be seen as an implementation of the *inverse optics* paradigm: it attempts to extract surface properties from the integration of image cues. It must be stressed that we never intended this framework to imply that precise surface properties such as dense, high resolution depth maps, must be delivered by the system. This extreme interpretation of inverse optics seems to be common, but was not the motivation of our project, which originally started with the name *Coarse Vision Machine* to emphasize the importance of computing qualitative, as opposed to very precise, properties of the environment.

Our second main goal in the Vision machine project will be Machine Learning. In particular, we have begun to explore simple learning and estimation techniques for vision tasks. We have succeeded in synthesizing a color algorithm from examples [Hurlbert & Poggio 1987] and in developing a technique to perform unsupervised learning [Sanger 1988] of other simple vision algorithms such as simple versions of the computation of texture and stereo. In addition, we have used learning techniques to perform integration tasks, such as labeling the type of discontinuities in a scene. We have also begun to explore the connections between recent approaches to learning, such as neural networks, genetic algorithms, and classical methods in approximation theory such as splines, Bayesian techniques, and Markov Random Field models. We have identified some common properties of all these approaches and some of the common limitations, such as sample complexity. As a consequence, we now believe that we can leverage our expertise in approximation techniques for the problem of learning in machine vision. Our future theoretical and computational studies will examine available learning techniques, their properties and limitations and develop new ones for the tasks of early vision, for the integration stage and for object recognition. The algorithms will be tested with the Vision Machine system and eventually incorporated into it. We will also pay attention to parallel network implementations of these algorithms: for this subgoal we will be able to leverage the work we are now doing in developing analog VLSI networks for several of the components of the Vision Machine. Towards the goal of achieving much higher flexibility in the Vision Machine we propose to explore (a) the synthesis of vision algorithms from a set of instances and (b) the refinement and tuning of preprogrammed algorithms, such as edge detection, texture discrimination, motion, color and calibration for stereo. We will also develop techniques to estimate parameters of the integration stage. Much of our effort will be focused on the new scheme for visual recognition of 3D objects, whose key component is the automatic learning of a large database of models. We aim to develop a prototype of a flexible vision system that can, in a limited way, learn from experience.

In the following, we outline some of the other directions of future development.

Labeling the physical origin of edges: Computing qualitative surface attributes

◇ Physical discontinuities

We classify edges according to the following physical events: discontinuities in surface properties, called *mark* or *albedo* edges (for example, changes in the color of the surface); discontinuities in the orientation of the surface patch, called *orientation* edges (for example, an edge in a polyhedron); discontinuities in the illumination, called *shadow* edges; *occluding boundaries*, which are discontinuities in the object space (a different object); and *specular* discontinuities, which exist for non-Lambertian objects.

◊ Integration via labeling with a linear classifier

Gamble, Geiger, Weinshall and Poggio have implemented a part of the general scheme. More specifically, they have used a simple linear classifier to label edges at pixels where there exists an intensity discontinuity, using the output of the line process associated with each low-level vision module. They use the fact that the modules' discontinuities are aligned, having being integrated with the intensity edges before, so that the nonexistence of a module discontinuity at a pixel is meaningful. The linear classifier corresponds to a linear network where each output unit is a weighted linear combination of its inputs (for a similar application to a problem of color vision, see Hurlbert and Poggio [1987]). The input to the network is a pixel where there exists an intensity edge and that feeds a set of qualitatively different input units. The output is a real value vector of each labels' support.

In the system we have so far implemented, we achieve a rather restricted integration, because each module is integrated only with the intensity module, and labeling is done via a simple linear classifier only. It is still unclear how successful labeling can be, using only local information.

Saliency, grouping, and segmentation

A grouping and segmentation module working on the output of the edge detection module is an important part of a vision system: humans can deal with monocular, still, black and white pictures devoid of stereo, motion and color. We are now developing techniques to find salient edges, to group them and thereby segment the image. These algorithms have not been integrated yet in the Vision Machine system.

◊ Saliency measure

Edge maps produced by most current edge detectors are cluttered with edge responses and may have edges caused by noise. This creates difficulties for higher level processing, because the combinatorics of these algorithms often depends on the number of edge primitives being examined. What is needed is a technique to focus attention on the "important" edges in a scene. We call such attention focusing techniques that measure the "importance" of an edge saliency measures. Shimon Ullman [Ullman & Sha'ashua 1988] has proposed two different kinds of saliency measures: local saliency and structural saliency. An edge's local saliency is entirely determined by features of that edge alone. For example, an edge's length, its average gradient magnitude, or the color of a bounding region serve as local saliency measures.

Structural saliency refers to more global properties of an edge—its relationships with other edges. Although two edges may not be locally salient, if there is a "nonaccidental" relationship between them, then the structure becomes salient. Examples of "nonaccidental" relationships, as pointed out by David Lowe, include collinearity, parallelism, and symmetry, among other things.

We have investigated local saliency measures applied to the output of the Canny edge detector [Beymer 1989]. The edge features we have considered include curvature, edge length, and gradient magnitude. The measure favors those edges that have low average curvature, long length, and a high gradient magnitude. The saliency measure eliminates many of the edges due to noise and many of the unimportant edges. The edges that remain are often the long, smooth boundaries of objects and significant intensity changes inside the objects. We expect that the salient edges will help higher level processes such as grouping (structural saliency) and model based recognition by allowing them to focus attention on regions of an image bounded by salient edges.

◊ T junctions: Their detection and use in grouping

In cluttered imagery, imagery containing many objects occluding one another, it is important to group together pieces of the image that come from the same object. In particular, given an edge map produced by the Canny edge detector, we would like to select and group together the edges from a particular object before running high level recognition algorithms on the edge data. This grouping stage helps reduce the combinatorics of the higher level stages, as they are not forced to consider false edge groupings as objects. Considering how occlusion cues can be used in grouping, we have investigated the detection of T junctions and grouping rules arising from the pairing of T junctions. When one object partially occludes another in a cluttered scene, a T junction is formed between the two objects. Beymer has developed algorithms for detecting T junctions as a postprocessing step to the Canny edge detector. The Canny edge detector, while very good at detecting edges, is particularly bad at detecting junctions. Indeed, it was designed to detect one dimensional events. This one dimensional characterization of the image breaks down at junctions because locally there are three or more surfaces in the image. We have investigated how one could use edge curvature and region properties of the image to reconstruct these "broken" junctions. Often the way Canny will fail at junctions is that one of the three curves belonging to the junction will be broken off from the other two. We have modified an existing algorithm and achieved promising results in restoring broken T junctions.

Fast vision: The role of time smoothness

The present version of the Vision Machine processes only isolated frames. Even our motion algorithm takes as input simply a sequence of two images. The reason for this is, of course, limitations in raw speed. We cannot perform all of the processing we do at video rate (say, 30 frames per second), though this goal is certainly within present technological capabilities. If we could process frames at video rate, we could exploit constraints in the time dimension similar to the ones we are already exploiting in the space domain. Surfaces, and even the brightness array itself, do not usually change too much from frame to frame. This is a constraint of smoothness in time, which is valid almost everywhere, but not *across* discontinuities in time. Thus one may use the same MRF technique, applied to the output of stereo, motion, color, and texture, and enforce continuity in time (if there are no discontinuities), that is, exploit the redundancy in the sequence of frames.

We believe that the surface reconstructed from a stereo pair usually does not need to be recomputed completely when the next stereo pair is taken a fraction of a second later. Of course, the role of the MRFs may be accomplished in this case by some more specific and more efficient deterministic method such as, for example, a form of Kalman filtering. Note that space-time MRFs applied to the brightness arrays would yield spatiotemporal interpolation and approximation of a kind already considered [Fahle & Poggio 1980; Poggio, Nielsen & Nishihara 1982; Bliss 1985].

A VLSI Vision Machine?

Our Vision Machine consists mostly of specialized software running on the Connection Machine. This is a good system for the present stage of experimentation and development. Later, once we have perfected and tested the algorithms and the overall system, it will make sense to compile the software into silicon in order to produce a faster, cheaper, and smaller Vision Machine. We are presently planning to use VLSI technologies to develop some initial chips as a first step toward this goal. In this section, we will outline some thoughts about VLSI implementation of the Vision Machine.

Algorithms and Hardware.   We realize that our specialized software vision algorithms are not, in general, optimized for hardware implementation. So, rather than directly "hardwiring algorithms" into standard computing circuitry, we will be investigating "algorithmic hardware" designs that utilize the local, symmetric nature of early vision problems. This will be an iterative process, as the algorithm influences the hardware design and as hardware constraints modify the algorithm.

Degree of Parallelism. Typical vision tasks require tremendous amounts of computing power, and are usually parallel in nature. As an example, biological vision uses highly parallel networks of relatively slow components to achieve sophisticated systems. However, when implementing our algorithms in silicon integrated circuits, it is not clear what level of parallelism is necessary. While biology is able to use three dimensions to construct highly interconnected parallel networks, VLSI is limited to $2\frac{1}{2}$ dimensions, making highly parallel networks much more difficult and costly to implement. However, the electrical components of silicon integrated circuits are approximately four orders of magnitude faster than the electrochemical components of biology. This suggests that pipelined processing or other methods of time-sharing computing power may be able to compensate for the lower degree of connectivity of silicon VLSI. Clearly, the architecture of a VLSI vision system may not resemble any biological vision systems.

Signal Representation. Within the integrated circuit, the image data may be represented as a digital word or an analog value. While the advantages of digital computation are its accuracy and speed, digital circuits do not have as high a degree of functionality per device as analog circuits. Therefore, analog circuits should allow much denser computing networks. This is particularly important for the integration of computational circuitry and photosensors, which will help to alleviate the I/O bottleneck typically experienced whenever image data are serially transferred between Vision Machine components. However, analog circuits are limited in accuracy, and are difficult to characterize and design.

Learning and parameter estimation

Using the MRF model involves an energy function which has several free parameters, in addition to the many possible neighborhood systems. The values of these parameters determine a distribution over the configuration-space to which the system converges, and the speed of convergence. Thus rigorous methods for estimating these parameters are essential for the practical success of the method and for meaningful results. In some cases, parameters can be learned from the data: for example, texture parameters [Geman & Graffigne 1987], or neighborhood parameters (for which a cellular automaton model may be the most convenient for the purpose of learning). There are general statistical methods which can be used for parameter estimation:

- A maximum likelihood estimate—one can use the indirect iterative EM algorithm [Dempster *et al.* 1977], which is most useful for maximum likelihood estimation from incomplete data (see Marroquin [1987] for a special case). This algorithm involves the iterative maximization (over the parameter space) of the expected value of the likelihood function given that the parameters take the values of their estimation in the previous iteration. Alternatively, a search constrained by some statistics for a minimum of an appropriate merit function may be employed (see Marroquin [1987]).

- A smoothing (regularization) parameter can be estimated using the methods of cross-validation or unbiased risk, to minimize the mean square error. In cross-validation, an estimate is obtained omitting one data point. The goal is to minimize the distance between the predicted data point (from the estimate above with the point omitted) and the actual value, for all points.

In the case of Markov Random Fields, some more specific approaches are appropriate for parameter estimation:

- Besag [1972] suggested conditional maximum likelihood estimation using coding methods, maximum likelihood estimation with unilateral approximations on the rectangular lattice, or "maximum pseudolikelihood"—a method to estimate parameters for homogeneous random fields (see Geman and Graffigne [1987]).
- For the MPM estimator, where a fixed temperature is yet another parameter to be estimated, one can try to use the physics behind the model to find a temperature with as little disorder as possible and still reasonable time of convergence to equilibrium (for example, away from "phase-transition").

An alternative asymptotic approach can be used with smoothing (regularization) terms: instead of estimating the smoothing parameter, let it tend to 0 as the temperature tends to 0, to reduce the smoothing close to the final configuration (see Geman and Geman [1987]).

In summary, we plan to explore three distinct stages for parameter estimation in the integration stage of the Vision Machine:

- **Modeling** from the physics of surfaces, of the imaging process and of the class of scenes to be analyzed and the tasks to be performed The range of allowed parameter values may also be established at this stage (for example, minimum and maximum brightness value in a scene, depth differences, positivity of certain measurements, distribution of expected velocities, reflectance properties, characteristics of the illuminant, etc.).
- **Estimating** of parameter values from a set of examples in which data and desired solution are given. This is a *learning stage*. We may have to use days of CM time and, at least initially, synthetic images to do this.
- **Tuning** of some of the parameters directly from the data (by using EM algorithm, cross-validation, Besag's work, or various types of heuristics).

The dream is that at some point in the future the Vision Machine will run all the time, day and night, looking about and learning on its own to see better and better.

References

Barrow, H. G., and J. M. Tenenbaum [1978], "Recovering Intrinsic Scene Characteristics from Images," in *Computer Vision Systems*, edited by A. Hanson, and E. Riseman, Academic Press, New York.

Bertero, M., T. Poggio, and V. Torre [1988], "Ill-Posed Problems in Early Vision," Report AIM-924 Artificial Intelligence Laboratory , Massachusetts Institute of Technology, Cambridge, MA.

Besag, J. [1972], "Spatial Interaction and the Statistical Analysis of Lattice systems," *J. Roy. Stat. Soc.*, vol. B34, pp. 75-83.

Beymer, David [1989], "Junctions: their detection and use for grouping in images," Massachusetts Institute of Technology, (in press).

Blake, A [1986], "On the Geometric Information Obtainable from Simultaneous Observation of Stereo Contour and Shading," Technical Report CSR-205-86, Dept. of Computer Science, University of Edinburgh.

Blelloch, G. E. [1987], "Scans as Primitive Parallel Operations," *Proc. Intl. Conf. on Parallel Processing*, pp. 355-362.

Bliss, J. [1985] "Velocity Tuned Spatio-Temporal Interpolation and Approximation in Vision," M.S. Thesis, Department of Electrical Engineering and Computer Science, Massachusetts Institute of Technology, Cambridge, MA.

Brooks, R. [1987], "A Robust Layered Control System for a Mobile Robot," *IEEE Journal of Robotics and Automation*, vol. RA-2, pp. 14-23.

Bülthoff H., and H. Mallot [1987], "Interaction of Different Modules in Depth Perception," *Proc. First Intl. Conf. on Computer Vision*, Computer Society of the IEEE, Washington, DC, pp. 295-305.

Bülthoff, H., and H. Mallot [1987], "Interaction of Different Modules in Depth Perception: Stereo and Shading," Report AIM-965, Artificial Intelligence Laboratory , Massachusetts Institute of Technology, Cambridge, MA.

Bülthoff, Heinrich H., and Hamspeter A. Mallot [1988], "Integration of depth modules: stereo and shading," *J. Opt. Soc. Am.*, vol. 5, pp. 1749-1758.

Bülthoff , Heinrich H. [1988], personal communication.

Bülthoff, Heinrich H., James J. Little, and Tomaso Poggio [1989], "A parallel algorithm for real-time computation of optical flow," *Nature*, vol. 337, pp. 549-553.

Canny, J. F. [1983], "Finding Edges and Lines," Report AI-TR-720, Artificial Intelligence Laboratory , Massachusetts Institute of Technology, Cambridge, MA.

Cornog, K. H. [1985], "Smooth Pursuit and Fixation for Robot Vision," M.S. Thesis, Department of Electrical Engineering and Computer Science, Massachusetts Institute of Technology, Cambridge, MA.

Dempster, A. P., N. M. Laird, and D. B. Rubin [1977], "Maximum Likelihood from Incomplete Data via the EM Algorithm," *J. Roy. Stat. Soc.*, vol. B39, pp. 1-38.

Drumheller, M., and T. Poggio [1986], "On Parallel Stereo," *Proc. Intl. Conf. on Robotics and Automation*, IEEE.

Fahle, M., and T. Poggio [1980], "Visual Hyperacuity: Spatiotemporal Interpolation in Human Vision," *Proc. Roy. Soc. Lond. B*, vol. 213, pp. 451-477.

Geman, D., and S. Geman [1987], "Relaxation and Annealing with Constraints," *Complex Systems Technical Report 35*, Division of Applied Mathematics, Brown University, Providence, RI.

Geman, S., and D. Geman [1984], "Stochastic Relaxation, Gibbs Distributions, and the Bayesian Restoration of Images," *IEEE Trans. Pattern Analysis and Machine Intelligence*, vol. 6.

Geman, S., and C. Graffigne [1987], "Markov Random Field Image Models and their Applications to Computer Vision," *Proc. Intl. Congress of Mathematicians*, preprint, edited by A. M. Gleason.

Gamble, E., and T. Poggio [1987], "Integration of Intensity Edges with Stereo and Motion," Report AIm-970, Artificial Intelligence Laboratory , Massachusetts Institute of Technology, Cambridge, MA.

Grimson, W. E. L. [1981], *From Images to Surfaces*, The MIT Press, Cambridge, MA.

Grimson, W. E. L. [1982], "A Computational Theory of Visual Surface Interpolation," *Phil. Trans. Roy. Soc. Lond. B*, vol. 298, pp. 395-427.

Grimson, W. E. L. [1984], "Binocular Shading and Visual Surface Reconstruction," *Computer Vision, Graphics and Image Processing*, vol. 28, pp. 19-43.

Hildreth, E. C. [1983], *The Measurement of Visual Motion*, The MIT Press, Cambridge, MA.

Hillis, D. [1985], "The Connection Machine," Ph.D. Thesis, Department of Electrical Engineering and Computer Science, Massachusetts Institute of Technology, Cambridge, MA.

Horn, B. K. P. [1986], *Robot Vision*, The MIT Press, Cambridge, MA.

Hurlbert, A. [1989], "The Computation of Color Vision," Ph.D. Thesis, Department of Brain and Cognitive Sciences, Massachusetts Institute of Technology, Cambridge, MA.

Hurlbert, A., and T. Poggio [1986], "Do Computers Need Attention?" *Nature*, vol. 321, p. 12.

Hurlbert, A., and T. Poggio [1987] "Learning a Color Algorithm from Examples," Report AIM-909, Artificial Intelligence Laboratory *Center for Biological Information Processing Paper 25*, Massachusetts Institute of Technology, Cambridge, MA.

Huttenlocher, D., and S. Ullman [1987], "Recognizing Rigid Objects by Aligning them with an Image," Report AIM-937, Artificial Intelligence Laboratory, Massachusetts Institute of Technology.

Huttenlocher, D., and T. Cass [1988], Proceedings of the Image Understanding Workshop.

Ikeuchi, K., and B. K. P. Horn [1981], "Numerical Shape from Shading and Occluding Boundaries" *Artificial Intelligence*, vol. 17, pp. 141-184.

Kender, J. R. [1979], "Shape from Texture: An Aggregation Transform that Maps a Class of Textures into Surface Orientation," *Proc. Sixth Intl. Joint Conf. on Artificial Intelligence*, Tokyo.

Kirkpatrick, S., C. D. Gelatt, Jr., and M. P. Vecchi [1983], "Optimization by Simulated Annealing," *Science*, vol. 220.

Kruskal, C. P., L. Rudolph, and M. Snir [1985], "The Power of Parallel Prefix," *Proc. Intl. Conf. on Parallel Processing*, pp. 180-185.

Lim, W. [1986] "Fast Algorithms for Labelling Connected Components in 2D Arrays," *Thinking Machines Corp. Technical Report NA86-1*, Cambridge, MA.

Little, J., G. E. Blelloch, and T. Cass [1987], "Parallel Algorithms for Computer Vision on the Connection Machine," *Proceedings Intl. Conf. on Computer Vision*, Los Angeles, pp. 587-591.

Little, J., H. Bülthoff, and T. Poggio [1987], "Parallel Optical Flow Computation," *Proc. Image Understanding Workshop*, edited by L. Bauman, Science Applications International Corp., McLean, VA, pp. 915-920.

Little, J., H. Bülthoff, and T. Poggio [in preparation], "Parallel Optical Flow Using Winner-Take-All Scheme," 1989.

Mahoney, J. V. [1987], "Image Chunking: Defining Spatial Building Blocks for Scene Analysis," M.S. Thesis, Department of Electrical Engineering and Computer Science, Massachusetts Institute of Technology, Cambridge, MA. Published as AI-TR-980, Artificial Intelligence Laboratory , Technical Report , Cambridge, MA.

Marr, D. [1982], *Vision*, Freeman, San Francisco.

Marr, D., and E. Hildreth [1980], "Theory of Edge Detection," *Proc. Roy. Soc. Lond. B*, vol. 207, pp. 187-217.

Marr, D., and T. Poggio [1976], "Cooperative Computation of Stereo Disparity," *Science*, vol. 194, pp. 283-287.

Marr, D., and T. Poggio [1979], "A Computational Theory of Human Stereo Vision," *Proc. Roy. Soc. Lond. B*, vol. 204, pp. 301-328.

Marroquin, J. L. [1987] "Deterministic Bayesian Estimation of Markov Random Fields with Applications to Computational Vision," *Proc. First Intl. Conf. on Computer Vision*, Computer Society of the IEEE, Washington, DC.

Marroquin, J. L. [1985], "Probabilistic Solutions of Inverse Problems," Report AI-TR-860, Artificial Intelligence Laboratory Technical Report , Massachusetts Institute of Technology, Cambridge, MA.

Marroquin, J. L. [1984], "Surface Reconstruction Preserving Discontinuities," Report AIM-792, Artificial Intelligence Laboratory , Massachusetts Institute of Technology, Cambridge, MA.

Marroquin, J. L., S. Mitter, and T. Poggio [1986], "Probabilistic Solution of Ill-Posed Problems in Computational Vision," *Proc. Image Understanding Workshop*, edited by L. Bauman, Scientific Applications International Corp., McLean, VA, 1986. A more complete version appears in *J. Amer. Stat. Assoc.*, vol. 82, pp. 76-89, 1987.

Metropolis, N., A. Rosenbluth, M. Rosenbluth, A. Teller, and E. Teller [1953], "Equation of State Calculations by Fast Computing Machines," *J. Phys. Chem.*, vol. 21.

Nishihara, H. K. [1984]. "PRISM: A Practical Real-Time Imaging Stereo Matcher," Report AIM-780, Artificial Intelligence Laboratory , Massachusetts Institute of Technology, Cambridge, MA.

Nishihara, H. K., and P. A. Crossley [1988], "Measuring Photolithographic Overlay Accuracy and Critical Dimensions by Correlating inarized Laplacian of Gaussian Convolutions," *IEEE Trans. Pattern Matching and Machine Intell.*, vol. 10.

Poggio, T., K. R. K. Nielsen, and H. K. Nishihara [1982], "Zero-Crossings and Spatiotemporal Interpolation in Vision: Aliasing and Electrical Coupling Between Sensors," Report AIM-675, Artificial Intelligence Laboratory , Massachusetts Institute of Technology, Cambridge, MA.

Poggio, G., and T. Poggio [1984], "The analysis of stereopsis," *Ann. Rev. Neurosci.*, vol. 7, pp. 379-412.

Poggio, T. [1985], "Early Vision: From Computational Structure to Algorithms and Parallel Hardware," *Computer Vision, Graphics, and Image Processing*, vol. 31.

Poggio, T. [1985], "Integrating Vision Modules with Coupled MRFs," Report AIW-285, Artificial Intelligence Laboratory Working Paper , Massachusetts Institute of Technology, Cambridge, MA.

Poggio, T., and staff [1985], "MIT Progress in Understanding Images," *Proc. Image Understanding Workshop*, edited by L. Bauman, Scientific Applications International Corp., McLean, VA.

Poggio T., and staff [1987], "MIT Progress in Understanding Images," *Proc. Image Understanding Workshop*, edited by L. Bauman, Scientific Applications International Corp., McLean, VA.

Poggio, T., H. L. Voorhees, and A. L. Yuille [1984], "Regularizing Edge Detection," Report AIM-776, Artificial Intelligence Laboratory , Massachusetts Institute of Technology, Cambridge, MA.

Poggio, T., V. Torre, and C. Koch [1985], "Computational Vision and Regularization Theory," *Nature*, vol. 317, pp. 314-319.

Richards, W., and D. D. Hoffman [1985], "Codon Constraints on Closed 2D Shapes," *Computer Vision, Graphics, and Image Processing*, vol. 32, pp. 265-281.

Reichardt W., and T. Poggio [1976], "Visual Control of Orientation in the Fly: I. A Quantitative Analysis," *Quart. Rev. Biophysics*, vol. 3, pp. 311-375.

Reichardt W., and T. Poggio [1976], "Visual Control of Orientation in the Fly: II. Towards the Underlying Neural Interactions," *Quart. Rev. Biophysics*, vol. 9, pp. 377-439.

Rock, I. [1973], *Orientation and Form*, Academic Press, New York.

Terzopoulos, D. [1986], "Integrating Visual Information From Multiple Sources," in *From Pixels to Predicates*, edited by A. P. Pentland, Ablex Publishing Corp., Norwood, NJ.

Tikhonov, A. N., and V. Y. Arsenin [1977], *Solution of Ill-Posed Problems*, Winston and Wiley Publishers, Washington, DC.

Torre, V., and T. Poggio [1984], "On Edge Detection," Report AIM-768, Artificial Intelligence Laboratory , Massachusetts Institute of Technology, Cambridge, MA.

Ullman S. [1979], *The Interpretation of Visual Motion*, The MIT Press, Cambridge, MA.

Ullman, S. [1984], "Visual Routines," *Cognition*, vol. 18.

Verri, A., and T. Poggio [1986], "Motion Field and Optical Flow: Qualitative Properties," Report AIM-917, Artificial Intelligence Laboratory , Massachusetts Institute of Technology, Cambridge, MA.

Voorhees, H. L., and T. Poggio [1987], "Detecting Textons and Texture Boundaries in Natural Images," *Proc Intl. Conf. on Computer Vision*, Computer Society of the IEEE, Washington, DC.

Waxman, A. [1987], "Image Flow Theory: A Framework for 3-D Inference from Time-Varying Imagery," in *Advances in Computer Vision*, edited by C. Brown, Lawrence Erlbaum Assocs, NJ.

Wyllie, J. C. [1979], "The Complexity of Parallel Computations," Technical Report pp. 79-387, Department of Computer Science, Cornell University, Ithaca, NY.

43

When AI people first wrote image-understanding programs, processing a 256 × 256 pixel image with even the simplest program would often take an hour. This limited not only what people did, but also what people thought about. Back in the days when the PDP-10 was the dominant AI computer, it was natural to think in terms of 3 × 3 filters and 4 × 4 filters and not as natural to think in terms of the massive computations that the human eye can deploy.

On the other hand, knowing that a blazingly-fast device can be built enables you to think about what you would do if you had it even before fully functional hardware takes shape. Once Knight had built a small 8 × 10 pixel chip for sensing images and producing the difference-of-Gaussian computation on them, vision researchers could get on with using difference-of-Gaussian computations. Even though that computation takes a long time on a serial machine, vision researchers realized that practical devices could be built if and when the difference-of-Gaussian computation proved to have important practical applications.

Now further advances in VLSI technology have enabled a new round of thinking about what sorts of image-oriented computations can be done on chips. The collection of ideas explained by Horn in this chapter, while not intended to be a thorough review, demonstrates nevertheless that it is reasonable to think in terms of silicon retinas without seriously overstressing the metaphorical sense of the word retina.

Parallel Networks for Machine Vision

Berthold K. P. Horn

The term "parallel networks" in the title of this chapter may appear to be redundant, because the computations at different nodes of an analog network naturally proceed in parallel. However, in several of the examples explored here a number of different interacting networks are used, and these do indeed operate "in parallel." We have to try and understand the kinds of computations that simple networks can perform and then use them as components in more complex systems designed to solve early vision problem.

Some of the ideas are first developed in continuous form, where we deal, for example, with resistive sheets instead of a regular grid of resistors. This is because the analysis of the continuous version is often simpler, and lends itself to well known mathematical techniques. Some thought must, of course, be given to what happens when we approximate this continuous world with a discrete one. This typically includes mathematical questions about accuracy and convergence, but also requires that the network be laid out on a two-dimensional plane, because today's implementations allow only very limited stacking in the third dimension. This can be a problem in the case where the network is inherently three-dimensional, or layered, or where several networks are used cooperatively. There are four major topics addressed here:

1   A Gaussian convolver for smoothing that operates continuously in time.
2   Coupled resistive networks for interpolation of image derived data.
3   Moment calculation methods for determining position and orientation.
4   Systems for recovering motion and shape from time-varying images.

In the process we touch on several important subtopics, including:

- Interlaced arrangements of the cells of the layers of a multi-resolution network on a two-dimensional surface.
- Tradeoffs between closed form solutions favored on serial computers and iterative or feedback methods better suited for analog networks.
- Laying out time as an extra spatial dimension so as to build a system in which information flows continuously.
- An equivalence between two apparently quite differently uses of a resistive network.
- Feedback methods for solving constrained optimization problems using gradient projection, normalization, and penalty functions.

Note, that the four sections of this chapter are fairly independent and not arranged in any particular order—for additional details see Horn [1988].

A Non-Clocked Gaussian Convolver for Smoothing

Gaussian convolution is a useful smoothing operation, often used in early vision, particularly in conjunction with discrete operators that estimate derivatives. There exist several digital hardware implementations, including one that exploits the separability of the two-dimensional Gaussian operator into the convolution of two one-dimensional Gaussian operators [Larson *et al.* 1981]. Analog implementations have also been proposed that use the fact that the solution of the heat-equation at a certain time is the convolution of a Gaussian kernel with the initial temperature distribution [Knight 1983].

One novel feature of the scheme described here is that data flows through continuously, with output available at any time. Another is an elegant way of interlacing the nodes of layers at several resolutions. First comes a brief review of why there is interest in Gaussian convolution.

Edge detection

The detection of step-edge transitions in image brightness involves numerical estimation of derivatives. As such it is an ill-posed problem [Poggio & Torre 1984; Torre & Poggio 1986]. All but the earliest efforts (see, for example, Roberts [1965]) employed a certain degree of smoothing before or after application of finite difference operators in order to obtain a more stable estimate. Equivalently, they used computational molecules of large support (see, for example, Horn [1971]). While most of the early work focused on the image brightness gradient, that is, the first partial derivatives of image brightness, there where some suggestion that second-order partial derivatives might be useful. Rotationally symmetric ones appeared particularly appealing and it was noted that the Laplacian is the lowest order linear operator that (almost) allows recovery of the image information from the result [Horn 1972, 1974].

It was also clear early on that smoothing filters should be weighted so as to put less emphasis on points further away than those nearby.[1] The Gaussian was popular for smoothing because of a number of its mathematical properties, including the fact that the two-dimensional Gaussian can be viewed as the product of two one-dimensional Gaussians, and, much more importantly, as the convolution of two one-dimensional Gaussians [Horn 1972]. This gave rise to the hope that it might be computed with reasonable efficiency, an important matter when one is dealing with an image containing hundreds of thousands of picture cells. Note that the Gaussian is the only function that is both rotationally symmetric and separable in this fashion [Horn 1972]. The separability property, which was the original impetus for choosing the Gaussian as a smoothing filter, was forgotten at times when proposals where made later to build hardware convolvers (but, see Larson *et al.* [1981]).

Multi-resolution techniques

There are other reasons for smoothing a discretized image, including suppression of higher spatial frequency components before subsampling. Subsampling of an image produces an image of lower resolution, one that contains fewer picture cells. Ideally, one would hope that this smaller image retains all of the information in the original higher resolution image, but this is, of course, in general not possible. The original image can be reconstructed only if it happens not to contain spatial frequency components that are too high to be represented in the subsampled version. This suggests suppressing higher frequency components before subsampling in order to avoid *aliasing* phenomena. An ideal low-pass filter should be used for this purpose.[2] While the Gaussian filter is a poor approximation to a low pass

---

[1]There was, however, intense disagreement about whether the composite edge operator should have a sharp transition in the middle or not. Some argued that the transition should be rapid, because a matched filter has an impulse response equal to the signal being detected, which in this case was assumed to be an ideal step transition. Others claimed that the aim was to suppress higher spatial frequencies to improve the signal to noise ratio. This latter argument took into account the fact that the signal drops off at higher frequencies while the noise spectrum tends to be fairly flat. The view of the edge operator as a composition of a smoothing filter and a finite difference approximation of a derivative finally reinforced the latter view.

[2]For an excellent finite support approximation to a low-pass filter look in Rifman and McKinnon [1974], Bernstein [1976], Abdou and Wong [1982].

filter, it has the advantage that it does not have any over- or undershoot in either the spatial or the frequency domain. Consequently, the Gaussian smoothing operator has been used in several multi-scale schemes, despite the fact that it is not a good approximation to a low-pass filter.

The difference of two spatially displaced Gaussians was used quite early on in edge detection [MacLeod 1970a, 1970b]. The idea of working at multiple scales occurred around about this time also (Rosenfeld and Thurston [1971, 1972] and Rosenfeld, Thurston and Lee [1972]). An elegant theory of edge detection using zero-crossings of the Laplacian of the Gaussian at multiple scales was developed by Marr and Hildreth [1980] and Hildreth [1980, 1983]). This reversed an earlier suggestion that a directional operator may be optimal [Marr 1976].

It has been shown, then, that the rotationally symmetric operators do have some drawbacks, including greater inaccuracy in edge location when the edge is not straight, as well as higher sensitivity to noise than directional operators (see, for example, Berzins [1984] and Horn [1986]). Operators for estimating the second derivative in the direction of the largest first derivative (the so-called *second directional derivative*) have been proposed Haralick [1984] (see also Hartley [1985] and Horn [1986]).[3] Recently, Canny developed an operator that is optimal (in a sense he defines) in a one-dimensional version of the edge detection problem [Canny 1983]. His operator is similar, but not equal to, the first derivative of a Gaussian. A straightforward (although *ad hoc*) extension of this operator to two-dimensions has recently become popular.

If we view the problem as one of estimating the derivatives of a noisy signal, we can apply Wiener's optimal filtering methods [Wiener 1966; Anderson & Moore 1979]. Additive white noise is uncorrelated and so has a flat spectrum, while images typically have spectra that decrease as some power of frequency, starting from a low-frequency plateau [Ahuja & Schachter 1983]. The magnitude of the optimal filter response ends up being linear in frequency at low frequencies, then peaks and drops off as some power of frequency at higher frequencies. Under reasonable assumptions about the spectra of the ensemble of images being considered, this response may be considered to match (very roughly) the transform of the derivative of a Gaussian.

All this suggests that while there is nothing really magical about the Gaussian smoothing filter, it has been widely accepted and has many desirable mathematical properties (although only a few of these were discussed here). It is thus of interest to find out whether convolutions with Gaussian kernels can be computed directly by simple analog networks. It is also desirable to find out whether the Laplacian of the convolution with a Gaussian, or the directional derivatives, can be computed directly.

---

[3]While the second directional derivative is a non-linear operator, it is coordinate-system independent, as is the Laplacian operator.

Binomial filters

In practice, we usually have to discretize and truncate the signal, as well as the filters we apply to it. If we sample and truncate a Gaussian, it loses virtually all of the interesting mathematical properties discussed above. In particular, truncation introduces discontinuities that assure that the transform of the filter will fall off only as the inverse of frequency at high frequencies, not nearly as fast as the transform of the Gaussian itself. Furthermore, while the transfer function of a suitable scaled Gaussian lies between zero and one for all frequencies, the transfer function of a truncated version will lie outside this range for some frequencies. These effects are small only when we truncate at a distance that is large compared to the spatial scale of the Gaussian.

In addition, when we sample, we introduce aliasing effects, because the Gaussian is not a low-pass waveform. The aliasing effects are small only when we sample frequently in relation to the spatial scale of the Gaussian. It makes little sense to talk about convolution with a "discrete Gaussian" obtained by sampling with spacing comparable to the spatial scale, and by truncating at a distance comparable to the spatial scale of the underlying Gaussian. The resulting filter weights could have been obtained by sampling and truncating many other functions and so it is not reasonable to ascribe any of the interesting qualities of the Gaussian to such a set of weights.

Instead, we note that the appropriate discrete analog of the Gaussian is the binomial filter, obtained by dividing the binomial coefficients of order n by 2^n so that they conveniently sum to one. Convolution of the binomial filter of order n with the binomial filter of order m yields the binomial filter of order $(n + m)$, as can be seen by noting that multiplication of polynomials corresponds to convolution of their coefficients. The simplest binomial smoothing filter has the weights:

$$\left\{ \frac{1}{2}, \frac{1}{2} \right\} .$$

Higher order filters can be obtained by repeated convolution of this filter with itself:

$$\left\{ \frac{1}{4}, \frac{2}{4}, \frac{1}{4} \right\} \otimes \left\{ \frac{1}{2}, \frac{1}{2} \right\} = \left\{ \frac{1}{8}, \frac{3}{8}, \frac{3}{8}, \frac{1}{8} \right\} .$$

The transform of the binomial filter of order n is simply $\cos^n \omega/2$, because the transform of the simple filter with two weights is just $\cos \omega/2$. This shows that the magnitude of the transform is never larger than one for any frequency, a property shared with a properly scaled Gaussian. Such a filter cannot amplify any frequency components, only attenuate them.

Analog implementation of binomial filters

Binomial filters can be conveniently constructed using charge coupled device technology [Sage 1984; Sage & Lattes 1987]. It is also possible to use potential dividers to perform the required averaging. Consider, for example, a uniform one-dimensional chain of resistors with inputs applied as potentials on even nodes and results read out as potentials on odd nodes. The potentials on the odd nodes clearly are just averages of the potentials at neighboring even nodes.[4]

One such resistive chain can be used to perform convolution with the simple two-weight binomial filter. To obtain convolution with higher-order binomial filters, we can reuse the same network, with inputs and outputs interchanged, provide that we have clocked sample-and-hold circuits attached to each node. At any particular time one half of the sample-and-hold circuits are presenting their potentials to the nodes they are attached to, while the other half are sampling the potentials on the remaining nodes.

But we may be more interested in non-clocked circuits, where outputs are available continuously. The outputs of one resistive chain can be applied as input to another, provided that buffer amplifiers are interposed to prevent the second chain from loading the first one. We can cascade many such resistive chain devices to obtain convolutions with binomial filters of arbitrary order.

It is possible to extend this idea to two dimensions. Consider nodes on a square grid, with each node connected to its four edge-adjacent neighbors by a resistor. Imagine coloring the nodes red and black, like the squares on a checker-board. Then the red nodes may be considered the inputs, where potentials are applied, while the black nodes are the outputs, where potentials are read out. Each output potential is the average of four input potentials, and each input potential contributes to four outputs.

Unfortunately, the spatial scale of the binomial filter grows only with the square root of the number of stages used. Thus, while a lot of smoothing happens in the first few stages, it takes many more stages later in the sequence to obtain significantly additional smoothing. Also, the smoothed data has lost some of its high frequency content and so can perhaps be represented by fewer samples. These considerations suggest a multi-scale approach, where the number of nodes decreases from layer to layer. Averaging of neighbors at a later layer involves connections between nodes corresponding to points that are far apart in the original layer. Thus the smoothing that results in one of the later layers is over a larger spatial scale. We discuss later how to efficiently interlace the nodes of several such layers of different resolution on a two-dimensional surface.

---

[4]The outputs in this case are offset by one half of the pixel spacing from the inputs, but this is not a real problem. In particular, an even number of such filtering stages produces results that are aligned with the original data.

The kind of network we are discussing here can also be approached in a different way, starting from the properties of continuous resistive sheets, and analog methods for solving the heat equation. For details of this approach see Horn [1988].

Multiple scales

The information is smoothed out more and more as it flows through the layers of this system. Consequently we do not need to preserve full resolution in layers further from the input. Very roughly speaking, the information is low-pass filtered and so fewer samples are required to represent it. This suggests that successive sheets could contain fewer and fewer nodes.

Note also that it would be difficult indeed to superimpose, in two dimensions, multiple layers of the three dimensional network described above, if each of them contained the same (large) number of nodes. Now if, instead, a particular layer contains only $1/k$ times as many nodes as the previous layer then the total number of nodes is less than $k/(k-1)$ times the number of nodes in the first layer, as can be seen by summing the appropriate geometric series. If, for example, we reduce the number of nodes by one half each time, then a network containing a finite number of layers has less than twice the number of nodes that the first layer requires. (If we reduce the number of nodes to a quarter each time, then the whole network has less than 4/3 times as many as the first layer.)

Growth of standard deviation with number of layers

If we define the *width* of the binomial filter as the standard deviation from its center position, while the *support* is the number of non-zero weights, then it turns out that width grows only as the square-root of the support. So another argument for subsampling is that, if all the layers and the interconnections are the same, then the width of the binomial filter grows only with the square root of the number of layers. One way to obtain more rapid growth of the width of the smoothing filter is to arrange for successive layers to contain fewer nodes. This can be exploited to attain exponential growth of the effective width of the smoothing filter with the number of layers.

In the case of a square grid of nodes, a simple scheme would involve connecting only one cell out of four in a given layer to the next layer. This corresponds to a simple subsampling scheme. Sampling, however, should always be preceded by low-pass filtering (or at least some sort of smoothing) to limit aliasing. A better approach therefore involves first computing the average of four nodes in a given 2×2 pattern in order to obtain a smoothed result for the next layer.[5] Each cell in the earlier layer contributes to only one of the averages being computed in this scheme.

The average could be computed directly using four resistors, but these would load down the network. The average can be computed instead using resistors connected to buffer amplifiers. Each cell in the earlier layer feeds a buffer amplifier and the output of the amplifier is applied to one end of a resistor. The other ends are tied together in groups of four and connected to the nodes in the next layer. Note that the nodes of the latter sheet should be thought of as corresponding to image locations between those of the earlier sheet, rather than lying on top of a subset of these earlier nodes. But this subtlety does not present any real problems.

Layout of interlaced nodes

A four-to-one reduction in number of nodes is easy to visualize and leads to rapid reduction in the number of nodes in successive layers, but it does not yield a very satisfactory subsampling operation. Aliasing can be reduced if the number of nodes is reduced only by a factor of two. Note that in this case the total number of nodes in any finite number of layers is still less than twice the number of nodes in the first layer. An elegant way of achieving the reduction using a square grid of nodes is to think of successive layers as scaled spatially by a factor of $\sqrt{2}$ and also rotated 45° with respect to one another. Once again, each of the new nodes is fed a current proportional to the difference between the average potential on four nodes in the earlier layer and the potential of the node itself. This time, however, each of the earlier nodes contribute to two of these averages rather than just one, as in the simple scheme described in the previous section. A node receives contributions from four nodes that are neighbors of its ancestor node in the earlier layer, but it receives no contribution directly from that ancestor.

An elegant partitioning of a square tessellation into subfields may be used in the implementation of this scheme in order to develop a satisfactory physical layout of the interlaced nodes of successive layers of this network (Robert Floyd drew my attention to this partitioning in the context of parallel schemes for producing pseudo grey-level displays on binary image output devices [Floyd 1987]). This leads to the interlaced pattern shown in figure 1, where each cell is labeled with a number indicating which layer it belongs to.

This scheme leads to an arrangement where the nodes of the first layer are thought of as the black cells in a checkerboard. The red cells form a

---

[5]Naturally, because this is not an ideal low-pass filter, some aliasing effects cannot be avoided. In fact, the resulting transfer function goes through zero not at the Nyquist frequency, but only at twice that frequency, but this is much better than not doing any smoothing at all.

```
0  1  3  1  5  1  3  1  7  1  3  1  5  1  3  1  9
1  2  1  2  1  2  1  2  1  2  1  2  1  2  1  2  1
3  1  4  1  3  1  4  1  3  1  4  1  3  1  4  1  3
1  2  1  2  1  2  1  2  1  2  1  2  1  2  1  2  1
5  1  3  1  6  1  3  1  5  1  3  1  6  1  3  1  5
1  2  1  2  1  2  1  2  1  2  1  2  1  2  1  2  1
3  1  4  1  3  1  4  1  3  1  4  1  3  1  4  1  3
1  2  1  2  1  2  1  2  1  2  1  2  1  2  1  2  1
7  1  3  1  5  1  3  1  8  1  3  1  5  1  3  1  7
1  2  1  2  1  2  1  2  1  2  1  2  1  2  1  2  1
3  1  4  1  3  1  4  1  3  1  4  1  3  1  4  1  3
1  2  1  2  1  2  1  2  1  2  1  2  1  2  1  2  1
5  1  3  1  6  1  3  1  5  1  3  1  6  1  3  1  5
1  2  1  2  1  2  1  2  1  2  1  2  1  2  1  2  1
3  1  4  1  3  1  4  1  3  1  4  1  3  1  4  1  3
1  2  1  2  1  2  1  2  1  2  1  2  1  2  1  2  1
9  1  3  1  5  1  3  1  7  1  3  1  5  1  3  1  6
```

Figure 1. A way to interlace nodes of several layers of a multi-scale network so they can be laid out on a two-dimensional surface. The network containing nodes labeled $(n + 1)$ has half as many nodes as the network whose nodes are labeled n. The total number of nodes is less than twice the number of nodes in the finest layer.

diagonal pattern with $\sqrt{2}$ times the spacing of the underlying grid. We can now consider this new grid as a checkerboard, turned $45°$ with respect to the first. The black cells in this checkerboard belong to the second layer. The remaining red cells form a square grid aligned with the underlying grid but with twice the spacing between nodes. Considering this as a checkerboard in turn, we let the black cells be the nodes of the third layer, and so on ....

Note that one half of the cells are labeled 1, one quarter are labeled 2, one eighth are labeled 3 and so on. The top left node, labeled 0, does not belong to any of the partitions. If we consider the nodes labeled with their row number i and there column number j, both starting at zero at the top left node, we find that a node belongs to layer k if the binary representation of $i^2 + j^2$ has $k - 1$ trailing zeros!

Coupled Poisson's Equation for Interpolation

Uniform resistive networks that solve Poisson's and Laplace's equations have many other applications. One is in interpolation, where data may be provided on just a few contours, as happens in the edge matching approach

to binocular stereo [Grimson 1981].[6] Many modern interpolation methods
are based on physical models of deformation of elastic sheets or thin plates.
So these are briefly reviewed here first.

Mathematical physics of elastic membranes

An elastic membrane takes on a shape that minimizes the stored elastic
energy. In two dimensions the stored energy is proportional to the change
in area of the membrane from its undisturbed shape, which we assume here
is flat. The area is given by

$$\iint_D \sqrt{1 + z_x^2 + z_y^2}\, dx\, dy \,,$$

where $z(x, y)$ is the height of the membrane above some reference plane. If
the slope components z_x and z_y are small,

$$\sqrt{1 + z_x^2 + z_y^2} \approx 1 + \frac{1}{2}\left(z_x^2 + z_y^2\right) \,.$$

Thus the membrane minimizes

$$\iint_D (z_x^2 + z_y^2)\, dx\, dy \,,$$

provided that the partial derivatives z_x and z_y are small. A unique minimum exists if the sheet is constrained to pass through a simple closed curve
∂D on which the height is specified. The Euler equation for this calculus
of variation problem yields

$$z_{xx} + z_{yy} = 0 \quad \text{or} \quad \Delta z = 0 \,,$$

except on the boundary where the height $z(x, y)$ is specified [Courant &
Hilbert 1953].

Interpolation by means of a thin plate

The above equation has been proposed as a means of interpolating from
sparse data specified along smooth curves, not necessarily simple closed

---

[6]The problem of interpolation is harder if data is given only on a sparse set of
points, as opposed to contours. Consider, for example, Laplace's equation with
some constant value specified on a simple closed curve with a different value
given at a single point inside the curve. The solution minimizes the integral
of the sum of squares of the first partial derivatives. It turns out that this
is not a well-posed problem, because there is not a unique solution. One of
the "functions" that minimizes the integral takes on the value specified on the
boundary everywhere except at the one point inside where a different value
is given. Clearly no "interpolation" is occurring here. This problem is not
widely discussed, in part because the discrete approximation does not share
this pathological behavior [Grzywacs & Yuille 1987].

contours. We explored the use of this idea, for example, in generating digital terrain models from contour maps in our work on automated hill-shading (Strat [1977] and Horn [1979, 1981, 1983]) as well as in remote sensing (Bachmann [1977], Horn and Bachmann [1978], and Sjoberg and Horn [1983]). Some undergraduate research project work was based on this idea [Mahoney 1980], as were the bachelor's theses of Goldfinger [1983], and Norton [1983]. Recently, a 48×48 cell analog chip has been built to do this kind of interpolation [Luo, Koch & Mead 1988].

The result of elastic membrane interpolation is not smooth, however, while height in the result is a continuous function of the independent variables, slope is not. Slope discontinuities occur all along contour lines, and the tops of hills and bottoms of pits are flat.[7]

This is why we decided to use thin plates for interpolation from contour data instead. The potential energy density of a thin plate is

$$A \left(\frac{1}{\rho_1^2} + \frac{1}{\rho_2^2} \right) + \frac{2B}{\rho_1 \rho_2} \,,$$

where A and B are constants determined by the material of the plate, while ρ_1 and ρ_2 are the principal radii of curvature of the deformed plate [Courant & Hilbert 1953]. Again, assuming that the slopes z_x and z_y are small, we can use the approximations

$$\frac{1}{\rho_1} + \frac{1}{\rho_2} \approx (z_{xx} + z_{yy}) \quad \text{and} \quad \frac{1}{\rho_1 \rho_2} \approx z_{xx} z_{yy} - z_{xy}^2 \,.$$

This allows us to approximate the potential energy of the deformed plate by a multiple of

$$\iint_D \left((z_{xx} + z_{yy})^2 - 2(1-\mu)(z_{xx} z_{yy} - z_{xy}^2) \right) \, dx \, dy \,,$$

where $\mu = B/A$. If the material constant μ happens to equal one, this simplifies to the integral of the square of the Laplacian:

$$\iint_D (\Delta z)^2 \, dx \, dy \,.$$

The Euler equations for this variational problem lead to the bi-harmonic equation

$$\Delta(\Delta z) = 0 \,,$$

except where the plate is constrained. This fourth-order partial differential equation has a unique solution when the height $z(x, y)$, as well as the normal derivative of $z(x, y)$ are specified on a simple closed boundary ∂D.

It turns out that the same Euler equation applies when the material constant μ is not equal to one, because $(z_{xx} z_{yy} - z_{xy}^2)$ is a divergence expression [Courant & Hilbert 1953]. Solution of the bi-harmonic equation, while

---

[7]Discontinuities in slope are not a problem for many applications of interpolated depth or range data. Shaded views of the surfaces, however, clearly show the discontinuities, because shading depends on surface orientation.

involving considerably more work than Laplace's equation, produces excellent results in interpolation from contours. Iterative methods for solving these equations are available (see for example Horn [1986]). Some obvious implementations may not be stable, particularly when updates are executed in parallel, so care has to be taken to ensure convergence. The problem is that computational molecules or stencils with negative weights are needed, and these can amplify errors with some spatial frequencies rather than attenuate them.[8] This issue is not pursued any further here. The proper way of dealing with boundary conditions is also not discussed here, for details, see the cited references.

The same methods were used in interpolation of surface depth from stereo data along brightness edges [Grimson 1981, 1982, 1983]. Grimson observed that the null-space of the quadratic variation $(z_{xx}^2 + 2z_{xy}^2 + z_{yy}^2)$ is smaller than that of the squared Laplacian $(\Delta z)^2$, and so decided to use the quadratic variation as the basis for his binocular stereo interpolation scheme. This corresponds to choosing $\mu = 0$. Note that this affects only the treatment of the boundary; one still solves the bi-harmonic equation inside the boundary.

The methods discussed here rapidly get rid of high spatial frequency components of the error, but may take many iterations to reduce the low frequency components. The number of iterations required grows quadratically with the width of the largest gap between contours on which data is available.

Efficient multiresolution algorithms were developed to speed up the iterative computation of a solution [Terzopoulos 1983]. This approach has also been applied these to variational problems other than interpolation [Terzopoulos 1984].

Resistive networks for the bi-harmonic equation

It is clear then that methods for solving the bi-harmonic equations are important in machine vision. Unfortunately, simple networks of (positive) resistances cannot be constructed to solve discrete approximations of this equation. Computational molecules or stencils [Horn 1986] for the bi-harmonic operator involve negative weights and connections to nodes two steps away.

It is of interest then to discover ways of using methods for solving Poisson's equation

$$\Delta z(x, y) = f(x, y)$$

in the solution of the bi-harmonic equation, because simple resistive networks can be constructed to solve Poisson's equation. One simple idea is

---

[8]The corresponding system of linear equations is not diagonally dominant.

to use the coupled system,

$$\Delta z(x,y) = u(x,y) \quad \text{and} \quad \Delta u(x,y) = f(x,y),$$

because here

$$\Delta(\Delta z) = \Delta u = f(x,y).$$

The constraints on $z(x,y)$ can be handled easily in this formulation, but constraints on the partial derivatives of $z(x,y)$ are harder to incorporate. This idea will not be pursued further here.

An alternative explored recently by Harris [1986] involves minimization of the functional

$$\iint_D \left((z_x - p)^2 + (z_y - q)^2 + \lambda(p_x^2 + p_y^2 + q_x^2 + q_y^2)\right) \, dx\, dy.$$

The Euler equations for this calculus of variation problem yield

$$\Delta z = p_x + q_y,$$
$$\lambda \Delta p = p - z_x,$$
$$\lambda \Delta q = q - z_y.$$

In this scheme, three coupled Poisson's equations are used, each of which can be solved using a resistive network. Constraints on both $z(x,y)$ as well as z_x and z_y can be incorporated.

The relationship to the problem of solving the bi-harmonic equation can be seen by expanding

$$\Delta(\Delta z) = \Delta(p_x + q_y),$$

and noting that differentiation and application of the Laplacian are linear operations, so that they can be interchanged:

$$\Delta(p_x) = (\Delta p)_x = (1/\lambda)(p - z_x)_x = (1/\lambda)(p_x - z_{xx})$$
$$\Delta(q_y) = (\Delta q)_y = (1/\lambda)(q - z_y)_y = (1/\lambda)(q_y - z_{yy})$$

and finally

$$\Delta(\Delta z) = (1/\lambda)\left((p_x + q_y) - (z_{xx} + z_{yy})\right) = 0,$$

since $\Delta z = (p_x + q_y)$. (Note that this does not necessarily imply that $p = z_x$ and $q = z_y$.)

This scheme is reminiscent of the one developed by Horn for recovering depth $z(x,y)$, given dense estimates of the components p and q of the gradient of the surface (as used in Ikeuchi [1984], and described in Horn and Brooks [1986]). There one minimizes

$$\iint_D (z_x - p)^2 + (z_y - q)^2 \, dx\, dy,$$

for which the Euler equation yields

$$\Delta z = p_x + q_y,$$

where p and q are here the given estimates of the components of the surface gradient. In Harris's scheme we do not have these estimates at all points, instead we are given z at some points, and some linear combination of p and q at some other points.

The above ideas can be extended to solving the *image irradiance equation* that occurs in the *shape from shading* problem [Horn 1989; Horn & Brooks 1989]. See Harris [1989] for other ideas on an analog implementations of the thin plate interpolation method.

Moment Calculations for Position and Orientation

Calculations of sums of products of image coordinates and functions of the picture cell grey-levels are useful in several early machine vision algorithms. These moments are easily calculated using many different architectures, including bit-sliced, pipelined, analog networks, and by means of charge coupled devices. Such methods have several applications. A new technique for directly estimating motion of the camera from first derivatives of image brightness, for example, depends on the calculation of such moments (as discussed in the next section).

In addition, a large fraction of all binary image processing methods involve the computation of the zeroth, first and second moments of the regions of the image considered to be the image of one object. Presently, most commercially available machine vision systems have only rudimentary mechanisms for dealing with grey-level images and are aimed mainly at binary images. These systems typically have digital means for computing the moments. While such systems are restricted in their application, they are widely available and well understood. They can be used, for example, to determine the position and orientation of an isolated, contrasting workpiece lying flat on a conveyor belt (see, for example, Chapter 3 in Horn [1986]). Once the position and orientation of the object is known, a robot hand with the appropriate orientation may be sent to the indicated position to pick up the part. A device that finds the centroid of a spot of light in the image can also be used as a high-resolution light-pen and a means of tracking a light source, such as a light bulb attached to an industrial robot arm.

A variety of methods is available for efficiently computing the zeroth- and first-order moments, including methods for working with projections of the image or run-length coded versions of the image. Less appears to be known about how to easily compute second- and higher-order moments, except that iterated summation can be used to avoid the implied multiplications.

Such ideas are used in special purpose digital chips that have been built for finding moments [Hatamian 1986, 1987]. We nevertheless explore analog networks for this task, partly to see whether they may have advantages over existing digital implementations and partly because they constitute a stepping stone on the way to some types of networks used in the recovery of motion from time-varying images [Horn 1988].

In this section several different methods are explored for computing moments using analog networks. It will be shown that some elegant methods exist that make it possible to obtain these moments using networks with relatively few components.

Use of first moments for position

Suppose that we have a characteristic function that indicates places in the image where the object region is thought to be. That is,

$$b(x,y) = \begin{cases} 1, & \text{if } (x,y) \text{ is in the region;} \\ 0, & \text{otherwise.} \end{cases}$$

Under favorable circumstances, such a characteristic function can be obtained by thresholding a grey-level image. The area of the object is obviously just the zeroth-order moment

$$A = \iint_D b(x,y)\, dx\, dy \, ,$$

where the integral is over the whole image.

The position of the object can be considered to be the location $(\bar{x}, \bar{y})$ of its center of area, defined in terms of the two first-order moments as follows:

$$A\,\bar{x} = \iint_D x\, b(x,y)\, dx\, dy \quad \text{and} \quad A\bar{y} = \iint_D y\, b(x,y)\, dx\, dy \, .$$

The center of area, or *centroid* is independent of the choice of coordinate system.[9]

Use of second moments for orientation

There are three second-order moments, and these can be used to define the orientation of the object as well as a shape factor. The orientation of the object may be taken to be specified by the direction of the axis of least inertia, which is independent of the choice of coordinate system axes.[10]

The inertia of a particle relative to a given axis is the product of the mass of the particle and the square of the perpendicular distance of

---

[9]That is, the position of the centroid relative to the object does not depend on the choice of coordinate used in the calculation.

[10]If we rotate the coordinate system, we find that the axis of least inertia determined in the new coordinate system is just the rotated version of the axis of least inertia in the original coordinate system.

the particle form the axis. So the inertia of an extended object about an arbitrary axis in the image plane can be defined as

$$I = \iint_D r^2(x, y)\, b(x, y)\, dx\, dy,$$

where

$$r(x, y) = x \sin \theta - y \cos \theta + \rho$$

is the distance of the image point (x, y) from the line with inclination θ (measured anti-clockwise form the x-axis) and perpendicular distance ρ from the origin.

It is easy to show that the axis of least inertia passes through the center of area, so it is convenient to compute the second-order moments with respect to the center of area (see, for example, Chapter 3 in Horn [1986]). Let

$$a' = \iint_D x'^2\, b(x, y)\, dx\, dy,$$

$$b' = \iint_D x'y'\, b(x, y)\, dx\, dy,$$

$$c' = \iint_D y'^2\, b(x, y)\, dx\, dy,$$

where $x' = (x - \bar{x})$ and $y' = (y - \bar{y})$. The inertia can then be expressed as a function of the angle of inclination of the axis in the form

$$I = \frac{1}{2}(a' + c') + \frac{1}{2}(c' - a') \cos 2\theta - b' \sin 2\theta.$$

Differentiating this with respect to θ and setting the result equal to zero yields

$$(c' - a') \sin 2\theta_0 + 2\, b' \cos 2\theta_0 = 0,$$

for the inclinations of the axes corresponding to extrema of inertia. Note that we do not actually need all three of the second-order moments to compute θ_0, only the combination $(c' - a')$ and b' are required. This observation is exploited later in a circuit designed to find the orientation of the axis of least inertia.

There is a two-way ambiguity here, since the equation is satisfied by $(\theta_0 + \pi)$ if it is satisfied by θ_0. This is to be expected, because we are only finding the line about which the region has least inertia. Higher order moments can be used to resolve this ambiguity, but we will not pursue this subject any further here.

The axis through the center of area yielding maximum inertia lies at right angles to the axis yielding minimum inertia. The maximum and minimum inertia themselves are given by

$$I_{\max} = \frac{1}{2}(a' + c') + \frac{1}{2}\sqrt{b'^2 + (c' - a')^2},$$

$$I_{\min} = \frac{1}{2}(a' + c') - \frac{1}{2}\sqrt{b'^2 + (c' - a')^2}.$$

The ratio of $I_{\min}$ to $I_{\max}$ is a factor that depends on the shape of the object. It will be equal to one for a centrally symmetric object like a circular disc and near zero for a highly elongated object. Note that we need all three second-order moments to compute a "shape factor."

So-called *moment invariants* are combinations of moments that are independent of translation and rotation of the object region in the image [Cagney & Mallon 1986]. The second order moment invariants are all combinations of the minimum and maximum inertia. There are thus only two degrees of freedom. One may choose any convenient combinations, such as

$$I_{\max} + I_{\min} = a' + c' \,,$$

$$(I_{\max} - I_{\min})^2 = b'^2 + (c' - a')^2 \,.$$

These invariants are sometimes used in recognition.

Additional comments and higher moments

In practice the double integrals that apply in the continuous domains are replaced by double sums, in the obvious way. So the area, for example, is just a multiple of

$$A = \sum_{i=1}^{n} \sum_{j=1}^{m} b_{i,j} \,.$$

The second-order moments a', b', and c', relative to the centroid $(\bar{x}, \bar{y})$, can be computed from the moments a, b, and c relative to the (arbitrary) origin of the coordinate system, provided that the zeroth and first-order moments are known:

$$a' = a - A\,\bar{x}^2, \quad b' = b - A\,\bar{x}\bar{y}, \quad \text{and} \quad c' = c - A\,\bar{y}^2 \,.$$

Still higher moments may be used to get more detailed descriptions of the shape. Also, as noted, the axis of least inertia leaves an ambiguity in orientation. The third-order moments can be used to disambiguate the two possibilities.

We have assumed so far that $b(x, y)$ can only take on two values. It should be obvious that the same analysis holds when $b(x, y)$ is not binary (yet independent of accidents of lighting and viewing geometry). This may be advantageous, for example, when one has a coarsely sampled image, in which case the position and orientation of the part may not be determined very accurately from a mere binary image because of aliasing problems. Intermediate grey-levels on the boundary of the object can provide information that allows one to determine the position and orientation to much higher precision.

Resistive networks for moment calculation

If area and center of area are all we are computing, then a very simple scheme can be used. Consider first a regular one-dimensional chain of N resistors each of resistance R. We can use such a simple resistive chain to generate potentials at each node linearly related to the position. This potential can then be used in further calculation—to generate a current injected into a global buss [Horn 1988]. Now consider a different way of using the very same chain. Suppose that the chain is grounded at each end, and that we can measure the currents I_l and I_r flowing into the ground at these points. There are k resistors to the left and $(N - k)$ to the right of the k-th node. Suppose a potential V develops at the k-th node when we inject a current I there. Clearly

$$I_l = \frac{V}{kR} \quad \text{and} \quad I_r = \frac{V}{(N - k)R},$$

while the total current is

$$I = I_l + I_r = \frac{N}{k(N - k)} \frac{V}{R},$$

so that

$$\frac{I_l}{I} = \frac{N - k}{N} \quad \text{and} \quad \frac{I_r}{I} = \frac{k}{N}.$$

We can compute the "centroid" of these two currents:

$$\bar{x} = x_l \frac{I_l}{I} + x_r \frac{I_r}{I} = x_l + \frac{k}{N}(x_r - x_l),$$

which is the x coordinate of the place where the current was injected. If we inject currents at several nodes, we can show, using superposition, that the computation above yields the centroid of the injected currents.

Now imagine a regular two-dimensional resistive grid grounded on the boundary. Current is injected at each picture cell where $b(x, y) = 1$. The currents to ground on the boundary from the network are measured. The total current obviously is proportional to the area, that is, the number of picture cells where $b(x, y) = 1$. More importantly, the center of area of the current distribution on the boundary yields the center of area of the injected current distribution.

To see why, consider a uniform resistive sheet covering the region D, grounded on the boundary ∂D. Current $i(x, y)$ per unit area is injected into the sheet at the point (x, y), where the potential is $v(x, y)$. The potential satisfies Poisson's equation

$$\Delta v(x, y) = -\rho\, i(x, y),$$

where ρ is the resistivity (per unit square). Now consider the current density per unit length extracted from the sheet at the boundary:

$$j(x, y) = -\rho \frac{\partial v}{\partial n},$$

where the normal derivative of the potential can be defined by

$$\frac{\partial v}{\partial n} = \frac{\partial v}{\partial x}\frac{dy}{ds} - \frac{\partial v}{\partial y}\frac{dx}{ds},$$

with the tangent tò the boundary given by

$$\left(\frac{dx}{ds}, \frac{dy}{ds}\right)^T.$$

It is clear that the total current injected into the sheet must equal the total current leaving through the boundary. We can show this formally using the two-dimensional version of Green's formula [Korn & Korn 1968]:

$$\iint_D (u\Delta v - v\Delta u)\, dA = \int_{\partial D}\left(u\frac{\partial v}{\partial n} - v\frac{\partial u}{\partial n}\right)ds,$$

with $v = v(x,y)$ and $u(x,y) = 1$. We obtain

$$\iint_D \Delta v\, dA = \int_{\partial D}\frac{\partial v}{\partial n}\, ds,$$

or

$$\iint_D i(x,y)\, dA = \int_{\partial D} j(x,y)\, ds.$$

This works, of course, even when the boundary is not grounded.

Now, if we instead use $u(x,y) = x$ in Green's formula, we obtain

$$\iint_D x\,\Delta v\, dA = \int_{\partial D}\left(x\frac{\partial v}{\partial n} - v\frac{\partial x}{\partial n}\right)ds,$$

which, since $v(x,y) = 0$ on the boundary, becomes just

$$\iint_D x\,\Delta v\, dA = \int_{\partial D} x\frac{\partial v}{\partial n}\, ds,$$

so that

$$\iint_D x\,i(x,y)\, dA = \int_{\partial D} x\,j(x,y)\, ds.$$

So the first-order moment in the x-direction of the boundary current is equal to the first-order moment in the x-direction of the injected current. Similarly,

$$\iint_D y\,i(x,y)\, dA = \int_{\partial D} y\,j(x,y)\, ds.$$

The same trick can be used with any harmonic function $u(x,y)$, that is, a function for which $\Delta u = 0$.

It is easy to see that xy and $(y^2 - x^2)$ are harmonic functions, so we can compute their integrals in this fashion also:

$$\iint_D (y^2 - x^2)\,i(x,y)\, dA = \int_{\partial D} (y^2 - x^2)\,j(x,y)\, ds,$$

and

$$\iint_D xy\,i(x,y)\, dA = \int_{\partial D} xy\,j(x,y)\, ds.$$

Now the first of these integrals corresponds to $(c - a)$, while the second corresponds to b in the calculation of orientation. This means that we can obtain the position and orientation of a region just from the currents on the boundary of the resistive network.

Note, however, that we cannot obtain all three second-order moments *independently* from the boundary currents. We only obtain one of the two second order moment invariants. Consequently, we also cannot compute a shape factor from the boundary currents.

The two-dimensional Laplacian operator can be written in polar form as

$$\Delta u = \frac{1}{r} \frac{\partial}{\partial r} \left(r \frac{\partial u}{\partial r} \right) + \frac{1}{r^2} \frac{\partial^2 u}{\partial \theta^2} \,,$$

so we see that

$$u_k = r^k \cos(k\theta) \quad \text{and} \quad v_k = r^k \sin(k\theta) \,,$$

are two families of harmonic functions. We have used the first few members of these sets already, namely,

$$1, \quad x = r \cos \theta, \quad y = r \sin \theta, \quad x^2 - y^2 = r^2 \cos 2\theta, \text{ and } 2xy = r^2 \sin 2\theta \,.$$

The next pair of harmonic functions one could use are the monkey-saddle functions

$$x^3 - 3xy^2 \quad \text{and} \quad 3x^2 y - xy^2 \,.$$

Continuing in this way, we see that one can compute two combinations of each of the $(n + 1)$ moments of n-th order from the boundary currents. We cannot compute all of the moments independently. For purposes of determining the position and orientation, however, we only need the first few.

Implementation details and previous work

To obtain the required combinations of moments, we have to integrate the product of the boundary current with

$$1, \quad x, \quad y, \quad (x^2 - y^2) \quad \text{and} \quad 2xy \,.$$

The first is just the total current flowing out of the resistive network. The computation of the rest will be affected somewhat by the shape chosen for the resistive network. In the case of a circular image region, for example, we multiply the currents by weights that vary as

$$1, \quad \cos \theta, \quad \sin \theta, \quad \cos 2\theta \quad \text{and} \quad \sin 2\theta \,,$$

where θ is the angle measured from the center of the image. Note that the weights are fixed for each point on the boundary. The computation may be simplified by using a square boundary, but at the cost of loss of rotational symmetry.

There has been considerable work on finding moments using digital means. Special purpose systems have been developed for tracking objects using these schemes [Gilbert *et al.* 1980; Gilbert 1981]. Also, a number of special purpose digital signal processing systems have been built to compute moments. Some of these systems have much of the required circuitry on a single digital chip [Hatamian 1986, 1987]. Furthermore, a discrete analog chip has been built that determines the centroid using a gradient descent method [DeWeerth & Mead 1988]. With considerable increase in circuit complexity this could perhaps be extended to also determine orientation using the approach described in the first part of this section.

There also exists a continuous analog light-spot position sensor that uses a method similar to the one described above (Selspot Systems). It consists of a single, large, square photo-diode and some electronics. Electrodes are attached on four edges of the "lateral effect" photo-diode and four operational amplifiers are used to measure the short-circuit current out of each of the four edges. The total current is just the integral of the signal. The ratio of the difference to the sum of the currents on opposite edges gives the position of the centroid in one direction. The currents in the other two edges give the other component of the centroid.

Apparently the possibility of computing combinations of higher moments from the boundary currents, and thus determining orientation also, has not previously been noted.

A network equivalence theorem

In the above we have discussed two apparently quite different ways of using a simple resistive network:

- Apply a given potential distribution along the edge of the network and use the open-circuit potentials at interiors nodes in further calculation, and

- Inject currents at interior nodes and use the measured short-circuit currents on the edge in further calculation.

There is an intimate relationship between these two ways of using a resistive network. In some cases one of the two schemes leads to much simpler implementation than the other, so it is important to understand the equivalence. This will now be explored in more detail for arbitrary networks of resistors.

Consider a resistive network with external nodes segregated into two sets A and B of size N and M respectively. Now perform two experiments:

1   Connect the nodes in group A to voltage sources with potentials V_n for $n = 1, 2, \ldots, N$ and measure the resulting open-circuit potentials on the nodes in group B. Let these be called v_m, for $m = 1, 2, \ldots, M$.

2   Connect the nodes in group B to current sources with currents i_m, for $m = 1, 2, \ldots, M$, and measure the short-circuit currents in the nodes of group A. Let these be called I_n for $n = 1, 2, \ldots, N$.

Then

$$\boxed{\sum_{n=1}^{N} I_n V_n = \sum_{m=1}^{M} i_m v_m}$$

Proof: Consider in case 1 that we apply a potential only to node n in group A, that is, $V_k = 0$ for $k \neq n$. Let the resulting open-circuit potential on node m in group B be called $v_{m,n}$. We note that superposition tells us that the potential on node m in group B when potentials are applied to *all* of the nodes in group A is

$$v_m = \sum_{n=1}^{N} v_{m,n} .$$

Next, consider in case 2 that we inject current only at node m in group B, that is $i_l = 0$ for $l \neq m$. Let the resulting short-circuit current at node n in group A be called $I_{n,m}$. We note that superposition tells us that the current in node n of group A when currents are injected into *all* of the nodes of group B is

$$I_n = \sum_{m=1}^{M} I_{n,m} .$$

The reciprocity theorem tells us that

$$I_{n,m} V_n = i_m v_{m,n} .$$

Now sum over all of the nodes in group A:

$$\sum_{n=1}^{N} I_{n,m} V_n = \sum_{n=1}^{N} i_m v_{m,n} ,$$

or

$$\sum_{n=1}^{N} I_{n,m} V_n = i_m \sum_{n=1}^{N} v_{m,n} = i_m v_m .$$

Then sum over all of the nodes in group B:

$$\sum_{m=1}^{M} \sum_{n=1}^{N} I_{n,m} V_n = \sum_{m=1}^{M} i_m v_m ,$$

or

$$\sum_{n=1}^{N} \sum_{m=1}^{M} V_n I_{n,m} = \sum_{n=1}^{N} V_n \sum_{m=1}^{M} I_{n,m} = \sum_{m=1}^{M} i_m v_m ,$$

or, finally

$$\sum_{n=1}^{N} I_n V_n = \sum_{m=1}^{M} i_m v_m .$$

Application

One application of this theorem is in the simplification of circuits for the analog computation of some weighted average. Suppose that we have a resistive network that is used to compute some quantities v_m (for example, a potential representing the x position in an image) from some fixed inputs V_n (for example, potentials representing x on the edge of the resistive network). These potentials are then used to compute a weighted average like

$$\bar{v} = \frac{\sum_{m=1}^{M} i_m v_m}{\sum_{m=1}^{M} i_m} ,$$

where the quantities i_m are the weights (for example, image brightness).

Then an equivalent way of obtaining the same result is to inject currents proportional to i_m into the resistive network, now grounded in the places where inputs where applied earlier. Let the currents at the places where the network is grounded be I_n. Then the same weighted average can be obtained by computing instead

$$\bar{V} = \frac{\sum_{n=1}^{N} I_n V_n}{\sum_{n=1}^{N} I_n} .$$

Which of the two schemes is simpler depends on details of the implementation, including the relative sizes of N and M.

Example

In the one dimensional version of the centroid-finding chip, a potential representing x is generated from two fixed input potentials applied at either end of a uniform resistive chain. An output current proportional to the product of the light intensity at a picture cell and the local value of x is injected into a global bus. The weighted average of the potentials at the picture cells can then be computed from this current and a current proportional to the total brightness

$$\bar{v} = \frac{\sum_{m=1}^{M} v_m i_m}{\sum_{m=1}^{M} i_m} .$$

This allows us to determine the x position of the centroid of the light spot

$$\bar{x} = \frac{(V_2 - \bar{v})x_1 + (\bar{v} - V_1)x_2}{V_2 - V_1} ,$$

where x_1 and x_2 are the coordinates at either end of the resistive chain, at the points where the potentials V_1 and V_2 are applied.

The computation can also be performed by injecting currents proportional to the brightness at each picture cell into the same uniform linear resistive chain now grounded at either end. The centroid can be computed from the currents flowing into ground at the ends:

$$\overline{x} = \frac{x_1 I_1 + x_2 I_2}{I_1 + I_2}.$$

In this particular case, the second scheme appears to be simpler.

For generalizations of these ideas to the continuous domain, see Horn [1988].

Short Range Motion Vision Methods

Attacks on the motion vision problem can be categorized in a number of ways. First of all, there is the question of how large a change between successive images the method is meant to deal with. Feature-based methods appear to be best suited for the so-called *long-range* motion vision problem, where there is a relatively large change between images. Conversely, these methods generally are not good at estimating motions with subpixel accuracy. Feature-based methods essentially solve the correspondence problem, which is the central problem in binocular stereo. Unfortunately, the problem in motion vision is typically even harder than the binocular stereo problem, because the search for a match is not confined to an epipolar line.

Gradient-based methods are better suited to situations where the motion between successive images is fairly small, that is, the *short-range* motion vision problem. Correlation methods appear to fall somewhere in between, because they cannot deal with significant changes in foreshortening or photometric changes, yet are not able to easily produce displacement estimates with subpixel accuracy.

There are several different approaches to the short-range motion vision problem. Here we briefly list some based directly on brightness derivatives rather than matching of isolated features or correlation. We first discuss several methods for recovering optical flow and then go on to methods for recovering rigid body motion directly, without using optical flow as an intermediate result.

All methods for recovering motion implicitly make some assumptions about how images change when the viewer moves with respect to the scene. Simple correlation methods, for example, assume that changes in foreshortening can be ignored. This is not a good assumption in wide-baseline binocular stereo nor in some long-range motion vision applications. Feature-based methods and correlation methods also assume that the brightness pattern does not change drastically with viewpoint. Fortunately, the brightness of many real surfaces does not depend significantly on the viewing direction for a fixed illumination geometry.

Methods based on brightness gradients implicitly assume that the variations in brightness at a particular point in the image due to motion are much larger than the brightness fluctuations induced by changes in viewpoint. This is a reasonable assumption unless the surface lacks markings and is illuminated by rapidly moving light sources. Most methods will be "fooled" by the motion of virtual images resulting from specular or glossy reflections of point light sources.

Recovering optical flow from brightness derivatives

The *motion field* is the projection in the image of velocities of points in the environment with respect to the observer. Observer motion and object shapes can be estimated from the motion field. The *optical flow* is a vector field in the image that indicates how brightness patterns move with time. The optical flow field is not unique, because the matching of points along an isophote in one image with an isophote of the same brightness in the other image is not unique. Additional constraints have to be introduced in order to select a particular "optical flow." Under favorable circumstances the optical flow so computed is a good estimate of the motion field. There are several algorithms of different complexity and robustness for estimating optical flow. At one end of the spectrum we have algorithms that assume the flow is constant over the image, at the other, there are algorithms that can deal with depth discontinuities. Many of the interesting variations are listed here in order of increasing complexity:

1   **Constant Optical Flow** [Nagel 1984; Weldon 1986]: Here the flow velocity, (u, v), is assumed to be constant over the image patch. This may be a good approximation for a small field of view. Several cameras aimed in different directions (spider head) could yield flow vectors that provide the information necessary to solve for the observer motion. Alternatively, this computation may be applied to (possibly overlapping and weighted) patches of one image. A basic least squares analysis leads to a simple algorithm. All that is required is:

    a   Estimation of the brightness derivatives E_x, E_y, and E_t.

    b   Accumulation of the sums of the products E_x^2, $E_x E_y$, E_y^2, $E_x E_t$, and $E_y E_t$, and,

    c   Solution of two linear equations in the two unknowns u and v. This last step could be done off-chip, using the totals accumulated on-chip. Alternatively, the computation can be done in an iterative or feedback mode on chip (as it is in

Tanner and Mead [1987]). The bandwidth going off-chip is very low in either case.

If the computation is done for many (possibly overlapping and weighted) image windows, then an optical flow vector field results (at resolution less than the full image resolution). Such a vector field can then be processed off-chip to yield camera motion and scene structure using a least-squares method (*a lá* Bruss and Horn [1983]).

2 **Basic Optical Flow** [Horn & Schunck 1981]: Here the velocity field is allowed to vary from place to place in the image, but is assumed to vary smoothly. Depth discontinuities are not treated, but elastic deformations, fluid flows and rigid body motions yield reasonable results. The calculus of variation problem here leads to a coupled pair of Poisson's equations for $u(x, y)$ and $v(x, y)$, the components of the optical flow. The right-hand sides of these equations (that is, parts not involving u and v) are computed from the brightness derivatives. One needs to be able to compute values such as $(\alpha^2 + E_x^2 + E_y^2)$ (or approximations thereto). The partial differential equations themselves, of course, can be conveniently solved on two interlaced resistive networks. The inputs may be currents injected at nodes, while the outputs are the potentials there. The boundaries have to be treated carefully. The algorithm is robust with respect to small random errors in the resistive network. (It is not robust against round-off error in the digital version, common when the number of bits available to representing u and v are limited). As usual, there is some small advantage to working on a hexagonal grid.

3 **Optical Flow with Multiplier** [Gennert & Negahdaripour 1987]: The basic optical flow algorithm is based on the assumption that the brightness of a small patch of the surface does not change as it moves. In practice there are small brightness changes, because the shading on the surface may change slowly as a patch moves into areas that are illuminated differently. When the surface is highly textured, brightness variations at a point in the image resulting from motion are much larger than those due to changes in shading and illumination, and so these can be safely ignored. If there is no strong texture on the surface, somewhat better results can be obtained if one takes account of these small changes in shading. One can do this using a simple multiplier model. Here the brightness of a patch in a frame of an image sequence is assumed to be a multiple of the brightness of the same patch in the previous frame. The multiplier (assumed to be near unity) is allowed to vary from point to point in the image, but is assumed to vary slowly with position. The resulting calculus of variation problem now leads to three coupled partial differential equations. The new algorithm is

not much more complex (about 50% more work) than the basic one, yet yields better results.

4   **Optical Flow with Discontinuities** [Koch, Marroquin & Yuille 1986; Gamble & Poggio 1987; Hutchinson, Koch, Luo & Mead 1987; Murray & Buxton 1987]: The notion of a *line process* for dealing with discontinuities in images originated with Geman and Geman [1984]. This idea was later applied to discontinuities in optical flow by Koch, Marroquin and Yuille [1986], Hutchinson, Koch, Luo and Mead [1987], and Murray and Buxton [1987]. To deal with discontinuities in the optical flow, which typically occur at object boundaries, one introduces line processes that cut the solution and prevent smoothing over discontinuities. The resulting penalty function to be minimized is no longer convex and the solution involves more than simply solving a set of coupled partial differential equations. It seemed at first that this approach was doomed to failure, because methods like simulated annealing for solving such nonlinear problems are hopelessly inefficient on an ordinary serial computer. However, a reasonably efficient method results if one gives up the demand for the absolute global minimum and instead is satisfied with a good solution, with cost close to the absolute minimum cost [Blake & Zisserman 1988]. It helps to base the decision about whether to introduce a line process at a particular place only on the local change in the cost of the solution [Geman & Geman 1984]. Further improvements in performance can be had if line processes are allowed only very near to discontinuities in brightness, that is, edges [Gamble & Poggio 1987]. This suggests integrating some edge finding algorithm on the same chip. The approach here leads to an analog network that interacts with some logic circuits implementing the line-process decision making (see figure 5 in Koch, Marroquin and Yuille [1986]).

Often there is a concern about the rate of convergence of simple methods for solving Poisson's equation. Multi-grid methods are suggested as a means of speeding up the process. This is fortunately not so much of a concern here because:

- It is rare to have no inputs (zero right-hand side) over large patches (that is, large patches of uniform brightness are rare).

- The analog networks ought to settle fairly rapidly, even when there are many nodes because the time-constant should be small.

- Excellent starting values are available from the solution for the previous frame.

Because it is difficult to get good estimates of optical flow from noisy image data, there has been a trend recently to go directly to the ultimately desired information, namely observer motion and object shape. Instead of computing these from a flow field, they are derived directly from image brightness and the partial derivatives of brightness. These methods also lend themselves to implementation in a parallel network (see next section). They do, however, assume rigid body motion. Thus these methods are of little use when we are dealing with elastic deformations and fluid flow. Consequently there is still strong interest in finding rapid, robust methods for estimating the optical flow.

Direct recovery of rigid body motion

It is possible to derive observer motion and object shape directly from brightness gradients using something like a least-squares approach. These methods are not as mature as those for estimating the optical flow, but may ultimately be of more interest. A number of special cases have been solved so far:

1   **Pure Rotation:**   [Alomoinos & Brown 1985; Horn & Weldon 1988] In the case of pure rotation, the motion field is particularly simple because it does not depend on the distances of the observer from the objects in the scene. In this case a simple least-squares analysis leads to a set of three linear equations in the three unknown components of the angular velocity vector $\omega = (A, B, C)^T$. The coefficients of these equations are once again sums over the whole image of products of brightness derivatives and image coordinates. The algorithm is remarkably robust with respect to noise in the brightness derivatives, because the problem is so highly overdetermined (three unknowns and hundreds of thousands of measurements).

2   **Pure Translation:**   [Horn & Weldon 1988] In the case of pure translation, the task is to recover the direction of the translation vector. The *focus of expansion* is the intersection of this vector with the image plane, that is, it is the image of the point towards which the observer is moving. Once the focus of expansion has been located, relative distances of selected points in the scene (where the brightness gradient is large enough in the direction towards the focus of expansion) can be estimated. (One simply divides the rate of change of brightness in the direction towards the focus of expansion by the time rate of change of brightness.) There are several methods for recovering the direction of translation. The most promising at this point requires eigenvector-eigenvalue decomposition of a 3×3 matrix constructed using sums of products of brightness derivatives and image coordinates. These sums could be computed on-chip, with the final analysis being done off-chip. This algorithm is not nearly as robust as the one for pure rotation, because there are now an enormous number of additional "unknowns,"

namely the distances to the scene at each picture cell. For the same reason this algorithm is much more interesting because it allows us to recover depth and thus obtain surface shape information.

3 **Planar Surface:**   [Horn & Negahdaripour 1987] If the scene consists of a single planar surface (perhaps an airport viewed from a landing aircraft), it is possible to compute the direction of translation, the orientation of the plane, the rotational velocity of the observer, as well as the time to impact, directly from certain sums accumulated over the whole image. There is a two-way ambiguity in the result that can be resolved using other sensory information or by waiting for new solutions based on subsequent frames. The sums required are "moments," products of the partial derivatives of brightness (E_x, E_y, and E_z) and the image coordinates x, and y. The final calculation involves eigenvector-eigenvalue decomposition of a 3×3 matrix constructed using these sums, but this can be done off-chip. Both closed form and iterative solutions are known. There are quite a large number of different sums needed, but each is relatively simple to compute.

4 **Other Constraints on Motion:**   E. J. Weldon and his students at the University of Hawaii have been investigating a number of other special restrictions on motion. A wheeled vehicle moving in contact with a smooth surface is confined to translation in the local tangent plane and rotation about the local normal. Thus the rotation vector has to be perpendicular to the translation vector. This constraint allows a solution of the motion vision problem that takes a form very similar to the one discussed above. Another interesting special case arises when the vehicle can rotate only about an axis parallel to the translational vector. There is also strong interest in exploiting fixation or tracking. If one fixates on a point in the moving environment, a constraint is introduced between the instantaneous rotational and translational velocities of the observer relative to the environment. This allows one to simplify the motion constraint equation and reduces the problem to something similar to that of pure translation.

The general case (arbitrary surface, both translation and rotation) has not been solved yet. Also, the pure translation solutions are not very robust, suggesting that one needs to continue the solution in time in order to get stable results (all of the methods discussed above work "instantaneously" using two image frames, and do not make much use of information in earlier frames).

   In the case of pure translation, depth is recovered only in places where the local brightness gradient is strong enough in the direction towards the focus of expansion. This suggests the need for a smooth interpolation process that fills in the rest. It might take the form of the solution of Poisson's equation or the bi-harmonic equation. A simple passive network will do for Poisson's equation, of course. If the higher order approach is taken, negative resistances and more connections are required. It is possible, however, as we saw earlier, to decompose the bi-harmonic equation into coupled Poisson's equations. The latter can then be solved using coupled resistive network.

Finally, to deal with depth-discontinuities, one can introduce line-processes once again. Naturally, we are now talking about a very complicated system!

Constant flow velocity

The method that assumes that optical flow is constant in a patch will be considered next, as a simple illustration of the kind of approach taken. First we review the brightness change constraint equation. Image brightness $E(x, y, t)$ is a function of three variables. If the brightness of a small patch does not change as it moves, we can write:

$$\frac{dE}{dt} = 0,$$

which can be expanded to yield:

$$\frac{\partial E}{\partial x}\frac{dx}{dt} + \frac{\partial E}{\partial y}\frac{dy}{dt} + \frac{\partial E}{\partial t} = 0,$$

or

$$uE_x + vE_y + E_t = 0,$$

where E_x, E_y are the components of the brightness gradient, while E_t is the time rate of change of brightness. This so-called *brightness change constraint equation* provides only one constraint on the two components of image flow, u and v. Thus image flow cannot be recovered locally without further information.

Suppose now that the image flow components u and v are constant over a patch in the image. Then we can recover them using a least squares approach: We minimize the total error

$$I = \iint_D (uE_x + vE_y + E_t)^2 \, dx \, dy.$$

Differentiation with respect to u and v leads to

$$\frac{dI}{du} = \iint_D (uE_x + vE_y + E_t) \, E_x \, dx \, dy,$$

$$\frac{dI}{dv} = \iint_D (uE_x + vE_y + E_t) \, E_y \, dx \, dy.$$

Setting these derivatives equal to zero, we obtain

$$u \iint_D E_x^2 + v \iint_D E_x E_y = - \iint_D E_x E_t \,,$$

$$u \iint_D E_y E_x + v \iint_D E_y^2 = - \iint_D E_y E_t \,.$$

These are two linear equations that can be easily solved for u and v.

$$D\, u = \iint_D E_y^2 \iint_D E_x E_t - \iint_D E_x E_y \iint_D E_y E_t \,,$$

and

$$D\, v = \iint_D E_x E_y \iint_D E_x E_t - \iint_D E_x^2 \iint_D E_y E_t \,,$$

where D is the determinant of the coefficient matrix, that is,

$$D = \iint_D E_x^2 \iint_D E_y^2 - \left(\iint_D E_x E_y \right)^2 \,.$$

The coefficients are easily calculated in parallel, if so desired.

While this closed form solution is very appealing in a sequential digital implementation, it involves division and other operations that are not particularly easily carried out in analog circuitry. In this case, an iterative or feedback strategy may be favored. Using a gradient descent approach, we arrive at

$$\frac{du}{dt} = -\alpha \iint_D \left(u E_x + v E_y + E_t \right) E_x \, dx \, dy \,,$$

$$\frac{dv}{dt} = -\alpha \iint_D \left(u E_x + v E_y + E_t \right) E_y \, dx \, dy \,.$$

At each picture cell, we estimate the derivatives of brightness, and compute the error in the brightness change constraint equation

$$e = \left(u E_x + v E_y + E_t \right) \,,$$

using global buses whose potentials represent u and v. Currents proportional to $-e\, E_x$ and $-e\, E_y$ are injected into the buses for u and v respectively. This is essentially how the constant flow velocity chip of Tanner [1986] and Tanner Mead [1987] works.

Special purpose direct motion vision systems

We have seen that in short-range motion vision one need not solve the correspondence problem. One can instead use derivatives of image brightness directly to estimate the motion of the camera. The time rate of change of image brightness at a particular picture cell can be predicted if the brightness gradient and the motion of the pattern in the image is known. This two-dimensional motion of patterns in the image, in turn, can be predicted if the three-dimensional motion of the camera is given. Given these facts, it should be apparent that the motion of the camera can be found by finding the motion that best predicts the time rate of change of brightness (t-derivative) at all picture cells, given the observed brightness gradients (x- and y-derivatives). Once the instantaneous rotational and translational motion of the camera have been found, one can determine the depth at points where the brightness gradient is large and oriented appropriately.

As discussed above, several special situations have already been dealt with, including the case where the camera is known to be rotating only, the case where the camera is translating only, and the case of arbitrary motion where the surface being viewed is known to be planar. The solution in the case of pure rotation is very robust against noise (because there are only three unknowns and thousands of constraints) and so well worth implementing. The solution in the case of arbitrary motion with respect to a planar surface is also quite robust, although it is subject to a two-way ambiguity. In this case there are eight unknowns (the rotational velocity, the translational velocity and the unit surface normal). The solution in the case of pure translation is more sensitive to noise (because there are about as many unknowns as constraints), but of great interest, because depth can be recovered. An elegant solution to the general case has not yet been found. It can, however, be expected that it will not be less robust than the pure translation case (because there are only three more unknowns).

We will now describe in detail a method for the solution of the pure rotation case and a method for the solution of the pure translation case. We saw earlier that if the brightness of a patch does not change as it moves, we obtain the brightness change constraint equation

$$uE_x + vE_y + E_t = 0 \,,$$

where E_x, E_y are the components of the brightness gradient, while E_t is the time rate of change of brightness. This equation provides one constraint on the image flow components u and v. Thus image flow cannot be recovered locally without additional constraint.

We are now dealing, however, with rigid body motion, where image flow is heavily constrained. The image flow components u and v dependent on the instantaneous translational and rotational velocities of the camera, denoted $\mathbf{t} = (U, V, W)^T$ and $\boldsymbol{\omega} = (A, B, C)^T$ respectively. It can be shown by differentiating the the equation for perspective projection [Longuett-Higgins & Prazdny 1980], that

$$u = \frac{-U + xW}{Z} + A\,xy - B(1 + x^2) + C\,y \,,$$

$$v = \frac{-V + yW}{Z} + A(1 + y^2) - B\,xy - C\,x \,,$$

where Z is the depth (distance along the optical axis) at the image point (x, y). Combining this with the brightness change constraint equation, we obtain [Horn & Weldon 1988]

$$E_t + \mathbf{v} \cdot \boldsymbol{\omega} + \frac{1}{Z} \mathbf{s} \cdot \mathbf{t} = 0 \,,$$

where

$$\mathbf{v} = \begin{pmatrix} +E_y + y(xE_x + yE_y) \\ -E_x - x(xE_x + yE_y) \\ yE_x - xE_y \end{pmatrix} \,,$$

and

$$\mathbf{s} = \begin{pmatrix} -E_x \\ -E_y \\ xE_x + yE_y \end{pmatrix} \,.$$

This is called the *rigid body brightness change constraint equation.*

Feedback computation of instantaneous rotational velocity

Horn and Weldon [1988] rediscovered a method apparently first invented by Alomoinos and Brown [1985] for direct motion vision in the case of pure rotation. This method uses integrals of products of first partial derivatives of image brightness and image coordinates and involves the solution of a system of three linear equations in three unknowns. When there is no translational motion, the brightness change constraint equation becomes just

$$E_t + \mathbf{v} \cdot \boldsymbol{\omega} = 0 \,.$$

This suggests a least-squares approach, where we minimize

$$I = \iint_D (E_t + \mathbf{v} \cdot \boldsymbol{\omega})^2 \, dx \, dy \,,$$

by suitable choice of the instantaneous rotational velocity $\boldsymbol{\omega}$. This leads to the simple equation

$$\left(\iint_D \mathbf{v}\mathbf{v}^T \, dx \, dy \right) \boldsymbol{\omega} = - \iint_D E_t \mathbf{v} \, dx \, dy \,.$$

This vector equation corresponds to three scalar equations in the three unknown components A, B, and C of the instantaneous rotational velocity vector. The system of linear equations can be solved explicitly, but this involves division by the determinant of the coefficient matrix. When considering analog implementation, it is better to use a resistive network to solve the equations. Yet another attractive alternative is to use a feedback scheme (not unlike the one used to solve for the optical flow velocity components in the case when they are assumed to be constant over the image patch being considered).

Finally, the solution can be obtained by walking down the gradient of the total error. The derivative with respect to $\boldsymbol{\omega}$ of the sum of squares of errors is just

$$\frac{dI}{d\boldsymbol{\omega}} = 2 \iint_D (E_t + \mathbf{v} \cdot \boldsymbol{\omega})\mathbf{v}\, dx\, dy\,.$$

This suggest a feedback scheme described by the equation

$$\frac{d\boldsymbol{\omega}}{dt} = -\alpha \iint_D (E_t + \mathbf{v} \cdot \boldsymbol{\omega})\mathbf{v}\, dx\, dy\,.$$

The idea revolves around a bus, with potential on three wires proportional to the present estimates of the components A, B and C of the instantaneous angular velocity $\boldsymbol{\omega}$. Estimates of the partial derivatives of image brightness (the components of the brightness gradient and the time rate of change of brightness) are computed at each picture cell. From them, and the position (x, y) of the cell, one can compute $\mathbf{v}$. The coordinates x and y can be made available to each cell using resistive chains that are connected to fixed potentials on the sides of the chip. (It may be useful also to directly supply xy, $(1 + x^2)$ and $(1 + y^2)$, because these are coefficients in the expression for $\mathbf{v}$).

Next, one computes the error term

$$e = E_t + \mathbf{v} \cdot \boldsymbol{\omega}\,,$$

which, in the absence of noise, is zero when the correct solution has been found. Currents are fed into the bus proportional to

$$-e\mathbf{v} = -(E_t + \mathbf{v} \cdot \boldsymbol{\omega})\mathbf{v}\,.$$

Each of the three bus wires is terminated in a capacitance. We now have a system that obeys an equation like

$$\frac{d\boldsymbol{\omega}}{dt} = -\alpha \iint_D (E_t + \mathbf{v} \cdot \boldsymbol{\omega})\mathbf{v}\, dx\, dy\,,$$

the steady state solution of which is

$$\iint_D (E_t + \mathbf{v} \cdot \boldsymbol{\omega})\mathbf{v}\, dx\, dy = \mathbf{0}\,,$$

or

$$\left(\iint_D \mathbf{v}\mathbf{v}^T\, dx\, dy\right)\boldsymbol{\omega} = -\iint_D E_t\mathbf{v}\, dx\, dy\,.$$

The feedback scheme involves considerably less computation than the closed form solution (for example, we do not have to compute the 3×3 matrix $\mathbf{v}\mathbf{v}^T$). Also, the feedback scheme can be shown to be stable (as long as the integral of $\mathbf{v}\mathbf{v}^T$ is not singular, that is, as long as there is sufficient contrast in the image texture).

The elementary components needed are the sensors, differential buffer amplifiers that estimate spatial derivatives, approximate time delays for estimating the temporal derivative, four-quadrant analog multipliers, and current sources. There also will be resistive chains to supply values of x and y at each image location.

Computation of instantaneous translational velocity

While the scheme described above for recovering the rotational velocity is very robust as shown both by sensitivity analysis and experimentation on computers with both synthetic and real images, it is does not allow us to recover depth. This is because there is no dependence of the brightness derivatives on depth when there is no translational motion. We now consider the other extreme, when there is only translational motion.

When there is no rotational motion, the brightness change constraint equation becomes just

$$E_t + (\mathbf{s} \cdot \mathbf{t})\frac{1}{Z} = 0\,.$$

Note that multiplying both Z and $\mathbf{t}$ by a constant does not perturb the equality. This tells us right away that there will be a scale factor ambiguity in recovering motion and depth. We take care of this by attempting only to recover the direction of motion. That is, we will treat $\mathbf{t}$ as a unit vector.

We can solve the constraint equation above for the depth Z in terms of the unknown motion parameters. We obtain

$$Z = -\frac{\mathbf{s} \cdot \mathbf{t}}{E_t}\,.$$

If our estimate of the instantaneous translational motion $\mathbf{t}$ is incorrect, we will obviously obtain incorrect values for the depth from this equation. Some of these values may be negative (which correspond to points on objects behind the camera), while others will be unexpectedly large. Some methods have been explored that to find a direction of translational motion that yields the smallest number of negative depth values when applied to the image brightness gradients [Horn & Weldon 1988]. Although these methods work, they have yet to show promise in terms of computational expediency. We consider another approach next.

In many cases, particularly in industrial robotics, the depth range is bounded and the occurrence of very large depth values is not normally anticipated. One method for estimating the instantaneous translation velocity makes use of this observation.[11] We essentially look for a translational velocity $\mathbf{t}$ that keeps Z small at most points in the image. Suppose, for example, that we find the translational velocity that minimizes

$$I = \iint_D Z^2 \, dx \, dy = \iint_D \frac{(\mathbf{s} \cdot \mathbf{t})^2}{E_t^2} \, dx \, dy\,,$$

subject to the constraint that $\mathbf{t}$ be a unit vector. We cannot measure brightness exactly, so there will be some error in our estimate of E_t. To avoid problems due to noise in places where E_t is almost zero, we may

---

[11]The derivation of the method in terms of a minimization of the integral of Z^2 is merely an explanatory artifice. There is a way of arriving at the same result in a way that does not appear to be this *ad hoc* [Horn & Weldon 1988].

introduce an offset in the denominator as follows:

$$I = \iint_D w(E_t) \, (\mathbf{s} \cdot \mathbf{t})^2 \, dx \, dy \,,$$

where $w(E_t) = 1/(E_t^2 + \epsilon^2)$. This integral can also be written in the form

$$I = \mathbf{t}^T \left(\iint_D w(E_t) \, \mathbf{s}\mathbf{s}^T \, dx \, dy \right) \mathbf{t} = \mathbf{t}^T S \, \mathbf{t} \,,$$

where S is a 3×3 matrix. The expression for I is clearly a quadratic form in $\mathbf{t}$. Given the constraint that $\mathbf{t}$ be a unit vector, such a quadratic form attains its minimum when $\mathbf{t}$ is the eigenvector of the matrix S corresponding to the smallest eigenvalue (see the discussion of Raleigh's quotient in Korn and Korn [1968]). Analog circuits can be devised to compute these eigenvectors [Horn 1988].

It is also possible to deal with a situation where motion can be arbitrary (that is, both rotation and translation), but the surface shape is constrained. While this problem has a closed form solution [Horn & Negahdaripour 1987], it turns out to be much easier to use gradient descent [Horn 1988]. The circuitry for this begins to be more complex, with several four-quadrant multipliers needed at each picture cell.

Gradient descent methods in general are very appealing when one is thinking about analog implementation. Fortunately it is possible to deal with *constrained* minimization as well as unconstrained minimization using either gradient projection [Horn 1988] or a reversal of the gradient component corresponding to the Lagrangian multiplier, combined with additional penalty functions [Platt & Barr 1988].

Summary and Conclusions

A number of problems in early vision have been explored here and shown to lead to interesting analog networks. The focus was on implementations involving resistive networks, perhaps with capacitors and analog multipliers, as well as simple amplifiers. In several cases, feedback schemes were shown to be considerably simpler to implement than circuits based on the closed form solutions usually sought for in digital implementations. Simple feedback networks with local connections can invert local operations [Horn 1974]. This is of interest because the inverses of local operations typically are global, and direct implementation of these inverses would require unimplementably high wiring densities.

A theorem giving an equivalence between two apparently quite different ways of using the same resistive network sometimes allows one to find a way of implementing a particular computation that is much simpler than the obvious direct implementation. Gradient projection was mentioned as a way of solving constrained minimization problems, although in several cases it was possible to avoid this added complication through judicious normalization of the terms to be minimized and addition of a penalty term.

Also described here is a novel way of interlacing the nodes of a three-dimensional multi-resolution network in a two-dimensional tessellation. The number of nodes decreases from layer to layer by subsampling after low-pass filtering. Each layer contains half the number of nodes in its predecessor.

Using a spatial dimension to represent time in a partial differential equation was shown to lead to new ways of implementing certain convolutional algorithms that would otherwise require a clocked architecture. In this alternate scheme, image data flows in continuously on one end, while processed information flows continuously out the other end.

It is clear that many early vision problems lend themselves to implementation in parallel analog networks. This applies particularly to so-called *direct* methods, as opposed to *feature-based* methods, because the direct methods deal mostly with quantities connected to measurements at individual picture cells as well as their relationship to values at neighboring picture cells. Work on analog methods for early vision, started more than twenty years ago. It has now received a strong new impetus from the more general availability of facilities for integrated circuit design and fabrication. This renewed interest is reflected in the pioneering work at Caltech in Carver Mead's group [Mead 1989]. But no one should think that the methods explored there, or the ideas collected here, comprise anything more than an extremely sparse sampling of what is yet to come.

References

Abdou, I. E., and K. Y. Wong [1982], "Analysis of Linear Interpolation Schemes for Bi-Level Image Applications," *IBM Journal of Research and Development*, vol. 26, no. 6, pp. 667–686, (see Appendix).

Ahuja, N., and B. J. Schachter [1983], *Pattern Models*, John Wiley, New York, NY.

Alomoinos, Y., and C. Brown [1984], "Direct Processing of Curvilinear Motion from Sequence of Perspective Images," *Proceedings of Workshop on Computer Vision Representation and Control*, Annapolis, Maryland.

The author wishes to acknowledge helpful discussions with Robert Floyd, John Harris, Christof Koch, Jim Little, Carver Mead, Tomaso Poggio, David Standley, and John Wyatt.

This chapter describes research done at the Artificial Intelligence Laboratory of the Massachusetts Institute of Technology. Support for this research was provided by a grant from the National Science Foundation, Number MIP-8814612 and by Du Pont Corporation.

Anderson, B. O., and J. B. Moore [1979], *Optimal Filters*, Prentice-Hall, Englewood Cliffs, NJ.

Bachmann, B. L. [1977], "Computer Correlation of Real and Synthetic Terrain Photographs," B.S. Thesis, Department of Electrical Engineering and Computer Science.

Bernstein, R. [1976], "Digital Image Processing of Earth Observation Sensor Data," *IBM Journal of Research and Development*, pp. 40-57, (see Appendᴄx).

Berzins, V. [1984], "Accuracy of Laplacian Edge Detectors," *Computer Vision, Graphics and Image Processing*, vol. 27, no. 2, pp. 195–210.

Blake, A., and A. Zisserman [1988], *Visual Reconstruction*, MIT Press, Cambridge, MA.

Bruss, A. R., and B. K. P. Horn [1983], "Passive Navigation," *Computer Vision, Graphics, and Image Processing*, vol. 21, no. 1, pp. 3–20.

Cagney, F., and J. Mallon [1986], "Real-Time Feature Extraction using Moment Invariants," *Proceedings of the SPIE Conference on Intelligent Robots and Computer Vision*, October 28–31, Cambridge, MA, vol. 726, pp. 120–124.

Canny, J. [1983], "Finding Edges and Lines in Images," Report AIM-720, Artificial Intelligence Laboratory, Massachusetts Institute of Technology, Cambridge, MA.

Courant, R., and D. Hilbert [1953], *Methods of Mathematical Physics*, vol. I, John Wiley and Sons, New York, NY.

DeWeerth, S. P., and C. A. Mead [1988], "A Two-Dimensional Visual Tracking Array," *Proceedings of the 1988 MIT Conference on Very Large Scale Integration*, MIT Press, Cambridge, MA, pp. 259–275.

Floyd, R. W. [1987], private communication, June.

Gamble, E., and T. A. Poggio [1987], "Visual Integration and Detection of Discontinuities: The Key Role of Intensity Edges," Report AIM-970, Artificial Intelligence Laboratory, Massachusetts Institute of Technology, Cambridge, MA.

Geman, S., and D. Geman [1984], "Stochastic Relaxation, Gibbs' Distributions, and the Bayesian Restoration of Images," *IEEE Transactions on Pattern Analysis and Machine Intelligence*, vol. 6, no. 6, pp. 721–741.

Gennert, M. and S. Negahdaripour [1987], "Relaxing the Constant Brightness Assumption in Computing Optical Flow," Report AIM-975, Artificial Intelligence Laboratory, Massachusetts Institute of Technology, Cambridge, MA.

Gilbert, A. L. [1981], "Video Data Conversion and Real-Time Tracking," *IEEE Computer*, pp. 50–56.

Gilbert, A. L., M. K. Giles, G. M. Flachs, R. B. Rogers, and Y. H. U [1980], *IEEE Transactions on Pattern Analysis and Machine Intelligence*, vol. 2, no. 1, pp. 47–56.

Goldfinger, A. M. [1983], "Smooth Interpolation of Digital Terrain Models from Contour Maps," B.S. Thesis, Department of Electrical Engineering and Computer Science, Massachusetts Institute of Technology.

Grimson, W. E. L. [1981], *From Images to Surfaces—A Computational Study of the Human Early Visual System*, MIT Press, Cambridge, MA.

Grimson, W. E. L. [1982], "A Computational Theory of Visual Surface Interpolation," *Philosophical Transactions of the Royal Society B*, vol. 298, pp. 395–427.

Grimson, W. E. L. [1983], "An Implementation of a Computational Theory of Visual Surface Interpolation," *Computer Vision, Graphics and Image Processing*, vol. 22, pp. 39–69.

Grzywacs, N., and A. Yuille [1987], "Massively Parallel Implementations of Theories for Apparent Motion," Report AIM-888, Artificial Intelligence Laboratory, Massachusetts Institute of Technology.

Hartley, R. [1985], "A Gaussian-Weighted Multi-Resolution Edge Detector," *Computer Vision, Graphics and Image Processing*, vol. 30, no. 1, pp. 70–83.

Haralick, R. M. [1984], "Digital Step Edges from Zero Crossings of Second Directional Derivatives," *IEEE Transactions on Pattern Analysis and Machine Intelligence*, vol. 6, no. 1, pp. 113–129.

Harris, J. G. [1986], "The Coupled Depth/Slope Approach to Surface Reconstruction," Report AIM-908, Artificial Intelligence Laboratory, Massachusetts Institute of Technology, Cambridge, MA. Also [1987] *Proceedings of the IEEE International Conference on Computer Vision*, London, England, pp. 277–283.

Harris, J. G. [1989], "An Analog VLSI Chip for Thin-Plate Surface Interpolation," *Proceedings of IEEE Neural Information Processing Systems Conference*, Denver, CO.

Hatamian, M. [1986], "A Real-Time Two-Dimensional Moment Generating Algorithm and Its Single Chip Implementation," *IEEE Transactions on Acoustics, Speech, and Signal Processing*, vol. 34, no. 3, pp. 546–553.

Hatamian, M. [1987], "A Fast Moment Generating Chip," *Proceedings of the International Conference on Digital Signal Processing*, Florence, Italy, pp. 230–234.

Hildreth, E. [1980], "Implementation of A Theory of Edge Detection," Report AIM-579.

Hildreth, E. [1983], "The Detection of Intensity Changes by Computer and Biological Vision Systems," *Computer Vision, Graphics and Image Processing*, vol. 22, no. 1, pp. 1–27.

Horn, B. K. P. [1971], "The Binford-Horn Linefinder," Report AIM-285, Artificial Intelligence Laboratory, Massachusetts Institute of Technology, Cambridge, MA.

Horn, B. K. P. [1972], "VISMEM: A bag of 'robotics' formulae," Report AIW-34, Artificial Intelligence Laboratory, Massachusetts Institute of Technology, Cambridge, MA.

Horn, B. K. P. [1974], "Determining Lightness from an Image," in *Computer Graphics and Image Processing*, vol. 3, no. 1, pp. 277–299.

Horn, B. K. P. [1979], "Automatic Hill-Shading and the Reflectance Map," *Proceedings of the Image Understanding Workshop*, Palo Alto, CA, pp. 79–120. Also AD-A098261 available from National Technical Information Service. Also SAI-80-895-WA available from Science Application Incorporated.

Horn, B. K. P. [1981], "Hill Shading and the Reflectance Map," *Proceedings of the IEEE*, vol. 69, no. 1, pp. 14–47. Also, same title [1982] *Geo-Processing*, vol. 2, pp. 65-146.

Horn, B. K. P. [1983], "The Least Energy Curve," *ACM Transactions on Mathematical Software*, vol. 9, no. 4, pp. 441–460.

Horn, B. K. P. [1986], *Robot Vision*, MIT Press, Cambridge, MA and McGraw-Hill, New York, NY.

Horn, B. K. P. [1988], "Parallel Networks for Machine Vision," Report AIM-1071, Artificial Intelligence Laboratory, Massachusetts Institute of Technology, Cambridge, MA.

Horn, B. K. P. [1989], "Height and Gradient from Shading," Report AIM-1150, Artificial Intelligence Laboratory, Massachusetts Institute of Technology, Cambridge, MA.

Horn, B. K. P., and B. L. Bachmann [1978], "Using Synthetic Images to Register Real Images with Surface Models," *Communications of the ACM*, vol. 21, no. 11, pp. 914–924.

Horn, B. K. P., and M. J. Brooks [1986], "The Variational Approach to Shape from Shading," *Computer Vision, Graphics and Image Processing*, vol. 33, no. 2, pp. 174–208. Also [1985] Report AIM-813, Artificial Intelligence Laboratory, Massachusetts Institute of Technology, Cambridge, MA.

Horn, B. K. P., and M. J. Brooks [1989], *Shape from Shading*, MIT Press, Cambridge, MA.

Horn, B. K. P., and S. Negahdaripour [1987], "Direct Passive Navigation: Analytical Solution for Planes," *IEEE Transactions on Pattern Analysis and Machine Intelligence*, vol. 9, no. 1, pp. 168–176.

Horn, B. K. P., and B. G. Schunck [1981], "Determining Optical Flow," *Artificial Intelligence*, vol. 16, no. 1–3, pp. 185–203.

Horn, B. K. P., and E. J. Weldon Jr. [1988], "Direct Methods for Recovering Motion," *International Journal of Computer Vision*, vol. 2, no. 1, pp. 51–76.

Hutchinson, J., C. Koch, J. Luo, and C. A. Mead [1988], "Computing Motion using Analog and Binary Resistive Networks," *IEEE Computers*, vol. 21, pp. 52-63.

Ikeuchi, K. [1984], "Reconstructing a Depth Map from Intensity Maps," *International Conference on Pattern Recognition*, Montreal, Canada, pp. 736–738. Also "Constructing a Depth Map from Images," Report AIM-744, Artificial

Intelligence Laboratory, Also AD-A135679 available from National Technical Information Service.

Knight, T. [1983], "Design of an Integrated Optical Sensor with On-Chip Pre-Processing," Ph.D. Thesis, Department of Electrical Engineering and Computer Science, Massachusetts Institute of Technology, Cambridge, MA.

Koch, C., J. Marroquin, and A. Yuille [1986], "Analog 'Neuronal' Networks in Early Vision," *Proceedings National Academy of Sciences, USA* (Biophysics), vol. 83, pp. 4263–4267. Also [1985] Report AIM-751, Artificial Intelligence Laboratory, Massachusetts Institute of Technology, Cambridge, MA.

Korn, G. A., and T. M. Korn [1968], *Mathematical Handbook for Scientists and Engineers*, McGraw-Hill.

Larson, N. G., K. Nishihara and B. K. P. Horn [1981], "Digital Gaussian Convolver," Patent Application, Registry no. 26192, April 22.

Longuett-Higgins, H. C., and K. Prazdny [1980], "The Interpretation of a Moving Retinal Image," *Proceedings of the Royal Society of London B*, vol. 208, pp. 385–397.

Luo, J., C. Koch, and C. Mead [1988], "An Experimental Subthreshold, Analog CMOS two-dimensional Surface Interpolation Circuit," *Proceedings of IEEE Neural Information Processing Systems Conference*, Denver.

MacLeod, I. D. G. [1970a], "A Study in Automatic Photo-Interpretation," Ph.D. Thesis, Department of Engineering Physics, Australian National University, Canberra, Australia.

MacLeod, I. D. G. [1970b], "On Finding Structure in Pictures," in *Picture Language Machines*, edited by S. Kaneff, Academic Press, London, England, pp. 231–256.

Mahoney, J. V. [1980], "Interpolation of a Contour Map of the Island of Mauritius using Elastic Membranes and Thin Plates," unpublished work in Undergraduate Research Opportunities Program, Massachusetts Institute of Technology.

Marr, D. [1976], "Early Processing of Visual Information," *Philosophical Transactions of the Royal Society B*, vol. 275, pp. 1377–1388.

Marr, D., and E. Hildreth [1980], "Theory of Edge Detection," *Proceedings of the Royal Society B*, vol. 207, pp. 187–217.

Mead, C. A. [1989], *Analog VLSI and Neural Systems*, Addison-Wesley, Reading, MA.

Murray, D. W., and B. F. Buxton [1987], "Scene Segmentation from Visual Motion Using Global Optimization," *IEEE Transactions on Pattern Analysis and Machine Intelligence*, vol. 9, no. 2, pp. 147–163.

Nagel, H. H. [1984], Unpublished Internal Report, University of Hamburg.

Norton, S. W. [1983], "Information Theoretic Surface Estimation Using Elevation Data," B.S. Thesis, Department of Electrical Engineering and Computer Science.

Platt, J. C., and A. H. Barr [1988], "Constrained Differential Optimization for Neural Networks," Technical Report TR-88-17, Computer Science Department, California Institute of Technology, Pasadena, CA. Also [1987] *Proceedings of IEEE Neural Information Processing Systems Conference.*

Poggio, T. A., and V. Torre [1984], "Ill-Posed Problems and Regularization Analysis in Early Vision," Report AIM-773, Artificial Intelligence Laboratory, Massachusetts Institute of Technology, Cambridge, MA.

Rifman, S. S., and D. M. McKinnon [1974], "Evaluation of Digital Correction Techniques—for ERTS Images," Report Number E74-10792, TRW Systems Group, July 1974 (see Chapter 4). Also Final Report TRW 20634-6003-TU-00, NASA Goddard Space Flight Center.

Roberts, L. G. [1965], "Machine Perception of Three-Dimensional Solids," in *Optical and Electro-Optical Information Processing*, edited by J. T. Tippet *et al.*, MIT Press, Cambridge, MA, pp. 159–197.

Rosenfeld, A. and M. Thurston [1971], "Edge and Curve Detection for Visual Scene Analysis," *IEEE Transactions on Computers*, vol. 20, no. 5, p. 562–569.

Rosenfeld, A., M. Thurston, and Y. H. Lee [1972], "Edge and Curve Detection: Further Experiments," *IEEE Transactions on Computers*, vol. 21, no. 7, p. 677–715.

Sage, J. P. [1984], "Gaussian Convolution of Images Stored in a Charge-Coupled Device," Solid State Research, Quarterly Technical Report for period from 1 August to 31 October 1983, MIT Lincoln Laboratory, pp. 53–59.

Sage, J. P., and A. L. Lattes [1987], "A High-Speed Two-Dimensional CCD Gaussian Image Convolver," Solid State Research, Quarterly Technical Report for period from 1 August to 31 October 1986, MIT Lincoln Laboratory, pp. 49–52.

Sjoberg, R. J., and B. K. P. Horn [1983], "Atmospheric Effects in Satellite Imaging of Mountainous Terrain," *Applied Optics*, vol. 22, no. 11, pp. 1702–1716.

Strat, T. M. [1977], "Automatic Production of Shaded Orthographic Projections of Terrain," B.S. Thesis, Department of Electrical Engineering and Computer Science.

Tanner, J. E. [1986], "Integrated Optical Motion Detection," Ph.D. Thesis, Computer Science Department, California Institute of Technology, Pasadena, CA. Technical Report 5223:TR:86

Tanner, J. E., and C. A. Mead [1987], "An Integrated Optical Motion Sensor," *VLSI Signal Processing II, (Proceedings of the ASSP Conference on VLSI Signal Processing)*, UCLA, pp 59–76.

Terzopoulos, D. [1983], "Multilevel Computational Processes for Visual Surface Reconstruction," *Computer Vision, Graphics and Image Processing*, vol. 24, no. 1, pp. 52–96.

Terzopoulos, D. [1984], "Efficient Multiresolution Algorithms for Computing Lightness, Shape from Shading, and Optical Flow," *International Joint Conference on Artificial Intelligence*, University of Texas, Austin, TX, pp. 314–317.

Torre, V., and T. A. P gio [1986], "On Edge Detection," *IEEE Transactions on Pattern Analysis and Machine Intelligence*, vol. 8, no. 2, pp. 147–163, Also [1984] Report AIM-768,Artificial Intelligence Laboratory, Massachusetts Institute of Technology, Cambridge, MA.

Weldon, E. J., Jr. [1986], Unpublished Internal Report, University of Hawaii, private communication.

Wiener, N. [1966], *Extrapolation, Interpolation, and Smoothing of Stationary Time Series with Engineering Applications*, MIT Press, Cambridge, MA.

Woodham, R. J. [1977], "A Cooperative Algorithm for Determining Surface Orientation from a Single View," *International Joint Conference on Artificial Intelligence*, Cambridge, MA, pp. 635–641.

Bibliography

Abdou, I. E., and K. Y. Wong [1982], "Analysis of Linear Interpolation Schemes for Bi-Level Image Applications," *IBM Journal of Research and Development*, vol. 26, no. 6, pp. 667–686.

Abu-Mostafa, Y. S., and D. Praltis [1987], "Optical neural computing," *Scientific American*, vol. 256, no. 3, pp. 66–73.

Adelson, E. H., and J. A. Movshon [1982], "Phenomenal coherence of moving visual patterns," *Nature (London)* vol. 300, pp. 523–525.

Adiv, G. [1984], "Determining 3-D Motion and Structure from Optical Flow Generated by Several Moving Objects," COINS TR 84-07, Computer and Information Science, University of Massachusetts, Amherst, MA.

Ahuja, N., and B. J. Schachter [1983], *Pattern Models*, John Wiley, New York, NY.

Albert, A. E. [1972], "Regression and the Moore-Penrose pseudoinverse," Academic Press, New York.

Albus, J. S. [1975a], "A New Approach to Manipulator Control: The Cerebellar Model Articulation Controller (CMAC)," *ASME J. Dynamic Systems, Meas., Control*, pp. 220-227.

Albus, J. S. [1975b] "Data Storage in the Cerebellar Model Articulation Controller (CMAC)," *ASME J. Dynamic Systems, Meas., Control*, pp. 228-233.

Aloimonos, Y., and C. Brown [1984], "Direct Processing of Curvilinear Motion from a Sequence of Perspective Images," *Proceedings of the Workshop on Computer Vision, Representation and Control*, Annapolis, Maryland.

Alt, F. Z. [1962], "Digital pattern recognition by moments," in *Optical Character Recognition*, edited by G. L. Fischer, D. K. Pollock, B. Raddack, and M. E. Stevens, McGregor & Werner Inc., Washington.

An, C. H., C. G. Atkeson, and J. M. Hollerbach [1988], *Model-Based Control of a Robot Manipulator*, MIT Press, Cambridge, MA.

Anderson, B. O., and J. B. Moore [1979], *Optimal Filters*, Prentice-Hall, Englewood Cliffs, NJ.

Andreev, G. Y., and N. M. Laktionev, [1969] "Contact stress during automatic assembly," *Russian Engineering Journal*, vol. 49, no. 11, p. 57.

Armstrong, B. [1987], "On finding 'exciting' trajectories for identification involving systems with non-linear dynamics," *Proc. IEEE Int. Conf. Robotics and Automation*, Raleigh, NC, pp. 1131-39.

Armstrong, Brian [1988], "Dynamics for Robot Control: Friction Modeling and Ensuring Excitation During Parameter Identification," Ph.D. Thesis, Department of Electrical Engineering, Stanford University, Stanford, CA.

Arnold, V. I. [1980], *Mathematical Methods of Classical Mechanics*, Springer-Verlag, New York, Heidelberg, Berlin.

Asada, H., and M. Brady [1985], "The curvature primal sketch," *IEEE PAMI* vol. 8, no. 1, pp. 2-14.

Asada, Haruhiko, Zeng-Dong Ma, and Hidekats Tokumaru [1987], "Inverse Dynamics of Flexible Robot Arms for Trajectory Control," *Modeling and Control of Robotic Manipulators,* ASME Winter Annual Meeting, pp. 329–336.

Aspinwall, D. M. [1980], "Acceleration Profiles for Minimizing Residual Response," *Journal of Dynamic Systems, Measurement, and Control,* vol. 102, no. 1, pp. 3–6.

Atkeson, C. G., E. W. Aboaf, J. McIntyre, and D. J. Reinkensmeyer [1988], "Model-Based Robot Learning," *Robotics Research: The Fourth International Symposium,* edited by Robert C. Bolles and Bernard Roth, MIT Press, Cambridge, MA, pp. 103-110.

Atkeson, C. G. [1989], "Learning Arm Kinematics And Dynamics," *Annual Review of Neuroscience,* vol. 12, pp. 157-183.

Ayache, N. J., and O. D. Faugeras [1982], "Recognition of partially visible planar shapes," *Proc. 6th Intl. Conf. Pattern Recognition,* Munich.

Ayache, N. J., and O. D. Faugeras [1986], "HYPER: A new approach for the recognition and positioning of two-dimensional objects," *IEEE Trans. Pattern Anal. Machine Intell.* PAMI, vol. 8 no. 1, pp. 44–54.

Bülthoff, Heinrich H., James J. Little, and Tomaso Poggio [1989], "A parallel algorithm for real-time computation of optical flow," *Nature,* vol. 337, pp. 549-553.

Bülthoff, Heinrich H., and Hamspeter A. Mallot [1988], "Integration of depth modules: stereo and shading," *J. Opt. Soc. Am.,* vol. 5, pp. 1749-1758.

Bachmann, B. L. [1977], "Computer Correlation of Real and Synthetic Terrain Photographs," B.S. Thesis, Department of Electrical Engineering and Computer Science.

Baird, H. [1986], *Model-Based Image Matching Using Location,* MIT Press, Cambridge, MA.

Baker H. H. [1982], "Depth from edge and intensity based stereo," Stanford University Technical Report STAN-CS-82-930.

Ballard, D. H., and H. Tanaka [1985], "Transformational form perception in 3D: Constraints, algorithms, implementation," *Proc. 9th Joint. Int. Conf. Art. Intel.,* pp. 964-968.

Ballard, D. H. [1981], "Generalizing the Hough transform to detect arbitrary patterns," *Pattern Recogn.,* vol. 13, no. 2, pp. 111–122.

Ballard, D. H. [1986], "Cortical connections and parallel processing: Structure and function," *Behavioral & Brain Sciences,* vol. 9, pp. 67-120.

Barlow, H. B. [1953], *J. Phsiol. Lond.,* vol. 119, pp. 69–88.

Barlow, H. B., R. Narasimhan, and A. Rosenfeld [1972], "Visual pattern analysis in machines and animals," *Science,* vol. 177, pp. 567-575.

Barlow, H. B. [1972], "Single units and sensation: A neuron doctrine for perceptual psychology?" *Perception, I.,* pp. 371-394.

Barnhill, R. E. [1977], "Representation And Approximation of Surfaces," in *Mathematical Software III,* edited by J. R. Rice, Academic Press, New York, pp. 69-120.

Barrow, H. G., and J. M. Tenenbaum [1978], "Recovering Intrinsic Scene Characteristics from Images," in *Computer Vision Systems*, edited by A. Hanson, and E. Riseman, Academic Press, New York.

Barrow, H. G., and J. M. Tennenbaum [1981], *Artificial Intelligence*, vol. 17, pp. 75–117.

Barto, A. G., R. S. Sutton, and C. W. Anderson [1983], "Neuronlike Adaptive Elements That Can Solve Difficult Learning Control Problems," *IEEE Transactions on Systems, Man, and Cybernetics*, vol. SMC-13, no. 5, pp. 834-845.

Bässler, Ulrich [1983], "Neural Basis of Elementary Behavior in Stick Insects," Springer-Verlag.

Bülthoff H., and H. Mallot [1987], "Interaction of Different Modules in Depth Perception," *Proc. First Intl. Conf. on Computer Vision*, Computer Society of the IEEE, Washington, DC, pp. 295-305.

Baum, E. B., J. Moody, and F. Wilczek [1988], "Internal Representations for Associative Memory," *Biological Cybernetics*, vol. 59, pp. 217-228.

Bayo, E. [1988], "Computed Torque for the Position Control of Open-Chain Flexible Robots," *Proceedings of the 1988 IEEE International Conference on Robotics and Automation*, pp. 316–321, Philadelphia, PA.

Bennett, M. V. L. [1977], in *Handbook of Physiology*, pp. 221–250 American Physiological Society, Bethesda.

Bennett, D. J., and J. M. Hollerbach [1988], "Self-calibration of single-loop, closed kinematic chains formed by dual or redundant manipulators," *Proc. 27th IEEE Conf. Decision and Control*, Austin, TX.

Bennett, D. J., and J. M. Hollerbach [1989a], "Identifying the kinematics of non-redundant serial chain manipulators by a closed-loop approach," *Proc. Fourth International Conference on Advanced Robotics*, Columbus, OH.

Bennett, D. J., and J. M. Hollerbach [1989b], "Identifying the kinematics of robots and their tasks," *Proc. IEEE Int. Conf. Robotics and Automation*, Scottsdale, AZ.

Bernstein, R. [1976], "Digital Image Processing of Earth Observation Sensor Data," *IBM Journal of Research and Development*, pp. 40-57.

Bertero, M. [1982], in *Problem non ben posti ed inversi*, Istituto di Analisi Globale, Firenze.

Bertero, M., C. Del Mol, and E. R. Pike [to appear], *J. Inverse Prob.*.

Bertero, Mario, Tomaso Poggio, and Vincent Torre [1988], "Ill-Posed Problems in Early Vision," *Proceedings of the IEEE*, vol. 76, pp. 869-889.

Berzins, V. [1984], "Accuracy of Laplacian Edge Detectors," *Computer Vision, Graphics and Image Processing*, vol. 27, no. 2, pp. 195–210.

Besag, J. [1972], "Spatial Interaction and the Statistical Analysis of Lattice systems," *J. Roy. Stat. Soc.*, vol. B34, pp. 75-83.

Besl, P. J., and R. C. Jain [1985], "Three-dimensional object recognition," *ACM Computing Surveys* vol. 17, no. 1, pp. 75–145.

Besner, D., and M. Coltheart [1975], "Same-different judgments with words and nonwords: The differential effect of relative size," *Memory & Cognition*, vol. 3, pp. 673-677.

Besner, D. [1978], "Pattern recognition: Are size and orientation additive factors?" *Perception & Psychophysics*, vol. 23, p. 93.

Besner, D. [1983], 'Visual pattern recognition: Size preprocessing reexamined," *Quat. J. Exp. Psychol.*, vol. 35A, pp. 209-216.

Beymer, David [1989], "Junctions: their detection and use for grouping in images," Massachusetts Institute of Technology, (in press).

Bhanu, B., and O. D. Faugeras [1984], "Shape matching of two-dimensional objects," *IEEE Trans. Pattern Anal. Machine Intell.*, PAMI, vol. 6, no. 3.

Biederman, I. [1985], "Human image understanding: Recent research and a theory," *Comp. Vis. Graph. Im. Proc.*, vol. 32, pp. 29-73.

Binford, T. O. [1971], "Visual perception by computer," presented to the *IEEE Conference on Systems and Control*, Miami.

Binford, T. O. [1982], "Survey of model-based image analysis systems," *Int. J. Robotics Research,* vol. 1, no. 1, pp. 18-64.

Bizzi, Emilio [1980], "Central and Peripheral Mechanisms in Motor Control," *Tutorials in Motor Behavior*, edited by G. E. Stelmach and J. Requin, North-Holland.

Blake, A., and A. Zisserman [1988], *Visual Reconstruction*, MIT Press, Cambridge, MA.

Blake, A. [1983], *Pattern Recognition Lett.*, vol. 1, pp. 393–399.

Blake, A [1986], "On the Geometric Information Obtainable from Simultaneous Observation of Stereo Contour and Shading," Technical Report CSR-205-86, Dept. of Computer Science, University of Edinburgh.

Blelloch, G. E. [1987], "Scans as Primitive Parallel Operations," *Proc. Intl. Conf. on Parallel Processing*, pp. 355-362.

Bliss, J. [1985] "Velocity Tuned Spatio-Temporal Interpolation and Approximation in Vision," M.S. Thesis, Department of Electrical Engineering and Computer Science, Massachusetts Institute of Technology, Cambridge, MA.

Bolles, R. C., and R. A. Cain [1982], "Recognizing and locating partially visible objects: The local-feature-focus method," *Int. J. Robotics Research,* vol. 1, no. 3, pp. 57-82.

Bolles, R. C., and P. Horaud [1986], "3DPO: A three-dimensional part orientation system," *Int. J. Robotics Res.*, vol. 5, no. 3, pp. 3–26.

Bobick, A. [1983], "A hybrid approach to structure-from motion," in *Proceedings of the ACM Interdisciplinary Workshop on Motion*, Toronto, Canada, pp. 91-109.

Bolz, Ray E., and George L. Tuve [1973], "CRC Handbook of Tables for Applied Engineering Science," CRC Press, Inc., p. 1071, Boca Raton, FA.

Braddick, O. J. [1974], "A short-range process in apparent motion," *Vision Research*, vol. 14, pp. 519-527.

Brady, J. M., G. E. Hinton, and T. J. Sejnowski [1983], *Nature*, vol. 306, pp. 21–26.

Brady M., J. Ponce, A. Yuille, and H. Asada [1985], "Describing surfaces," Report AIM-882, Artificial Intelligence Laboratory, Massachusetts Institute of Technology, Cambridge, MA.

Braunstein, M. L. [1976], *Depth Perception through Motion*, Academic Press, New york.

Braunstein, M. L., G. J. Andersen, M. W. Rouse, and J. S. Tittle, "Recovering viewer-centered depth from disparity, occlusion, and velocity gradients," *Perception and Psychophysics*, vol. 40, pp. 216-224, 1986.

Brock, D. L. [1984], "Strain Gage Based Force and Tactile Sensors," B.S. Thesis, Department of Mechanical Engineering, Massachusetts Institute of Technology, Cambridge, MA.

Brock, D. L. [1987], "Enhancing the Dexterity of a Multi-Fingered Hand Through Controlled Slip Manipulation," M.S. Thesis, Department of Mechanical Engineering, Massachusetts Institute of Technology, Cambridge, MA.

Brooks, R. A. [1981], "Symbolic reasoning among 3-dimensional models and 2-dimensional images," *Artificial Intel.*, vol. 17, pp. 285–349.

Brooks, R. A. [1982], "Symbolic error analysis and robot planning," *Int. J. Robotics Research*, vol. 1, no. 4.

Brooks, Rodney, A. [1984], "Aspects of Mobile Robot Visual Map Making," in *Robotics Research 2*, edited by Hanafusa and Inoue, MIT Press, pp. 369–375.

Brooks, R. A. [1985], "Visual Map Making for a Mobile Robot," *IEEE Conference on Robotics and Automation*, St Louis, pp. 824–829.

Brooks, Rodney A. [1986], "A Robust Layered Control System for a Mobile Robot," *IEEE Journal of Robotics and Automation*, RA-2, pp. 14–23.

Brooks, Rodney A., and Jonathon H. Connell [1986], "Asynchronous Distributed Control System for A Mobile Robot," *Proceedings SPIE*, Cambridge, MA, pp. 77–84.

Brooks, R. A., and T. Lozano–Pérez [1982], *A Subdivision Algorithm in Configuration Space for Findpath with Rotation*, Report AIM-684 Artificial Intelligence Laboratory, Massachusetts Institute of Technology.

Brown, C. M. [1984], *Science*, vol. 224, pp. 1299–1305.

Bruss, A. R., and B. K. P. Horn [1983], "Passive Navigation," *Computer Vision, Graphics, and Image Processing*, vol. 21, no. 1, pp. 3–20.

Buckley, S. J. [1987], "Planning and teaching compliant motion strategies," Report AI-TR–936, Massachusetts Institute of Technology, Artificial Intelligence Laboratory.

Bundesen, C., and A. Larsen [1975], "Visual transformation of size," *J. Exp. Psychol., HP&P*, vol. 1, pp. 214-220.

Burdick, J. W. [1988], *Kinematic analysis and design of redundant manipulators*, Ph.D. Thesis, Stanford University.

Bülthoff', Heinrich H. [1988], personal communication.

CWRP [1981], Committee of Wire Rope Producers, *Wire Rope Users Manual*, American Iron and Steel Institute, Washington, DC.

Cagney, F., and J. Mallon [1986], "Real-Time Feature Extraction using Moment Invariants," *Proceedings of the SPIE Conference on Intelligent Robots and Computer Vision*, October 28–31, Cambridge, MA, vol. 726, pp. 120–124.

Canny, J. F. [1983], "Finding Edges and Lines," Report AI-TR-720, Artificial Intelligence Laboratory, Massachusetts Institute of Technology, Cambridge, MA.

Canny, J. F. [1988], *The complexity of robot motion planning*, MIT Press.

Cerella, J. [1986], "Pigeons and perceptrons," *Pattern Recognition*, vol. 19, no. 6, pp. 431–438.

Cheng, P. E. [1984], "Strong Consistency of Nearest Neighbor Regression Function Estimators," *Journal of Multivariate Analysis*, vol. 15, pp. 63-72.

Childress, D. S. [1972], "Artificial Hand Mechanisms," *ASME Mechanisms Conference and International Symposium on Gearing and Transmissions*, San Francisco.

Chiu, S. L. [1985], "Generating Compliant Motion of Objects with an Articulated Hand," M.S. Thesis, Department of Mechanical Engineering, Massachusetts Institute of Technology, Cambridge, MA.

Chun, Hon M., James D. Turner, and Jer-Nan Juang [1985], "Disturbance-Accommodating Tracking Maneuvers of Flexible Spacecraft," *Journal of the Astronautical Sciences*, vol. 33, no. 2, pp. 197-216.

Cleveland, W. S. [1979], "Robust Locally Weighted Regression and Smoothing Scatterplots," *Journal of the American Statistical Association*, vol. 74, pp. 829-836.

Clocksin, W. F. [1980], "Perception of surface slant and edge labels from optical flow: a computational approach," *Perception*, vol. 9, pp. 253-269.

Clowes, M. B. [1967], "Perception, picture processing, and computers," in *Machine Intelligence*, edited by N. L. Collins, and D. Michie, vol. 1, pp. 181–197, Oliver & Boyd, Edinburgh.

Cole, K. S. [1968], *Membranes, Ions and Impulses*, University of California Press, Berkeley.

Connell, J. H. [1985], "Learning shape descriptions: Generating and generalizing models of visual objects," Report AIM-853, Artificial Intelligence Laboratory, Massachusetts Institute of Technology, Cambridge, MA.

Connell, Jonathan H. [1988], "A Behavior-Based Arm Controller," Report AIM-1025, Artificial Intelligence Laboratory, Massachusetts Institute of Technology, Cambridge, MA.

Cooper, L. A. [1976], "Demonstration of a mental analog of an external rotation," *Perception & Psychophysics*, vol. 1, pp. 20–43.

Corballis, M. C., N. J. Zbrodoff, L. I. Schetzer, and P. B. Butler, [1978], "Decisions about identity and orientation of rotated letters and digits," *Memory & cognition*, vol. 6, pp. 98–107.

Corballis, M. C., and B. A. Nagourney [1978], "Latencies to categorize disoriented alphanumeric characters as letters or digits," *Canad. J. Psychol.*, vol. 32, pp. 186-188.

Corcoran, D. W. J. [1971], *Pattern Recognition*, Penguin Books.

Cornog, K. H. [1985], "Smooth Pursuit and Fixation for Robot Vision," M.S. Thesis, Department of Electrical Engineering and Computer Science, Massachusettes Institute of Technology, Cambridge, MA.

Costello, G. A., and G. J. Butson [1982], "Simplified Bending Theory for Wire Rope," Proceedings of the American Society of Civil Engineers, vol. 108, no. EM2.

Costello, G. A. [1978], "Analytical Investigation of Wire Rope," Applied Mechanics Reviews, vol. 31, no. 7.

Courant, R., and D. Hilbert [1953], *Methods of Mathematical Physics*, vol. I, John Wiley and Sons, New York, NY.

Cover, T. M. [1968], "Estimation by the Nearest Neighbor Rule," *IEEE Transactions on Information Theory,* vol. IT-14, pp. 50-55.

Crain, I. K., and B. K. Bhattacharyya [1967], "Treatment of nonequispaced two dimensional data with a digital computer," *Geoexploration,* vol. 5, pp. 173-194.

Crowley, James L. [1985], "Navigation for an Intelligent Mobile Robot," *IEEE Journal of Robotics and Automation,* RA-1, pp. 31-41.

Cutting, J. E., and L. T. Kozlowski [1977], "Recognizing Friends by Their Walk: Gait Perception Without Familiarity Cues," *Bull. Psychonometric Soc.,* vol. 9, no. 5, pp. 353-356.

Dane, C., and R. Bajcsy [1982], "An object-centered three-dimensional model builder," *Proc. 6th Int. Conf. Pat. Recog.,* Munich, West Germany, pp. 348-350.

Davidon, W. C. [1968], "Variance algorithm for minimization" *The Computer Journal,* vol. 10, pp. 406-413.

Davis L. S. [1982], "Hierarchical generalized Hough transforms and line-segment based generalized Hough transforms," *Pattern Recognition,* vol. 15, pp. 277.

Davis, L. [1979], "Shape matching using relaxation techniques," *IEEE Trans. Pattern Anal. Machine Intell.,* PAMI, vol. 1, no. 1, pp. 60-72.

Dempster, A. P., N. M. Laird, and D. B. Rubin [1977], "Maximum Likelihood from Incomplete Data via the EM Algorithm," *J. Roy. Stat. Soc.,* vol. B39, pp. 1-38.

Denavit, J., and R. S. Hartenberg [1955], "A kinematic notation for lower pair mechanisms based on matrices," *J. Applied Mechanics,* vol. 22, pp. 215-221.

Devroye, L. P. [1978], "The Uniform Convergence of Nearest Neighbor Regression Function Estimators and Their Application in Optimization," *IEEE Transactions on Information Theory,* vol. IT-24, pp. 142-151.

Devroye, L. P. [1981], "On the Almost Everywhere Convergence of Nonparametric Regression Function Estimates," *The Annals of Statistics,* vol. 9, no. 6, pp. 1310-1319.

DeWeerth, S. P., and C. A. Mead [1988], "A Two-Dimensional Visual Tracking Array," *Proceedings of the 1988 MIT Conference on Very Large Scale Integration,* MIT Press, Cambridge, MA, pp. 259-275.

DiPietro, D. M. [1988]," Development of an Actively Compliant Underwater Manipulator," M.S. Thesis, Woods Hole Oceanographic Institution Joint Program in Oceanography and Oceanographic Engineering.

Diamond, R., and S. Carey [1986], "Why faces are and are not special: an effect of expertise," *Journal of Experimental Psychology; General* vol. 115, no. 2, pp. 107-117.

Doherty, J. K. [1976], *Track and Field Omnibook,* Tafnews Press, Los Altos, CA.

Donald, B. R. [1987], "Error detection and recovery for robot motion planning with uncertainty," Report AI-TR-982, Massachusetts Institute of Technology, Artificial Intelligence Laboratory.

Drake, S. H. [1977], "Using Compliance in Lieu of Sensory Feedback for Automatic Assembly," Ph.D. Thesis, Mechanical Engineering Department, Massachusetts Institute of Technology.

Drumheller, M., and T. Poggio [1986], "On Parallel Stereo," *Proc. Intl. Conf. on Robotics and Automation*, IEEE.

Drumheller, M. [1987], "Mobile robot localization using sonar," *IEEE Trans. Pat. Anal. Mach. Intel.*, vol. 9, no. 2, pp. 325–332.

Duda, R. O., and P. E. Hart [1973], *Pattern Classification and Scene Analysis*, John Wiley, New York.

Dufay, B., and J. C. Latombe [1983], "An Approach to Automatic Robot Programming Based on Inductive Learning," *International Symposium on Robotics Research*, Bretton Woods.

Duffy J. [1980], *Analysis of Mechanisms and Robot Manipulators*, Edward Arnold Ltd., London.

Eberman, B. S., and J. K. Salisbury [1989], "Determination of Manipulator Contact Information from Joint Torque Measurements," *Proceedings of the First International Symposium on Experimental Robotics*, Montréal, Canada.

Eberman, B. S. [1989], "Whole Arm Manipulation: Kinematics and Control," M.S. Thesis, Department of Mechanical Engineering, Massachusetts Institute of Technology, Cambridge, MA.

Eden, M. [1962], "A three-dimensional optical illusion," *MIT Research Laboratory of Electronics Quarterly Progress Report*, vol. 64, pp. 267-274.

Ehrlich, A. [1928], "Vehicle Propelled by Steppers," Patent Number 1-691-233.

Eigen, M. [1974], in *The Neurosciences: 3rd Study Program*, edited by F. O. Schmitt, and F. G.Worden) xix–xxvii, MIT Press, Cambridge, MA.

Eley, M. G. [1982], "Identifying rotated letter-like symbols," *Memory & Cognition*, vol. 10, pp. 25-32.

Elfes, Alberto, and Sarosh N. Talukdar [1983], "A Distributed Control System for the CMU Rover," *Proceedings IJCAI, Karlsruhe, West Germany*, pp. 830–833.

Engel, F. L. [1974], "Visual conspecuity and selective background interference in eccentric vision," *Vision Research* vol. 14, pp. 459–471.

Erdmann, M. A. [1986], "Using backprojections for fine-motion planning with uncertainty," *International Journal of Robotics Research*, vol. 5, no. 1, pp. 19–45.

Ernst, H. A. [1961], *A computer-controlled mechanical hand*, Ph.D. Thesis, Massachusetts Institute of Technology.

Eubank, R. L. [1988], *Spline Smoothing and Nonparametric Regression*, Marcel Dekker, New York, pp. 384-387.

Evarts, E. V., E. Bizzi, R. E. Burk, M. Delong, W. T. Thach, Jr. [1971], "Central control of movement," *Neurosciences Research Progress Bulletin* vol. 9 PP. 1-169.

Fahle, M., and T. Poggio [1953], *Proc. R. Soc.*, vol. B213, pp. 451–477.

Fahle, M., and T. Poggio [1980], "Visual Hyperacuity: Spatiotemporal Interpolation in Human Vision," *Proc. Roy. Soc. Lond. B*, vol. 213, pp. 451-477.

Falconer, K. J. [1971], "A general purpose algorithm for contouring over scattered data points," *Nat. Phys. Lab.*, Report NAC 6.

Farmer, J. D., and J. J. Sidorowich [1988], "Exploiting Chaos to Predict the Future and Reduce Noise," Technical Report LA-UR-88-901, Los Alamos National Laboratory, Los Alamos, New Mexico.

Farrenkopf, R. L. [1979], "Optimal Open-Loop Maneuver Profiles for Flexible Spacecraft," *Journal of Guidance and Control,* vol. 2, no. 6, pp. 491–498.

Farwig, R. [1987], "Multivariate Interpolation of Scattered Data by Moving Least Squares Methods," in *Algorithms for Approximation,* edited by J. C. Mason and M. G. Cox, Clarendon Press, Oxford, pp. 193-211.

Faugeras, O. D., and M. Hebert [1983], "A 3-D recognition and positioning algorithm using geometrical matching between primitive surfaces," in *Proc. Eighth Int. Joint Conf. Artificial Intell.,* Karlsruhe, W. Germany, pp. 996–1002.

Faugeras, O. D. [1984], "New steps towards a flexible 3-D vision system for robotics," *Proc. 7th Int. Conf. Pat. Recog.,* Montreal, Canada, pp. 796-805.

Faugeras, O. D., and M. Hebert [1986], "The representation, recognition, and location of 3-D objects," *Int. J. Robotics Research* vol. 5, no. 3, pp. 27–52.

Fennema, C. L., and W. B. Thompson, [1979], "Velocity determination in scenes containing several moving objects," *Computer Graphics and Image Processing,* vol. 9, pp. 301-315.

Fischler, M. A., and R. C. Bolles [1981], "Random sample consensus: a paradigm for model fitting with application to image analysis and automated cartograph," *Communication of the ACM* vol. 24, no. 6, pp. 381–395.

Fix, E., and J. L. Hodges, Jr. [1951], "Discriminatory analysis, Nonparametric regression: consistency properties," Project 21-49-004, Report No. 4. USAF School of Aviation Medicine Randolph Field, Texas. Contract AF-41-(128)-31.

Fix, E., and J. L. Hodges, Jr. [1952], "Discriminatory analysis: small sample performance," Project 21-49-004, Rep. 11 USAF School of Aviation Medicine Randolph Field, Texas.

Flynn, Anita [1985], "Redundant Sensors for Mobile Robot Navigation," *M.S. Thesis,* Department of Electrical Engineering and Computer Science, Massachusettes Institute of Technology.

Foster, D. H., and R. J. Mason [1979], "Transformation and relational-structure schemes for visual pattern recognition," *Biol. Cyber.* vol. 32, pp. 85-93.

Frank, A. A. [1970], "An approach to the dynamic analysis and synthesis of biped locomotion machines," *Medical and Biological Engineering,* vol. 8, pp. 465–476.

Franke, R., and G. Nielson [1980], "Smooth Interpolation of Large Sets of Scattered Data," *International Journal Numerical Methods Engineering,* vol. 15, pp. 1691-1704.

Franke, R. [1952], "Scattered Data Interpolation: Tests of Some Methods," *Mathematics of Computation,* vol. 38, no. 157, pp. 181-200.

Freeman, W. J. [1979], "EEG Analysis gives model of neuronal template matching mechanism for sensory search with olfactory bulb," *Biological Cybernetics* vol. 35, pp. 221–234.

Freuder, E. C. [1978], "Synthesizing constraint expressions," *Comm. of the ACM,* vol. 21, no. 11, pp. 958–966.

Freuder, E. C. [1982], "A sufficient condition for backtrack-free search," *J. ACM,* vol. 29, no. 1, pp. 24–32.

Friedman, J. H., J. L. Bentley, and R. A. Finkel [1977], "An Algorithm for Finding Best Matches in Logarithmic Expected Time," ACM Trans. on Mathematical Software, vol. 3, no. 3, pp. 209-226.

Frohlich, C. [1979], "Do springboard divers violate angular momentum conservation?" *American Journal of Physics* vol. 47 pp. 583–592.

Frohlich, C. [1980], "The physics of somersaulting and twisting," *Scientific American* vol. 242, pp. 154–164.

Fu, K. S. [1974], *Syntactic Methods in Pattern Recognition* Academic Press, New York.

Gamble, E., and T. Poggio [1987], "Integration of Intensity Edges with Stereo and Motion," Report AIM-970, Artificial Intelligence Laboratory, Massachusetts Institute of Technology, Cambridge, MA.

Gamble, E., and T. A. Poggio [1987], "Visual Integration and Detection of Discontinuities: The Key Role of Intensity Edges," Report AIM-970, Artificial Intelligence Laboratory, Massachusetts Institute of Technology, Cambridge, MA.

Garey, M. R., and D. S. Johnson [1979], *Computers and Intractability*, Freeman, San Francisco.

Geman, S., and D. Geman [1984], "Stochastic Relaxation, Gibbs' Distributions, and the Bayesian Restoration of Images," *IEEE Transactions on Pattern Analysis and Machine Intelligence*, vol. 6, no. 6, pp. 721–741.

Geman, S., and D. Geman [1984], *IEEE Trans. Pattern Analysis Machine Intelligence*, vol. 6, pp. 721–741.

Geman, D., and S. Geman [1987], "Relaxation and Annealing with Constraints," *Complex Systems Technical Report 35*, Division of Applied Mathematics, Brown University, Providence, RI.

Geman, S., and C. Graffigne [1987], "Markov Random Field Image Models and their Applications to Computer Vision," *Proc. Intl. Congress of Mathematicians*, preprint, edited by A. M. Gleason.

Gennert, M., and S. Negahdaripour [1987], "Relaxing the Constant Brightness Assumption in Computing Optical Flow," Report AIM-975, Artificial Intelligence Laboratory, Massachusetts Institute of Technology, Cambridge, MA.

George, G. S. [1980], *Biomechanics of Women's Gymnastics* Prentice-Hall Inc., Englewood Cliffs, NJ.

Gibson, J. J. [1950], *The perception of the visual world.* Houghton Mifflin, Boston.

Gibson, J. J. [1979], *The ecological approach to visual perception*, Houghton Mifflin, Boston.

Gibson, J. J., and E. J. Gibson, [1957] "Continuous perspective transformations and the perception of rigid motion," *Journal of Experimental Psychology*, vol. 54, pp. 129-138.

Gieck, Kurt [1983], "Engineering Formulas," McGraw-Hill Book Company, Inc., New York, pp. E4.

Gilbert, A. L. [1981], "Video Data Conversion and Real-Time Tracking," *IEEE Computer*, pp. 50–56.

Gilbert, A. L., M. K. Giles, G. M. Flachs, R. B. Rogers, and Y. H. U [1980], *IEEE Transactions on Pattern Analysis and Machine Intelligence*, vol. 2, no. 1, pp. 47–56.

Giralt, Georges, Raja Chatila, and Marc Vaisset [1983], "An Integrated Navigation and Motion Control System for Autonomous Multisensory Mobile Robots," in *Robotics Research 1*, edited by Brady and Paul, MIT Press, pp. 191–214.

Goad, C. [1983], "Special purpose automatic programming for 3d model-based vision," *Proceedings of DARPA Image Understanding Workshop.*

Goldberg, K. Y., and B. Pearlmutter [1988], "Using a Neural Network to Learn the Dynamics of the CMU Direct-Drive Arm II," Technical Report CMU-CS-88-160, Carnegie-Mellon University.

Goldfinger, A. M. [1983], "Smooth Interpolation of Digital Terrain Models from Contour Maps," B.S. Thesis, Department of Electrical Engineering and Computer Science, Massachusetts Institute of Technology.

Gordon, W. J., and J. A. Wixom [1978], "Shepard's Method of Metric Interpolation to Bivariate and Multivariate Interpolation," *Mathematics of Computation*, vol. 32, no. 141, pp. 253–264.

Gosh, S. K. [1972], *Theory of Stereophotogrammetry*, Ohio State University Bookstores.

Goto, T., K. Takeyasu, and T. Inoyama [1980], "Control algorithm for precision insert operation robots," *IEEE Trans. Systems, Man, Cybernetics*, vol. SMC-10, no. 1, pp. 19–25.

Graubard, K., and W. H. Calvin [1979], in *The Neurosciences: 4th Study Program*, edited by F. O. Schmitt, and F. G. Worden, pp. 317–332, MIT Press, Cambridge, MA.

Green, B. F. [1961], "Figure coherence in the kinetic depth effect," *Journal of Experimental Psychology*, vol. 62, pp. 272–282.

Grimsdale, R. L., F. H. Sumner, C. J. Tunis, and T. Kilburn [1959], "A system for the automatic recognition of patterns," *Proc. Inst. Elec. Eng.*, vol. 106, no. 26, pp. 210–221.

Grimson, W. E. L. [1981], *From Images to Surfaces—A Computational Study of the Human Early Visual System*, MIT Press, Cambridge, MA.

Grimson, W. E. L. [1981], *Phil. Trans. R. Soc.*, vol. B298, pp. 395–427.

Grimson, W. E. L. [1982], "A Computational Theory of Visual Surface Interpolation," *Philosophical Transactions of the Royal Society B*, vol. 298, pp. 395–427.

Grimson, W. E. L. [1983], "An Implementation of a Computational Theory of Visual Surface Interpolation," *Computer Vision, Graphics and Image Processing*, vol. 22, pp. 39–69.

Grimson, W. E. L. [1984], "Binocular Shading and Visual Surface Reconstruction," *Computer Vision, Graphics and Image Processing*, vol. 28, pp. 19–43.

Grimson, W. Eric L. [1985], "Computational Experiments with a Feature Based Stereo Algorithm," *IEEE Transactions on Pattern Analysis and Machine Intelligence*, PAMI-7, pp. 17–34.

Grimson, W. E. L., [1986a], "The combinatorics of local constraints in model-based recognition and localization from sparse data," *J. ACM* vol. 33, no. 4, pp. 658–686.

Grimson, W. E. L., [1986b], "Sensing Strategies for Disambiguating Among Multiple Objects in Known Poses", *IEEE Journal of Robotics and Automation,* vol. 2, pp. 196–213.

Grimson, W. E. L. [1988], "The Combinatorics of Object Recognition in Cluttered Environments using Constrained Search", Report AIM-1019, Artificial Intelligence Laboratory, Massachusetts Institute of Technology, Cambridge, MA.

Grimson, W. E. L. [1989a], "On the recognition of curved objects in two dimensions," *IEEE Trans. Pat. Anal. Mach. Intel.,* vol. 11, no. 6, pp. 632–643.

Grimson, W. E. L. [1989b], "On the recognition of parameterized 2d objects," *International Journal of Computer Vision,* vol. 3, pp. 353–372.

Grimson, W. E. L. [1989c], "The combinatorics of object recognition in cluttered environments using constrained search," *Artificial Intelligence,* to appear. See also Report AIM-1019, Artificial Intelligence Laboratory, Massachusetts Institute of Technology, Cambridge, MA.

Grimson, W. E. L. [1989d], "The combinatorics of heuristic search termination for object recognition in cluttered environments," Report AIM-1111, Artificial Intelligence Laboratory, Massachusetts Institute of Technology, Cambridge, MA.

Grimson, W. E. L., and D. P. Huttenlocher [1989a], *On the sensitivity of the Hough transform for object recognition,* IEEE Pattern Analysis and Machine Intelligence.

Grimson, W. E. L., and D. P. Huttenlocher [1989b], "On the Verification of Hypothesized Matches in Model-Based Recognition," Report AIM-1110, Artificial Intelligence Laboratory, Massachusetts Institute of Technology, Cambridge, MA.

Grimson, W. E. L., and T. Lozano-Pérez [1984], "Model-based recognition and localization from sparse range or tactile data," *Int. J. Robotics Res.,* vol. 3, no. 3, pp. 3–35.

Grimson, W. E. L., and T. Lozano-Pérez [1984], "Model-based recognition and localization from sparse range or tactile data," *Int. J. Robotics Res.,* vol. 3, no. 3, pp. 3–35.

Grimson, W. E. L., and T. Lozano-Pérez [1987], "Localizing overlapping parts by searching the interpretation tree," *IEEE Trans. Patt. Anal. and Mach. Intel.,* PAMI, vol. 9, no. 4, pp. 469–482.

Grzywacs, N., and A. Yuille [1987], "Massively Parallel Implementations of Theories for Apparent Motion," Report AIM-888, Artificial Intelligence Laboratory, Massachusetts Institute of Technology.

Guilleman, V., and A. Pollack [1974], *Differential Topology,* Prentice Hall, Inc., Englewood Cliffs, NJ.

Gupta, Narendra K. [1980], "Frequency-Shaped Cost Functionals: Extension of Linear-Quadratic-Gaussian Design Methods," *Journal of Guidance and Control,* vol. 3, no. 6, pp. 529–35.

Gurfinkel, V. S., E. V. Gurfinkel, A. Yu. Shneider, E. A. Devjanin, A. V. Lensky, and L. G. Shitilman [1981], "Walking robot with supervisory control," *Mechanism and Machine Theory,* vol. 16, pp. 31–36.

Gusev, A. S. [1969], "Automatic assembly of cylindrically shaped parts," *Russian Engineering Journal,* vol. 49, no. 11, pp. 53.

Hadamard, J. [1923], *Lectures on the Cauchy Problem in Linear Partial Differential Equations*, Yale University Press.

Hanafusa, H., and H. Asada [1977], "A Robot Hand with Elastic Fingers and its Application to Assembly process," *IFAC Symposium on Information and Control Problems in Manufacturing Technology*, Tokyo, pp. 127–138. Reprinted in *Robot Motion*, edited by M. Brady *et al.*, MIT Press, 1983.

Haralick, R. M. [1984], "Digital Step Edges from Zero Crossings of Second Directional Derivatives," *IEEE Transactions on Pattern Analysis and Machine Intelligence*, vol. 6, no. 1, pp. 113–129.

Haralick, R. M., and G. Elliott [1980], "Increasing tree search efficiency for constraint satisfaction problems," *Artificial Intelligence*, vol. 14, pp. 263–313.

Haralick, R. M., and L. G. Shapiro [1979], "The consistent labeling problem: Part I," *IEEE Transactions on Pattern Analysis Machine Intelligence*, PAMI, vol. 1, no. 4, pp. 173–184.

Harris, J. G. [1986], "The Coupled Depth/Slope Approach to Surface Reconstruction," Report AIM-908, Artificial Intelligence Laboratory, Massachusetts Institute of Technology, Cambridge, MA. Also [1987] *Proceedings of the IEEE International Conference on Computer Vision*, London, England, pp. 277–283.

Harris, J. G. [1989], "An Analog VLSI Chip for Thin-Plate Surface Interpolation," *Proceedings of IEEE Neural Information Processing Systems Conference*, Denver, CO.

Hartenberg, R. S., and J. Denavit [1964], *Kinematic Synthesis of Linkages*, McGraw-Hill Book Co., New York, NY.

Hartley, R. [1985], "A Gaussian-Weighted Multi-Resolution Edge Detector," *Computer Vision, Graphics and Image Processing*, vol. 30, no. 1, pp. 70–83.

Hatamian, M. [1986], "A Real-Time Two-Dimensional Moment Generating Algorithm and Its Single Chip Implementation," *IEEE Transactions on Acoustics, Speech, and Signal Processing*, vol. 34, no. 3, pp. 546–553.

Hatamian, M. [1987], "A Fast Moment Generating Chip," *Proceedings of the International Conference on Digital Signal Processing*, Florence, Italy, pp. 230–234.

Hay, C. J. [1966], "Optical motions and space perception—an extension of Gibson's analysis," *Psychological Review*, vol. 73, pp. 550-565.

Hayati, S. A. [1983], "Robot arm geometric link parameter estimation," *Proc. 22nd IEEE Conf. Decision and Control*, San Antonio, pp. 1477-1483.

Hemami, H., and C. L. Golliday Jr. [1977], "The inverted pendulum and biped stability," *Mathematical Biosciences*, vol. 34, pp. 95–110.

Herrnstein, R. J. [1984], "Objects, categories, and discriminative stimuli," in *Animal Cognition*, edited by H. L. Roitblat, T. G. Bever, and H. S. Terrace, Lawrence Erlbaum Assoc., Hillsdale NJ.

Higdon, D. T., and R. H. Cannon Jr. [1963], "On the control of unstable multiple-output mechanical systems," *ASME Winter Annual Meeting*.

Hildreth, E. [1980], "Implementation of A Theory of Edge Detection," Report AIM-579.

Hildreth, E. [1983], "The Detection of Intensity Changes by Computer and Biological Vision Systems," *Computer Vision, Graphics and Image Processing*, vol. 22, no. 1, pp. 1–27.

Hildreth, E. C. [1983], *The Measurement of Visual Motion*, The MIT Press, Cambridge, MA.

Hildreth, E. C. [1984a], *Proc. R. Soc.*, vol. B221, pp. 189–220.

Hildreth, E. C. [1984b], *The Measurement of Visual Motion*, MIT Press, Cambridge, MA.

Hillis, W. D. [1982], "A high resolution image touch sensor," *Int. Journ. Robotics Research*, vol. 1, no. 2, pp. 33–44.

Hillis, W. D. [1985], *The Connection Machine*, MIT Press, Cambridge.

Hinton, G. F. [1981], "Shape representation in parallel systems," *Proc. 7th Joint Int. Conf. Art. Intel.*, pp. 964-968.

Hinton, G. E. [1986], "Learning in massively parallel nets," *Proceedings: AAAI-86: 5th National Conference on Artificial Intelligence*, Philadelphia, PA, p. 1149.

Hinton, G. E., and T. J. Sejnowski [1983], *Proc. IEEE 1983 Conf. Computer Vision and Pattern Recognition*, Washington, DC.

Hirose, S. [1984], "A study of design and control of a quadruped walking vehicle," *International J. Robotics Research*, vol. 3, pp. 113–133.

Hirose, S., and Y. Umetani [1980], "The basic motion regulation system for a quadruped walking vehicle," *ASME Conference on Mechanisms*.

Hodgins, J. K. [1989], "Legged Robots on Rough Terrain: Experiments in Adjusting Step Length," Ph.D. Thesis, Computer Science Department, Carnegie Mellon University.

Hodgins, J. K., J. Koechling, and M. H. Raibert [1985], "Running experiments with a planar biped," *Third International Symposium on Robotics Research*, MIT Press, Cambridge, MA.

Hodgins, J., J. Koechling, M. H. Raibert [1986], "Running experiments with a planar biped," *Third International Symposium on Robotics Research*, MIT Press, Cambridge, MA.

Hodgins, J. K., and M. H. Raibert [1987], "Planar Biped Goes Head Over Heels," *ASME Winter Annual Meeting*, Boston.

Hoffman, D. [1983], "The interpretation of visual illusions," *Scien. Am*, vol. 249, no. 6, pp. 154-162.

Hoffman, D., and B. E. Flinchbaugh [1982], "The interpretation of biological motion," *Biological Cybernetics*, vol. 42, pp. 195-204.

Hoffman, D., and W. Richards [1986], "Parts of Recognition," in *From Pixels to Predicates*, edited by A. P. Pentland, Ablex Publishing Corp., Norwood NJ.

Hollars, Michael G., and Robert H. Cannon [1985], "Initial Experiments on the End-Point Control of a Two Link Manipulator with Flexible Tendons," *ASME Winter Annual Meeting*,.

Hollerbach, J. M. [1985], "Optimum kinematic design for a seven degree of freedom manipulator," *Robotics Research: The Second International Symposium*, edited by H. Hanafusa and H. Inoue, MIT Press, Cambridge, MA, pp. 349-356.

Hollerbach, J. M. [1988], "A survey of kinematic calibration," *Robotics Review*, edited by O. Khatib, J. J. Craig, and T. Lozano-Perez, MIT Press, Cambridge, MA.

Hollerbach, J. M. [1988], "A survey of kinematic calibration," *The Robotics Review 1988*, edited by O. Khatib, J. J. Craig, and T. Lozano-Perez, MIT Press, Cambridge, MA.

Hollerbach, J. M., and D. J. Bennett [1988], "Automatic kinematic calibration using a motion tracking system," *Robotics Research: the Fourth International Symposium*, edited by R. Bolles and B. Roth, MIT Press, Cambridge, MA, pp. 191-198.

Hollerbach, J. M., and K. C. Suh [1985], "Redundancy resolution of manipulators through torque optimization," *IEEE Int. Conf. Robotics and Automation*, St. Louis, pp. 1016-1021.

Hopfield, J. J. [1982], "Neural networks and physical systems with emergent collective computational abilities," *Proc. Nat. Acad. Sci. USA 79*, pp. 2554-2558.

Hopfield, J. J. [1984], *Proc. Natn. Acad. Sci. U.S.A.*, vol. 81, pp. 3088-3092.

Horn, B. K. P. [1971], "The Binford-Horn Linefinder," Report AIM-285, Artificial Intelligence Laboratory, Massachusetts Institute of Technology, Cambridge, MA.

Horn, B. K. P. [1972], "VISMEM: A bag of 'robotics' formulae," Report AIW-34, Artificial Intelligence Laboratory, Massachusetts Institute of Technology, Cambridge, MA.

Horn, B. K. P. [1974], "Determining Lightness from an Image," in *Computer Graphics and Image Processing*, vol. 3, no. 1, pp. 277–299.

Horn, B. K. P. [1974], *Computer Graphics Image Processing*, vol. 3, pp. 111-299.

Horn, B. K. P. [1979], "Automatic Hill-Shading and the Reflectance Map," *Proceedings of the Image Understanding Workshop*, Palo Alto, CA, pp. 79–120.

Horn, B. K. P. [1981], "Hill Shading and the Reflectance Map," *Proceedings of the IEEE*, vol. 69, no. 1, pp. 14–47. Also, same title [1982] *Geo-Processing*, vol. 2, pp. 65-146.

Horn, B. K. P. [1983], "The Least Energy Curve," *ACM Transactions on Mathematical Software*, vol. 9, no. 4, pp. 441–460.

Horn, B. K. P. [1986], *Robot Vision*, The MIT Press, Cambridge, MA.

Horn, B. K. P. [1988], "Parallel Networks for Machine Vision," Report AIM-1071, Artificial Intelligence Laboratory, Massachusetts Institute of Technology, Cambridge, MA.

Horn, B. K. P. [1989], "Height and Gradient from Shading," Report AIM-1150, Artificial Intelligence Laboratory, Massachusetts Institute of Technology, Cambridge, MA.

Horn, B. K. P, and B. G. Schunck [1981], "Determining optical flow," *Artificial Intelligence*, vol. 17 pp. 185-203.

Horn, B. K. P., and B. L. Bachmann [1978], "Using Synthetic Images to Register Real Images with Surface Models," *Communications of the ACM*, vol. 21, no. 11, pp. 914–924.

Horn, B. K. P., and E. J. Weldon Jr. [1987], "Computationally efficient methods of recovering translational motion," *International Conference on Computer Vision*, London, England, pp. 8–11.

Horn, B. K. P., and E. J. Weldon Jr. [1988], "Direct Methods for Recovering Motion," *International Journal of Computer Vision*, vol. 2, no. 1, pp. 51–76.

Horn, B. K. P., and M. J. Brooks [1985], Report AIM-813, Artificial Intelligence Laboratory, Massachusetts Institute of Technology, Cambridge, MA.

Horn, B. K. P., and M. J. Brooks [1986], "The Variational Approach to Shape from Shading," *Computer Vision, Graphics and Image Processing*, vol. 33, no. 2, pp. 174–208. Also [1985] Report AIM-813, Artificial Intelligence Laboratory, Massachusetts Institute of Technology, Cambridge, MA.

Horn, B. K. P., and M. J. Brooks [1989], *Shape from Shading*, MIT Press, Cambridge, MA.

Horn, B. K. P., and S. Negahdaripour [1987], "Direct Passive Navigation: Analytical Solution for Planes," *IEEE Transactions on Pattern Analysis and Machine Intelligence*, vol. 9, no. 1, pp. 168–176.

Hough, P. V. C. [1962], "Methods and means for recognizing complex patterns," U.S. Patent 3069654.

Hubel, D. G., and T. N. Wiesel [1962], "Receptive fields, binocular interaction, and functional architecture in the cat's visual cortex," *Journal of Physiology (London)*, vol. 160, pp. 106-154.

Hubel, D. H., and T. N. Wiesel [1968], "Receptive fields and functional architecture of monkey striate cortex," *Journal of Physiology (London)*, vol. 195, pp. 215-243.

Huberman, B. A., and T. Hogg [1984], "Adaptation and self-repair in parallel computing structures," *Phys. Rev. Let.* vol. 52, no. 12, pp. 1048-1051.

Hurlbert, A. [1985], Report AIM-814, Artificial Intelligence Laboratory, Massachusetts Institute of Technology, Cambridge, MA.

Hurlbert, A. [1989], "The Computation of Color Vision," Ph.D. Thesis, Department of Brain and Cognitive Sciences, Massachusetts Institute of Technology, Cambridge, MA.

Hurlbert, A., and T. Poggio [1986], "Do Computers Need Attention?" *Nature*, vol. 321, p. 12.

Hurlbert, A., and T. Poggio [1987] "Learning a Color Algorithm from Examples," Report AIM-909, Artificial Intelligence Laboratory*Center for Biological Information ProcessingPaper 25*, Massachusetts Institute of Technology, Cambridge, MA.

Hutchinson, J., C. Koch, J. Luo, and C. A. Mead [1988], "Computing Motion using Analog and Binary Resistive Networks," *IEEE Computers*, vol. 21, pp. 52-63.

Huttenlocher, D. P. [1988], "Three-dimensional recognition of solid objects from a two-dimensional image", Ph.D. Thesis, Department of Electrical Engineering and Computer Science, Massachusetts Institute of Technology, Cambridge, MA.

Huttenlocher, D. P., and S. Ullman [1987], "Object recognition using alignment," *Proc. First International Conference on Computer Vision*, London, pp. 478–484.

Huttenlocher, D., and S. Ullman [1987], "Recognizing Rigid Objects by Aligning them with an Image," Report AIM-937, Artificial Intelligence Laboratory, Massachusetts Institute of Technology.

Huttenlocher, D., and T. Cass [1988], Proceedings of the Image Understanding Workshop.

Ikeuchi K. [1981], "Determining surface orientations of specular surfaces by using the photometric stereo method," *IEEE Trans. Pattern Analysis and Machine Intelligence*, vol. 3, no. 6, pp. 661–669.

Ikeuchi, K. [1984], "Reconstructing a Depth Map from Intensity Maps," *International Conference on Pattern Recognition*, Montreal, Canada, pp. 736–738. Also "Constructing a Depth Map from Images," Report AIM-744, Artificial Intelligence Laboratory,

Ikeuchi, K. [1987], "Generating an interpretation tree from a CAD model for 3D-object recognition in bin-picking tasks," *Int. Journ. Computer Vision*, vol. 1, no. 2, pp. 145–166.

Ikeuchi, K., and B. K. P. Horn [1981], "Numerical Shape from Shading and Occluding Boundaries" *Artificial Intelligence*, vol. 17, pp. 141-184.

Inoue, H. [1974], "Force feedback in precise assembly tasks," Report AIM-308, Artificial Intelligence Laboratory, Massachusetts Institute of Technology. Reprinted in *Artificial Intelligence: An MIT Perspective*, edited by P. H. Winston, and R. H. Brown, MIT Press.

Jack, J. J., D. Nobel, and R. W. Tsien [1975], *Electric Current Flow in Excitable Cells*, Clarendon, Oxford.

Jacobs, D. [1988], *The Use of Grouping in Visual Object Recognition*, MS. Thesis, Department of Electrical Engineering and Computer Science, Massachusetts Institute of Technology.

Jacobsen, S. C. [1987], *et al.*, "Design of the Utah/MIT Dexterous Hand," *Proceedings IEEE International Conference on Robotics and Automation*, San Francisco.

Jansson, G., and G. Johansson [1973], "Visual perception of bending motion," *Perception*, vol. 2, pp. 321-326.

Johansson, G. [1964], "Perception of motion and changing form," *Scandinavian Journal of Psychology*, vol. 5, pp. 181-208.

Johansson, G. [1973], "Visual Perception of Biological Motion and a Model for Its Analysis," *Perception and Psychophysics*, vol. 14, no. 2, pp. 201-211.

Johansson, G. [1974], "Visual perception of rotary motion as transformation of conic sections—a contribution to the theory of visual space perception," *Psychologia*, vol. 17, pp. 226-237.

Johansson, G. [1978], "Visual event perception," in *Handbook of Sensory Physiology*, edited by R. Held, H. W. Liebowitz, H-L. Teuber, Springer, Berlin.

Johansson, G., and G. Jansson [1968], "Perceived rotary motion from changes in a straight line," *Perception and Psychophysics*, vol. 4, pp. 165-170.

Jolicoeur, P. [1985], "The time to name disoriented natural objects," *Memory & Cognition*, vol. 13, no. 4, pp. 289-303.

Jolicoeur, P. [1987], "A size-congruency effect in memory for visual shape," *Mem. & Cog.*, vol. 15, no. 6, pp. 531-543.

Jolicoeur, P., and D. Besner [1987], "Additivity and interaction between size ratio and response category in the comparison of size-discrepant shapes," *J. Exp. Psychol., HP&P*, vol. 13, no. 3, pp. 478-487.

Jolicoeur, P., and M. Landau [1984], "Effects of orientation on the identification of simple visual patterns," *Canad. J. Psychol.* vol. 38 no. 1, pp. 80-93.

Juang, Jer-Nan, James D. Turner, and Hon M Chun [1985], "Closed-Form Solutions for Feedback Control with Terminal Constraints," *Journal of Guidance and Control,* vol. 8, no. 1, pp. 39–43.

Julesz, B. [1971], *Foundation of Cyclopean Perception,* University of Chicago Press, Chicago.

Junkins, John L., James D. Turner [1986], *Optimal Spacecraft Rotational Maneuvers,* Elsevier Science Publishers, New York.

Kanade, T., and J. R. Kender [1983], "Mapping image properties into shape constraints: Skewed symmetry, affine-transformable patterns and the shape from texture paradigm," in *Human and Machine vision* edited by J. Beck, B. Hope, and A. Rozenfeld, Academic Press, New York.

Kanayama, Yutaka [1983], "Concurrent Programming of Intelligent Robots," *Proceedings IJCAI,* Karlsruhe, West Germany, pp. 834–838.

Kato, T., A. Takanishi, H. Jishikawa, and I. Kato [1983], "The realization of the quasi-dynamic walking by the biped walking machine," *Fourth Symposium on Theory and Practice of Robots and Manipulators,* edited by A. Morecki, G. Bianchi, and K. Kedzior, Polish Scientific Publishers, Warsaw, pp. 341–351.

Kawato, M., K. Furukawa, and R. Suzuki [1987], "A Hierarchical Neural-Network Model for Control and Learning of Voluntary Movement," Biol. Cybern. vol 57, pp. 169-185.

Kazmierczak, H., and K. Steinbuch [1963], "Adaptive Systems in Pattern Recognition," *IEEE Trans. on Electronic Computers,* EC-12, pp. 822-835.

Kender, J. R. [1979], "Shape from Texture: An Aggregation Transform that Maps a Class of Textures into Surface Orientation," *Proc. Sixth Intl. Joint Conf. on Artificial Intelligence,* Tokyo.

Khatib, Oussama [1983], "Dynamic Control of Manipulators in Operational Space," *Sixth IFTOMM Congress on Theory of Machines and Mechanisms,* New Delhi.

Khatib, O. [1986], "Real-time obstacle avoidance for robot manipulator and mobile robots," *The International Journal of Robotics Research,* vol. 5, no. 1, pp. 90–98.

Kirkpatrick, S., C. D. Gelatt, Jr., and M. P. Vecchi [1983], "Optimization by Simulated Annealing," *Science,* vol. 220.

Klein, Charles A. [1983], Karl W. Olson, and Dennis R. Pugh, "Use of Force and Attitude Sensors for Locomotion of a Legged Vehicle," *International Journal of Robotics Research,* vol. 2, no. 2, pp. 3–17.

Knight, T. [1983], "Design of an Integrated Optical Sensor with On-Chip Pre-Processing," Ph.D. Thesis, Department of Electrical Engineering and Computer Science, Massachusetts Institute of Technology, Cambridge, MA.

Koch, C., and T. Poggio [1983], *Proc. R. Soc.,* vol. B218, pp. 455–477.

Koch, C., and T. Poggio [1987], "Biophysics of computational systems: neurons, synapses, and membranes," *Synaptic Function,* edited by G. M. Edelman, W. E. Gall, and W. M. Cowan, John Wiley and Sons, New York, pp. 637-697.

Koch, C., T. Poggio, and V. Torre [1982], *Phil. Trans. R. Soc.*, vol. B298, pp. 227–268.

Koch, C., J. Marroquin, and A. Yuille [1986], "Analog 'Neuronal' Networks in Early Vision," *Proceedings National Academy of Sciences, USA*, (Biophysics), vol. 83, pp. 4263–4267. Also Report AIM-751 [1985], Artificial Intelligence Laboratory, Massachusetts Institute of Technology, Cambridge, MA.

Koenderink, J. J., and A. J. van Doorn [1975], "Invariant properties of the motion parallax field due to the motion of rigid bodies relative to the observer," *Optica Acta*, vol. 22, pp. 773-791.

Koenderink, J. J., and A. J. van Doorn [1979], "The internal representation of solid shape with respect to vision," *biol. Cybernetics*, vol. 32, pp. 211–216.

Kohonen, T. [1978], *Associative Memory: A System Theoretic Approach*, Springer Verlag, Berlin.

Kohonen, T. [1980], *Content-Addressable Memories,* Springer-Verlag, New York, NY.

Kohonen, T. [1984], *Self-Organization and Associative Memory*, Springer, Berlin.

Koozekanani, S. H., and R. B. McGhee [1973], "Occupancy problems with pairwise exclusion constraints—an aspect of gait enumeration," *J. Cybernetics*, vol. 2 pp. 14–26.

Korn, G. A., and T. M. Korn [1968], *Mathematical Handbook for Scientists and Engineers*, McGraw-Hill.

Kotnik, P. T., S. Yurkovich, and U. Ozguner [1988], "Acceleration Feedback for control of a flexible Manipulator Arm," *Journal of Robotic Systems,* vol. 5, no 3.

Kreithen, Melvin L. [1983],"Orientational Strategies in Birds: A Tribute to W. T. Keeton," in *Behavioral Energetics: The Cost of Survival in Vertebrates,* Ohio State University Press, pp. 3–28.

Kruskal, C. P., L. Rudolph, and M. Snir [1985], "The Power of Parallel Prefix," *Proc. Intl. Conf. on Parallel Processing*, pp. 180-185.

Kuffler, S. W. [1953], *J. Neurophysiol.*, vol. 16, pp. 37–68.

Laktionev, N. M., and G. Y. Andreev [1966], "Automatic assembly of parts," *Russian Engineering Journal*, vol. 46, no. 8, p. 40.

Lamdan, Y., J. T. Schwartz, and H. J. Wolfson [1987], "On recognition of 3-d objects from 2-d images," New York University, Courant Institute Robotics Report, no. 122.

Lamdan, Y., J. T. Schwartz, and H. J. Wolfson [1988], "Object recognition by affine invariant matching," *Proc. Comp. Vision and Patt. Recog.*, pp. 335–344.

Lancaster, P., and K. vol. Salkauskas [1981], "Surfaces Generated by Moving Least Squares Methods", *Mathematics of Computation,* vol. 37, no. 155, pp. 141-158.

Lancaster, P., and K. vol. Salkauskas [1986], *Curve And Surface Fitting*, Academic Press, New York.

Land, E. H. [1984], *Proc. Natn. Acad. Sci. U.S.A.*, vol. 80, pp. 5163–5169.

Lappin, J. S., J. F. Doner, and B. l. Kottas [1980], "Minimal conditions for the visual detection of structure and motion in three dimensions," *Science*, vol. 209, pp. 717-719.

Lappin, J. S., and M. A. Fuqua [1983], "Accurate visual measurement of three--dimensional moving patterns," *Science*, vol. 221, pp. 480-482.

Larsen, A., and C. Bundesen [1978], "Size scaling in visual pattern recognition," *J. Exp. Psychol., HP&P,* vol. 4, no. 1, pp. 1-20.

Larsenv, A. [1985], "Pattern matching: Effects of size ratio, angular difference in orientation, and familiarity," *Perception & Psychophysics,* vol. 38, pp. 63-68.

Larson, N. G., K. Nishihara and B. K. P. Horn [1981], "Digital Gaussian Convolver," Patent Application, Registry no. 26192, April 22.

Lee, D. N. [1976], "A theory of visual control of braking based on information about time to collision," *Perception*, vol. 5, pp. 437-459.

Lee, D. N. [1980], "The optic flow field: the foundation of vision," *Philosophical Transactions of the Royal Society of London, Series B*, vol. 290, pp. 169-179.

Leeuwenberg, E. L. J., and H. f. J. M. Buffart [1978], (editors) *Formal ·Theories of Visual Perception*, J. Wiley & Sons, Chichester.

Lewis, R. A., and A. R. Johnston [1977], "A scanning laser range finder for a robotic vehicle," *Fifth Intl. Joint Conf. on Artificial Intell.*, pp. 762–768.

Li, K. C. [1984], "Consistency for Cross-Validated Nearest Neighbor Estimates in Nonparametric Regression," *The Annals of Statistics*, vol. 12, pp. 230-240.

Lim, W. [1986] "Fast Algorithms for Labelling Connected Components in 2D Arrays," *Thinking Machines Corp. Technical ReportNA86-1*, Cambridge, MA.

Lindsay, P. H., and D. A. Norman [1977], "Human Information Processing," (2nd edition) Academic Press, New york.

Liston, R. A. [1970], "Increasing vehicle agility by legs: The quadruped transporter," *38th National Meeting of the Operations Research Society of America.*

Liston, R. A., and R. S. Mosher [1968], "A versatile walking truck," *Proceedings of the Transportation Engineering Conference*, Institution of Civil Engineers, London.

Little, J., H. Bülthoff, and T. Poggio [1987], "Parallel Optical Flow Computation," *Proc. Image Understanding Workshop*, edited by L. Bauman, Science Applications International Corp., McLean, VA, pp. 915-920.

Little, J., H. Bülthoff, and T. Poggio [1989], "Parallel Optical Flow Using Winner-Take-All Scheme," in preparation.

Little, J., G. E. Blelloch, and T. Cass [1987], "Parallel Algorithms for Computer Vision on the Connection Machine," *Proceedings Intl. Conf. on Computer Vision*, Los Angeles, pp. 587-591.

Lodwick, G. D., and J. Whittle [1970], "A technique for automatic contouring field survey data," *Australian Computer Journal*, vol 2, pp. 104-109.

Loftsgaarden, D. O., and C. P. Quesenberry [1965], "A Nonparametric Estimate of a Multivariate Density Function," *Annals of Mathematical Statistics,* vol. 36, pp. 1049-1051.

Longuett-Higgins, H. C., and K. Prazdny [1980], "The Interpretation of a Moving Retinal Image," *Proceedings of the Royal Society of London B*, vol. 208, pp. 385–397.

Lorenz, E. N. [1969], "Atmospheric Predictability as Revealed by Naturally Occurring Analogues", *Journal of the Atmospheric Sciences,* vol. 26, pp. 636–646.

Loucks, C. S., *et al.* [1987], "Modeling and Control of the Stanford/JPL Hand," *Proceedings IEEE International Conference on Robotics and Automation,* Raleigh, NC.

Lowe, D. G. [1985], *Perceptual Organization and Visual Recognition.* Kluwer Academic Publishers, Boston.

Lowe, D. G. [1986], "Three-dimensional object recognition from single two-dimensional images," *Robotics Research Technical Report 202,* Courant Institute of Math. Sciences, New York University.

Lowe, D. G. [1987], "Three-dimensional object recognition from single two-dimensional images," *Artificial Intelligence*, vol. 31, pp. 355–395.

Lozano–Pérez, T. [1976], *The design of a mechanical assembly system* Report AI-TR-397, Artificial Intelligence Laboratory, Massachusetts Institute of Technology. Reprinted in part in *Artificial Intelligence: An MIT Perspective,* edited by P. H. Winston, and R. H. Brown, MIT Press, 1979.

Lozano–Pérez, T. [1981], "Automatic planning of manipulator transfer movements," *IEEE Trans. Systems Man Cybernetics,* vol. SMC–11, no. 10, pp. 681–689. Reprinted in *Robot Motion,* edited by M. Brady, *et al.,* MIT Press, 1983.

Lozano–Pérez, T. [1983], "Spatial planning: a configuration space approach," *IEEE Trans. Computers,* vol. C-32, no. 2.

Lozano-Pérez, T. [1987], "A simple motion planning algorithm for general robot manipulators," *IEEE Journal of Robotics and Automation,* RA-3 no. 3, pp. 224–238.

Lozano-Pérez, T., J. L. Jones, E. Mazer, P. A. O'Donnell, W. E. L. Grimson, P. Tournassoud, and A. Lanusse [1987], "Handey: A robot system that recognizes, plans, and manipulates," *IEEE Computer Society Int. Conf. on Robotics and Automation,* Raleigh, NC, pp. 843–849.

Lozano-Pérez, T., M. T. Mason, and R. H. Taylor [1984], "Automatic synthesis of fine-motion strategies for robots," *International Journal of Robotics Research,* vol. 3, no. 1, pp. 3–24.

Lozano-Pérez, T., and R. H. Taylor [1988], "Geometric issues in planning robot tasks," in *Robotics Science,* edited by J. M. Brady, MIT Press.

Lozano-Pérez, T., W. E. L. Grimson, and S. J. White [1987], "Finding cylinders in range data," *IEEE Computer Society Int. Conf. on Robotics and Automation,* Raleigh, NC, pp. 202–207.

Lucas, E. [1984], "Huitieme recreation—la machine a marcher," *Recreations Mathematiques*, vol. 4 pp. 198–204.

Luo, J., C. Koch, and C. Mead [1988], "An Experimental Subthreshold, Analog CMOS two-dimensional Surface Interpolation Circuit," *Proceedings of IEEE Neural Information Processing Systems Conference,* Denver.

Müller, H. G. [1987], "Weighted Local Regression and Kernel Methods for Non-parametric Curve Fitting," *Journal of the American Statistical Association*, vol 82, pp. 231-238.

MacLeod, I. D. G. [1970a], "A Study in Automatic Photo-Interpretation," Ph.D. Thesis, Department of Engineering Physics, Australian National University, Canberra, Australia.

MacLeod, I. D. G. [1970b], "On Finding Structure in Pictures," in *Picture Language Machines*, edited by S. Kaneff, Academic Press, London, England, pp. 231–256.

Macauley, F. R. [1931], *The Smoothing of Time Series*, National Bureau of Economic Research, New York.

Mackworth, A. K. [1977], "Consistency in networks of constraints," *Artificial Intelligence*, vol. 8, pp. 99–118.

Mackworth, A. K., and E. C. Freuder [1985], "The complexity of some polynomial network consistency algorithms for constraint satisfaction problems," *Artificial Intelligence*, vol. 25, pp. 65–74.

Mahoney, J. V. [1980], "Interpolation of a Contour Map of the Island of Mauritius using Elastic Membranes and Thin Plates," unpublished work in Undergraduate Research Opportunities Program, Massachusetts Institute of Technology.

Mahoney, J. V. [1986], "Image chunking: defining spatial building blocks for scene analysis," M.S. Thesis, Department of Electrical Engineering and Computer Science, Massachusetts Institute of Technology, Cambridge, MA.

Mahoney, J. V. [1987], "Image Chunking: Defining Spatial Building Blocks for Scene Analysis," M.S. Thesis, Department of Electrical Engineering and Computer Science, Massachusetts Institute of Technology, Cambridge, MA. Published as AI-TR-980, Artificial Intelligence Laboratory.

Maki, R. [1986], "Naming and locating the tops of rotated pictures," *Canad. J. Psychol.*, vol. 40, no. 4, pp. 368-387.

Marder, E. [1984], *Trends Neurosci.* vol. 7, pp. 48–53.

Marr, D. [1976], "Early Processing of Visual Information," *Philosophical Transactions of the Royal Society B*, vol. 275, pp. 1377–1388.

Marr, D. [1982], *Vision*, Freeman, San Francisco.

Marr, D., and E. Hildreth [1980], "Theory of Edge Detection," *Proceedings of the Royal Society B*, vol. 207, pp. 187–217.

Marr, D., and H. K. Nishihara [1978], "Representation and recognition of the spatial organization of three-dimensional shapes," *Proc. Roy. Soc. B.*, *200*, pp. 269-291.

Marr, D., and S. Ullman [1981], *Proc. R. Soc.*, vol. B211, pp. 151–180.

Marr, D., and T. Poggio [1976], "Cooperative Computation of Stereo Disparity," *Science*, vol. 194, pp. 283-287.

Marr, D., and T. Poggio [1979], "A Computational Theory of Human Stereo Vision," *Proc. Roy. Soc. Lond. B*, vol. 204, pp. 301-328.

Marroquin, J. L. [1984], "Surface Reconstruction Preserving Discontinuities," Report AIM-792, Artificial Intelligence Laboratory, Massachusetts Institute of Technology, Cambridge, MA.

Marroquin, J. [1985], Report AIM-839, Artificial Intelligence Laboratory, Massachusetts Institute of Technology, Cambridge, MA.

Marroquin, J. L. [1985], "Probabilistic Solutions of Inverse Problems," Report AI-TR-860, Artificial Intelligence LaboratoryTechnical Report, Massachusetts Institute of Technology, Cambridge, MA.

Marroquin, J. L. [1987] "Deterministic Bayesian Estimation of Markov Random Fields with Applications to Computational Vision," *Proc. First Intl. Conf. on Computer Vision*, Computer Society of the IEEE, Washington, DC.

Marroquin, J. L., S. Mitter, and T. Poggio [1986], "Probabilistic Solution of Ill-Posed Problems in Computational Vision," *Proc. Image Understanding Workshop*, edited by L. Bauman, Scientific Applications International Corp., McLean, VA, 1986. A more complete version appears in *J. Amer. Stat. Assoc.*, vol. 82, pp. 76-89, 1987.

Mason, M. T. [1981], "Compliance and force control for computer controlled manipulators," *IEEE Trans. Systems, Man and Cybernetics*, vol. SMC-11, no. 6, pp. 418–432. Reprinted in *Robot Motion*, edited by M. Brady, *et al.*, MIT Press, 1983.

Mason, M. T. [1982], "Manipulator Grasping and Pushing Operations," Technical Report, Artificial Intelligence Laboratory, Massachusetts Institute of Technology.

Mason, M. T. [1983], "Compliant Motion," Reprinted in *Robot Motion*, edited by M. Brady, *et al.*, MIT Press.

Mason, M. T. [1984], "Automatic planning of fine motions: correctness and completeness," in *IEEE International Conference on Robotics and Automation*, pp. 492–503, Atlanta.

Mason, M. T., and J. K. Salisbury [1985], *Robot Hands and the Mechanics of Manipulation*, MIT Press, Cambridge, MA.

Matsuoka, K. [1980], "A mechanical model of repetitive hopping movements," *Biomechanisms*, vol. 5, pp. 251–258.

Mayhew, J. E. W., and J. P. Frisby [1981], "Psychophysical and computational studies towards a theory of human stereopsis," *Artificial Intelligence*, vol. 17, pp. 349-386.

McCallion, H., and P. C. Wong [1975], "Some thoughts on the automatic assembly of a peg and a hole," *Industrial Robot*, vol. 2, no. 4, pp. 141-146.

McGhee, R. B. [1968], "Some finite state aspects of legged locomotion," *Mathematical Biosciences*, vol. 2 pp. 67–84.

McGhee, R. B. [1983], "Vehicular legged locomotion," *Advances in Automation and Robotics*, edited by G. N. Saridis, JAI Press.

McGhee, R. B., and A. A. Frank [1968], "On the stability properties of quadruped creeping gaits," *Mathematical Biosciences*, vol. 3, pp. 331–351.

McGhee, R. B., and A. K. Jain [1972], "Some properties of regularly realizable gait matrices," *Mathematical Biosciences*, vol. 13 pp. 179–193.

McGhee, R. B., and M. B. Kuhner [1968], "On the dynamic stability of legged locomotion systems," *Advances in External Control of Human Extremities*, M. M. Gavrilovic, A. B. Wilson, Jr., (editors), Jugoslav Committee for Electronics and Automation, Belgrade, pp. 431–442.

McLain, D. H. [1974], "Drawing Contours From Arbitrary Data Points", *The Computer Journal,* vol. 17, no. 4, pp. 318-324.

Mead, C. A. [1989], *Analog VLSI and Neural Systems,* Addison-Wesley, Reading, MA.

Meckl, Peter H. [1988], "Control of Vibration in Mechanical Systems Using Shaped Reference Inputs," *Ph.D. Thesis, Department of Mechanical Engineering, MIT.* Also Report AI-TR-1018, Artificial Intelligence Laboratory, Massachusetts Institute of Technology, Cambridge, MA, 1988.

Meckl, Peter H., and Warren P. Seering [1988], "Controlling Velocity–Limited Systems to Reduce Residual Vibration," *Proceedings of the 1988 IEEE International Conference on Robotics and Automation,* Philadelphia, PA.

Meckl, P., and W. Seering [1985], "Active Damping in a Three-Axis Robotic Manipulator," *Journal of Vibration, Acoustics, Stress, and Reliability in Design,* vol. 107, no. 1, pp. 38-46.

Meckl, P., and W. Seering [1985], "Minimizing Residual Vibration for Point-to-point Motion," *ASME Journal of Vibration, Acoustics, Stress, and Reliability in Design,* vol. 107, no. 4, pp. 378-382.

Meckl, Peter H., and Warren P. Seering [1986], "Feedforward Control Techniques To Achieve Fast Settling Time in Robots," *Proceedings of The American Controls Conference,* Seattle, WA.

Meckl, Peter H., and Warren P. Seering [1987], "Reducing Residual Vibration in Systems with Time Varying Resonances," *Proceedings of the 1987 IEEE International Conference on Robotics and Automation,* pp. 1690-1695, Raleigh, NC.

Merlin, P. M., and D. J. Farber [1975], "A parallel mechanism for detecting curves in picture," *IEEE Trans. Comput.,* vol. 24, pp. 96–98.

Metropolis, N., A. Rosenbluth, M. Rosenbluth, A. Teller, and E. Teller [1953], "Equation of State Calculations by Fast Computing Machines," *J. chem. Phys.,* vol. 21, no. 6, pp. 1087–1092.

Michie, D., and R. A. Chambers [1968], "Boxes: An Experiment in Adaptive Control," *Machine Intelligence 2,* Oliver and Boyd, London, pp. 137-152.

Miles, W. R. [1931], "Movement interpretations of the silhouette of a revolving fan," *American Journal of Psychology,* vol. 43, pp. 392-405.

Miller, W. T., F. H. Glanz, and L. G. Kraft [1987], "Application of a general learning algorithm to the control of robotic manipulators," *International Journal of Robotics Research,* vol. 6, pp. 84-98.

Milner, P. M. [1974], "A model for visual shape recognition," *Psychol. Rev.,* vol. 81, no. 6, pp. 521-535.

Minsky, M., and S. Papert [1969], *Perceptrons: An Introduction to Computational Geometry,* MIT Press, Cambridge, MA.

Miura, H., and I. Shimoyama [1984], "Dynamic walk of a biped," *International J. Robotics Research,* vol. 3 pp. 60–74.

Miura, H. [1986], "Biped Locomotion Robots," Unpublished videotape.

Montanari, U. [1974], "Networks of constraints: Fundamental properties and applications to picture processing," *Inform. Sci.,* vol. 7, pp. 95–132.

Mooring, B. W., and G. R. Tang [1984], "An improved method for identifying the kinematic parameters in a six-axis robot," *ASME Proc. Int. Computers in Engineering Conf.*, Las Vegas, pp. 79-84.

Moravec, Hans P. [1983], "The Stanford Cart and the CMU Rover," *Proceedings of the IEEE*, vol. 71, pp. 872–884.

Morozov, V. A. [1984], *Methods for Solving Incorrectly Posed Problems*, Springer, New York.

Morrison, R. A. [1968], "Iron mule train," *Proceedings of Off-Road Mobility Research Symposium*, International Society for Terrain Vehicle Systems, WA, pp. 381–400.

Morton, J. [1969], "Interaction of information in word recognition," *Psychological Review*, vol. 76, pp. 165–178.

Movshon, J. A., E. H. Adelson, M. S. Gizzi, and W. T. Newsome [1984], in *Pattern Recognition Mechanisms*, edited by C. Chagas, R. Gattar, and C. G. Gross, pp. 95–107, Vatican, Rome; *Expl. Brain Res.*, to appear.

Murphy, K. N., and M. H. Raibert [1985], "Trotting and bounding in a planar two-legged model," *Fifth Symposium on Theory and Practice of Robots and Manipulators*, edited by A. Morecki, G. Bianchi, and K. Kedzior, MIT Press, Cambridge, MA, pp. 411–420.

Murray, D. W., and B. F. Buxton [1987], "Scene Segmentation from Visual Motion Using Global Optimization," *IEEE Transactions on Pattern Analysis and Machine Intelligence*, vol. 9, no. 2, pp. 147–163.

Murthy, S. S., and M. H. Raibert [1983], "3D balance in legged locomotion: modeling and simulation for the one-legged case," *Inter-Disciplinary Workshop on Motion: Representation and Perception*, ACM.

Muybridge, E. [1957], *Animals in Motion*, Dover Publications, NY. First edition, Chapman and Hall, Ltd., London, 1899.

Muybridge, E. [1955], *The Human Figure in Motion*, Dover Publications, NY. First edition, Chapman and Hall, Ltd., London, 1901.

Nagel, H. H. [1984], Unpublished Internal Report, University of Hamburg.

Nakamura, Y., and H. Hanafasu [1985], "Task priority based redundancy control of robot manipulators," *Robotics Research: The Second International Symposium*, edited by H. Hanafusa and H. Inoue, MIT Press, Cambridge, MA, pp. 155-162.

Narasimhan, S., D. M. Siegel, and J. M. Hollerbach [1988], "Condor: A Revised Architecture for Controlling the UTAH-MIT hand," *Proceedings of the 1988 IEEE International Conference on Robotics and Automation*, Philadelphia, PA.

Nashed, M. Z. [1976], (editor), *Generalized Inverses and Applications*, Academic, New York.

Negahdaripour, S. [1986], "Direct Methods for Structure from Motion," Ph.D. Thesis, Mechanical Engineering, Massachusetts Institute of Technology.

Negahdaripour, S., and B. K. P. Horn [1987], "A Direct Method for Locating the Focus of Expansion," Report AIM-939 Artificial Intelligence Laboratory, Massachusetts Institute of Technology, Cambridge.

Negahdaripour, S., and B. K. P. Horn [1987], "Direct Passive Navigation," *IEEE Trans. Pattern Analysis and Machine Intelligence*, vol. 9, no. 1, pp. 168–176.

Neisser, U. [1966], *Cognitive Psychology*, Appelton-Century-Crofts, New York.

Niemeyer, G., and J. J. Slotine [1989], "Performance in Adaptive Manipulator Control," Submitted to *1989 IEEE International Conf. on Robotics and Automation*, Scottsdale, AZ.

Nilsson, N. [1980], *Principles of Artificial Intelligence*, Tioga Publishing, California.

Nilsson, Nils J. [1984], "Shakey the Robot," *SRI AI Center Technical Note 323*.

Nishihara, H. K. [1984], "PRISM: A Practical Real-Time Imaging Stereo Matcher," Report AIM-780, Artificial Intelligence Laboratory, Massachusetts Institute of Technology, Cambridge, MA.

Nishihara, H. K., and P. A. Crossley [1988], "Measuring Photolithographic Overlay Accuracy and Critical Dimensions by Correlating inarized Laplacian of Gaussian Convolutions," *IEEE Trans. Pattern Matching and Machine Intell.*, vol. 10.

Nitzan, D., A. E. Brain, and R. O. Duda [1977], "The measurement and use of reflectance and range data in scene analysis," *Proc. of IEEE*, vol. 65, pp. 206–220.

Norton, S. W. [1983], "Information Theoretic Surface Estimation Using Elevation Data," B.S. Thesis, Department of Electrical Engineering and Computer Science.

Norton, J. P. [1986] *An Introduction to Identification*, Academic Press, Orlando, FL.

Ogata, Katsuhiko [1970], *Modern Control Engineering,* Prentice-Hall, Inc., Englewood Cliffs, NJ, p. 234.

Ohwovoriole, M. S., B. Roth, and J. Hill [1980], "On the Theory of Single and Multiple Insertions in Industrial Assemblies," *Proceedings 10th Int. Symp. Industrial Robots*, Milan, Italy, pp. 545–558.

Ohwovoriole, M. S., and B. Roth [1981], "A theory of parts mating for assembly automation," *Proceedings Ro. Man. Sy.*, Warsaw, Poland.

Omohundro, S. M. [1987], "Efficient Algorithms with Neural Network Behavior," *J. Complex Systems*, vol. 1, no. 2, pp. 273-347.

Oster, G. F., A. Perelson, and A. Katchalsky [1971], *Nature*, vol. 234, pp. 393–399.

Overton, K. J., and T. Williams [1981], "Tactile sensation for robots," *Proc. IJCAI*, Vancouver, Canada, pp. 791–795.

Palmer, J. A. B. [1969], "Automated mapping," *Proc. 4th Australian Computer Conference,* vol. 6, pp. 463-466.

Palmer, S. E. [1975], "The effects of contextual scenes on the identification of objects," *Memory & Cognition*, vol. 3, no. 5, pp. 519–526.

Palmer, S. E. [1977], "Hierarchical structure in perceptual representation," *Cognitive Psychology*, vol. 9, pp. 441–474.

Palmer, S. E. [1978], "Structural aspects of visual similarity," *Memory & Cognition*, vol. 6, no. 2, pp. 91–97.

Palmer, S. E. [1983], "The psychology of perceptual organization: A transformational approach," in *Human and Machine Vision*, edited by J. Beck, B. Hope, and A. Rosenfeld, Academic Press, New York.

Paul, B. J. [1987], "A Systems Approach to the Torque Control of a Permanent Magnet Brushless Motor," M.S. Thesis, Department of Mechanical Engineering, Massachusetts Institute of Technology, Cambridge MA.

Paul, R. P., and B. Shimano [1976], "Compliance and control," *Proceedings Joint Automatic Control Conference*, San Francisco, pp. 694–699. Reprinted in *Robot Motion*, edited by M. Brady, *et al.*, MIT Press, 1983.

Pelto, C. R., T. A. Elkins, and H. A. Boyd [1968], "Automatic contouring of irregularly spaced data," *Geophysics,* vol. 33, pp. 424-430.

Perrett, D. I., P. A. J. Smith, D. D. Potter, A. J. Mistlin, A. S. Head, A. D. Milner, and M. A. Jeeves [1985], "Visual cells in the temporal cortex sensitive to face view and gaze direction," *Proc. Roy. Soc. B,* vol. 223, pp. 293-317.

Petersik, J. T. [1979], "Three-dimensional object constancy: coherence of a simulated rotating sphere in noise," *Perception & Psychophysics*, vol. 15, pp. 328-335.

Petersik, J. T. [1980], "The effect of spatial and temporal factors on the perception of stroboscopic rotation simulations," *Perception*, vol. 9, pp. 271-283.

Pfeiffer, F., and B. Gebler [1988], *Proceedings of the 1988 IEEE International Conference on Robotics and Automation*, Philadelphia, PA, pp. 2–8.

Pinker, S. [1984], "Visual cognition: an introduction," *Cognition,* vol. 18, pp. 1-63.

Pitts, W., and W. S. McCulloch [1947], "How we know universals: The perception of auditory and visual forms," *Bulletin of Math. Biophysics* vol. 9, pp. 127-147.

Platt, J. C., and A. H. Barr [1988], "Constrained Differential Optimization for Neural Networks," Technical Report TR-88-17, Computer Science Department, California Institute of Technology, Pasadena, CA. Also [1987] *Proceedings of IEEE Neural Information Processing Systems Conference.*

Poggio, T. [1985], "Early Vision: From Computational Structure to Algorithms and Parallel Hardware," *Computer Vision, Graphics, and Image Processing,* vol. 31.

Poggio, T. [1985], "Integrating Vision Modules with Coupled MRFs," Report AIW-285, Artificial Intelligence LaboratoryWorking Paper, Massachusetts Institute of Technology, Cambridge, MA.

Poggio, T., and The Staff [1985], "MIT Progress in Understanding Images," *Proc. Image Understanding Workshop*, edited by L. Bauman, Scientific Applications International Corp., McLean, VA.

Poggio T., and The Staff [1987], "MIT Progress in Understanding Images," *Proc. Image Understanding Workshop*, edited by L. Bauman, Scientific Applications International Corp., McLean, VA.

Poggio, T., and A. Hurlbert [1984], Report AIW-264, Artificial Intelligence Laboratory, Massachusetts Institute of Technology, Cambridge, MA.

Poggio, T., and C. Koch [to appear], *Proc. R. Soc.,* vol. B.

Poggio, T. A., and V. Torre [1984], "Ill-Posed Problems and Regularization Analysis in Early Vision," Report AIM-773, Artificial Intelligence Laboratory, Massachusetts Institute of Technology, Cambridge, MA.

Poggio, T., V. Torre, and C. Koch [1985], "Computational Vision and Regularization Theory," *Nature,* vol. 317, pp. 314-319.

Poggio, T., K. R. K. Nielsen, and H. K. Nishihara [1982], "Zero-Crossings and Spatiotemporal Interpolation in Vision: Aliasing and Electrical Coupling Between Sensors," Report AIM-675, Artificial Intelligence Laboratory, Massachusetts Institute of Technology, Cambridge, MA.

Poggio, T., H. L. Voorhees, and A. L. Yuille [1984], "Regularizing Edge Detection," Report AIM-776, Artificial Intelligence Laboratory, Massachusetts Institute of Technology, Cambridge, MA.

Poggio, T., H. Voorhees, and A. Yuille, Report AIM-833, Artificial Intelligence Laboratory, Massachusetts Institute of Technology, Cambridge, MA.

Poggio, G., and T. Poggio [1984], "The analysis of stereopsis," *Ann. Rev. Neurosci.*, vol. 7, pp. 379-412.

Pollard S. B., J. E. W. Mayhew, and J. P. Frisby [1985], "PMF: A stereo correspondence algorithm using a disparity gradient limit," *Perception*, vol. 14, pp. 449–470.

Potmesil, M. [1983], "Generating models of solid objects by matching 3D surface segments," *Proc. 8th Int. Joint Conf. Art. Intell.*, Karlsruhe, West Germany, pp. 1089-1093.

Potter, M. C. [1975], "Meaning in visual search," *Science*, vol. 187, pp. 965-966.

Preparata, F. P, and M. I. Shamos [1985], *Computational Geometry* Springer–Verlag, New York.

Raibert, M. H. [1984], "Hopping in Legged Systems—Modeling and Simulation for the Two-Dimensional One-Legged Case," *IEEE Transactions on Systems, Man, and Cybernetics*, vol. SMC-14, no. 3, pp. 451-463.

Raibert, M. H. [1986], "Symmetry in running," *Science*, vol. 231 pp. 1292–1294.

Raibert, M. H. [1986a], *Legged Robots That Balance*, MIT Press, Cambridge, MA.

Raibert, M. H. [1986b], "Running with symmetry," *Int. J. of Robotics Research*, vol. 5, no. 4.

Raibert, M. H. [1986c], "Symmetry in running," *Science,* vol. 231, pp. 1292–1294.

Raibert, M. H., and H. B. Brown, Jr. [1984], "Experiments in balance with a 2D one-legged hopping machine," *ASME J. Dynamic Systems, Measurement, and Control*, vol. 106 pp. 75–81.

Raibert, M. H., H. B. Brown Jr., and M. Chepponis [1984], "Experiments in balance with a 3D one-legged hopping machine," *International J. Robotics Research*, vol. 3 pp. 75–92.

Raibert, M. H., J. Hodgins, H. B. Brown, M. Chepponis, K. Goldberg, J. Koechling, J. Miller [1986], *Dynamically Stable Legged Locomotion–Progress Report: January 1985–August 1986*, Robotics Institute, Carnegie-Mellon University.

Raibert, M. H., and J. E. Tanner [1982], "Design and implementation of a VLSI tactile sensing computer," *Int. Journ. Robotics Research.*, vol. 1, no. 3, pp. 3–18.

Raibert, M. H., and F. C. Wimberly [1984], "Tabular Control of Balance in a Dynamics Legged System," *IEEE Transactions on Systems, Man, and Cybernetics*, vol. SMC-14, no. 2, pp. 334-339.

Raibert, M. H., and J. J. Craig [1981], "Hybrid position/force control of manipulators," *J. Dynamic Systems, Measurement, Control*, vol. 102. Reprinted in *Robot Motion*, edited by M. Brady, *et al.*, MIT Press, 1983.

Raibert, M. H., M. Chepponis, and H. B. Brown Jr. [1986], "Running on four legs as though they were one," *IEEE J. Robotics and Automation*, vol. 2.

Reed, S. K. [1973], *Psychological Processes in Pattern Recognition*, Academic Press, New York.

Reichardt W., and T. Poggio [1976], "Visual Control of Orientation in the Fly: I. A Quantitative Analysis," *Quart. Rev. Biophysics*, vol. 3, pp. 311-375.

Reichardt W., and T. Poggio [1976], "Visual Control of Orientation in the Fly: II. Towards the Underlying Neural Interactions," *Quart. Rev. Biophysics*, vol. 9, pp. 377-439.

Reif, J. H. [1987], "Complexity of the generalized mover's problem," in *Planning, Geometry, and Complexity of Robot Motion*, edited by J. T. Schwartz, M. Sharir, and J. Hopcroft, Ablex Publishing.

Richards, W., and D. D. Hoffman [1985], "Codon Constraints on Closed 2D Shapes," *Computer Vision, Graphics, and Image Processing*, vol. 32, pp. 265-281.

Rifman, S. S., and D. M. McKinnon [1974], "Evaluation of Digital Correction Techniques—for ERTS Images," Report Number E74-10792, TRW Systems Group, July 1974. Also Final Report TRW 20634-6003-TU-00, NASA Goddard Space Flight Center.

Roberts, L. G. [1965], "Machine Perception of Three-Dimensional Solids," in *Optical and Electro-Optical Information Processing*, edited by J. T. Tippet *et al.*, MIT Press, Cambridge, MA, pp. 159–197.

Rock, I. [1973], *Orientation and Form*, Academic Press, New York.

Rock, I., J. DiVita [1987], "A case of viewer-centered object perception," *Cog. Psychol.*, vol. 19, pp. 280–293.

Rock, I., J. DiVita, and R. Barbeito [1981], "The effect on form perception of change of orientation in the third dimension" *J. Exp. Psychol. H.P.& P.*, vol. 7, no. 4, pp. 719–733.

Rosch, E., C. B. Mervis, W. D. Gray, D. M. Johnson, and P. Boyes-Braem [1976], "Basic objects in natural categories," *Cog. Psychol.*, vol. 8, pp. 382–439.

Rosenfeld, A., and M. Thurston [1971], "Edge and Curve Detection for Visual Scene Analysis," *IEEE Transactions on Computers*, vol. 20, no. 5, p. 562–569.

Rosenfeld, A., M. Thurston, and Y. H. Lee [1972], "Edge and Curve Detection: Further Experiments," *IEEE Transactions on Computers*, vol. 21, no. 7, p. 677–715.

Roth, B. [1984], "Screws, motors, and wrenches that cannot be bought in a hardware store," *Robotics Research: The First International Symposium*, edited by M. Brady, and R. Paul, MIT Press, Cambridge, MA, pp. 679-693.

Royall, R. M. [1966], "A class of nonparametric estimators of a smooth regression function," Ph.D. Thesis and Tech Report No. 14, Public Health Service Grant USPHS-5T1 GM 25-09, Department of Statistics, Stanford University, 1966.

Rumelhart, D. E., J. L. McClelland [1986], and the PDP Research Group, *Parallel Distributed Processing: Explorations in the Microstructure of Cognition, Volume 1: Foundations*, MIT Press, Cambridge, MA.

Russell, M., Jr. [1983], and I. Odex, "The first functionoid," *Robotics Age* vol. 5 pp. 12–18.

Sabin, M. A. [1980], "Contouring – A Review of Methods for Scattered Data," in *Mathematical Methods in Computer Graphics and Design,* edited by K. W. Brodlie, Academic Press, New York, pp. 63-86.

Sage, J. P. [1984], "Gaussian Convolution of Images Stored in a Charge-Coupled Device," Solid State Research, Quarterly Technical Report for period from 1 August to 31 October 1983, MIT Lincoln Laboratory, pp. 53–59.

Sage, J. P., and A. L. Lattes [1987], "A High-Speed Two-Dimensional CCD Gaussian Image Convolver," Solid State Research, Quarterly Technical Report for period from 1 August to 31 October 1986, MIT Lincoln Laboratory, pp. 49–52.

Sagi, D., and B. Julesz [1985], ""Where" and "what" in vision," *Science*, vol. 228, pp. 1217–1219.

Salisbury, J. K. [1980], "Active stiffness control of a manipulator in Cartesian coordinates," *IEEE Conference Decision and Control*, Albuquerque, New Mexico.

Salisbury, J. K. [1984], "Interpretation of Contact Geometries from Force Measurements," *Proceedings of the 1st International Symposium on Robotics Research*, Bretton Woods, NH, MIT Press, Cambridge, MA.

Salisbury, J. K. [1987], "Whole-Arm Manipulation," *Proceedings of the 4th International Symposium on Robotics Research*, Santa Cruz, CA, MIT Press, Cambridge MA.

Salisbury, J. K., and J. J. Craig [1982], "Articulated Hands: Force Control and Kinematic Issues," *International Journal of Robotics Research,* vol. 1, no. 1, MIT Press, Cambridge, MA.

Salisbury, K., D. L. Brock, and S. L. Chiu [1985], "Integration of Language, Sensing and Control for a Robot Hand", *Proceedings 3rd ISRR*, Gouvieux France, MIT Press, Cambridge, MA, 1986.

Salisbury, J. K., W. T. Townsend, B. S. Eberman, and D. M. DiPietro [1988], "Preliminary Design of a Whole-Arm Manipulation System (WAMS)," *Proceedings of the 1988 IEEE International Conf. on Robotics and Automation*, Philadelphia, PA.

Scalettar, R., and A. Zee [1988], "Emergence of Grandmother Memory in Feed Forward Networks: Learning With Noise and Forgetfulness," in *Connectionist Models and Their Implications: Readings From Cognitive Science,* edited by D. Waltz and J. A. Feldman, Ablex Publishing, Norwood, NJ, pp. 309-327.

Schaefer, J. F., and R. H. Cannon Jr. [1966], "On the control of unstable mechanical systems," *International Federation of Automatic Control*, London, vol. 6c, pp. 1–13.

Schmitt, F. D. [1984], *Neuroscience*, vol. 13, pp. 991–1002.

Schmitt, F. O., P. Dev, and B. H. Smith [1976], *Science*, vol. 193, pp. 114–120.

Schwartz, J. T., and M. Sharir [1987], "Identification of partially obscured objects in two and three dimensions by matching noisy characteristic curves," *Int. Journ. Robotics Research*, vol. 6, no. 2, pp. 29–44.

Sehitoglu, H., and J. H. Aristizabal [1986], "Design of a Trajectory Controller for Industrial Robots Using Bang-Bang and Cycloidal Motion Profiles," *Robotics: Theory and Applications,* ASME Winter Annual Meeting, Anaheim, CA, pp. 169–175.

Seifert, H. S. [1967], "The lunar pogo stick," *J. Spacecraft and Rockets*, vol. 4 pp. 941–943.

Sekuler, R., and D. Nash [1972], "Speed of size scaling in human vision," *Psychonomic Sci.,* vol. 27, pp. 93-94.

Selfridge, O. G., [1959], "Pandemonium: A paradigm for learning," in, *The Mechanization of Thought Processes,* H.M. Stationary Office, London.

Shepard, D. [1968], "A two-dimensional function for irregularly spaced data," *Proceedings of 23rd ACM National Conference*, pp. 517-524.

Shepard, R. N., and J. Metzler [1971], "Mental rotation of three-dimensional objects," *Science,* vol. 171, pp. 701-703.

Shepard, R. N., and L. A. Cooper [1982], *Mental Images and Their Transformations*, MIT Press/Bradford Books, Cambridge, MA.

Shigley, R. [1957], *The Mechanics of Walking Vehicles*, Land Locomotion Laboratory, Report 7, Detroit, MI.

Shirai, Y., and M. Suwa [1971], "Recognition of polyhedrons with a range finder," *Second Intl. Joint Conf. on Artificial Intelligence.*

Shwartz, S. P. [1981], "The perception of disoriented complex objects." *Proc. 3rd Conf. Cog. Sci.*, Berkeley, pp. 181-183.

Silberberg, T. M., D. A. Harwood, and L. S. Davis [1986], "Object recognition using oriented model points," *Computer Vision, Graphics, and Image Processing*, vol. 35, pp. 47–71.

Silberberg, T. M., L. S. Davis, and D. A. Harwood [1984], "An iterative Hough procedure for three-dimensional object recognition," *Pattern Recognition*, vol. 17, no. 6, pp. 612–629.

Simon, Herbert A. [1969], *Sciences of the Artificial*, MIT Press, Cambridge, MA.

Simons, J., H. van Brussel, J. de Schutter, and J. Verhaert [1982], "A self-Learning Automaton with Variable Resolution for High Precision Assembly by Industrial Robots," *IEEE Transactions on Automatic Control*, vol. AC-27, no. 5.

Simunovic, S. N. [1975], "Force information in assembly processes," *Proceedings 5th Int. Symp. Industrial Robots*, Chicago, pp. 415-431.

Simunovic, S. N. [1979], Ph.D. Thesis, "An Information Approach to Parts Mating" Mechanical Engineering Department, Massachusetts Institute of Technology.

Singer, Neil C., and Warren P. Seering [1988], "Using Acausal Shaping Techniques to Reduce Robot Vibration," *Proceedings of the 1988 IEEE International Conference on Robotics and Automation*, Philadelphia, PA.

Singer, Neil C. [1988], "Residual Vibration Reduction in Computer Controlled Machines," *Ph.D. Thesis, Department of Mechanical Engineering, Massachusetts Institute of Technology,*. Also Report AI-TR-1030, Artificial Intelligence Laboratory, Massachusetts Institute of Technology, Cambridge, MA, 1988.

Sinha, N. K., and B. Kuszta [1983], *Modeling and Identification of Dynamic Systems*, Van Nostrand Reinhold Co., New York, NY,

Sitek, G. [1976], "Big Muskie," *Heavy Duty Equipment Maintenance*, vo. 4, pp. 16–23.

Sjoberg, R. J., and B. K. P. Horn [1983], "Atmospheric Effects in Satellite Imaging of Mountainous Terrain," *Applied Optics*, vol. 22, no. 11, pp. 1702–1716.

Sklansky, J. [1978], "On the Hough Technique for curve detection," *IEEE Trans. Comput.*, vol. 27, pp. 923–926.

Smith, O. J. M. [1958], *Feedback Control Systems*, McGraw-Hill Book Company, Inc., NY, p. 338.

Snell, E. [1974], "Reciprocating Load Carrier," Patent Number 2-430-537.

Sperling, G., M. Pavel, Y. Cohen, M. S. Landy, and B. J. Schwartz [1983] in *Physical and Biological Processing of Images*, edited by O. J. Braddick, and A. C. Sleigh, Springer, Berlin.

Spivak, M. [1965], *Calculus on Manifolds*, W. A. Benjamin, Inc., New York.

Stanfill, C., and D Waltz [1986], "Toward Memory-Based Reasoning," *Communications of the ACM*, vol. 29 no. 12, pp. 1213-1228.

Steinbuch, K., and B. Widrow [1965], "A Critical Comparison of Two Kinds of Adaptive Classification Networks," *IEEE Trans. on Electronic Computers*, vol. EC-14, pp. 737-740.

Steinbuch, K., and U. A. W. Piske [1963], "Learning Matrices and Their Applications," *IEEE Trans. on Electronic Computers*, vol. EC-12, pp. 846-862.

Stentz, A. [1983], "Behavior during stance," in *Dynamically Stable Legged Locomotion—Third Annual Report*, M. H. Raibert *et al.*, Robotics Institute, Carnegie-Mellon University, CMU-RI-TR-83-20, pp. 106–110.

Stockman, G., and J. C. Esteva [1984], "Use of geometrical constraints and clustering to determine 3D object pose.", TR84-002, East Lansing, Michigan State University, Department of Computer Science.

Stockman, G. [1987], "Object recognition and localization via pose clustering," *Comp. Vision, Graphics, and Image Proc.*, vol. 40, pp. 361–387.

Stone, C. J. [1975], "Nearest Neighbor Estimators of a Nonlinear Regression Function," *Proc. of Computer Science and Statistics: 8th Annual Symposium on the Interface*, pp. 413-418.

Stone, C. J. [1977], "Consistent Nonparametric Regression," *The Annals of Statistics*, vol. 5, pp. 595-645.

Stone, C. J. [1982], "Optimal Global Rates of Convergence for Nonparametric Regression," *The Annals of Statistics*, vol. 10, no. 4, pp. 1040-1053.

Strat, T. M. [1977], "Automatic Production of Shaded Orthographic Projections of Terrain," B.S. Thesis, Department of Electrical Engineering and Computer Science.

Suen, C. Y., M. Berthod, and S. Mori [1980], "Automatic recognition of hand-printed & characters—the state of the art," *Proc. IEEE* vol. 68, no. 4, pp. 469–487.

Sugimoto, K., and J. Duffy [1982], "Applications of linear algebra to screw systems," *Mechanisms and Machine Theory*, vol. 17, no. 1, pp. 73-83.

Sugimoto, K., and T. Okada [1985], "Compensation of positioning errors caused by geometric deviations in robot system," *Robotics Research: The Second International Symposium*, edited by H. Hanafusa and H. Inoue, MIT Press, Cambridge, MA, pp. 231-236.

Sugimoto, K., and T. Okada [1985], "Compensation of positioning errors caused by geometric deviations in robot system," *Robotics Research: The Second International Symposium*, edited by H. Hanafusa and H. Inoue, MIT Press, Cambridge, MA, pp. 231-236.

Sutherland, I. E., and M. K. Ullner [1984], "Footprints in the asphalt," *International J. Robotics Research*, vol. 3, pp. 29–36.

Sutherland, N. S. [1959], "Stimulus analyzing mechanisms," in *The Mechanization of Thought Processes*, H.M. Stationary Office, London.

Sutherland, N. S. [1968], "Outline of a theory of visual pattern recognition in animal and man," *Proc. Royal Society, B*, vol. 171, pp. 297–317.

Swigert, C. J. [1980], "Shaped Torque Techniques," *Journal of Guidance and Control*, vol. 3, no. 5, pp. 460–467.

Taar, M. J., and S. A. Pinker [1988], "Viewer-centered and object-centered representations for visual object recognition,"

Tanner, J. E. [1986], "Integrated Optical Motion Detection," Ph.D. Thesis, Computer Science Department, California Institute of Technology, Pasadena, CA. Technical Report 5223:TR:86

Tanner, J. E., and C. A. Mead [1987], "An Integrated Optical Motion Sensor," *VLSI Signal Processing II, Proceedings of the ASSP Conference on VLSI Signal Processing*, UCLA, pp 59–76.

Taylor, R. H. [1976], "The synthesis of manipulator control programs from task-level specifications," Report AIM-282, Artificial Intelligence Laboratory, Stanford University.

Terzopoulos, D. [1983], "Multilevel Computational Processes for Visual Surface Reconstruction," *Computer Vision, Graphics and Image Processing*, vol. 24, no. 1, pp. 52–96.

Terzopoulos, D. [1983], *Computer Graphics Image Processing*, vol. 24, pp. 52–96.

Terzopoulos, D. [1984], "Efficient Multiresolution Algorithms for Computing Lightness, Shape from Shading, and Optical Flow," *International Joint Conference on Artificial Intelligence*, University of Texas, Austin, TX, pp. 314–317.

Terzopoulos, D. [1985], Report AIM-800, Artificial Intelligence Laboratory, Massachusetts Institute of Technology, Cambridge, MA.

Terzopoulos, D. [1986], "Integrating Visual Information From Multiple Sources," in *From Pixels to Predicates*, edited by A. P. Pentland, Ablex Publishing Corp., Norwood, NJ.

Thompson, D. W., and J. L. Mundy [1987], "Three dimensional model matching from an unconstrained viewpoint," *Proc. IEEE Int. Conf. on Robotics and Automation*, Raleigh, N.C., pp. 208–220.

Thompson, D. W., and J. L. Mundy [1987], "Three-dimensional model matching from an unconstrained viewpoint," *Proc. IEEE International Conference on Robotics and Automation,* Raleigh, N.C., pp. 208–220.

Tikhonov, A. N., and V. Y. Arsenin [1977], *Solutions of Ill-Posed Problems,* Winston, Washington, DC.

Tikhonov, A. N. [1963], *Sov. Math. Dokl.,* vol. 4, pp. 1035–1038.

Tikhonov, A. N., and V. Y. Arsenin [1977], *Solution of Ill-Posed Problems,* Winston and Wiley Publishers, Washington, DC.

Tomita, F., and T. Kanade [1985], "A 3D vision system: Generating and matching shape description in range images," in *Robotics Research 2,* edited by H. Hanafusa and H. Inoue, MIT Press, Cambridge, pp. 35–42.

Tonry, D. [1983], *Tumbling,* Harper and Row, New York.

Torre, V., and T. A. Poggio [1986], "On Edge Detection," *IEEE Transactions on Pattern Analysis and Machine Intelligence,* vol. 8, no. 2, pp. 147–163, Also [1984] Report AIM-768,Artificial Intelligence Laboratory, Massachusetts Institute of Technology, Cambridge, MA.

Tou, J. T., and R. C. Gonzalez [1974], *Pattern Recognition Principles,* Addison-Wesley, Reading, MA.

Tournassoud, P., T. Lozano-Pérez, and E. Mazer [1987], "Regrasping," *IEEE International Conference on Robotics and Automation,* Raleigh.

Townsend, W. T., and J. K. Salisbury [1987], "The Effect of Coulomb Friction and Stiction of Force Control," *Proceedings IEEE International Conference on Robotics and Automation,* Raleigh, NC.

Townsend, W. T., and J. K. Salisbury [1988], "The Efficiency Limit of Belt and Cable Drives," *ASME Journal of Mechanisms, Transmissions, and Automation in Design,* vol. 110, no. 3.

Townsend, W. T. [1988], "The Effect of Transmission Design on Force-Controlled Manipulator Performance," Ph.D. Thesis, Department of Mechanical Engineering, Massachusetts Institute of Technology, Cambridge MA, also Report AI-TR-1054, Artificial Intelligence Laboratory, MIT.

Treisman, A., and G. Gelade [1980], "A feature integration theory of attention," *Cog. Psychol.,* vol. 12, pp. 97-136.

Tsai, R. Y, and T. S. Huang [1982], "Uniqueness and estimation of three-dimensional motion parameters of rigid objects with curved surfaces," University of Illinois at Urbana-Champaign Coordinated Science Laboratory Report R-921.

Tsuji, Saburo [1985], "Monitoring of a Building Environment by a Mobile Robot," in *Robotics Research 2,* edited by Hanafusa and Inoue MIT Press, pp. 349–356.

Turney, J. L., T. N. Mudge, and R. A. Volz [1985], "Recognizing partially occluded parts," *IEEE Trans. Pat. Anal. Mach. Intel.,* vol. 7, no. 4, pp. 410–421.

Uhr, L. (editor) [1966], *Pattern Recognition,* Wiley, NY.

Uhr, L. [1973] *Pattern Recognition, Learning, and Thought,* Englewood Cliffs, Prentice-Hall, NJ.

Ullman, S. [1979], *Computer Graphics Image Processing,* vol. 9, pp. 115–125.

Ullman, S. [1979a], *The Interpretation of Visual Motion*, MIT Press, Cambridge, MA.

Ullman, S. [1979b], "The interpretation of structure from motion," *Proceedings of the Royal Society of London, Series B*,vol. 203, pp. 405-426.

Ullman, S. [1979c], "Relaxation and constrained optimization by local processes," *Computer Graphics and Image Processing*, vol. 9, no. 6, pp. 115-125.

Ullman, S. [1983], "Recent computational results in the interpretation of structure from motion," in *Human and Machine Vision*, edited by A. Rosenfeld, and J. Beck, Academic Press, New york, pp. 459-480.

Ullman, S. [1984], "Visual routines," *Cognition*, vol. 18, pp. 97-159.

Ullman, S., and E. Hildreth [1983], "The measurement of visual motion," in *Physical and Biological Processing of Images*, edited by O. J. Braddick, and A. C. Sleigh, Springer,Berlin.

Urschel, W. E. [1949], "Walking Tractor," Patent Number 2-491-064.

Veitschegger, W. K., and C-H. Wu [1987], "A method for calibrating and compensating robot kinematic errors," *Proc. IEEE Int. Conf. Robotics and Automation*, Raleigh, NC, pp. 39-44.

Verri, A., and T. Poggio [1986], "Motion Field and Optical Flow: Qualitative Properties," Report AIM-917, Artificial Intelligence Laboratory, Massachusetts Institute of Technology, Cambridge, MA.

Voorhees, H. L., and T. Poggio [1987], "Detecting Textons and Texture Boundaries in Natural Images," *Proc Intl. Conf. on Computer Vision*, Computer Society of the IEEE, Washington, DC.

Vukobratovic, M., and Y. Stepaneko [1972], "On the stability of anthropomorphic systems," *Mathematical Biosciences*, vol. 14, pp. 1–38.

Wahba, G. [1980], Report TR-595, University of Wisconsin.

Waldron, K. J., V. J. Vohnout, A. Pery, and R. B. McGhee [1984], Configuration design of the adaptive suspension vehicle, *International J. Robotics Research*, vol. 3, pp. 37–48.

Wallace, H. W. [1942], "Jumping Tank Vehicle", Patent Number 2-371-368.

Wallach, H., and D. N. O'Connell [1953], *J. Exp. Psychol.*, vol. 45, pp. 205–217.

Wallach, H, A. Weisz, and P. A. Adams [1956], "Circles and derived figures in rotation," *American Journal of Psychology*, vol. 69, pp. 48-59.

Wallach, H., D. N. O'Connell, and U. Neisser[1953], "The memory effect of visual perception of 3-D form," *Journal of Experimental Psychology*, vol. 45, pp. 360-368.

Wallach, H., and D. N. O'Connell [1953], "The kinetic depth effect," *Journal of Experimental Psychology*, vol. 45, pp. 205-217.

Waltz, D. L. [1987], "Applications of the Connection Machine", *Computer,* vol. 20, no. 1, pp. 85-97.

Waltz, D. [1975], "Understanding line drawings of scenes with shadows," in *The Psychology of Computer Vision*, edited by P. H. Winston, McGraw Hill, New york, pp. 19–91.

Wang, S., T. C. Hsia, and J. L. Wiederrich [1986], "Open-Loop Control of a Flexible Robot Manipulator," *International Journal of Robotics and Automation* vol. 1, no. 2, pp. 54–57.

Watson, G. S. [1964], "Smooth Regression Analysis," *Sankhyā: The Indian Journal of Statistics, Series A,* vol. 26, pp. 359-372.

Waxman, A. [1987], "Image Flow Theory: A Framework for 3-D Inference from Time-Varying Imagery," in *Advances in Computer Vision,* edited by C. Brown, Lawrence Erlbaum Assocs, NJ.

Waxman, A. M., and K. Wohn [1985], "Contour Evolution, Neighborhood Deformation, and Global Image Flow: Planar Surfaces in Motion," *The International Journal of Robotics Research,* vol. 4, no. 3, pp. 95–108.

Waxman, A. M., and S. Ullman [1985], "Surface Structure and 3-D Motion from Image Flow: A Kinematic Analysis." *The International Journal of Robotics Research,* vol. 4, no. 3, pp. 72–94.

Weldon, E. J., Jr. [1986], Unpublished Internal Report, University of Hawaii, private communication.

Webb, J. A., and J. K. Aggarwal [1981], "Visually interpreting the motions of objects in space," *Computer,* vol. 14, no. 8, pp. 40-49.

White, M. J. [1980], "Naming and categorization of tilted alphanumeric characters do not require mental rotation," *Bulletin of the Psychonomic Society,* vol. 15 no. 3, pp. 153–156.

White, B. W., and G. E. Mueser [1960], "Accuracy in reconstructing the arrangement of elements generating kinetic depth displays," *Journal of Experimental Psychology,* vol. 60, pp. 1-11.

Whitney, D. E. [1972], "The mathematics of coordinated control of prosthetic arms and manipulators," *ASME Journal of Dynamic Systems, Measurement, Control,* pp. 303-309.

Whitney, D. E. [1977], "Force feedback control of manipulator fine motions," *J. Dynamic Systems, Measurement, Control,* pp. 91–97.

Whitney, D. E. [1982], "Quasi-static assembly of compliantly supported rigid parts," *J. Dynamic Systems, Measurement, Control* vol. 104, pp. 65–77. Reprinted in *Robot Motion,* edited by M. Brady, *et al.* MIT Press, 1983.

Whittaker, E., and G. Robinson [1924], *The Calculus of Observations,* Blackie and Son, London.

Widrow, B., and F. W. Smith [1964], "Pattern recognizing control systems," *Computer and Information Sciences,* edited by J. T. Tou and R. H. Wilcox, Clever Hume Press.

Wiener, N. [1966], *Extrapolation, Interpolation, and Smoothing of Stationary Time Series with Engineering Applications,* MIT Press, Cambridge, MA.

Will, P. M., and D. D. Grossman [1975], "An experimental system for computer controlled mechanical assembly," *IEEE Trans. Computers* vol. C-24, no. 9, pp. 879–888.

Willshaw, D. J., O. P. Buneman, and H. C. Longuet-Higgins [1969], "Non-holographic associative memory," *Nature,* vol. 222, pp. 960–962.

Wilson, Donald M. [1980], "Insect Walking," *Annual Review of Entomology,* vol. II, 1966, reprinted in "The Organization of Action: A New Synthesis," C. R. Gallistel, Lawrence Erlbaum.

Winston, Patrick Henry [1970], "Learning structural descriptions from examples," Ph.D. Thesis, Massachusetts Institute of Technology, Cambridge, MA.

Also in *The Psychology of Computer Vision*, edited by P. H. Winston [1975], McGraw-Hill, New York.

Wiser, M. [1981], "The role of intrinsic axes in shape recognition," *Proc. 3rd Conf. Cog. Sci.*, Berkeley, pp. 184-186.

Witkin, A. P., and J. M. Tenenbaum [1983], "On the role of structure in vision," in *Human and Machine Vision*, edited by J. Beck, B. Hope, and A. Rosenfeld, Academic Press, New York, pp. 481-543.

Wolf, P. R. [1983], *Elements of Photogrammetry*, McGraw-Hill, New York.

Woodham, R. J. [1980], "Photometric method for determining surface orientation from multiple images," *Optical Engineering*, vol. 19, no. 1, pp. 139–144.

Woodham, R. J. [1977], "A Cooperative Algorithm for Determining Surface Orientation from a Single View," *International Joint Conference on Artificial Intelligence*, Cambridge, MA, pp. 635–641.

Wyllie, J. C. [1979], "The Complexity of Parallel Computations," Technical Reportpp. 79-387, Department of Computer Science, Cornell University, Ithaca, NY.

Yuille, A. [1983], Report AIM-724, Artificial Intelligence Laboratory, Massachusetts Institute of Technology, Cambridge, MA; *Advances in Artificial Intelligence*, edited by T. M. M. O'Shea, Elsevier, Amsterdam, (to appear).

Zunse, L. [1970], *Visual Perception of Form*, Academic Press, New York.

Index

D

K

L

J

N

O

X, Y, Z

Contributions

8   **Recognizing a Program's Design** by Charles Rich and Linda Wills, is a revision of a paper originally published in *IEEE Software* [1990], vol. 7, no. 1. Copyright ©1990 IEEE, reprinted with permission.

9   **Logical vs. Analogical or Symbolic vs. Connectionist or Neat vs. Scruffy** by Marvin Minsky, appeared in *Artificial Intelligence at MIT: Expanding Frontiers*, edited by Patrick H. Winston with Sarah A. Shellard [1990] vol. 1, ch. 9, pp. 218–243, MIT Press, Cambridge, MA. Copyright ©1990 Marvin Minsky.

10 **Excerpts from The Society of Mind** by Marvin Minsky is a collection of excerpts from *The Society of Mind* [1987], Simon and Schuster. Copyright ©1987 Simon and Schuster, reprinted with permission.

11 **HyperBF: A Powerful Approximation Technique for Learning** by T. Poggio and F. Girosi, appeared in *Artificial Intelligence at MIT: Expanding Frontiers*, edited by Patrick H. Winston with Sarah A. Shellard [1990] vol. 1, ch. 11, pp. 270–285, MIT Press, Cambridge, MA. Copyright ©1990 MIT Press.

12 **Principle-Based Parsing: Natural Language Processing for the 1990s** by Robert C. Berwick and Sandiway Fong, contains portions from *Proceedings of the First International Workshop on Parsing* [1989], Carnegie-Mellon University. Copyright ©1990 Robert C. Berwick and Sandiway Fong, reprinted with permission.

13 **Machine Translation:'A Principle-Based Approach** by Bonnie J. Dorr, is a substantially revised vision of a paper titled "Conceptual Basis of the Lexicon in Machine Translation," first published in *Proceedings of the First Annual Workshop on Lexical Acquisition, IJCAI-89* [1989]. Copyright ©1989 Morgan Kaufmann Publishers, reprinted with permission.

14 **Repairing Learned Knowledge using Experience** by Patrick H. Winston and Satyajit Rao, appeared in *Artificial Intelligence at MIT: Expanding Frontiers*, edited by Patrick H. Winston with Sarah A. Shellard [1990] vol. 1, ch. 14, pp. 362–379, MIT Press, Cambridge, MA. Copyright ©1990 Patrick H. Winston and Satyajit Rao.

15 **Model-Based Reasoning: Troubleshooting** by Randall Davis and Walter C. Hamscher, appeared in *Exploring Artificial Intelligence*, edited by H. E. Shrobe, Morgan Kaufmann Publishers [1988]. Copyright ©1988 Morgan Kaufmann Publishers, reprinted with permission.

16 **Invention From First Principles: An Overview** by Brian Williams, appeared in *Artificial Intelligence at MIT: Expanding Frontiers*, edited by Patrick H. Winston with Sarah A. Shellard [1990] vol. 1, ch. 16, pp. 430–463, MIT Press, Cambridge, MA. Copyright ©1990 Brian Williams.

17 **Mathematical Knowledge Representation** by David Allen McAllester, is a series of extracts taken from *Ontic: A Knowledge Representation System for Mathematics*, by David A. McAllester [1989] MIT Press, Cambridge, MA. Copyright ©1989 MIT Press, reprinted with permission.

18 **Three Universal Relations** by David Allen McAllester, appeared in *Artificial Intelligence at MIT: Expanding Frontiers*, edited by Patrick H. Winston with Sarah A. Shellard [1990] vol. 1, ch. 18, pp. 486–497, MIT Press, Cambridge, MA. Copyright ©1990 MIT Press.

19 **An Architecture for Mostly Functional Languages** by Tom Knight, appeared in *Proceedings of the Lisp and Functional Programming Conference* [1986]. Copyright ©1986 ACM, reprinted with permission.

20 **Performance Analysis of k-ary n-cube Interconnection Networks** by William J. Dally, is a revision of a paper first published in *Proceedings of the 1987 Stanford Conference on Advanced Research in VLSI, IEEE Transactions on Computers*. Copyright ©1987 IEEE, reprinted with permission.

21 **The J-Machine System** by William J. Dally, appeared in *Artificial Intelligence at MIT: Expanding Frontiers*, edited by Patrick H. Winston with Sarah A. Shellard [1990] vol. 1, ch. 21, pp. 520–547, MIT Press, Cambridge, MA. Copyright ©1990 MIT Press.

22 **Guarded Horn Clause Languages: Are They Deductive and Logical?** by Carl Hewitt and Gul Agha, appeared in *International Conference on Fifth Generation Computer Systems* [1988] ICOT, Tokyo. Copyright ©1988 Carl Hewitt and Gul Agha, reprinted with permission.

23 **Organizations are Open Systems** by Carl Hewitt, appeared in *ACM Transactions on Office Information Systems* [1986] vol. 4, no. 3. Copyright ©1986 ACM, reprinted with permission.

24   **A Robust Layered Control System for a Mobile Robot** by Rodney A. Brooks, is a substantially revised version of a paper first published in *IEEE Journal of Robotics and Automation* [1986], vol. RA-2 no. 1. Copyright ©1986 IEEE, reprinted with permission.

25   **A Robot that Walks: Emergent Behaviors from a Carefully Evolved Network** by Rodney A. Brooks, appeared in *Neural Computation 1:2* [1989], pp. 253-262, MIT Press. Copyright ©1989 MIT Press, reprinted with permission.

26   **Task-Level Planning of Pick-and-Place Robot Motions** by Tomás Lozano-Pérez, Joseph L. Jones, Emmanuel Mazer, and Patrick A. O'Donnell, appeared in *IEEE Computer* [1989], vol 22, no 3. Copyright ©1989 IEEE, reprinted with permission.

27   **Automatic Synthesis of Fine-Motion Strategies for Robots** by Tomás Lozano-Pérez, Matthew T. Mason, and Russell H. Taylor, appeared in *International Journal of Robotics Research* [1984], vol. 3, no 1. Copyright ©1984 MIT Press, reprinted with permission.

28   **Using Associative Content-Addressable Memories to Control Robots** by Christopher G. Atkeson and David J. Reinkensmeyer, appeared in *Artificial Intelligence at MIT: Expanding Frontiers*, edited by Patrick H. Winston with Sarah A. Shellard [1990], vol. 2, ch. 28, pp. 102–127, MIT Press, Cambridge, MA. Copyright ©1990 Christopher G. Atkeson and David J. Reinkensmeyer.

29   **Preshaping Command Inputs to Reduce System Vibration** by Neil C. Singer and Warren P. Seering, appeared in *ASME Journal of Dynamic Systems, Measurement, and Control* [1990], vol. 112, no. 1. Copyright ©1990 ASME, reprinted with permission.

30   **Legged Robots** by Marc H. Raibert, is revised version of a paper first published in *Communications of the ACM* [1986], vol. 29, no. 6. Copyright ©1986 ACM, reprinted with permission.

31   **Biped Gymnastics** by Jessica K. Hodgins and Marc H. Raibert, appeared in *International Journal of Robotics Research* [1990], vol. 8, no. 2. Copyright ©1990 MIT Press, reprinted with permission.

32   **Using an Articulated Hand to Manipulate Objects** by Kenneth Salisbury, David Brock, and Patrick O'Donnell, appeared in *Proceeding of the SDF Benchmark Symposium on Robotics Research* [1987], Santa Cruz, CA. Copyright ©1987 MIT Press, reprinted with permission.

33 **An Experimental Whole-Arm Manipulator** by Kenneth Salisbury, Brian Eberman, Michael Levin, and William Townsend, appeared in *Robotics Research: The Fifth International Symposium* [1989], Tokyo, Japan. Copyright ©1990 MIT Press, reprinted with permission.

34 **Calibrating Closed Kinematic Chains** by David J. Bennett and John M. Hollerbach, appeared in *Artificial Intelligence at MIT: Expanding Frontiers*, edited by Patrick H. Winston with Sarah A. Shellard [1990], vol. 2, ch. 34, pp. 250–267, MIT Press, Cambridge, MA. Copyright ©1990 MIT Press.

35 **Identifying the Kinematics of Robots** by David J. Bennett and John M. Hollerbach, appeared in *Artificial Intelligence at MIT: Expanding Frontiers*, edited by Patrick H. Winston with Sarah A. Shellard [1990], vol. 2, ch. 35, pp. 268–285, MIT Press, Cambridge, MA. Copyright ©1990 MIT Press.

36 **Object Recognition by Constrained Search** by W. Eric L. Grimson, appeared in *Machine Vision—Acquiring and Interpreting the 3D Scene* edited by Herbert Freeman, Academic Press [1990]. Copyright ©1990 Academic Press, reprinted with permission.

37 **On the Recognition of Parameterized 2D Objects** by W. Eric L. Grimson, is a revised version of a paper first published in *International Journal of Computer Vision* [1988], vol. 3, pp. 353–372. Copyright ©1988 Kluwer Academic Publishers, reprinted with permission.

38 **Aligning Pictorial Descriptions** by Shimon Ullman, appeared in *Cognition* [1989], vol. 32, no. 3, pp. 193-254. Copyright ©1989 North-Holland Publishers, reprinted with permission.

39 **Maximizing Rigidity: Recovery of 3-D Structure from Motion** by Shimon Ullman appeared in *Perception* [1984], vol. 13, pp. 255-274. Copyright ©1984 Pion Publishers, reprinted with permission.

40 **Direct Methods for Recovering Motion** by Berthold K. P. Horn and E. J. Weldon Jr., appeared in *International Journal of Computer Vision* [1988], no. 2, pp. 51-76, Kluwer Academic Publishers. Copyright ©1988 Kluwer Academic Publishers, reprinted with permission.

41 **Computational Vision and Regularization Theory** by Tomaso Poggio, Vincent Torre, and Christof Koch, appeared in *Nature* [1985],

vol. 317, no. 26. Copyright ©1985 Macmillan Journals, reprinted with permission.

42 **The MIT Vision Machine** by T. Poggio, J. Little, E. Gamble, W. Gillett, D. Geiger, D. Weinshall, M. Villalba, N. Larson, T. Cass, H. Bülthoff, M. Drumheller, P. Oppenheimer, W. Yang, A. Hurlbert, D. Beymer, and P. O'Donnell, appeared in *Proceedings of the Image Understanding Workshop* [1988], edited by L. Bauman, SAI Corp., McLean,VA. Copyright ©1988 Morgan Kaufmann Publishers, reprinted with permission.

43 **Parallel Networks for Machine Vision** by Berthold K. P. Horn, appeared in *Artificial Intelligence at MIT: Expanding Frontiers*, edited by Patrick H. Winston with Sarah A. Shellard [1990], vol. 2, ch. 43, pp. 530–573, MIT Press, Cambridge, MA. Copyright ©1990 MIT Press.

The MIT Press, with Peter Denning, general consulting editor, and Brian Randell, European consulting editor, publishes computer science books in the following series:

ACM Doctoral Dissertation Award and Distinguished Dissertation Series

Artificial Intelligence, Michael Brady, Daniel Bobrow, and Randall Davis, editors

Charles Babbage Institute Reprint Series for the History of Computing, Martin Campbell-Kelly, editor

Computer Systems, Herb Schwetman, editor

Exploring with Logo, E. Paul Goldenberg, editor

Foundations of Computing, Michael Garey and Albert Meyer, editors

History of Computing I, Bernard Cohen and William Aspray, editors

Information Systems, Michael Lesk, editor

Logic Programming, Ehud Shapiro, editor; Fernando Pereira, Koichi Furukawa, and D. H. D. Warren, associate editors

The MIT Electrical Engineering and Computer Science Series

Research Monographs in Parallel and Distributed processing, Christopher Jesshope and David Klappholz, editors

Scientific Computation, Dennis Gannon, editor

Artificial Intelligence

Patrick Henry Winston and J. Michael Brady, founding editors. J. Michael Brady, Daniel G. Bobrow, and Randall Davis, current editors.

Artificial Intelligence: An MIT Perspective, Volume I: Expert Problem Solving, Natural Language Understanding, Intelligent Computer Coaches, Representation and Learning, edited by Patrick Henry Winston and Richard Henry Brown, 1979.

Artificial Intelligence: An MIT Perspective, Volume II: Understanding Vision, Manipulation, Computer Design, Symbol Manipulation, edited by Patrick Henry Winston and Richard Henry Brown, 1979.

NETL: A System for Representing and Using Real-World Knowledge, Scott Fahlman, 1979.

The Interpretation of Visual Motion, by Shimon Ullman, 1979.

A Theory of Syntactic Recognition for Natural Language, Mitchell P. Marcus, 1980.

Turtle Geometry: The Computer as a Medium for Exploring Mathematics, Harold Abelson and Andrea di Sessa, 1981.

From Images to Surfaces: A Computational Study of the Human Visual System, William Eric Leifur Grimson, 1981.

Robot Manipulators: Mathematics, Programming, and Control, Richard P. Paul, 1981.

Computational Models of Discourse, edited by Michael Brady and Robert C. Berwick, 1982.

Robot Motion: Planning and Control, edited by Michael Brady, John M. Hollerbach, Timothy Johnson, Tomás Lozano-Pérez, and Matthew T. Mason, 1982.

In-Depth Understanding: A Computer Model of Integrated Processing for Narrative Comprehension, Michael G. Dyer, 1983.

Robotic Research: The First International Symposium, edited by Hideo Hanufusa and Hirochika Inoue, 1985.

Robot Hands and the Mechanics of Manipulation, Matthew T. Mason and J. Kenneth Salisbury, Jr., 1985.

The Acquisition of Syntactic Knowledge, Robert C. Berwick, 1985.

The Connection Machine, W. Daniel Hillis, 1985.

Legged Robots that Balance, Marc H. Raibert, 1986.

Robotics Research: The Third International Symposium, edited by O. D. Faugeras and Georges Giralt, 1986.

Machine Interpretation of Line Drawings, Kokichi Sugihara, 1986.

ACTORS: A Model of Concurrent Computation in Distributed Systems, Gul A. Agha, 1986.

Knowledge-Based Tutoring: The GUIDON Program, William Clancey, 1987.

AI in the 1980's and Beyond: An MIT Survey, edited by W. Eric L. Grimson and Ramesh S. Patil, 1987.

Visual Reconstruction, Andrew Blake and Andrew Zisserman, 1987.

Reasoning about Change: Time and Causation from the Standpoint of Artificial Intelligence, Yoav Shoham, 1988.

Model-Based Control of a Robot Manipulator Chae H. An, Christopher G. Atkeson, and John M. Hollerbach, 1988.

A Robot Ping-Pong Player: Experiment in Real-Time Intelligent Control, Russell L. Andersson, 1988.

Robotics Research: The Fourth International Symposium, edited by Robert C. Bolles and Bernard Roth, 1988.

The Paralation Model: Architecture-Independent Parallel Programming, Gary Sabot, 1988.

Concurrent System for Knowledge Processing: An Actor Perspective, edited by Carl Hewitt and Gul Agha, 1989.

Solid Shape, Jan J. Koenderink, 1989.

Automated Deduction in Nonclassical Logics: Efficient Matrix Proof Methods for Modal and Intuitionistic Logics, Lincoln Wallen, 1989.

3D Model Recognition from Stereoscopic Cues, edited by John E. W. Mayhew and John P. Frisby, 1989.

Shape from Shading, edited by Berthold K. P. Horn and Michael J. Brooks, 1989.

Artificial Intelligence at MIT: Expanding Frontiers, edited by Patrick Henry Winston with Sarah Alexandra Shellard, 1990.